Russian Cultural Studies

Russian
Cultural Studies

An introduction

Edited by Catriona Kelly
and David Shepherd

OXFORD UNIVERSITY PRESS

1998

Oxford University Press, Great Clarendon Street, Oxford OX2 6DP

Oxford New York

Athens Auckland Bangkok Bogotá Buenos Aires Calcutta
Cape Town Chennai Dar es Salaam Delhi Florence Hong Kong Istanbul
Karachi Kuala Lumpur Melbourne Mexico City Mumbai
Nairobi Paris São Paolo Singapore Taipei Tokyo Toronto Warsaw

and associated companies in
Berlin Ibadan

Oxford is a registered trade mark of Oxford University Press

Published in the United States
by Oxford University Press Inc., New York

British Library Cataloguing in Publication Data

Data available

Library of Congress Cataloging in Publication Data

Data available

ISBN 0–19–871510–2
ISBN 0–19–871511–0 (Pbk.)

1 3 5 7 9 10 8 6 4 2

Typeset by Graphicraft Typesetters Ltd., Hong Kong
Printed in Great Britain
on acid-free paper by
Biddles Ltd.,
Guildford and King's Lynn

Acknowledgements

The editors wish to record their especial gratitude to Andrew Lockett of OUP for entrusting them with this project, and for his patience during its gestation.

Similarity between the proposal for a book and the end product is often, if not coincidental, at least distant. This is the second of two books arising from a single volume first mooted in 1992 (the first, *Constructing Russian Culture in the Age of Revolution, 1881–1940*, is also published by OUP). In part this development results from changes in the understanding of Russian culture which have taken place since then, and which we have tried to reflect, and in part from the helpful suggestions of anonymous readers. But it is also in large measure the fruit of a workshop on the theme of Russian Cultural Studies held at the School of Slavonic and East European Studies, University of London, in July 1995, with the generous support of the British Academy and the Leverhulme Trust. Discussions at the workshop opened new avenues and provided fresh impetus; especially import-ant were the frequent contributions made by Robin Aizlewood, Martin Dewhirst, Sheila Fitzpatrick, Maria Gough, Julian Graffy, Barbara Heldt, Geoffrey Hosking, Lindsey Hughes, Robert Service, and Tony Swift. The workshop could not have succeeded in this way without Radojka Miljevic's organizational skills.

The slightly unorthodox genesis of this book has its counterpart in matters of presentation. This is not a traditional volume of essays, each by an individual author. Rather, in the interests of narrative and thematic coherence, material submitted by contributors has in some cases been combined, often with greater than usual editorial inter-vention, to form lengthy chapters which are credited in their entirety to the authors. The willingness of contributors to accept this uncon-ventional procedure is greatly appreciated.

Thanks are also due to Laurence Waters for his assistance in preparing the illustrations.

Finally, the editors owe heartfelt thanks to Ian Thompson and Jeff Denton for practical and, above all, moral support.

Contents

List of Illustrations

List of Contributors

Lynne Attwood: Lecturer in Russian Studies at the University of Manchester. She is the author of *The New Soviet Man and Woman: Sex-Role Socialisation in the USSR* (1990), and editor of *Red Women on the Silver Screen* (1993). She is currently working on the construction of gender identity in the USSR, focusing on the changing representations of women in the press and in films.

Mark Banting: Freelance writer, researcher, and speaker on all aspects of homosexuality in modern society, whose special interest is (homo)sexuality in Soviet and post-Soviet Russia.

Birgit Beumers: Lecturer in the Department of Russian at the University of Bristol. Her research interests are in Russian culture, theatre, and cinema of the post-war period. Her *Yury Liubimov at the Taganka Theatre (1964–1994)* was published in 1997.

Frank Ellis: Lecturer in Russian at the University of Leeds, and the author of *Vasily Grossman: The Genesis and Evolution of a Russian Heretic* (1994). He is currently working on a book examining the changes in the Russian media since 1991.

Jane Ellis: Freelance scholar based in Oxford. She is the author of *The Russian Orthodox Church: A Contemporary History* (1986) and *The Russian Orthodox Church: Triumphalism and Defensiveness* (1996), and for six years was editor of the journal *Religion in Communist Lands*. She is currently completing a doctoral thesis on the Russian Orthodox Church between 1985 and 1994, and a monograph on the Moscow Patriarchate's attitude towards Protestant missionaries.

Anna Ferenc: Assistant Professor of Music at Dalhousie University, and author of the dissertation 'Investigating Russian Musical Modernism: Nikolai Roslavets and his New System of Tone Organization'. Her current research interests include modernist expression in the music of Arthur Lourié, Alexander Mosolov, and Alexander Skriabin.

Julian Graffy: Senior Lecturer in Russian Language and Literature at the School of Slavonic and East European Studies, University of London. He is co-editor, with Geoffrey Hosking, of *Culture and the Media in the USSR Today*

(1989), and, with Ian Christie, of *Protazanov and the Continuity of Russian Cinema* (1993). He is currently researching a study of the role of the foreigner in Russian cinema.

Catriona Kelly: Reader in Russian and Tutorial Fellow at New College, University of Oxford. She is the author of *Petrushka: The Russian Carnival Puppet Theatre* (1990) and *A History of Russian Women's Writing, 1820–1992* (1994), editor of *An Anthology of Russian Women's Writing, 1777–1992* (1994), and co-editor, with David Shepherd, of *Constructing Russian Culture in the Age of Revolution, 1881–1940* (1998). She is currently working on a monograph entitled *Refining Russia: Gender, Manners and Morals from Catherine to Yeltsin.*

Peter Kenez: Professor of History at the University of California at Santa Cruz. His books include *The Birth of the Propaganda State: Soviet Methods of Mass Mobilization, 1917–1929* (1985), *Cinema and Soviet Society, 1917–1953* (1992), and *A History of the Soviet Union from the Beginning to the End* (forthcoming). He is also co-editor, with Abbot Gleason and Richard Stites, of *Bolshevik Culture: Experiment and Order in the Russian Revolution* (1985).

Stephen Lovell: Ph.D. student at the School of Slavonic and East European Studies, University of London. He is the author of articles published in *Slovo* and in *Europe–Asia Studies*, and is currently working on the myths and reality of reading in Soviet Russia.

Gerard McBurney: Divides his time between composing, arranging, teaching, writing, and broadcasting about music. He has made many programmes for BBC Radio 3, and has written and researched documentary films for British and German television. His recent music includes *A Winter's Walk round the Park at Troitse-Lykovo* for the 1995 Spitalfields Festival, *3 Antiphons of Hildegard of Bingen* (1996) for the Kronos Quartet, and the music for the 1997 RNT/Théatre de Complicité production of *Caucasian Chalk Circle*.

Rosalind Marsh: Professor of Russian Studies at the University of Bath and President of the British Association for Slavonic and East European Studies. She is the author of *Soviet Fiction since Stalin: Science, Politics and Literature* (1986), *Images of Dictatorship: Stalin in Literature* (1989), and *History and Literature in Contemporary Russia* (1995), and editor of *Women in Russia and Ukraine* (1996) and *Gender and Russian Literature: New Perspectives* (1996).

Robin Milner-Gulland: Professor of Russian and East European Studies at the University of Sussex. He is the author of *Cultural Atlas of Russia* (1980) and *The Russians* (1997), and co-author, with John Bowlt, of *An Introduction to Russian Art and Architecture* (1980). The editor and translator of N. N. Zabolotsky, *The Life of Zabolotsky* (1994), he has also edited *Soviet Russian Verse: An Anthology* (1964) and, with Martin Dewhirst, *Russian Writing Today* (1977). He is currently working on a comprehensive history of Russian art and architecture.

Hilary Pilkington: Senior Lecturer in Russian Politics and Society at the Centre for Russian and East European Studies, University of Birmingham. Her research interests are in changing socio-cultural identities in late Soviet and post-Soviet Russia, and she is currently working on the impact of globalization on Russian youth culture. She is author of *Russia's Youth and Its Culture: A Nation's Constructors and Constructed* (1994) and *The 'Other' Russians: Migration, Displacement and Identity in Post-Soviet Russia* (forthcoming), and editor of *Gender, Generation and Identity in Contemporary Russia* (1996).

James Riordan: Professor of Russian Studies in the Department of Linguistic and International Studies, University of Surrey. He is the author of *Sport, Politics and Communism* (1991), and co-editor, with Igor Kon, of *Sex and Russian Society* (1993), and, with Christopher Williams and Igor Ilyinsky, of *Young People in Post-Communist Russia and Eastern Europe* (1995). His current research is concerned with sexuality, young people, and sport in Russia, Eastern Europe, and China.

David Shepherd: Professor of Russian and Director of the Bakhtin Centre at the University of Sheffield. He is the author of *Beyond Metafiction: Self-Consciousness in Soviet Literature* (1992), editor of *Bakhtin, Carnival, and Other Subjects* (1993) and *The Contexts of Bakhtin* (1998), and co-editor, with Catriona Kelly, of *Discontinuous Discourses in Modern Russian Literature* (1989). His current research is focused on the intellectual contexts of the Bakhtin Circle.

Vadim V. Volkov: Lecturer in and Dean of the Faculty of Political Sciences and Sociology of the European University at St Petersburg. In 1995 he received his Ph.D. from Cambridge University for a thesis entitled 'The Forms of Public Life: The Public Sphere and the Concept of Society in Imperial Russia', and is currently writing a book on this subject. His research interests are in social theory, historical sociology, Russian social history, and issues of civil society.

Stephen White: Professor of Politics at the University of Glasgow, and President of the British Association for Slavonic and East European Studies from 1994 to 1997. His recent publications include *Russian Goes Dry* (Cambridge, 1996) and (with several co-authors) *How Russia Votes*. He is currently completing a book on the political élite in the Soviet period based on interview as well as printed and archive material.

Translation and Transliteration

Unless otherwise stated, translations are by the contributors or editors. With the exception of some commonly occurring names, in particular of composers, Russian words are transliterated according to the Library of Congress system (without diacritics). Gorky (now once again Nizhnii Novgorod) is distinguished from Gor'kii (the writer who gave it its temporary name).

Introduction: Why Cultural Studies?

CATRIONA KELLY

HILARY PILKINGTON

DAVID SHEPHERD

VADIM VOLKOV

Of Binarisms and Polarities

As Western culture's nearest, if not necessarily most significant, 'other', Russia has inspired centuries of almost obsessive commentary and analysis by Western travellers and armchair observers. In the pre-Petrine period, visitors such as Giles Fletcher and Adam Olearius remarked on the Muscovites' propensity for bibulousness, bigotry, and buggery, as well as on their appalling taste in music, entertainments, and table manners, beginning a long tradition of attributing to Russians practices held repellent in the West (though often evident there too). Since the rise of academic study of Russia in the late nineteenth century, expressions of rank distaste have been partly forced out by more considered and nuanced representations of the country (though the former still have their place in popular attitudes towards the 'Soviet Union', if not 'Russia'). However, there still exists a conviction that it is possible to encapsulate the essence of the country, to lay it bare in an aphoristic formulation, normally as contradiction or paradox. James Billington's magisterial study of the 1960s, *The Icon and the Axe*, for example, saw Russian history as a long struggle between the wild and the tame on the one hand, and violence and the cult of beauty on the other.

One suspects that arguments of this kind would command little respect if applied to French, German, British, or American history; yet with regard to Russian history they appear peculiarly seductive. After all, if Russia is 'a riddle wrapped in a mystery inside an enigma', it must be possible to find a solution, to crack the code. Russian observers too seem to have sensed the need to solve the riddle in ways of their own: the notion of Russia as torn between warring poles underlies, for example, many of the sophisticated and intense studies of cultural history produced by the 'Tartu school', the renowned scholar Iurii Lotman and his pupils during the 1960s, 1970s, and 1980s.[1] Within this model the binary oppositions of East and West, high and low, major and minor, perennial and ephemeral, old and new, political and apolitical, are highlighted, scrutinized, but in the final reckoning left intact.

The usefulness of binary schematizations in depicting and understanding Russia's symbolic reality is not, of course, to be underestimated. Dualism in propaganda, literature, and texts of all kinds is ubiquitous and overt, cropping up, for instance, even in such unexpected places as language classes for non-native speakers (where the recognition of antonyms is a standard technique in instruction and testing alike). Dualistic analyses of Russian culture are therefore not without foundation, and have proved especially appealing in analysing the most self-consciously symbolic eras of Russian history—the regimes of Peter the Great and Joseph Stalin. Vladimir Papernyi's 1985 study *Culture '2'* (*Kul'tura '2'*) is an especially rich and persuasive survey of high Stalinism, a culture so obsessed with outward forms that it became an offence, for example, to speak of 'Kautskii and Lenin' (because this meant relegating the Soviet leader to second place), and in which shape and object were so closely related that the marble used for decorating public buildings was seen to enhance prosperity by a sort of sympathetic magic, while the interior space in the great statue of Stalin at the All-Soviet Agricultural Exhibition was used for displaying—a maquette of the very same statue of Stalin. Papernyi posits an unusually complex binary model of differentiation between this culture and 'Culture 1'. Culture 1 was scientific, whereas Culture 2 propagated a 'mysticism of science', lyrical (i.e. word- and experience-based) where the latter was 'epic', martial rather than philoprogenitive and domestic, mechanistic rather than 'humanistic' (in Culture 2 even buildings were given 'skins' of flesh-coloured tiles), asexual and fraternal rather than family-based (with the return of the nuclear family during Culture 2 manifested by an upsurge in the manufacture of double beds, and also by the introduction of 'wives' councils' in place of 'Party women's sections').

Despite the fascinating insights offered on a range of details, from red carpets to cinema exit signs, Papernyi's book does share some of the problems of binary historiography (or mythography) in general. Culture again emerges as the product of reified or even demonized abstract forces reasserting themselves periodically in a manner not

1 See B. Gasparov, 'Introduction', in *The Semiotics of Russian Cultural History: Essays by Iurii M. Lotman, Lidiia Ia. Ginsburg, Boris A. Uspenskii*, ed. A. D. Nakhimovsky and A. S. Nakhimovsky (Ithaca, NY, 1985), 21.

subject to human control. Both the real circumstances of production, and especially the real circumstances of consumption, are beyond Papernyi's purview, as he himself acknowledges.[2] Furthermore, Stalinism is seen by Papernyi as perfectly harmonious, a 'unified culture' distinguished, above all, by its refusal to separate what are normally perceived as polarities—especially aesthetics and function. Yet the 'unitariness' of high-Stalinist culture could have sat at best uneasily with another important feature of the culture, according to Papernyi's own description: the hierarchization of every element and item, so that, for instance, only the main streets and squares of cities were fully beautified, and only the most important towns dignified by being named after Party leaders.[3]

Even when they lack the comparative theoretical sophistication of Papernyi's, such binaristic models do not preclude the accumulation of important and intriguing historical data (just as Billington's book is still valuable for, among other things, its meticulous account of religious philosophies and cults). But it is perhaps time to recognize that Russian history is neither more nor less complex and illogical than the histories of other European countries; that causative processes have been diverse and unpredictable here as elsewhere; and that these processes may not be subsumed into easy conflicts between 'intelligentsia' and 'people', 'Westernizers' and 'Slavophiles', or into generalizations about 'autocratic' and 'totalitarian' societies. The indisputable fact that Russia has never (yet) had an Anglo-American style democracy should not be elevated into proof of the country's eternal capacity for repression. Some at least of the mechanisms of government under both tsars and Soviets, such as bribery or patron–client networks, are found in other European countries too (from Ireland to Italy). Many other European societies shared some of Russia's social upheavals: civil war, rapid industrialization, the existence of a large migrant labour population. Russia, like most other European countries, has been shaped by the pervasive influence of Christianity (a sturdy anti-clerical and secular intellectual tradition during the last two centuries notwithstanding). And the cultural artefacts produced even in the most isolationist periods of post-Petrine history have been broadly similar, in form and function, to those produced in many Western countries, even if the context in which they circulated was different.

Western Approaches to Russian Culture

There has, in recent years, been a striking growth in culturally oriented studies of Russian and, especially, Soviet history. This reflects

2 V. Papernyi, *Kul'tura '2'* (Ann Arbor, 1985), 207.

3 Some of these difficulties are addressed in S. Boym, 'Paradoxes of a Unified Culture', in T. Lahusen and E. Dobrenko (eds.), *Socialist Realism without Shores* (South Atlantic Quarterly, 94 (1995)), 821–36.

more general trends in historical research in the West and the impact of new research agendas opened up by the quest to uncover previously unspoken histories, most notably women's history, black history, and gay history. Yet despite the interesting work already done in these areas, the hegemony of political history in our discipline has proved extraordinarily tenacious. One reason for this is clearly the highly charged political environment of the post-war period, which entrenched rather than undermined binaristic models. The positing of the USSR as the 'other' against which the West must struggle, now in overtly economic, ideological, and moral terms, was encapsulated in the totalitarian model widely applied in the analysis of Soviet development. Whereas political scientists used the totalitarian model rather crudely but at least comparatively, historians adopting a totalitarian model of Soviet development stressed the unique nature of the country's path. While arguing that only they fully took account of Russia's cultural peculiarity, they simultaneously fell into the same kind of cultural isolationism as the Soviet Union itself. In contrast, modernization theorists, whose focus was more social and economic than political, in their determination to highlight the commonality of experience between the Soviet Union and the West laid themselves open to criticism of crude economic determinism and cultural insensitivity.

It is not only the grand theories within which research is framed that have inhibited the emergence of an informative Russian 'cultural studies' analogous to the discipline, or nexus of disciplines, that goes under that name in other areas. To the extent that the social sciences from which cultural studies grew (anthropology and sociology) attempt a relativistic, or relational, account of the phenomena that they observe, cultural studies would seem well suited to offer new perspectives on Russian history. But a further inhibiting factor was precisely the minimal opportunity, until recently, for firsthand data-gathering. In the virtual absence of opportunities for sustained fieldwork, social scientists were left with the daunting prospect of scouring media texts and government statements for minute changes in policy. This has inevitably bred a top-down approach to the study of society and culture, one which reduces cultural production to a binary model (underlying truth plus superficial distortion), while the processes of cultural reception and practice have remained virtually unanalysed.

Such a top-down approach to culture has traditionally dominated Anglophone accounts of what has always been seen as the primary expression of Russian culture, literature. These accounts tend to operate with an imaginary, but powerful, distinction between 'literature'

Catriona Kelly, Hilary Pilkington, David Shepherd, Vadim Volkov

and 'society', 'text' and 'context'. On the one hand, it has been widely acknowledged that 'external' forces such as literary institutions (most notably censorship) play a larger role in Russia than elsewhere. On the other hand, there has been a tendency to regard such forces as peripheral to the composition of all but 'minor' works. One critic, for example, has recently defined socialist realism as 'a literary practice that produced the overwhelming majority of Soviet literature, minus, of course, the well-known "dissident" exceptions and the "returned" masterpieces'.[4] According to this binary opposition, then, 'society' is what produces inferior literature, while great literature, literature in a full sense, originates (and is, by implication, consumed) somewhere outside the ordinary conditions of production. What is more, even those literary histories that attempt to integrate 'major' works into the context of their production (such as Ronald Hingley's *Russian Writers and Soviet Society*, 1979) have generally viewed Russian culture according to a paradigm that emphasizes the importance of institutional and Party control. This produces a history in which questions about the relative popularity of literary texts, or other cultural artefacts, are not asked, and where popular cultural forms play a role only in so far as they impinge upon the production of 'culture' proper.

In post-Soviet Russian studies there has been a surge in social and cultural studies, many inspired by gender-aware approaches. However, this theory-grounded work, drawing as it does on small-scale research and with no base on which to build has not yet proved able to displace the grand old theories of Russian and Soviet studies. Consequently the field remains dominated by reworkings of totalitarian and modernization theories. The former suggest that the collapse of the Soviet system proved its inherent unreformability, while the latter speak of 'mismodernization' and call for a new programme to rectify the mistakes of the past.[5] Thus, although some attention is ostensibly paid to the role of the media revolution and *glasnost'* in bringing about the collapse of the state, in reality it is the political that is once again interpreted as the moving force of society.[6] This is true also of the recent attention paid to political culture—symbolized by that figment of a sociologist's imagination, Homo Sovieticus[7]—which has been mobilized to expose the cultural impediments to democratization, or to account for the socio-cultural legacy of the Soviet period more generally. Needless to say this kind of approach fails to penetrate the complex nature of identity formation and cultural practice in the post-war Soviet period, and instead reduces Soviet social and cultural relations to a fictitious generalized average, based on public opinion-polling methods, and is employed primarily to predict what paths to the future might be suitable for Russia.

4 T. Lahusen, 'Socialist Realism in Search of its Shores: Some Historical Remarks on the "Historically Open Aesthetic System of the Truthful Representation of Life" ', in Lahusen and Dobrenko (eds.), *Socialist Realism*, 661.
5 For examples of approaches based on totalitarian models, see Z. Brzezinski, *The Grand Failure: The Birth and Death of Communism in the Twentieth Century* (New York, 1989), and M. Malia, 'To the Stalin Mausoleum', *Daedalus*, 1 (Winter 1990), 295–344. On 'mismodernization', see R. Sakwa, *Russian Politics and Society* (London, 1993), 399–400.
6 See e.g. R. Karklins, 'Explaining Regime Change in the Soviet Union', *Europe–Asia Studies*, 46 (1994), 29–45.
7 See e.g. Iu. Levada (ed.), *Sovetskii prostoi chelovek: Opyt sotsial'nogo portreta na rubezhe 90-kh godov* (Moscow, 1992).

In a recent study of the emergence of cultural studies in Britain, Ioan Davies has linked it to the collapse of empire and the end of the particular forms of social hegemony characterizing the imperial age. It would be a theoretically unsustainable position to argue that the collapse of the Soviet empire ought to lead to precisely analogous consequences (that would be taking the rejection of binary oppositions much too far—and Davies rightly cautions against trying to transplant models across national and cultural boundaries).[8] However, new cultural studies in, or of, Russia might well seek to have recourse to some of the theoretical agenda of contemporary cultural studies in the West, such as the study of globalization and localization; domination and subordination; identity formation; and even those totemic terms of postmodernity, diversity, difference, and fragmentation.

Of course sceptics may argue that attempts to apply questions raised by postmodernity to post-Soviet society may simply repeat the mistakes of those who sought earlier to apply modernization theories. And it would certainly be wrong to suggest that theories and hypotheses developed by cultural studies taking Western cultures as its object should be applied wholesale to Russia. Inevitably, much will not fit. Moreover, for obvious if not always convincing reasons, we must anticipate resistance to or rejection of the broadly Marxist approach at the heart of, at least, British cultural studies. For example, it is difficult to imagine that the following account of cultural production, based on the work of Lukács's pupil Sandor Radnoti, would find much favour among Russianists:

all cultural production is dependent on the market, not simply in an economic sense but in the broader sense that it is in principle subordinated to a common standard of value that allows the difference between cheap and valuable art to be determined. It is dependent upon a *general* and uniform economy of value. Given the impossibility of such an economy, however (since value is a domain of dispute, not of consensus), the self-understanding of modern art can only ever give rise to debate about value, in a constant attempt to maintain its distinction from its mass-cultural other.[9]

There are a number of reasons why such a relational account of the crucial question of cultural value might raise the hackles of students of Russia and the Soviet Union. There is still a lingering sense that value is something self-evident, will always out, and that it is what demarcates high culture from its low antipode, rather than connecting the two. Moreover, notwithstanding the insistence that the notion of 'market' is not used exclusively in its literal economic sense, the whole passage recalls Soviet vulgar Marxism, with its insistence on the primacy of the economic over all other factors.

8 See I. Davies, *Cultural Studies and Beyond: Fragments of Empire* (London, 1995), 170–1.
9 J. Frow, *Cultural Studies and Cultural Value* (Oxford, 1995), 19.

Russian Approaches to Culture

It is true that cultural studies may be even less likely to be embraced by Western and post-Soviet Russian scholars alike precisely because of the dominant emphasis of the study of culture in the Soviet Union—even though, paradoxically, this emphasis did not in fact entail a privileging of the economic. Not long ago a Western academic, announcing in Russian that s/he worked on 'culture', might well have risked giving the impression to non-social scientists that s/he was a biologist or agronomist seeking to improve the fertility of grain, fruit, or some other agricultural crop. This strongly materialist association of the term 'culture' clearly reflects the fundamental Marxist understanding of culture as the changing of nature by humanity. However, in the Soviet Union this materialism was offset by a no less robust reflexive idealism. When applied to human endeavour, 'culture' essentially referred to 'high culture', and thus invited exactly the same (Marxist or Marxian) critique that lies at the heart of cultural studies projects in the West. In this sense—and this is a well-enough established point—there was considerable continuity between dominant pre- and post-Revolutionary understandings of culture.

Until the 1880s the term 'culture' (*kul'tura*) was not current in Russian society. It is not to be encountered in the language of Pushkin. Nor did Dobroliubov, Chernyshevskii, and Pisarev, the prominent radical literary critics of the 1860s, use the word. Belinskii did mention it occasionally in 1845, speaking of a 'literary culture'; otherwise, the term was used in its original etymological meaning, in relation to agriculture.[10] The first mention of *kul'tura*, however, is registered in the lexicon by Zimmerman in 1807; and Tatishchev's dictionary of 1826 translates the French *culture* as *obrazovannost'* (educatedness).[11] In Western Europe, a range of terms such as *courtoisie*, *civilité*, *Bildung*, *cortezia*, and some others were used to denote different cultural phenomena, and later, in the eighteenth century, they evolved into either 'culture' or 'civilization'. In the absence of *kul'tura* in the language of Russian society, the general meaning of this term was conveyed by the words 'enlightenment' (*prosveshchenie*), 'education', 'civilization', 'literature', or 'spirituality' (*dukhovnost'*). For the characterization of individuals words such as 'educated' (*obrazovannyi*), 'well-bred' (*vospitannyi*), and the like were used in the same way as 'cultured' (*kul'turnyi*) came to be used later.

The emergence of *kul'tura* in the discourse of the Russian intelligentsia is usually connected with German influence. The German

10 See R. Budagov, *Istoriia slov v istorii obshchestv* (Moscow, 1971), 128.
11 See N. Shanskii, *Etimologicheskii slovar' russkogo iazyka*, ii (Moscow, 1982), headword *kul'tura*.

Kultur referred to the original national spirit as opposed to the alien French influence expressed by the concept of *Zivilisation*. *Kultur* was also central to the self-identity of German middle-class intellectuals, as they sought to distinguish themselves from the superficially refined aristocracy, whom they associated with *Zivilisation*.[12] The Russian Slavophiles, who constructed a similar opposition between the true national spirit of pre-Petrine Russia and the Westernized élite, employed 'enlightenment' and 'educatedness' respectively. According to Pavel Miliukov, culture (*kul'tura*) and civilization (*tsivilizatsiia*) emerged as oppositional terms in the discourse of the Slavophiles of the 1880s, most prominently in the writings of Konstantin Leontiev, who associated the authentic and rich *kul'tura* with the earlier period of exuberant growth and complexity, and *tsivilizatsiia* with the age of secondary simplification and decline of a national culture. In his *Essays on the History of Russian Culture*, first published in 1892–5, Miliukov tried to avoid the opposition set by Leontiev, suggesting a broad definition of *kul'tura* as a specific relationship between the material culture and spiritual culture of the nation. He argued that the cleavage between traditional culture and the culture of the educated élite in Russia was not a sign of crisis or decline, but the result of the historical transition from spontaneous cultural development to the reflexive stage characteristic of any mature nation. Sharing the hopes of contemporary liberals, Miliukov predicted that the cleavage between the two cultures would be gradually eliminated through the 'transmission of the cultural achievements from the intelligentsia to the masses'.[13]

It was in connection with the missionary idea of the transmission of education and culture to the backward masses, and in the context of the first attempts, in the late 1870s, to put it into practice that the term *kul'tura* and its derivatives *kul'turnyi* and *kul'turnost'* began to gain prominence. The materialist and abstract connotations of the word were both activated as the seeds of culture were sown. Liberals working in *Zemstvo* schools for peasant education, teachers at Sunday schools for workers and peasants, and intellectuals (liberals as well as Populists) studying popular reading habits, as well as other groups involved in similar activities, saw themselves as doing cultural work (*kul'turnaia rabota*) and, accordingly, were sometimes referred to as *kul'turniki*.[14] Through their activity *kul'tura* came to be understood as a kind of value that could be accumulated, then purposefully transferred to and acquired by wider groups of the population. This genetic relationship with the nascent practices of mass policy constitutes a subtle difference between *kul'tura* and the earlier cultural phenomena denoted by other terms.

12 See N. Elias, *The Civilizing Process*, i. *The History of Manners*, tr. E. Jephcott (Oxford, 1978), 4.
13 P. Miliukov, *Ocherki po istorii russkoi kul'tury*, ii (Paris, 1937), 980.
14 See B. Bank, *Izuchenie chitatelei v Rossii (XIX v.)* (Moscow, 1969).

The effects of such policy came to be denoted by the term *kul'turnost'*. Formally, the term can only be used in relation to a person or a group, and points to a relative level of personal culture and education. It is unclear whether it acquired widespread currency or significance in Imperial Russia, or whether it was used by groups other than the Marxists, for the only pattern of contextual usage given by Soviet dictionaries comes from Plekhanov's *The Russian Worker in the Revolutionary Movement*, first published in the 1890s: 'The more I got to know Petersburg workers, the more I was impressed by their *kul'turnost'*.'[15] The centrality of *kul'tura* and *kul'turnost'* to the post-1917 period is beyond any doubt: *kul'tura* was at the core of Soviet cultural policy, while *kul'turnost'* was of a semi-official order and referred to the realm of everyday practice. If *kul'tura* gradually came to constitute one of the central spiritual values of Soviet civilization, if it became firmly rooted in official discourse and in the consciousness of the intelligentsia, it is because its specific use-value was, under certain historical circumstances, rediscovered and employed by the Soviet authorities.

Thus Soviet notions of culture, far from being based on a vulgar Marxist conception of the cultural sphere as little more than a reflection of the economic base of society, emphasized the centrality of the cultural sphere in shaping and facilitating economic development. Post-Revolutionary radical cultural campaigns (against illiteracy, religion, superstition, and bourgeois morality) were highly interventionist, precisely in pursuit of this agenda. Of course, far from all of Soviet society was converted to the modernist dream, and resistance to cultural campaigns in the countryside, as well as the violent cultural politics of the 1920s and 1930s, evidence the contested nature of cultural progress in the pre-war years. It was in the cultural sphere that 'progressive' ideas did battle with negative, reactionary ideas. Whilst in the official version of events, the former always won, as time would tell, the ideological commitment to the equal distribution of the benefits of modernity and the emphasis on collective rather than individual experience of the modern world would come to encourage the manifestation of collective resistance to the negative consequences of modernization. As the latter accumulated, so political change in the USSR became increasingly unavoidable.

The apotheosis of this dominance of the cultural over the economic might be considered to be the period of high Sovietism (the late-Brezhnev era), when the 'Soviet way of life' (*sovetskii obraz zhizni*) was declared to be the source of the superiority of the socialist system. The individual in developed socialist society was declared to be an 'all-round personality', having been able, in a non-exploitative society, to

15 Quoted in *Slovar' sovremennogo russkogo iazyka*, v (Moscow, 1956), headword *kul'turnost'*.

develop all his/her qualities and capabilities. The creation of such an individual, it was argued, had been facilitated by rapid urbanization, which had broken down old, and reactionary, ties of collectivity. Moreover, towns and cities were focal points for key social institutions (political and social organizations, theatres and cinemas, museums and clubs, scientific and educational establishments) which helped socialize the individual correctly. Indeed in the Brezhnev years the 'cultural achievements' of Soviet society were measured by the number of clubs, palaces of culture, theatres, cinemas, libraries, and sports complexes that had been built. Another central area in which modernization was proclaimed to have produced great cultural progress was in the sphere of ethnic relations. Rapid industrialization and the remedial modernization of formerly 'backward' republics, it was claimed, had created a 'new historical community of people' (the Soviet people, *sovetskii narod*) marking an integration of nations and nationalities into a single community and thus, for the first time in history, creating a truly multinational culture. This did not mean that all national distinctions had disappeared, or indeed that they should disappear, but that they were mutually enriching, and that, as everyday life became increasingly internationalized, so there would be a continuing drawing together of peoples.

The problem for Soviet analysts, therefore, was not that they were bound to a strict, and crude, Marxist understanding of culture, but rather that, in post-Revolutionary Soviet society, determinist Marxist understandings of social and cultural processes of change could not be applied. The motor of history (class struggle) had apparently been immobilized by the Revolution, and practitioners of the discipline known as culturology (*kul'turologiia*) were above all concerned with explaining the new mechanism by which *socialist* society progressed. To this end two key terms were employed: continuity (*preemstvennost'*) and inheritance (*nasledovanie*). The latter had two forms: genetic inheritance (necessary for the physical reproduction of society), and social inheritance, indicating the transfer of norms, values, customs, and skills necessary for the cultural reproduction of society. What is remarkable about this notion of cultural process is of course its skin-deep dialectics, beneath which lay an extremely conservative notion of cultural change; the best in society is simply passed down from generation to generation in a smooth process of cultural inheritance. Cultural change in Soviet society was symbolically represented in the form of a relay race, in which the baton was smoothly passed between team members, each representing a new generation whose task it was to overcome the unique obstacles confronted during the successful completion of their lap of the race to communism. There was, apparently, no struggle on either the horizontal level (over what constitutes that worthy of inheritance) or the vertical level (between generations). Thus, cultural politics were rendered non-existent, and progress was achieved through the social inheritance of the cultural values of the previous generation. These values, moreover, have much in common with those of the capitalist modernization project: urban superiority, the rule of rationality, science, and technology, and a belief in harnessing nature in the interests of the social good.

From the very beginning of *perestroika* the cultural sphere was identified as a key site of change, something made manifest in Gorbachev's call for the 'activation of the human factor' and constant reference to the need for a *perestroika* of the individual. Indeed the whole *glasnost'* campaign indicated the centrality of new media and information technologies to the restructuring programme, thus implying a recognition of the cultural sphere as a revitalized site of production integral to future Soviet economic development. Thus the stagnation period was criticized for having restricted the functions of culture to those of leisure or amusement (passive phenomena), thereby suppressing culture's creative and active element. Past ideologues (most culpable was Zhdanov in the immediate post-war period) were accused of having promoted theories of cultural uniformity which had led to the emphasis in the 1970s on stability and incremental socio-cultural change. This, it was argued, had effectively held back cultural innovation even more than the bureaucratic administrative system had held back economic development, by producing a standardized consciousness and a utilitarian approach to cultural phenomena.

The antidote was revival of the voluntarist approach to culture. Above all, this entailed emphasizing that culture was not only determined by social factors but also *confronted* them. It thus allowed for an explanation of why the personality cult of Stalin had been resisted, and positive cultural values renewed, despite the onslaught on true Soviet values that the cult had signified. Secondly, there was a new recognition of the polyphony and dynamism of culture in the *perestroika* period. The villain of the piece was technocratism, which had devalued human input, turning Soviet citizens into cogs and culture into no more than a branch of the economy financed according to the residual principle. Finally, the cultural isolationism of the past system was criticized, since it had meant that the USSR had missed out on the 'all-human values and achievements of world literature and art', while false internationalism had achieved only a levelling-down of different national cultures.

The *perestroika* debate, however, did not fundamentally change the paradigm within which culture was interpreted; it simply switched the balance back to intervention rather than reflection. It called for the release of the creative potential of the individual, but this was to be channelled towards a specific task: the revitalization of Soviet society and its accelerated movement towards its (unaltered) predetermined goal. The modernity project was not dislodged, but new goals set by late modernity were recognized, and a plan devised to facilitate their achievement.

'Culturology' and Cultural Studies

There was thus not only considerable continuity within the official culturological project throughout the whole history of the Soviet Union, but also a significant degree of overlap between that project and Western understandings of culture; hence the post-Soviet 'return' to traditional—aesthetic rather than political—approaches represents a shift of emphasis (a significant one, to be sure) more than an out-and-out break with the past. Nor does the alternative understanding of 'culturology' which grew out of the Tartu school from the 1960s onwards represent anything like a radical break with either Soviet or Western conceptions. Mikhail Epstein, the foremost Russian theorist of the postmodern (site of cultural studies *par excellence*) has recently defined culturology's proper object of study as 'culture as the *integral* system of various cultures—national, professional, racial, sexual, etc.' Culturology itself

represents our culture's self-determination, including its ability for self-criticism, self-denial, and the formation of various countercultures. Indeed, countercultures become possible only within the context of a highly developed culture, as evidence of its ripeness and sacrificial fullness, like an individual who has reached the highest level of attainment and can do nothing more than give of him- or herself to others (a thought of Dostoevsky's).

This model contains enough to justify Epstein's assertion that 'The closest English equivalent of "culturology" is no doubt the term "cultural studies".' It allows for the study of previously un- or undervalued cultural products and identities, and requires that the relationship between the cultural and the political be examined to the extent that 'politics is one of the constitutive parts of culture and is itself subject to culturological analysis and justification'. But the Lotmanesque emphasis on wholeness, totality, and integration; the leading role granted to high culture as top-down producer, but never product, of counterculture (there is a certain inevitability about the parenthetical reference to Dostoevskii, the uniquely gifted individual offering us an insight into what it is to be a uniquely gifted, that is, culturally accomplished individual); and the insistence that reflection on culture is precisely self-reflection made possible by the existing achievements of high culture—all combine to produce a version of cultural studies that is almost entirely within the familiar paradigm. Hence 'to live within society *and* to be free of it—this is what culture is about. It enters the blood and bone of society, in order to liberate individuals from the constraints of their social existence.'[16] Ultimately, just as the Tartu school essays no Galilean heresy about the disposition of the major bodies in its cultural-semiotic universe, so Epsteinian culturology sets out to insert a wealth of new details within long-established outlines. It thereby, at the very moment it offers to embrace hitherto disparaged or disregarded cultural practices and phenomena, reinforces their exclusion from consideration as part of culture 'proper'.

This book seeks to adopt a position closer to Western-style cultural studies, or of culturology as characterized in a recent Russian higher-education textbook which explicitly eschews privileging of 'artistic culture' in favour of a broad, inclusive approach: 'the most important thing in culture is the study of the human being's active connections with the world, and these connections are revealed through study of **way of life, the social and cultural roles of the individual** [*lichnost'*], **cultural identity** [*identichnost'*], **types of culture**'.[17] In this respect the present volume is a companion to *Constructing Russian Culture in the Age of Revolution, 1881–1940* not only chronologically, but also methodologically—indeed, the two books arose from a single commission. They share a focus on 'various sites of cultural production . . . and numerous examples of cultural product . . . in order to establish links between aspects of Russian society that are not usually considered together'.[18] They also have in common an emphasis on the problematic relationship between cultural production and cultural consumption, and on the often fraught processes by which individual, class, and national identities have been imposed and negotiated. As a result we are less concerned to accept or reject established assessments of cultural value and hierarchical relations than to explore the development of concepts of cultural value, hierarchy, and identity. This is not, of course, a matter of saying that all cultural artefacts are equi-valent. Rather it is a matter of trying to offer an account of the complex processes which result in the articulation of particular value judgements, of trying to show how and why value comes to be ascribed. Our emphasis is relational, not relativistic.

16 See M. Epstein, 'Culture—Culturology —Transculture', in *After the Future: The Paradoxes of Postmodernism and Contemporary Russian Culture*, tr. and ed. A. Miller-Pogacar (Amherst, Mass., 1995), 284–8.
17 V. V. Agenosov et al., *Kul'turologiia: Teoriia i istoriia kul'tury* (Moscow, 1996), 5; emboldening in original. In the light of this characterization of culturology, the statement on the textbook's copyright and cataloguing page that it has been prepared 'on the basis of new state standards' cries out to be submitted to culturological analysis.
18 C. Kelly and D. Shepherd, 'Introduction: Literature, History, Culture', in Kelly and Shepherd (eds.), *Constructing Russian Culture in the Age of Revolution, 1881–1940* (Oxford, 1998), 4.

The thrust of this common approach is especially well illustrated by the discussion in the Epilogue of *Constructing Russian Culture* of the 'programmes for identity' elaborated and implemented in the first twenty years or so of the Soviet Union's existence, and in particular of the role played by the concept of *kul'turnost'* mentioned above. This depended to a large extent on retention of the market and aspects of consumer culture, notwithstanding the abundantly documented hostility towards commercialism which predated the Revolution, and which after it found expression in some left thinkers' hopes that the market would be abolished, and in protests against the New Economic Policy as a sell-out rather than a tactical retreat. Appeasement of consumer demand continued even after the end of NEP and the inauguration of central planning in 1928. The programme to inculcate *kul'turnost'*, for all that it changed subtly throughout the 1930s, fulfilled the constant function of legitimating the idea of a 'prosperous life' by equating material and cultural goods, polite behaviour, and the old idea of 'cultivation' as an intellectual entity. It endowed 'objects and symbols of private life' with overdetermined significations, and shaped the word and thought of those who sought to become cultured. Although, in Vera Dunham's now canonical discussion, *kul'turnost'* was associated with 'petit-bourgeois values', it in fact extended much further, acting as a promoter of social cohesion; this was reflected in, for example, Soviet intellectuals' idealization of the home, as well as in popular life. However, the campaign to instil *kul'turnost'* was typical of Soviet programmes for identity in its ultimate contradictoriness:

> Eventually, the very success of the *kul'turnost'* campaign was to prove its undoing. The idea of material acquisition as a perfectly justifiable reward for honest toil cut across a key tenet of Soviet labour ideology: that work should be its own reward. Progressively, the doctrine of *kul'turnost'*, supposedly both spiritual and material in character, undermined the disinterested, purely spiritual doctrine of labour as self-sacrifice that was propounded in other areas of Soviet propaganda.[19]

Production, consumption, cultural value, social identity, and, not least, tension between policy and its outcome: these are what provide, whether explicitly or, more often than not, implicitly, the framework for the discussion of post-Revolutionary Russian culture in this volume.

A few words about the extent of the volume's coverage are in order. It is not intended to be an encyclopaedia of Russian culture since 1917, offering blanket coverage of every area that might be described as 'culture'. Some areas of Russian life—for example, the

19 See C. Kelly and V. Volkov, 'Directed Desires: *Kul'turnost'* and Consumption', in Kelly and Shepherd (eds.), *Constructing Russian Culture*, 291–313 (312). See also V. Dunham, *In Stalin's Time: Middleclass Values in Soviet Fiction* (London, 1976; repr. Cambridge 1979).

world of high politics—concern us very little, partly because such extensive analyses of them are available elsewhere, and partly because of our ambition to provide a more bottom-up account. Conversely, coverage has been constrained by the low availability of substantial secondary studies in some key areas, such as literary sociology, working-class life between 1930 and 1991, or the culture of the Russian emigration. Finally, the existence of numerous excellent studies of popular culture in the Soviet period, and the substantial Epilogue devoted to the period 1917–1940 in *Constructing Russian Culture*, justify, we believe, the brief treatment of, or absence of reference to, *inter alia*, public festivities and street festivals, architecture, and popular music. Reference is made at appropriate points to sources that will enable these gaps to be filled. The book that has emerged is intended, in time-honoured scholarly tradition, as much to point the direction of future research as to summarize existing scholarship, to raise questions as well as to answer them. We hope, as much as anything else, to stimulate new investigations into areas such as attitudes to sexuality and the body, women's history, or popular attitudes to authority.

The book is divided into five parts, each of which in turn is made up of varying numbers of chapters. The principle of division is thematic rather than chronological, since this was deemed more appropriate to the theoretical and methodological aims pursued. Within chapters, of course, chronology does play an important part in the organization of material, although exemplification takes priority over exhaustiveness: not all chapters cover the full span from 1917 to the present, and particular periods do not receive equal treatment in the discussion of different topics. The year of Stalin's death, 1953, does feature repeatedly as an end- and starting-point: this reflects less a conventional belief in the capacity of key political events to have immediate and unmediated cultural effects than a concern with what might be called the 'symbolic' import of the end of the Stalin era, and with the subsequent attempts to understand not only that era's connections with the periods preceding and following it, but also the true nature of its relationship with the personality whose name it bears.

Chapters are sufficiently self-contained to be read in isolation when desired, although their ordering, like the succession of parts, is designed to maximize their inter-illumination. The focus of Part I might seem to confirm the traditional primacy of literary culture, but in fact the intention is to demonstrate from the outset that literaturo-centric approaches have established literature's primacy in part by leaving out of consideration some of the most problematic aspects of the 'literary process', and also to displace literature from the centre of attention. Part II sees a gradual move away from the verbal text with its chapters on theatre (where performance rather than text is emphasized), music, the visual arts, and the political poster; in all cases, however, assumptions about the unmediated relationship between policy and practice continue to be interrogated. Part III deals with cultural forms new to the twentieth century—cinema, radio, and television—as well as with the newspapers and advertising whose functions have affected and been affected by those new forms; it ends with an overview of the pervasiveness throughout post-Stalinist 'high culture' of the 'commercialism' usually seen as the province of the new forms. In Part IV the emphasis shifts to explicit consideration of the negotiation of identities, and in particular of three key sites of individual and institutional opposition to and accommodation with the Soviet regime: populism, religion (in particular Russian Orthodoxy), and emigration. Issues of identity loom equally large in Part V, where the history of sexuality after the Revolution is presented as a further illustration of the conflicts and contradictions of the period, rather than of a putative transition to a society in which personal identity was meekly subject to manipulation from above. The chapter dealing with the representation of gender roles in post-Stalin cinema continues this theme by illustrating how a cultural form perceived by the Soviet leadership as its most powerful tool of identity-formation was no less capable of undermining official precepts. Finally, the discussion of youth culture shows how this concept has now been all but abandoned in favour of a consideration of youth cultural practice as the meeting of two moments: youth's positioning in discourse, and youthful negotiations of this positioning, the creation and reworking of identities.

The overall arrangement of the volume thus mimics the shift in the traditional understanding of the relationship between the central and the marginal, the need for which is one of its theoretical premisses. The current and potential contours of this changing relationship within cultural practice receive brief consideration in the Conclusion, which examines, first, the senses of 'Russianness' which have begun to emerge since the collapse of the Soviet Union in 1991, and, second, the prominence in Russia of postmodernism, a term used to denote not only the instability within, and constant reconfiguration of, contemporary cultural practice, but also a methodological framework within which the diversity and contradictoriness of that more or less scandalous practice can be accounted for.

Finally, although a project of this kind is something relatively new to study of Russia (as the perplexed or indignant reactions of some colleagues, particularly literary specialists, has confirmed for us), we would not wish to overstate the novelty of the material contained in this volume. As the annotations to the text make abundantly clear, all of us are much indebted, for material and methodology alike, to such pioneers as Vera Dunham, Laura Engelstein, Sheila Fitzpatrick, Richard Stites, Denise Youngblood, and many others whose work has done so much to bring about significant shifts in our ways of talking about Russian culture. Nor, notwithstanding this volume's overall pursuit of a cultural studies project, would we wish to claim for it the kind of unity or unanimity in diversity which was once proclaimed a hallmark of Soviet culture and nationhood. A book distinguished by such a large number of contributors is bound to contain differences of style, emphasis, methodology, and, not least, politics. Some contributors find themselves here in company different from that which they are accustomed to keeping. But that, and the possible accompanying tensions, are, of course, entirely within the spirit of cultural studies itself; and for the editors to have attempted a top-down elision of differences would have meant traducing that spirit.

The Politics of Literature

'Revolutionary' Models for High Literature: Resisting Poetics

PETER KENEZ

DAVID SHEPHERD

Bolshevik Views of Culture: Modernization and Patronage

Lenin and his comrades were great modernizers. As Marxists they took it for granted that all societies go through the same well-established stages of social development, and that according to this scheme Russia was backward. They had little respect for or interest in traditional Russian culture; for them the particular customs of the Russian peasantry were simply manifestations of backwardness. For Bolshevik theorists, leading a revolution in the most backward major country in Europe presented problems. They explained the embarrassing fact (for a Marxist) that the revolution took place first in a country where capitalism had hardly developed, by means of the theory of the weakest link in the chain of imperialism. That is, as they saw it, the task of the Russian revolutionaries was merely to break the chain of imperialism; they confidently expected that once that happened the entire rotten capitalist system would unravel.

On the one hand, instinctive revolutionaries as they were, the Leninists could not miss the chance offered by the confusion that followed the collapse of the Romanov monarchy, but on the other, they were more bothered by the Menshevik criticism that Russia was not ready for a socialist revolution than they were themselves willing to admit. The solution in principle was simple. The revolutionaries, while fighting their enemies, had to accomplish what capitalism had failed to do: to raise the cultural level of the people to rival that of Western Europeans. Proletarian Russia had to go through a cultural revolution. Lenin, who had paid little attention to popular education before 1917, believing that this issue was not a proper concern for Bolsheviks, once in power took an altogether different view. During the last years of his life, the necessity of raising the cultural level of the peoples of the new socialist state became a significant motif in his writings. He wrote:

Our opponents told us repeatedly that we were rash in undertaking to implant socialism in an insufficiently cultured country. They base themselves on theory (the theory of all pedants) in saying that we started at the wrong end. In our country the political and social upheaval turned out to be a precondition for that cultural revolution that is ahead of us at the moment. This cultural revolution will be sufficient to make our country into a fully socialist one. But it presents immense difficulties in purely cultural terms (for we are illiterate) and also in a material sense (for us to become cultured it is necessary to have a certain material base).

A few days later he addressed again the same issue in connection with his reading of Sukhanov's work on the Revolution:

If for the creation of socialism it is necessary to attain a certain level of culture (though no one can say exactly what that level is) why can we not start by acquiring with revolutionary means the preconditions of this cultural level and then on the basis of worker-peasant power and Soviet system proceed to overtake other nations?[1]

One gets the impression that Lenin would have preferred to lead a nation in Western Europe where there was only political power to be conquered. Lenin, like so many members of the Russian intelligentsia, was ambivalent about his Russian heritage. On the one hand he never properly understood or felt at home in Western Europe; on the other he admired values that he associated with the advanced, industrialized countries. This most Russian person had no respect for Russian ways and wanted to Europeanize Russia, but by carrying out his revolution and cutting his country off from the West, he started it on a separate road, and as time went on the distance between it and the West widened. With considerable insight and yet contrary to Marxist logic, he claimed that precisely because the bourgeoisie created a higher level of civilization, the conquest of political power would prove more difficult in Western Europe.

When Lenin wrote about culture he had in mind not just high culture or its low, or popular, antipode, but also technical civilization, material achievements. This understanding was not idiosyncratic, but was shared by most of the Russian intelligentsia. In this sense electrification, an efficient postal system, trains running on time, good roads, personal hygiene, and so on were obviously aspects of culture. Culture also meant an internalization of the industrial discipline that

1 V. I. Lenin, 'O kooperatsii', in *Polnoe sobranie sochinenii*, 5th edn., xlv (Moscow, 1970), 376–7.

Lenin very much admired in the West, and especially in the United States. By contrast, Lenin associated with backward Russia the opposite of discipline, spontaneity (*stikhiinost'*), and greatly distrusted it. For the Bolsheviks bringing education to the masses and acquainting them with the achievements of Western civilization were inseparable.

The goal was to remake society and in the process remake humanity. People had to be made to understand the correctness of Bolshevik views; they had to become workers and fighters for the socialist cause. The primary means for achieving these goals were education, enlightenment, and culture. Whatever the reasoning, the Bolsheviks, given the extraordinarily harsh circumstances in which they had to operate, became remarkably interested in and generous sponsors of 'culture'.

The story of this sponsorship has been told more than once, and while each telling has its own nuances, the story itself is remarkably stable. It charts the successive stages of the process by which the Communist Party arrogated to itself exclusive jurisdiction over the theory and practice of culture, annihilating opposition, driving it underground or into exile, to the point where within the Soviet Union itself barely a whisper of protest could be heard to challenge the deafening, preposterous assertions of Soviet culture's superiority. And it is a story with a moral, warning against the politicization of an essentially apolitical, autonomous sphere of human activity. The history of Soviet culture stands, for many, as proof that the phrase 'cultural politics' is not an acceptable collocation.

It is difficult, not to say irresponsible, to question most aspects of this story: to suggest that things were not always quite what they appeared to be in the Soviet period is to seem to espouse not so much the whimsical elusiveness of a Gogolian narrator as the altogether more perverse posturings of a Baudrillard seeking, both before and after the event, to question the reality of the Gulf War.[2] If the narrative that follows in this chapter is revisionist, then it is so emphatically not in the sense that it seeks to deny, or to put a positive gloss on, the most reprehensible acts and utterances of the Soviet leadership and its accomplices. But in places it does seek to revise, or to question, certain abiding assumptions about the success of the top-down, *dirigiste* Soviet approach to cultural theory and practice, arguing not only that the sites of resistance to this approach were more varied and less marginal than is often acknowledged, but also that the theory and practice themselves, for all their apparent self-assurance, were fraught with contradictions more interesting than those that are usually spoken of, and more instructive than many of the lessons traditionally drawn from the Soviet experience. If it is true that, as Richard Stites contends, 'Cultural politics, which exists always and

2 For an account and critique of Baudrillard's arguments, see C. Norris, *Uncritical Theory: Postmodernism, Intellectuals and the Gulf War* (London, 1992), 11–31.

everywhere in attenuated or unconscious forms, became for [the Bolsheviks] a reified agenda',[3] then it is important that a critique of this reification should not be founded upon equally reified notions of culture.

If scholarship on Russian literature continues to be overwhelmingly based on the conviction that the value and quality of the greatest works are in inverse proportion to the obtrusiveness of their conditions of production, one need look no further for an explanation of this than the shabby history of Soviet literary institutions. Nothing here, it would seem, conforms to our sense of what is normal or natural either in the identity which was stamped on to literature, or in the identities that literature was called upon to help shape. Our reaction to what was done to and in the name of Soviet literature might be that anticipated by Lenin in 1905:

Emerging from the captivity of the feudal censorship, we have no desire to become, and shall not become, prisoners of bourgeois-shopkeeper literary relations. We want to establish, and we shall establish, a free press, free not simply from the police, but also from capital, from careerism, and what is more, free from bourgeois-anarchist individualism.

These last words may sound paradoxical, or an affront to the reader. What! some intellectual, an ardent champion of liberty, may shout. What, you want to impose collective control on such a delicate, individual matter as literary work! You want workmen to decide questions of science, philosophy or aesthetics, by a majority of votes! You deny the absolute freedom of absolutely individual ideological work!

Calm yourselves, gentlemen! First of all, we are discussing party literature and its subordination to party control. Everyone is free to write and say whatever he likes, without any restrictions.[4]

We will later, in Ch. 10, see how this document, with its strict delimitation of 'freedom of criticism', became a keystone of subsequent Soviet theory and practice of the media, something that will reinforce the scepticism that may be induced by the final sentence quoted here. Moreover, Lenin's failure, within even a text as brief as this one, to maintain a rigorous distinction between party literature, understood as straightforward political journalism and propaganda, and literature, understood as novels and other fictional products of 'individual ideological work', strengthens the temptation to read the document as a blueprint for the eventual collapsing of this distinction in socialist realism, as of course does its status within Soviet literary theory as *ex post facto* justification for the prominence within socialist realism of Party-mindedness (*partiinost'*).

However, precisely because such a straight line came to be drawn in Soviet accounts, we would do well not to succumb to their beguiling

3 R. Stites, *Russian Popular Culture: Entertainment and Society since 1900* (Cambridge, 1992), 38.
4 Lenin, 'Party Organisation and Party Literature', in C. Vaughan James, *Soviet Socialist Realism: Origins and Theory* (London, 1973), 104–5.

appeal, condemning cynicism where they praised far-sightedness. First, Lenin's blurring of the generic and functional distinctions between publicistic writing and *belles-lettres* may be read as just one more expression (an unusually stark one, it must be acknowledged) of the dominant nineteenth-century view of literature as inconceivable without reference to its overdetermined status as medium of social critique. Second, the fact that the literary institutions installed in the Soviet Union by the 1930s were, to put it mildly, scarcely free of 'careerism', or indeed of 'capital', does not necessarily diminish the force of Lenin's critique of pre-Revolutionary institutions. When he writes 'One cannot live in a society and be free from society. The freedom of the bourgeois writer, artist or actress is simply masked (or hypocritically masked) dependence on the money-bag, on corruption, on prostitution',[5] Lenin may undercut his own argument with rhetorical overkill, but he makes a point about the existence of connections between economies of publishing and economies of literary value which is pertinent for pre- and post-Revolutionary periods alike.[6] Finally, this text, exemplifying both the theory and, we must assume, the practice of 'party literature', bears the stamp of a certain 'individual ideological work'. There is no mistaking the man or the style. The text is utterly characteristic of Lenin, exemplifying that combination of 'on the one hand, a tone of irony and mockery, and, on the other, a tone of categorical, energetic affirmation' identified by Boris Eikhenbaum as a constant of his language.[7] It is an irony that would not have been lost on Lenin himself that his language should have attracted the attention of Formalist critics whose principal concern, we should recall, was to define the distinctiveness of the literary, of *literaturnost*'.[8]

If Lenin's article is a founding text of Soviet cultural politics, then it is not only by virtue of its anticipation of the theory and practice of Soviet literature, but also by virtue of its internal contradictions, its unwitting promotion of categories which it seeks to repress. In this it shares the qualities identified by Lenin in his articles on Tolstoi, particularly the notorious piece in which he describes the writer as a mirror of the Russian Revolution. The usual dismissal of Lenin's description of Tolstoi as a vulgarizing misappropriation of the work of a writer whose anti-revolutionary views were beyond any doubt is questioned by Pierre Macherey's masterly analysis of these articles. Macherey contends that, according to Lenin's conception 'The work is perhaps a mirror precisely because it registers the partiality of its own reflections,' and that 'there is a conflict within the text between the text and its ideological content', so that Tolstoi's work 'reveals both the contradictions of his age and the deficiencies involved in his

5 Ibid. 105.
6 Cf. the discussion of late 19th-c. literary culture's silence on its 'own involvement with the commercial culture that it critiqued', in S. Smith and C. Kelly, 'Commercial Culture and Consumerism', in Kelly and D. Shepherd (eds.), *Constructing Russian Culture in the Age of Revolution, 1881–1940* (Oxford, 1998), 139–44 (139).
7 B. Eikhenbaum, 'Osnovnye stilevye tendentsii v rechi Lenina', *Lef*, 1 (1924), 58. The same issue also contained articles on Lenin's language by Shklovskii and Tomashevskii.
8 On the resonance and significance of this category, see N. Cornwell and F. Wigzell, '*Literaturnost*': Literature and the Market-place', in Kelly and Shepherd (eds.), *Constructing Russian Culture*, 37–49.

partial view of those contradictions.'[9] In the same way Lenin's 1905 article might be said to mirror the contradictory impulses of subsequent literary theories (both official and unofficial) which pretended to totality of comprehension, but in proclaiming this laid bare the gaps and *non-dits* of that comprehension. Analysing the concern with 'modern high culture' of the intelligentsia in 'backward or underdeveloped countries', David Joravsky has postulated the presence of three recurrent and contrarily directed impulses, towards prophecy, political praxis, and professionalization. In post-1917 Russia, 'The most explosive friction, as it turned out, was *within* the Communist mentality, where all three trends contended with each other as inarticulate self-contradictions, which found expression, as they were brought toward conscious expression, in delusions, anger, even violence.'[10]

It is the exploration of some of these gaps, *non-dits*, and self-contradictions that will be our principal concern in what follows. There already exist so many histories of Soviet literature in the period 1921–53 that there is no need for yet another attempt at an exhaustive roll-call of the heroes and villains, high points and low points, expressions of delusion, anger, and violence which marked the Soviet state's increasingly brutal resistance to poetic tradition and traditional poetics. The constraints on that resistance, from both within and without, require attention—not so that it can be in any way downplayed or justified, but so that it can be better understood.

NEP: Economic and Cultural Diversity?

The 'tactical' return to market economics that was the New Economic Policy transformed the life of the country and made post-Civil War reconstruction possible. It also had far-reaching ideological implications: the revolutionary government now accepted that socialism would be built gradually. But economic liberalization was not accompanied by political reforms designed to make possible greater openness in discussing the social and political problems that preceded and accompanied that liberalization. The Bolsheviks gave economic concessions because they believed that they had no alternative. In order to feed the population, restrictions on peasants marketing their produce had to be loosened, but there was no comparable pressure for political reforms or for extending intellectual freedom. The end of the Civil War did not allay the fears of the new rulers. In their view the time was not propitious for broadening the public sphere; on the contrary, the moment was particularly dangerous. On the one hand, they had to watch their enemies growing stronger, and on the other

9 P. Macherey, *A Theory of Literary Production*, tr. G. Wall (London, 1978), 121–2, 124, 115.
10 D. Joravsky, 'Cultural Revolution and the Fortress Mentality', in A. Gleason, P. Kenez, and R. Stites (eds.), *Bolshevik Culture: Experiment and Order in the Russian Revolution* (Bloomington, Ind., 1985), 97.

they feared that the best activists would now become disenchanted. To make matters worse, revival of the economy required a return to principles of financial orthodoxy. Expenditure had to be cut, and consequently subsidies for cultural work, and for propaganda and indoctrination, had to be seriously curtailed. In the new economic environment there was no longer scope for free distribution of books and newspapers. The government, which had contributed a great deal to the literacy drive in the preceding years, now attempted to shift the burden on to society. Hundreds of literacy schools had to be closed down.[11]

The principles of NEP were introduced in publishing, but only with some delay. The leaders understood that this industry was not exactly like others, and that it required careful oversight; they were determined to protect themselves from ideological and political damage. Only in August 1921 did the Moscow city Soviet rescind its previous municipalization order, allowing private publishing houses to be licensed once again. At the same time, however, the Politburo ordered agencies of state control to follow carefully what was printed and distributed.[12] The Bolsheviks sought to prevent the spread of religious literature, pornography, and 'counterrevolutionary works'. In the political climate of 1921 they considered the writings of Socialist Revolutionaries to represent the greatest threat, and therefore their fellow socialists were most likely to suffer the effects of censorship.

Paradoxically, however, the cultural activities of the élite were less directly touched than those of the masses. The Bolsheviks understood that what influenced the political outlook of the masses was far more significant than writings aimed at an élite audience. They had little respect for popular culture, believing that people should read not what interested them, but what was good for them. In Richard Stites's words, 'It was only when the Bolsheviks came to power that state authorities took upon themselves the onerous and arrogant task of regulating the people's tastes in a serious way.'[13] As a consequence the type of literature that was most popular in tsarist Russia—*lubki*, lives of saints, stories about bandits—almost disappeared. It is most likely that in spite of the painfully slow spread of literacy, the peasants, the majority of Russians, actually read less than they had before the Revolution.

The authorities ensured that libraries catering to the masses were purged of what might have appeared ideologically dubious. Narkompros, the People's Commissariat for Enlightenment, periodically issued circulars requiring the purging of village libraries and book collections kept by the cultural departments of trade unions. These lists were extraordinarily comprehensive. They included Plato and Kant, but also, absurdly, some works by Lenin that had appeared

11 See P. Kenez, *The Birth of the Propaganda State* (Cambridge, 1985), 146.
12 See A. Nazarov, *Oktiabr' i kniga* (Moscow, 1968), 234–5.
13 R. Stites, *Russian Popular Culture: Entertainment and Society since 1900* (Cambridge, 1992), 36.

under a pseudonym, 'outdated' agitational pamphlets, adventure stories, and lives of saints.[14]

Yet for all their determined pursuit of continuity in the policing of the public sphere, justification of this continued censorship was problematic for the Bolshevik leaders following the end of the Civil War, when the literary and theatrical censorship bodies Glavlit and Glavrepertkom were established (in 1922 and 1923 respectively). There were considerable differences among the leaders; some were more comfortable with the present situation than others. Lenin and his ideological comrades proudly claimed censorship as a legitimate weapon in class struggle. Trotskii's position was close to Lenin's. He had supported censorship in 1918 as a temporary imperative, and now advanced new arguments. In 1922 in his reply to Kautskii's criticism of the Red terror and the suppression of newspapers, he maintained that it was wrong to equate bourgeois and communist suppression of the press, for the bourgeoisie was a dying class and was merely attempting to retard history, whereas Bolshevik suppression simply accelerated the historical process.[15] On another occasion, in a less polemical vein, Trotskii expressed himself more moderately:

If the Revolution has the right to destroy bridges and art monuments whenever necessary, it will stop still less from laying its hand on any tendency in art, which, no matter how great its achievement in form, threatens to dis-integrate the revolutionary environment or to arouse the internal forces of the revolution, that is the proletariat, the peasantry and the intelligentsia, to a hostile opposition to one another. Our standard is clearly political, imperat-ive and intolerant. But for this very reason, its must define the limits of its activity clearly. For a more precise expression of my meaning, I will say: we ought to have a watchful revolutionary censorship, and a broad and flexible policy in the field of art, free from petty partisan maliciousness.[16]

By contrast other leading figures, such as Lunacharskii, evidently felt uncomfortable in the new and unaccustomed role of censor. The Commissar of Enlightenment wrote in a most interesting article of 1921:

The person who tells us that censorship is necessary even when it prevents the publication of great works of art when these hide obvious counter-revolution, is correct. So is the one who says that we must choose, and we must give only third, or fourth, priority to undoubtedly necessary works in comparison with books for which we have the greatest need. But the person who says 'Down with all those prejudices about the freedom of expression. State leadership in literature corresponds to our new, communist order. Censorship is not a terrible component of our time of transition, but a regu-lar part of socialist life', the person who draws the conclusion that criticism should be turned into some kind of denunciation and that artistic work

14 See Kenez, The Birth, 248–9.
15 The Writings of Leon Trotsky, ed. I. Howe (New York, 1963), 152.
16 L. Trotsky, Literature and Revolution (London, 1991), 248.

should be turned into primitive, revolutionary slogans, that person only shows that under the communist exterior, if you scratch him a little, you will actually discover 'Derzhimorda' [Shut-yer-gob].[17]

Lunacharskii here came as close to an explicit defence of the freedom of expression as any Bolshevik leader was to come in the early 1920s. And under his ultimate authority, the state publishing house Gosizdat (which was part of Narkompros) rejected few of the manuscripts submitted for inspection by the private publishing houses over which it had supervisory authority. In Petrograd, for example, private publishers submitted 190 manuscripts in the course of the first three months of 1922, of which only ten were rejected; in Moscow Gosizdat disallowed thirty-one out of 813 manuscripts.[18] Although private publishing houses printed only a small and ever-declining share of the total output of books during the 1920s, they nevertheless made a contribution to the variety available for the Soviet reader, bringing out a considerable portion of books on philosophy and psychology, as well as translations and *belles-lettres*.

The small number of rejections might give a misguided impression about the laxity of censorship, for there is no way to count the number of authors who decided not to submit their works in anticipation of rejection. That said, during the early stages of NEP many authors whose pro-Soviet credentials were less than impeccable, such as Dmitrii Merezhkovskii, Nikolai Berdiaev, S. L. Frank, and N. O. Losskii, were published in Soviet Russia. And while freedom of expression was by no stretch of the imagination total during NEP, the years from 1921 to 1928 are by common consent regarded as the period in which an approximation of such freedom was enjoyed. Anthony Kemp-Welch provides a succinct expression of this view:

NEP permitted considerable freedom to Russia's brilliant élites, which led the world in many areas of intellectual endeavour. Through their pioneering work, new disciplines appeared: developmental economics, peasant studies, the sociology of law, and new branches of educational psychology. Institutes such as the Communist Academy and its numerous publications built up a body of original thought whose implications are not yet exhausted in our day. . . . Cultural experiment was equally exuberant—constructivism, suprematism, utopian architecture and innovative theatre—offering an artistic counterpart to the political revolution. But the position of the intelligentsia as a whole was uncertain. On the one hand, it was officially encouraged as an essential agency on the path to socialism. . . . On the other hand, the party held over it the threat, implicit at first, but becoming more overt as the decade proceeded, of eventual dispossession.[19]

This accurate account of the intellectual and cultural practice of the NEP period also brings into focus the difficult question of the

17 A. Lunacharskii, 'Svoboda knigi i revoliutsiia', *Pechat' i revoliutsiia*, 1 (1921), 8.
18 See N. L. Meshcheriakov, 'O rabote chastnykh izdatel'stv', *Pechat' i revoliutsiia*, 1 (1922), 128–34.
19 A. Kemp-Welch, *Stalin and the Literary Intelligentsia, 1928–39* (Basingstoke, 1991), 34–5.

nature of the relationship between the richness of that practice and the political and economic circumstances of NEP. If the threat of 'dispossession' was one that the Party could realistically make throughout the period, then clearly it was justifiably confident of both its right and its capacity to impose or withhold invigilation and constraint. In this case the Party, ironically, deserves much of the credit for the flourishing practice of the NEP period—the 'counterpart' to its political project. Even if the threat of dispossession was more perceived than real, given the existence of well-documented disagreement within the Party on such matters as censorship, and the difficulty of imposing institutional control throughout the differentiated, unstable society of NEP, the same causal relationship seems to obtain: skilful masking of the moments when 'oversight' signified not surveillance, but its absence, allowed the Party to exploit fear of dispossession as a significant and even positive force driving intellectual and cultural activity (witness the frequent dramatization in 1920s literature of the traditional intelligentsia's interrogation at the hands of both opponents and its own reflexive proclivities). These two alternative interpretations of NEP culture are in fact both predicated on an opposition between control (residing with Party or state institutions) and freedom (understood as negotiation or evasion, licensed or unlicensed, of this control). They leave at best implicit, at worst out of the reckoning, the controls and constraints exercised by the market forces of NEP which, as the case of private publishers suggests, were not necessarily synchronized with those of Party and state. Also bracketed out are the forces exerted by individuals or organizations whose own relationship with Party and state was oblique or tense. Finally, they leave insufficient space for the possibility that the Party should not be given exclusive credit for fostering the sense of its capacity to dispossess: that sense was surely the product of processes far more complex than top-down directives evincing greater or lesser repressive intent.

If, as Richard Stites argues, 'Just as NEP was an economic hybrid, so the popular cultural scene was one of uncertainty, unclarity, and ambivalence',[20] then the same can largely be said of the scene of high literature—without, however, assuming that the complexities of that scene were a direct, unmediated consequence of the complexities of NEP. Perhaps the greatest importance of NEP is that it offers a concentrated example of the myriad forms of mediation which have to be taken into account in discussing the culture of any period, whether in Russia or elsewhere. It may not be possible to give an exhaustive and coherent account of these forms of mediation and their effects, but it is important not to ignore them or attempt to elide them from our discussions. To do that would be to repeat the sins of omission of much

20 Stites, *Russian Popular Culture*, 61.

of the 1920s debate about literature, which, as we will now see, was vitiated by its fetishizing of the immediate.

Class, Culture, and the 'Will to Victory'

The tendency for this fetishizing of the immediate to override ac-knowledgement of the importance of mediation is nowhere clearer than in the theory and practice of the various proletarian writers' movements. A fine example is G. Lelevich's theoretical introduction to an upbeat assessment of the state of proletarian literature in 1924:

The work of art acts principally on the feelings of the reader, viewer, or listener, in precisely the same way as a scientific work acts principally on the intellect [*myshlenie*]. Art organizes the feelings, organizes the psyche, system-atizes them at the same time as science systematizes thoughts.

. . . In our society both the artist's sense of the world and the demands of the reader are immediately [*neposredstvenno*] conditioned by the various class character of the former and the latter. The artist creates (consciously or unconsciously—it makes no difference) in accordance with his class nature, under pressure (whether conscious or unconscious—it makes no difference) from his class-specific audience. These two moments determine both the character of the work, and the character of that work's effect on the reader, and the character of the system into which the work organizes the feelings of its audience.

Each social class, as it develops historically, gradually achieves mastery over art, this powerful weapon of class struggle. . . . This all takes place slowly, gradually, step by step, often insufficiently consciously, occurring in a way instinctively, spontaneously [*stikhiino*], of its own accord [*samotekom*], but it is nevertheless an historical law whose effect no class has yet avoided.[21]

Lelevich's vulgar-Marxist view of the directly defining role of class, sovereign over any other conscious or unconscious impulse or inten-tion, means that even as he outlines a complex, multi-dimensional model of the relationship between literary creation and reception he reduces it to a single dimension. The orientation of the artist and of the work towards the anticipated response of its audience, and the consequent potential for contradiction and conflict, are cancelled out by the systematic disposition of 'feelings' to which consumption of the work leads with apparent inevitability.

Moreover, in this Plekhanovist scheme of things it becomes difficult to distinguish between cause and effect. Does the hegemony of a given social class lead to the flowering of art which gives immedi-ate and organized expression to that class's feelings, or does art's immediate organization of feelings in its readership produce and underwrite the hegemony of that class? The obvious answer to this

21 G. Lelevich, 'Puti proletarskoi literatury', *Oktiabr'*, 1 (1924), 179–80.

question would be that the process was a dialectical one, but there is little sign of dialectical thinking in Lelevich's article, where one would be hard pressed to distinguish between thesis and antithesis in a model of ill-differentiated artistic production and consumption that is all synthesis.

This is in large measure a consequence of the overinvestment in the organizational capacities of art which Lelevich, speaking here on behalf of the Moscow Association of Proletarian Writers (MAPP), shares with Aleksandr Bogdanov, the founder of the movement from which MAPP sought to differentiate itself, Proletkul't. To some extent that differentiation is achieved by Lelevich's distinction between the emotions and the intellect as the respective provinces of art and science. For Bogdanov, art was able to affect both cognition and emotion, and as such was 'the most powerful weapon for the organization of collective forces, and, in a class society, of class forces'.[22] The power granted to art by Bogdanov is extraordinary; it is little wonder that Lenin and the Party should have looked with such suspicion on a movement which allied robust insistence on its autonomy from Party and state control to a transformative and organizational mission difficult to distinguish from that of the Party.[23] But if by 1924 Proletkul't, weakened by in-fighting as well as by its absorption into Narkompros in 1920, was eclipsed by MAPP and other proletarian writers' organizations, its thinking, notwithstanding apparent modulations such as Lelevich's, was still shaping the agenda for those organizations.

This agenda was pithily characterized in 1920 by Nikolai Chuzhak, a prominent theorist of the left-art movement, as a 'will to victory'.[24] The problem for the theorists of proletarian culture was that this will, ostensibly the driving force behind their endeavours to build a distinctive proletarian culture, was prone to be translated into wishful thinking about victory already attained or about to be achieved, because guaranteed by the teleology of history. At the risk of seeming to elide differences and mediations between proletarian theory and practice, we may identify this translation in the paradigmatic proletarian 'iron-psalm' (*zhelezopsalm*) 'We Grow out of Iron' by Aleksei Gastev, in which the poet describes his merger with the metal construction of his factory:

В жилы льется новая, железная кровь.
Я вырос еще.
У меня самого вырастают стальные плечи и безмерно сильные руки. Я слился с железом постройки.
Поднялся.
Выпираю плечами стропила, верхние балки, крышу.

22 A. Bogdanov, 'Proletariat i iskusstvo', in N. L. Brodskii (ed.), *Literaturnye manifesty*, i. *Ot simvolizma k Oktiabriu. Sbornik materialov* (Moscow, 1929; repr. Munich, 1969), 130.
23 See Lenin, 'On Proletarian Culture', and 'On the Proletkults (Letter from the Central Committee, R. C. P.)', in James, *Soviet Socialist Realism*, 112–15; see also L. Mally, *Culture of the Future: The Proletkult Movement in Revolutionary Russia* (Berkeley and Los Angeles, 1990), pp. xviii, xxviii.
24 N. F. Chuzhak, 'Proletarskaia kul'tura', in *K dialektike iskusstva: Ot realizma do iskusstva, kak odnoi iz proizvodstvennykh form. Teoretichéski-polemicheskie stat'i* (Chita, 1921), 55.

Ноги мои еще на земле, но голова выше здания.

Я еще задыхаюсь от этих нечеловеческих усилий, а уже кричу:

—Слова прошу, товарищи, слова!

Железное эхо покрыло мои слова, вся постройка дрожит нетерпением. А я поднялся еще выше, я уже наравне с трубами.

И не рассказ, не речь, а только одно мое железное я прокричу:

«Победим мы!»

[New iron blood pours into my veins.
And I'm growing taller.
Steel shoulders and immeasurably strong arms grow out from me. I merge with the building's iron.
Then I stretch myself.
With my shoulders I push out the rafters, the highest girders and the roof.
My feet are still on the ground, but my head is above the building.
I'm out of breath from this superhuman effort, but I'm already shouting:
'Let me speak, Comrades! Let me speak!'
The iron echo has drowned my words; the whole structure is trembling with impatience. And I've risen still higher, I'm on a level with the smokestacks.
And I'm going to shout—not a story, not a speech, but one single iron phrase:
'The victory will be ours!']²⁵

This movement of fusion or synthesis between poet and factory mimics (or rather, given that the poem was composed in 1914 and published in 1918, anticipates) the aporetic synthesis within proletarian theory whereby the concrete conditions of class-specific being as organizer of class-specific artistic activity (the poet 'grows out of iron') become indistinguishable from class-specific artistic activity as organizer of class-specific being. The impasse to which this leads is figured in the poet's climactic pronouncement, which is neither a story nor a speech, but a bald affirmation of the 'will to victory' whose 'iron echo' is somewhat hollow.

Further, the tension resulting from Gastev's combination of the organicist trope of growth with the metonym of proletarian being-as-labour, iron, makes explicit another major problematic of the whole proletarian episode, the use of the 'classical heritage'. This is notwithstanding Gastev's own declared conviction that the form of proletarian art should be every bit as revolutionary as its content, something which set him apart from the view with which the majority of proletarian writers associated themselves, or were associated by others.²⁶ This position was outlined by Bogdanov in 1917 in the founding declaration of Proletkul't principles:

25 A. Gastev, 'My rastem iz zheleza', Russian text and translation (here modified slightly) in V. Markov and M. Sparks (eds.), *Modern Russian Poetry* ([London], 1966), 698–9.
26 See K. Johansson, *Aleksej Gastev: Proletarian Bard of the Machine Age* (Stockholm, 1983), 69–70.

The treasures of the old art should not be received passively. If they were they would educate the working class in the spirit of the culture of the dominant classes, and thus in a spirit of subordination to the structures of life created by those classes. The proletariat must take the treasures of the old art in a critical light, in their new interpretation revealing their hidden collective foundations and their organizational meaning. In this way they will form a valuable inheritance for the proletariat, a weapon in its struggle against the very old world which produced them . . .[27]

This positive attitude towards the literature of the past has traditionally been seen, in Western scholarship, as a rare saving grace in a proletarian project otherwise vitiated by its attachment to political theory in general and communist ideology in particular. For contemporary critics the matter was more controversial. An early reviewer of the book in which Gastev's 'We Grow' was published expressed disquiet at the disparity between the originality of its content and the derivativeness of its form, citing its Whitmanesque qualities.[28] Evgenii Zamiatin, deliberately and notoriously 'heretical' in his theory and practice, made Gastev's emphasis on the collective and on Taylorist theories of labour a target of his dystopian novel *We*, and dismissed all proletarian writing as 'the most revolutionary content and the most reactionary form'.[29] In this Zamiatin, no friend of the left-art movement, nevertheless echoed its strident opposition to proletarian movements, an opposition born of repressed awareness of shared origins in the theories of Bogdanov, and shared goals in the determination to ensure that art played a role in the transformation of life. On this point the left artists were more consistent than the proletarian writers, since their espousal of constructivism and production art as means of 'building life' (*zhiznestroenie*) meant that there was little danger of the confusion of cause and effect that beset their opponents. On the question of the classical heritage, too, they showed exemplary rigour, extending the infamous Cubo-Futurist desire to throw classical writers overboard from the ship of contemporary life to contempt for the representatives of Proletkul't, who 'thought . . . that the revolutionary character [of literature] was exhausted by agitational content alone and remained thoroughly reactionary in the area of form [*oformlenie*]', and for the 'bureaucratic language and parrotting of political basics' of later proletarian writers.[30]

There was a good deal of posturing in the left-art movement's attacks, from a position of relative weakness, on proletarian writers; at times debate was drowned out by the two sides' exchange of 'prolier-than-thou' protestations. But there were occasions when the critique of the proletarian project from left-art positions did cast revealing light on its contradictions. In 1928 V. Pertsov, commenting

27 Bogdanov, 'Proletariat i iskusstvo', 130–1.
28 F. Kalinin, 'Put' proletarskoi kritiki i *Poetika rabochego udara* A. Gasteva', *Proletarskaia kul'tura*, 4 (1918), 13–18, quoted in Johansson, *Aleksej Gastev*, 100–1.
29 E. Zamyatin, 'I am Afraid', in *A Soviet Heretic: Essays*, ed. and tr. M. Ginsburg (Chicago, 1970), 56.
30 'Za chto boretsia Lef', *Lef*, 1 (1923), 4, 6.

on the current predilection of the All-Union Association of Proletarian Writers (VAPP, shortly to become RAPP, the Russian Association of Proletarian Writers which was to dictate much of the agenda for the next few years), for 'learning from the classics' and 'realism', wrote:

All these discussions of 'learning' and 'realism' are dominated by a naked formalistic approach to literature. The literary work is understood as a pure form which can be transferred into any social sphere. However these people who fail to comprehend the social function of the work of art taken as a whole refer to themselves—as VAPPists, On-Guardists, Voronskians, and so on—whatever name is taken by those who fail to understand the uniqueness of the effect of the literary work in concrete historical circumstances, fail to see the historical conflicts in the development of the craft of literature, they are all dangerous, superficial formalists and idealists. War to the death must be declared on them.

For some reason these people think that the classics they call upon us to learn from were 'classics' from birth.[31]

Leaving aside, for the moment, Pertsov's chilling expression of his own 'will to victory', we may identify the principal concern of his onslaught as, once again, immediacy. By highlighting the dangers immanent in the naïve gesture of dividing form and content, he shows how, once proletarian theory had lost sight of the distinction between social organization as cause and as effect of literary work, its projected 'critical assimilation' of the cultural heritage materialized as mere imitation and epigonism. The impasse to which this led was most effectively demonstrated by the famous and absurd hunt for that emblem of literature devoid of history, a 'Red Lev Tolstoi'.

Pertsov's critique of proletarian theory and practice has much in common with that articulated by representatives of the Party, most notably Trotskii. As early as 1923 Trotskii had mounted a trenchant attack on the proletarian project and its misplaced confidence in the powers of class and organization:

It would be childish to think that every class can entirely and fully create its own art from within itself, and, particularly, that the proletariat is capable of creating a new art by means of closed art guilds or circles, or by the Organization for Proletarian Culture [Proletkul't], etc. Generally speaking, the artistic work of man is continuous. Each new rising class places itself on the shoulders of its preceding one. But this continuity is dialectic, that is, it finds itself by means of internal repulsions and breaks.

Hence, while endorsing the proletariat's aim of 'conquering power' in the political sphere, Trotskii reproached it for willing an unnecessary victory in the sphere of culture: 'The proletariat acquires power for the purpose of doing away forever with class culture and to make way for human culture. We frequently seem to forget this.'[32]

31 V. Pertsov, 'Kul't predkov i literaturnaia sovremennost'', *Novyi Lef*, 1 (1928), 9.
32 Trotsky, *Literature and Revolution*, 207, 215.

Having thus ruled out of court the objective and strategy of the proletarian writers, Trotskii opens the way for his definition and defence of 'fellow-travellers', writers who in their public positions and practice body forth the transitional, mediated and mediating character of post-Revolutionary literature. The intermediary character of fellow-traveller writing within a dialectic of literary history insisted on by Trotskii is rather different from the in-betweenness of ironic detachment and intellectual scepticism for which fellow-travellers are customarily admired. Indeed, notwithstanding the irreducible variety of stances taken by fellow-travellers as individuals and/or as members of literary groups, they shared a conviction that their intermediate position was the result of their very immediate access to a writerly identity that was not in the final reckoning bound to, in Pertsov's terms, their 'concrete historical circumstances'. This conviction is, in turn, shared by the majority of commentators on Soviet literature of the 1920s, for whom the fellow-travellers are valuable despite, not because of, their relationship to those circumstances. The intuitive 'art of seeing the world' which Aleksandr Voronskii, editor of one of the major outlets for fellow-traveller work, the thick journal *Krasnaia nov'* (*Red Virgin Soil*), saw as defining the genuine writer is yet another category by which immediacy is restored. Hence it is neither surprising nor entirely without logical justification that Voronskii, himself a constant target of the 'frenzied zealots' of the proletarian writers' movement, should be arraigned alongside them by Pertsov on a charge of dehistoricizing the 'craft of literature'.[33]

Whereas Trotskii disallowed both the end and the means of the proletarian writers, the official Party line endorsed the end but questioned the means. While acknowledging that the proletariat would in time achieve hegemony within literature, the Party's 1925 statement of its policy for literature refused to grant the proletarian writers' movement a 'monopoly', arguing that 'this would mean, above all, the destruction of proletarian literature'. Rather than underwrite the theoretical arguments of the likes of Lelevich, the Party's document emphasized that 'the class nature of art in general and literature in particular is expressed in forms that are infinitely more varied than, for instance, in politics', recognized the importance of the 'interstitial ideological forms' of fellow-traveller writing, and called (in the spirit of NEP) for 'free competition between the various groupings and streams in this sphere'. It also reminded the proletarian writers of the need for critical assimilation of the cultural heritage rather than its uncritical adoption.[34]

However, we should not of course be overcome with admiration for the apparent theoretical sophistication with which the Party

33 See A. Voronskii, 'Iskusstvo videt' mir', in *Iskusstvo videt' mir: Sbornik statei* (Moscow, 1928), 110–14. For an account of the persecution of Voronskii by RAPP, see S. I. Sheshukov, *Neistovye revniteli: Iz istorii literaturnoi bor'by 20-kh godov*, 2nd edn. (Moscow, 1984), and R. A. Maguire, '*Red Virgin Soil': Soviet Literature in the 1920's* (Princeton, 1968).
34 'On the Party's Policy in the Field of Literature (Resolution of the Central Committee of the R. K. P. (b), 18 June 1925)', in James, *Soviet Socialist Realism*, 116–19.

rebuts the claims of the proletarian writers' movement. The fact remains that the Party shared with that movement a certainty that immediacy was the order of the day in one crucial area, that of reception. When the declaration speaks of the need to 'make use of all the technical achievements of the old masters to work out an appropriate form, intelligible *to the millions*', it betrays an assumption that, however mediated and sophisticated the processes by which the work of literature is produced, the processes by which it is received are correspondingly straightforward, entailing a passive assimilation of the ideological positions expressed in the work. Critical assimilation is the task of the writer and of the critic; once this has taken place, there is no room or necessity for a critical stance on the part of the reader, whose class outlook remains as susceptible to direct manipulation as in the crudest of Proletkul't models. This is a clear continuation of the pre-Revolutionary pattern whereby intellectuals 'both attempted to provide workers and peasants with the means of thinking independently, and resented it when they did'.[35]

By this stage, however, a further element had been added: the possibility of acting on this resentment. Given the importance attached by the Party to the shaping of identity as a precondition for the realization of its own 'will to victory', it could hardly fail to be concerned if literary work did not achieve mass intelligibility. And if this did not result from 'free competition of ideologies', then a more *dirigiste* approach to the production of literature would need to be adopted. For many commentators, the 1925 resolution contains the promise, or rather the threat, of such an approach. Drafted by Bukharin and Lunacharskii (well-known to be conservative in his tastes and thus conciliatory towards the fellow-travellers), but also by the uncompromising Lelevich, 'Far from enshrining neutrality, as sometimes suggested, [the] text makes much more sense when interpreted as a step towards intervention.'[36] On this reading the resolution may be seen as a continuation of the agenda set by Lenin in 1905, with the debates of the intervening years about the organizational capacities of literature adding a new dimension to his yoking of Party organization and Party literature: all literature, it is implied, will not only be organized by and for the Party, but will also organize by and for the Party. Yet it makes most sense to see the 1925 resolution as riven by the same sort of tensions as is Lenin's article. These result not only from the different ideological stances of its authors, but also from, precisely, its failure to recognize that the principles of mediation identified as operating in the sphere of literary production must also affect that of reception. That being so, any attempt to impose by administrative diktat the immediate organizational effects sought by the proletarian

35 L. McReynolds and C. Popkin, 'The Objective Eye and the Common Good', in Kelly and Shepherd (eds.), Constructing Russian Culture, 70.
36 Kemp-Welch, Stalin and the Literary Intelligentsia, 34.

writers' movement could not succeed. In a sense, then, whether the 1925 resolution is or is not an assertion of the right to intervene, or indeed the first instance of intervention, is of secondary importance. The resolution is important first and foremost because it offers further confirmation of the limits on the Party's capacity to grasp, literally and figuratively, the literary process in all its complexity. These limits were never to be fully overcome even in the long years of the Party's uncontested hegemony.

Cultural Revolution

The very term 'cultural revolution' encapsulates the tension between continuity and rupture, actual and theoretical control, that has been our concern so far in this chapter. It appeared almost in passing in the 1925 statement of Party policy on literature as 'a prerequisite for further movement towards a communist society', a Leninist designation of 'an enormous growth in cultural enquiry and demands' as both empirical fact and political imperative.[37] But the expansion of this 'zone', as it was termed in 1925, during the period from 1928 to 1931 entailed transformations in both quantity and quality. The repudiation of NEP and the shift to central economic planning brought a declaration of war on newly targeted 'class enemies'. As 'NEP-men' were dispossessed in the cities, and kulaks crushed in the countryside, the traditional intelligentsia, freshly branded as remnants of the bourgeois order, faced vicious assaults in the name of the creation of a new, 'proletarian intelligentsia'.

What Sheila Fitzpatrick has termed a 'switch to a class-war concept of cultural revolution', 'initiated as a revolution from above', surely signalled an end to the Party's readiness to tolerate opposition to, or competition with, its organizational objectives. But, as Fitzpatrick has pointed out, this period in fact saw 'a cultural upheaval, some aspects of which were directly manipulated by the Party leadership, others outside the range of leadership vision'. It is precisely in those aspects of cultural revolution that eluded the controlling gaze of the Party that it is possible to locate the greatest continuity with preceding practice. A major aim of the 1925 resolution had been to reprimand the proletarian writers' movement for presuming to speak in the name of the Party. Three years later little had changed:

By 1928 RAPP, still lacking a formal mandate, had assumed leadership in the campaign to unmask the 'rightist danger' in the arts and scholarship. Between 1928 and 1932, the RAPP leaders exercised a repressive and cliquish

37 'On the Party's Policy', 116.

dictatorship over literary publication and criticism. This dictatorship, supposedly in the name of the proletarian Party, was in fact not under effective Central Committee control.[38]

RAPP's agenda during the cultural revolution might be broadly described as first, abandoning, on behalf, if not with the blessing, of the Party, the latter's acceptance that there was a greater variety of forms in literature than in politics; and second, imposing homology between the literary and the political. The most striking organizational expression of this was a process of outreach, reminiscent of, and as fraught with difficulty as, the nineteenth-century Populist 'going to the people': writers would read their works to audiences of factory workers and travel, singly or, more in the spirit of the times, in brigades to learn and write about flagship projects of socialist construction, thereby, in the case of fellow-travellers, promoting their own reconstruction (the word *perestroika* received one of its periodic airings).[39] RAPPist critics, in their turn, would deploy their full resources of invective to excoriate failures of aspiration to make the transition from the position of fellow-travelling (*poputnichestvo*) to that of alliance (*soiuznichestvo*). Instead of 'patiently assisting these inevitably numerous forms [of fellow-travelling] to return to full health in the process of an increasingly close and comradely cooperation with the cultural forces of Communism',[40] the self-appointed implementers of Party policy extended the 1925 resolution's curative imagery into a full-blown somatic rhetoric of disease, degeneracy, and death. Thus one recalcitrant fellow-traveller, Konstantin Vaginov, found himself characterized in 1929 as the 'undertaker-in-chief', inspired by a 'necrophiliac muse', of a group of poets whose works gave expression to 'the voice of the class enemy', then accused a year later of offering his readers 'personally and socially gelded characters', and of portraying Soviet writers as 'gravediggers and degenerates'.[41]

Yet RAPP itself, as a body, was not without its dysfunctions. On the one hand there was the majority who adhered to established proletarian positions on questions of form. By this stage these had been distilled down to three slogans: 'learning from the classics' (*ucheba u klassikov*), 'the living man' (*zhivoi chelovek*), and 'Red Lev Tolstoi' (*krasnyi Lev Tolstoi*). The first designated general good practice; the second, the anticipated result of implementing this good practice in relation to the portrayal of contemporary character; and the third the yet-to-appear writer whose work would, by exemplifying the first two, represent the recapitulation of the highest achievements of nineteenth-century critical realism, complete with the 'dialectics of the soul' for which Chernyshevskii had so admired Tolstoi. On the

38 S. Fitzpatrick, 'Cultural Revolution as Class War', in Fitzpatrick (ed.), *Cultural Revolution in Russia, 1928–1931* (Bloomington, Ind., 1984), 9, 12, 21, 29.
39 See K. Clark, 'Little Heroes and Big Deeds: Literature Responds to the First Five-Year Plan', in Fitzpatrick (ed.), *Cultural Revolution*, 198.
40 'On the Party's Policy', 118.
41 See D. Shepherd, *Beyond Metafiction: Self-Consciousness in Soviet Literature* (Oxford, 1992), 92, 113.

other hand there was the minority Litfront (Literary Front) group, less favourably disposed towards traditional fictional forms and more inclined to advocate a dissolution of the distinction between journalistic writing and *belles lettres*. This was a transformation in the identity of literature for which implicit justification might be found in Lenin's 1905 article on Party organization, which in turn was following the logic of nineteenth-century literature's functional fluidity; and it was a transformation which on the face of it would make literature a medium more suited to the project of transforming individual and collective identities.

It is no surprise that the literary practice of the cultural revolution cannot be traced straightforwardly back to the theories and demands of RAPP. Production novels in which collectives and construction sites, rather than individuals or 'living men', were heroes, competed for plaudits with semi-factual sketches (*ocherki*) whose proliferation was testimony to the authority exerted by Litfront. As Katerina Clark has argued, 'RAPP's power was not a cause but a symptom of the prevailing atmosphere of extremism.' Thus although, through its trinity of slogans, RAPP was arguing for a return to traditional modes of writing, 'literature as traditionally understood seemed to be withering away'. However,

It should not be glibly assumed that this 'withering away' was a purely artificial process generated from above. There was a genuine, if very diffuse, desire on the part of many writers to transform their own status in some way, to participate in the construction of the new society and to achieve a more direct link with the masses.[42]

It is generally agreed that the most extreme movement to flourish in this 'atmosphere of extremism' was the revived Left Front of the Arts (LEF), which went further than its RAPPist near-namesake in arguing for a 'literature of fact', on the grounds that contemporary reality offered such a rich diversity of conflict and character as to render fictional versions of reality, especially those which had recourse to nineteenth-century methods, superfluous. For the 'factographers', fiction, once progressive as a counter to the repressiveness of Nicholas I and subsequent autocrats, had lost this quality, indeed could be regressive in a post-revolutionary context; and, as the call to arms against RAPP by Pertsov quoted earlier indicates, they yielded nothing to RAPP in the ferocity with which they condemned those whose theories and practices were not compatible with their own.[43] For one recent commentator LEF stood out among other literary movements of the cultural revolution in that there was no contradiction between its theory and its practice, an ostensible strength which was in fact an

42 Clark, 'Little Heroes', 194, 198.
43 See N. F. Chuzhak, 'Pisatel'skaia pamiatka', in Chuzhak (ed.), *Literatura fakta: Pervyi sbornik materialov rabotnikov LEFa* (Moscow, 1929; repr. Munich, 1972), 9–28.

'Achilles' heel' lying in the 'failure to understand the mechanisms through which reality is technically processed by the modern means of communication that register it', and the blindness to the fact that art was secondary in relation to 'ideology and its immediate manifestations in the form of party decrees, instructions, and theses'.[44] In other words, the poetics, or rather anti-poetics, of LEF represent a rare achievement of the goal of immediacy pursued but unattained by other movements.

In fact LEF theory and practice is no freer from the effects of mediation than any other, and if anything is distinguished by its combination of resistance to mediation, shared with other movements, with a more unusual awareness of its inevitability and the benefits of acknowledging this. Pertsov's critique of the failure of RAPP and others to see the mediating role played by reception is a case in point. And the notorious concept of social commission (*sotsial'nyi zakaz*), for which LEF is held responsible (or culpable), is not, in LEF theory, the blunt instrument for describing and ensuring appropriate political commitment that it is generally taken for. Although it emerged as part of left-art theory in the first half of the 1920s, the social commission assumed particular importance during the cultural revolution, when 'society' actually did commission writers, not without coercion, to provide literary representations of socialist construction. But Osip Brik's contribution to a journal discussion of social commission made it clear that for LEF this was an unacceptable, reductionist instantiation of a complex idea:

The fact of the matter is that when they talk of commission, members of LEF do not mean a commission which is given by individual representatives of a class, or even by individual institutions which express the will of that class; they are talking about an autonomous understanding of this social commission as possibly contradicting the actual commission given by individual representatives of a class. . . . The social significance of an artist is determined not by his social origins, but by the social significance of the tasks which he sets himself.[45]

Two years earlier, Brik had highlighted the untenability of approaches that sought to explain effects in terms of the most obvious and easily identifiable causes:

The vulgar confusion of the ideological nature of the author with the ideological effect of the work of art reveals in our critics an elementary failure to understand the laws of artistic creation. They persist in the misguided idea that the work of art is no more than a direct expression by the author of his cherished thoughts and emotions. They still think that a work of art can be decoded in terms of authorial consciousness, with nothing left over.

44 B. Groys, *The Total Art of Stalinism* (Princeton, 1992), 28, 29, 30.
45 O. Brik, 'Ne teoriia, a lozung', *Pechat' i revoliutsiia*, 1 (1929), 29, 31.

Of course we cannot say that the role of the author in his work is no greater than the role of a skilled worker in a metallurgical plant. But in just the same way as the ideology expressed in a shell produced in a big-gun factory tells us nothing about the imperialist intentions of the workers who have produced that shell, so this or that ideology expressed in a literary work tells us nothing about the ideology of its author.[46]

Here, as elsewhere, Brik comes close to squandering the enormous theoretical potential of his argument through polemical overstatement; there is also an undertone of zealotry recalling the rhetoric of his colleague Pertsov, whose call for a war to the death over questions of literary history drowns out the modulations of his argument, thus creating the impression that it outdoes the RAPPist nostrums against which it is directed in stridency rather than in subtlety. That is LEF theory at its worst. At its best, however, it displays a sophistication notable for its absence elsewhere. And, however regretfully, the LEFists brought this sophistication to bear on their own practice. For all that they proclaimed the freedom of factual genres from the mediating conventionality (*uslovnost'*) of fiction, the factographers consistently recognized that their practice shared with fiction manifold procedures of selection and combination of material, adoption of specific and limited viewpoints, and so forth.[47] The negligible quantity of factographical writing produced speaks volumes for the unrealizability of the movement's aims, while in the few instances available for scrutiny the protestations of a total break with literary tradition are the very site of continuity with it. Take, for example, the following passage from the Sergei Tret'iakov's introduction to his 'bio-interview' with a Chinese student:

> The invented story and composed novel are loathsome.
>
> The once honourable title of writer has an offensive ring in our times.
>
> Today's true craftsman is a 'discoverer of new material', a careful giver of shape to it without distortion.
>
> The book *Den Sy-Khua* has been made by two people. Den Sy-Khua himself was the supplier of raw material, I was the one who gave it form.
>
> To see what surrounds you, to make out one's life in detail, is a high-grade skill. It comes from extensive training, and writing for journals and newspaper reporting are the best engineers.
>
> I can think of no other term for what I have given form to than 'interview'. But this interview takes in the life of an individual, and it is for that reason that I have added to it the particle 'bio'.
>
> This book is only a few chapters of a genuine human life. It will break off with the words 'to be continued'.[48]

The moments at which the writing confronts and resists tradition as embodied in fictional genres and their armoury of techniques

46 Brik, 'Uchit' pisatelei', *Novyi Lef*, 10 (1927), 34.
47 See Shepherd, *Beyond Metafiction*, 85–6.
48 S. Tret'iakov, 'Den Sy-Khua (Bio-interv'iu)', *Novyi Lef*, 7 (1927), 14–15.

(metaphor, figurative language, careful selection and arrangement of material) are the moments at which it reinscribes and revalorizes that tradition, so that the 'chapters of a genuine human life' are chapters both literal and figurative: conventional, artificial divisions of a narrative, and metaphors for the stages of that life, a life whose open-endedness in (f)actuality is conveyed by a formula, 'to be continued' (*prodolzhenie sleduet*), associated with the serialized—and thus susceptible to ultimate closure—lives of fictional characters.

This invites us to speculate upon a possible, if (appropriately enough, in the light of Brik's arguments), unintended relationship of congenerity between literature of fact and the late nineteenth-century pursuit of 'objectivity' in fiction: both projects were forced to confront their own impossibility as they encountered, and gave expression to, the always-already-mediatedness of the reality they sought to transcribe. And there is much more than just piquant irony in the fact that a Chekhovian problematic should have been re-engaged by a group of writers who would no doubt have consigned the fact-obsessed doctor and his card indexes to the same deep as his less 'dispassionate' predecessors.[49] It suggests that even when reinvented as a form of class war, and even in its most anti-traditional hypostasis, 'cultural revolution' did not entirely lose its Leninist connotations of disseminating rather than curtailing tradition. Each of the two principal meanings of the term is presupposed by and in its other.

Authority versus Autonomy: Socialist Realism

The end of the cultural revolution came in June 1931 when, in a typical volte-face, Stalin began once again to court and promote the very bourgeois intellectuals who had been its principal victims. The return from exile shortly before this of Maksim Gor'kii, his conservative cultural predilections intact, to assume the role now written for him of patriarch of Soviet letters, was the principal harbinger of an end to the upheavals in the literary world.[50] In April 1932 a brief Central Committee resolution announced the dissolution of all existing literary and artistic organizations, to be succeeded by unitary, All-Union bodies. The most common interpretation of this resolution is that 'it is apparent that this is the moment at which Soviet writers are ordered to become "artists in uniform"', at which 'the Party had reorganized literature on its own terms . . . the fist had closed on Soviet literature'.[51] The unruly RAPP had fulfilled the task which, though not assigned by the Party, had suited its interests, and so could now be

49 On Chekhov and late 19th-c. debates about objectivity, see McReynolds and Popkin, 'The Objective Eye', 93–8.

50 See Fitzpatrick, 'Cultural Revolution', 37–8, and Clark, 'Little Heroes', 203.

51 Kemp-Welch, *Stalin and the Literary Intelligentsia*, 115, and E. J. Brown, *The Proletarian Episode in Russian Literature, 1928–1932* (New York, 1953), 218. An English translation of the resolution is in James, *Soviet Socialist Realism*, 120.

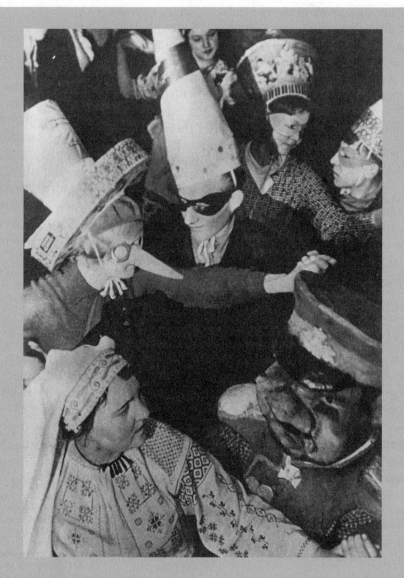

1 Carnival in Moscow, 1936 (from *Nashi dostizheniia*).

The massive street demonstrations begun after the Bolshevik Revolution continued into the 1930s in rather different form, with less emphasis on the art and choreography of professional artists, and more on the 'spontaneous' participation of working people. There is no doubt that many occasions (such as the opening of culture parks and exhibitions) still were genuine popular festivals; on the other hand, both the imagery of the celebrations (as here) and the darkening political context in which they were held could give them a sinister flavour like that of the Inquisition-dominated *auto da fé*, a connotation that was not lost on the Russian cultural critic Mikhail Bakhtin, who began his study of carnival culture, in the work of François Rabelais in the 1930s.

discarded along with the remnants of the other movements it had helped destroy. However, this view is open to challenge:

Western commentators have seen these events as a final nail in the coffin of literary autonomy. There is, however, a good deal of evidence to suggest that the Party's action in dissolving RAPP was prompted by a desire to halt RAPP's persecution of independent writers' groups and of non-Party writers in particular; and that the intention was not to oppress the literary profession but to rid it of ugly and counterproductive faction fighting. Certainly the relatively broad composition of the initial Writers' Union committees lends support to such an interpretation.[52]

The very fact that two such different interpretations of the resolution can be advanced reveals, yet again, the dangers of assuming that the intentions of the Party can be read directly off from its official statements, and of assuming that those intentions were translated into institutional effects 'with nothing left over', in Brik's words. Of course things had changed since the years of NEP, when factors militating against both the formulation and the implementation of an uncompromising and uncompromised top-down policy flourished. Stalin's consolidation of power, not least as a consequence of the cultural revolution, made the achievement of such an agenda more possible, and to suggest that he did not pursue this goal would be to ignore overwhelming evidence. Most prominent among this evidence is the official 'method' for Soviet literature and art, intensively debated after the end of the cultural revolution, and proclaimed at the First Congress of the Soviet Writers' Union in 1934. None the less, the genesis of socialist realism, and its inglorious history, do offer counter-evidence that the gap between theory and practice, although perhaps narrower than before, was as impossible to close as ever, and continued to function as both product and cause of tension.

Nowhere is this gap more provocatively exposed than in Boris Groys's contention that the origins of socialist realism are to be found not in Party committees and decrees, but in the movement whose representatives were excluded from those committees and derided in those decrees, the avant-garde. In what looks like a classic case of repression in the Freudian sense, the avant-garde, and in particular the left-art movement, were pushed out to and beyond the margins of cultural history following the cultural revolution, and indeed during it, because the Party recognized in them both itself and the basis of its new project. For Groys, the 1932 resolution meant that 'The avant-garde's dream of placing all art under direct party control to implement its program of life-building (that is, "socialism in one country") had now come true'—but the dream was dreamt, and interpreted, by a hostile other:

52 Clark, 'Little Heroes', 204.

In these new circumstances Socialist Realism put into effect practically all the fundamental watchwords of the avant-garde: it united the artists and gave them a single purpose, erased the dividing line between high and utilitarian art and between political content and purely artistic decisions, created a single universal and easily recognisable style, liberated the artist from the service of the consumer and his individual tastes and from the requirement to be original, became part of the common cause of the people and set itself not to reflect reality but to project a new and better reality.[53]

Thus, despite its attachment to the kind of formal experimentation anathematized by socialist realism, and despite the fact that many of its most prominent figures shared the same professional and personal fate as writers and artists of more traditional cast, the avant-garde turns out to be responsible for, or rather culpable in, the most dismal expression of cultural politics in the Soviet period.

Such insistence on the complex, far from immediate connections between cause and effect is very much in the spirit of this chapter; but it is in the same spirit to ask whether Groys's model is not itself sustained by repression. His description of what the aesthetic of socialist realism led to is damning and in most respects accurate. But in seeking to locate the origins of this aesthetic in a marginal movement, and thus to reinforce the virtually universal sense that socialist realism was a grotesque distortion of the natural relations between the margins and the centre of culture, he goes too far in exempting the centre from responsibility. We have seen how LEF's literature of fact sought to be what Groys claims socialist realism was, and how in the very act of placing itself outside literary tradition it betrayed its connections with the naturalistic, objectivity-oriented writing of the late nineteenth century. In this sense socialist realism's alleged avant-garde inspiration partook of what Régine Robin has called the 'realist obsession' which constituted the 'discursive base' of the post-Revolutionary years. Originating in the nineteenth century with 'fundamental utterances on aesthetics and realism' by the radical critics Belinskii, Chernyshevskii, Dobroliubov, and Pisarev,

53 Groys, The Total Art, 34, and 'The Birth of Socialist Realism from the Spirit of the Russian Avant-Garde', in H. Günther (ed.), The Culture of the Stalin Period (Basingstoke, 1990), 134.
54 R. Robin, Socialist Realism: An Impossible Aesthetic?, tr. C. Porter (Stanford, Calif., 1992), 109–10.

this discursive base traverses the revolutionary whirlwind, and . . . the discussions of the late 1920's, from Voronskii and Pereval to the RAPP . . . from the proletarian leaders to Gor'kii—all the discussions on the need to renew realism and to surpass the critical realism of the nineteenth century, the discussions about the new formula being sought, 'partisan realism', 'monumental realism', 'social realism', 'revolutionary realism', finally 'socialist realism'—all these discussions reformulate and refashion the base discursive memory . . . in the open contradictory tension of questions raised but not resolved.[54]

The avant-garde was by no means the only, or even the dominant, medium by which socialist realism was connected to this discursive base. The word 'realism' does not represent a cynical attempt by the Party to graft its new method on to a tradition with which it has less in common than it claims; rather, it is the denotation of the method's unstable identity and fraught relationship to a tradition whose own identity was always something sought rather than achieved.

Hence it is no longer possible to see the First Congress of the Soviet Writers' Union as a kind of military parade at which writers, conscripted to a cause many or most of them did not believe in, and kitted out in their new uniforms, received their orders from the Party hierarchy to go forth and provide the 'truthful, historically concrete representation of reality in its revolutionary development' which was the foundation of the new method. Robin's unsurpassed account of the two-week Congress demonstrates how it emerges even from the official printed version as a time and a place of the most intensive debate, agreement, disagreement, compliance with and resistance to fixed positions articulated from both above and below. From this 'great cacophony that was striving to be a symphony' came a will to unanimity every bit as powerful as the will to victory of the proletarian writers in the 1920s, 'a compromise . . . between the *savoir faire* of the fellow travelers . . . and the *vouloir faire* of the proletarians': 'Socialist realism arose *at one and the same time* (and in the greatest ambiguity) from the base of Soviet intellectual society and from the summit of the Communist Party, which oriented the direction of the research, giving a name to what had been nameless.'[55]

The 'revolutionary' credentials of socialist realism are thus inseparable from its 'conservative' affiliations. It is no coincidence that the inauguration of socialist realism should have come shortly before official efforts to inculcate *kul'turnost'* began to emphasize the importance of acquiring a knowledge of canonical literature, both Russian and foreign.[56] But the definition of socialist realism was not entirely accomplished by the debates at the 1934 Congress. If what followed 'was a peculiar variety of didactic middlebrow literature whose rules quickly migrated to statuary, film, radio drama, and song . . . a tortuous compromise between the art of old masters, folk culture, ideology, and some elements of popular commercial art', this is not because this is what the Congress decided would happen, but because 'The various forms of popular culture have marked Soviet society from below to above just as the forms of inculcation of official ideology have marked it from above to below.'[57] Socialist realism was not imposed unilaterally from above by the Congress of the Soviet Writers' Union any more than it was imposed unilaterally from above

55 Ibid. II, 212, 48.
56 See C. Kelly and V. Volkov, 'Directed Desires: *Kul'turnost'* and Consumption', in Kelly and Shepherd (eds.), *Constructing Russian Culture*, 291–313.
57 Stites, *Russian Popular Culture*, 67; R. Robin, 'Stalinism and Popular Culture', in Günther (ed.), *The Culture of the Stalin Period*, 37; and E. Dobrenko, 'The Disaster of Middlebrow Taste, or: Who Invented Socialist Realism?', in T. Lahusen and Dobrenko (eds.), *Socialist Realism without Shores* (*South Atlantic Quarterly*, 94 (1995)), 773–806.

on that Congress. It both defined and was defined by theories and practices of high and low culture alike.

However, it is impossible to ignore the contrast between the complex syncretic processes by which socialist realism was defined and the indisputably top-down uses to which it rapidly came to be put. Writers were called to account for ideologically unsound works, forced to undergo the public humiliation of self-vilification (*samokritika*), hounded, arrested, imprisoned, exiled, murdered, directly or indirectly in the name of socialist realism. Compliance with the method demanded that the mandatory qualities of *narodnost'* (reflection and promotion of the viewpoint and interests of the people) and *ideinost'* (ideological soundness) be collapsed into the third category of the trinity, *partiinost'* (Party-mindedness): after all, the Party was the guardian of the people's interests, and of ideological rectitude, so it was only logical that its always correct line should be faithfully reflected in the work of the writers and artists whose activities it subsidized and sponsored, thereby guaranteeing correctness in other respects. Heroes whose 'positiveness' was in direct proportion to their Party-mindedness became *de rigueur*. The representation of 'reality in its revolutionary development' came to signify an almost entirely anticipatory portrayal of the notorious 'bright future' as the method's historical affiliations with the 'discursive base' of realism were occluded, and mythology, identified by Gor'kii at the 1934 Congress as a key antecedent of socialist realism, was transformed into its principal objective. Katerina Clark's account of the Soviet novel as the repository of the Soviet Union's myths about itself remains the most compelling analysis of socialist realist practice.[58]

That the Party possessed in socialist realism and the Union of Soviet Writers tools for *dirigisme* and repression of unprecedented scope is beyond any doubt.[59] What we must be wary of, however, is the assumption that, because these were the ends to which socialist realism became a means, they were ends which were inscribed within the method from its very beginnings, that they were an unmediated and planned result of the theory. To assume this would be to succumb to the very same temptations of dehistoricization for which socialist realist practice and Soviet accounts of it are rightly ridiculed. To close the gap, remove the tension, between theory and practice and posit an unmediated connection between them is to execute a move squarely within the traditions of socialist realist practice.

In other words, we should not read socialist realism in terms of the categories it would have us employ. It may have striven to expunge ambiguity and unpredictability, to conform to what Clark calls the 'Master Plot' of its mythological narrative of pre-ordained truth. But,

58 See K. Clark, *The Soviet Novel: History as Ritual*, 2nd edn. (Chicago, 1985).
59 On the Union, see J. Garrard and C. Garrard, *Inside the Soviet Writers' Union* (London, 1990).

just as we refuse to accept the nonsensical assertion that all literature should be measured in terms of its conformity to these criteria, so we should be sceptical about whether such conformity is in fact possible. The difficulty of imposing definitive closure on fictional narrative, even if that were accepted to be a desirable goal, was acknowledged at the Congress: the theory formulated there recognized the inevitability of ambiguity, uncertainty, contradiction. True, for many this was a reluctant recognition, a source of anxiety: in Robin's words, a 'fear of not being able to *control* the meaning of fiction, and still less its reception, is at the heart of the aesthetic established at the First Soviet Writers' Congress'.[60] This fear was what drove the Party to police literary practice with increasing vigilance; and the more it strove to abolish the source of its fear and to control the production and the reception of literary meaning, the more it confirmed that the fear was well-founded. It is possible to read even the most tedious, conformist socialist realist novels 'against the grain', to show how, even as they strive to fulfil the myth-making and myth-bearing functions allotted to them with ever more insistence, they exert, like many of the founding theoretical documents of Soviet literature, a powerful 'textual resistance', reveal the contradictions inscribed within their project as they seek to suppress them.[61]

This kind of deconstructive analysis offers scant compensation for those writers (and readers) on whom the Party's fear of loss of control was taken out, first in the repressions of the *ezhovshchina* of the late 1930s, and then again in the years after the Great Patriotic War. Between 1941 and 1945 'All sources attest to the relative loosening of intellectual and creative controls in the years of the German occupation and the life and death struggle for national and state survival'; and although 'it was the unofficial and semiofficial culture that rose to ascendance after the initial shock and best expressed the feelings of a people at war',[62] official culture did benefit from a relaxation of constraints on expression, and offered a platform even for figures marginalized since the advent of socialist realism and earlier. But hopes that this wartime retreat from extreme censoriousness would continue were dashed in the immediate aftermath of victory, when the period of the most sustained and successful *dirigisme* in literature and all the arts began.

The decision was made at the highest level that rigid discipline was to be reimposed in all aspects of the life of the nation. Some Western historians have argued that this tightening was the consequence of the break with the West: it was necessary to mobilize the country to face a new enemy. More likely it was the other way round: the Stalinists, fearing social disintegration and aware of the great weaknesses of the

60 Robin, *Socialist Realism*, 62.
61 See ibid., esp. pt. 3, ch. 4, and D. Shepherd, 'Canon Fodder? Problems in the Reading of a Soviet Production Novel', in C. Kelly, M. Makin, and Shepherd (eds.), *Discontinuous Discourses in Modern Russian Literature* (London, 1989), 39–59.
62 R. Stites, 'Introduction: Russia's Holy War', in Stites (ed.), *Culture and Entertainment in Wartime Russia* (Bloomington, Ind., 1995), 5, 4.

regime, recognized that continued friendly relations with the West were too dangerous and might have a subversive effect on Soviet society. They needed the Cold War.

The major turning point occurred in August and September, 1946, when a series of resolutions were published under the authority of the Central Committee of the Communist Party. This tightening was not limited to the intellectual sphere—during the same period a regulation concerning 'strengthening discipline in the collective farms' was published—but its impact was perhaps more devastating in this sphere than in any other. The cumulative effect of the condemnations of and brutal attacks on individual intellectuals was to narrow further than ever the sphere of the permissible in intellectual life. Since Andrei Zhdanov, the man responsible for ideology within the Politburo, was the most visible spokesman for the new policies in the two years between 1946 and his death in August 1948, this period came to be known as the *zhdanovshchina*—but of course Zhdanov was no more the 'onlie begetter' of the *zhdanovshchina* than Ezhov had been of the repressions to which his name was given. The victims of Zhdanov's denunciations did not lose their lives, and after Zhdanov's fall and death in 1948 both the intellectual climate and terror became worse.

The best known and the most significant of the staged events was in literature. The method here as elsewhere was to single out exemplary targets, thereby defining the limits of the permissible and conveying to others in the most concrete terms what was expected. Hence the infamous assault on the two Leningrad journals *Leningrad* and *Zvezda* (*The Star*), and on two writers whose works they had continued to publish after the war, Anna Akhmatova and Mikhail Zoshchenko. The closure of *Leningrad*, the change in editorial personnel of its sister journal, and the expulsion of the two writers from the Writers' Union marked the beginning of a period when Party intervention in literary life knew no limits and brooked no opposition. That the intention of the Party was to do more than merely scapegoat two writers became clear two weeks later with the condemnation of the repertoire of Soviet theatres as apolitical and containing too many second-rate Western plays. In the months which followed it was the turn of the film-makers. One of the main motifs in the attacks on the artists was that they had paid excessive attention to personal problems rather than to social issues: a Soviet artist was not to waste his time by worrying about such personal matters as love, jealousy, or death. The other point made by the critics was that the artists painted too gloomy a picture of Soviet reality. Soviet artists, in other words, were expected to widen even further the gap between the world as depicted by them and reality. The socialist realist artist was enjoined once more to see the germs of the beautiful future in the less than perfect present; the distinction between the 'is' and the 'ought' was to be abolished.[63]

The clearest expression of the Party's intensified intervention was its micro-management of the writing of fiction in terms of constantly changing requirements. The best known example is the insistence that Aleksandr Fadeev rewrite his novel *The Young Guard* (*Molodaia Gvardiia*, 1946–51) to highlight, in defiance of historical fact, the leading role played by the Party in the partisan movement whose activities the novel portrayed. The same rationale lay behind the often radical rewriting of works published up to twenty years earlier.[64] Yet even here it is possible to identify instances where literary practice exceeded the limits of theory. The tensions generated by the Party's iron grip surfaced in the official condemnations, in the early 1950s, of the 'conflictlessness' (*beskonfliktnost'*) and 'varnishing of reality' (*lakirovka deistvitel'nosti*) which had characterized the sanitized representations of Soviet reality in the preceding years. But Party approbation did not necessarily guarantee conformity. A case in point is Viktor Nekrasov's *In the Trenches of Stalingrad* (*V okopakh Stalingrada*, 1946), awarded a Stalin Prize in 1947, but replete with double-edged references to Stalin's conduct of the war which made it 'a mine-field of innuendo'.[65] This is not a simple question of ambiguity secreted in the text by the author in defiance of censorship, and uncovered by the reader or critic; rather, it is a question of the impossibility of exercising total control over the reception of a text, as well as over its production, which the Party had every reason to continue to fear.

Such celebrations of unavoidable textual ambiguity may seem irresponsible in the light of the treatment handed out to Zoshchenko, Akhmatova, and others. There is little to be gained from showing how the Central Committee's assertion that 'The power of Soviet literature, the most progressive of any literature in the world, consists in the fact that it is a literature which neither has, nor can have, any other interest besides the interest of its people and its state'[66] is just one more expression of a will to a victory still unachieved and unachievable. But our condemnation of the *zhdanovshchina* and its consequences gains rather than loses from an analysis that insists on the continuing 'impossibility', in Robin's terms, of the socialist realist project as understood by the Party at that time. For this project was founded on the erroneous assumption that the discourse of fiction was sufficiently pliable for writers to be able to do what they were told, to express the Party ideology which they were forced to espouse as their own in their works, 'with nothing left over'. The fact that there was always something left over means that to the heroic

63 See P. Kenez, *Cinema and Soviet Society* (Cambridge, 1992), 215–20.

64 See M. Friedberg, 'New Editions of Soviet Belles-Lettres: A Study in Politics and Palimpsests', *American Slavic and East European Review*, 13 (1954), 72–88, and Shepherd, 'Canon Fodder?', 51–2.

65 D. Piper, 'Soviet Union', in H. Klein (ed.), *The Second World War in Fiction* (London, 1984), 141.

66 *The Central Committee Resolution and Zhdanov's Speech on the Journals 'Zvezda' and 'Leningrad'*, tr. F. Ashbee and I. Tidmarsh (Royal Oak, Mich., 1978), 43.

resistance of those writers who refused to conform is added the resistance to conformity of poetics itself.

Two Types of Autonomy

On numerous occasions, of course, especially in the 1920s, the resistance of poetics had operated in tandem with, rather than despite the absence of, the resistance of the writer to produce powerful defences of 'the traditional role of the autonomous artist who maintained an aesthetic distance to reality and was therefore capable of independently observing and recording it', a role which 'suited neither the avant-garde nor the party'.[67] Much of the metafictional writing that flourished during the cultural revolution combined this reassertion of writerly autonomy with declarations of the independence of literary and cultural value from political or ideological context and contagion. However, such writing also showed that poetics offered resistance not only to proletarian, Party, and avant-garde programmes for culture, but also and at the same time to the traditions to which and by which those programmes were opposed, and which it itself promoted.[68] This may sound like an argument in favour of even-handed treatment of two positions whose relative merits invite greater discrimination. In fact, as a brief reading of an exemplary text will show, it is a further argument against being ensnared by the crude, binaristic models with which the theory and practice of socialist realism are associated.

The text in question is Mikhail Bulgakov's *The Master and Margarita* (*Master i Margarita*). Begun in 1928 and worked on until its author's death in 1940, this is a novel whose own history seems to underwrite the validity of the truths it professes. Its sudden appearance in the most inauspicious of times (1966–7, when the re-Stalinization of literary politics under Brezhnev had brought the trial of Siniavskii and Daniel') and the most inauspicious of places (the conservative journal *Moskva* (*Moscow*)) invites interpretation as confirmation of its most famous line, the assertion that great literary works, whatever the obstacles placed in their way, will always out: 'manuscripts don't burn'. The opposition of the great writer and great literature to their hack counterparts is the novel's principal concern. In its portrayal of Soviet writers as careerists whose sole concern is their status and the perquisites brought by membership of the organization MASSOLIT, the novel offers a devastating indictment of the infighting, compromises, and corruption endemic in the organization on which

67 Groys, *The Total Art*, 38.
68 See Shepherd, *Beyond Metafiction*.

MASSOLIT is based, the Moscow branch of RAPP, and, by extension, in the Soviet Writers' Union. Standing out against this background is the master, justly described by the visiting Devil Woland as 'thrice romantic': for the master writing is a calling, not a profession; he is a seeker after truth, and a visionary; and he deliberately sets himself apart from the world, and is persecuted for his difference, driven to the despairing (and supremely romantic) gesture of burning the manuscript of his unpublishable novel about Christ. The fact that his novel survives this burning to be returned to him by Woland suggests that it, like its author, transcends the time and place of its making, belongs in the tradition of perennially valuable literature to which other writers in the novel can never aspire.

There can be little doubt that this reassertion of a literary tradition, and set of literary values, denied by Soviet literary politics is what *The Master and Margarita* sets out to achieve. Yet the novel, unremitting in its critique of the institutional consequences of that politics, consistently undermines its own proffered solution. The master's romantic credentials are treated ironically. If he is able to treat his writing as a calling rather than as a profession, it is only because he has had the good fortune to win the state lottery—like those he despises and invites the reader to despise, he depends on state patronage. And he inhabits not the traditional garret of the romantic writer, but a basement apartment. But the greatest irony accompanies the most powerful assertion of his place in the Russian literary tradition, his association with Pushkin.

The pervasiveness of Pushkin in Russian culture is conveyed through the travails of one of the victims of Woland's exposure of Muscovite materialism, Nikanor Ivanovich Bosoi. Although he has never read a word of Pushkin in his life, but has simply taken the poet's name in vain in flippant remarks about paying the rent or the bill for boiler-fuel, Bosoi, his equilibrium disturbed by Woland, dreams the text of one of Pushkin's *Little Tragedies*, 'The Covetous Knight'. There is no getting away from Pushkin, who functions as a natural, omnipresent literary—and, indissociably from this, moral—reference-point. But the single most important reference to Pushkin is the 'peace' or 'rest' (*pokoi*) with which the master is finally rewarded by Woland, acting at the behest of Ieshua as transmitted by Matthew the Levite: ' "He has not earned light, he has earned rest". '[69] This 'rest' is a recurrent obsession in Pushkin's lyric poetry, and perhaps the most famous expression of the poet's yearning for it is the 8-line poem of 1834 beginning 'It's time, my friend, it's time! My heart asks for rest', and ending with these four lines:

69 M. Bulgakov, *The Master and Margarita*, tr. M. Glenny (London, 1988), 406.

На свете счастья нет, но есть покой и воля.
Давно завидная мечтается мне доля—
Давно, усталый раб, замыслил я побег
В обитель дальнюю трудов и чистых нег.

[There is no happiness in the world, but there is rest and freedom.
I have long dreamed of an enviable lot.
Long ago I, a weary slave, conceived my flight
To a distant dwelling of labours and pure bliss.][70]

These lines describe accurately the cosy corner in eternity to which the master will retire with Margarita, to write and commune with fellow artists. Bulgakov's master is thus granted, although not in the world (*na svete*: the use of the word *svet* in its other meaning of 'light' in Matthew's words to Woland reinforces the link with the poem), the peace so strongly desired by Pushkin's poetic persona.

This connection with Pushkin provides the finishing touch to the portrayal of the master as a writer unlike his peers. Even though his major work is unpublished, he proves able to effect the kind of moral transformation of a (potential) reader which Pushkin achieves in the case of Bosoi, and which is, according to received wisdom and standard critical accounts, the aspiration and achievement of major Russian writers since the nineteenth century. But the peace earned by the 'thrice romantic' master is in Pushkin indissociable from the post-romantic, or anti-romantic, development of Pushkin's work in particular and Russian literature in general in the 1830s and subsequently: the overcoming of romantic poetics and romantic conceits is Pushkin's principal theme. Romantic notions of inspiration and difference are often treated ironically; and Pushkin was one of the first Russian writers of his age to welcome the professionalization of the writer's craft. The mockery of romantic conceit and positive attitude towards professionalization are combined as early as 1824 in his 'Conversation Between a Bookseller and a Poet', where the poet thinks back wistfully to a time when 'A carefree poet, I wrote | From inspiration, not for payment'. The bookseller responds with a detailed encomium to the benefits of the marketplace, climaxing with 'Let me speak plainly: | Inspiration cannot be sold, | But a manuscript can. | Why delay?'. The poet gives in to the bookseller's blandishments, shifting significantly into prose to say 'You are quite right. Here is my manuscript. Let us agree our terms.'[71] In the light of this it would seem that the choice of Pushkin as the master's model undermines, rather than reinforces, any notion that the master's fate underwrites romantic notions about the autonomy of the writer and of literature.

None of this is meant to imply that the tribulations of the master, or of his author Bulgakov, should be belittled. On the contrary: the

70 A. S. Pushkin, 'Pora, moi drug, pora', in *Sobranie sochinenii v desiati tomakh*, 4th edn., iii (Leningrad, 1977), 258.
71 Pushkin, 'Razgovor knigoprodavtsa s poetom', ibid. ii. 174, 179.

complex narrative structure and intertextual affiliations of *The Master and Margarita* steer us away from the danger of subscribing to simplistic ideas that would not do justice to the tragedy of either character or author. The Pushkinian opposition of inspiration which is not for sale and a manuscript which is requires a careful consideration of the nature and limits of autonomy, which can be understood in two ways: freedom from direction from above, from political tutelage and censorship; and freedom from ties to one's time, as well as from the marketplace in which all cultural products, high or low, must circulate. These two senses of autonomy are too often conflated. But the need for autonomy in the first sense may be asserted and defended at the same time as its impossibility in the second sense is proclaimed. More than this, to treat the second sense as a necessary corollary of the first is to weaken the grounds on which the first may be defended. *The Master and Margarita* combines passionate asseveration of the artist's inalienable right to be free of political tutelage with a demonstration that this freedom does not, cannot bring exemption from 'the body and pressure of time'. This is what makes this most un-Soviet of novels such an important contribution to the debates conducted by the likes of Lenin, Lelevich, and LEF.

3

STEPHEN LOVELL

ROSALIND MARSH

Culture and Crisis: The Intelligentsia and Literature after 1953

The many historians and analysts of the Russian intelligentsia have few points in common, but they would all surely agree that the intelligentsia in Russia always occupies an intermediate position between political authority (*vlast'*) and people (*narod*). To fall between these two stools may at times be inconvenient and embarrassing, for example when a programme of political action needs to be implemented in the name of the people, but it also carries with it certain advantages. The educated stratum is necessary and privileged under Soviet-style state socialism. As well as its role in administering the state bureaucracy, it is also entrusted with a significant cultural mission: to act as the bearer of enlightenment and the instiller of a particular state-sanctioned model of culturedness.[1] By the last two decades of the Soviet Union's existence, the section of society engaged in what went under the name of 'intellectual labour' enjoyed cultural hegemony along with a certain amount of prestige and security. Members of the intelligentsia could read and write books and journals, work away in research institutes, stage plays, make films, and—in the privacy of their own homes—hold long vodka-driven philosophical debates, without for a second doubting that these were important, socially constructive, and financially viable activities. This is not to suggest that truly free-thinking and independent-minded intellectuals felt anything other than stifled in Brezhnev's Soviet Union; it is just that such free-thinkers, as in any large sample of intellectuals, were in the minority.

The gradual disillusionment of the intelligentsia, including the majority which had by and large been prepared to carry out the role allotted to it, with the Soviet regime between the death of Stalin and the accession of Gorbachev can be traced with reference to important political events and the worst acts of repression of the post-Stalin era, all of them played out in a very public manner. These included the two periods of freeze provoked by the overenthusiastic reaction to the thaws inaugurated by Khrushchev's Secret Speech at the Twentieth Party Congress of 1956 and his subsequent public denunciation of Stalin at the Twenty-Second Party Congress of 1961; the Siniavskii–Daniel' trial of 1966; the invasion of Czechoslovakia in 1968; the dismissal in 1970 of Aleksandr Tvardovskii as editor of *Novyi mir*, which in the years 1958–70 had enjoyed a reputation as the most liberal literary journal; the deportation of Solzhenitsyn in 1974; the reprisals against the unofficial journal *Metropol'* in 1980; and the renewed repression which characterized the short reigns of Andropov (1982–4) and Chernenko (1984–5). If most of these events and acts are traditionally described with reference first and foremost to literature, this is not necessarily an overreductive approach; as the critic Aleksandr Ageev has argued, 'Russian culture of recent times is clearly literocentric'.[2] Each of these successive crises was preceded and accompanied by a surge of creativity across the spectrum of the arts, which demonstrated the great vitality of a Russian culture operating independently of the Party's dictates. This vitality was evident not only in the questioning of official ideology, but also in the increasing influence of postmodernism, despite the Party's continuing propagation of socialist realism.

For this reason the tendency to denigrate virtually all the achievements of writers, film-makers, and artists whose works appeared in Soviet Russia before Gorbachev's inauguration of *glasnost'* in the late 1980s is one of the least attractive aspects of cultural life in post-Communist Russia.[3] It has become fashionable for iconoclastic Russian critics to attack 'liberals' or 'dissidents' of the critical-realist tradition from various different angles: either because of the conventional structure and style of their work; the conservative, Russian nationalist viewpoint espoused by some; the political or cultural compromises some artists were obliged to make under the Soviet regime; or because many ended up (whether by choice or compulsion) in emigration. In the 1990s, vociferous adherents of alternative literature have belittled virtually any cultural product of the post-Stalin era which displays the moral or political concerns of its creator.

However, such a blanket condemnation of all culture produced within or beyond the borders of the Soviet Union before 1991 (or even

1 On the vicissitudes in the development of the intelligentsia's *mission civilisatrice* in the Soviet period, see S. Fitzpatrick, *The Cultural Front: Power and Culture in Revolutionary Russia* (Ithaca, NY, 1992); C. Kelly, 'New Boundaries for the Common Good', in Kelly and D. Shepherd (eds.), *Constructing Russian Culture in the Age of Revolution, 1881–1940* (Oxford, 1998), 238–55; and Kelly and V. Volkov, 'Directed Desires: *Kul'turnost'* and Consumption', ibid. 291–313.

2 A. Ageev, 'Conspectus on the Crisis: Sociocultural Conditions and the Literary Process', in E. E. Berry and A. Miller-Pogacar (eds.), *Re-Entering the Sign: Articulating New Russian Culture* (Ann Arbor, 1995), 172. For a more detailed discussion of Soviet literary politics in this period, see R. Marsh, *Soviet Literature since Stalin: Science, Politics and Literature* (London, 1986), 10–22.

3 One of the most influential articles of this kind was V. Yerofeev [Erofeev], 'Soviet Literature: In Memoriam', *Glas*, 1 (1991), 225–34; see also Iu. Bondarev, *Literaturnaia Rossiia*, 14 Dec. 1990, 2–4, and M. Kharitonov, 'Apologiia literatury', *Literaturnaia gazeta*, 19 June 1991, 11.

before 1985) cannot do justice to the complex and heterogeneous processes of post-Stalin culture, which can in no sense be regarded as a monolithic block of artistic propaganda concerned only to conform to or react against the tenets of socialist realism. The breakdown of the public consensus of the Stalin period and the emergence of new forms of consensus among the Russian intelligentsia cannot be satisfactorily encompassed simply by the notions of 'thaw', or later, of *perestroika* and *glasnost'*. Whereas the timing of the publication of literary works, or the exhibition of paintings, in Russia has been heavily dependent on changing political circumstances, the actual writing of literature and production of cultural artefacts have followed their own laws and their own timetable, which have frequently borne little relation to politics.

Beginnings of Diversity and Dissent

Even in the Stalin era, when opposition to official socialist realist doctrine could mean persecution, imprisonment, or even death, critical works of high artistic quality were nevertheless being written, such as Mandel'shtam's epigram on Stalin, Akhmatova's *Requiem*, Chukovskaia's *Sof'ia Petrovna*, Bulgakov's *The Master and Margarita*, and Pasternak's *Doctor Zhivago*. Even in the bleakest period for Soviet literature inaugurated by the repressive *zhdanovshchina* of 1946–8, veiled references to Stalinist repression were appearing in writing ostensibly for children, such as Lev Kassil's *Tale of the Three Master Craftsmen* (*Povest' o trekh masterakh*, 1949); in historical films, notably the second part of Eisenstein's *Ivan the Terrible* (1946; released only in 1968); and in some literature published in *Novyi mir* in the early 1950s, such as Valentin Ovechkin's sketch *Weekdays of a District* (*Raionnye budni*, 1952), which highlighted the problems in Soviet agriculture, and Vasilii Grossman's *For the Just Cause* (*Za pravoe delo*, 1952), which drew an oblique parallel between Nazi and Stalinist obscurantism.[4]

The death of Stalin in 1953 ended the paralysing terror which had previously been the Party's main instrument of control over Soviet writers, and lessened the fear that frankness would lead to arrest or repression. The Party's initial cautious dethronement of Stalin in the early 1950s stimulated writers to depict what they considered to be the deficiencies in Soviet society, facilitating the publication of works such as Part One of Il'ia Erenburg's *The Thaw* (*Ottepel'*, 1954), which advocated universal human values divorced from political categories. Another result of such greater openness was that the divisions among the Soviet cultural intelligentsia began to surface in public for the first time: at the Second Writers' Congress of December 1954 it became

4 For further discussion, see E. R. Frankel, *Novy Mir: A Case Study in the Politics of Literature, 1952–1958* (Cambridge, 1981), 9–14.

evident that two camps, which became known as 'liberals' and 'conservatives', now existed in Soviet literature.

However, as many memoirs attest, it was not until Khrushchev's Secret Speech selectively denouncing Stalin at the Twentieth Party Congress of February 1956 that a fatal blow was struck at many writers' hitherto unthinking faith in Stalin and the myth of the Party's infallibility.[5] The second thaw which occurred in the wake of the Twentieth Congress, from 1956 to early 1957, witnessed the publication of some even more controversial works, such as Vladimir Dudintsev's *Not by Bread Alone* (*Ne khlebom edinym*, 1956) and Granin's *Personal Opinion* (*Sobstvennoe mnenie*, 1956), which depicted a lone inventor's struggle against an all-pervasive bureaucracy. However, the most significant literary event of 1956 was the attempt by a group of writers to establish an independent organization of Moscow writers outside the Party-controlled Soviet Writers' Union, which led to the publication of two volumes of the anthology *Literaturnaia Moskva* (*Literary Moscow*).

The expectations aroused by Khrushchev's de-Stalinization campaign and the Party's erratic procedure of alternating thaws and freezes led to the emergence of literary dissidence, a term used to describe those who ventured beyond permissible ideological, political, and aesthetic limits, even in the more liberal atmosphere of the thaw. Two new literary phenomena developed: *samizdat* ('self-publishing', the unofficial copying and circulation of underground manuscripts); and *tamizdat* (publication 'over there', that is, in the West). One of the earliest examples of *tamizdat* occurred in 1956, when a hitherto unknown anonymous writer adopting the Jewish pseudonym 'Abram Terts' (who later proved to be Andrei Siniavskii), sent two works abroad for publication: *On Socialist Realism* (*O sotsialisticheskom realizme*, 1960) a devastating critique of the concepts and methods of Soviet literary theory; and *The Trial Begins* (*Sud idet*, 1960), a surrealistic depiction of the late Stalin period, and an indictment of the view that the ends justify the means.

It has not generally been acknowledged that Khrushchev's revelations at the Twentieth Congress had a considerable impact on women writers as well as men in the generation that subsequently became known as the *shestidesiatniki* (people of the 1960s), since Soviet critics have not usually expected women writers to be interested in political events. However, two unpublished memoirs of 1993 by the St Petersburg writer Nina Katerli, 'Sovok—moi geroi i moi chitatel'' ('Homo Sovieticus—my hero and my reader') and 'Kto ia?' ('Who am I?'), attest to the importance of the Twentieth Congress in changing her world-view.

5 See R. Medvedev, *Let History Judge: The Origins and Consequences of Stalinism*, rev. and exp. edn., ed. and tr. G. Shriver (New York, 1989), 5; E. Yevtushenko, *A Precocious Autobiography*, tr. A. MacAndrew (London, 1963), 123; and K. Simonov in *Soviet Weekly*, 18 July 1987, 5. For a selection of quotations on this subject, see S. F. Cohen, 'The Stalin Question since Stalin', in Cohen (ed.), *An End to Silence: Uncensored Opinion in the Soviet Union* (New York, 1982), 29.

Katerli speaks very honestly about the firm Stalinist convictions with which she was inculcated during her youth, even though her uncle had been shot and her aunt was in a prison camp: 'I belong to the generation of *shestidesiatniki*, who had been formed inwardly in Stalin's time. Until the moment of his exposure by Khrushchev I was an absolute Stalinist, and perceived the death of the "Leader of the Peoples" as a tragedy.' Although she admits that she only 'tried to sob' at Stalin's funeral, she was obsessed with the one thought: 'what could I devote my life to, so that He would be resurrected?' It was not until three years after his death that her faith in Stalin was completely shaken: 'Khrushchev's speech exposing "Stalin's personality cult", and the *samizdat* and *tamizdat* which followed, liberated me from the evil magic fairly easily and rapidly. The world turned upside-down, I saw *where* I was living, understood *how* I had lived before, rose from my knees, and gradually became a normal human being.' She compares her own feelings and those of many of her generation to those of a person who had been liberated from a lifetime's imprisonment in a narrow, dark box: 'That person got out of the box, stretched his numb body, opened his eye wide—and only then for the first time understood how terrible his situation had been and what happiness freedom is. I think that many of my contemporaries, "people of the 1960s generation", felt the same way.'[6] However, she admits that the process of liberation was far from easy, and that de-Stalinization led not to intellectual autonomy and freedom of thought, but to a mere dogmatic inversion of previous values—a psychological development which was to become fairly typical of the dissident Soviet intellectual: 'This does not mean that I got completely rid of a Soviet approach to reality—it was simply that at a particular moment, from being a pro-Soviet person I became anti-Soviet, although it is natural to be just a person, something which is rarely available to my contemporaries.'[7]

Khrushchev's public denunciation of Stalin at the Twenty-Second Party Congress of February 1961 speeded up the process of de-Stalinization and led to the publication of some literary works that demonstrated the undermining of writers' confidence in the Party's chosen historical path. The previously unknown Aleksandr Solzhenitsyn, a provincial schoolteacher who had been writing in secret both in prison camp and after his release in 1953, sent his manuscript *One Day in the Life of Ivan Denisovich* (*Odin den' Ivana Denisovicha*) to Tvardovskii's *Novyi mir*. Its publication in October 1962, sanctioned by Khrushchev himself, created a sensation: it was the first work published in the Soviet Union to reveal the daily misery of an inmate of a Soviet prison camp, and, through the symbol of the 'Socialist Way of Life' settlement which the prisoners are obliged to

6 N. Katerli, 'Sovok —moi geroi i moi chitatel'', unpublished memoir read at the conference 'Women in Russia and the Former USSR', University of Bath, Mar.–Apr. 1993, 2, and 'Kto ia', 6, 10.
7 Katerli, 'Sovok—moi geroi', 3. Katerli's view coincides with the opinions of some Western critics, who have called realist dissidents such as Solzhenitsyn and Maksimov 'inverted socialist realists' who arrive at different conclusions from orthodox Soviet writers, but 'have taken over in all essentials the Socialist Realist aesthetic': see G. Hosking, *Beyond Socialist Realism: Soviet Fiction since Ivan Denisovich* (London, 1980), 123, and A. Besançon, 'Solzhenitsyn at Harvard', *Survey*, 24 (1979), 134.

build, hinted that the entire Soviet Union in Stalin's time had been one enormous prison camp. Solzhenitsyn's main theme is not simply physical survival, but the survival of a human being's moral integrity even in the harshest conditions.[8]

Other significant anti-Stalin works to appear in the early 1960s were Evtushenko's poem 'Stalin's Heirs' ('Nasledniki Stalina', published in *Pravda* on 21 October 1962) which suggested that Stalin's spirit still communicated with his successors, and Sergei Zalygin's novel *On the Irtysh* (*Na Irtyshe*, 1964), which presented collectivization as a national catastrophe. The publication of these works marked the climax of de-Stalinization in the USSR until the accession of Gorbachev, since a ban was placed on the many other manuscripts describing Stalinist society and life in exile, prisons, and camps that began to inundate Soviet journals and publishing houses.

Whereas prose published in the Soviet Union in the early 1960s remained predominantly realist, experimentation in language and style became the province of poetry. The originality and virtuosity of such young poets as Voznesenskii and Evtushenko attested to their revulsion against the debasement of language in the Stalin era. The revival of poetry in the early 1960s reflected the growing spiritual emancipation of young Soviet people, whose enthusiasm for verse was so great that the Luzhniki sports stadium in Moscow could be packed by almost 15,000 people for a poetry recital. Another new genre which flourished in the early 1960s was 'youth prose', contributed to the journal *Iunost'* (*Youth*) by such writers as Aksenov, Gladilin, Bitov, Iskander, and Nagibin, which dealt with the problems of rebellious adolescents influenced by the idiom and culture of Western teenagers. Young Soviet people also listened avidly to rock-and-roll music, first broadcast to the USSR in the 1950s by Voice of America, and to the new genre of 'authors' songs' or 'guitar-poetry' (words and music written and performed by the author himself) which had been introduced by Bulat Okudzhava in 1956.[9] All these developments signalling the emergence of an autonomous youth culture aroused the implacable hostility of Party bureaucrats.

Unofficial artists such as Zheltovskii and Nikonov and sculptors such as Ernst Neizvestnyi began to experiment with abstract forms, but their attempt to exhibit their work in the Manège Gallery in Moscow in 1962 came to grief when Khrushchev visited the exhibition and, horrified by the 'blotches' on display which he attributed to 'pederasts', once again initiated a repressive policy towards the arts.[10] In this uncongenial atmosphere Solzhenitsyn's second story *Matrena's House* (*Matrenin dvor*, 1963), one of the pioneering works of 'village prose', was lambasted for its depiction of the poor conditions on

8 For the history of the work's publication, see A. Solzhenitsyn, *The Oak and the Calf: Sketches of Literary Life in the Soviet Union*, tr. H. Willetts (London, 1980), 16–46.
9 For further discussion, see G. S. Smith, *Songs to Seven Strings: Russian Guitar Poetry and Soviet 'Mass Song'* (Bloomington, Ind., 1993); J. Riordan, *Soviet Youth Culture* (Bloomington, Ind., 1989); and R. Stites, *Russian Popular Culture: Entertainment and Society since 1900* (Cambridge, 1992).
10 For a full transcript of Khrushchev's speech, see P. Johnson, *Khrushchev and the Arts: The Politics of Soviet Culture, 1962–1964* (Cambridge, Mass., 1965), 101–5.

collective farms, the greed and corruption of the peasantry, and the 'un-Soviet' virtues of charity and humility displayed by its heroine.

The Brezhnev Era

After Khrushchev's fall in October 1964, the KGB became more active in its investigation of literary dissidents, but there was no public crackdown on cultural activities until the trial of Andrei Siniavskii and Iulii Daniel' in February 1966. This was the first trial of Soviet writers in which the main evidence against them was their own literary work, and the sentences of 7 and 5 years' hard labour respectively proved to be the catalyst which speeded up the process of disaffection of many liberal Soviet writers from the regime. This trial was followed by another, that of the dissidents Iurii Galanskov and Aleksandr Ginzburg, who had compiled a *White Book* containing transcripts of the Siniavskii–Daniel' trial, which were circulated in typescript and made available to Western correspondents. This technique was subsequently employed in the establishment of an underground journal, *The Chronicle of Current Events* (*Khronika tekushchikh sobytii*) in 1968, and the formation of the full-scale human rights movement, in which writers continued to play a major role.

The great indignation created by these trials in the Soviet Union and throughout the world led the Brezhnev regime to adopt a more flexible cultural policy: the encouragement of the publication of mediocre, ideologically correct writing for the masses; an attempt to prevent the circulation of works which might be construed as openly anti-Soviet; and moves to pacify the liberal intelligentsia by permitting the selective and small-scale publication of some outstanding and controversial works. These included pre-Revolutionary and early post-Revolutionary literature such as the 1979 edition of Andrei Belyi's novel *Petersburg*, or the 1973 editions of Bulgakov's novels and Mandel'shtam's poetry; and foreign literature in translation, including selections of the trinity of writers who had previously been bywords for the decadence of Western modernism, Kafka, Proust, and Joyce. A similar approach was adopted in relation to the visual arts: after the scandal caused by the Soviet authorities' decision to bulldoze an exhibition of unofficial art in Izmailovo Park in 1974, a second exhibition was allowed to take place unhindered in early 1975.

Not only was the intelligentsia offered these instances of nonconformist cultural practice to fuel its discussions (and try to divert its attention from other matters); it was also given access to a greater range of discourses within which to frame its discussions. In some

2 Photograph of the poet Boris Kornilov (1907–1938), with his wife, the poet Ol'ga Berggol'ts, their daughter, Kornilov's parents and sister, taken in the late 1920s.

Like all those who perished during the Great Purges, Kornilov had been unmention-able in print for the two decades after his death (his most famous poem, set to music by Shostakovich, was passed off as a piece of folklore), but literary rehabilitation was brought about by publication of an edition of his work under the Poet's Library (Biblioteka poeta) imprint in 1966. The Poet's Library, famous among academics, bib-liophiles, and poetry-lovers alike, was set up in the 1930s, but reached the pinnacle of its influence in the late 1950s and early 1960s, when annotated editions in uniform mid-blue covers propagated a new canon of Russian and Soviet literature, including the works of formerly denigrated writers. Every volume was illustrated, and some authors' photographs, particularly those of Pasternak and Akhmatova, were to become icons. Kornilov was never one of the inner circle of Russian poetic martyrs, but this photograph is historically intriguing, demonstrating as it does the social mobility (from village schoolteacher to metropolitan writer) that was so characteristic of the 1920s.

cases these were, like the works of previously proscribed Russian writers, returns to the past, such as the criticism of the aristocratic historian of Russian literature, D. S. Mirsky. In others they were ostensible new departures, such as Mikhail Bakhtin's studies of Dostoevskii (1963) and Rabelais (1965), with an array of categories such as polyphony, carnival, Menippean satire, and 'gay relativity' which, although thirty years on they are the subject of continuing, and sometimes sophisticated and important, debate as to their true signification and significance, in the 1960s and 1970s offered exciting new ways of locating and characterizing oppositional, even utopian-revolutionary, subtexts in a variety of cultural products. Also new was the structuralism, followed by the cultural semiotics, of the Moscow–Tartu school of criticism headed by Iurii Lotman. If Bakhtin's theories threatened hegemonic critical and political discourses (a threat that could, however, be easily contained within the institutional fora in which exploration of the (sub)textual expressions of challenges to hierarchy took place), then the Tartu school, while by no means supinely conformist, and often dazzling with its explication of the workings of cultural 'secondary modelling systems', or with the jewels prised from hitherto neglected archives, did not set out, in its accounts of Russian cultural history, to overturn the hierarchies of high and low, enduring and ephemeral, valuable and dispensable, with which official Soviet aesthetics, rooted as it was in an Aristotelian conservatism easily discernible beneath the sickly luxuriance of its displays of revolutionary radicalism, had operated since the 1930s. This, together with the geographical marginality of Tartu, helped ensure that while, like Bakhtin, the school left an indelible imprint on the post-1960s Soviet critical idiom, it was never in a position to supplant the dominant discourses.

Notwithstanding these concessions, the great majority of cultural products, and accounts of them, which appeared in the USSR from 1964 to 1985 continued to conform to socialist realist canons. Prominent examples of 'secretarial literature' by literary bureaucrats were Georgii Markov's Lenin Prize-winning novel *Siberia* (*Sibir'*, 1971–3) and the epic war novels rehabilitating Stalin, Aleksandr Chakovskii's *Blockade* (*Blokada*, 1969–75) and Ivan Stadniuk's *War* (*Voina*, 1971–4), which were published in huge print-runs, though frequently left by an indifferent public to gather dust on the shelves. Of far greater appeal to a mass audience were television, which had become almost universal in the USSR by the late 1970s, middle-brow literature, such as science fiction, the detective stories of Iulian Semenov and the historical novels of Valentin Pikul', and Hollywood-style films propagating patriotic and patriarchal values, such as Sergei

Bondarchuk's *War and Peace* (1966–7) and Aleksandr Men'shov's *Moscow Doesn't Believe in Tears* (*Moskva slezam ne verit*, 1980).

Published Literature

Even in the repressive atmosphere of the Brezhnev era, control over culture and the media proved to be imperfect, and not all liberal cultural influences could be suppressed. *Glasnost'* has shed new light on the submerged pluralism which existed in Soviet cultural life before Gorbachev's accession, demonstrating that the Brezhnev era was far from being a 'period of stagnation' in the arts. Many Russian writers and artists who remained in the USSR, such as Fedor Abramov and Vladimir Tendriakov, died before their most outspoken works achieved publication: Abramov's *Journey into the Past* (*Poezdka v proshloe*, 1989), Tendriakov's 'Bread for the Dog' ('Khleb dlia sobaki') and 'Donna Anna' (both 1988). Others, such as Daniil Granin, Anatolii Rybakov, and Boris Mozhaev, expressed ideas in literature written secretly 'for the drawer' which could only be hinted at in their published works: Granin's *Bison* (*Zubr*, 1987), Rybakov's *Children of the Arbat* (*Deti Arbata*, 1987), Mozhaev's *Peasant Men and Women* (*Muzhiki i baby*, 1987).

The Brezhnev era witnessed the intensification of many trends which had begun under Khrushchev, not least the division into published and underground literature. However, the relationship between the arts on the surface and in the underground was more complex than might appear at first sight. The very existence of uncensored literature and art obliged the government from time to time to make concessions, to allow a measure of autonomy to certain talented cultural figures. In turn, uncensored literature, widely read in the literary community, at least in Moscow and Leningrad, exerted a significant influence on certain writers, encouraging them to tackle controversial, or even formerly forbidden themes. This practice may partially explain the publication and wide readership of such interesting writers as Rasputin, Trifonov, Shukshin, Bykau (Bykov), Okudzhava, Tendriakov, and others who continued to act as a moral opposition in the pre-Gorbachev era.

One genre which helped to keep humane values alive was the unheroic, pacifist war literature which continued to be published during the Brezhnev period, such as Grigorii Baklanov's *July 1941* (*Iiul' 1941 goda*, 1965) and Vasil' Bykov's *The Dead Feel No Pain* (*Mertvym ne bol'no*, 1966) and *The Mark of Doom* (*Znak bedy*, 1982), although patriotic themes were again promoted in 1978 by Brezhnev's ghost-written memoir *Little Earth* (*Malaia zemlia*, 1979), for which he was awarded the Lenin Prize for Literature in the year of its publication. Certain interesting works of historical fiction also occasionally achieved publication, such as Iurii Trifonov's anti-Stalinist novel *The House on the Embankment* (*Dom na naberezhnoi*), which appeared at the height of *détente* in 1976. However, the historical establishment sometimes intervened to condemn liberal works of which they disapproved, as in the case of Mikhail Shatrov's play *This is How We Will Conquer!* (*Tak pobedim!*, 1982), which praised the New Economic Policy of the 1920s.[11]

One of the most important genres of the Brezhnev era was 'village prose' (*derevenskaia proza*), which, albeit sometimes of high literary quality, managed to achieve publication largely because it reflected many of the nationalistic values of the Brezhnevite establishment. It deplored the poverty and spiritual disorder of modern life, evinced a marked distrust of modern technology which threatened to devastate the natural environment, and advocated a return to an imaginary rural paradise. Two particularly outstanding works were Vasilii Belov's *Business as Usual* (*Privychnoe delo*, 1966), which portrays an ordinary peasant, Ivan Afrikanovich, who lives in harmony with nature, but, when persuaded by a relative to go to the nearest town to earn enough money to feed his family, becomes completely disoriented; and Valentin Rasputin's *Farewell to Matera* (*Proshchanie s Materoi*, 1976), which depicts the gradual decline and apocalyptic destruction of a whole community, the island village of Matera on the Angara River in Siberia (a name evocative of Mother Russia) which is due to be flooded by the completion of a hydroelectric power scheme.

Another interesting genre was 'everyday prose' (*bytovaia proza*), generally set in a contemporary urban environment. The main exponent of this tendency was Iurii Trifonov, who depicted the moral compromises, grasping materialism, uneasy relationships, and breakdown of communication typical of the Soviet urban middle class in the 'era of stagnation'.[12] A variation on this trend was Natal'ia Baranskaia's *A Week like Any Other* (*Nedelia kak nedelia*, 1969), a realistic account of the everyday hardship of a Soviet woman attempting to combine work, domestic duties, and motherhood, which aroused a tremendous response from Soviet women. It was widely interpreted in the West as a feminist work, although this has always been denied by the author herself. It was not until 1980 that explicitly feminist writings appeared in the Soviet Union, with the publication of the underground journals *Zhenshchiny i Rossiia* (*Women and Russia*) and *Mariia*, which emphasized the persistent discrimination against women in Soviet society, venturing beyond the sanitized, pro-natalist

11 M. Shatrov in *Literaturnaia gazeta*, 8 May 1988, relates that academician A. Egorov, then Director of the Institute of Marxism-Leninism, wrote to Andropov on 27 Jan. 1982 in his capacity as head of the KGB, recommending that the play should be removed from the repertoire of the Moscow Arts Theatre.
12 For a full discussion of Trifonov's work, see D. Gillespie, *Iurii Trifonov: Unity through Time* (Cambridge, 1992), and N. Kolesnikoff, *Yury Trifonov: A Critical Study* (Ann Arbor, 1991).

treatment of women's issues characteristic of the Brezhnev era. A number of the journals' contributors were arrested, and several leaders of the movement, Tat'iana Mamonova, Tat'iana Goricheva, and Iuliia Voznesenskaia, emigrated in 1980. Other outstanding writings by women in the 1970s and 1980s, such as the 'cruel prose' (*zhestokaia proza*) of Liudmila Petrushevskaia, which provides a grim evocation of the moral disintegration of Russian society, and the ornamentalist prose of Tat'iana Tolstaia, which highlights the conflict between reality and illusion, remained largely unpublished until the Gorbachev era.

Nevertheless, even during the clampdown of the early 1980s some liberal influences still surfaced through the writings of the so-called 'generation of the 40-year-olds', such as Vladimir Makanin and Anatolii Kurchatkin; while talented works by new dramatists such as Petrushevskaia, Nina Sadur, and Viktor Slavkin were first produced in small studio theatres in uncensored amateur productions.

The relationship between the Party leaders and the cultural intelligentsia remained a complex and changing one. Whereas the limits of official tolerance had been overstepped in January 1979 with the unofficial printing in eight copies of *Metropol'*, a collection of hitherto unpublished Soviet writings compiled by Aksenov, Bitov, Iskander, and others, underground writers were sometimes accorded a surprising degree of semi-official tolerance. In the early 1980s Vasilii Zakharov, the secretary in charge of the Leningrad Region (*oblast'*) Party Committee (later promoted to Minister of Culture under Gorbachev) permitted the publication of the semi-official literary journal *Chas* (*Hour*) and the meetings of the literary club, Klub-81, which produced the almanac *Krug* (*Circle*).[13]

The impact of certain liberal literary works was felt even at the highest levels of the Party. Gorbachev, who had begun his Party career in the Khrushchev era and attended the reforming Twenty-Second Congress of 1961, was on record as saying that the Kirghiz writer Chingiz Aitmatov was his favourite author.[14] Gorbachev's subsequent desire to fill the blank spots of Soviet history may well have been influenced by Aitmatov's novel *The Day Lasts Longer than a Hundred Years* (*I dol'she veka dlitsia den'*, 1980), which exposes the destruction of the past by the Soviet regime. Aitmatov depicts strange characters called *mankurts* who, according to a Central Asian legend, were prisoners who had been turned into slaves by having their heads wrapped in camel skins which under the hot sun dried as tight as a steel band. A *mankurt* was a dehumanized creature who did not remember his tribe, his family, or even his own name; not surprisingly, the image of the *mankurt* was frequently used by critics and publicists

13 See N. Condee and V. Padunov, 'The Outposts of Official Art: Recharting Soviet Cultural History', *Framework*, 34 (1987), 87–8.
14 See D. Doder and L. Branson, *Gorbachev: Heretic in the Kremlin* (New York, 1990), 17.

in the Gorbachev era as a symbol of the collective loss of memory of the Soviet people.[15] Gorbachev's sympathy for Aitmatov's work was publicly acknowledged in 1990, when Aitmatov became a member of Gorbachev's Presidential Council.

Political and Literary Dissidence

During the Brezhnev era dissidence began to emerge as a full-scale socio-political movement, and many of the shades of opinion on historical and political topics which subsequently came to be publicly expressed under *glasnost'* already existed in embryo. Sometimes the differences of opinion between liberals and Russian nationalists surfaced in public, as in the debate of 1969–70 between the nationalist journal *Molodaia gvardiia* (*Young Guard*) and the liberal *Novyi mir*; similarly, in 1982 the nationalist tendency of *Nash sovremennik* (*Our Contemporary*), associated with Suslov, came into conflict with the internationalist, technocratic tendency associated with Andropov. However, it was mainly in *samizdat* and *tamizdat* that significant divergences of opinion in the interpretation of Soviet history and society came to the fore.

Important tendencies within the dissident movement included the liberal Marxist viewpoint of the historian Roy Medvedev; Andrei Sakharov's advocacy of human rights, democracy, and an eventual convergence between the communist and Western systems; and the neo-Slavophile views of Solzhenitsyn and his supporters, who appealed to the traditions of Russian Orthodoxy and distinctively Russian forms of social organization.[16] Other more extreme nationalist, even fascist, views were expressed in *samizdat* journals such as *Veche* and *Slovo natsii*.

Literary dissidence also grew in intensity from the end of the 1960s. In 1967 Solzhenitsyn sent a passionate appeal against censorship to the delegates of the Fourth Writers' Congress, but the Congress was prohibited from discussing this or any other important issue. The Soviet invasion of Czechoslovakia in 1968 finally set in motion a series of repressive measures which compelled liberals to fall silent, adversely affected the quality of published literature, and forced dissidents underground. In late 1969 Solzhenitsyn was expelled from the Writers' Union, and the editorial board of *Novyi mir* was disbanded. From 1969 until the accession of Gorbachev in 1985, the KGB employed a policy of selective terror against dissident artists, largely relying on cultural bureaucrats and editors to police their own cultural scene.

15 See e.g. G. Volkov in *Sovetskaia kul'tura*, 4 July 1987.
16 See A. Sakharov, 'Progress, Coexistence and Intellectual Freedom' (1968), in *Sakharov Speaks*, ed. H. E. Salisbury (London, 1974), 56–114, and A. Solzhenitsyn et al., *From Under the Rubble*, tr. A. M. Brock et al. (London, 1975).

By the late 1960s Solzhenitsyn had become convinced that his works could no longer be published in the Soviet Union. His two major novels, *Cancer Ward* (*Rakovyi korpus*) and *The First Circle* (*V kruge pervom*), were published in the West in 1968. Like *Ivan Denisovich*, both use the device of a closed society—a hospital and one of Stalin's special prisons for scientists respectively—in order to juxtapose characters from many different walks of life and paint a vivid picture of Soviet society as a whole. *August 1914* (*Avgust chetyrnadtsatogo*), the first volume of Solzhenitsyn's historical cycle on the Revolution, *The Red Wheel* (*Krasnoe koleso*), appeared in 1971, followed by *The Gulag Archipelago* (*Arkhipelag Gulag*, 1973–5), a monumental history of the Soviet prison-camp system, which attributes its origins to Lenin. This proved the final straw for the Soviet authorities, and Solzhenitsyn was forcibly deported in 1974, not to return to Russia until twenty years later, in May 1994.

Many of the most interesting works by other Russian writers produced in these years, both in the metropolis and emigration, were also published only in *samizdat* or *tamizdat* and frequently smuggled back into the Soviet Union. Guitar-poetry continued to be an intimate medium for the frank expression of the singer's inmost thoughts to a small audience, a means of bypassing the scrutiny of editor and censor. The songs of Okudzhava, Galich, and Vysotskii, satirizing the Stalinist past and the Brezhnevite present, were widely disseminated through the new genre of *magnitizdat* (clandestine tape recordings). Another new method of circulating literary texts in the 1970s and 1980s was *khamizdat* (from the word *kham*, 'boor'), which developed from the practice of printing a limited number of copies of a controversial work for the Central Committee, or sometimes just for the Politburo. Since the children of top officials sometimes sympathized with the democratic movement and copied the forbidden books they obtained from their parents, a number of sensational works confiscated by the KGB were able to find their way abroad in this way.

The partial rehabilitation of Stalin within the USSR after 1964, and the ban imposed on any discussion of questions of guilt and responsibility for past crimes, meant that a major theme in dissident literature continued to be an exploration of Stalin, Stalinism, and the falsification of history, which were treated in countless works of fiction and memoirs. Prominent examples were Nadezhda Mandel'shtam's memoir *Hope against Hope* (1971), a perceptive account of the effect of Stalinism on the Soviet intelligentsia in the 1930s; Varlam Shalamov's *Kolyma Tales* (*Kolymskie rasskazy*, 1978), a collection of concise, polished short stories exploring the worst camps in Stalin's Gulag system and the depths that the human spirit can plumb; Iurii Dombrovskii's

The Faculty of Unnecessary Things (*Fakul'tet nenuzhnykh veshchei*, 1978), whose non-communist hero opposes Stalinist tyranny through the power of thought and moral courage; and Vladimir Voinovich's *The Life and Extraordinary Adventures of Private Ivan Chonkin* (*Zhizn' i neobychainye prikliucheniia soldata Ivana Chonkina*, 1976), a good-humoured satire on Stalin's role as a war leader, the inefficiency of the commanders, and the ignorance of the ordinary soldiers. A further taboo was broken by Grossman's *Everything Flows* (*Vse techet*, 1970), an extensive reappraisal of the Soviet myth about Lenin, which presents his political philosophy and role in Russian history as an extension of the age-old Russian traditions of autocracy and non-freedom.

Another important theme in dissident literature was an exposure of the contemporary workings of the Soviet internal security system, which encompassed prison-camp literature such as Anatolii Marchenko's *My Testimony* ('Zhivi kak vse' and 'Ot Tarusy do Chuny', 1969), Siniavskii's *Voice from the Chorus* (*Golos iz khora*, 1973) and Irina Ratushinskaia's *Grey is the Colour of Hope* (*Seryi—tsvet nadezhdy*, 1988); works dealing with the incarceration of political offenders in mental hospitals, such as Valerii Tarsis's *Ward No. 7* (*Palata no. 7*, 1965) and Zhores Medvedev's *A Question of Madness* (1971); or with the persecution of writers, such as Efim Etkind's *Notes of a Non-Conspirator* (*Zapiski nezagovorshchika*, 1978), Voinovich's *The Ivankiad* (*Ivan'kiada*, 1979), and Solzhenitsyn's *The Oak and the Calf* (*Bodalsia telenok s dubom*, 1975).

The philosopher Aleksandr Zinov'ev, in a series of works combining documentary realism and formidable satirical talent, provided the most complete and devastating indictment of the corruption and spiritual emptiness of Soviet society in Brezhnev's time. Other dissident and *émigré* writers such as Joseph Brodsky and Vladimir Maksimov took as their theme the affirmation of spiritual and religious values; while other works proved unacceptable in the USSR before *glasnost'* either because they treated erotic themes, such as the novels of Eduard Limonov and Iuz Aleshkovskii, or employed modernist, fantastic, or surrealistic devices: for example, Andrei Bitov's *Pushkin House* (*Pushkinskii dom*, 1978), Sasha Sokolov's *School for Fools* (*Shkola dlia durakov*, 1976), Vasilii Aksenov's *The Steel Bird* (*Stal'naia ptitsa*, 1966) and *The Burn* (*Ozhog*, 1988). One particularly popular work of this type was Venedikt Erofeev's *Moscow to the End of the Line* (*Moskva–Petushki*, 1969); a comic evocation of an alcoholic's imaginary journey, which symbolizes both the complete disaffection of Soviet people from official ideology, and human destiny in general.

Anti-utopian fiction, such as Siniavskii's *Liubimov* (1963), the Strugatskii brothers' *Snail on the Slope* (*Ulitka na sklone*, 1966–8),

Zinov'ev's *Yawning Heights* (*Ziaiushchie vysoty*, 1976), Aksenov's *Crimea Island* (*Ostrov Krym*, 1981), Voinovich's *Moscow 2042* (*Moskva 2042*, 1987), and Iskander's *Rabbits and Boa Constrictors* (*Kroliki i udavy*, 1988), became a particularly prominent dissident genre, reflecting writers' growing disillusionment with the entire Soviet experiment, a pre-occupation which has persisted until the end of the Soviet period and beyond. The disintegration of the totalitarian system also found vivid expression in the *sots-art* (socialist art) of Vitalii Komar and Aleksandr Melamid (both of whom emigrated in the 1970s), who ironically appropriated the signs of communist ideology in their parodies of socialist realist paintings.

In the twenty years after Brezhnev's accession the most famous and vocal political and literary dissidents were imprisoned, sent to psychiatric hospitals, internally exiled, permitted or forced to emigrate. Yet persecution simply meant that the great variety of views on historical, political, and cultural subjects which existed in the USSR was suppressed, not eliminated altogether, only to re-emerge with great force after 1985. The emigration of many prominent writers in the 1970s and early 1980s engendered an entire third wave of Russian *émigré* literature, although most of the concerns of these writers remained related to the Soviet Union, and their ties with the homeland remained much closer than those of earlier generations of exiles.

The Gorbachev Era: Breakdown of Consensus

The announcement of a new Party line in 1986 gave intellectuals hopes that they could not only act as the passive, if respected, transmitters of cultural values, but actually enter the political arena as the Party's equal partners in reform. In the words of one of Gorbachev's most valued advisers, Aleksandr Iakovlev, 'Perestroika is impossible without the intelligentsia because perestroika is also the intellectualization of society.'[17] The assumption was that, once the intelligentsia was free to air democratic ideas in public rather than just at the kitchen table, it would carry the rest of society along with it and turn the Soviet Union into a civilized and democratic place.

Literature was perhaps the most important, but certainly not the only, beneficiary as Soviet intellectuals made impressive use of the opportunities afforded them under *glasnost'*. The late 1980s were for several of them a glamorous and exciting time. A group of journalists, historians, economists, and literary critics now carried the fight to the Stalinists, who still maintained a strong presence in Soviet organizations. Liberal intellectuals kept up a high public profile as

17 Quoted in S. Cohen and K. vanden Heuvel, *Voices of Glasnost: Interviews with Gorbachev's Reformers* (New York, 1989), 64. For further discussion of Iakovlev's role, see R. Marsh, *History and Literature in Contemporary Russia* (Basingstoke, 1995), 12, 13, 14; R. Pittman, 'Perestroika and Soviet Cultural Politics: The Case of the Major Literary Journals', *Soviet Studies*, 42 (1990), 113–14; and J. Wishnevsky, 'Aleksandr Yakovlev and the Cultural "Thaw"', *Radio Free Europe/Radio Liberty Research Bulletin*, 6 (5 Feb. 1987), art. no. 51, 1–4.

they stood for election to the Congress of People's Deputies and threw themselves into independent democratic groupings, all the while carrying on furious polemics with those they considered reactionaries. Gorbachev's turn to the right in 1990–1 was greeted by renewed polemics between reformist and Soviet-preservationist camps. The defeat of the August 1991 coup was experienced with elation as a moment when intelligentsia and people acted together in defence of shared beliefs. One of the most striking images of August reaffirmed the passionate moral commitment of the intelligentsia: while Yeltsin bestrode his tank and crowds mounted a vigil outside the White House, the cellist Rostropovich, after Sakharov's death perhaps the epitome of *intelligentnost'*, was photographed awkwardly cradling a machine-gun inside the Russian government building.

But the charged atmosphere of the *glasnost'* years could not forever obscure a more fundamental change in Soviet society that must, with hindsight, lead us to interpret the 1980s as the end of a cultural model rather than a bright democratic new dawn. The fatal weakening of the Soviet system had unpleasant side effects. The intelligentsia suffered considerable material hardship and loss of social prestige as Soviet institutions went into decline. A Soviet higher education no longer guaranteed a job for life. Post-Soviet Russia was left with a large number of well-qualified and experienced people who could not be gainfully employed or paid even a half-decent wage. Middle-aged women with higher education were particularly at risk: chemists and engineers formed long queues at the newly created job centres (*birzhi truda*), which for the most part sought only labourers and cleaning-ladies.

However oppressive the intelligentsia's material situation may have become in the 1990s, the causes of its malaise ran still deeper. The intelligentsia was forced to rethink radically its relationship to the two groups which, as mentioned above, have always defined its identity: the *narod* and the government. The intelligentsia's existence actually depends on strong state power, and on a high degree of tension between state and society. Under these conditions, the intelligentsia is not called upon to perform the functions of a Western-style technical élite, but to act as mediator between state and society. On the one hand, it implements and interprets commands from the top downwards; on the other, it articulates values from below and represents embryonic interest groups. The collapse of the Soviet Union was the logical result of the efforts of the liberal-minded intelligentsia, but it was also the intelligentsia's death warrant. When *glasnost'* gave way to cacophony, interest groups were no longer in need of mediators: they could speak for themselves. The intelligentsia's relationship to political power was likewise transformed: before, politically minded Soviet intellectuals, whether conformist or oppositionist, would always define their ideological orientation by referring to the single political authority in the country. In post-Soviet Russia, however, knee-jerk support or opposition was not an adequate response to the challenges—social, economic, and political—facing the would-be nation state.

Despite this fundamental change in the nature of their relationship, intelligentsia and government have not yet learned to live apart. In 1993 Boris Yeltsin formed a Presidential Council which included the literary scholars Marietta Chudakova and Iurii Kariakin. When the White House was shelled in October 1993, intellectuals saw an opportunity to take up their usual positions on either side of the ideological barricades—to express either their full support for Yeltsin or their absolute condemnation of his actions. However, the old style of ideological confrontation was no longer interesting to a population that had grown increasingly indifferent to politics. Moreover, it was becoming harder to see politics in black and white when the Russian political spectrum admitted so many shades of red, brown, green, and even Thatcherite blue.

Post-Soviet intellectuals clearly felt politically disoriented. But even more fatal to the intelligentsia's self-esteem and sense of purpose was the loss of its belief in the instrumentality of ideas, and more specifically in the capacity of its liberal propaganda to achieve cultural consensus. For the first time the Soviet intelligentsia came face-to-face with the *narod* in whose name it so often spoke, and the experience was profoundly disturbing. The Soviet intelligentsia's detachment from the real values of the Soviet peoples can clearly be seen in its neglect—or alternatively demonization—of national sentiment. *There is No Other Way* (*Inogo ne dano*, 1988), a collection of essays which is practically the manifesto of the reformist intelligentsia, contains not a single contribution on the national conflicts that were about to erupt in full view of the world.

Another striking example of the intelligentsia's social dislocation is its response to popular culture. As a case study in the emergence of popular culture in Russia, let us take the socially prestigious activity of reading, and begin with the effects of Gorbachev's policies on Russian literature. Gorbachev did not, of course, introduce *glasnost'* for the love of Russian literature, but in order to contribute to his policy of *perestroika*. He wished to release information about the legacy of the Stalinist and Brezhnevite past and the abuses and shortcomings in contemporary society in order to gain the support of the intelligentsia and promote his policies of economic and political reform; literature was, as ever, an especially propitious medium for what was a traditional Soviet-style top-down programme. However, by 1987–8 liberal writers and editors were escaping from official control and following their own agendas, which went far beyond what Gorbachev and the other Party leaders originally had in mind.

To a great extent, the Gorbachev period was concerned with the continuation of 'unfinished business' inherited from the Khrushchev era, and the belated restoration of their cultural heritage to the Russian public. The first stage of *glasnost'* in 1986–7, closely associated with Iakovlev, witnessed the publication of works by writers who had remained in the USSR, some of which had narrowly escaped publication in the Khrushchev era. Initially, these were works already well-known in the West, written by writers who were now dead, such as Bek, Akhmatova, and Tvardovskii, who were less controversial than the living; but by 1987 unknown, previously censored works by living writers, such as Rybakov's *Children of the Arbat*, Shatrov's *The Peace of Brest-Litovsk (Brestskii mir)*, and Anatolii Pristavkin's *A Golden Cloud Spent the Night (Nochevala tuchka zolotaia)*, had begun to appear.

Works by writers who had lived or died in the Soviet Union were published in an order commensurate with the amount of controversy they aroused.[18] To some extent this was a function of the generation to which the authors belonged, and, in some cases, of how recently they had been persecuted by the regime. In the first place, in the years 1986–8 many works appeared by writers of the older generation whose careers had begun in the period of Russian modernism before the Revolution: the most famous were Bulgakov, Pasternak, Mandel'shtam, and Gumilev. By 1988 editors were beginning to test the limits of *glasnost'* by sanctioning the first appearance in print of works by writers of the next generation who still lived in the USSR, including frank memoirs by former victims of Stalinism such as Anatolii Zhigulin and Lev Razgon. Works also appeared by writers who had been imprisoned or expelled from the Writers' Union in the post-Stalin era, such as Siniavskii and Daniel'. Another step forward was the publication of writers imprisoned since the inauguration of *perestroika*, such as Leonid Borodin, who had been released as late as 1987.

It became evident that *glasnost'* in literature had entered a new phase when many *émigré* writers appeared in print for the first time in the USSR. Works by *émigrés* were also published in stages. First came famous works by writers of the first wave of emigration after the Revolution, such as Nabokov and Zamiatin. The question of publishing *émigrés* of the third wave who had emigrated in the 1970s and 1980s was a much more controversial issue, because they were still alive and

18 For further discussion of the order in which 'returned literature' was published under *glasnost'*, see J. Graffy, 'The Literary Press', in Graffy and G. Hosking (eds.), *Culture and the Media in the USSR Today* (Basingstoke, 1989), 107–57, and R. Marsh, 'Glasnost and Russian Literature', *Australian Slavonic and East European Studies*, 6 (1992), 21–9.

able to comment on *perestroika*. However, from late 1987 onwards, when some of Brodsky's poems were published in the USSR after he had won the Nobel Prize for Literature, a constant flood of works by *émigré* writers and interviews with *émigrés* appeared in literary journals.

Third-wave writers were also published in order of controversiality, demonstrating the eagerness of editors to test and broaden the limits of the permissible. It was not until 1989, after much discussion and initial opposition from Gorbachev, that Solzhenitsyn's writings finally returned to his homeland: *The Gulag Archipelago* was published first, in accordance with the writer's own wishes. In 1990–1, while the reformer Nikolai Gubenko was Minister of Culture, *émigré* works appeared which it once would have seemed inconceivable to see in the Soviet Union: Eduard Limonov's erotic novel *It's Me, Eddie* (*Eto ia, Edichka*, 1979; translated as *Fuck Off, America*, 1982), and works of a religious, nationalist nature by Vladimir Maksimov, the editor of the anti-Soviet journal *Kontinent* (based in Paris until 1992, when it moved to Moscow). The final obstacle to the free publication of literary works appeared to have fallen in 1991, when some of Zinov'ev's works satirizing the entire communist system began to appear. Even before the failure of the coup in August 1991 there seemed almost nothing that could not be published and discussed in Russia.

Apart from the publication of many famous, new, and forgotten writers, the Gorbachev era was also remarkable for the gradual opening up of new themes for treatment in literature. Nowhere can this be observed more strikingly than in the case of literature on historical subjects, which, hand-in-hand with publicistic writing in the press, has gradually delved deeper and deeper into twentieth-century Russian history, challenging historians to produce a more truthful analysis of their country's past.[19]

In 1987 writers and publicists were able to initiate a serious analysis of Stalin and Stalinism, treating such subjects as collectivization and the purges; by 1988 graphic descriptions of tortures and prison camps were allowed, and Grossman's monumental novel *Life and Fate* (*Zhizn' i sud'ba*), which provides a radical reassessment of the Great Patriotic War and compares the anti-Semitism of Stalin and Hitler, unexpectedly achieved publication. However, it was not until the end of 1988 that satirical descriptions of Stalinism by *émigré* writers such as Voinovich and Georgii Vladimov were permitted. 1989 was the year when it became possible to publish highly critical comments about Lenin in works such as Grossman's *Everything Flows* and Solzhenitsyn's *Gulag Archipelago*. From 1990 many works appeared which provide a reappraisal of the Bolshevik Revolution, the Red

19 For further discussion of the historical fiction newly published in the Gorbachev era, see Marsh, *History and Literature in Contemporary Russia*.

20 On the problems of young writers in the Gorbachev era, see T. Tolstaia in *Knizhnoe obozrenie*, 1 (1988), 4, and the discussion between E. Popov and S. Chuprinin in *Literaturnaia gazeta*, 3 Aug. 1988, 3. On the narrow range of new writers whom journals wished to publish, see A. Ageev, 'Posle shoka', *Literaturnaia gazeta*, 3 June 1991, 4. For evidence that young writers still faced problems in post-Soviet Russia, see the comments of Evgenii Sidorov, the new Minister of Culture, in I. Rishina, 'Aktery ushli so stseny. V roli ministra—Evgenii Sidorov', *Literaturnaia gazeta*, 12 Feb. 1992, 3.
21 The term 'forgotten generation' was used by the poet Larisa Miller in 'Mertvyi sezon prodolzhaetsia', an article which the Soviet press refused to print, dated 25 Oct. 1990. For evidence of partial resolution of the problem, see e.g. Miller, 'Oknami na voliu', *Novyi mir*, 8 (1990), 19–20, and in *Literaturnaia gazeta*, 17 July 1991, 12.
22 New journals and almanacs included *Vestnik novoi literatury*, *Solo*, *Zolotoi vek*, *Russkoe bogatstvo*, *Glas*, *Vest'*, *Zerkala*, *Leksikon*, *Vstrechnyi khod*, *Slovo*, *Pushkinskaia ploshchad'*, *Laterna magica*; see also R. Marsh, ' "Alternative literature" in Russia: An Interview with Mikhail Berg', *Rusistika*, 4 (1991), 16–18. In 1992 *Vestnik novoi literatury* and *Solo* were awarded a prize of £2,500 established by an anonymous sponsor to encourage publishers of contemporary literature: see A. Nemzer

Terror, and Civil War, such as Gor'kii's *Untimely Thoughts* (*Nesvoevremennye mysli*), Bunin's *Accursed Days* (*Okaiannye dni*), and Denikin's *History of Russian Discord* (*Ocherki russkoi smuty*); and Solzhenitsyn's *Red Wheel* cycle, which began to be published in the USSR in 1990, reinterprets the February Revolution and the fall of tsarism. By the end of the Gorbachev period the ghost of Stalinism appeared to have been exorcized once and for all (although some lamented the absence of any public trial), and writers and film-makers had called into question the whole seventy years of Soviet power.

The great attention paid to the rehabilitation of 'returned literature' in the Gorbachev period meant that insufficient space remained in journals for works by new, younger writers.[20] Until 1990–1 little opportunity existed either for writers of the forgotten generation of 50 and under who had been unable to publish in the Brezhnev era, but had neither suffered persecution in the past nor had any desire to treat political issues or sensational themes in their current work. It was not until the late 1980s and early 1990s, when the store of returned literature was beginning to run out, that this problem was being at least partially resolved.[21] A number of new literary almanacs publishing young and formerly neglected writers sprang up;[22] and in 1991 one of the established journals, *Znamia*, published at least eight new writers in their twenties or thirties. Alternative prose by such writers as Viktor Erofeev and Evgenii Popov, who eschewed the social or civic role formerly assigned to literature by both socialist and dissident realists, began to appear in print, as did works by a number of talented, previously largely unknown women poets and prose writers who had formerly been unable to publish, such as Ol'ga Sedakova, Elena Shvarts, Larisa Miller, Bella Ulanovskaia, and Liudmila Ulitskaia.[23]

By 1990, Russian literature no longer consisted of only two main ideologically opposed strands; the literary repertoire had become very eclectic, and the readership too had become highly differentiated. According to the critic Mikhail Zolotonosov, the formerly monolithic structure of Soviet literature had splintered into a variety of literary subcultures, each with its own aesthetics, morality, readership, and relationship to the authorities, whose representatives were in conflict with one another. Zolotonosov distinguishes at least ten different subcultures, ranging from the Great Writers of the Russian Land (former socialist realist classics, such as Georgii Markov and Petr Proskurin) to experimental literature and aesthetic épatage, represented by such writers as Dmitrii Prigov, Viktor Krivulin, and Lev Rubinshtein.[24]

Such cultural pluralism in the late- and post-Soviet period has been regarded by some Russian commentators not as a normal result of artistic individualism, but as a reflection of the general chaos and disintegration of moral and political values in contemporary Russian society. Certainly it is an aspect of a fundamental shift which took place during the *glasnost'*-driven process of literary rediscovery. During *perestroika* the circulations of the major literary journals shot up to several million; in 1988 it seemed that everyone wanted to read Zamiatin, Grossman, and Pasternak. But this proved only a temporary surge of interest. Naturally, Soviet society wanted to turn over the hidden pages of its own history, and, as always, it preferred to do this via the medium of fiction.[25] However, once people had satisfied their immediate curiosity, they had little inclination to delve into the finer aesthetic and historiographical points of interpretation. When several of Solzhenitsyn's major works appeared in 1990, the popular response was disappointingly muted when compared to the enthusiastic reception of more lightweight writers a couple of years earlier.

What the intelligentsia finally discovered in this period, to its immense chagrin, was that the Soviet people was rather more concerned to develop a mass culture than to plug the many gaps in its knowledge of high culture. This interest in mass culture was nothing new, but it was only in the 1990s that it was permitted to find open expression. The Soviet people may have been 'the best-read in the world' (*samyi chitaiushchii v mire*), but it also read a high proportion of what was, in the view of the intelligentsia, bilge.[26] Soviet culture was always a bizarre (to a Western understanding) mixture of high and low. Culture had the elevated task of inculcating moral and social virtues in its audience, and yet at the same time, to justify its existence in a 'socialist' society, it had to have genuine mass appeal. These were not always incompatible aims: in the 1960s Tvardovskii's *Novyi mir* did achieve the difficult feat of acting as bearer of both high and popular (*narodnyi*) culture (the publication of Solzhenitsyn's *One Day* in 1962 is the outstanding example of this). However, by the late 1980s these twin aims of Soviet culture were proving hard to achieve simultaneously. The journalism of *perestroika* tried to combine mass appeal (*massovost'*) with the moral authority traditionally associated with the written word in Russia. The pro-*perestroika* weekly *Ogonek* tried to create something approaching a hybrid of the *Guardian* (a leftish intellectual broadsheet) and the *Daily Mail* (a right-wing tabloid). As we saw in the discussion of the literary politics of the 1920s, the Soviet cultural model—the transmission of socially necessary qualities to the masses through the medium of the printed word—posited an inert and unsophisticated audience without any strongly formed tastes of its own. The Soviet people had once read, with genuine pleasure, Gor'kii, Nikolai Ostrovskii, Sholokhov, and a range of Soviet

in *Nezavisimaia gazeta*, 10 Dec. 1992, 1.

23 Information about women writers' inability to publish, or their unwillingness even to try to publish, some of their work in the Brezhnev and Gorbachev eras comes from R. Marsh's personal interviews with Sedakova, Miller, Elena Chizhova, Katerli, Ulanovskaia, and Ulitskaia.

24 M. Zolotonosov, 'The Fountain at Rest: A Small Monograph on Postsocialist Realism', in Berry and Miller-Pogacar (eds.), *Re-Entering the Sign*, 159–60.

25 The Soviet reading public's predilection for *belletristika* from the 1920s onwards is analysed in A. Reitblat, 'Osnovnye tendentsii razvitiia massovogo chteniia v SSSR', in N. Kartashov (ed.), *Tendentsii razvitiia chteniia v sotsialisticheskikh stranakh* (Moscow, 1983), 119–45.

26 See K. Mehnert, *The Russians and their Favorite Books* (Cambridge, Mass., 1983).

hacks; now it was expected to read, with equal pleasure, Bulgakov, Pasternak, and Solzhenitsyn. However, the Soviet reader of the early 1990s was rather different from the one the literary intelligentsia had constructed in its imagination.

In fact, the Soviet reading public changed fundamentally from the 1960s onwards. First of all, it got a lot bigger—an important precondition for a mass culture. In the 1940s and 1950s the inculcation of *kul'turnost'* produced only a comparatively thin cultured stratum; in the 1960s urbanization, wider access to education, improved living conditions, and increased leisure time all had the effect of creating a new, broader class of habitual readers. The prestige of books increased significantly, as did the size of private collections. Now readers were more likely to quench their thirst for the printed word in the privacy of their own homes; public libraries, which had functioned effectively as bringers of mass enlightenment in the 1920s and 1930s, were failing to meet the public demand for light reading.[27] An interesting role in the changing social function of reading was played by the *makulatura* scheme, introduced in 1974, whereby unwanted newspapers and magazines could be exchanged for books. This experiment was, of course, introduced as an attempt to solve the perennial Soviet paper shortage, but as a side-effect it went some way to forming mass taste. Large sections of the population which had previously been uninterested in the printed word outside newspapers were now introduced to the idea of the book as something valuable to be acquired; they were also encouraged to build a library of ideologically neutral and highly readable literature. Foreign writers of historical fiction such as Dumas and Druon accordingly became all the rage: they were printed and reprinted throughout the 1970s, and are still to be found on the bookshelves of many post-Soviet families.[28]

Perhaps the most extraordinary phenomenon in home-grown Soviet popular culture in the 1970s and 1980s was also a writer of historical fiction, Valentin Pikul', who lived most of his life in Soviet Latvia and died in 1990. He was the best-selling author of more than twenty historical novels encompassing 300 years of European history, but set principally in the eighteenth century. At the height of his career, his novels received a minimum print-run of 150,000 hardbacks, which would typically be sold out within a week. In 1991 alone the combined print-run of his novels came to nearly 8 million. Most of his novels were filmed, which made him into a rouble multi-millionaire, although this did not alter his austere lifestyle. Pikul''s most controversial novel was *At the End of the Line* (*U poslednei cherty*, 1979), an unprecedentedly detailed portrayal of the private life of Nicholas II and the Empress Alexandra up to the summer of 1918, emphasizing

27 See G. Walker, 'Readerships in the USSR: Some Evidence from Post-War Studies', *Oxford Slavonic Papers*, 19 (1986), 158–73, and V. Stel'makh (ed.), *Kniga i chtenie v zerkale sotsiologii* (Moscow, 1990).

28 See A. Levinson, 'Makulatura i knigi: Analiz sprosa i predlozheniia v odnoi iz sfer sovremennoi knigotorgovli', in V. Stel'makh (ed.), *Chtenie: Problemy i razrabotki* (Moscow, 1985), 63–88.

the role of Rasputin and his adventures with high-society women. Pikul' advanced a historical interpretation unusual at that time, attributing the fall of the tsarist empire to the disintegration and debauchery of the ruling élite rather than to the success of the revolutionaries. In this novel Pikul' for the first time expressed his own political views, those of a strongly right-wing Russian nationalist, accusing Jews of bringing about communism, the suppression of the Orthodox Church, and the complete destruction of the country. Before Solzhenitsyn in *The Red Wheel*, Pikul' treated Petr Stolypin, Prime Minister from 1906 to 1911, with respect, and presented his murder as a tragedy for Russia. Pikul''s novel created a sensation among the Russian reading public, although he was berated for alleged anti-Semitism (a charge he always denied, calling himself a true Russian patriot), low-brow style, and superficial, sensationalist approach to historical events. A contrary opinion was, however, expressed by the Soviet historian Nikolai Molchanov, who called him 'a major historian of Russia'.[29]

The enormous popularity of Pikul''s novel suggests that it not only satisfied the Soviet public's demand for escapist fiction, but also its long-suppressed yearning for information about the tsarist past, especially the life of the last tsar, and that its nationalist values appealed to a large constituency in late-Soviet Russia. This became even more evident in 1989, when huge public interest in the fate of the last tsar and his family resurfaced after reports of the alleged discovery of their burial site. Fascination with the Romanov dynasty and reverence for Nicholas II have increased in the post-Communist period; and since the ethos of Pikul''s novel corresponded closely to the resurgent nationalism of the 1990s, it was republished in 1992 under the title *Evil Force* (*Nechistaia sila*) with formerly excised passages restored.

Although in the 1970s and early 1980s some steps were taken to provide the mass reader with suitably entertaining reading matter, this reader was never exposed to genuine mass literature. Western thrillers and romantic novels were strictly out of bounds. Such neglect was determined not only by ideological illwill but also by the structure of Soviet publishing. The mechanisms of supply and demand were not in place: publishing was highly centralized and, with occasional exceptions such as the works of Pikul', produced unwanted books in absurdly large print-runs. A writer's popularity was always less important than his or her status in the Soviet Writers' Union. Moreover, the sociology of reading was poorly developed: little interest was taken in the private book-owners whose forays into public libraries were becoming increasingly rare. The boom in the number of readers from the 1960s onwards created a book culture based on

29 Negative response in *Pravda*, 8 Oct. 1979; for Pikul''s claim that his novel also provoked personal assault, see the interview in *Nash sovremennik*, 2 (1989), 184–92. Molchanov quoted in J. Vronskaya's obituary, *Independent*, 21 July 1990. For a more detailed discussion of Pikul''s novels, see Mehnert, *The Russians*, 155–60.

shortages: a large number of readers chased after an insufficient number of desirable books on a flourishing black market. Some people clearly had greater access to this market than others: in 1989 it was estimated that 7 per cent of families owned 40 per cent of books.[30] The cultural diversity of the reading public was never properly taken into account: the number of titles published went down, books became thicker, and their print-runs larger. All this had the prophylactic effect of blocking cultural dynamism and diversity.

When Soviet readers were able to satisfy their yearning for good, diverting stories by reading novels that sought to do nothing else but meet this need, they abandoned the thick journals and 'forgotten' novels of the *glasnost'* period. However, the transition from a Soviet to a mass culture is not as clear-cut as this might suggest. Whether or not a book belongs to a mass or mainstream culture depends on the way it is read by real readers in a particular society at a particular time. Hence Rybakov's *Children of the Arbat* may be regarded as a work of mass culture *avant la lettre*. Within the intelligentsia it provoked a huge polemic about the historical roots of Stalinism, but the novel's enormous popularity with the wider public was due to its engrossing plot and the immediacy of its depiction of the 1930s. Rybakov's fictional portraits of Stalin and Kirov were regarded as of questionable accuracy by critics, but they must surely have exercised considerable fascination on most general readers. Vladimir Dudintsev's *Robed in White* (*Belye odezhdy*), another novel written before *glasnost'* but previously unpublished, was adapted for television in a way that emphasized its love interest rather than its account of Stalin's assault on the natural sciences. And Nikita Mikhalkov's Oscar-winning *Burnt by the Sun* (*Utomlennye solntsem*), had it been released five years earlier, would probably have been assessed—and found wanting—for its contribution to the historical debate on the 1930s; in 1994, though, it could be appreciated for its account of the personal tragedy of an old Bolshevik and its psychological drama.

The arrival of mass literature in Russia has had a disruptive effect on the sedate literary process of post-Soviet cultural life. Books have literally been displaced—they are now sold in large quantities on the streets and at wholesale markets such as the one to be found at the Olympic sports centre in Moscow. Street bookstalls (*lotki*) are perhaps the surest indicator of popular demand in the emerging book market. Most sellers make sure to cater for Russia's new professionals: there is a large number of textbooks on business, management, law, and accountancy, as well as on foreign languages. These aids to professional advancement are joined by the slightly more unexpected subjects of religion, occultism, and pets—three pillars of psychological

30 L. Gudkov and B. Dubin, *Literatura kak sotsial'nyi institut* (Moscow, 1994), 265; this volume is full of information and insights on the sociology of reading in the USSR.

support in post-Soviet Russia. There has in fact been a boom in books on psychology, covering anything from body language to teenage rebellion. Pornography is a predictable ingredient in most large bookstalls, although there is reckoned to be less of it now than in the early 1990s.

It seems, nevertheless, that in the face of all this diversity fiction has still managed to cling to its predominant position in Russian print culture. Adventure stories, romantic novels, and thrillers all appear to sell fast. In 1993–4 the genre of historical fiction underwent a resurgence, recapturing some of the ground it had lost to sex and violence. The ever-popular Pikul' has been joined by other writers who have an opinion to offer on the lives of the Russian tsars, the history of the nobility, or Eurasianist interpretations of Russia's origins. Publishers tested the waters in 1990–1 by bringing out new editions of Soviet historical fiction, for example works by Aleksei Iugov, Arkadii Perventsev, and even the highly ideologized Georgii Markov. These were soon joined on the book market by some late nineteenth-century historical fiction: Vsevolod Solov'ev's epic *Chronicle of Four Generations* (*Khronika chetyrekh pokolenii*) and *The Young Emperor* (*Iunyi imperator*, about Peter II), and Vsevolod Krestinskii's *bytovye romany* (novels of everyday life), all saw the light of day. By 1995 publishers were confident enough in their analysis of popular taste to commission works of historical fiction from contemporary writers. The publishing house Armada put out a series entitled 'The Romanovs: A Dynasty in Novels', consisting of nearly a dozen volumes, each with a print-run of over 100,000. This seems to suggest that history, and especially historical fiction, has a significant role to play in articulating a post-Soviet national identity.[31]

Another notable trend in 1994–5 was a move away from foreign novels to domestic produce. In part this was motivated by financial considerations: in 1973 the Soviet Union joined the Universal Copyright Convention, and so a Russian publishing house has to pay for the rights to any foreign work written since then. However, there are also signs of Russian authors mastering formula genres such as the romantic novel (known as *zhenskii roman*, women's novel). Crime novels are flourishing too. Many have a topical flavour, often to the extent of featuring Boris Yeltsin as the principal character.[32] And the novels in Viktor Pronin's *Banda* series (thrillers detailing a detective's no less topical struggle with the mafia in a provincial Russian city) regularly appear at the top of the best-seller lists published in the weekly newspaper *Knizhnoe obozrenie* (*Book Review*). Yet it is not clear that the Western notion of best-seller is applicable to Russian publishing in the 1990s. The claims of Russian best-sellers are based on

31 For more detail see A. Arkhangel'skii, 'Gei, slaviane!', *Novyi mir*, 7 (1995), 213–24.
32 See D. Babich, 'Double Trouble in Yeltsin Dystopia', *Guardian*, 10 Apr. 1996, 12.

a minute sample of retail outlets: the Russian system of book promotion and distribution is not developed enough for any novel to reach a truly mass audience. Perhaps, in the absence of a comfortably off middle class, there is no prospect of a mass book market in the immediate future.

However, these considerations are unlikely to deter writers in Russia. There may well be no internationally applicable blueprint for a best-seller, but the search for a specifically Russian model is certainly under way: writing popular fiction is a potentially lucrative activity in a country where over 100,000 people attended the Ninth Moscow International Book Fair in September 1995; in the West such an occasion would attract few outside the publishing business. It seems highly probable that the Russian best-seller, when it arrives, will neglect the 'accursed questions' of Russian intellectual history while in some way exuding confidence in what tomorrow will bring (*uverennost' v zavtrashnem dne*). Writers have thus far had more trouble meeting the latter requirement: many of them have achieved an abrupt break with the spiritual concerns of the Russian literary tradition, but have discovered that to replace *dukhovnost'* with violence, cynicism, and *chernukha* (*verismo*) is insufficient for commercial success. What post-Soviet citizens appear to want is reading matter that does not remind them of the malaise of their own society, and at the same time projects a fundamentally stable moral universe. This hypothesis perhaps goes some way to explaining the quite spectacular success of South American soaps on Russian television in recent years; it might also shed some light on why, of all contemporary, non-popular Russian writers, the anecdotal *émigré* Sergei Dovlatov appears to be most in demand.

The commercialization of culture was a necessary concomitant of the freedom of speech that was formally recognized in the Law on the Press of June 1990 (a similar law for the new Russia was passed in December 1991). The idea that culture would have to exist without state support was met with (often well-founded) alarm by the intelligentsia. Writers resented a (seemingly new, but actually rather venerable) kind of commission (*zakaz*)—that of the market. It is a sad irony that freedom of speech indirectly brought an end to the vigorous independence of the *samizdat* publications that had multiplied in the late 1980s. *Nezavisimaia gazeta* (*The Independent*), which started as a breakaway venture by journalists from the *perestroika* flagship *Moskovskie novosti* (*Moscow News*) and rapidly gained a reputation as the most dynamic investigative newspaper in Russia, in time found its independence and very existence threatened by harsh economic realities. It temporarily ceased publication in 1995 and seemed on the verge of closure, although it eventually found a backer. The Russian press has had to resign itself to never recapturing the mass appeal of the *perestroika* years. Now most Russians prefer local newspapers to the central press. Indeed, it could be argued that, with the possible exceptions of *Komsomol'skaia pravda* and *Argumenty i fakty* (*Arguments and Facts*), there are no truly national newspapers left. It is surely significant that both these papers are weeklies: they leave the business of intensively monitoring political developments to dailies and other media, and instead offer a judicious blend of down-to-earth social and political comment, sensationalism, and pure entertainment.

Towards a New Pluralist Consensus?

There are signs that leading members of the intelligentsia are beginning to learn the lessons of recent years, and to attempt to use mass culture as an arena for their kind of moral and political debate. In 1995 Solzhenitsyn and Voinovich chose to resort to television rather than to literature in order to get their views across to a wider public: Solzhenitsyn was allowed to appear regularly on the government-sponsored Channel One, engaging in direct addresses to his fellow-countrymen under the title 'Meetings with Aleksandr Solzhenitsyn', until his broadcasts were banned in the run-up to the elections of December 1995; and Voinovich was writing a hilarious, satirical television series entitled 'The New Russians'.[33] And if, notwithstanding the unprecedented cultural and spiritual renaissance of 1987–8, by 1991 it had become commonplace to speak of the death of not only Soviet, but also Russian, literature, by 1995 the apocalyptic mood seemed to have passed. Some interest in serious contemporary fiction was aroused by the establishment of the Booker Prize in Russia in 1992.[34] And the Russian publishing market has become able to accommodate a bewildering variety of genres: alongside the boom in home-grown thrillers, horror stories, and erotica, those 'thick journals' which still remain in business are competing with publishing houses to keep interesting contemporary Russian literature alive in the post-Communist period.

Postmodernism, a concept interpreted more widely in Russia than by Western theorists such as Jean Baudrillard, Jean-François Lyotard, or Fredric Jameson, is now regarded by many Russian critics as the dominant form of post-Soviet literature. In the words of the influential young critic Viacheslav Kiritsyn, 'Post-modernism today isn't simply a fad, it's part of the atmosphere; you can like it or not like it, but precisely it and only it is relevant at the moment.'[35] By 1995 there

33 For a discussion of Solzhenitsyn's broadcasts, see K. Kedrov, 'Poniatna tol'ko bol'', *Izvestiia*, 20 Sept. 1995, 5; on their banning, see V. Turovskii, '6 versii o prichinakh zakrytiia "Versii", i ne tol'ko . . .', *Izvestiia*, 26 Sept. 1995, 1–2. The information about Voinovich comes from a Sept. 1995 meeting where he read extracts from his new script 'Novye russkie' to an audience of Moscow schoolchildren and teachers.

34 See D. Bykov in *Rossiiskaia gazeta*, 8 Dec. 1992, 7; A. Nemzer in *Nezavisimaia gazeta*, 10 Dec. 1992, 1; and A. Latynina in *Literaturnaia gazeta*, 16 Dec. 1992, 7. On the limitations of the Russian Booker Prize novels, see S. Dalton-Brown, 'Lucrative Literature: The Booker Prize in Russia', in M. Pursglove (ed.), *The New Russia* (Oxford, 1995), 23–34, and A. Tait, 'The Awarding of the Third Booker Prize', *Modern Language Review*, 92 (1997), 660–77.

35 V. Kuritsyn, 'Postmodernism: The New Primitive Culture', in Berry and Miller-Pogacar (eds.), *Re-Entering the Sign*, 53.

was some evidence that (post-)Soviet postmodernism may have been only a transient phenomenon, or, as in the West, a persistent, but strictly minority genre appealing only to a narrow intellectual élite. The disillusionment of many ordinary Russian readers with obscure postmodernist texts is reflected in the resurgence of realistic novels such as Vladimov's *The General and his Army* (*General i ego armiia*), which won the Booker Prize in 1995; and the continuing significance of documentary prose genres, such as the novel-essay.[36]

It is undeniably true that Russian literature will never be the same as it was before Gorbachev's accession. *Glasnost'* gave new authors and works a central place in the Russian literary canon, and destroyed the reputations of former Soviet classics. The critic Mikhail Zolotonosov emphasized this process in his ironic article 'IАIТSАТUРER as a Phenomenon of Soviet Culture' (the strange word is *reputatsiia* (reputation) spelt backwards).[37] By the end of the Soviet period, the formerly official literature of socialist realism was in decline (although it continued to enjoy cult status among former communists, and by 1994 was still much in demand as a form of escapism, or a 'tranquillizer');[38] the genre of village prose had lost the great popularity it achieved in the Brezhnev era (even though the nationalistic and patriarchal values it propagated were by no means dead); and the 'liberal' anti-Stalin literature published in 1987–8 already seemed outdated (although it was still being produced). The former emphasis on Soviet values had been replaced by an interest in Russian literature and philosophy, both of the pre-Revolutionary and *émigré* varieties, and Russian culture had re-established its links with world culture.

Whereas in the Brezhnev era heated debates used to rage among Western critics and Russian *émigrés* about whether there was 'one Russian literature or two',[39] the cultural revolution of the *glasnost'* era swept away all rigid distinctions between liberal and dissident writers, between literature written in the metropolis and the emigration, or between realist and postmodernist prose. It could be argued that all these trends can now be regarded as component parts of the complex diversity of modern Russian literature, which encompasses a wide range of political views (from liberal democracy to conservative nationalism), a variety of opinions on sexual morality (from puritanism to extreme licence), and a multitude of literary forms covering the entire spectrum from conventional realism (both Soviet and anti-Soviet) to diverse forms of postmodernist experimentation. However, the emergence of such pluralism does not mean that all conflicts between individuals or groups of writers have been eradicated or are treated with greater tolerance. By 1995, when the failure of post-Soviet 'democracy' and the rise of nationalism and anti-Semitism in

36 See Vladimov's defence of realism in 'Govoriat laureaty fonda "Znameni"', *Znamia*, 3 (1995), 196–8, and P. Basinskii, 'Sumerki realizma', *Literaturnaia gazeta*, 27 Sept. 1995, 4. On the novel-essay, see A. Melikhov, 'Pliuralizm, no v meru', *Literaturnaia gazeta*, 29 Mar. 1995, 4. For more on postmodernism in Russia, see below, Conclusion.
37 M. Zolotonosov, 'IАIТSАТUРER kak fenomen sovetskoi kul'tury', in V. D. Oskotskii and E. A. Shklovskii (eds.), *Vzgliad: Kritika, polemika, publikatsii*, iii (Moscow, 1991), 274–91.
38 See S. Chuprinin, 'Perechen' primet', *Znamia*, 1 (1995), 190.
39 See e.g. O. Matich (ed.), *The Third Wave: Russian Literature in Emigration* (Ann Arbor, 1984), 23–50.

Russia had become evident, there were signs that a new division was emerging in Russian literature: some *émigré* writers such as Zinovii Zinik had come to feel that their works were ignored just as much by the public of the new Russia as by the previous Soviet regime.[40]

40 We are grateful to Julian Graffy for this information based on interviews with Zinik.

Suggested further reading

Literature, 1917–1953:

Brown, E. J., *Russian Literature since the Revolution*, rev. edn. (Cambridge, Mass., 1982).

Clowes, E. W., *Russian Experimental Fiction: Resisting Ideology after Utopia* (Princeton, 1993).

Crouch, M., and Porter, R. (eds.), *Understanding Soviet Politics Through Literature: A Book of Readings* (London, 1984).

Erlich, V., *Modernism and Revolution: Russian Literature in Transition* (Cambridge, Mass., 1994).

Hingley, R., *Russian Writers and Soviet Society, 1917–1978* (London, 1979).

Janecek, G., *The Look of Russian Literature: Avant-Garde Visual Experiments 1900–1930* (Princeton, 1984).

Kasack, W., *Dictionary of Russian Literature since 1917* (New York, 1988).

Kelly, C., *A History of Russian Women's Writing, 1820–1991* (Oxford, 1994).

Maguire, R. A., *'Red Virgin Soil': Soviet Literature in the 1920's* (Princeton, 1968).

Mathewson, R., *The Positive Hero in Russian Literature*, 2nd edn. (Stanford, Calif., 1975).

Moser, C. C. (ed.), *The Cambridge History of Russian Literature* (Cambridge, 1992).

Shepherd, D., *Beyond Metafiction: Self-Consciousness in Soviet Literature* (Oxford, 1992).

Struve, G., *Russian Literature under Lenin and Stalin: 1917–1953* (London, 1972).

Thomson, B., *The Premature Revolution: Russian Literature and Society, 1917–1946* (London, 1972).

Cultural and literary policy:

Borland, H., *Soviet Literary Theory and Practice During the First Five-Year Plan* (New York, 1950).

Brown, E. J., *The Proletarian Episode in Russian Literature, 1928–1932* (New York, 1953).

Dewhirst, M., and Farrell, R. (eds.), *The Soviet Censorship* (Metuchen, NJ, 1973).

Dunham, V., *In Stalin's Time: Middleclass Values in Soviet Fiction* (London, 1976; repr. Cambridge 1979).

Eastman, M., *Artists in Uniform: A Study of Literature and Bureaucratism* (London, 1934).

Fitzpatrick, S. (ed.), *Cultural Revolution in Russia, 1928–1931* (Bloomington, Ind., 1984).

Garrard, J., and Garrard, C., *Inside the Soviet Writers' Union* (London, 1990).

Gleason, A., Kenez, P., and Stites, R. (eds.), *Bolshevik Culture: Experiment and Order in the Russian Revolution* (Bloomington, Ind., 1985).

Grayson, J., and Hosking, G. A. (eds.), *Ideology and Russian Literature* (London, 1990).

Günther, H. (ed.), *The Culture of the Stalin Period* (Basingstoke, 1990).

Hahn, W., *Postwar Soviet Politics: The Fall of Zhdanov and the Defeat of Moderation, 1946–1953* (Ithaca, NY, 1982).

Kemp-Welch, A., *Stalin and the Literary Intelligentsia, 1928–39* (Basingstoke, 1991).

Kenez, P., *The Birth of the Propaganda State* (Cambridge, 1985).

Mally, L., *Culture of the Future: The Proletkult Movement in Revolutionary Russia* (Berkeley and Los Angeles, 1990).

Rosenberg, W. G. (ed.), *Bolshevik Visions: First Phase of the Cultural Revolution in Soviet Russia* (Ann Arbor, 1984).

Stites, R., *Revolutionary Dreams: Utopian Vision and Experimental Life in the Russian Revolution* (New York, 1989).

—— *Russian Popular Culture: Entertainment and Society since 1900* (Cambridge, 1992).

—— (ed.), *Culture and Entertainment in Wartime Russia* (Bloomington, Ind., 1995).

Swayze, H., *Political Control of Literature in the USSR, 1946–59* (Cambridge, Mass., 1962).

Trotsky, L. D., *Literature and Revolution*, tr. Rose Strumsky (London, 1991).

Vickery, W. N., *The Cult of Optimism* (Bloomington, Ind., 1963).

Socialist realism:

Chung, H. (ed.), *The Party Spirit: Socialist Realism and Literary Practice in the Soviet Union, East Germany and China* (Amsterdam, 1996).

Clark, K., *The Soviet Novel: History as Ritual*, 2nd edn. (Chicago, 1985).

Ermolaev, H., *Soviet Literary Theories 1917–1934: The Genesis of Socialist Realism* (Los Angeles, 1963).

Gorky, M., *et al.*, *Soviet Writers' Congress 1934: The Debate on Socialist Realism and Modernism in the Soviet Union* (London, 1977).

Groys, B., *The Total Art of Stalinism* (Princeton, 1992).

Hosking, G., 'The Socialist Realist Tradition', in *Beyond Socialist Realism: Soviet Fiction since Ivan Denisovich* (London, 1980), 1–28.

James, C. V., *Soviet Socialist Realism: Origins and Theory* (London, 1973).

Lahusen, T., and **Dobrenko, E.** (eds.), *Socialist Realism without Shores* (*South Atlantic Quarterly*, 94 (1995)).

Luker, N., 'Introduction', in Luker (ed.), *From Furmanov to Sholokhov: An Anthology of the Classics of Socialist Realism* (Ann Arbor, 1988), 11–38.

Robin, R., *Socialist Realism: An Impossible Aesthetic*, tr. C. Porter (Stanford, Calif., 1992).

Literature after 1953:

Aiken, S. H., **Barker, A. M.**, **Koreneva, M.**, and **Stetsenko, E.**, *Dialogues/Dialogi: Literary and Cultural Exchanges between (ex) Soviet and American Women* (Durham, NC, 1994).

Berry, E. E., and **Miller-Pogacar, A.** (eds.), *Re-Entering the Sign: Articulating New Russian Culture* (Ann Arbor, 1995).

Brown, D., *Soviet Russian Literature since Stalin* (Cambridge, 1978).

—— *The Last Years of Soviet Russian Literature: Prose Fiction 1975–91* (Cambridge, 1993).

Brown, E. J., *Russian Literature since the Revolution*, rev. edn. (Cambridge, Mass., 1982).

Clyman, T. W., and **Greene, D.** (eds.), *Women Writers in Russian Literature* (Westport, Conn., 1994).

Erofeyev, V. (ed.), *The Penguin Book of New Russian Writing* (Harmondsworth, 1995).

Garrard, J., and **Garrard, C.**, *Inside the Soviet Writers' Union* (London, 1990).

Glas: New Russian Writing (Moscow, 1991–).

Goscilo, H. (ed.), *Balancing Acts: Contemporary Stories by Russian Women* (Bloomington, Ind., 1989).

—— (ed.), *Fruits of her Plume: Essays on Contemporary Russian Women's Culture* (Armonk, 1993).

—— (ed.), *Lives in Transit: Recent Russian Women's Writing* (Ann Arbor, 1993).

—— and **Lindsey, B.** (eds.), *Glasnost: An Anthology of Russian Literature* (Ann Arbor, 1990).

Graham, S. D. (ed.), *New Directions in Soviet Literature* (Basingstoke, 1992).

Hingley, R., *Russian Writers and Soviet Society, 1917–1978* (London, 1979).

Hosking, G., *Beyond Socialist Realism: Soviet Fiction since Ivan Denisovich* (London, 1980).

Kelly, C., *A History of Russian Women's Writing, 1820–1992* (Oxford, 1994).

Lakshin, V., *Solzhenitsyn, Tvardovsky and 'Novyi Mir'*, tr. and ed. M. Glenny (Cambridge, Mass., 1965).

Loseff, L., *On the Beneficence of Censorship: Aesopian Language in Modern Russian Literature* (Munich, 1984).

Mal'tsev, Iu., *Vol'naia russkaia literatura: 1955–1975* (Frankfurt-am-Main, 1976).

Marsh, R., *Soviet Fiction since Stalin: Science, Literature and Politics* (London, 1986).

—— *Images of Dictatorship: Stalin in Literature* (London, 1989).

—— *History and Literature in Contemporary Russia* (Basingstoke, 1995).

Porter, R., *Russia's Alternative Prose* (Oxford, 1994).

Shneidman, N. N., *Soviet Literature in the 1970s: Artistic Diversity and Ideological Conformity* (Toronto, 1979).

—— *Soviet Literature in the 1980s: Decade of Transition* (Toronto, 1989).

Solzhenitsyn, A., *The Oak and the Calf: Sketches of Literary Life in the Soviet Union*, tr. H. Willetts (London, 1980).

Svirski, G., *A History of Post-War Soviet Writing: The Literature of Moral Opposition*, tr. and ed. R. Dessaix and M. Ulman (Ann Arbor, 1981).

Postmodernism and experimentation:

Berry, E. E., and **Miller-Pogacar, A.** (eds.), *Re-Entering the Sign: Articulating New Russian Culture* (Ann Arbor, 1995).

Clowes, E. W., *Russian Experimental Fiction: Resisting Ideology after Utopia* (Princeton, 1993).

Epstein, M., *After the Future: The Paradoxes of Postmodernism and Contemporary Russian Culture*, tr. and ed. A. Miller-Pogacar (Amherst, Mass., 1995).

Theatre, Music, Visual Arts

4

Performing Culture: Theatre

BIRGIT BEUMERS

Russian theatre practice of the twentieth century has been dominated both by a controversy over the function of theatre in society, reflected in changes of theatre administration and management, and also by conflicting theories about the relationship between theatre and the spectator, expressed in the competing concepts of demonstration (*predstavlenie*) and emotional experience (*perezhivanie*). Furthermore, not only did theories about the function of theatre determine a Soviet director's approach to the spectator; the absence of a consistent theory of the role of culture in socialism meant that, in the Soviet Union, theatres depended on the understanding of culture provided by a given leader, or by functionaries in charge of ideology.

For Lenin, theatre was a means of ideological agitation, experimental in form and politically engaged; during the Stalin era and, to a lesser extent, throughout the years of stagnation under Brezhnev, officially acceptable theatre was held to be that which created on stage the perfect illusion of a perfect society; during Khrushchev's thaw and Gorbachev's *glasnost'* the theatre again functioned as a tool for propaganda, this time to expose errors on a human and moral scale, to criticize human behaviour in order to improve the behaviour of man in a socialist society. Therefore, at certain times in Soviet history, the method of demonstration, appealing intellectually to the audience and inviting it to think critically about social developments, was rejected in favour of the less challenging method based on emotional identification with characters inhabiting a perfect world.

I shall examine first the history of theatre as an institution, and then discuss the main theatre practices in Soviet Russian theatre with a special emphasis on the text in performance, and its relationship to the audience.

Theatre as a Cultural Institution

Although theatre had played an important role in pre-Revolutionary Russian culture, the Bolsheviks were swift to realize its potential for agitation among the masses and the propagation of socialist ideas. In fact, during the Civil War the development of its rival, the cinema, was halted because of a lack of funds and film stock, and the theatre remained the most accessible and wide-reaching cultural institution, until in 1922 Lenin declared cinema 'the most important of all arts'[1] and directed funds primarily to the movie industry.

Immediately after the Revolution, Anatolii Lunacharskii was appointed Commissar of Enlightenment (head of Narkompros). He faced the task of reorganizing the entire theatrical administration, placing the former Imperial theatres under state control, and transforming private enterprises into municipal theatres. In Moscow this task was delegated to Vsevolod Meyerhold (Meierkhol'd) who, between 1920 and 1921, was in charge of the Moscow Theatre Section of the Commissariat, having previously made his name as director of numerous lavish productions in St Petersburg. During the initial years of the Soviet state, many theatre directors actively supported the revolutionary cause: apart from Meyerhold, these included Nikolai Evreinov and Sergei Eisenstein (Eizenshtein), forming part of a loose grouping commonly known as Theatrical October. Theatrical October rejected the theatrical traditions of the past, and directors embarked on projects that manifested a theatricalization of recent historical events, and were monumental in style, such as the 1920 mass spectacle of *The Storming of the Winter Palace* (*Vziatie Zimnego dvortsa*), staged by Evreinov to commemorate the October Revolution and involving 8,000 participants and 100,000 spectators. These directors demanded a break with the style Stanislavskii had developed at the Moscow Arts Theatre (MKhAT), based on psychological realism, emotional experience, and verisimilitude.

In 1920–1 theatres were reorganized and numbered by Meyerhold, who abolished the reference to patrons in the names of theatres (e.g. Korsh, Nezlobin, Sohn), and subordinated theatres to the Russian Federation. Meyerhold's was the RSFSR Theatre No. 1 (merger of Exemplary and Free Theatres, 1920), while the Nezlobin Theatre

1 Lenin in 1922, quoted in P. Kenez, *Cinema and Soviet Society 1917–1953* (Cambridge, 1992), 29.

merged with the Red Army Theatre to form RSFSR Theatre No. 2, and the Korsh Theatre became RSFSR Theatre No. 3. Like many artists of the left, Meyerhold was dismayed when the New Economic Policy was introduced in 1921; at the same time, control over theatres was assumed by the Department for Political Education (Glavpolitprosvet), a move which downgraded the roles of Lunacharskii and Meyerhold. In 1923, the RSFSR Theatre No. 1 was reorganized into the Meyerhold Theatre, in a reversion to the old principle of linking theatres to their founders. In 1919 many theatres had been awarded the status of 'academic', a move that served as a formal approval of their—largely realistic—tradition.[2] On a purely practical level, academic theatres were protected from the zeal of Meyerhold, who attempted to turn theatres into institutions serving the revolutionary purpose, since they came directly under Lunacharskii's control and were placed on a higher budget. New theatres were founded in an attempt to bring the theatre closer to specific groups of the working population: in 1918 the Proletkul't had begun to operate theatres in which the spectator could turn into an actor and participate or perform in the show. The Theatre of the Revolution and the Theatre of the Soviet Workers' Unions were founded in 1922, followed in the late 1920s by the Theatre of Young Workers.[3] In the early 1920s, the Moscow Arts Theatre operated a number of studios, in which Stanislavskii offered other directors the possibility of experimenting. The studio headed by Evgenii Vakhtangov, who explored fantastic realism and the grotesque, received theatre status as the Third Studio in 1921, and in 1926 became the Vakhtangov Theatre. The potential for diversity was reflected in the establishment of such theatres as the Moscow State Jewish Theatre (GOSET, 1920) and the Satire Theatre (1924). However, control of the widely accessible medium of theatre had to be ensured; and for this purpose, Glavrepertkom was instituted in 1923 to censor theatre repertoires.

The 1930s saw a reversal of the proliferation of theatres that had taken place during the early 1920s: the state and Party eradicated almost all those theatres and directors who had developed a more 'formalist' approach to the text and who strove, in different ways, towards a synthesis of artistic forms on the stage. Mikhail Chekhov, founder of the Second Moscow Arts Theatre Studio, had worked towards a new acting method that would draw on the actor's energy rather than (as in Stanislavskii's method) on character psychology. This, as well as his ideas of collective authorship for productions, encountered opposition within the theatre around 1927. Chekhov emigrated in 1928, and the studio was closed in 1936. The Proletkul't

2 Academic theatres (former Imperial theatres) included the Bol'shoi, Moscow Arts, Malyi, and Vakhtangov theatres in Moscow, and the Aleksandrinskii (Pushkin), Mariinskii (Kirov), and Mikhailovskii (Malyi Operatic) theatres in St Petersburg/Leningrad.
3 All three were to undergo politically significant changes of name at politically significant moments: the Theatre of the Revolution (1922–43) became the Moscow Theatre of Drama (1943–54), then the Maiakovskii Theatre (1954–present); the Theatre of the Soviet Workers' Unions (1922–38) became the Mossovet Theatre (1938–present); and the Theatre of Young Workers (1927–38) became the Theatre of the Lenin Komsomol (1938–present) (see R. Leach, Revolutionary Theatre (London, 1994), 61, and Teatral'naia entsiklopediia (Moscow, 1961–7)).

theatres, rejecting the notion of professionalism in acting, had been closed as early as 1932; Nikolai Okhlopkov was removed from his post as Artistic Director of the Realistic Theatre, and the company merged with Aleksandr Tairov's Kamernyi (Chamber) Theatre in 1938. The Meyerhold Theatre was closed in 1938, and Meyerhold was arrested and shot in 1940. The elevation of Stanislavskii's 'system' as the only acceptable method for actors' training in 1938 was the clearest possible indication of where rectitude was to lie.

All this, of course, suggests a preference for 'realism' in theatrical performance of a kind compatible with the socialist realism increasingly expected of written texts. In line with the tendency, examined above (see Ch. 2), of official discussions to leave out of the reckoning the reception of cultural products, debates about drama at the 1934 Congress of the Soviet Writers' Union focused overwhelmingly on the nature of the dramatic text rather than theatrical performance. The keynote address by Kirpotin contains a sideswipe at the 'rationalistic, abstract form' which 'repeats today the creative practice (historically justified in its day) of Maiakovskii in the drama and Meyerhold in the theatre', and which represents 'a mortal danger both for dramaturgy and for theatre'. What is striking is the brevity of Kirpotin's comments, and their reduction of a whole tradition of experimentation to two names; this suggests an unshakeable confidence in the capacity of new dramatic texts to generate appropriate theatrical forms and practices more or less fully in accord with the precepts of Stanislavskii, whom Kirpotin cites approvingly and at length. It is, however, possible to detect discordant notes in the proceedings of the Congress—further confirmation that 1934 did not represent the end of all room for manœuvre. So, four years before being condemned (though, unlike Meyerhold, not executed) for 'formalism', Tairov began his contribution by pointedly acknowledging that the days when theatre practitioners could claim that plays were mere pretexts for their work had now gone, and went on to draw applause with his assertion that dramatists and theatre practitioners alike were equally subordinate to the new 'idea of the building of a new society, the birth of a new human consciousness'; but his praise for the technical mastery of the Soviet theatre and criticism of the 'inadequate growth, inadequate technical armoury, inadequate creative scope and force of our dramaturgy' leave little doubt about his disagreement with Kirpotin's assessment of the relationship between text and performance. (This is borne out by Tairov's masterly management of his own performance: notwithstanding his text's lengthy reproach to Soviet playwrights, its peroration was met with suitably climactic 'noisy applause'.)[4]

4 See 'Doklad V. Ia. Kirpotina o sovetskoi dramaturgii' and 'Rech' A. Ia. Tairova', in *Pervyi Vsesoiuznyi s"ezd sovetskikh pisatelei, 1934: Stenograficheskii otchet* (Moscow, 1934; repr. 1990), 375–84 (379) and 420–3.

During the war many theatres were temporarily closed and actors drafted to serve the war effort. The late 1940s saw the opening of a number of new theatres: the Moscow Drama Theatre (Malaia Bronnaia) and the Moscow Theatre of Drama and Comedy (Taganka) in 1946, the Stanislavskii Drama Theatre in 1948, and the Pushkin Drama Theatre in 1950. GOSET and the Kamernyi Theatre were closed in 1949, both victims of the anti-Semitic campaign against 'rootless cosmopolitans' that was orchestrated in the aftermath of the *zhdanovshchina*.[5]

The liberal cultural policies associated with the post-Stalin thaw affected the theatre as well as other cultural practices. In 1953 the Ministry of Culture assumed the responsibility for repertoire control previously exercised by Glavrepertkom, but delegated responsibility for municipal theatres to the Moscow City Council. The need for diversity in the arts was asserted; in the theatre this entailed an assault on the canonization of the Stanislavskii system, and Meyerhold was rehabilitated. A number of appointments were made to the artistic directorship of reputable theatres in Moscow and Leningrad: Mariia Knebel' (Mikhail Chekhov's pupil) to the Central Children's Theatre (1955), where she helped Oleg Efremov and Anatolii Efros with their debuts as actor and director; Meyerhold's pupil Valentin Pluchek to the Satire Theatre (1957); Georgii Tovstonogov to the Bolshoi Drama Theatre (BDT) in Leningrad (1956); Anatolii Efros to the Theatre of the Lenin Komsomol (1963); and Iurii Liubimov to the Taganka Theatre (1964). In 1957 Oleg Efremov, together with young Moscow Arts School graduates, founded the Sovremennik Studio, which obtained theatre status in 1965. For a theatre that had suffered an almost fatal blow with the absence of distinguished dramatic writing since the promulgation of socialist realism in 1934, and the 'theory of no conflict' or *beskonfliktnost'* (commonly attributed to the writers Nikolai Virta and Boris Lavrenev) propounded in the late 1940s, these changes revived interest in the performing arts, and the diversity of the theatre was fully explored. The tour of the Berliner Ensemble to the Soviet Union in 1957 encouraged a debate over Brecht's epic theatre, and Brecht was to be a major influence in Soviet theatre during the late 1950s and 1960s (notable productions included Liubimov's version of *The Good Person of Szechwan*).

During the late 1960s and 1970s, however, theatrical life stagnated, both administratively and artistically. No new theatres emerged in the major cities. Censorship interfered heavily with the creation of repertoires, especially in the late 1960s. During the Twenty-Third Party Congress of 1966, several controversial productions were banned. In 1967, Efros was dismissed for 'ideological shortcomings' from his

5 On the *zhdanovshchina*, see above, Part I. The campaign against 'cosmopolitans' (euphemism for Jews) began as a campaign against the liberal course of some, mostly Jewish, theatre critics.

post at the Lenin Komsomol Theatre and given the inferior job of staff director at the Malaia Bronnaia Theatre. The editor of the journal *Teatr*, Iurii Rybakov, was relieved of his duties after he had published a series of positive reviews of controversial and banned productions. Young directors were granted almost no opportunity to work in the established theatre; in order to help them, many large theatres opened 'small stages' in the late 1970s for experimental work. Generally, though, the massive political and artistic censorship exercised after 1968 infringed the artistic licence of almost every theatre director, and inflicted yet another crushing blow on theatrical activity.

Throughout the 1960s and 1970s opposition to official demands or requests by the censors was possible, but carried an element of greater or lesser risk, depending on a number of external and internal, political and personal factors. Anniversaries of the Revolution, Party Congresses, or international events such as the Olympic Games in 1980 usually called for tighter rules to be applied. Party membership and the location of the theatre could influence decisions: Efros, not a Party member, was dismissed for his interpretations of Chekhov, while Liubimov, a Party member, was merely threatened with dismissal for his production of *The Life of Fedor Kuzkin* (*Zhivoi*) in the same season (1967/8). Efros's absurdist version of Chekhov's *Three Sisters* (*Tri sestry*) in Moscow was banned, while Party member Tovstonogov's *Three Sisters* was passed in Leningrad. Acts of censorship were ideologically inconsistent, and often reactions depended on the spur of the moment: Voznesenskii's *Protect Your Faces* (*Beregite vashi litsa*) was banned from the repertoire of the Taganka Theatre in 1971 because of a reference to the moon, taken as an allusion to the American superiority in space after their successful manned moon missions; the production would probably have been permitted in the 1960s. Control was delegated to low-ranking officials, and decisions were often motivated by their personal taste rather than ideological criteria. Directors could appeal to higher organs (the Central Committee, or the Ministry of Culture), as was the case with Liubimov's *Vysotskii*, which was granted special permission from the Central Committee in 1982 to be shown to a selected audience on the anniversaries of the birth and death of the poet and actor Vladimir Vysotskii.

After 1986, the Russian theatre benefited greatly from Gorbachev's reforms. Gorbachev replaced the hardliners in key positions in the cultural sector of state and Party[6] and encouraged a process of liberalization in the arts. The theatres supported, indeed promulgated, Gorbachev's policies of openness (*glasnost'*) and reform (*perestroika*) with great zeal and determination. On an organizational level,

6 Vasilii Zakharov succeeded Petr Demichev as Minister of Culture; Boris Yeltsin took over the Moscow Party Committee from Viktor Grishin; in the Central Committee, Egor Ligachev succeeded Mikhail Zimianin as Secretary for Ideology, Aleksandr Iakovlev followed Evgenii Tiazhel'nikov as Head of Agitprop, and Iurii Voronov succeeded Vasilii Shauro as Head of the Culture Section.

Gorbachev's economic reforms (the introduction of *khozraschet*, or independent budgeting) transformed theatres from institutions financially managed by the state and ideologically controlled by the Party, into independent theatres with autonomous administrations. The All-Russian Theatre Society (VTO) was disbanded, on the initiative of Oleg Efremov, and reorganized into the Theatre Workers' Union (STD): this removed the power of control over theatres from the Moscow City Council. At the same time the Artistic Councils (advisory boards) of theatres were endowed with substantial power over artistic and administrative matters, which led to the splitting of the Moscow Arts Theatre in 1987 (into the Chekhov MKhAT of Oleg Efremov, and the Gor'kii MKhAT of Tat'iana Doronina); to the division of the Taganka Theatre (one section headed by ex-Minister of Culture Nikolai Gubenko, the other by Liubimov); the separation of the Ermolova Theatre (one group led by Vladimir Andreev, the other run by the theatre's Artistic Council). All these were early side-effects of democratization.

The experiment allowing theatres to run their own budgets proved especially beneficial to the studio theatres.[7] They were able to obtain official status and claim subsidies from the local authorities; consequently, their number grew rapidly. The studios enjoyed enormous popularity in the late 1980s. From 1991 new conditions of management were introduced by law:[8] theatres were encouraged to seek alternative sources of funding, while the subsidies remained fixed and a contract system ensured that only essential staff would be kept on the payroll. A variety of forms of ownership became possible: theatres could be municipal or federal institutions, or private enterprises. Producers' agencies were established to finance productions. Many theatres are now commercial not only in that they are run for profit, but also in that they offer entertainment in the form of musicals or revues; experimentation remains possible only on the small stages or in studio theatres, many of which, however, have failed to sustain the reputation for innovation that they established in the late 1980s.

Audiences now had choices not previously available; during the 1960s and 1970s tickets for theatres in demand (Taganka, Sovremennik) had been difficult to acquire and were often sold only in conjunction with a ticket for an undersubscribed theatre, or obtained by *blat* (networking, exchange of favours). Freedom of choice initially increased the popularity of the studios, then interest in the theatre dropped altogether in favour of TV serials and political debates in the late 1980s and early 1990s. Theatres now play to small audiences, although the interest in theatre art has revived. The spectator of the 1990s is more and more overtly pushed into the role of a

7 *Prikaz Ministerstva kul'tury SSSR*, 330, 6 Aug. 1986.
8 *Postanovlenie soveta ministrov RSFSR*, 297, 31 May 1991.

consumer, which is an inevitable side-effect of the move towards a market-oriented state.

Text in Performance: 1917–1953

At the Moscow Arts Theatre Konstantin Stanislavskii (1863–1938) had aimed at creating an illusion of reality on stage, and wished the theatre to mirror reality. The actor in his theatre created roles on the basis of psychological realism so that the audience could identify and experience with the actor the emotions of the character. Stanislavskii's actor motivated his words psychologically, and the text therefore was sacrosanct in such a theatre. Vsevolod Meyerhold (1874–1940), by contrast, perceived the function of theatre as that of a magnifying glass, which would enhance certain fragments or episodes from reality. Meyerhold restructured plays into fragments and episodes which would rouse the audience rationally rather than (as in Stanislavskii's method) emotionally. He staged both classics, such as Crommelynck's *The Magnanimous Cuckold* (*Velikodushnyi rogonosets*) and Sukhovo-Kobylin's *Tarelkin's Death* (*Smert' Tarelkina*) (both 1922) and contemporary plays, such as Maiakovskii's *The Bath-House* (*Bania*) and *The Bedbug* (*Klop*). The sets were constructivist in style, the costumes resembling factory wear (set and costume designs were made by such artists as Liubov' Popova, Aleksandr Rodchenko, and Varvara Stepanova) in order to bring art closer to the worker. Meyerhold perceived theatre as having a social and political function; he went out to factories to perform plays, and closely monitored audience response in order to heighten the comical and agitational elements in his productions.[9] The spectator, he held, should always be aware of being in a theatre, and should never be deluded by a pretence of verisimilitude. Meyerhold used placards for locations as a stylization device, citations from documentary evidence, and cinematic features such as screens, slogans, and projections to draw parallels with real life. His actors were trained in biomechanics (the science of rational movement), so that movements on stage would be choreographed and paced (rather than motivated by psychological identification) and bring man closer to a perfect, machine-like state; he created types rather than characters with psychological depth. Meyerhold's was a theatre of demonstration (*predstavlenie*) rather than of identification and experience (*perezhivanie*), a theatre of stylization (*uslovnost'*) rather than realism (*byt*).

Between these polar opposites fell a number of directors such as Evgenii Vakhtangov (1883–1922), one of Stanislavskii's favourite

9 See L. Kleberg, *Theatre as Action: Soviet Russian Avant-Garde Aesthetics* (London, 1993), 94–100.

pupils, who emphasized the need for an imaginative interpretation of the text (rather than an obsession with the word, as in Stanislavskii, or a restructuring of the text into episodes outside narrative, as in Meyerhold) and for enhancing the grotesque aspect of reality. His style of fantastic realism was best captured in his 1922 production of *Princess Turandot*. Vakhtangov died prematurely, leaving no direct successor. Aleksandr Tairov (1885–1950) developed at the Kamernyi Theatre (1914–49) an actor-based approach, focusing on choreography in space and musicality in movement. Tairov remained politically uncommitted, drawing on the classical heritage of Western and Eastern theatre. He relied on the actor to control voice, gesture, and movement, and to synthesize all art forms into an aesthetic unity. His productions were carefully choreographed and musically paced, exploring the expressive possibilities of gesture in the free space of a stage which was occupied by the minimalist geometry of sets by Aleksandra Ekster (until her emigration in 1924) and the Stenberg brothers.

Throughout the 1930s and 1940s a restriction of the forms of artistic expression, elevating Stanislavskii's psychological realism to a system and making it the only valid form of actors' training, limited the diversity of theatrical approaches which had flourished during the first post-Revolutionary decade. The constructivist experiments of Meyerhold and the choreographic quests of Tairov were banned from theatrical theory and practice, as were the pursuits of actor-pedagogues. But some diversity was still possible. Mikhail Kedrov (1893–1972) explored those areas which had begun to influence Stanislavskii in the 1930s when he moved away from rigid psychologism towards a method of physical action. Mikhail Chekhov (1891–1955) was influenced by the anthroposophic ideas of Rudolf Steiner and applied the insights of meditation to his acting methods. But from the late 1940s, the *zhdanovshchina* as manifest in the 1948 decrees against diversity in repertoires, followed by propagandization of the notion that drama should be conflictless, all but paralysed the Soviet theatre. The need to reform the theatre was first expressed by critics, playwrights, and newspaper editors even before the death of Stalin, but theatre practitioners began to speak out only in 1956, when the Stanislavskii system was openly challenged by the Vakhtangov Theatre's directors Boris Zakhava and Ruben Simonov, who called for a synthesis of the acting methods of *perezhivanie* (experience) and *predstavlenie* (representation). The appointment of new directors during the thaw can be seen as a response on the part of state and Party officials to this quest for innovation.

Text in Performance: After 1953

Most important of all the changes was the formation in 1957 of a new theatre. The Sovremennik (Contemporary) emerged from a course of the MKhAT School headed by Oleg Efremov (b. 1927), at a time when the Arts Theatre was signally failing to make contact with contemporary audiences. The Sovremennik's audience, actors, and playwrights all belonged to the younger generation. Efremov built on the psychological realism of Stanislavskii in his productions of plays, choosing mainly texts with young protagonists, so that both actor and audience could identify psychologically with the characters. He rejected the trappings of external verisimilitude (make-up, costume), and relied instead on the actor to bring his personality into the role: an actor's personality would always remain visible as he identified psychologically with the character in a process of psychological fusion. Group homogeneity was vital for the theatre, which defined itself as a collective institution, and regarded a production as a collective artistic achievement. Efremov largely refrained from breaking down the 'fourth wall' (the barrier between stage and auditorium); actors shared experiences rather than space with the audience, creating a mental and psychological rather than a physical link. Efremov consciously combined stylization (*uslovnost'*), as exemplified in the non-realistic sets he used, with mimetic acting techniques, and demonstrated his closeness to the traditions of psychological realism, while dissociating himself from external verisimilitude. In 1970 he was appointed artistic director of the Moscow Arts Theatre, where he faced the task of reviving a theatre staffed by a *galère* of ageing actors and with a repertoire consisting of even older productions. Although he met this challenge very effectively to begin with, Efremov's success suffered when the Arts Theatre moved to a new building on Tverskoi Boulevard, too enormous in capacity to permit the bond with the audience which was so vital for Efremov's approach. Despite his efforts, the Arts Theatre ossified entirely.

In Leningrad, the post-war theatre scene was dominated almost exclusively by Georgii Tovstonogov (1913–89) who headed the Bol'shoi Drama Theatre (BDT) in Leningrad from 1957 until his death. He merged the concepts of Stanislavskii and Meyerhold, mixing authenticity (*dostovernost'*) with stylization (*uslovnost'*), and combining psychological analysis with figurativeness. Tovstonogov refrained from imposing his idea of a particular role on the actor: he saw the director's role as being to evolve a concept of the production as a whole. His productions showed a harmony between the past and the present, between the objective and the subjective, the political and the personal. Attracted by the possibilities of polyphonic structures, Tovstonogov favoured non-dramatic literature, and perceived the text as a scenario or a musical score. He employed cinematic devices, such as cuts (black-outs) used to separate episodes, and voice-overs (voices fade as a commentator resumes the narrative). Tovstonogov's *Three Sisters* (1965) was a landmark in the interpretation of Chekhov on the Soviet stage. Each of the sisters was alone with her predicament, and had nobody to share it with: everything between the sisters had been said before the curtain went up. Communication had no purpose, but underlined rather the absurdity of their existence. Tovstonogov refrained from challenging this absurdity, though, and showed sympathy and compassion for the sisters. At the end, he spatially united the sisters with the audience, bringing them into the auditorium on a revolving platform. In the 1970s Tovstonogov began to work with the set designer Eduard Kochergin (b. 1937), who creates monochrome spaces from natural material. Their successful collaboration was marked by the adaptation in 1975 of Tolstoi's *Strider—The Story of a Horse* (*Kholstomer*). Sackcloth was draped around the stage, with patches at the sides which could be opened; the costumes were made of the same material and were suggestive rather than naturalistic. Strider, played by Evgenii Lebedev, acted both as protagonist and narrator. Tovstonogov read the condition of the exploited horse as a tragic metaphor for human life, refraining from explicit social criticism. He remained throughout his career an uncontroversial figure in Soviet theatre, unlike Iurii Liubimov and Anatolii Efros.

After an immensely successful student production of Brecht's *The Good Person of Szechwan* (1964), Iurii Liubimov (b. 1917) was put in charge of the Taganka Theatre of Drama and Comedy. This and subsequent Taganka productions contained a strong socio-political element, building contacts with the audience: the theatre perceived society as a generator of social and political change. Liubimov combined devices from Brecht's epic theatre (placard, song) with Meyerhold's stylization, Eisenstein's montage, and Vakhtangov's fantastic realism, but, to placate the official view, included in the portrait gallery at his theatre a picture of Stanislavskii. Liubimov creates his own scenarios from poetry, prose, drama, and factual documents. His is an author's theatre (*avtorskii teatr*) in which the director composes the text and imposes his or her personal interpretation on the production. Liubimov wishes to create an awareness in spectators that they are in the theatre; the actor should not pretend or artificially evoke emotions in him- or herself, but instead react both to the role and to the audience. In Liubimov's theatre, the actor is

3 *Ten Days that Shook the World* in Performance, Taganka Theatre, Moscow, 1965.

Based on John Reed's famous account, Liubimov's spectacle rendered the atmosphere and force of the 1917 Revolution through a wide range of theatrical devices. Buffoonery, accompanied by verbal irony or satire, was a vital component for the portrayal of counter-revolutionary and bourgeois scenes. In this scene, 'Meeting of the US Senate Commission', the senators interrogating Reed stood in front of an animated portrait of Wilson, with only their hands and faces emerging from behind their robes (a device used in Meyerhold's 1906 production of Blok's *The Little Fairground Booth*). This reduction of the senators to insignificant men hiding behind their profession and position was reinforced by ridicule at the textual level. The interrogation was followed by a song sung by Wilson from behind his animated portrait, and by an ensemble of music-hall singers emerging in hats, red boots, black fishnet tights, shorts, and waistcoats, with portraits of President Coolidge attached to their bottoms.

subordinated to the production concept, and is an executor of the director's will.

The range of theatrical devices available to Liubimov was fully displayed in *Ten Days that Shook the World* (1965), a spectacle loosely based on John Reed's account of the 1917 Revolution. As in Eisenstein's films of the 1920s, the real protagonists are the common people (*narod*): they are active and energetic, a driving force of the Revolution. The people represent contrasting forces in history, and achieve by their action a historical synthesis: revolution. The model of two opposing forces informs the aesthetic principle for the representation of reactionary and revolutionary forces in comic and tragic, grotesque and pathetic, satirical and serious terms. Pantomime, rehearsed with the help of circus artists, represented the Revolution in symbols or images, as in the rise of the red flame of revolution, or the beating of the anvil as a symbol for the power of the workers, sparking off the revolutionary fire. The imprisonment of revolutionaries was represented by the prisoners' holding their arms in the form of a rectangle around their faces, which were lit by a spot, creating the impression of heads behind bars. Shadow-play showed the 'shades of the past': several typical members of the old society passed behind a huge white screen which covered the entire height of the stage. Three Red Guard soldiers had their shadows enlarged to a size that even extended over the screen, almost wiping away all the 'elements' of the past. A 'light curtain' (light projected from the stage floor to the balcony) distanced stage events and marked scene changes (like cuts between cinema scenes). Brecht's devices for alienation proved valuable: songs commented on the action; projections of Lenin created a documentary atmosphere; placards indicated the place of action. The production started in the foyer, decorated with red banners bearing revolutionary slogans; the tickets were impaled on bayonets by Red Guards. The audience was asked upon leaving to vote for or against the production by inserting their tickets into either a red or a black box. The integration of the audience into the festive revolutionary atmosphere served to deprive history of its magnificence and private life of its seclusion. As such, *Ten Days* clearly marks Liubimov's allegiance to the tradition of Meyerhold and Brecht in the theatricalization of history, the stylization (and reduction to grotesqueness) of characters, and the intellectual demands placed upon the audience.

Liubimov's productions of the 1970s reflected the era of political stagnation: the individual was perceived as tragically alone in a hostile and evil society, while in the 1980s the isolated individual withdrew into himself and investigated his past through his conscience. Many Taganka actors were active in literature, film, or music as well as the theatre; among them was Vladimir Vysotskii (1938–80), best-known as a guitar poet, whose songs were illegally circulated on tapes (*magnitizdat*). With designer David Borovskii (b. 1934) Liubimov reached a perfect symbiosis: Borovskii worked with natural material and authentic objects, working out from a central metaphor that condensed the main idea in Liubimov's often overflowing theatricality into a straightforward formal image, without which the productions would not work. Thus, for example, the curtain in *Hamlet* (1971), woven of thick yarn, represented fate: it swayed across the stage with such force as to sweep people off the stage.

In contrast to Liubimov (the *enfant terrible* of Russian theatre because of his resistance to official demands for cosy psychological depth rather than challenging ideas and stylistic strategies), Anatolii Efros (1925–87) has to this day been neglected in Western accounts of Russian theatre history. At the beginning of his career he investigated the theme of children on their way to adulthood as represented in Viktor Rozov's plays. At the Theatre of the Lenin Komsomol he continued to build his repertoire almost entirely on contemporary drama. Efros worked with the concept of psychophysics, according to which movement makes inner psychological changes visible; the *mise-en-scène* expresses the inner conflict of the characters. The scenic space was stylized and neutral, giving no exact location. The actor actively created his role which was built in 'demonstrations' (*pokazy*), in which the actor showed his part to the director following a structural analysis. Towards the end of the 1960s Efros's interpretations of two Chekhov classics proved so controversial that he was dismissed from the theatre. *The Seagull* (Theatre of the Lenin Komsomol, 1966) was condemned for its unorthodox interpretation of Chekhov in terms of 'lack of communication', presenting Chekhov as a predecessor of the Western theatre of the absurd. Whereas in Tovstonogov's production lack of communication reflected the despair and isolation of the sisters, in Efros's, which centred on an understanding of non-communication as stemming from social atomization rather than from isolation of particular individuals for idiosyncratic reasons, all the characters were deprived of love, and of a meaning in life, and therefore relationships were dominated by the impossibility of communication. Efros thus challenged the assumption of socialist realism that man by definition has a meaning in life. Furthermore, the set was un-Chekhovian, made of new wooden boards—the product of the trees cut down in *The Cherry Orchard* (design by Sosunov and Lalevich). Similarly, in *Three Sisters* (Malaia Bronnaia Theatre, 1967) bitterness and disappointment pervaded the characters, who indulged in existential despair. The set was designed (by V. Ia. Durgin) in the

Russian *style moderne*, repeating the ornamentation of the Arts Theatre interior and thus making an ironic reference to the outmoded Arts Theatre productions of Chekhov. After his transfer to the Malaia Bronnaia Theatre, Efros also worked mainly on classical drama, always dwelling on the tragic dimension of a text.

These four directors have dominated Soviet theatre since the Second World War, perhaps because of their dependence on 1920s practice. Few new directors have emerged from their 'master-classes'. Indicative here are the cases of two directors who began in the pre-*glasnost'* period and are still working. Mark Zakharov (b. 1933), artistic director of the Theatre of the Lenin Komsomol since 1973, has created a wide-ranging repertoire and built up an ensemble with many actors known for their work in the cinema. The rock-opera *Perchance* (*Iunona i Avos'*, 1981) by Voznesenskii and Rybnikov attracted crowds to the theatre. Zakharov was highly regarded for his political engagement in the early *perestroika* period when he was one of the first to catch the spirit of reform, challenging in his articles the interference of bureaucrats. In his productions, he tackled historical issues with a hitherto unknown openness, as in Mikhail Shatrov's *The Dictatorship of Conscience* (*Diktatura sovesti*, 1985), which for the first time mentioned suppressed political figures, such as Bukharin and Trotskii, banned from Soviet history books. Lev Dodin has created a substantial repertoire at the Malyi Drama Theatre, Leningrad, mainly adapting prose for the stage. A trilogy based on Fedor Abramov's village prose (*The House* (*Dom*) and *Brothers and Sisters* (*Brat'ia i sestry*)), won him world-wide acclaim. His style is much influenced by Liubimov, and his devices often echo those used in Taganka productions. Although highly popular in the West, Dodin has not developed further the approach of stylization and demonstration he took over from Meyerhold and Liubimov; much of his work is derivative at heart.

Anatolii Vasiliev (b. 1942) is probably the most important and influential director in Russia today. A pupil of Mariia Knebel', he uses the actor like wax in his hands, creating a psychologically and physically real character on stage, behind which the personality of the actor is effaced. His production of Viktor Slavkin's *A Young Man's Grown-Up Daughter* (*Vzroslaia doch' molodogo cheloveka*, 1979) was spectacular because of its use of jazz music, condemned as decadent in the 1950s and 1960s. The play (about the meeting of old university friends, now in their forties, who were once jazz fans and *stiliagi*, or teddy boys) contrasts the present of the 1970s with the past of the 1950s (expressed through jazz music). On the small stage of the Taganka Theatre, Vasiliev rehearsed for several years Slavkin's next play, *Cerceau* (*Serso*, 1985) which was a landmark in Russian theatrical history and an emblem of the spirit of *glasnost'*. *Cerceau* is a product of lived experience together with material from a variety of sources: from Thomas Cook's train timetable to Nikolai Gogol'; from the brochure *How to Play Cerceau* to Anton Chekhov; from remarks made by the Swedish cultural attaché Lars Kleberg (the model for the figure of Lars in the play) to Pushkin. The play tells of the mid-life crisis suffered by a group of 40-year-olds. 'Rooster' (Petushok) invites some colleagues, neighbours, and chance acquaintances for a weekend at a dacha. All the characters lead their own lives without revealing their true feelings. After a series of excursions into the past, the tragic isolation of each person becomes apparent, and yet they are incapable of sharing more of their lives with each other. The production brought together seven actors, stars of the Russian theatre and cinema: the film stars Natal'ia Andreichenko and Aleksei Petrenko; Al'bert Filozov, Liudmila Poliakova, and Iurii Grebenshchikov from the Stanislavskii Theatre; and Dal'ian Shcherbakov and Boris Romanov from the Taganka Theatre. As such, it was the first production with an independent group of actors rather than a fixed company. Performances stopped in 1991 because there was no venue available, and the group disbanded. Vasiliev's production elevated a patchwork play to a sophisticated 4-hour performance. It showed a work dominated by past hopes and present despair, transformed to a glimpse of hope through memories of the past and of a youth that has never really faded. The world on the stage is a perfect illusion, and not only of immediate reality; it also allows for the recreation of the past through costumes and properties (the sticks and hoops of the game 'Cerceau', a cache of letters discovered in the dacha). Vasiliev deliberately creates a barrier between the stage world and the audience. In later productions he was to reject totally the external reality of the Moscow of the 1990s.

In 1987 Vasiliev set up his own theatre, the School of Dramatic Art. He has since focused on the process of rehearsal rather than the result, and therefore has not completed any production in Moscow, although he has directed a number of plays abroad. Instead, he invites each individual spectator to attend open rehearsals, or watch *Lament of Jeremiah* (*Plach Eremeia*, 1995), a choral performance which he choreographed. Initially experimenting with improvisation (Pirandello), he then worked on dialogue structures in philosophical treatises (Plato, Thomas Mann). His main concern is the expression of ideas and the relationship of the idea to the speaker. Although Vasiliev is without doubt one of the most influential theorists and teachers in Russia, as a practitioner he has not been able to live up to the degree of perfection he achieved in *Cerceau*.

Performance in the Post-Soviet Theatre

Vasiliev's concern with theory is an exception in the present Russian theatre. Directors of the 1960s and 1970s have left behind few theoretical writings. Petr Fomenko (b. 1932) is an exception: having moved from Moscow to Leningrad after the banning of several productions in 1968, he returned to Moscow in the 1980s to teach at the State Institute for Theatre Arts (Gosudarstvennyi institut teatral'nogo iskusstva, GITIS; now Rossiiskaia akademiia teatral'nogo iskusstva, RATI). His work as a pedagogue is as outstanding as are his productions in the professional theatre. He has set up a workshop (the Fomenko Studio, Masterskaia P. Fomenko), where his former students produce excellent work in a realistic vein. At the Vakhtangov Theatre he staged Ostrovskii's *Guilty without Guilt* (*Bez viny vinovatye*), the first act of which takes place in the foyer, and the second in the buffet, so that the action is ostensibly removed from the theatrical environment. Although Fomenko's strength is his work with the actor, he creates powerful images for individual scenes, never losing sight, though, of the overall idea of his production.

In the absence of censorship and control, directors are for the first time since the Revolution free again to experiment, and to return both artistically and financially to pre-Revolutionary structures, enriched by the contributions of Soviet directors and influences from the West. Innovative work is largely taking place on small stages and in studios, and taking shape in independent projects. The most impressive of these independent projects have been organized by the Meyerhold Centre, where Valerii Fokin (b. 1946) directed Kafka's *Metamorphosis* and *A Room in a Hotel in the City of N* (based on Gogol''s *Dead Souls*). Fokin reduces the scenic space of his productions to a minimum and forces the audience to share the pessimism and despair of his protagonists by physical closeness. The theatrical agency BOGIS (set up by BOGoliubova and ISaeva; Isaeva has left and runs a film actors' agency), with director-manager Galina Bogoliubova, has produced independent projects with actors Oleg Men'shikov and Aleksandr Feklistov (*N—Nijinsky* and *Bashmachkin*—an adaptation of Gogol''s 'The Overcoat'), both staged without a director. In her latest production, *The Last Night of the Last Tsar* (*Posledniaia noch' poslednego tsaria*, 1996), Bogoliubova assembled star names on the bill, with Fokin directing Mikhail Ul'ianov, Aleksandr Zbruev, Irina Kupchenko, and Evgenii Mironov, performing in a play by Eduard Radzinskii. Despite affordable ticket prices, the infrequent performances are not sold out.

The recent success of commercial theatres is best represented by the theatre of Roman Viktiuk, who established his reputation with a most controversial production of *The Maids* by Jean Genet. Himself homosexual, Viktiuk cast men in the parts of the maids and produced a show influenced by dance-theatre. He mixes elements of dance, music-hall, and cabaret in a magic theatre where the performer and spectator are led into a space situated between a recognizable reality and a world with dream-like qualities. For Viktiuk theatre is a metaphor for life, and he realizes in his productions what is impossible in reality, both in moral and aesthetic terms. Things morally wrong and socially not permissible are subjected to ornamentation until sin becomes, aesthetically speaking, so beautiful that it is unrecognizable as such. He perceives the world as an aesthetic phenomenon and stylizes at the expense of content. Viktiuk often relies on star names to attract audiences.

The diversity in Russian theatre has clearly unfolded after the reforms of the 1980s and the collapse of the Soviet state, which has allowed the theatre to assume a number of functions, commercial as well as educational, from platforms for philosophical debate to all-out entertainments, and to show a wide range of plays, from those raising hope to those evoking pessimism. However, the names of prominent directors belong mainly to the older generation: Vasiliev, Fomenko, Fokin, Zakharov, and Dodin are all over 50, and only in St Petersburg have some younger directors, notably Vasiliev's pupils, been granted access to established theatres. Moreover, little work is being done that lays the foundations for new methods of acting, with the exception of Vasiliev, who fails to translate his methods into practice. It is in this area that the Russian theatre is still struggling, trying to pick up the threads of the past where they were cut off in the 1930s rather than develop genuinely new concepts of theatre based both on the 'golden age' of the 1920s and the techniques of Western directors such as Jerzy Grotowski, Eugenio Barba, Giorgio Strehler, Peter Stein, or Peter Brook.

5

Music in the Socialist State

ANNA FERENC

Modernism and Proletkul't, 1921–1932

In discussing initial musical developments under proletarian dictatorship in Russia, one must distinguish between the political structuring
of the art on the one hand and, on the other, actual music-making.
From the political point of view, the year 1921 marks a relatively
significant victory for the state in its bid for more control in the
cultural arena once the autonomous and in part reactionary forces
of the Proletkul't had been disbanded in October 1920. However, the
absence of a clear ideological programme for the proletarianization
of music, confusion over the abstract nature of the art, and the need
to rely on fellow-travellers for leadership allowed for the continuation
of agendas that had existed before 1921 and, in some respects, even
before 1917. This situation combined with improvement in economic
conditions under the New Economic Policy (NEP) and Lenin's position that 'cultural problems cannot be solved as quickly as political
and military problems'[1] to yield a musical eclecticism that would play
itself out only on the eve of the next decade.

Western scholarship has traditionally acknowledged that music
thrived under NEP despite various material shortages. The period has
generally been associated with 'a lessening of revolutionary militancy,
a relaxation of ideological tensions [and] a greater permissiveness in
matters of musical taste and style'.[2] For example, with the resumption
of Western contacts interrupted since 1914, the NEP period saw a
re-emergence of activities reminiscent of the pre-Revolutionary Evenings of Contemporary Music. These were concerts in St Petersburg

1 V. Lenin, *New Economic Policy* (New York, 1937), 274, quoted in B. Schwarz, *Music and Musical Life in Soviet Russia, 1917–1981*, enlarged edn. (Bloomington, Ind., 1983), 42.
2 Schwarz, *Music and Musical Life*, 43.

sponsored by the World of Art group from 1902 onwards. Under the guidance of Viacheslav Karatygin, they presented Russian audiences with works by Western composers such as Mahler, Strauss, and Ravel, together with works by contemporary Russian composers such as Skriabin, Rachmaninov, and Medtner. Debussy, Reger, and Schoenberg made personal appearances at these Evenings, and it was at one of these concerts in 1909 that Diaghilev was introduced to the music of Stravinsky, an encounter that led him to commission *The Firebird* (*Zhar-ptitsa*). In the same way, in the NEP period foreign artists were invited to perform in Russia, and foreign composers of new music, among them Paul Hindemith, Darius Milhaud, and Franz Schreker, conducted Russian premières of their own works. Between 1925 and 1927, Leningrad audiences witnessed performances of Igor' Stravinsky's *Pulcinella* (*Pul'chinella*) and *Renard* (*Baika pro lisu, petukha i baraban*), Ernst Krenek's *Der Sprung über den Schatten*, Arnold Schoenberg's *Gurre-Lieder*, and Berg's *Wozzeck*. A reciprocal interest in contemporary Russian music emerged in the West. The works of modern Soviet composers, such as Samuel Feinberg, Aleksandr Mosolov, and Nikolai Miaskovskii, were played at the prestigious music festivals of the International Society of Contemporary Music (ISCM). In addition, under a special arrangement with the Soviet State Publishing House, new Russian scores were issued by Universal Edition in Vienna.

These events represent but one facet of musical life in the 1920s and, by the end of the decade, a distinctly less modernist, more proletarian-oriented stance began to dominate the musical arena. This and other developments during the period can best be understood in terms of existing factions in the musical community, their competitive attempts to provide the new social order with an appropriate cultural response, and the changing political strengths of players in key administrative positions committed to particular aesthetic platforms. The definition and implementation of an ideologically correct musical agenda was debated vehemently throughout the 1920s. But these polemical battles essentially propagated factionalism that arose during the Civil War.

In part, factionalism was allowed to develop under Lunacharskii's leadership of Narkompros (the People's Commissariat of Enlightenment). As a Bolshevik intellectual, Lunacharskii encouraged artists to pursue 'revolutionary inspiration' in their art, but also defended pre-Revolutionary cultural achievements as the legitimate inheritance of the proletariat and, so as to entice co-operation from highly skilled, politically independent professionals, recognized the need for creative freedom and individuality of expression. His choice of Arthur

Lourié (Artur Lur'e) to head the Commissariat's music division (Muzo) reflects this liberal policy. Lourié actively promoted the cause of modern music and thought the art form to be essentially an apolitical medium. As reported later by critic and musicologist Leonid Sabaneev:

Due to the good fortune that the first music 'minister' of Soviet Russia was Arthur Lourié, himself an ultra-modernist and follower of Stravinsky and Schoenberg, the modern school of thought predominated in the musical bureaucratic circle, entirely to the disadvantage of the representatives of moderate and conservative trends. A strong promotional propaganda was organized for the modernists; their works were published by the State, an act that doubtlessly represented a positive aspect of this period.[3]

Other music specialists who allied themselves with the Narkompros agency included the composers and modernist sympathizers Vladimir Shcherbachev and Nikolai Miaskovskii; the musicologists Pavel Lamm, Nadezhda Briusova, and Boris Asafiev; the critics Vladimir Derzhanovskii and Viacheslav Karatygin; the pianists Konstantin Eiges and Konstantin Igumnov; and the violinist Lev Tseitlin, who in 1922 founded a successful conductorless orchestra, Persimfans, which gave impressive performances of not only the standard classical repertoire, but also challenging contemporary scores. Within an additional 'academic' subsection in Muzo, which in October 1921, became Russia's first State Institute of Musical Science (Gosudarstvennyi institut muzykal'nykh nauk, GIMN), music researchers such as Sabaneev, Nikolai Ianchuk, Petr Zimin, and Mikhail Ivanov-Boretskii pursued scholarly and educational interests. Lourié's exclusionary professional aesthetic, however, soon elicited complaints from the revolutionary-minded Trade Union of Art Workers (Rabis) and was the cause of his early dismissal and replacement by the more moderate former Proletkul't member Boris Krasin in 1921.

During the Civil War, musicians took part in 'enlightenment' programmes for workers that yielded a proliferation of military bands and amateur choral studios. Insisting that artistic creativity be ideally limited to events and subjects 'by, for and about workers',[4] the more militant faction of these Proletkul't organizations can be seen as a precursor of the movement to proletarianize music in the 1920s. However, the primary focus of the Proletkul't's music studios involved familiarizing workers with the classics of Russian and Western art music as well as the Russian folksong, and relied on the expertise of highly trained musicians such as Boris Krasin, Nadezhda Briusova, and Aleksandr Kastalskii.[5] In addition to the

3 L. Sabaneev, 'Die Musik und die musikalischen Kreise Russlands in der Nachkriegszeit', Muzikblätter des Anbruchs, 7 (1925), 106.
4 L. Mally, Culture of the Future: The Proletkult Movement in Revolutionary Russia (Berkeley and Los Angeles, 1990), 122.
5 See A. Nelson, 'Music and the Politics of Culture in Revolutionary Russia, 1921–30', Ph.D. thesis (Michigan, 1993), 32.

focus on working with the masses, the Moscow Proletkul't's music division afforded a place for a small avant-garde group eager to break with the conventions of the past in an attempt to forge truly new forms of musical expression. Perhaps the most iconoclastic product to emerge from this effort was Arsenii Avraamov's *Symphony of Hooters* (*Simfoniia gudkov*), which was executed in Baku harbour to mark the anniversary of the Revolution in 1922, and recreated less successfully in Moscow the following year. The instruments of the orchestra in Baku included navy ship sirens and whistles, bus and car horns, a machine gun battery, and cannons, as well as a complex, specially designed 'whistle main' (*magistral'*). The composition involved the superposition of cannon volleys, sirens, horns, and whistles with renditions of the *Internationale*, the *Marseillaise*, and the *Varshavianka* by a mass band and choir.[6]

Avraamov also experimented with microtonal compositional possibilities, and eventually developed a 48-part octave subdivision at GIMN. His microtonal interests were shared early on by Lourié and Ivan Wyshnegradsky and predated the establishment in Petrograd of a Society for Quarter-Tone Music in 1923 by Georgii Rimskii-Korsakov (a nephew of the well-known composer, Nikolai). The interest in quarter-tone composition received a favourable assessment from Lunacharskii even as the first electronic instrument, the 'Termenvox' or 'Theremin', invented by the acoustics engineer Lev Termen (known abroad as Leon Theremin) attracted praise from Lenin in 1922. The Theremin was to have far-reaching applications, making its way into compositions by Joseph Schillinger, Edgard Varèse, the soundtrack of Hollywood films, and even American popular music culture.

In 1923, an Association for Contemporary Music (Assotsiatsiia sovremennoi muzyki, ASM) was established in Moscow, and for a time also served as the Russian chapter of the ISCM. Aiming to promote contemporary Russian works at home and abroad and to enhance Soviet musical life with performances of some of the latest compositions from the West, it represented highly trained musicians of progressive, if not modernist, orientation. Under the administrative leadership of Derzhanovskii and fellow-critic Viktor Beliaev, the Association counted among its adherents Miaskovskii, Lamm, Feinberg, Sabaneev, Konstantin Saradzhev, and Nikolai Roslavets. Asafiev and Shcherbachev became involved in a similar though separate organization by the same name in Leningrad. The positions occupied by many of these individuals in conservatories, State agencies, and all divisions of Narkompros in particular allowed them to achieve their objectives and to influence and encourage a younger

6 See Nelson, 'Music and the Politics of Culture', 31.

generation of composers that included Aleksandr Mosolov, Leonid Polovinkin, Vissarion Shebalin, Vladimir Deshevov, and Dmitrii Shostakovich. The ASM published periodicals and sponsored a series of chamber and orchestral concerts that featured the music of European composers such as Hindemith, Milhaud, Bela Bartok, Artur Honegger, Eric Satie, and Karol Szymanovski, as well as compositions by the Russians Feinberg, Miaskovskii, Roslavets, Mosolov, Polovinkin, and Shebalin.

Within the modernist circle, two composers are particularly noteworthy: Nikolai Roslavets (1881–1944) and Aleksandr Mosolov (1900–73). Representing the older generation, Roslavets was a leading figure in the most avant-garde sphere of the modernist cause, a relatively prolific composer during the 1920s, and initially a dedicated Communist who held positions in Rabis, the Moscow Proletkul't, the Administration of Professional Education (Glavprofobr) in Narkompros, and the State Publishing House (Gosizdat) among others. Between 1913 and 1919, he developed a new system of tone organization, which he continued to apply to his chamber and orchestral compositions throughout the next decade. Based on the manipulation of synthetic chords, it resembles Skriabin's late compositional practice, and its complexity attracted comparison at home and later abroad with the dodecaphonic work of Arnold Schoenberg.[7] After the Revolution, Roslavets naïvely defended his pre-Revolutionary compositional creed by drawing an analogy between his emancipation of music from outdated conventions and the new socialist structuring of society. His formalism, however, soon proved to be unacceptable, and, by the early 1930s, his music was silenced and his name disappeared from reference sources.

Mosolov, on the other hand, was a promising young composer who gained international notoriety in the late 1920s and early 1930s for his orchestral piece *The Iron Foundry* (*Zavod*), the first movement of a suite excerpted from the ballet *Steel* (*Stal'*), which was never staged. Often associated with constructivism, the composition's portrayal of machines in motion through a layering of motoric, dissonant, and percussive ostinatos actually has much in common with the earlier Cubo-Futurist aesthetic. First performed along with Roslavets's Cantata 'October' and Shostakovich's Second Symphony at an ASM concert in 1927 to commemorate the tenth anniversary of the Revolution, *The Iron Foundry* was subsequently acclaimed at the ISCM festival in Liège in 1930 and was featured at the Hollywood Bowl in 1932.

In 1923, the Association of Proletarian Musicians (later the Russian Association of Proletarian Musicians, or RAPM) was founded by

7 See e.g.
N. Miaskovskii, 'Nikolai Roslavets. I. *Tri sochineniia* dlia peniia i fortepiano. II. *Grustnye peizazhi* dlia peniia i fortepiano', *Muzyka*, 197 (1914), 542–4, and D. Gojowy, 'Nikolai Andreevic Roslavets, ein früher Zwölftonkomponist', *Die Musikforschung*, 22 (1969), 22–38.

members of the propaganda division (*agitotdel*) of the State Publishing House. Originally consisting of individuals who were 'just beginning musical training or had been more active in revolutionary politics than in the mainstream of musical life',[8] it was committed to promoting music that was readily accessible and ideologically clear in the manner of revolutionary songs and mass choruses. The organization was firmly set against modernism and rejected cultivation of any ties with the West. Consequently, in its struggle for power and influence, the RAPM targeted the alliance between the musical establishment and the agencies of Narkompros by accusing the ASM of propagating 'decadent', 'bourgeois', 'formalist' ideology. While members of the RAPM produced music of little lasting value, the efforts of the Production Collective at the Moscow Conservatoire (Prokoll) founded in 1925 were a little more successful. Embracing the proletarian cause, but distancing itself from the simplistic, militant rhetoric of the RAPM, Prokoll aimed to operate as a collective, though its best work was accomplished by the gifted student, Aleksandr Davidenko.

Confusion over defining and developing a truly Soviet music for the new uneducated proletarian audience fuelled growing ideological debates in which the communist membership of proletarian forces eventually gained the upper hand. In 1929, Lunacharskii left his post in Narkompros, and the ASM ceased its activities shortly thereafter. To escape the increasing political turmoil, certain composers such as Roslavets and Mosolov spent time in Central Asia composing music based on indigenous folk melodies. Miaskovskii, on the other hand, having emerged as the foremost Soviet symhonist, abandoned the ASM. In the twilight of NEP culture, a cry for central intervention in musical affairs was raised in all quarters. Guidance came on 23 April 1932, in the form of the Party resolution 'On the Reformation of Literary and Artistic Organizations'. This dissolved all existing proletarian organizations, replaced them with unions containing a communist faction, and instituted the elusive aesthetic doctrine of 'socialist realism', advocating the portrayal of an idealistic reality in its 'revolutionary development'.[9] In so doing, the resolution ended a period of flexibility and began an era of state-controlled cultural regimentation.

Music after 1932: Centralization and Cultural Control

A single Union of Soviet Composers (Soiuz sovetskikh kompozitorov) for composers and musicologists was established in 1932 in

Moscow and Leningrad. By 1940, branches existed in many other urban centres throughout most of the republics. An Organizational Committee (Orgkomitet), directed by such recognized composers as Shostakovich, Reinhold Glière, Iurii Shaporin, Dmitrii Kabalevskii, Aram Khachaturian, and Viktor Belyi, was set up in 1939 to co-ordinate activities in Moscow. Its mouthpiece was the periodical *Sovetskaia muzyka* (*Soviet Music*), founded in 1933, whose aim was to oppose 'the ideology of modernists as well as the leftist interpretation of Marxism' and to promote 'the development of a Marxist-Leninist musicology'.[10] In the musical community, the goal from now until the death of Stalin in 1953 would be to uphold the directives of the 1932 resolution and, with help from the central authority, to root out counter-revolutionary, formalist (read 'modernist') tendencies.

In the midst of these new developments, Prokof'ev returned to Moscow from his sojourn abroad. After many extended visits that began in 1932, his repatriation was completed in 1936. Overtaken by nostalgia for his homeland and a desire to compose for the Russian people, Prokof'ev was not entirely averse to writing music that was more accessible as long as it did not lead to 'provincialism'. In adjusting to Soviet musical sensibilities, Prokof'ev welcomed the challenge of composing for a proletarian audience. Though several of his works dating from the 1930s were unsuccessful, others, such as the orchestral suite from *Lieutenant Kije* (*Podporuchik Kizhe*, 1934), the ballet *Romeo and Juliet* (*Romeo i Dzhul'etta*, 1935–6), the symphonic tale *Peter and the Wolf* (*Petia i volk*, 1936), and the Second Violin Concerto (1935) brought him much repute. *Semen Kotko*, premièred in 1940, was Prokof'ev's first attempt at composing a Soviet opera. His search for an appropriate middle ground between aria and recitative produced a melodic style that was unacceptable to the authorities, who ultimately discarded the work.

The artistic versatility displayed by the young Shostakovich worked at first to his advantage. Although his training under Glazunov linked him with pre-Revolutionary traditions, as a graduate of the Leningrad Conservatoire in 1925, Shostakovich belonged to the first generation of musicians educated under Soviet rule. His first symphony and graduation piece, which was premièred in 1926, launched him immediately into an international career. It was followed by such inventive compositions as his first Piano Sonata (1926), a collection of piano miniatures titled *Aphorisms* (*Aforizmy*), and the opera *The Nose* (*Nos*)—a satirical masterpiece after Gogol' conceived in 1928 and first performed in 1930. At the same time, Shostakovich paid homage to the proletarian side of musical developments in his two subsequent symphonies. Written to commemorate the tenth

10 Schwarz, *Music and Musical Life*, 114.

anniversary of the Revolution in 1927, the Second Symphony was dedicated 'To October', while the Third Symphony of 1929 was subtitled 'The First of May'. Both are single-movement compositions that include choruses on revolutionary texts set in a sharply-contrasting, straightforward fashion. Thus, while proletarian critics denigrated *The Nose* for its misguided experimentation and lack of appropriate ideological content, they found signs of promise in the composer's symphonies and film music.

Shostakovich's second opera accomplished what had heretofore been frustratingly unattainable: the creation of a Soviet opera of high quality that reflected contemporary realities and aspirations. *Lady Macbeth of Mtsensk* (*Ledi Makbet Mtsenskogo uezda*, also known as *Katerina Izmailova*, composed in 1930–2) was premièred in Leningrad in 1934 to critical and popular acclaim. In addition to nearly 200 Russian performances, the work was exported internationally to New York, London, Stockholm, Prague, Zurich, Ljubljana, and Copenhagen. However, although originally hailed as 'a great achievement of Soviet culture',[11] it was soon officially condemned for its vulgarity by an article in *Pravda* on 28 January 1936 headlined 'Muddle instead of Music' ('Sumbur vmesto muzyki'). Stalin, who had attended a performance of the opera, is known to have regarded Nikolai Leskov's story of lust, greed, rape, and murder in pre-Revolutionary provincial Russia as entirely inappropriate subject-matter for Soviet art. The *Pravda* editorial (no doubt composed at his behest) criticized the dissonance and confusion of Shostakovich's musical setting, and also its 'pornographic' qualities. A week later, a second article in *Pravda* singled out ideological shortcomings in Shostakovich's ballet, *The Limpid Stream* (*Svetlyi ruchei*).

Though the strategic assault targeted one composer, it was appropriately interpreted as a warning to the entire musical community. In subsequent Union meetings that took place to discuss the official pronouncement, few composers came to Shostakovich's defence. It became clear that, as Stalin's control tightened and the cultural purges heightened, adherence to the Party line was mandatory and that any sign of modernism was intolerable. Shostakovich responded by withdrawing his Fourth Symphony from performance and writing a Fifth—the subtitle, 'A Soviet Artist's Response to Just Criticism', was not Shostakovich's, but he never repudiated it—which was well-received at its première in 1937 and restored the composer's status until the next cultural onslaught in 1948.

While *Lady Macbeth* was removed from the stage (it was rehabilitated in 1963), the opera *The Quiet Don* (*Tikhii Don*) by Ivan Dzerzhinskii rose to fame on Stalin's personal approval. Dzerzhinskii's work was

11 Schwarz, *Music and Musical Life*, 119.

patriotic and uncomplicated, and featured melodies reminiscent of revolutionary songs. It became the prototype of a new genre of song opera of which Tikhon Khrennikov's *Into the Storm* (*V buriu*, 1939) counts as the most successful example. As composers began to avoid abstract music for safety's sake, a parallel development in the orchestral repertoire became the song symphony, which included simple, politically correct vocal passages within large-scale symphonic forms. Alternatively, indigenous folk music became an invaluable compositional resource. The work of the Georgian-born Armenian composer, Aram Khachaturian, is particularly noteworthy in this regard for its effective infusion of traditional forms with elements of Armenian folk music. Many composers also turned to writing film music. None were as fortunate here as Prokof′ev, whose collaboration with Sergei Eisenstein produced such classics as *Aleksandr Nevskii* (1938) and *Ivan the Terrible* (*Ivan Groznyi*, 1942–5). However, Isaak Dunaevskii's scores for G. Aleksandrov's musical comedies *Circus* (*Tsirk*, 1936), *The Cheerful Lads* (*Veselye rebiata*, 1939), *The Shining Path* (*Svetlyi put′*, 1940), and *Volga-Volga* (1941) were some of the greatest popular successes of all time, with a number of songs from the films (especially 'Song of the Motherland') becoming known to every Soviet citizen, and loved by a great many.

The German invasion of the Soviet Union in 1941 brought, as we have seen, a certain relaxation in artistic ideological constraints. Faced with the real possibility of national annihilation, the protection of culture was paramount, but policing it for potential formalist deviation was trivial. All significant cultural institutions of Moscow and Leningrad, as well as such leading musical figures as Miaskovskii, Feinberg, Shaporin, Prokof′ev, Shostakovich, and Khachaturian, were evacuated. Musicians took up arms, continued to perform, supplied a repertoire of patriotic war songs, and composed works of more lasting artistic value.

Of all the compositions written during the war, including the notable war symphonies of Prokof′ev, Miaskovskii, and Khachaturian, the most celebrated at home and abroad was Shostakovich's Seventh or Leningrad Symphony. Written in the heat of battle, its direct emotional appeal struck a chord in both Russians and their allies. Completed in December 1941, the symphony was premièred in Kuibyshev early in 1942 by the evacuated Bol′shoi Theatre Orchestra. Even before the work made its Leningrad debut in August of that year, it was conducted in London and performed in the United States under Toscanini on a national radio broadcast. The symphony continued to be heard throughout the war and, for Russians, it transcended musical boundaries to become a symbol of the nation's struggle and indomitable will to survive. By contrast, the Eighth and Ninth Symphonies that followed elicited mixed reactions. Whereas the Seventh Symphony offered a heroic depiction of the war, the Eighth, composed in 1943, represented a grim contemplation of its horrors. Most striking and powerful, but also most disappointing, was the composition's anti-climactic ending, which undermined any sense of triumph by deliberately avoiding resolution of tension built up over the five movements. The Ninth Symphony, written to mark the end of the war and premièred in 1945, surprised listeners who were expecting a heroic, monumental, apotheosis to reflect images of a glorious, hard-won victory. Instead, Shostakovich presented a brief, exuberant, light-hearted orchestral piece with no grand choruses and no extra-musical programme.

Following on the heels of the Great Patriotic War, the Cold War and the Iron Curtain marked a return to Party vigilance in cultural affairs through the launching of even harsher ideological campaigns, supervised from 1946–8 by Andrei Zhdanov. During this period of *zhdanovshchina*, the cultural policies established in the 1930s were revisited and so militantly enforced that they remained intact even after Zhdanov's unexpected death in August 1948. Particularly objectionable, from the Party's viewpoint, was the prevalence after the war of non-programmatic instrumental music at the expense of vocal genres. This trend towards the abstract in music was deemed antithetical to the aesthetic needs of the people. Such critically independent and ideologically misguided expressions as Shostakovich's latest symphonies were unacceptable.

Three Party resolutions in 1946 concerning literature, theatre, and film foreshadowed the blow eventually dealt to music on 10 February 1948 by the resolution 'On the Opera *The Great Friendship* by V. Muradeli'. Muradeli's opera was conceived as a tribute to Stalin's native Georgia, and was the major musical work composed to celebrate the thirtieth anniversary of the Revolution. However, Zhdanov did not approve of either the music or the libretto. Using the work as a point of departure, the 1948 resolution set out to subjugate all musical creativity once and for all to the dictates of a Marxist-Leninist doctrine according to Stalin's interpretation. It targeted specifically the work of Prokof'ev, Miaskovskii, Shebalin, Khachaturian, Gavriil Popov, and, again, Shostakovich. These pillars of the musical community were found guilty of 'formalistic distortions and anti-democratic tendencies . . . alien to the Soviet people and its artistic taste'.[12] For them, the official alienation translated into loss of employment, cancellation of performances, and delays in future endeavours. At the Composers' Union, the leadership of the Orgkomitet was deposed

12 Schwarz, *Music and Musical Life*, 219.

and Tikhon Khrennikov was appointed to the post of the Union's General Secretary which he was to hold for many years. A similar censuring of musicologists ensued. In the following year, Russia's best musical scholars were reproached for their interest in foreign music, for approaching Russian music with Western concepts, and for their own associations with composers now out of favour, and were forced to rethink historical developments in light of the official Party line.

The resolution of 1948 'initiated a musical witch-hunt and stifled creativity', and also 'exposed the cultural policy of the Soviet Union to world-wide ridicule and contempt'.[13] The setback suffered by the musical community was certainly great. In Prokof'ev's case, his failing health during his last five years made him more apt to co-operate than to protest. His late works, such as the ballet *The Tale of the Stone Flower* (*Kamennyi tsvetok*, 1948–50), the Cello Sonata (1949), the Seventh Symphony (1951–2), and the Oratorio *On Guard for Peace* (*Na strazhe mira*, 1950) are characterized by lyricism and conventionality. Though he continued until 1952 to revise his masterpiece opera *War and Peace* (*Voina i mir*), begun in 1941, a complete performance of it, albeit with cuts, did not take place until 1957, four years after the composer's death. Shostakovich, on the other hand, responded to the situation by working in two musical idioms: one, represented by patriotic film scores, choruses, and the oratorio *Song of the Forests* (*Pesn' o lesakh*), conscientiously avoided controversy; the other was a clandestine expression of his artistic voice in such works as the first Violin Concerto (1947–8), the Fourth String Quartet (1949), and the song-cycle *From Jewish Folk Poetry* (*Iz evreiskoi narodnoi pesni*, 1948), all of which were deliberately withheld from performance until well after Stalin's death in 1953.

On the eve of the ensuing cultural thaw, it seemed that the musical community finally understood the ideological path it was to follow. However, a younger generation would soon discover that they were not entirely cut off from foreign ideas. In 1946, the Rumanian-born musicologist and composer, Filip Herschkowitz (Gershkovich) arrived in Moscow. Having studied with Alban Berg and Anton Webern in Vienna, he fled east to escape Nazi persecution. Barred from the Composers' Union, he nevertheless had opportunities to pass on the teachings of the Second Viennese School through private instruction to such future luminaries as Edison Denisov, Alfred Schnittke, Sof'ia Gubaidulina, Valentin Sil'vestrov, Leonid Hrabovsky, Alexander Vustin, and Elena Firsova. When a Party resolution in 1958 rehabilitated the masters condemned ten years earlier, those embarking on a similar path found support for cultivating their own individual voices.

13 Ibid. 227.

6

GERARD
MCBURNEY

Soviet Music after the Death of Stalin: The Legacy of Shostakovich

Unquestionably the dominant figure in Soviet music from 1953 onwards was Dmitrii Shostakovich. Over the previous two decades, Sergei Prokof'ev had been the only creative personality comparable in range, technique, and achievement. But Prokof'ev died, by a curious irony, on the same day as Stalin. And although there were other composers such as Aram Khachaturian (1903–78), Iurii Shaporin (1887–1966), and Boris Liatoshinskii (1895–1968), who made their reputations before or during the Stalinist period and continued to write music thereafter, it was Shostakovich who became the emblem of the Soviet composer.

Shostakovich died in 1975, but nearly a quarter of a century later his reputation remains immense, and is still growing within his own country and abroad. The influence of his distinctive musical language and the perceived example of his life cast long shadows over the history of Soviet music, right up until the end of the Soviet Union; and even today he exerts a strong fascination for many Russian musicians, a fascination stimulated by much recently published material shedding new light on his character and private opinions. Shostakovich remains an artist who provokes interesting questions and in certain quarters scepticism. This is partly because, although his music gives obvious and compelling evidence of rare powers of invention, originality of construction, and profundity of thought, its appeal has been significantly enhanced by what some have considered its extramusical associations.

Prominent among these is the undoubted emotional aura which has gathered around the composer's personality. In particular, his public humiliations in 1936 and 1948 endowed him, especially in the eyes and ears of his sympathetic compatriots, with a moral authority of a kind not usually associated with writers of music. As Sof'ia Gubaidulina (b. 1931) puts it:

Shostakovich is of utmost importance to people of my generation, not only because of the influence he exerted as a composer, but also as a person . . . Despite his outward irony, and his manner of expressing himself in paradoxes, he felt and understood the suffering that Russians are doomed to endure, and the manner in which it defines their behaviour and relationships. In this way Shostakovich belongs to the Russian humanitarian tradition.[1]

Combine such an idealistic image of the man with his characteristic and peculiarly rhetorical manner of musical expression, especially in his symphonies, and the result is an art that is perceived by the sympathetic listener as capable of carrying a far greater emotional and symbolic meaning than the sound and construction of the notes alone would seem to suggest. This is why, especially when it was listened to by those who lived with the restrictions of freedom of expression typical of the Soviet period, Shostakovich's music could give the impression of being possessed of overwhelming moral and prophetic significance.

The composer himself, particularly in later years, did not discourage this way of listening to his work. This is clear from the pieces themselves, from numerous details of syntax, organization, and instrumentation, and from the composer's audible fondness for symbolic structures, especially in such major works as the Tenth and Eleventh Symphonies (1953 and 1957), the Eighth String Quartet (1960), and the two Cello Concertos (1959 and 1966). But it is also clear from evidence from outside the music, from the anecdotal accounts of memoirs and letters, and from Shostakovich's careful choice of texts. One might note, for example, the documentary intentions of his Thirteenth Symphony (1962), setting new poems including the notorious *Babii Iar* by the young Evgenii Evtushenko; or his Fourteenth Symphony (1969), with its dramatic and politically suggestive arrangement of fragments by Lorca, Apollinaire, Küchelbecker, and Rilke.

Solomon Volkov's supposed memoirs of Shostakovich suggest—and this is borne out in private and unpublished memories—that the composer liked to identify his role as an artist with that of the *iurodivyi* (fool-in-Christ) from *Boris Godunov* (in Musorgskii's developed version of this character, rather than in Pushkin's slighter original).[2] And in several of his more important works, starting with

1 Quoted in E. Wilson, *Shostakovich: A Life Remembered* (London, 1994), 305–6.
2 S. Volkov (ed.), *Testimony: The Memoirs of Shostakovich* (London, 1979).

the last movement of the Fifth Symphony (1937), he quotes deliberately and obviously from Musorgskii's memorable orchestral accompaniment to the opening of Pimen's monologue from the monastery scene in *Boris*, as though to suggest that his own music should be understood, like the monk's manuscript, as nothing less than a political and moral chronicle designed to preserve 'these truthful stories' so that 'the descendants of the true believers may learn the past history of their native land'.[3] It was perhaps as a result of Shostakovich's fondness for this particular quotation that, during the heady days of the early Gorbachev period, it became something of a cliché to hear distinguished Soviet musicians, on radio, in preconcert talks, and at reform-inspired meetings at the Composers' Union, refer to Shostakovich as 'Pimen nashego vremeni' ('the Pimen of our time').

Perhaps not surprisingly, voices have been raised, both in and outside Russia, by those who consider there to be something suspect, manipulative, and even sentimental about music, which, it is assumed, depends for its full effect on audiences and performers sharing an awareness of possible extra-musical meanings which are not spelt out in the score, but for which the music is none the less supposed to be a significant metaphor. And suspicion has also been directed against the rhetorical devices by which Shostakovich distorts the detail of his musical discourse so that we are constantly reminded of his ironic and ulterior intentions. These devices include deliberate banality, coarseness, tawdriness, parody, quotation, echoes of film music, and so on, all of which carry the problematic possibility that they might actually be what they appear to be.

In the West a strong distaste for this aspect of Shostakovich's art was already being expressed by Stravinsky well before the Second World War, and has been vigorously maintained by others since. In a letter to Ernest Ansermet of April 1935, Stravinsky describes Shostakovich's opera *Lady Macbeth of Mtsensk* (*Ledi Makbet Mtsenskogo uezda*) in terms remarkably similar to those used in the celebrated *Pravda* attack, 'Muddle instead of Music' ('Sumbur vmesto muzyki') of the following year: 'The work is lamentably provincial, the music plays a miserable role as illustrator, in a very embarrassing realistic style . . . I regret being so hard on Shostakovich, but he has deeply disappointed me, intellectually and musically.'[4] And Stravinsky's attitude to Shostakovich did not grow warmer in later years.

At the same time, it is understandable that in the middle and later Soviet period, when artistic expression was subject to a variety of controls, Shostakovich's personal discovery of the ironic and implicative possibilities of music was a crucial one. Music, not obviously mimetic,

3 Translation adapted from P. Davidson's, included in the 1991 Berlin Philharmonic recording, S3K 58 977.
4 I. Stravinsky, letter to Ernest Ansermet, 4 Apr. 1935, in *Selected Correspondence*, ed. R. Craft, i (London, 1982), 224.

has always been a hard art to police. And Russia, which from the mid-nineteenth century onwards played enthusiastic host to one of the most inventive musical cultures in the Western world, had still in the Soviet period a large, well-educated, and expectant audience, by no means confined to Leningrad and Moscow, and, for political reasons, likely to be highly responsive to music offering so obvious a possibility of subversive interpretation. Zoia Tomashevskaia recalls Anna Akhmatova's immediately sympathetic reaction to Shostakovich's controversial use of nineteenth-century prisoners' songs and twentieth-century revolutionary songs as the thematic material of his Eleventh Symphony: 'Those songs were like white birds flying against a terrible black sky.'[5]

In any case, while the debate about Shostakovich continues apace and at times with mounting irritation,[6] his principal works, including many written between 1953 and his death (most notably, the Tenth, Eleventh, Thirteenth, Fourteenth, and Fifteenth Symphonies, the two cello concertos, the last ten of his fifteen string quartets, and his monumental song-cycles on poems by Tsvetaeva and Michelangelo), have established themselves at the end of the twentieth century as part of the standard repertoire of international music-making. This fact alone would seem to be evidence enough of their continuing hold on the collective musical imagination.

Division and Interdependence: Official and Avant-Garde Music after 1953

As well as the dominance of one outstanding talent, there were also a number of other important factors which affected Soviet music from 1953 to 1991 and made it noticeably distinct from music written in Western Europe and North America during the same period. And chief among these were the various and sometimes peculiar political pressures to which composers were subject.

One of the most interesting results of these pressures was that, already in the wake of the Khrushchev thaw of the late 1950s, and well before Shostakovich's death in 1975, 'Soviet classical' composers,[7] like other Soviet artists, had separated themselves into two different and fairly clearly defined camps: those writing 'official' music (memorably renamed 'secretarial music' by Edison Denisov, because so much of it was written by composers who were secretaries of the various branches of the Union), sanctioned, nourished, and supported by the Composers' Union; and those writing 'left', 'avant-garde', or 'underground' music, who regarded themselves as existing in a state

5 Quoted in Wilson, Shostakovich, 319.

6 See e.g. I. MacDonald, The New Shostakovich (Oxford, 1991), or R. Taruskin, 'Public Lies and Unspeakable Truth: Interpreting Shostakovich's Fifth Symphony', in D. Fanning (ed.), Shostakovich Studies (Cambridge, 1995), 17–56.

7 The concept of 'Soviet classicism' or 'Soviet classics' (there is some overlap between the two ideas) is one frequently encountered in official and semi-official journalism emanating from within the pale of the Composers' Union.

of critical opposition to the tedious and academic orthodoxies which continued to be propagated by the Union right up until the Gorbachev period. (The three terms used to denote unofficial music, all of which have historical origins much earlier in the Soviet period, were used right up to the end of the Soviet Union, not only as terms of abuse by those who represented and spoke for the Composers' Union, but also in conversation by those who regarded themselves as part of the avant-garde.)

Although these two camps viewed themselves as opposed to each other, it must not be thought that they were unconnected; indeed, the enmity between them is best understood as part of a complex pattern of interdependence. For example, from the late 1950s until the early 1990s, the tone and political direction of the Union of Soviet Composers was constantly stimulated and affected by its need to clarify its hostile reaction to left and avant-garde tendencies. This can be seen especially clearly in the key-note speeches made at the various Union Congresses of the 1960s and 1970s by Tikhon Khrennikov, politically active within the Union from the 1930s, and First Secretary from 1948 until the Union's dissolution in 1991. Typically, Khrennikov in these speeches would castigate the 'errors' of 'modernistic' composers such as Arvo Pärt (b. 1935), Alfred Schnittke (b. 1934), and Edison Denisov (b. 1929) and insist on the need for the Union to maintain 'vigilance' and 'discipline' (key Leninist watchwords).[8] He would be particularly sharp about those composers who he considered had 'hobnobbed with foreigners' in order to get their music performed outside the USSR.[9] At the same time, the developing musical interests of composers of the left, and the impressive degree of solidarity that they could sometimes display in the face of official criticism, give evidence of the degree to which their own agenda was also shaped by the immediate need to confront and oppose the oppressive aesthetic assumptions and demands of the Union.

Moreover, the majority of composers of the left, however their careers and prospects were restricted by the Union authorities, remained Union members right through the later Soviet period. And for the most part they retained access to Union privileges including the much-valued possibility of staying, for little cost, at the Union's various Houses of Creation (*Doma tvorchestva*) at Repino, Ruza, Sortavala, Ivanovo, and elsewhere. Several of the most outspoken representatives of the left, including Edison Denisov and Nikolai Karetnikov (1930–94), lived in city apartments in blocks owned by the Union. And, especially in the 1980s, some of the most adventurous experimental concerts in Moscow and Leningrad actually took place in the Union's own concert-halls.

8 References to, and extracts from, some of these speeches can be found in B. Schwarz, *Music and Musical Life in Soviet Russia, 1917–1981*, enlarged edn. (Bloomington, Ind., 1983).

9 See N. Karetnikov, *Temy s variatsiiami* (Moscow, 1990), 71–3.

There were, too, a number of composers who attempted a political game enabling them to hold high office in the Union and still write music of a kind that would be deemed avant-garde enough to achieve foreign performances and win the approval of those who were enthusiastic supporters of modernism. Perhaps the best-known such figure was Rodion Shchedrin (b. 1932) a talented musician who built his politically respectable career (including appointment in 1974 to the post of First Secretary of the Composers' Union of the RSFSR) on the back of his long association with the Bol'shoi Theatre, an association cemented by his marriage to the world-famous ballerina Maia Plisetskaia. It was this that provoked Filip Gershkovich, in one of his celebrated *bons mots*, to refer to Shchedrin as 'Saltykov-Plisetskii', in derisive reference to the famous nineteenth-century writer and satirist Saltykov-Shchedrin. In the early summer of 1985, Edison Denisov was summoned by Tikhon Khrennikov and angrily rebuked for attempting to promote a performance of his piece, *The Blue Notebook* (*Golubaia tetrad'*), setting texts by the then banned writers Daniil Kharms and Aleksandr Vvedenskii. When Denisov remonstrated: 'Why do you always pick on me? Why don't you say the same things to Shchedrin?', Khrennikov, caught off guard, 'snarled back at me: "Rodion writes the same shit you do!" '[10] In playing this game, the likes of Shchedrin were, in some people's eyes, only following the example of Shostakovich himself, who joined the Communist Party in 1960 and was decorated with honours and Union titles. There is a difference, however. The pressures to conform that were applied to composers of the generation of Shchedrin, or even to those a good deal younger than him, can hardly be said to have been as prolonged or as severe as those which were applied to Shostakovich.

It is also worth pointing out that, beyond the immediate concerns of both official and left musicians, there lay other quite different musical worlds such as those of traditional Soviet light music (*estrada*), jazz, and, later, rock, as well as the more literary traditions of bards and guitar-poets. But these too still reflected the fundamental division of the classical composers into two camps. Leading musicians working in the fields of *estrada*, military music, educational music, and mass song nearly all had close links with the ruling hierarchy of the Union, while the mostly unofficial jazz and rock musicians and guitar-poets, if they did not share the particular musical interests of the classical avant-garde, seem to have felt themselves at least to have been part of the same underground.[11]

Perhaps one of the most curious aspects of the sometimes questionable symbiotic relationship between official composers and those on the left is to be found in the way that both of them, from the

10 Interview with G. McBurney, 1985.
11 On guitar poetry, see Smith, *Songs to Seven Strings Russian Guitar Poetry and Soviet 'Mass Song'* (Bloomington, Ind., 1993); on jazz, see S. F. Starr, *Red and Hot: The Fate of Jazz in the Soviet Union* (New York, 1993); on estrada, see R. Stites, *Russian Popular Culture: Entertainment and Society since 1900* (Cambridge, 1992), chs. 5, 6, and 7.

early 1960s to the 1990s, and despite profound differences of musical language, continued to be haunted by the almost overpowering influence of Shostakovich. Indeed it would almost be possible to write a history of serious music inside the Soviet Union from the death of Stalin to 1991 solely in terms of the variety of ways in which different composers reacted to Shostakovich's example.

The story of how official Soviet composers fell so heavily under the influence of an artist whom they had several times done their best to destroy is a confusing one, with roots in the causes and effects of the campaigns by Zhdanov and others in the 1930s and 1940s to force music into the arbitrary frame of socialist realism. But at its heart is a curious and rather bald paradox: that the official composers who so frequently attacked Shostakovich, and indeed Prokof'ev, found that when they themselves tried to write music, it was difficult for them to escape the influence of the very same formalists they purported to despise. This was partly because Prokof'ev and Shostakovich were quite simply the strongest musical personalities around. But it was also because, at least by 1948, both composers had evolved styles that already fulfilled most of the pseudo-musical demands that Zhdanov was to insist on (a clear distinction between melody and accompaniment, traditionally recognizable formal and tonal signposts, and so on). The only thing these two great composers had failed to do was to use their hard-won and recently simplified later styles exclusively in the cause of 'optimistic' propaganda. In most other respects it was precisely their music, rather than that of their tormentors, which provided the most obvious models of what the new socialist realist music ought to sound like.

This helps to explain why, especially in the course of the 1960s and 1970s, the operas, symphonies, and concertos[12] of such high-ranking officials of the Composers' Union as Khrennikov, Dmitrii Kabalevskii (1904–87), or Andrei Eshpai (b. 1925) (all of them pupils of the distinguished Nikolai Miaskovskii, who, along with Shostakovich and Prokof'ev, had been one of the principal victims of the Union's wrath in 1948), became so cluttered with obvious and usually deplorable imitations of Shostakovich's most rhetorical and cinematic gestures, as well as of the distorted modal harmonies and banally conventional accompaniment figures that were such typical surface features of his language even in his most serious works of the 1940s and 1950s. There is an important distinction to be made, however, between Shostakovich's intentions and those of his imitators. In Shostakovich's music, features of this kind were in the main intended to play an ironic or alienating role. In the music of his imitators, we are asked to take such things at face value. What may appear to be banal in

12 One of the odder aspects of the resolutions that ended the 1948 Union Congress was their repeated insistence that the most important musical task ahead was the creation of new Soviet versions of all the most traditional large-scale genres of Western music, including the opera and the symphony.

Shostakovich's music is, in the music of Khrennikov, always and only just that, i.e. banal. Indeed, listening to Soviet music of the 1950s and 1960s in chronological order, one might sometimes imagine that Shostakovich were parodying *in advance* what his hapless imitators were yet to write.

By contrast, the influence of Shostakovich on the music of left or underground composers is a different matter, one not of style and technique, but of symbolic intention. What composers such as Schnittke, Denisov, and Gubaidulina took from Shostakovich was not the sound of his music but what it was meant to signify beyond the sound, its implied extra-musical content—precisely that aspect of his art that has provoked irritation and suspicion, especially from Western musicians.

In an interview in 1989, a distinguished performer of contemporary Russian and Soviet music, the cellist and commentator Aleksandr Ivashkin, attempted to place this matter in a wider historical context:

Russian music was always slightly different from European, and most importantly in a certain non-musical content . . . This was always true, perhaps beginning with Glinka and the Mighty Handful, and it was particularly so with Skriabin . . . But it is more observable now for a number of reasons . . . perhaps more social reasons than artistic ones . . . For many years we could not speak or demonstrate what we really thought, and therefore there arose a very strange phenomenon, where something would reveal itself only a little on the surface while the rest of it would remain under water. It's like a great iceberg of which only a small part appears on the surface.

And this is how there appeared the symbolism that is now typical of Russian music . . . a symbolism, as a rule, of very simple elements. And this is why for many musicians abroad new Soviet music seems very strange, especially the music of Schnittke and Gubaidulina . . .

It's important to understand this, to understand how the very simple elements which are really there in our music, seem to us to be symbolical. This tradition comes from Shostakovich, and especially from his late works, where something very simple isolates itself, an interval, a sound or a rhythm, and becomes a symbol behind which lies a meaning which the listener conjectures for themselves [*sic*].

That is to say, the music is more the occasion of meditation and philosophical generalization than an end in itself . . . it was never simply a construction in sound, never![13]

One of the things that makes the work of left composers of the post-Shostakovich generations interesting is precisely the variety of ways they found to incorporate a Shostakovichian symbolism of the kind Ivashkin describes into new musical languages that borrowed little or nothing from the sound of his music. And this is especially true of those works written in the 1960s and early 1970s by younger

13 Int. with McBurney, BBC TV, London, June 1989.

composers who had embraced elements of what, to them, was the entirely new language of Western European radical modernism.

Finding Lost Connections: The Modernist Revival after 1953

The first arrival of European modernism in the Soviet Union at the end of the 1950s was in some senses a rediscovery of the past. For the first thirty years of the century Russia had had an active modernist movement in music as in the other arts, and had produced composers such as Skriabin, Stravinsky, and the young Prokof'ev and Shostakovich, who had played prominent roles on what may be loosely called the international modernist scene. Moreover there was, in the 1920s, a rich internal world of experimental music by such composers as Mosolov, Roslavets, and others, which reflected a sophisticated awareness of what was going on beyond Soviet borders. This situation changed in 1932 with Stalin's abrupt reorganization and regimentation of the arts into Unions, and with the repression that followed. As a result, for nearly thirty years Soviet musicians were effectively cut off from information about or contact with the manifold changes and developments taking place in Western music.

Some idea of how the Soviet musical educational process attempted to deal with the existence of vast swathes of music considered not worth performing or even actively pernicious can be gleaned by perusing V. Gorodinskii's tellingly titled and intriguing 1950 volume *The Music of Spiritual Poverty*. This consists of a shrill condemnation of most Western music of the first half of the twentieth century, including American jazz. Ironically, it became something of a collector's item with music students in the 1950s, as it was the unintentional source of otherwise unobtainable information on figures such as Schoenberg, Stravinsky, and Bartok. Edison Denisov described this period in 1990: 'When I entered the Moscow Conservatoire in 1951, it was a very dark time for all the arts in our country, and for music in particular. People were expelled from the Conservatoire just for mentioning the names of Debussy, Ravel, and Stravinsky.'[14]

The re-establishing of lines of communication with modern Western music and musicians was therefore a crucial development of Soviet musical life in the late 1950s and early 1960s. And it is a development in which a number of different people played important roles. In the first place there were still in the 1950s those among the older generation of musicians and music teachers, including Shostakovich himself, who well remembered the musical world before 1932 and

14 See V. Gorodinskii, *Muzyka dukhovnoi nishchety* (Moscow, 1950); Denisov, int. with McBurney, BBC TV, 1990.

could discreetly reintroduce into the educational process the names of composers and pieces of music whose very existence had at times been denied. Shostakovich, for example, made a four-hand version of Stravinsky's *Symphony of Psalms* to enable his students in Moscow to get to know this otherwise unavailable work. And in Kiev the elderly Boris Liatoshinskii encouraged his pupils to gather in his apartment to listen to broadcasts of new music from the Warsaw Autumn Festival.

However, there were two individuals who played a particularly important role at this time. One was Filip Gershkovich, [15] a composer and music-theorist of Rumanian-Jewish origin, who studied in Vienna before the Second World War with Alban Berg and Anton Webern. In 1940, he fled Rumania for the USSR, where he lived until 1987, when, after many refusals, he finally received permission to leave for Vienna. Gershkovich was admitted to the Composers' Union in 1942 but was subsequently expelled in 1949 and spent most of the rest of his life in Moscow in great poverty. He held no official position, but taught many students privately, including Karetnikov, Denisov, Schnittke, Gubaidulina, Viktor Suslin (b. 1942), and, later, Elena Firsova (b. 1950) and Dmitrii Smirnov (b. 1948), the last of whom has written an important unpublished account of Gershkovich's teachings, *A Book about Gershkovich (Kniga o Gershkoviche)*.[16]

In a recent interview, Viktor Suslin has summed up his personal view of Gershkovich's importance:

I think that without Gershkovich we would not have had (from the formal point of view) such interesting compositions as those of Schnittke and Gubaidulina. It would all have been quite different. [Gershkovich] was like a seed. I personally would say that Gershkovich can be considered a sort of apostle sent by Webern to work among the barbarians . . . Thanks to Gershkovich, a number of Moscow composers received a direct line from Webern, Schoenberg, and Berg.[17]

Despite Suslin's last comment, it should be stressed that Gershkovich did not teach his pupils to write in the style of the Second Viennese School and he always refused the requests of those Soviet composers who went to him asking to learn how to compose with twelve-note rows. His lessons were based, like those of Schoenberg and Webern, almost exclusively on the close analysis of Bach and Beethoven, but in a manner far removed from the primitive analytical style of the Moscow Conservatoire.

The other figure who played an important role at this period was Andrei Volkonskii. He was born in the West in 1933. As a child he showed talent as a composer and keyboard player, and as a result came into contact with several key figures of the French musical world

15 'Gershkovich' is a transliteration of the Russian spelling of this name. In Western literature the name appears variously in its German form, Philip Herschkowitz, and its Romanian form, Filip Herscovici.
16 Gershkovich's collected writings have been published since his death: see F. Gershkovich, *O muzyke* (Moscow, 1991).
17 Int. with McBurney, BBC 2, London, June 1989.

including, apparently, Louis Aubert, Olivier Messiaen, and Dinu Lipatti. (The various references to Volkonskii in Western and Russian publications do not always agree on exactly whom he studied with: there have been suggestions that as well as coming into contact with the musicians named, he also worked with the Schoenberg disciple René Leibowitz.) In the late 1940s his parents decided to return to the USSR, and by the early 1950s Volkonskii was a student, albeit a rebellious one, at the Moscow Conservatoire.

The personal accounts of numerous composers of the same generation as Volkonskii give eloquent evidence of his importance as a link with an outside world of which little or nothing had been known before, as well as of his ability to stimulate others to try new compositional techniques. These included, crucially, serial techniques based not only on the officially condemned models of Schoenberg, Webern, and Berg, but also on the absolutely unknown early experiments of young post-war composers in Paris including Pierre Boulez. Volkonskii's own music, in such works as *Musica Stricta* for piano (1956, the first notable attempt at serial music by a Soviet composer from this period) and the Lorca cycle for voice and chamber ensemble, *The Suite of Mirrors* (*Siuita zerkal*, 1959), had an audible effect on the early serial attempts of his contemporaries.[18]

Volkonskii also had an effect on Soviet musical life outside the world of young composers. He was already writing criticism for the Union's official organ *Sovetskaia muzyka* in 1954, and was able to mount a much-needed defence in its pages of Shostakovich's newly released and controversial Tenth Symphony.[19] In 1958 he was a co-founder, with the conductor and viola-player Rudol'f Barshai, of the Moscow Chamber Orchestra, the ensemble for which Shostakovich was later inspired to write one of his greatest works, the Fourteenth Symphony (1969). And in 1964 he founded the Ensemble Madrigal to enable the performance of European 'early music', a repertoire previously almost completely ignored in Soviet concerts and recordings.

Volkonskii spent about twenty-five years inside the Soviet Union, before re-emigrating to the West in 1973, worn out by official harassment and increasing restrictions on his work as a performer and as a composer. The experimental musical honeymoon of the Khrushchev years was long since over. As he commented bitterly to the *New York Times* in June of that year: 'I was just a speck of dirt in the grand marble palace of Soviet culture.'[20] Since the fall of the USSR in 1991, Volkonskii, who still plays and composes, has also become one of the leading lights of the Belyayeff Foundation. In this capacity he has devoted himself to giving material and practical help to Russian composers in difficulties, both those still in Russia and those now in the West.

18 Material from interviews held in the late 1980s and early 1990s by McBurney includes tributes to Volkonskii's importance from Schnittke, Denisov, Sil'vestrov, Karetnikov, and Tigran Mansurian (b. 1939), as well as notes of conversations with Arvo Pärt, Alemdar Karamanov (b. 1934), and Roman Ledenev (b. 1930).
19 See Schwarz, *Music and Musical Life*, 283–6.
20 Ibid. 543.

As well as significant and influential individuals from inside the Soviet Union such as Gershkovich and Volkonskii, there were also a number of Western musicians who visited the country at this period, bringing with them crucial news and information and even the possibility of contact with Western composers. First and most famous of these was the Canadian pianist Glenn Gould, who, during a concert-tour of the USSR in 1957, gave an informal master-class to students in the Small Hall of the Moscow Conservatoire, in the course of which he described the twelve-note techniques of Schoenberg and his followers and played music by Berg, Webern, and Krenek.[21] This incident, legendary among older Moscow musicians and often described in press interviews by both Alfred Schnittke and Edison Denisov, was recalled in 1990 by Nikolai Karetnikov:

When he played Webern, it was a revelation because not one of us could have imagined that such music existed in the world. As a result we had to think and draw our own conclusions. This was very complicated, because we had no literature to help us . . . and so all the rules had to be drawn directly from the music, we had to determine for ourselves what was most important about this music . . .[22]

Other visitors who affected the outlook of young composers included that distinguished leader of the Italian avant-garde (and member of the Italian Communist Party) Luigi Nono, who brought presents of scores and recordings which formed the original source of much of what became a small but important musical *samizdat*; and, in 1967, Pierre Boulez, who conducted the BBC Symphony Orchestra in performances of, among other things, his own *Éclat* and Webern's Variations for Orchestra. But the most politically significant visit of these years was undoubtedly that of the greatest Russian composer of the twentieth century, Stravinsky, who was finally persuaded to revisit his homeland in 1963 for the first time since 1912.

Stravinsky's visit was treated by the Soviet state, and by Tikhon Khrennikov and the Union of Composers, as a propaganda coup. The years of Stravinsky's vilification as a 'traitor to the homeland' were quietly and hypocritically forgotten. But for young composers, Stravinsky's visit had a deeper significance. Here was living proof of the significance and seriousness of the real, pre-Soviet Russian tradition. Stravinsky's very presence gave promise of the previously unimaginable possibility of rebuilding those links with the Russian past that had been torn down by Stalin, the Composers' Union, and the doctrines of socialist realism.

Not surprisingly, under what seemed the welter of new information to which young composers were subjected at this period, the

21 Nearly all concerts in the USSR were recorded as a matter of course, and so in 1984 Melodiia was able to issue Gould's lecture recital on LP with the number M10 45963 009.
22 Int. with McBurney, BBC TV.

music that was written by those who were trying to make sense of what they were only just learning reflects a marked and at times bewildering eclecticism and stylistic uncertainty. At the same time one should not mistake or overstate this situation. Eclecticism and uncertainty were also features of the work of many Western composers at this period, as can be observed in the music of such signally different talents as Luciano Berio in Italy, Peter Maxwell Davies in Britain, and Bernd Alois Zimmermann in West Germany. And as far as Soviet composers were concerned, the real discovery of this eclecticism or play with new stylistic and technical possibilities was that it could so quickly be absorbed into characteristic patterns of Russian music-making, becoming yet another means of articulating what Aleksandr Ivashkin has described as the typical symbolic concerns of Russian and Soviet music.

To put it crudely, in the Soviet context it was inevitable that any newly borrowed style or musical device carried symbolic meaning. If you quoted from or suggested the style of or an idea from, say, Schoenberg, Debussy, Boulez, or Cage, you were, whether you intended so or not, making a politically symbolic statement. So the left composer's task at this period became not so much the simple absorption of new information, but the use of this new musical material as a weapon in the continuing confrontation with the enemy, the Union and its official composers. The terms of the confrontation were already decided; this was just a new weapon that came to hand.

The single work that most vividly sums up the position of the younger generation of nonconformist composers at this period is Schnittke's First Symphony, which was given its belated world première in Gorky (now Nizhnii Novgorod) in October 1974. Gorky was at that time a city closed to foreigners, which is perhaps why the Union allowed the piece to be performed there, having refused permission for it to be given in Moscow. It is not hard to see why they should have been nervous of allowing the piece to be performed at all. The symphony is a gigantic canvas, more than an hour long. The outer two of its four movements in particular are constructed as an elaborate and noisy tissue of quotation, parody, and imitation of a whole mass of other music by composers from many different historical periods and cultures. At several points there are sharp caricatures of official Soviet music, often played side by side with, or even at the same time as, self-consciously touching fragments of favourite moments from the music of the greatest masters, such as Bach, Mozart, and Beethoven. And in the centre of the symphony there is an extended free cadenza for two jazz musicians (from the 1930s onwards, as we have seen, jazz had frequently figured in Union propaganda as an example of what was most decadent in Western music).

But perhaps the most obvious and telling detail is the structural and theatrical device that frames the whole symphony. At the beginning of the work the entire orchestra wanders on to the stage, improvising as they go. After several minutes of mere noise, the exuberance and chaos of this improvisation is then suddenly cut short by the appearance of the conductor, who imposes order. At the end of the symphony, the whole charade, with its all too obvious representation of matters outside the concert-hall, is then repeated in an extended form. The effect of this framing device, though certainly crude, remains a strong one, not least because of the impractical absurdity of trying to get nearly 100 musicians on and off stage while playing their instruments at the same time. And the gesture is carefully enough planned in relation to the rest of the music that the whole piece can still make a powerful impression even now, twenty years later and in a different political environment.

For many Soviet composers of the next generation after Schnittke, those who were born in the late 1940s or in the 1950s, his First Symphony remains a key document of the declining years of the Soviet Union. Viktor Suslin has described the piece as the 'Gulag Archipelago in music',[23] which comment, if hyperbolic in the opinion of those for whom Schnittke's music does not rate highly, at least suggests something of the power of the work's effect on a younger generation who were searching for a new musical lead to replace that of the dying Shostakovich.

On the other hand, if Suslin and his contemporaries were looking for this Symphony to be the harbinger of something new, they were to be disillusioned. As it turned out, this powerful and dramatic piece was to be an ending rather than a beginning, a grandiose summing up of the previous decade and a half of rebellious experimentation and interest in things Western long hidden and denied. What followed in the later 1970s and in the 1980s was a period not of experiment and discovery, but of retrenchment and, when the music was at its best, refinement.

Rediscovering the Past: Historicism and Nostalgia after 1975

In retrospect, the seeds of this retrenchment can be identified already a year or two before the appearance of Schnittke's First Symphony, when certain composers who had previously played a notable part in

23 Int. with McBurney, BBC TV, London, 1989.

the exploration of radical new compositional techniques from the West began to turn back towards an interest in rediscovering some of the older traditions of both Russia and the West. In particular, they were interested in those native traditions from within the Soviet Union which had, like Western modernism, been restricted, derided, distorted, or simply unacknowledged in the business of creating the new 'Soviet music'.

In 1970, the Ukrainian Valentin Sil'vestrov began work on a large piece for piano trio, *Drama*, which he finished the following year. The 'drama' in question was the profound change that was taking place inside the composer's own view of the kind of music he wanted to write. *Drama*'s three movements chart a journey from a delicately modernist language inspired by Webern and his successors, through a territory of random noise and improvisation, to the emergence of a neo-romantic language indebted to nothing so much as the early songs and chamber music of Glinka. At about the same time, Sil'vestrov's close friend, the Estonian Arvo Pärt, was working on his Third Symphony (1971), in which he endeavoured a self-conscious and somewhat nervous orchestral exploration of some of the oldest traditions of European and Russian church music.

These at first surprising experiments of Pärt and Sil'vestrov turned out to be but the beginning of what was to become a surge of interest on the part of composers from all over the Soviet Union in reviving and developing musical languages from the past. Some composers, following in Sil'vestrov's path, turned to earlier and often specifically Slavic forms of classical music. Others seemed more interested in the ancient non-classical music of the different ethnic populations of the USSR. Still others concentrated their attention on the music of the different religious traditions, both from inside the country and from outside. Some, including the Georgian Giya Kancheli (b. 1935), attempted to synthesize in their music material from both religious and secular sources. What all these endeavours had, and still have, in common was their focus on earlier musical sources of a kind that had been misrepresented or even completely repressed by the official Soviet version of musical history.

It is not hard, of course, to understand the ease with which a new interest in religious music was awakened in the 1970s. During the Stalin period, and for some time afterwards, most forms of religious music had remained fairly inaccessible to performers and composers. So, almost inevitably, the rediscovery of such material at the beginning of the 1970s seemed to offer alluringly expressive and symbolic possibilities. In this, musicians were no different from other Soviet artists such as writers, painters, and film-makers, in whose work the same religious interests began to surface at about the same time. And, perhaps understandably, there has subsequently been a good deal of scepticism, especially in the West, from those who feel there to be something modish and even exploitative about the resulting proliferation of what is all too easily seen as art that is merely posing at being religious.

At the same time, it should be pointed out that when they engaged with religious ideas and texts and with religious musical imagery, composers such as Schnittke, Denisov, Gubaidulina, and Karetnikov undoubtedly felt and (in the case of the first three) still feel that they were addressing subjects which have always provided legitimate material for the arts in Russia.[24] Composers such as these regarded themselves as simply returning to a subject-matter that had been artificially kept from them since 1917.

It is interesting to observe in this context the work of one of the most distinctive and unusual of all the many Russian composers of religious music to emerge in the last years of the Soviet Union, Galina Ustvol'skaia. Ustvol'skaia was born in 1919, and began serious composition as early as the 1940s, when she was a student of Shostakovich. But she counts as a recent figure because her music remained almost completely isolated and unknown, even in Russia, until the 1990s. This situation was partly a result of Ustvol'skaia's character, for until recently she shunned the attention of those who have taken an interest in her music. But it is also because of the nature of her musical language, which is not only possessed by startlingly obvious and highly unconventional religious intentions, but rhythmically and harmonically is one of the most abrasive and unexpected of any composer working now.

It is true that Ustvol'skaia's overtly religious music begins only with her *Composition 1—Dona Nobis Pacem* (*Kompozitsiia No. 1 'Dona Nobis Pacem'*) of 1971, but she herself would claim that all her acknowledged music, from as far back as the First Piano Sonata of 1947, is religious in inspiration and intent. And indeed even at that stage her preoccupation with the structure and intonations of early Orthodox chant is fairly obvious. (It would be interesting to know where, in the 1940s, Ustvol'skaia managed to find out about early religious music and Russian chant: her youth and musical studies took place at a time when information about such matters was highly restricted.) But the essence of Ustvol'skaia's art is that she neither quotes nor stylizes. There is nothing nostalgic, easily appealing, or retrospective about her intentions, and her music, with its harsh and relentless processions of tone-clusters and hammer blows, yields nothing to conventional assumptions about what makes sense or what might sound

24 Religious works by these composers include: Schnittke's *Requiem* (1975), Symphony No. 2 (1979), and Symphony No. 4 (1984); Denisov's *Requiem* (1980) and *Life of Jesus* (1992); Gubaidulina's *Seven Last Words* (1982) and *Offertorium* (1986); and Karetnikov's *Mystery of St Paul* (1971–85) and *Eight Spiritual Songs in Memory of Boris Pasternak* (1969–89).

aesthetically pleasing. For better or for worse, what she writes is less music, in the ordinary sense, than, in the words of the Leningrad pianist Oleg Malov, 'a sermon, a spiritual address'.[25]

At the opposite extreme from the music of Ustvol'skaia, it is worth observing that, by the late 1980s, the fashionable fascination of Soviet composers with religion had become so widespread that it could be heard operating almost equally in the music of left composers and of official composers. Indeed, especially after 1990 or so, astonishing was the spectacle of erstwhile officials of the Soviet Union, such as Andrei Eshpai, clambering on to the bandwagon of religious music to scribble liturgies and requiems. The distinguished Moscow-based percussionist Mark Pekarskii summed up the new situation in 1992: 'One has the impression that the same old bandits, who had found themselves sitting on an old train travelling very slowly in one direction, have simply jumped off on to another old train moving equally slowly in the opposite direction.'[26]

The various musical journeys of different composers to rediscover (or reinvent) the national or tribal past have proceeded with much the same energy and intensity as the similar rediscoveries of the religious past. Since the appearance of such works as Valentin Sil'vestrov's *Drama* in the early 1970s, many (especially Slavic) composers have participated in the development of what became known familiarly as 'retro', many trying their hand at copying and sometimes distorting the styles of Russian composers of the nineteenth and early twentieth centuries. Even a composer as distinct as Denisov has been affected by this tendency, notably in his Pushkin and Blok song-cycles, which attempt a bizarre fusion of the manner of a Glinka romance with his own largely heterophonic and atonal idiom.

As with the composers of religious music, this movement towards a reinvention of the musical roots of the nation has had the effect of bringing an unexpected *rapprochement* between composers of the official school and those who would once have regarded themselves as of the left. This is particularly true of the group of younger composers including Roman Ledenev, who surround the curious figure of Georgii (or Iurii) Sviridov (b. 1915). Sviridov was a Shostakovich pupil, who shocked and irritated his erstwhile master[27] by his drift, as early as the 1940s, towards a self-consciously reactionary and would-be Slavophile musical idiom, based on close imitation of the manner of such composers as Tchaikovsky, Borodin, and Rachmaninov. Especially in the new world of post-Soviet politics, Sviridov's right-wing stance has drawn understandable criticism, similar to that which has been directed at the painter Il'ia Glazunov or the writer Valentin Rasputin.

25 Int. with McBurney, BBC TV, 1990.
26 Int. with McBurney, 1992.
27 For evidence of this, see I. Glikman, *Pis'ma k drugu* (Moscow, 1993).

But the nationalist nostalgia of Sviridov and others like him, with its unsavoury suggestions of racial intolerance and isolationism, should not be confused with the genuine freshness and originality of a composer such as Sil'vestrov, whose excursions into the past are driven not by a simple desire to retreat from the present, but by a far more creative and complex endeavour to explore the constructive and imaginative connections *between* the past and the present. In fact, as much as anything, Sil'vestrov's music is about the impossibility of recreating the past.

The language Sil'vestrov has evolved over the last twenty-five years or so takes as its point of departure the music of Russia's amateur composers of the early nineteenth century. This apparently whimsical choice of focus must be understood as driven by the historical symbolism of such figures as Varlamov, Gurilev, Aliabev, and Glinka, rather than by the actual music they wrote, which, with the exception of Glinka's later work, is entirely limited by the conventions of the *biedermeier* drawing-room romance. The meaning of composers such as these, hardly known outside Russia and often forgotten even there, lies in the fact that they were the musical contemporaries of Pushkin, Del'vig, Küchelbecker, and Baratynskii, whose poetry they so often set; that several of them, including Aliabev, were Decembrists; and that their music, frail though it seems to us, is the sound of one of the key moments in the history of Russian culture, the birth-time of Russian romanticism and of a particular view of the identity and destiny of the tribe.

Sil'vestrov, in works like his enormous vocal cycle *Quiet Songs* (*Tikhie pesni*, 1974–7) and his masterly Fifth Symphony (1980–2) has constructed, with ever-increasing refinement and sensitivity, something like a musical echo-chamber. Half-familiar fragments and wistful evocations of music from nearly 200 years ago hover against the background of an elaborately wrought acoustic field, at times so hushed that it lies at the very edge of audibility. Listening to his music, we find ourselves straining to catch suggestions of what we might imagine we ought to have been able to remember, but find to be beyond our grasp. The subject of his music, unlike that of so many of his contemporaries, is not the presence of the past, but its absence, its irretrievable loss.

7

CATRIONA KELLY

ROBIN MILNER-
GULLAND

Building a New Reality:
The Visual Arts, 1921–1953

Avant-Gardists versus Realists

As the dust settled after Revolution and Civil War, it became clear to practitioners of the visual arts, design, and architecture that an uncertain future, but one replete with novel and exciting opportunities, had opened up before them. A few major cultural figures, who were abroad at the time of the Revolution, remained outside Russia (Mikhail Larionov and Natal'ia Goncharova, as well as Léon Bakst, Sergei Diaghilev, and Igor' Stravinsky, in France, Il'ia Repin in Finland). In the 1920s, they were joined in emigration by several 'World of Art' painters, such as Filipp Maliavin, Alexandre Benois (Benua), and Mstislav Dobuzhinskii. Others who left Russia in that decade were Wassily (Vasilii) Kandinsky and Marc Chagall—who already had reputations in the West—and some younger figures such as Pavel Mansurov and Naum Gabo, and the futurist David Burliuk.[1] But most artists, whatever their politics—including initially the five just mentioned—threw themselves wholeheartedly into rebuilding the arts in the new revolutionary state. The old patrons had gone, but the new authorities seemed keen to encourage a cultural life appropriate to the radical character of their ideology. Quite how this would be realized in practice took many years—till the mid-1930s—to become evident; nobody doubted that the Party could or should have an artistic policy, but at first it took care not to favour any of the sharply competing tendencies exclusively.

Of course the detailed configuration of such tendencies, and the groups they spawned, was different in the 1920s from the situation in the 1910s. The symbolists who had played such a remarkable role in the birth of Russian modernism around the turn of the century were a spent force (unless one includes in their number one or two highly idiosyncratic newcomers, such as Vasilii Chekrygin or Aleksandr Tyshler). The followers of the original Wanderers (*Peredvizhniki*), rebels in their time, had made their peace with the world of authority in the late nineteenth century, and by the early Soviet period represented traditional values and academicism.[2] Repin—who lived on till 1930—was a considerable influence in the reassertion of realism (eventually, socialist realism). The deliberately shocking neo-primitivism favoured around 1910 gave way to a subtler reassessment of what folk-based stylizations and thematics could offer sophisticated art (whether in, for example, the vibrant Armenian scenes of Matiros Sar'ian, or the marvellously intricate engravings of Vladimir Favorskii).

The broad distinction between, on the one hand, a highly diverse, provocative, and self-conscious avant-garde, many of whose representatives had turned their backs on figuration, indeed on old concepts of art generally, and were looking for new worlds to conquer, and a conglomeration of traditionalistic forces on the other, remained in force after the Revolution as before. But an interesting development of the 1920s was the emergence of figures who to some extent bridged the gap, often representing a Russian equivalent to the contemporary German *Neue Sachlichkeit* (new objectification); without giving up traditional painterly concerns and methods, its practitioners were unmistakably of the twentieth century. Such important and varied figures as Aleksandr Deineka, Iurii Pimenov, and Kuz'ma Petrov-Vodkin came into this category. In the second half of this section, we shall look more closely at the last of these, and juxtapose his work with that of a most characteristic socialist-realist painter of the Stalin period, Gerasimov. Before that, we can usefully, if briefly, follow the careers of the major avant-gardists in the 1920s and 1930s.

Though the heroic days of the modern movement in Russia are really the 1910s, it is worth remembering that its leaders—Kazimir Malevich, Vladimir Tatlin, Pavel Filonov, Larionov, as well as important figures such as Goncharova, Liubov' Popova, Aleksandra Ekster, Ol'ga Rozanova, David Burliuk, and others—were all still in their thirties at the time of the Revolution (Aleksandr Rodchenko and El Lissitzky were in their twenties), and at the peak of their activity.

Having made their mark in opposition to bourgeois aesthetics and values before 1917, the avant-gardists unexpectedly found themselves in a position where, with the dominance of the formerly powerful Academy of Arts brought to an end, previous constraints had been

1 See Ch. 12.

2 See R. Bartlett and L. Edmondson, 'Collapse and Creation: Issues of Identity in the Russian *Fin de Siècle*', in C. Kelly and D. Shepherd (eds.), *Constructing Russian Culture in the Age of Revolution, 1881–1940* (Oxford, 1998), 180–5.

removed and they could fulfil what they saw to be their public role. Like the futurist writers with whom they closely co-operated (including Velimir Khlebnikov and Vladimir Maiakovskii), they considered that their vision had an added authority because they had anticipated the Revolution spiritually. Most of the Bolshevik leaders were people of staider tastes (though the Commissar of Enlightenment, Lunacharskii, had been a symbolist playwright), and did not accept the avant-gardists' pretensions; still, they created the circumstances in which such ideas could be experimentally developed and publicized, above all by setting up a series of new institutions for the arts. Most important among these were SVOMAS (Free State Art Studios), which later became VKhUTEMAS and VKhUTEIN; its Petrograd equivalent PEGOSKhUMA, the Academy of Artistic Sciences; the great art school at Vitebsk run by Chagall until he was ousted by Malevich; and above all INKhUK (the Institute of Artistic Culture) in Moscow. This last served as a laboratory for art research and educational ideas, contributed much to the development of constructivism (on which more below), and through figures such as Kandinsky, Malevich, and Lissitzky had an impact on the Bauhaus in Germany and on Western avant-garde art generally. Russian modernism had never been merely rebellious or committed to art for art's sake, but had always had a didactic, cognitive undercurrent, and many avant-gardists—as well as artists of less radical convictions—threw themselves into teaching in the liberated atmosphere of the new studios, open to all.

No one played a more deliberately public role, in a variety of fields where art shaded into either visionary or utilitarian projects, than Vladimir Tatlin. Though rather shy and gauche, he was an inspirational teacher, expounding in particular the 'culture of materials'. He was put in charge of carrying out Lenin's decree on 'monumental propaganda' (April 1918), to replace tsarist monuments; but more congenially, he developed, in the years from 1919, his own 'monument without a beard', as Maiakovskii put it, dedicated first to the Revolution, then to the Third International. Tatlin's Tower, as the unrealized project was known, was to have been the headquarters of the thing commemorated, a vast double spiral (containing revolving chambers) in 'the materials of modern classicism', skewed to the angle of the Pole Star; it was an answer to the Eiffel Tower and indeed to the whole tradition of monumental building from the legendary Tower of Babel onwards. Subsequently, Tatlin designed clothing, a stove, and other objects of use; he spent many years working on a machine (*Letatlin*, a pun on the Russian verb *letat'*, to fly, and his own name), that would give individual humans the power of flight. Though considered the founder of constructivism, Tatlin in fact disliked the constructivists' rationalism, angularity, and imposition of straight lines onto nature; his own vision was of fluidity, dynamism, organicism. He and his followers were not so much persecuted as sidelined under Stalin; Tatlin himself did some stage-design and book illustration, then went back to easel-painting for his own satisfaction (as did Rodchenko, with remarkable results anticipating the work of Jackson Pollock).

Tatlin's colleague and rival, Malevich, had developed 'suprematism', a breakthrough into a new conceptual sphere of non-figurative art, before the Revolution. After it, as well as teaching, he experimented with non-functional ideal architectural projects (as a response, perhaps, to Tatlin's Tower) and wrote an important text, *The Non-Objective World*. Before his death in 1935, he had returned to paintings featuring the highly stylized human form, sometimes picking up the stark images of peasant toil characteristic of his early work, transfigured through suprematist techniques (the use of brightly coloured geometrical forms as schematic representations of bodily parts). Pavel Filonov, by contrast, greeted the revolutionary years with a series of paintings celebrating 'universal flowering', and then developed, for himself and his disciples (the Filonov School) a highly original 'method', analytic art, based on the concept of *sdelannost'*. This concept, literally 'madeness', signified unremitting hard work on the art object, so that every atom and predicate of the thing portrayed could be symbolized. As late as 1933, his Collective of Masters of Analytic Art could collaborate on an ambitious project to illustrate the Finnish epic, the *Kalevala*; but his great retrospective exhibition at the Leningrad Russian Museum (1930) was dismantled without ever being opened to the public, and he too was sidelined in the 1930s.

Filonov's personal example was significant beyond the visual arts. After 1917, believing true art belonged to the people, he neither signed nor sold any of his pictures; like a sage or saint, he lived extremely frugally, not even possessing an overcoat. He died during the Siege of Leningrad, was written out of the Soviet record until the late 1960s, and became a cult figure among the few who knew of him. His reluctance to sell his work meant that he was effectively unknown in the West, but most of his surviving work finished up in the storerooms of the Russian Museum, inaccessible to most Russians or Westerners until *perestroika*. For the Soviet regime, an ultra-leftist such as Filonov was ideologically more alarming than any number of 'bourgeois' artists.

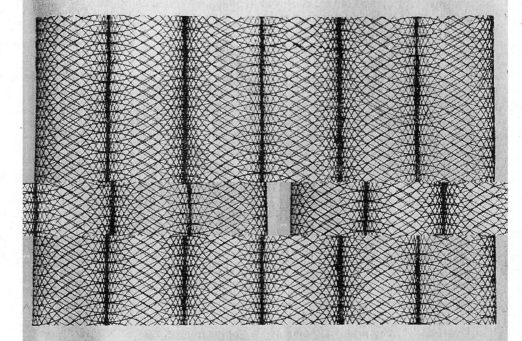

ТЕКСТИЛЬНОЙ ПРОМЫШЛЕННОСТИ.

РОДЧЕНКО

Ситец.

4 Textile design by Aleksandr Rodchenko, from the journal of the avant-garde LEF (Left Front of Arts), 1924.

LEF, with which such prominent modernists as Maiakovskii and the critic Osip Brik were associated, had a role analogous to that of the German Bauhaus in assiduously propagandizing the utilitarian principles of the constructivists. Apart from textile designs by Rodchenko, Popova, and others, constructivist items appearing in LEF's journal included folding beds (highly practical, given the living-space shortages of the 1920s), tables, and modernist newspaper kiosks.

The Triumph of Constructivism

The starting point of this section, 1921, marked a genuine break-through in the avant-gardists' quest for a significant role in the new society: it was in that year that the first constructivist exhibition was held. From now until the 1930s, constructivism would be the most compelling force in avant-garde art, its novelty such as to make even the remarkable works of the early modernists seem quaint and nostalgia-laden. Constructivism represented the first arrival on Russian soil of a true machine-age aesthetic, with painterly values of shading and tonality eschewed in favour of rigidity and hard lines. Moreover, as one expert on the movement has argued, 'from the start, the Constructivists were concerned not merely to promote a new aesthetic but to demonstrate their potential capabilities as designers of real objects and structures'.[3] Not merely artworks, the new 'con-structions' were intended as design prototypes, and their makers, such as Rodchenko, Stepanova, Ioganson, and the Stenberg brothers, worked with factories in order to produce the new fabrics, clothing, furnish-ings, and objects that signalled the new Soviet style to the world. Their participation was evident in every section of Soviet cultural life, from the most permanent (architecture and monumental sculpture) to the most transient (theatre design and fashion). Limited financial resources meant that their far-reaching plans could not always be realized to the extent, or in the manner, that they had envisaged. But their audacious designs, particularly their remarkable contributions to the graphic arts, made their work seem, above all in the eyes of foreigners, the most important expression of this confident, modern, and forward-looking new society.

Between 1921 and 1923, the constructivists' close relationship with Narkompros, and their strong representation in the art workshops where many Soviet artists trained, meant that representatives of alternative tendencies had to face a choice: to retreat into isolation, to engage in polemic with the constructivists, or to search for power bases of their own. The first course was adopted by, for example, Nina Simonovich-Efimova and Robert Falk, who simply pursued their own artistic impulses without justifying these through manifestos. The second course began to be adopted by a number of groups in the early 1920s, as the constructivists' ideas themselves came under assault from artists with similar political views, but rather different ideas about the best way of propagandizing them in the new society. The 'projectionists', for example, argued that transforming society via objects was an absurd project: far better was to attempt perfecting

3 C. Lodder, 'The Transition to Constructivism', in *The Great Utopia: The Russian and Soviet Avant-Garde, 1915–1932* (Guggenheim Museum, New York, 1992), 276; see also Lodder's pion-eering study, *Russian Constructivism* (New Haven, 1983).

machines themselves. Like the pioneer of documentary cinema, Dziga Vertov, they also preached a realism that would not be simply mimetic, but would actively engage with society in order to change it and shape it into a new Utopia.[4] The various strands of non-objective art—Malevich's suprematism, the 'analytic art' of Pavel Filonov and his followers, and the geometrical abstractionism of Matiushin—arose from different conceptions of the nature of art, based on analogies between the arts and biological sciences or higher mathematics, rather than physics and mechanics. But the constructivists' most dangerous opponents were those coming into the third category, above all the Comfut painters and other post-impressionists, and the realists' caucus, the Association of Artists of Revolutionary Russia, founded in 1922 by a group of discontents frustrated by the stale attitudes held by the rump of the Wanderers movement.

Constructivism was never merely an art movement; it represented (like symbolism a few decades earlier) a whole way of looking at the world and of living in a manner appropriate to the new age—almost an ideology. The five participants in its inaugural exhibition ('5 × 5 = 25') renounced easel-painting; its first propagandist, Aleksei Gan, author of *Konstruktivizm* (1922), proclaimed that 'Art is dead.' What this signified in practice was an attempt to get beyond the artificialities of style into a realm of pure, unornamented validity. Constructivist goals and methods had much in common with those of the French architect Henri Le Corbusier, who, indeed, designed an important Moscow building and took part in the ill-fated competition (1932–5) for the design of a grandiose Palace of Soviets (the authorities' decision to opt for a neo-classical project marked a turn away from official support of modernism). But, though many of its projects were unrealized, constructivism actually had considerable impact on the built environment in 1920s Russia. Individual constructivist structures include the great Moscow radio mast and Lenin's Mausoleum (no less)—but more characteristic and forward-looking are extensive integrated areas of townscape, bringing together the living, working, and recreational environment, as in the enormous Likhachev car-works occupying the territory and vicinity of the old Simonov monastery in south-east Moscow. Constructivism reached into cinema, photography, theatre, clothing, fabric- and book-design, sculpture, industrial design, even (tentatively) into literature and music. Unlike other avant-gardist tendencies, it touched on the lives of virtually every citizen. Even after the 'anti-constructivist counter-revolution' of the early 1930s, constructivism's after-effects lingered on in Soviet posters and some other design areas, such as graphic arts, photography, experimental theatre production, and indeed some

4 See I. Lebedeva, 'The Poetry of Science: Projectionism and Electroorganism', in *The Great Utopia*, 441–9.

aspects of the grandiose scheme of the Moscow Metro (for example, the Maiakovskii Station, plain and streamlined as against the Stalinist ornateness characterizing most of the network, or the design of the trains, escalators, and other functional parts of the system). Furthermore, it was a part of the Soviet heritage that could be revived and carried forward in the thaw of the 1950s, as the full range and stature of the modernist achievement in Russia began to be revealed, and to be given hesitant official recognition.

AKhRR: The Origins of Socialist Realism

If the constructivists came to seem the most important grouping in the Soviet art world after 1921, their prominence was largely symbolic. It was post-impressionist easel-painters such as Pavel Kuznetsov and his wife Elena Bebutova, and David Shterenberg (a specialist in intense still-lifes) who dominated Narkompros, controlling exhibition selections, teaching and administrative posts, and the allocation of subsidies. Even so far as collaboration with industry went, the constructivists did not have it all their own way: the important revolutionary ceramics produced by the former Imperial Porcelain Factory in Petrograd/Leningrad were designed by a team under the control of Sergei Chekhonin (a former World of Arts member and exquisite, but traditional, draughtsman).[5] While Anatolii Lunacharskii remained Commissar of Enlightenment, the moderate left was unassailable in the visual arts, and realism made far less headway here than in literature or even cinema, hard though Proletkul't (a relatively impotent force, especially after 1920) and AKhRR (Assotsiatsiia khudozhnikov revoliutsionnoi Rossii, Association of Artists of Revolutionary Russia, a more effective one) might push. With Shterenberg in charge, Soviet representation at international exhibitions, such as the much-admired Soviet pavilion at the 1925 Paris Exhibition, covered a wide range of different modernist trends, and Soviet artists kept in close touch with what their fellows were doing abroad, themselves contributing to magazines as well as exhibiting at shows.

Rather than trying to win over the People's Commissariat of Enlightenment, then, the AKhRR set its sights on easier and better-funded targets. Influential and wealthy bodies, such as the Red Army and the trades-union movement, responded well to the content and form of AKhRR canvases (neo-realist treatments of workers and soldiers, or mythologizations of Soviet history, such as Isaak Brodskii's *The Shooting of the 26 Baku Commissars* of 1925). Especially

5 See N. Lobanov-Rostovsky, *Revolutionary Ceramics: Soviet Porcelain, 1917–1927* (New York, 1990).

from the mid-1920s, AKhRR carried out a fierce propaganda war with its opponents, even going so far as to send Brodskii as envoy to secure the approval of his old teacher, the doyen of Russian realists, Il'ia Repin, then living in Finland.[6]

The onset of the cultural revolution in 1928 at first appeared to bring about a boost in AKhRR's fortunes: the Association's Tenth Exhibition was accorded the exceptional honour of a visit by Stalin, no enthusiast for painting (unlike the movies). But at the same time cracks begin to show within AKhRR itself, as a splinter group of 'proletarian' painters attacked the leadership for its bourgeois tastes. And if the dissolution of all existing artistic, as well as literary, groupings in 1932 represented a definite defeat for the constructivists and other representatives of non-figurative tendencies in arts, it was no immediate triumph for the hardline realists. AKhRR artists were only lightly represented at first in the Union of Soviet Artists, set up in 1932 as a loose co-ordinating body for the various regional and republican Unions. However, from the appointment of the realist painter and leading light of AKhRR, Aleksandr Gerasimov, as president of the Moscow Union of Artists, and then, in 1938, as first president of the Organizational Committee of the Union of Soviet Artists—a steering body meant to develop the Union as a more powerful instrument of overall control—the authority of the Association was consolidated. The point was reinforced in 1947 when the Academy of Arts, closed down after the October Revolution, was refounded, with Gerasimov, again, as its first director.

From the late 1930s, and especially from 1947, then, academicism— but the academicism of the late nineteenth century, after it had come under the influence of the Wanderers' national-populist (narodnye) enthusiasms—was the direction in which Russian painters were supposed to work. Three genres were particularly favoured: the portrait, above all of political or military leaders; the historical painting; and the genre painting (workers on the production line, collective farmers bringing in the harvest, or other such public scenes—domestic scenes figured only briefly, in the late 1940s and early 1950s). Continuity with the past was evident more in the handling of themes than in the themes themselves (the Wanderers' earlier paintings of human wretchedness, before they became 'establishment' artists at the end of the nineteenth century, would not have been passed for exhibition in the Stalin era, and historical scenes now depicted key moments of the Soviet past, rather than the seventeenth-century motifs that the Wanderers had often used in order to comment obliquely on present oppressions). But socialist-realist painters grouped their figures symmetrically, in neat patterns—pyramids, parallelograms—and

6 See E. Valkenier, *Il'ia Repin and the World of Russian Art* (New York, 1990), ch. 8.

used colour contrasts discreetly, whether working in sombre or in warm tones (bravura treatment was reserved for the most heroic subjects, such as Boris Iakovlev's lurid painting of a triumphant Marshal Zhukov on his white stallion before the flaming ruins of Berlin). Varnish was applied thickly to create an impeccably smooth and shiny surface, and the laws of geometrical perspective were not disrupted.

Interpretations of Socialist Realism: Petrov-Vodkin versus Gerasimov

There was, all the same, some room for personal interpretations of the new directives, as the contrasting cases of two painters, Kuz'ma Petrov-Vodkin and Aleksandr Gerasimov, illustrate. From similar provincial working-class backgrounds, and born at roughly the same time (in 1878 and 1881 respectively), the two had career paths that intersected at certain points, but diverged widely at others. Both received their formal training at the Moscow College of Painting, Sculpture, and Architecture, and both had connections with AKhRR (Petrov-Vodkin sent work to its Tenth Exhibition in 1928, while Gerasimov was a member from 1925). Both contributed to the construction of the Soviet art establishment (Petrov-Vodkin was involved in reorganizing the Academy of Art's training school in Petrograd immediately after the Revolution, and was first president of the Leningrad Union of Artists from 1932; Gerasimov, as mentioned earlier, was on the presidium of the Moscow Union of Artists from 1932, and went on to even higher things later). Both won high state honours (Petrov-Vodkin became an 'honoured arts activist' in 1930, Gerasimov in 1936). Both were talented painters who have often been cited as instances of the sadly detrimental and standardizing effects of socialist realism. 'Petrov-Vodkin abandoned his complex method of composition after 1932', according to Elizabeth Valkenier, while the author of a pioneering Western study of Gerasimov, Matthew Cullerne Bown, asserts that 'the requirement of the leader-genre for a pedantic, academic finish and dumb, uncontroversial composition had taken the edge off [Gerasimov's] work [by the early 1940s]'.[7] Yet in fact the later work of each painter is far from devoid of visual interest, and bears traces of the significant differences, as well as of the similarities, in their world-views.

Gerasimov was a man of defensively anti-aesthetic tastes even before the Revolution, whose humble background had given him a sense of inferiority towards confident metropolitan intellectuals. He made his first trip abroad as late as 1934, smugly asserting afterwards

7 E. Valkenier, *Russian Realist Art* (New York, 1977), 172, and M. C. Bown, 'Aleksandr Gerasimov', in Bown and B. Taylor (eds.), *Art of the Soviets: Publishing, Sculpture and Architecture in a One-Party State, 1917–1992* (Manchester, 1993), 131–2.

that the experience had been of no interest. Taught by the impressionist painter Korovin at the Moscow School of Painting, he himself developed into a capable impressionist painter rather in the manner of Serov or Leonid Pasternak, able to handle light and shade contrasts adeptly, and to suggest the plasticity of human figures. Very much a painter of physical reality, he seems to have been left wholly unmoved by the icons that would have been the most common visual images in the town where he grew up, teaching himself to draw, as a boy, by copying magazine illustrations. Petrov-Vodkin, on the other hand, though apparently without any more social advantages, was far more open to different intellectual and artistic currents. A remarkable writer as well as a painter, he had travelled widely both in the Russian Empire and outside, spending eighteen months living and working in Paris from 1906 to 1908. Far from being shy of 'aesthetes', he exhibited at their most important forum, the World of Art shows. Both his early work and his post-Revolutionary canvasses combine post-impressionist impulses with compositional and intonational motifs drawn from the Russian icons in which he, a far more metaphysically oriented painter than Gerasimov, had taken a strong interest as he was growing up.[8]

The paintings that Gerasimov executed after the Revolution were described by Lunacharskii as expressing above all *zhizneradostnost'* (joy in life),[9] and this central quality of socialist-realist painting was certainly foreshadowed in the upbeat poses, saturated lighting, bright colours, and energetic brushwork of his 1920s and 1930s canvasses. In contrast, 'joy in life' is notably absent from many of Petrov-Vodkin's paintings of the 1920s and 1930s, especially from those on revolutionary subjects, which concentrate on the tragedy of the emerging Revolution and its aftermath. A religious believer whose pre-Revolutionary output had, however, included some frescoes uncanonical enough to incur the wrath of the Orthodox Church authorities, Petrov-Vodkin had a highly personal and mystical view of revolutionary history, choosing to present it as a myth of self-sacrifice and martyrdom. In the years immediately after the Revolution, Christian imagery, overt or sublimated, informs many of his most impressive works. This is perhaps not too surprising in the famous canvas titled *1918 in Petrograd*, known alternatively and more descriptively as *The Petrograd Madonna*, where the use of a mother-and-child pairing to represent the Russian nation was sanctioned by parallels in the official iconography of the day.[10] It is much more startling in *Death of a Commissar* (1927), where the male revolutionary, rather than dropping heroic and resolute in mid-battle, is shown slumped in the foreground, lying in the arms of a soldier comrade, his eyes closed and on the point of sliding passively

8 On Gerasimov, see Bown, 'Aleksandr Gerasimov', 127–39. On Petrov-Vodkin, see Y. Rusakov, *Kuzma Petrov-Vodkin* (Leningrad, 1986), and K. S. Petrov-Vodkin, *Pis'ma. Stat'i. Vystupleniia. Dokumenty*, ed. E. N. Selizarova (Moscow, 1991).
9 Bown 'Aleksandr Gerasimov', 126.
10 See E. Waters, 'The Female Form in Soviet Political Iconography, 1917–32', in B. A. Clements, B. A. Engel, and C. D. Worobec (eds.), *Russia's Women: Accommodation, Resistance, Transformation* (Berkeley, 1991), 225–42.

5 Design for a 1924 calendar by Kuz'ma Petrov-Vodkin, 1923.

The calendar was published in an edition of a million copies by the State Publishing Company. The blank space at the bottom is to allow a tear-off calendar pad to be attached. The composition of Petrov-Vodkin's rider on his red horse is based on traditional icons of warrior saints, such as St George and St Demetrios. The syncretic image not only answered Petrov-Vodkin's own tastes as a religious believer who supported the Revolution, but was appropriate to a Soviet mass audience, given that church calendars had been one of the most popular forms of printed book before the Revolution.

into death. Both the Commissar and his soldier companion, a slender and androgynous figure (despite his pencil moustache), whose cartridge belt looks from one angle more like an ecclesiastical stole than an item of military equipment, gaze off-canvas as if looking into worlds unseen, although in different directions in order to signify the parting that is about to take place. The background of the painting, in Petrov-Vodkin's 'spherical perspective', is a distorted oval of figures that resembles a displacement to the horizontal of the angled sphere that is used to represent the heavenly domain in icons of the Dormition and of Christ Enthroned in Glory. The revolutionary *pietà* is not at all heroic in its effects, and a good deal less triumphalist than the painter's First World War image, *On the Firing Line of 1915–1916*, which shows a charge by resolute bayoneteers against the background of a sunny and smiling valley.

Another example of Petrov-Vodkin's 1920s syncretism was his design for a 1924 wall calendar, in which a mounted, androgynous figure on a red horse bears a strong resemblance to traditional portrayals of warrior saints, such as St George and St Demetrios, in Russian and Byzantine icons, the heavy hatching on the drapes being particularly suggestive. But the figure is without wings or aureole, and the red horse on which it is mounted was used elsewhere as a symbol of radical peasant self-assertion (for example, in *Fantasy* (1925), and *The Bathing of the Red Horse* (1912)). In fact, the calendar, like much of Petrov-Vodkin's work in the 1920s, can be seen as an embodiment in one text of Walter Benjamin's description of Moscow's Sukharevka Market in 1926, with a kiosk of religious prints jostled by booths of political posters 'like a prisoner between two policemen'.[11] To Petrov-Vodkin's pride, his calendar was printed in a run of a million copies (100 times the number allowed for a lithograph of his *Lenin Lying in State* a year later).[12]

Even when not invoking religious motifs so directly, as in his work of the 1930s, Petrov-Vodkin was still capable of handling canonical socialist-realist subjects in a manner that was both painterly and disturbing. In his *House-Warming Party* (1936) he shows a group of working-class Petrograders who have just taken possession of a room in a bourgeois flat. Details support the cheerful, celebratory air that such a scene should have—tea is being drunk, food has been placed on a sideboard—but the final effect is uneasy. The new inhabitants and their friends are placed along the fringes of the room, perched on their chairs stiffly as though not fully settled, clamping their lips or peering at the unfamiliar objects; one man even squinnies round the side of the stove-chimney as though looking in from outside the scene. Shadows clutter the corners, and bright lights from windows

11 W. Benjamin, *Moskauer Tagebuch* (Frankfurt-am-Main, 1980), 100.
12 See Petrov-Vodkin, letters to A. P. Petrova-Vodkina of 25 Dec. 1923 and 15 Apr. 1924, in *Pis'ma*, 226, 229.

somewhere in front of the canvas are reflected in the uncurtained panes at the back. In the left-hand corner, an empty frame with a lamp underneath it and a bunch of dried catkins (the 'palms' of Russian Palm Sunday) stuck through, hangs in the 'fair corner' (*krasnyi ugol*) where icons would traditionally have been placed.

House-Warming Party was described by a late Soviet biographer as 'monotonous, flat . . . verbose and circumstantial [in its] character-isation . . . rhythmically, not too well organised'.[13] Yet it is also a haunting work, eerie in its sense of emptiness, tense with foreboding rather than anticipating a bright future. It illustrates that socialist realism was not incompatible with sophistication. Petrov-Vodkin's relatively early rehabilitation (he was given a major retrospective in 1969, nearly a decade before Malevich or Kandinskii were brought up from museum stores) has made him seem a safer painter than he in fact was—both before the Revolution, when his original draughts-manship annoyed conventional art amateurs such as Nabokov's uncle Konstantin Dmitrievich, and between his death in 1939 and 1954, when his work was shown only very occasionally at exhibitions, and when only about fifteen major paintings were acquired by Soviet museums.[14]

In contrast to Petrov-Vodkin's, Gerasimov's work was not only regularly exhibited after 1940, but also regularly honoured. From the late 1930s, the painter became one of the most assiduous artistic acolytes of the cult of personality, responsible for such famous leader icons as *Stalin and Voroshilov in the Kremlin* (1938), *Stalin at the Telegraph* (1941), as well as the memorably echolalic *Stalin and Gor'kii at Gorki* (1939). Gerasimov was, besides, a leading exponent of the new aca-demicism, eschewing any panache and daring in his brushwork, observing the most careful conventionalism in his composition, and employing the requisite thick coats of properly glossy varnish. Any subversion in his imagery must surely have been unintentional, a matter of chance: witness the bathetic fate of his *The First Cavalry Army* (1936), which became unexhibitable shortly after its completion because many of the heroes it depicted had just been executed in the purges.

Certainly, there is no evidence in Gerasimov's later paintings that he intended to unsettle the canons whose most powerful overseer he himself was. Nothing could be more different, either in atmosphere or in handling, from *House-Warming Party* than his enormous post-war canvas, *Stalin at a Meeting with Commanders*. It is a smooth, bland representation of a high point in military history, rather than an edgy delineation of a most ambiguous episode in the reshaping of private culture. The lighting is brightly harmonious, its source easily

13 Rusakov, *Kuzma Petrov-Vodkin*, 230.
14 See letter of K. D. Nabokov to K. I. Chukovskii, Apr. 1910, in *Chtenie v dorevoliutsionnoi Rossii: Sbornik nauchnykh trudov* (Moscow, 1995), 144; for 1939–54 institutional history, see Rusakov, *Kuzma Petrov-Vodkin*, 253–93 (catalogue raisonné of works and exhibitions). Petrov-Vodkin was not, of course, the only artist to produce interesting and challenging work after 1932: others include the painters Deineka, Tatlin, Filonov, and Malevich, and the sculptors Sergei Konenkov and Vera Mukhina.

establishable as the long windows at the back of the palatial, pillared room where Stalin and his subordinates sit. The expected viewpoint is obvious: the spectator, rather than feeling under interrogation by the figures, is invited to complete the circle of generals sitting round Stalin. The painting's central contrast is easily interpretable: Stalin's modest outfit, without medals or braid, stands out clearly against the glittering uniforms of the men surrounding him, the gilt chandeliers and the gilded pillars, all captured with wearisomely regular highlights. The ultimate dictator, we are given to understand, is not a man to whom personal aggrandizement is important, but a man more accessible, less beset with fussiness, than many of his underlings.

There are for all that, though, elements in the painting that are less obvious, that give it a greater visual interest than might at first appear. A vast bust of Stalin placed directly above the leader is a carefully planted visual clue, emphasizing his dual nature, both unpretentious and above ordinary life. More oddly, a group of strikingly swarthy generals is clustered in a triadic motif immediately around Stalin, drawing surreptitious attention to the leader's non-Russian otherness. Finally, the painting functions as an intriguing reworking of a famous painting by Repin, *Formal Session of the State Council, 7 May 1901* (1903), which also shows a formal assembly in a similar pillared and chandeliered room. Repin, like Gerasimov, plays off the modest figure of the ruler (here Nicholas II) against his oversized icon (here, a vast full-length portrait). Like Gerasimov, Repin shows a circle of functionaries round the ruler, one of whom is reading aloud with his back to the viewer. There are, however, two striking differences between the images. The gilt and red brocade *fauteuils* on which the State Councillors sit have been replaced, in Gerasimov's work, by ungainly, rough-hewn wooden seats, like school chairs, jarring incongruously with their glamorous surroundings. And the invitation to the spectator to place him- or herself in the inner circle of commanders acquires particular force when set against the complete, closed circle of the State Council, which does its work without the need, or desire, for external observation or participation.

There can be no doubt that, though sharing a similar commemorative purpose, Gerasimov's painting is a vastly inferior work to Repin's. The figures in it are identikit masks of stern valour, without the liveliness of the State Councillors—some paunchy, some scrawny, some suavely handsome, others with crinkled faces and port-wine complexions. Their poses are stiff and predictable, and the handling of the paint is flat and uninspired. Though preferable to the vulgar bravura of Khmelko, Ioganson, or Iakovlev, Gerasimov's 1940s painting is neither memorable nor (to a detached viewer) emotive. But

Stalin and the Commanders none the less illustrates that even high-Stalinist mythic icons painted by servile conformists could depend for their effectiveness on intertextual references and visual puzzles that were not always obvious at first sight. Both this, and the utterly different instance of Petrov-Vodkin's *House-Warming Party*, are cases, as with many other socialist-realist works, where the use of a convenient label has prevented Western critics from looking much more closely than their Soviet colleagues (who had rather more excuse for their myopia) were prepared to look.

STEPHEN WHITE

The Art of the Political Poster

Maiakovskii called them 'flowers of the revolution'; and for the critic Viacheslav Polonskii, who helped to organize their production during the Civil War, they were 'more powerful than cannon and bullets' in achieving the Bolshevik victory.[1] It was certainly difficult to avoid the presence of the political poster in early post-Revolutionary Russia, as a succession of visitors could testify. A German doctor, Alfons Goldschmidt, in Moscow in the spring of 1920, found 'posters on all the walls, in thousands of shops, on telegraph poles, in pubs, in factories, everywhere'.[2] The radical British journalist H. N. Brailsford, in the small town of Vladimir, 120 miles to the east, found 'posters in colour, posters in print and clever stencilled drawings, imprinted in black on the whitewashed walls', which 'formed your mind for you, as you walked, by their reiterated suggestion'.[3] By 1922, Polonskii remarked, there was something like 'postermania', with designs of some kind being produced by 'virtually every institution with an agitational or educational function'.[4]

There was certainly no doubt that if the new Soviet government wanted to appeal for popular support it would have to rely on non-literary means. According to the 1897 census, only 28 per cent of the population of the Russian Empire aged between 9 and 49 could read and write. By 1920, when the next census was taken, things had improved somewhat, but still no more than 40 per cent were literate.[5] In any case the printing industry had ground to a halt because of the lack of fuel and spare parts, public transport was in chaos, and stocks of paper were very low. There was every reason, under these circumstances, for the Bolshevik leaders to give priority to a form of communication that made its appeal in graphic terms, and that could be seen by the largest possible numbers: and this form was above all the political poster, more than 3,600 of which were issued during the first years after the Revolution in millions of copies—and when paper ran out, stencilled directly onto walls and pavements.[6]

It was argued, until recently, that the political poster was a spontaneous phenomenon, 'born of October' with the regime itself. There was, in fact, a considerable Russian poster tradition, with the same emphases as in other European countries—urging those who saw them to subscribe to monthly journals or encyclopedias, or to buy biscuits or cognac.[7] A few drew attention to the political issues of the day, such as the war between Russia and Japan in 1904–5. And when the First World War began there were posters calling for support for the boys at the front, often in the form of contributions to war loans. Boris Kustodiev's *Freedom Loan*, one of the most famous, was the winner of a competition for posters of this kind sponsored by the Provisional Government. Another famous poster, Leonid Pasternak's *The Price of Blood* (1918), was one of the first to be issued by the new regime: it was simply a reissue of a poster Pasternak had produced in 1914 in aid of war victims, with a change of title (and, the poet's father discovered to his chagrin, without payment).[8]

The first years after the Revolution, however, saw the emergence of a poster art of a vigour and effectiveness that went far beyond anything that had existed in pre-Revolutionary times; and this, to a large extent, was the achievement of Dmitrii Moor (1883–1946). The 'commissar of propagandistic revolutionary art', as a contemporary described him,[9] Moor was born to a Cossack family in southern Russia and then moved to Moscow with his family in early childhood. He became involved in newspaper cartoon work while a law student at university, but received no formal artistic training. Moor's most famous work was *Have You Volunteered?*, with its finger-stabbing Red Army man. Produced in a single night in 1920, it was indirectly influenced by Alfred Leete's Lord Kitchener of 1914, but became in its turn a point of reference for poster artists in the USSR and abroad. Moor himself produced a poster along very similar lines at the start of the Second World War, and later still the same device was being used for the front covers of Soviet magazines, asking, 'What have you done for *perestroika*?' As privatization began in the early 1990s, the question was, 'Have you got your voucher?' Then, as new arrangements for income tax were introduced, it was the turn of Deputy Premier Anatolii Chubais to ask, 'Have you filed your declaration?'[10]

1 V. P. Polonskii, *Russkii revoliutsionnyi plakat* (Moscow, 1925), 76.
2 A. Goldschmidt, *Moskau 1920* (Berlin, 1920), 57.
3 H. N. Brailsford, *The Russian Workers' Republic* (London, 1921), 40.
4 V. Polonskii, 'Russkii revoliutsionnyi plakat', *Pechat' i revoliutsiia*, 5 (1922), 61.
5 See *Gramotnost' v Rossii* (Moscow, 1922), 10.

6 For the total see S. S. Khromov, *Grazhdanskaia voina i voennaia interventsiia v SSSR: Entsiklopediia* (Moscow, 1983), 459.
7 N. I. Baburina, *Russkii plakat (konets XIX–nachalo XX veka)* (Leningrad, 1988).
8 L. O. Pasternak, *Zapisi raznykh let* (Moscow, 1975), 84.
9 D. S. Moor, *Ia—bol'shevik* (Moscow, 1967), 108.
10 See respectively *EKO*, 5 (1986), front cover; *Komsomol'skaia pravda*, 1 Oct. 1992, 1; and (for Chubais) *Izvestiia*, 29 Jan. 1997, 6.

6 Dmitrii Moor, *The Red Soldier at the Front is Without Footwear and Clothing* (propaganda poster, 1920).

Moor was the most prominent of the artists who engaged in poster work during the Russian Civil War, and the one whose work was most closely associated with military themes. Most of it, during these years, was commissioned by the military publishing house and distributed at the front. As in other countries during times of war, a major poster theme was assistance for the war effort, either to enrol directly (as in Moor's own *Have You Volunteered?* of June 1920), or to provide the resources that were needed. Moor's appeal, issued as the Civil War was coming to an end but the struggle with Poland was still in progress, asked viewers to 'open their trunks' (the traditional storage place for treasures among the peasantry and working classes) and 'hand over everything that they could to their defender'.

Moor enjoyed a comparable success with his *Help!*, a stark appeal for assistance prompted by the famine in the Volga basin during the late summer of 1921.

Moor was one of a group of talented artists who gave their energies to the political poster during these Civil War years. Another was Viktor Deni (1893–1946), whose career had begun in the satirical journals of the early years of the century. Another still was Nikolai Kochergin (1897–1974), a Muscovite who graduated from the Stroganov Art School and moved into military camouflage and then propaganda work, first in Moscow and then in the Caucasus (he was especially celebrated for his use of colour). A further distinctive contribution was made by Maiakovskii and the Siberian artist Mikhail Cheremnykhy (1890–1962), who jointly devised the comic-strip 'Rosta Windows' named after the news agency that sponsored their production.[11] The Windows, Maiakovskii later wrote, were a 'fantastic thing . . . It meant news sent by telegraph immediately translated into posters, decrees into couplets.'[12] The Moscow studio alone produced more than 1,600 Rosta Windows, and more than fifty other centres were involved in their production between 1919 and 1922.[13]

These were years of experiment, in the poster as in other forms. The hammer and sickle had emerged earlier in 1917 as a symbol of the social forces that the new regime sought to represent;[14] it became the official emblem of the RSFSR in the constitution that was adopted in the summer of 1918 ('a golden sickle and hammer, with handles pointing downward, against a red background of the rays of the sun'). The five-pointed star emerged during the Civil War, representing (it was suggested) the five continents, and it became the emblem of the newly formed Red Army; it was added to the state emblem of the newly formed USSR in 1924. The artists of these early years, however, borrowed freely from the classical and even Christian traditions. There were posters that depicted red angels bringing peace to the world, others that rehearsed the 'ten commandments of the proletarian', and others still that employed the imperial eagle. One of the most popular adaptations saw a mounted Trotskii as St George, cutting off the head of a bourgeois serpent; on at least one occasion the paint wore off, revealing the icon that lay underneath.[15]

If the Civil War brought forth the military and heroic poster, the posters of the later 1920s and 1930s reflected a more practical concern with social and economic development. Illiteracy, once the Civil War had ended, became one of the main targets of the new government, and many posters of the mid- and later 1920s popularized reading-rooms and newspapers themselves, or warned of the dangers that lay in wait for the uninstructed. Public health was another concern:

11 See W. Duwakin, *Rosta-Fenster: Majakowski als Dichter und bildender Kuenstler*, 2nd edn. (Dresden, 1975).

12 V. V. Maiakovskii, 'Tol'ko ne vospominaniia' (1927), in *Polnoe sobranie sochinenii*, xii (Moscow: 1961), 153.

13 K. N. Suvorova (comp.), *V. V. Maiakovskii: Opisanie dokumental'nykh materialov*, i. '*Okna' ROSTA i Glavpolitprosveta, 1919–22* (Moscow, 1964), 4; B. Stykalin, *Okna satiry ROSTA* (Moscow, 1976), 34–5.

14 *Agitatsionno-massovoe iskusstvo pervykh let Oktiabr'skoi revoliutsii: Katalog vystavki* (Moscow, 1967), 19.

15 The instance is recalled in A. Platonov, *Izbrannoe* (Moscow, 1966), 49 (omitted in some edns.). The political poster of the Civil War years is given extensive treatment in S. White, *The Bolshevik Poster* (New Haven, 1988); the later period is considered in V. Bonnell, *Iconography of Power: Soviet Political Posters under Lenin and Stalin* (Berkeley, 1997).

there were posters urging inoculations against typhoid, encouraging cleanliness and fresh air, and propagating better forms of child care. In the late 1920s the tempo quickened once more: five-year plans had to be fulfilled, preferably 'ahead of time', and the countryside had to be collectivized, in principle (although certainly not in practice) on a voluntary basis. Gustav Klutsis (1895–1944), a Latvian of German origin, pioneered the use of photomontage in some of these posters in much the same way John Heartfield was doing in Germany. Klutsis was one of those who contributed to an emerging emphasis upon Stalin and the political leadership in the later 1930s; he perished himself in one of the prison camps that had been established during these years.[16]

The Second World War saw a new peak of poster production, with a greater freedom of artistic initiative and a cause with which regime and artists could readily identify.[17] Some of the older artists, such as Moor and Deni, returned to the fray. And younger artists began to receive recognition, among them Iraklii Toidze (1902–84), a Georgian, and the Kukryniksy, a collective pseudonym/acronym for three Moscow artists—Mikhail Kupriianov, Porfirii Krylov, and Nikolai Sokolov. Toidze's best-known poster was *The Motherland Calls* (1941), produced just after the USSR had been invaded by Nazi Germany. According to his widow, Toidze was working in his studio when she heard on the radio that war had been declared. She felt, she recalled, 'as though the world was falling apart'. Alarmed above all for their children, she rushed into the studio and cried out the single word 'War!' Toidze looked at her and said: 'Stand still! Don't move!' The following day she had been incorporated into one of the most famous of all Soviet wartime posters.[18]

The Kukryniksy, who had worked together as well as separately from the late 1920s, achieved their greatest fame during the war with a series of sharply satirical posters at the expense of the Nazi leaders, particularly Hitler and Goebbels. Their poster *We Shall Mercilessly Defeat and Expose the Enemy* was produced within a few days of the declaration of war, and more than 100 of their posters and cartoons had appeared by the time the war ended. The first Tass Windows had similarly begun to appear within a week of the Nazi invasion; they were produced almost daily throughout the war.

The end of the war, once again, brought a change of subject, away from military themes and back to social change and economic reconstruction. Viktor Ivanov (1909–68), a Moscow artist who had come to prominence during the Second World War, was active throughout this period; his work included several posters devoted to the maintenance of peace as well as a celebrated series of posters on Lenin, produced during the years that led up to the centenary of the

16 On Soviet photomontage more generally, see A. Zhitomirskii, *Iskusstvo politicheskogo fotomontazha* (Moscow, 1983).
17 A good representative collection is available in *Sovetskie plakatisty—frontu* (Moscow, 1985).
18 *Moskovskie novosti*, 41 (1988), 9.

Soviet leader's birth in 1970. The maintenance of peace remained a prominent poster theme in later years, with Leonid Brezhnev, wearing the Lenin Peace Prize that he had awarded himself, often its principal exponent. So too did elections, with voters being invited to the polls almost every year (although not, until the late 1980s, to make a choice of candidate or party); election posters were typically fronted by workers (men, carrying hammers) and collective farmers (women, carrying sickles), with members of the intelligentsia behind them wearing glasses for ease of identification.

The shift from Brezhnevite complacency to the years of *glasnost'* and *perestroika* brought a further change in the character of Soviet posters, away from the trumpeting of plans fulfilled and towards a more open acknowledgement of the social problems that still remained.[19] One of the most notable of these was alcohol abuse: the main cause of premature death, industrial accidents, and family breakdown, it became the subject of a full-scale campaign in the first years of the Gorbachev leadership.[20] Another theme was environmental conservation—clean air and water, and respect for nature—in the face of evidence that up to 60 per cent of the population lived in conditions that were harmful to their health. There were the problems of orphans and neglected children, and the wounded veterans of the Afghan war. Still another problem was AIDS, and the wider question of drug abuse.

Even in the late *perestroika* years, there were gaps and misrepresentations in Soviet poster art. The position of women, with their 'double burden', was rarely addressed. Nor was the ethnic unrest that, in the end, overwhelmed the state itself. And many of the posters that did appear fell entirely within the framework of regime myth. One well-known design showed Gorbachev conducting the country to a score by the founder of the Soviet state, reflecting the official orthodoxy that the task of the new leadership was to return to 'healthy Leninist foundations'; another showed Lenin looking through a fogged-up window labelled 1985, the year of Gorbachev's accession to the leadership.[21] But there were posters that raised the sensitive issue of privilege, and others that suggested that *glasnost'* was no substitute for a fully-fledged freedom of information. Posters were more likely to be harnessed to Party purposes than the other arts, and the main publishing house, Plakat, was itself a part of the Central Committee apparatus. But posters were more than a propaganda art: they had to reflect the concerns of ordinary life, they could mobilize in times of crisis, and by the late 1980s they were part of a society that was reconsidering its future at the same time as it re-evaluated its contradictory past.

19 See e.g. *Plakat perestroiki* (Moscow, 1988); *Plakat v rabochem stroiu* (Moscow, 1988); and *Les Affiches de la glasnost et de la perestroika* (Paris, 1989). 20 For the campaign itself—with a selection of illustrations—see S. White, *Russia Goes Dry: Alcohol, State and Society* (Cambridge, 1996). 21 Both are illustrated in *Les Affiches* (nos. 131 and 1).

Suggested further reading

Theatre:

General

Benedetti, J., *Stanislavsky: An Introduction* (London, 1982).

Braun, E., *The Director and the Stage: From Naturalism to Grotowski* (London, 1982).

Chekhov, M., *To the Actor* (New York, 1953).

—— *To the Director and Playwright*, comp. C. Leonard (New York, 1984).

Fulop-Miller, R., and Gregor, J., *The Russian Theatre: Its Character and History, with Especial Reference to the Revolutionary Period*, tr. P. England (London, 1930).

Glenny, M., 'The Soviet Theatre', in R. Auty and D. Obolensky (eds.), *Companion to Russian Studies*, ii (Cambridge, 1977), 271–85.

Golub, S., *The Recurrence of Fate: Theater and Memory in Twentieth-Century Russia* (Iowa City, 1994).

Leach, R., *Revolutionary Theatre* (London, 1994).

—— and Borovsky, V. (eds.), *Cambridge History of Russian Theatre* (Cambridge, 1997).

Roose-Evans, J., *Experimental Theatre: From Stanislavsky to Peter Brook* (London, 1989).

Stanislavski, K., *Building a Character* (London, 1979).

—— *An Actor Prepares* (London, 1980).

—— *My Life in Art* (London, 1980).

—— *Creating a Role* (London, 1981).

—— *Stanislavski's Legacy* (London, 1981).

Worrall, N., *The Moscow Arts Theatre* (London, 1996).

1917–53

Braun, E., *The Theatre of Meyerhold: A Revolution on the Modern Stage* (London, 1979; rev. edn. 1995).

—— (ed. and tr.), *Meyerhold on Theatre* (London, 1969).

Clark, K., *Petersburg: Crucible of Cultural Revolution* (Cambridge, Mass., 1995), ch. 4.

Kelly, C., *Petrushka: The Russian Carnival Puppet Theatre* (Cambridge, 1990), ch. 5.

Kleberg, L., *Theatre as Action: Soviet Russian Avant-Garde Aesthetics* (London, 1993).

Leach, R., *Vsevolod Meyerhold* (Cambridge, 1989).

Russell, R., *Russian Drama of the Revolutionary Period* (Basingstoke, 1988).

Vendrovskaia, L., and Kaptereva, G. (eds.), *Vakhtangov* (Moscow, 1982).

Worrall, N., *Modernism to Realism on the Soviet Stage: Tairov—Vakhtangov—Okhlopkov* (Cambridge, 1989).

1953–present

Beumers, B., *Yury Lyubimov: Thirty Years at the Taganka Theatre* (New York, 1997).

Efros, A., 'Energy, Enervation and the Mathematics of Intrigue', *Theatre Quarterly*, 7 (1977), 28–33.

Golub, S., 'Acting on the Run: Efros and the Contemporary Soviet Theatre', *Theatre Quarterly*, 7 (1977), 18–28.

Szewcow, M., 'Anatolij Efros Directs Chekhov's *The Cherry Orchard* and Gogol's *The Marriage*', *Theatre Quarterly*, 7 (1977), 34–46.

160

Music:

Abraham, G., *et al.* (eds.), *Russian Masters 2* (New Grove Dictionary of Music and Musicians; London, 1986).

Craft, R., *Stravinsky: Selected Correspondence*, i (London, 1982).

Fanning, D. (ed.), *Shostakovich Studies* (Cambridge, 1995).

Feigin, L. (ed.), *Russian Jazz: New Identity* (London, 1985).

Gerlach, H., *Fünfzig sowjetische Komponisten* (Leipzig, 1984).

Gershkovich, F., *O muzyke* (Moscow, 1991).

Glikman, I., *Pis'ma k drugu* (Moscow, 1993).

Gorodinskii, V., *Muzyka dukhovnoi nishchety* (Moscow, 1950).

Hulme, D. C., *Dmitri Shostakovich: A Catalogue, Bibliography, and Discography* (Oxford, 1991).

Ivashkin, A., *Besedy s Al'fredom Shnitke* (Moscow, 1994).

Karetnikov, N., *Temy s variatsiiami* (Moscow, 1990).

Krebs, S. D., *Soviet Composers and the Development of Soviet Music* (New York, 1970).

Lemaire, F. C., *La Musique du XXe siècle en Russie et dans les anciennes Républiques Soviétiques* (Paris, 1994).

MacDonald, I., *The New Shostakovich* (Oxford, 1991).

Nelson, A., 'Music and the Politics of Culture in Revolutionary Russia, 1921–30', Ph.D. dissertation (University of Michigan, 1993).

Restagno, E. (ed.), *Gubajdulina* (Turin, 1991).

—— (ed.), *Schnittke* (Turin, 1993).

Ryback, T. W., *Rock Around the Bloc: A History of Rock Music in Eastern Europe and the Former Soviet Union* (New York, 1990).

Schwarz, B., *Music and Musical Life in Soviet Russia, 1917–1981*, enlarged edn. (Bloomington, Ind., 1983).

Sikorski, H. (ed.), *Alfred Schnittke zum 60. Gerburtstag: Eine Festschrift* (Hamburg, 1944).

Smith, G. S., *Songs to Seven Strings: Russian Guitar Poetry and Soviet 'Mass Song'* (Bloomington, Ind., 1993).

Starr, S. F., *Red and Hot: The Fate of Jazz in the Soviet Union* (New York, 1993).

Tsenova, V., and **Barskii, V.** (eds.), *Muzyka iz byvshego SSSR* (Moscow, 1994).

Vanni, J. di, *1953–1983: Trente ans de musique soviétique* ([Arles], 1987).

Volkov, S., *Testimony: The Memoirs of Shostakovich* (London, 1979).

Wilson, E., *Shostakovich: A Life Remembered* (London, 1994).

Zeifas, N., *Pesnopeniia: O muzyke Gii Kancheli* (Moscow, 1991).

Visual arts:

Bird, A., *A History of Russian Painting* (Oxford, 1982), chs. 11–13.

Bowlt, J. (ed.), *Russian Art of the Avant Garde: Theory and Criticism* (New York, 1976).

Bown, M. C., and **Taylor, B.** (eds.), *Art of the Soviets: Painting, Sculpture and Architecture in a One-Party State* (Manchester, 1993).

Compton, S., *Russian Avant-Garde Books, 1917–1934* (London, 1992).

Cooke, C. (ed.), *Russian Avant-Garde Art and Architecture* (New York, 1983).

Efimova, A., and **Manovich, L.** (ed. and tr.), *Tekstura: Russian Essays on Visual Culture* (Chicago, 1993).

Golomstock, I., *Totalitarian Art* (London, 1989).

Gray, C., *The Russian Experiment in Art, 1863–1922*, rev. and exp. edn. (London, 1986).

The Great Utopia: The Russian and Soviet Avant-Garde, 1915–1932 (Guggenheim Museum, New York, 1992).

Khan-Magomedov, S. O., *Pioneers of Soviet Architecture: The Search for New Solutions in the 1920s and 1930s*, ed. C. Cooke (London, 1987).

Lebedev, P. I., *Bor'ba za realizm v iskusstve 20-kh godov: Materialy. Dokumenty. Vospominaniia*, (Moscow, 1962).

Lobanov-Rostovsky, N., *Revolutionary Graphics: Soviet Porcelain, 1917–1927* (New York, 1990).

Lodder, C., *Russian Constructivism* (New Haven, 1983).

Russkaia sovetskaia khudozhestvennaia kritika 1917–1941: Khrestomatiia (Moscow, 1982).

Sarabianov, D. V., and Adaskina, N. L., *Popova* (New York, 1990).

Strizhenova, T., *Soviet Costumes and Textiles, 1917–1945* (Moscow, 1991).

Stupples, P., *Pavel Kuznetsov: His Life and Art* (Cambridge, 1989).

Valkenier, E., 'The Native Roots of Socialist Realism', in *Russian Realist Art* (New York, 1989), 164–95.

Yablonskaya, M. N., *Women Artists of Russia's New Age* (London, 1990).

Zhadova, L., *Malevich: Suprematism and Revolution in Russian Art, 1910–1980* (London, 1978).

—— (ed.), *Tatlin* (London, 1988).

Posters:

Bonnell, V., *Iconography of Power: Soviet Political Posters under Lenin and Stalin* (Berkeley, 1997).

White, S., *The Bolshevik Poster* (New Haven, 1988).

Cinema, Media, the Russian Consumer

9

Cinema

JULIAN GRAFFY

From the Beginnings to the Revolution

In 1896, only months after its first public demonstration in Paris, the French theatrical entrepreneur Charles Aumont brought the Lumière brothers' cinematograph to Russia. It was seen at the All Russian Fair in July of that year by the young Maksim Gor'kii, who memorably captures the perceptual confusions experienced by audiences by describing the experience as a visit to 'the kingdom of shadows'.[1] Though the first Russian amateur films also date from 1896, for the next decade distribution and exhibition of films was in the hands of French companies such as Pathé and Gaumont, who established offices in Russia in 1904 and 1905, and began to make films especially for the Russian market. The first Russian film company was set up in 1906 by Aleksandr Khanzhonkov, and from 1908 the Khanzhonkov company began to produce films on Russian national subjects, including the first full-length feature film in the world, *The Defence of Sebastopol* (*Oborona Sevastopolia*, 1911). The Khanzhonkov studio would go on to shoot over 300 films with many of the leading directors and actors of the period.[2] Khanzhonkov's main rival was Aleksandr Drankov, who set up the first Russian film studio in St Petersburg in 1907, and shot a scene from Pushkin's *Boris Godunov*. This was followed in 1908 by *Sten'ka Razin*, based on the life of the leader of a seventeenth-century peasant revolt, now usually described as 'the first Russian feature film'.[3]

By the end of 1913 Russian producers had made over 300 films and controlled 10 per cent of the market. The outbreak of the First World

1 M. Gor'kii, 'The Lumière Cinematograph', in R. Taylor and I. Christie (eds.), *The Film Factory: Russian and Soviet Cinema in Documents 1896–1939* (London, 1988), 25.

2 On Khanzhonkov, see S. Skovorodnikova, 'Aleksandr Alekseevich Khanzhonkov', in P. Cherchi Usai *et al.* (eds.), *Silent Witnesses: Russian Films 1908–1919* (London, 1989), 568–70.

3 On Drankov, see R. Yangirov, 'Aleksandr Osipovich Drankov', ibid. 554–60.

4 For film production figures, here and later, see 'Segida-info', *Iskusstvo kino*, 4 (1996), 73–6 (75).

5 For a pioneering analysis of the social history of pre-Revolutionary Russian cinema, see Iu. Tsiv'ian, *Istoricheskaia retseptsiia kino: Kinematograf v Rossii 1896–1930* (Riga, 1991); rev. Eng. language edn. as Y. Tsivian, *Early Cinema in Russia and its Cultural Reception* (London, 1994) (on the role of the foyer, see 44–8).

6 See Table 1, 'Cinema installations and their distribution in the Russian Empire and USSR, 1914–41', in Taylor and Christie (eds.), *Film Factory*, 423; and V. Kepley, Jr., '"Cinefication": Soviet Film Exhibition in the 1920s', *Film History*, 6 (1994), 263.

7 On Kholodnaia, see esp. B. B. Ziukov (comp.), *Vera Kholodnaia: K 100-letiiu so dnia rozhdeniia* (Moscow, 1995).

War imposed difficulties on the importation of foreign films and consequently boosted the Russian industry—a further 330 films were made in 1914, 440 in 1915, and 500 in 1916. The proportion of foreign films on Russian screens fell to 20 per cent.[4]

In their first years, cinema shows were put on in a variety of rented premises, but as early as 1903 permanent cinema halls were being opened, and in the cities cinema-going was quickly established as a popular form of entertainment. Because of the very short length of the early films, attendance was casual, and cinema-going was valued more as a social experience than for the intrinsic interest of the films themselves. Cinema-going is widely reported in memoirs as a 'democratic' activity that transcended class boundaries. As the films themselves became longer and the idea of the film programme was established, the role of the cinema foyer as gathering place became increasingly important, a function it would continue to fulfil into the Soviet period.[5] By 1914 there were 1,412 permanent cinema installations in the Russian Empire, of which 1,279 were in cities.[6]

The achievements of the pre-Revolutionary Russian cinema, so long overshadowed by the productions of the 1920s avant-garde, have recently been rediscovered. The animator Wladislaw Starewicz made a succession of remarkable films set in the world of insects. Perhaps the most extraordinary is *The Cameraman's Revenge* (*Mest' kinematograficheskogo operatora*, 1912), which, as well as being a parody of the adulterous triangles so beloved of bourgeois theatre and cinema, is also, through its projectionist protagonist and its scene of cinema-going, the first investigation of the role of the cinema in people's lives, the first metafilm. Evgenii Bauer, formerly a theatrical designer, joined Khanzhonkov's company in 1913, and made eighty-two films before his untimely death in 1917. His urban melodramas of doomed love, class relations, and tainted money are distinguished by an unprecedented attention to lighting and to the placing of the actors in the frame. One of his masterpieces, *A Life for a Life* (*Zhizn' za zhizn'*, 1916), starred Vera Kholodnaia, whose beauty and tragic roles made her the greatest star of the era, the 'queen of the screen'.[7] A third prolific director of the period, Iakov Protazanov, made seventy-three films before the Revolution, including *The Departure of a Great Old Man* (*Ukhod velikogo startsa*, 1912), about the last days of Tolstoi, and a number of films with the mesmerizing Ivan Mozzhukhin, the greatest male star of the period, including a haunting version of Pushkin's *The Queen of Spades* (*Pikovaia dama*, 1916), the proto-expressionist *Satan Triumphant* (*Satana likuiushchii*, 1917), and a version of Tolstoi's *Father Sergius* (*Otets Sergii*, 1918).

The Revolutions of 1917 brought major disruption to the Russian film industry and led to a wave of emigrations of directors, actors, and other film personnel. Both Starewicz and Mozzhukhin subsequently carved out substantial careers in France. Protazanov, who at the time of the Revolution was working for the Ermol'ev company, joined them in moving to Paris. Other Russian film-makers moved to Berlin and even to Hollywood.

From Revolution to Cultural Revolution

The new Bolshevik regime was quick to realize the importance of control of the cinema. In August 1918 the first agit-train left Moscow for Kazan, and most agit-trains in the ensuing years had a film section showing *agitki* or agitational films.[8] On 27 August 1919 Lenin signed a decree nationalizing private cinema enterprises, and on 1 September 1919 the State School for Cinematic Art began work in Moscow, headed by the pre-Revolutionary director Vladimir Gardin. In October 1919 the All-Russian Photographic and Cinematic Section of Narkompros, the People's Commissariat of Enlightenment, published a collection of articles on the cinema, in which Lunacharskii, the People's Commissar, asserted that 'the main task of cinema in both its scientific and feature divisions is that of propaganda'.[9] In 1920 Lenin told Clara Zetkin that the Soviet state must be the 'protector', 'customer', and 'guide' of artists. On 17 January 1922 he directed that all film programmes should contain a 'definite proportion' of 'entertainment' and 'propaganda' films, later enshrined as the 'Leninist proportion' of 75 per cent to 25 per cent, and in February of that year, in conversation with Lunacharskii, he stressed that 'of all the arts for us the most important is cinema'.[10]

If these words of Lenin are perhaps the most famous statement of arts policy by a Soviet leader, he was by no means the only leading politician to take an interest in cinema. Trotskii, in 'Vodka, the Church and the Cinema', an article published in *Pravda* on 12 July 1923, recognized the unprecedented accessibility of cinema, an 'innovation [which] has cut into human life with a successful rapidity never experienced in the past'. Seeing its potential both as a weapon of propaganda and as a source of revenue, he concluded: 'Here is an instrument which we must secure at all costs!'[11] And Stalin, speaking at the Thirteenth Party Congress in May 1924, insisted that 'Cinema is the most important means of mass agitation. Our task is to take it into our hands.'[12]

8 On the agit-trains, see R. Taylor, *The Politics of the Soviet Cinema 1917–1929* (Cambridge, 1979), 52–63. A mock-up of an agit-train is on view in London's Museum of the Moving Image.
9 Taylor and Christie (eds.), *Film Factory*, document 10, p. 47.
10 Ibid., doc. 11, p. 50; doc. 12, p. 56; and doc. 13, p. 57.
11 Ibid., doc. 32, pp. 95, 97.
12 G. Mar'iamov, *Kremlevskii tsenzor: Stalin smotrit kino* (Moscow, 1992), 3.

The early 1920s also saw the rapid articulation of film theory in Russia. Pioneering in this respect was Lev Kuleshov, who had begun his career before the Revolution as a designer and actor for Bauer, and in an article of March 1918 had stressed the importance to cinema of the montage lessons already learned by American film-makers: 'Montage is to cinema what colour composition is to painting or a harmonic sequence of sounds is to music.'[13] Kuleshov set up a workshop in the State School for Cinematic Art in 1920. His core students were the future directors Vsevolod Pudovkin (who would later write: 'We make films. Kuleshov made cinema'), Boris Barnet, and Sergei Komarov, and the actors Aleksandra Khokhlova, Porfirii Podobed, and Vladimir Fogel'. In 1921 Kuleshov and his 'model actors' (*naturshchiki*, a term he used to stress that the actor should express emotion through physical action) shot film experiments involving the fabrication by montage of a created landscape (*tvorimaia zemnaia poverkhnost'*) and a created person (*tvorimyi chelovek*). In 1922 Kuleshov moved his group out of the State School so as to increase their scope for experiment.[14] They also attended performances of American films to assess audience response. An article Kuleshov wrote in August 1922, 'Americanism', found the success of Hollywood films to lie in their 'cinema specificity', their stress on movement, and their 'organic link with contemporary life', and again concluded that the 'organisational basis' of cinema was in the juxtaposition and interrelation of filmed fragments, that 'the essence of cinema, its method of achieving maximum effect' is montage.[15] The collective's first feature film, *The Extraordinary Adventures of Mr West in the Land of the Bolsheviks* (*Neobychainye prikliucheniia mistera Vesta v strane bol'shevikov*, 1924), was described by Kuleshov as a verification of the group's working methods,[16] and stands as a vindication both of his work with model actors and of his montage experiments. It is also, influentially, one of the first Soviet films to base its plot around the subject of 'coming to revolutionary consciousness', a motif that would be extraordinarily productive in the cinema of the next two decades.

Another new group that attracted attention through the radicalism of its vision of cinema was the documentarist Cine-Eye group consisting of Dziga Vertov, his brother and cameraman Mikhail Kaufman, and his wife and editor Elizaveta Svilova, the so-called 'Soviet of three'. In their 'We: A Version of a Manifesto' of August 1922 they find the whole of existing cinema 'absurd', 'insubstantial', 'leprous', and proclaim the 'death of "cinematography"' . . . so that the art of cinema may live', seeking in the poetry of the machine a way forward to the 'new man', the 'perfect electric man'. The Cine-Eye is here described as 'the art of organising the necessary movements of

13 Taylor and Christie (eds.), *Film Factory*, doc. 9, p. 46.
14 On Kuleshov's early career, see esp. M. Yampolsky, 'Kuleshov's Experiments and the New Anthropology of the Actor', in R. Taylor and I. Christie (eds.), *Inside the Film Factory: New Approaches to Russian and Soviet Cinema* (London, 1991), 31–50; V. Kepley, Jr., 'The Kuleshov Workshop', *Iris*, 1 (1986), 5–23, and 'Mr Kuleshov in the Land of the Modernists', in A. Lawton (ed.), *The Red Screen* (London), 1992, 132–47; and E. Khokhlova, 'Novoe ob "effekte Kuleshova"', *Iskusstvo kino*, 6 (1992), 21–5.
15 Taylor and Christie (eds.), *Film Factory*, doc. 22, p. 73.
16 Ibid., doc. 38, p. 108.

objects in space and time'.[17] In the 1923 'The Cine-Eyes: A Revolution', Vertov again pronounces a death sentence on existing fiction films ('legitimised myopia') and calls for a revolution through newsreel. Again stressing that the camera is more perfect than the human eye, he underlines the crucial role of montage in time and space: 'I am the cine eye. I construct things . . . I the machine show you the world as only I can see it.'[18] The experimental newsreels created by Vertov's group, the Kino-Pravda, which 'observes and records life *as it is*', were seen as the means by which fiction film would be defeated. 'We shall blow up the Tower of Babel that is art.'[19]

A third major group emerged in Leningrad in 1922, the FEKS, the Factory of the Eccentric Actor, led by the young Grigorii Kozintsev and Leonid Trauberg, who would go on to form one of the most productive partnerships in Soviet cinema. Their Eccentric Manifesto stressed the value of popular art forms such as circus, music-hall, and cabaret, of Americanism, tricks, action, movement, stunts. They chose 'Charlie's arse, not Eleonora Duse's hands!'[20] Kozintsev and Trauberg's brilliantly iconoclastic film version of Gogol''s *The Over-coat* (*Shinel'*, 1926), made from a script by the formalist critic and literary theorist Iurii Tynianov, combines elements from a wide range of Gogol''s works with an explicit homage to Chaplin. Chaplin is also invoked in one of the first articles by the young Sergei Eisenstein (Eizenshtein), who in 1922 allotted him 'the eighth seat in the Coun-cil of the Muses'.[21] In an article of the following year, Eisenstein developed his theory of the 'montage of attractions', in which he described his montage as having a 'specific final thematic effect' and insisted that the 'school for the montageur is cinema'.[22] In a later article on *The Battleship Potemkin* (*Bronenosets 'Potemkin'*) he reiterated that 'the expressive effect of cinema is the result of juxtapositions' and emphasized the *collective* nature of the film-making process.[23] It was through the application of his montage method in *The Strike* (*Stachka*, 1924) and *The Battleship Potemkin* (1925), further developed in *October* (*Oktiabr'*, 1927) that Eisenstein allied Kuleshovian experiment with historico-revolutionary subject-matter and explicit ideological intent. In 1925 he described a work of art as 'a tractor ploughing over the audience's psyche in a particular class context',[24] and a year later he said that 'by "film" I understand tendentiousness and nothing else'.[25] Eisenstein's 1920s revolutionary trilogy is the most concentrated, most artistically ambitious, and most effective expression of the coming-to-consciousness thematics. The pioneering work of Kuleshov, Kozintsev and Trauberg, Vertov, Eisenstein, and later of Pudovkin and Dovzhenko was enormously admired by influential critics, especially in the West, and it is their achievement that has formed

17 Ibid., doc. 21, pp. 69–72.
18 Ibid., doc. 31, pp. 89–94.
19 Ibid., doc. 41, pp. 112–14.
20 The Eccentric Manifesto is doc. 15, ibid. 58–64.
21 S. Eisenstein and S. Yutkevich, 'The Eighth Art: On Expressionism, America, and, of course, Chaplin', in S. Eisenstein, *Selected Works* i. *Writings, 1922–34*, ed. and tr. R. Taylor (London, 1988), 29.
22 S. Eisenstein, 'The Montage of Attractions', ibid. 34–5.
23 Eisenstein, 'Béla Forgets the Scissors', ibid. 80.
24 Eisenstein, 'The Problems of the Materialist Approach to Form', ibid. 62.
25 Eisenstein, 'Eisenstein on Eisenstein, the Director of *Potemkin*', ibid. 75.

the kernel of traditional assessments of the role of cinema in the Soviet Union in the 1920s. Ironically, however, theirs were not the films that found most success with Soviet audiences.

The nationalization of cinema enterprises in 1919 was more of a symbolic expression of intent than a practical measure. The cinematic process had been disrupted by Revolution and Civil War and production had been decimated. Whereas 500 feature films had been made in Russia in 1916, only 148 were made in the period between 1918 and 1923.[26] In 1922 cinemas grossed only 27,000,000 roubles by comparison with takings of 142,000,000 in 1915. Only four cinemas in all of Moscow remained open throughout 1921.[27] A succession of measures was taken by the government to reorganize the administration of the industry. In December 1922 the Photographic and Cinematic Section of the Commissariat of Enlightenment was reconstituted as the Central State Cinematic Enterprise (Goskino) and given a monopoly on the organization of distribution. In September 1923 the Mantsev Commission was set up to examine the overall organization of Soviet cinema.[28] The All-Union Conference on Cinematic Affairs in March 1924, the final Mantsev Commission report in April, and the Resolution on Cinema of the Thirteenth Party Congress in May were followed by the replacement of Goskino by Sovkino in June 1924.[29] But the state had no money to give to the cinema and the industry was required to be self-financing. Most of the capital revenues came from urban exhibition. Nationalized cinemas had been leased out from 1921, and trade delegations sent abroad in search of spare parts. A film trading initiative of 1922–3 authorized by Lenin allowed for Soviet films to be sold abroad and Western films to be imported, and soon 85 per cent of films showing in commercial cinemas were imported.[30] Thus the takings from imported foreign films played a crucial role in funding the regeneration of Soviet cinema. Russian audiences had always had a taste for foreign products. The most popular film in both Moscow and Petrograd cinemas at the time of the October Revolution was Enrico Guazzoni's version of Sienkiewicz's novel of Rome in the time of Nero, *Quo vadis*?[31] A print of Griffith's *Intolerance* was shown in Petrograd in 1918 and in Moscow in 1919. On seeing it Pudovkin abandoned science for the cinema. Its success was so great that in 1921 it had a special Petrograd run to raise money for the victims of the Civil War famine.[32] In 1924, at the height of the import of films, 366 foreign films were shown on Soviet screens as opposed to seventy-six Soviet ones. Though the number declined after this, and by 1927 more Soviet films were shown than foreign ones, figures for the whole decade show a preponderance of foreign films.[33] At the beginning of the decade they were mainly German, and the comic

26 'Segida-info', 75–6.
27 Kepley, 'Cinefication', 264.
28 On the Mantsev Commission, see Taylor, *The Politics of the Soviet Cinema*, 77–82.
29 Taylor and Christie (eds.), *Film Factory*, doc. 40, p. 111, and doc. 42, pp. 114–15.
30 On the market in the 1920s, see V. Mikhailov, '20-e gody: Uroki rynka v sovetskom kino', in D. Dondurei (ed.), *Otechestvennyi kinematograf: Strategiia vyzhivaniia* (Moscow, 1991), 56–67.
31 M. Turovskaia, 'K probleme massovogo fil'ma v sovetskom kino', *Kinovedcheskie zapiski*, 8 (1990), 73.
32 On *Intolerance*, see V. Kepley, Jr., '*Intolerance* and the Soviets: A Historical Investigation', in Taylor and Christie (eds.), *Inside the Film Factory*, 52–3.
33 See the charts in D. Youngblood, *Movies for the Masses: Popular Cinema and Soviet Society in the 1920s* (Cambridge, 1992), 20, and V. Kepley, Jr. and B. Kepley, 'Foreign Films on Soviet Screens, 1922–1931', *Quarterly Review of Film Studies*, 4 (1979), 431. On the role of foreign films in general, see ibid. 429–42; Youngblood, *Movies for the Masses*, 19–21, 50–67; and P. Kenez, *Cinema and Soviet Society, 1917–1953* (Cambridge, 1992), 72–5.

actor Harry Piel was a particular favourite.[34] From 1924 onwards American films predominated. They were popular with audiences for the very qualities of narrative simplicity and incisiveness, believable characters, and the inclusion of star actors which Kuleshov and others had recognized. The American film *The Thief of Baghdad*, starring Douglas Fairbanks, was the most popular film of the 1920s, more than 1,700,000 viewers seeing it in the first six months of its run.[35] More than forty Chaplin films were shown in the Soviet Union during the decade, as were several Tarzan films.[36] Before *The Battleship Potemkin* opened in January 1926, another Fairbanks vehicle, *Robin Hood*, was showing at eleven of the twelve first-run cinemas in central Moscow, and *Potemkin* was quickly withdrawn. When it was re-released in June after its success in Germany it was again replaced, first by Buster Keaton in *Our Hospitality*, and then again by *Robin Hood*, which achieved one and a half more screen days in Moscow in 1926 than *Potemkin*.[37] The visit of Fairbanks and Mary Pickford to Moscow in July 1926 produced adulatory crowds, and the State Theatrical and Cinematic Publishing House issued an accompanying pamphlet *They are Here* in an edition of 45,000 copies.[38] At the same time the most popular exported Soviet films were Konstantin Eggert's *The Bear's Wedding* (*Medvezh'ia svad'ba*, 1926), a Gothic horror story about a were-bear based on Merimée (which also outperformed *Potemkin* in the USSR), and Zheliabuzhskii and Moskvin's *The Station Master* (*Kollezhskii registrator*, also known as *Stantsionnyi smotritel'*, 1925), based on one of Pushkin's *Tales of Belkin*; both were sold to far more foreign countries than was *Potemkin*.[39] Thus cinema during the NEP period remained popular entertainment, and the tastes of Soviet audiences were similar to those of the rest of the world.

As well as making money from exhibition, the organizers of the new Soviet industry were eager to encourage foreign investment in Soviet production. In general these overtures were not heeded, except in the case of the Workers' International Relief organization, set up in Berlin under the leadership of the communist entrepreneur Willi Münzenberg. Early activity collecting money for famine relief in Russia in the early 1920s was followed by fund-raising to support the making of documentary films, the purchase of film stock and equipment for the Russians, and the importation into the Soviet Union of American and Western European films. Finally, on 1 August 1924, Workers' International Relief signed a contract with the Rus' studio, the only surviving pre-Revolutionary film company, and Mezhrabpom-Rus' was founded.[40] Gradually Mezhrabpom bought more of the company's stock, and the studio was renamed Mezhrabpom-fil'm in 1926. While centralization of film production

34 For the popular appeal of Harry Piel and later attacks on his cult, see Youngblood, *Movies for the Masses*, 53–4, 61–2.
35 See ibid. 20, and Kepley and Kepley, 'Foreign Films', 437. For further corroboration of the popularity of this film, see the lines 'Ia Mishu vstretila na klubnoi vecherinochke, | Kartinu stavili togda *Bagdadskii vor*' in the song 'Smotrite, grazhdane, ia zhenshchina neschastnaia', which forms part of ch. 15 of Konstantin Vaginov's 1933 novel *Garpagoniada* (K. Vaginov, *Kozlinaia pesn': Romany* (Moscow, 1991), 473).
36 Kepley and Kepley, 'Foreign Films', 437.
37 See Taylor, *The Politics of the Soviet Cinema*, 95, and Turovskaia, 'K probleme massovogo fil'ma', 74.
38 See Youngblood, *Movies for the Masses*, 54, and, on the pamphlet *Oni u nas*, Taylor, *Politics of the Soviet Cinema*, 115–16. Footage from the visit was later included in Sergei Komarov's 1927 hit comedy *The Kiss of Mary Pickford* (*Potselui Meri Pikford*).
39 See M. Turovskaia, 'I gusti del pubblico agli inizi degli anni trenta', in A. Crespi and S. de Vidovich (eds.), *Prima dei codici: Il cinema sovietico prima del realismo socialista 1929–1935* (Venice, 1990), 31.
40 On Mezhrabpom, see V. Kepley Jr., 'The Workers' International Relief and the Cinema of the Left, 1921–1935', *Cinema Journal*, 1 (1983), 7–23, and A. Kherroubi and V. Posener (eds.), *Le*

Studio Mejrabpom ou
l'aventure du cinéma privé
au pays des bolcheviks
(Paris, 1996).

continued, Mezhrabpom-fil'm was allowed to continue to function until the mid-1930s: its studios were taken over by the new Children's Studio, Soiuzdetfil'm, on 8 June 1936. Mezhrabpom's unique combination of foreign capital, pre-Revolutionary expertise, and an eye for the market meant that it produced a succession of popular hits. A poll in the late 1920s showed that it had produced half of the ten most popular films of the decade.[41] Its first great hit was *Aelita* (1924), directed by Iakov Protazanov, whom Moisei Aleinikov, the director general of Rus', had met during his Berlin negotiations with Münzenberg and persuaded to return. *Aelita* is remembered as the first Soviet science-fiction film, and for the extraordinary constructivist sets and costumes of its Martian scenes, based upon the designs of Aleksandra Ekster; but it is also a remarkably blunt exposure of the vacuousness of utopian visions.[42] It was followed by *The Station Master* and *The Bear's Wedding*, and the adventure comedy, *Miss Mend* (1926, directed by Fedor Otsep and Boris Barnet), all of which set box-office records.[43] Later in the decade the studio released the lyrical comedies of Boris Barnet such as *The Girl with the Hatbox* (*Devushka s korobkoi*, 1927) and *The House on Trubnaia* (*Dom na Trubnoi*, 1928), and a succession of hits by Protazanov. But it was also responsible for Pudovkin's trilogy of coming to ideological consciousness, *The Mother* (*Mat'*, 1926), *The End of St Petersburg* (*Konets Sankt Peterburga*, 1927), and *Storm over Asia* (*Potomok Chingiz-Khana*, 1928). It made the first Soviet sound film, Nikolai Ekk's *The Path to Life* (*Doroga v zhizn'*), which was released on 1 June 1931. However, this mix of ideology, profitability, and sound was not enough to protect the studio from the gathering ideological clouds.

By 1928 there were 7,331 cinema installations in the USSR. Of these, 4,942 were in towns. Of the 2,389 in villages, 1,305 were mobile installations.[44] Though the urban commercial houses were considerably outnumbered in terms of capacity (17 per cent by 1930), the fact that they showed first run features, and in particular foreign hits, meant that they brought in 80 per cent of the profits. Workers' clubs, more numerous than commercial cinemas, nevertheless in the late 1920s brought only one third of the viewers.[45] The clubs developed through the 1920s as places combining relaxation (which it was impossible to enjoy in the cramped living conditions of the urban working class) and cultural improvement. In 1923 only 25 per cent of clubs had regular film showings, but they proved the most popular of the entertainments provided, and by the end of the decade facilities were available in 89 per cent of clubs.[46] A film showing at a workers' club forms the frame of Dziga Vertov's 1928 documentary of life in the idealized Soviet city, *The Man with the Movie Camera* (*Chelovek s*

41 Kepley, 'The Workers' International Relief', 21–2 (n. 21).
42 On *Aelita*, see I. Christie, 'Down to Earth: *Aelita* Relocated', in Taylor and Christie (eds.), *Inside the Film Factory*, 80–102.
43 M. Turovskaia, 'The Tastes of Soviet Moviegoers during the 1930s', in T. Lahusen and G. Kuperman (eds.), *Late Soviet Culture: From Perestroika to Novostroika* (Durham, NC, 1993), 99.
44 Taylor and Christie (eds.), *Film Factory*, 423.
45 Mikhailov, '20-e gody', 65.
46 On the workers' clubs, see V. Kepley, Jr., 'Cinema and Everyday Life: Soviet Workers' Clubs of the 1920s', in R. Sklar and C. Musser (eds.), *Resisting Images: Essays on Cinema and History* (Philadelphia, 1990), 108–25, and 'Cinefication', 262–77, from which this information is taken.

kinoapparatom). Nevertheless, since clubs could manage to show films only twice a week and had access to only 10 per cent of foreign product, workers preferred to frequent the more expensive commercial cinemas. In the later 1920s more and more attention was also paid to 'cinefying' the countryside.[47] The number of projection units serving the villages rose to 4,340 by the spring of 1929, of which 3,477 were portable.[48] Nevertheless village exhibition was so heavily subsidized that though rural cinemas were using half the prints in distribution they made very little profit.

During the 1920s Soviet studios made 670 feature films. Their key themes have been summarized as: (1) adaptations of literary classics; (2) films set abroad; (3) Civil War epics; (4) Revolutionary epics; and (5) the most productive theme of all, dramas of everyday life set during the NEP.[49] Everyday life evoked a succession of major works by Barnet, Protazanov, and Fridrikh Ermler, and also what is perhaps the master work of the genre, *Bed and Sofa* (*Tret'ia Meshchanskaia, Third Meshchanskaia Street*, 1927, dir. Abram Room), a film explicitly intended by its director as a 'concentrated, condensed' work, a reaction against films worked on a 'major scale', a work whose slogan was aesthetic economy.[50] Like Protazanov's *Aelita*, *Bed and Sofa* is an extraordinarily daring dissection of the new Soviet reality and its philosophical underpinnings, and it concludes that the new era has made no place for women. Its message was not lost on ideologically motivated critics and it was withdrawn after showing in Moscow for a week in March 1927.[51] For by the end of the decade the ideological watchmen were making ever more confident judgements about what could and what could not be filmed.

From the Cultural Revolution to the Second World War

At the Fifteenth Party Congress in December 1927 plans were announced for the collectivization of agriculture. 1928 saw the end of NEP and the beginning of the First Five-Year Plan with its programme of rapid industrialization. The period was also explicitly seen as a time of cultural change intended to produce 'proletarian hegemony' in the cultural professions, and the term 'cultural revolution' was used to denote a political confrontation between the proletarian communists and the bourgeois intelligentsia leading to the creation of a new 'proletarian intelligentsia' through 'class war'.[52] Intervention in the running of the artistic professions increased. The Resolution of the First All-Union Party Conference on Cinema, held in March 1928,

47 See e.g. A. Goldobin, 'Our Cinema and Its Audience', in Taylor and Christie (eds.), *Film Factory*, doc. 45, pp. 124–5.

48 See Kepley, 'Cinefication', 269, and 'Cinema and Everyday Life'.

49 On the themes of 1920s films, see the tables in M. Tsikounas, *Les Origines du cinéma soviétique: un regard neuf* (Paris, 1992), 217–18.

50 See ' "Tret'ia Meshchanskaia" (Beseda s rezhisserom A. M. Roomom)', first in *Kino*, 14 Sept. 1926, 1–2, repr. in V. Zabrodin (comp.), *Abram Matveevich Room, 1894–1976: Materialy k retrospektive fil'mov* (Moscow, 1994), 13–15.

51 On the film, see J. Mayne, *Kino and the Woman Question* (Columbus, Ohio, 1989), 110–29; on its release see D. Youngblood, 'The Fiction Film as a Source for Soviet Social History: The *Third Meshchanskaia Street* affair', *Film and History*, 3 (1989), 56. On gender issues in other films, see L. Attwood and C. Kelly, 'Programmes for Identity: The "New Man" and the "New Woman" ', in Kelly and D. Shepherd (eds.), *Constructing Russian Culture in the Age of Revolution, 1881–1940* (Oxford, 1998), 273–85.

52 See S. Fitzpatrick, 'Cultural Revolution as Class War', in Fitzpatrick (ed.), *Cultural Revolution in Russia, 1928–1931* (Bloomington, Ind., 1978), 8–40 (8). See also Ch. 2, above.

stressed the cinema's role in 'cultural revolution' and 'socialist construction'. It insisted that cinema could not be apolitical, and proposed themes such as socialist construction and industrialization, the collectivization of agriculture, the battle against the bureaucrats, the strengthening of defence readiness, and the role of youth. In December of that year the Sovkino Workers' Conference reiterated that production must be linked to the Party line, and emphasized the need for ideological guidance. This was to be instigated by strengthening the role of Party cadres in production, and on 11 January 1929 a Party Central Committee decree ordered the implementation in film schools of what came to be known as the 'proletarian quota' of 75 per cent.[53] The call for films that showed 'all our achievements in industry and agriculture, all the victories of the working class on the front of socialist construction' was again invoked at the stage-managed First Workers' Conference on Cinema in July 1929, and in the RAPP resolution on cinema of September 1929.[54] But a corollary of this increased desire to direct the content of films was an increased incidence of the banning of scripts or of completed films, and references to the 'script crisis' recur in the 1928–9 resolutions. In February 1930 an editorial in the journal Na literaturnom postu (On Literary Guard) calling for the reconstruction of the Soviet cinema reported that whereas only 3 per cent of Soviet films were banned in 1928, in the first quarter of 1929–30 the figure rose to 38 per cent, including 55 per cent of Sovkino films and 75 per cent of Vostokkino films.[55] The number of films made in the USSR fell from 128 in 1930 to 29 in 1933, and would not reach the 1930 total again until 1959.[56]

In February 1930 the Soviet film industry was reorganized as Soiuzkino, and in December of that year the Old Bolshevik Boris Shumiatskii was made its head. Attempts to streamline the industry continued. In February 1933 Soiuzkino was replaced by the State Directorate for the Cinematic and Photographic Industry (GUKF). At the First Congress of the Soviet Writers' Union in August 1934 there was further criticism of Soviet cinema, and yet more changes were instituted. In September GUKF was subdivided into smaller units from which the Mosfil'm and Lenfil'm studios emerged, and in October the first Union of Film and Photographic Workers of the USSR was established. The extent to which film-makers had now been cowed is apparent in a craven letter to Stalin on the seventeenth anniversary of the Revolution signed by 65 leading directors, actors, and others.[57] In January 1935 the All-Union Creative Conference of Workers in Soviet Cinema was held to celebrate the fifteenth anniversary of the nationalization decree of August 1919, and in its attacks on the 1920s pantheon of Eisenstein, Kuleshov, Vertov, and Dovzhenko

53 Taylor and Christie (eds.), Film Factory, doc. 83, p. 211; doc. 96, pp. 241–5; and doc. 100, p. 254.
54 See Youngblood, Movies for the Masses, 157, and Taylor and Christie (eds.), Film Factory, doc. 110, pp. 275–80 (277).
55 Ibid., doc. 114, pp. 290–2.
56 'Segida-info', 76.
57 Taylor and Christie (eds.), Film Factory, doc. 133, pp. 335–7.

174   Julian Graffy

it completed the transition begun at the March 1928 conference.[58] It was followed in February by the first Moscow International Film Festival.

This time of redefinition for the Soviet film industry was also, not unconnectedly, the period of the move to sound. Sound came to Soviet cinema more slowly than in the West, but its fundamental consequences were recognized as early as 1928 by Eisenstein, Aleksandrov, and Pudovkin, who in their 'Statement on Sound Cinema' spoke of the 'danger' of the 'illusionism' and 'inertia' of talking pictures, arguing rather for a 'contrapuntal' use of sound to suit the montage nature of cinema.[59] Debates about the role of sound continued over the following years,[60] but when it was introduced it had precisely the consequences feared by Eisenstein. The introduction of dialogue increased the length of shots and militated against rapid montage. Dialogue also destroyed the internationalism of cinema (and played its part in the diminution of the number of imports). It increased the interest of the censors, since it led to greater plot articulation. But it also facilitated increased identification of audiences with screen heroes and led to the introduction of new genres.[61] The first sound film, Ekk's *The Path to Life*, released in June 1931, the story of the re-education of orphans in a post-Revolutionary work commune, was an enormous popular success. But the introduction of sound also made possible the inauguration of one of the most popular 1930s genres, the musical. The first Soviet musical, *The Accordion* (*Garmon'*, 1934, dir. Igor' Savchenko) is set in a village and shows how a Young Communist League (Komsomol) member uses his music to defeat the machinations of the kulaks. The same year saw the release of the first of a series of musicals directed by Grigorii Aleksandrov and starring his wife, Liubov' Orlova. In *The Merry Lads* (*Veselye rebiata*), an allegorical representation of the Soviet state's self-image, the untapped musical talent of a simple shepherd from a collective farm and a housemaid leads them to triumph at the Bol'shoi Theatre. The film was singled out for praise by Boris Shumiatskii in his 1935 book *Kinematografiia millionov* (*A Cinema for the Millions*), a kind of primer of what Soviet cinema could achieve, where he noted its 'cheerfulness' and 'joie de vivre', and emphasized that 'the victorious class wants to laugh with joy . . . Soviet cinema must provide the audience with this joyful Soviet laughter'.[62] Aleksandrov and Orlova repeated their success in *The Circus* (*Tsirk*, 1936), in which Orlova plays Marion Dixon, an artiste thrown out of an American circus for having a black child. Brought to Moscow by a sinister German entrepreneur, she achieves success in three areas at once: her show is a popular triumph; she falls in love with a Soviet hero; and she manages a transition to

58 Ibid., doc. 138, pp. 349–55.
59 Ibid., doc. 92, pp. 234–5.
60 See e.g. ibid., docs. 105, 108, 115, 120, 121, 122.
61 For sophisticated analyses of the role of sound, see I. Christie, 'Making Sense of Early Soviet Sound', in Taylor and Christie (eds.), *Inside the Film Factory*, 176–92, and E. Margolit, *Sovetskoe kinoiskusstvo: Osnovnye etapy stanovleniia i razvitiia. (Kratkii ocherk istorii khudozhestvennogo kino)* (Moscow, 1988), 24–31, a volume that I have found extremely valuable in compiling this survey.
62 B. Shumiatskii, *Kinematografiia millionov*, quoted in Taylor and Christie (eds.), *Film Factory*, doc. 140, p. 369.

political consciousness. The film ends with the cast marching through Red Square singing the 'Song of the Motherland', which would become the most popular song of the Soviet period. Shumiatskii, while less unstinting in his praise than for *The Merry Lads*, admired its 'original plot' and 'great mastery'.[63]

Further variations on the model followed, *Volga-Volga*, reputedly Stalin's favourite film, in 1938, and *The Radiant Path* (*Svetlyi put'*, 1940, originally, and tellingly, called *Cinderella* (*Zolushka*), a title that any of these films could have borne), and Orlova was established as the greatest star of the period. At the end of the 1930s and into the 1940s the director Ivan Pyr'ev elaborated a rural variant of the genre, with roots in popular culture and ritual, in his collective farm musicals such as *The Rich Bride* (*Bogataia nevesta*, 1937), *Tractor Drivers* (*Traktoristy*, 1939), and *The Swineherd and the Shepherd* (*Svinarka i pastukh*, 1941), all starring his wife, Marina Ladynina. In *Tractor Drivers* Ladynina plays the Stakhanovite, medal-winning leader of a female tractor brigade who, after several misunderstandings, wins the love of a heroic Red Army tank driver, who has meanwhile licked the feckless male brigade into shape, making them as handy on a tank as on a tractor.

All these films contain within them the motif of coming to consciousness, a consciousness both of the rightness of the Soviet system and of the individual's worth within it and contribution to it. This motif was also found in tales of collectivization, a subject 'suggested' to film-makers by Party spokesmen in the late 1920s, and the challenge was taken up by leading directors. But Eisenstein's *The Old and the New* (*Staroe i novoe*, 1929), with its excessive attention to physiology, Dovzhenko's *Earth* (*Zemlia*, 1930), which saw the coming of the collective in the eternal context of the Ukrainian peasant's oneness with the land, and Medvedkin's eccentric, anarchic *Happiness* (*Schast'e*, 1934) all fell foul of the authorities, and it was not until the fairy-tale versions of Pyr'ev that the genre was safely established.[64]

The path to consciousness is also at the centre of the key film of the 1930s, the Vasil'ev brothers' (they were not in fact related) *Chapaev* (1934), based upon a semi-autobiographical novel by Dmitrii Furmanov, which tells the tale of Commissar Furmanov's ideological inoculation of heroic, but spontaneous and undisciplined, Red Army Commander Chapaev. This film above all was taken up by the Party as a fertile model. Shumiatskii described it as 'the best film produced by Soviet cinema',[65] and it was aggressively marketed by *Pravda*, which ran an editorial in November 1934 entitled 'The Whole Country Will Watch Chapaev'.[66] Hundreds of copies of the film were made, including silent copies for areas without sound equipment.[67] Yet ironically, the film's success with the public owed as much to

63 Shumiatskii, *Kinematografiia millionov*, quoted in Taylor and Christie (eds.), *Film Factory*, doc. 142, p. 376.
64 Pyr'ev would return to the subject after the Second World War and produce his most varnished version of collective-farm life in his *Cossacks of the Kuban'* (*Kubanskie kazaki*, 1949). After Stalin's death a new realism would enter into treatments of the subject.
65 Shumiatskii, *Kinematografiia millionov*, quoted in Taylor and Christie (eds.), *Film Factory*, doc. 140, p. 358.
66 Christie and Taylor (eds.), *Film Factory*, doc. 132, pp. 334–5 (where the title is erroneously translated in the present tense).
67 On the 'marketing' of the film, see Turovskaia, 'I gusti', 34.

7 Scene from Nikolai Ekk's *The Little Nightingale* (*Grunia Kornakova,* 1936).
Ekk's film is devoted to a strike in a pre-Revolutionary porcelain factory. The subject of
strikes was a popular one in politically committed 1920s cinema, most famously articulated by Eisenstein, whose films are directly quoted in *The Little Nightingale*. But Ekk
dilutes his revolutionary propaganda with large doses of adventure and entertainment.
The still shows the women workers preparing for the glorious rout of the tsarist police
sent to break up their strike, a victory in which their only weapons are thousands of
plates and other pieces of crockery.

non-ideological as to ideological factors, and it is notable that once Furmanov has performed his act of ideological insemination he is unceremoniously dumped from the film, which settles into a tragic Western in praise of old Russian values of loyalty, family, love of the land, and sacrifice. A similar effect is visible in the first Soviet colour feature film, Nikolai Ekk's *The Little Nightingale* (*Solovei-solovushko, Grunia Kornakova*) of 1936. Built around a pre-Revolutionary strike in a women's porcelain factory, it borrows freely from both *The Strike* and *The Battleship Potemkin*, but treats the subject more as an adventure story and ends with a glorious extended sequence in which the women defeat the tsarist police armed only with thousands of plates.

The motif of 'coming to consciousness' is repeated in other genres of the period such as films about socialist construction, and explains the popularity of film trilogies, such as the films by Kozintsev and Trauberg about the pre-Revolutionary worker Maksim (1934–8), or Mark Donskoi's screen version of Gor'kii's autobiographical trilogy (1938–9). Gradually the cinema created a pantheon of heroes, what Liliia Mamatova has called an 'iconostasis of Bolshevik godheads'.[68] There were films about historical leaders, notably Eisenstein's *Aleksandr Nevskii* (1938), Petrov's *Peter the Great* (*Petr pervyi*, 1937–9), and Pudovkin and Doller's *Suvorov* (1940). There were films about Revolutionary leaders, of which the most important were Mikhail Romm's *Lenin in October* (*Lenin v oktiabre*, 1937) and *Lenin in 1918* (*Lenin v 1918 godu*, 1939), but also Ermler's *The Great Citizen* (*Velikii grazhdanin*, 1937–9), about Kirov. There were films about heroic fliers, such as Raizman's *The Pilots* (*Letchiki*, 1935), and about explorers, such as Gerasimov's *The Brave Seven* (*Semero smelykh*, 1936) and Kalatozov's *Valerii Chkalov* (1941). As the decade went on the motif of defending the motherland against its enemies became more insistent in a variety of genres, from the historical epic to the musical.

Between 1928 and 1940 ticket sales tripled and the number of cinema installations quadrupled.[69] Yet the number of films being made had fallen vertiginously and foreign imports had almost disappeared.[70] Consequently a far larger number of copies of a smaller number of films were circulated, which led to a narrowing of viewer choice. Yet the need to use the cinema as a place of entertainment in the absence of others was as great as ever, so people went to 'the cinema' rather than to a particular film, just as they had done before the Revolution. But as Maia Turovskaia's researches into popular taste have shown, there was still room for the expression of individual preference, and in 1937 the returns *per copy in circulation* of films drawn from children's classics such as Artashez Ai-Artian's *Karo* (based on Gaidar) and Vladimir Legoshin's *The Lone White Sail* (*Beleet*

68 L. Mamatova, 'Model' kinomifov 30-kh godov: Genii i zlodeistvo', *Iskusstvo kino*, 3 (1991), 96. On the creation of the heroes and the myths of 1930s cinema, see also Mamatova, 'Model' kinomifov 30-kh godov', *Iskusstvo kino*, 11 (1990), 103–11; M. Iampol'skii, 'Tsenzura kak torzhestvo zhizni', *Iskusstvo kino*, 7 (1990), 97–104; and H. Günther, 'Geroi v totalitarnoi kul'ture', in H. Gassner and E. Petrova (comps.), *Agitatsiia za schast'e: Sovetskoe iskusstvo stalinskoi epokhi* (Düsseldorf-Bremen, 1994), 71–6.

69 See Taylor and Christie (eds.), *Film Factory*, 423, and Kenez, *Cinema and Soviet Society*, 132.

70 See the chart in Turovskaia, 'The Tastes', 95.

parus odinokii, based on Kataev) actually outweighed those of the outright box-office leader for that year, Romm's *Lenin in October*, whose receipts were garnered from five times as many copies.[71]

Boris Shumiatskii led a delegation of Soviet film-makers to Europe and Hollywood in late 1935, and on his return he drew up plans to set up a Soviet Hollywood in the Crimea. The plans were approved by Stalin after his thirty-eighth viewing of *Chapaev*, but came to nothing.[72] His failure to increase production led to attacks on Shumiatskii and he was eventually dismissed, arrested, and executed in 1938.[73] He was briefly replaced by Semen Dukel'skii, under a new State Committee for Cinematic Affairs, but he in turn was replaced in June 1939 by Ivan Bol'shakov, who would head the Soviet industry throughout the war. The immediate pre-war period saw further reorganization and further campaigns against films which failed some ideological test, notably Stolper and Ivanov's *The Law of Life* (*Zakon zhizni*, 1940), attacked in *Pravda* on 16 August 1940 as a 'false film' and then discussed by the Central Committee in September. Plans for reorganization continued into 1941, but on 22 June 1941 the German army invaded the Soviet Union.

The Second World War

In September 1941 the Central United Film Studio (TsOKS) was set up in Alma-Ata, and in October the evacuation of the Mosfil'm and Lenfil'm studios to Central Asia, to studios in Alma-Ata, Tashkent, Ashkhabad, and Stalinabad (Dushanbe) was begun. The Soviet film industry was mobilized, and at the start of the war concentrated on the production of newsreels and other documentary material. The material shot by front-line cameramen was edited by documentary film-makers who remained in Moscow. Feature film production initially concentrated on short films collected together as *Fighting Film Collections* (*Boevye kinosborniki*), of which twelve collections were made in 1941–2.[74] One of the first full-length films about the war, Pyr'ev's *The Secretary of the Regional Party Committee* (*Sekretar' Raikoma*), released at the end of 1942, follows partisan resistance to Hitlerite occupation and stars Marina Ladynina, familiar to audiences from Pyr'ev's pre-war collective farm trilogy. Of the seventy films made by studios between 1942 and 1945, forty-eight were war films and twenty-one were on historical subjects or drawn from classical Russian literature.[75] Since these films were made in Central Asian studios, but also because of a desire to represent the war as an experience that united the whole country in suffering and resistance, few

71 Analysis provided by Turovskaia, ibid. 103. On popular taste in the 1930s, see also Youngblood, *Movies for the Masses*, 171–9.
72 See ' "Daesh' Gollivud!" ', publ. and intr. Iu. Murin, *Iskusstvo kino*, 11 (1992), 91.
73 For an excellent survey of Shumiatskii's career, see R. Taylor, 'Ideology as Mass Entertainment: Boris Shumyatsky and Soviet Cinema in the 1930s', in Taylor and Christie (eds.), *Inside the Film Factory*, 193–216.
74 For a detailed analysis of wartime production, see Kenez, *Cinema and Soviet Society*, 186–206, and 'Black and White: The War on Film', in R. Stites (ed.), *Culture and Entertainment in Wartime Russia* (Bloomington, Ind., 1995), 157–75.
75 Figures taken from Kenez, *Cinema and Soviet Society*, 195.

wartime films were set at the front, scarcely any attention was paid to the actions of military and political leaders, and far more of them were devoted to the experience of partisan groups. It is also notable how many wartime films were centred on the experiences of women, including Iulii Raizman's *Mashen'ka* (1942), the story of a young telegraphist drafted as a nurse and forced to postpone the chance of personal happiness; Ermler's *She Defends the Motherland* (*Ona zashchishchaet rodinu*, 1943), in which the heroine Praskov'ia, whose husband and son have been killed, leads resistance to Nazi occupation; Mark Donskoi's *The Rainbow* (*Raduga*, 1944), set in an occupied Ukrainian village; and Lev Arnshtam's *Zoia* (1944), a version of the heroic death of the young partisan Zoia Kosmodem'ianskaia.[76] All these films stress the closeness of their heroines to the Russian or Ukrainian people and motherland (Praskov'ia refuses to believe that Moscow can have fallen). Wartime films also boosted morale by casting actors who were hugely popular from their pre-war roles. The comic central triangle of players from *Tractor Drivers*, for example, were now seen heroically enduring the privations of war: Ladynina in *The Secretary of the Regional Committee*, Nikolai Kriuchkov as a wounded tank driver in Stolper and Ivanov's *A Lad from Our Town* (*Paren' iz nashego goroda*, 1942), and Boris Andreev as one of the *Two Warriors* (*Dva boitsa*) in Leonid Lukov's 1943 film, in which the other, Mark Bernes, sang one of the most popular songs of the war, 'Temnaia noch'' ('A Dark Night'), full of nostalgia for home.

The historical films of the period served the same function of stressing Russian military and state achievement, and thus contributing to wartime optimism. The martial exploits of the Napoleonic wars were revisited in Vladimir Petrov's *Kutuzov* (1943), and the formation of a great national leader in Eisenstein's *Ivan the Terrible* (*Ivan Groznyi*), Part One (1944), which won a State Prize in 1946.

From the End of the War to the Death of Stalin

Notoriously, the end of the war brought a new tightening of the ideological control of the country, and the arts and science were singled out for attack in a period that came to be known, after Stalin's ideological henchman, Andrei Zhdanov, as the *zhdanovshchina*.[77] Attacks on film-makers began on 4 September 1946 with a Central Committee decree attacking part two of Lukov's film *The Great Life* (*Bol'shaia zhizn'*), part two of Eisenstein's *Ivan the Terrible* (not released until 1958), and other films. In December another decree referred to 'major shortcomings in the organization of film production', which it

76 On the manipulation of reality in the cause of keeping up the wartime spirit in this film, see R. Sartorti, 'On the Making of Heroes, Heroines and Saints', in Stites (ed.), *Culture and Entertainment in Wartime Russia*, 185–6, 190.

77 See Ch. 2 above.

blamed not on the state control and pervasive censorship that consistently vitiated attempts to meet production targets, but on 'theft' and 'wrecking'.[78] Concern abut the paucity of films being made was restated in a decree of the Soviet of Ministers of the USSR in June 1948, which, trying to make a virtue out of a disaster, called for 'fewer films, but of higher quality'.[79] The combination of the disruption caused to the industry by the war and the rigorous post-war censorship brought the number of films made to a catastrophically low level—in 1951 the total was only nine—and led to the so-called 'film hunger'. In these circumstances—and with an awareness of the receipts they might bring in—the Party authorized the distribution of (mostly German) 'trophy films', which were to be released with interpretative introductory texts and suitably doctored subtitles.[80] The glamour of some of these films proved extremely attractive to Soviet audiences: one of them, *The Girl of My Dreams* (*Die Frau meiner Träume*, 1944, dir. Georg Jacoby), a musical starring the Hungarian actress Marika Rökk, made five times as much per copy in circulation in 1947 as the year's overall biggest money-spinner, Boris Barnet's wartime thriller *The Scout's Exploit* (*Podvig razvedchika*), and in 1949 the German pictures in distribution took 94 per cent of the receipts.[81]

A new wave of repressions hit the cinema in 1949, and the ghastly nadir of intimidation is apparent in the minutes of a meeting of cinema workers held at the Moscow House of Cinema in February 1949, in which directors such as Pudovkin and Aleksandrov accused their Jewish colleagues of 'bourgeois cosmopolitanism' and other crimes.[82]

Of the films that did get made during these years, a considerable number were conventional biographical studies of great men—historical leaders, composers, writers, scientists, filmed in an anonymous style, or actually filmed performances of plays and operettas (thirty-one in 1952–3 alone). The fashion for filming the lives of composers (Musorgskii, Rimskii-Korsakov, *two* lives of Glinka) can be put down both to Stalin's inordinate love of *The Great Waltz*, Julien Duvivier's 1938 Hollywood life of Johann Strauss, and to the relative ideological safety of music rather than words. The war theme continued to be popular, but there was also a new 'cold war' thematics, with a new, this time American, enemy, in films such as Aleksandrov's *Meeting on the Elbe* (*Vstrecha na El'be*, 1949) and Romm's *The Secret Mission* (*Sekretnaia missiia*, 1950).[83]

The post-war period also saw the apotheosis of the Stalin cult in Soviet cinema. If Lenin had recognized the crucial propaganda role of cinema, it was Stalin (who said of cinema that though it was an illusion it 'dictated its laws to life')[84] who, for over two decades, had taken an active role in its functioning. Stalin's interventions in the cinema

78 This document was published by D. Kantor and E. Levin in ' ". . . imeiutsia krupneishie nedostatki . . ." ', *Iskusstvo kino*, 12 (1989), 107–9.

79 Published in E. Levin, 'Piat' dnei v 49-m. "Vse vyshe, i vyshe, i vyshe . . ." ', *Iskusstvo kino*, 1 (1990), 97–8.

80 A Politburo session of 31 Aug. 1948, for example, gave permission for the wide or limited release of fifty listed films: see O. Bulgakowa (ed.), *Die ungewöhnlichen Abenteur des Dr Mabuse im Lande der Bolschewiki: Das Buch zur Filmreihe 'Moskau-Berlin'* (Berlin, 1995), 257. There is a list of thirty-five German films that were actually distributed, with their Soviet release dates, in A. Demenok and E. Khokhlova (comps.), *Kino totalitarnoi epokhi (1933–1945)* (Moscow, 1989), 45–6.

81 Turovskaia, 'The Tastes', 104.

82 See I. Levin, 'Piat' dnei v 49-m', *Iskusstvo kino*, 1 (1990), 93–9; 2 (1990), 93–101; and 3 (1990), 77–91.

83 On the Cold War films, see M. Turovskaya, 'Soviet Films of the Cold War', in R. Taylor and D. Spring (eds.), *Stalinism and Soviet Cinema* (London, 1993), 131–41.

84 'Kino—ne chto inoe, kak illiuzion, no zhizni diktuet svoi zakony', quoted by D. Volkogonov in his 'Triumf i tragediia: Politicheskii portret I. V. Stalina', *Oktiabr'*, 11 (1988), 87.

industry ranged from assessing screenplays and suggesting alternative titles for films to the now legendary viewing sessions at the
Kremlin upon which the decision whether to pass a film for release
depended (Eisenstein and Cherkasov were summoned to the Kremlin
late one night in February 1947 to hear of his dissatisfaction with *Ivan
the Terrible*, Part Two).[85] He also took a very close interest in how he
himself was portrayed on screen, and the post-war years saw the
appearance of two of the most notorious cult films, both made by the
Georgian director Mikhail Chiaureli and starring the Georgian actor
Mikhail Gelovani as Stalin. If *The Vow* (*Kliatva*, 1946) seems to provide
the *ne plus ultra* of the cult, showing Stalin communing with the dead
Lenin to the music of Tchaikovsky, vowing faithfulness to his programme, and then organizing the development of the Soviet Union
from the First Five-Year Plan and industrialization to victory in the
Second World War, *The Fall of Berlin* (*Padenie Berlina*, 1949) shows
him celebrating that victory and promising to build the future in an
epic (and mythological) final scene that is the apogee of the Stalinist-
monumentalist style in art. But Stalin's cinematic star would not
remain in the ascendant for very long. As early as 1950 the French
critic André Bazin dismantled the myth of Stalin as superman and
concluded: 'The only difference between Stalin and Tarzan is that
films about the latter make no pretence of documentary accuracy.'[86]
And when cult films such as Romm's *Lenin in October* and *Lenin in 1918*
were re-edited during the thaw, Stalin would end up on the cutting
room floor.

The Khrushchev Period

85 The fullest of the
many surveys of Stalin's
involvement in Soviet
cinema is Mar'iamov,
Kremlevskii tsenzor. See
also O. Bulgakova,
'Povelitel' kartin: Stalin
i kino, Stalin v kino',
in Gassner and Petrova
(comps.), *Agitatsiia za
schast'e*, 65–70.
86 A. Bazin, 'Le
Mythe de Staline dans
le cinéma soviétique',
Esprit, July–Aug. 1950;
this quotation taken
from the Russian
translation, 'Mif Stalina
v sovetskom kino',
Kinovedcheskie zapiski, 1
(1988), 162.

Party concern that in 1951 only a quarter of the films in circulation
were Soviet led to a special resolution at the Nineteenth Party
Congress in October 1952 to increase both the number of films made
and the number of cinema installations. At the same time, even before
Stalin's death there were signs of stirring in Soviet art, mounted under
the banner of such words as 'authenticity', 'sincerity', and 'truthfulness'. This led to the appearance of a number of works of a kind of
documentary fiction, portraying the ordinary lives of Soviet people.
Gradually the process spread to Soviet cinema, aided by the lessons
learnt from viewing newly accessible European films, such as the
works of the Italian neo-realists, or the films shown at the Week of
French Cinema held in Moscow in October 1955. The renewal of
the Moscow International Film Festival in 1959 would give a further
boost to this opening up. Films such as *The Rumiantsev Case* (*Delo*

Rumiantseva, 1955, dir. Iosif Kheifits), in which a young chauffeur is tricked by a gang of crooks, or *Spring on Zarechnaia Street* (*Vesna na Zarechnoi ulitse*, 1956, dir. Feliks Mironer and Marlen Khutsiev), set among young workers, brought a new attention to everyday life visible in the settings, in the acting style (new actors replaced the stars of the 1930s and 1940s), even in the way the characters looked. This division in the visual style of Soviet cinema was accompanied by the destruction of the audience cohesion that had lasted for two decades, and was symptomatic of the global changes affecting Soviet society. A crucial symbolic stage in this development was the 'de-Stalinizing' Twentieth Party Congress in February 1956, noted for Khrushchev's 'secret speech'. One practical consequence of the Congress was an increase in the funding available to film-makers, and the number of films made per year, which had already begun to increase, reached 137 in 1959, another factor contributing to the fragmentation of audience taste. A moral consequence was the impulse towards a new 'de-Stalinized' treatment of the Second World War, and some of the most remarkable films of the Khrushchev period were war films. *The Cranes are Flying* (*Letiat zhuravli*, 1957, directed by the veteran Mikhail Kalatozov) is as innovative in its sympathetic treatment of its heroine, whose life is fractured by war and who betrays her soldier lover, as in its hand-held camerawork by Sergei Urusevskii, and this originality won it the 1958 Cannes Grand Prix. The same stress on the tragic experience of the individual and the same ignoring of the role of 'leaders', both military and political, is apparent in Sergei Bondarchuk's *The Fate of Man* (*Sud'ba cheloveka*, 1959), Grigorii Chukhrai's *The Ballad of a Soldier* (*Ballada o soldate*, 1959), and Andrei Tarkovskii's feature debut *Ivan's Childhood* (*Ivanovo detstvo*, 1962), one of several films which sited their innovative vision in the world of childhood.

In the early 1960s a new generation of film-makers (the students of older masters such as Romm and Donskoi), notably Tarkovskii, Vasilii Shukshin, and Elem Klimov, began their careers, and there were also several films about the lives of young people, including Georgii Daneliia's lyrical *I Walk Around Moscow* (*Ia shagaiu po Moskve*, 1963), Marlen Khutsiev's *The Il'ich Gate* (*I am Twenty*) (*Zastava Il'icha* (*Mne dvadtsat' let*), 1964), which includes a public reading by the new poets, Evtushenko, Voznesenskii, and Akhmadulina, and Klimov's debut, *Welcome, or No Unauthorized Admission* (*Dobro pozhalovat', ili Postoronnim vkhod vospreshchen*, 1964), set in a pioneer camp, which had the temerity to poke fun at a number of cherished Khrushchevian ideals such as the space race and the virgin-lands campaign.

But the thaw period was by no means unambiguous, and the dependence of state artistic policy upon political events caused a kind of schizophrenia, apparent for example in late 1962 when the publication in *Novyi mir* of Aleksandr Solzhenitsyn's *One Day in the Life of Ivan Denisovich* (*Odin den' Ivana Denisovicha*) (the symbolic high point of Khrushchevian liberalism) coincided with the Cuban missile crisis and was followed by Khrushchev's notorious remarks at the Thirty Years of Moscow Art exhibition at which he called contemporary artists 'pederasts' and their paintings 'dog shit'.[87] Film-makers were not immune to Khrushchev's artistic narrow-mindedness (carefully fuelled by conservatives), and Khutsiev's *The Il'ich Gate*, the most ambitious analysis of the moods and desires of the new, post-war generation was attacked by Khrushchev in March 1963 for portraying 'morally sick people' who could not be relied upon to build a communist society.[88] The uncensored version of the film would not be released for almost twenty-five years.[89]

The Brezhnev Period

The search for a new truthfulness and the expression of an individual vision continued through the 1960s, and is apparent in such films as Andrei Tarkovskii's most ambitious work, his disquisition on man, history, country, art, and God in *Andrei Rublev* (1964), or Larisa Shepit'ko's *Wings* (*Kryl'ia*, 1966), an examination of a woman fighter-pilot's difficult adjustment to the dullness of her post-war life. It also contributed to the flowering of a new, visually innovative 'poetic cinema' in the national republics, exemplified by the films of Sergei Paradzhanov in the Ukraine (*Shadows of Our Forgotten Ancestors* (*Teni zabytykh predkov*), 1964) and Armenia (*The Colour of Pomegranates* (*Tsvet granata*), 1969), and by a new Georgian cinema headed by Tengiz Abuladze. In the early 1960s, too, films assessing Soviet history or the Soviet present with greater directness continued to win audiences. But as the decade passed, and the new conservative line in the arts became established, so the role of the cinema and its relationship with its audience changed again. More and more films were now being made (an average of 140–50 per year throughout the Brezhnev period), and more purely entertainment films were being imported. In 1966 the only Marilyn Monroe film distributed in the USSR, *Some Like It Hot*, attracted 211,000 viewers per copy in circulation (against an average figure that year of 25–30,000), a sign, yet again, of a taste for the eroticism that Soviet cinema could not supply.[90]

In the 1970s the role of the cinema as the main entertainment medium was usurped by television (Central Television went over fully to colour transmission in 1978) and audiences fell drastically, as

87 'Khrushchev on Modern Art', doc. 3 of P. Johnson and L. Labedz (comps.), *Khrushchev and the Arts: The Politics of Soviet Culture, 1962–64* (Cambridge, Mass., 1965), 105, 103.
88 'Khrushchev Speaks Again', ibid., doc. 8, p. 154.
89 For an analysis of the cinema of the thaw period, see esp. V. Troianovskii (ed.), *Kinematograf ottepeli: Kniga pervaia* (Moscow, 1996), which also contains the testimonies of many participants; and M. Martin, 'Le Dégel', in his *Le Cinéma soviétique de Khrouchtchev à Gorbatchev (1955–1992)* (Lausanne, 1993), 19–66.
90 M. Turovskaia, 'Evoliutsiia zritel'skikh predpochtenii: Zakonomernosti sprosa', in Dondurei (ed.), *Otechestvennyi kinematograf,* 71.

did the average age of cinema-goers (on the development of television, see Ch. 10 below). Entertainment cinema could still draw very large audiences, for example the comedies of Leonid Gaidai, who attracted 76.7 million viewers to *The Diamond Hand* (*Brilliantovaia ruka*) in 1969 and 60.7 million to *Ivan Vasil'evich Changes Profession* (*Ivan Vasil'evich meniaet professiiu*) in 1973.[91] The absolute box-office champion of the period was B. Durov's *Pirates of the Twentieth Century* (*Piraty XX veka*, 1979), with 104,000,000 viewers, closely followed by Vladimir Men'shov's *Moscow Doesn't Believe in Tears* (*Moskva slezam ne verit*, also 1979) with 98,000,000. It is symptomatic of the accommodation of Soviet popular cinema to international genres and tastes during this period that this sentimental, conservative fairy tale was widely seen as an appropriation of Hollywood genre norms and went on to win a Hollywood Oscar as Best Foreign Language Film of 1980. By comparison the attendance figures for the films by Andrei Tarkovskii released during the Brezhnev period are 2.9 million for *Andrei Rublev*, 10.5 million for *Solaris* (*Soliaris*), 2.2 million for *Mirror* (*Zerkalo*), and 4.1 million for *Stalker*. Indeed, the fate of the new authorial cinema of the Brezhnev years, with its disturbing readiness to question society's norms, was usually failure at the box office, and often relegation to limited exhibition on the cinema club circuit. Yet hard-hitting analyses of serious subjects also continued to be made, in films about the Second World War (Shepit'ko's *The Ascent* (*Voskhozhdenie*), 1976, Aleksei German's *Roadcheck* (*Proverka na dorogakh*), 1971 and *Twenty Days Without War* (*Dvatdsat' dnei bez voiny*), 1976), or about an individual's relationship to society's norms and values. A series of films by the director Vadim Abdrashitov and the scriptwriter Aleksandr Mindadze, beginning with *A Word for the Defence* (*Slovo dlia zashchity*) in 1977, examined the crises in the lives of protagonists forcibly deprived of their illusions about the state they lived in.

But the other most fundamental aspect of the experience of filmmakers during the Brezhnev years was banning. Films had regularly been banned throughout the Soviet period,[92] but in the Brezhnev period banning was practised on an unprecedented scale. Sometimes directors or actors were allowed, or encouraged, to emigrate, as in the cases of Tarkovskii, Konchalovskii, and the Georgian Otar Ioseliani, but linguistic problems and the sheer expense and collective effort involved in making films meant that emigration for film-makers was a far more disruptive and potentially disastrous experience than for writers or musicians, dancers or painters, and few careers survived the uprooting. Perhaps for this reason, emigration was not a favoured option, and most film-makers remained in the country where their

91 Figures from 'Semidesiatye . . . Sinkhronisticheskie tablitsy', *Kinovedcheskie zapiski*, 11 (1991), 6–20. This issue of the journal is devoted to analysis of 1970s Soviet cinema. For the tastes of 1970s viewers, see M. Turovskaia, 'Zritel'skie predpochteniia 70-kh', ibid. 94–6.
92 For a fascinating documentary catalogue of the banned films of earlier years, see E. Margolit and V. Shmyrov (comps.), (*Iz"iatoe kino.*) *Katalog sovetskikh igrovykh kartin, ne vypushchennykh vo vsesoiuznyi prokat po zavershenii v proizvodstve ili iz"iatikh iz deistvuiushchego fil'mofonda v god vypuska na ekran* (1924–1953) (Moscow, 1995).

films were shelved—a term used to refer both to complete banning and to relegation to a minimal category of circulation. The full extent of the devastation of Soviet cinema during this period emerged after the Fifth Congress of the Union of Film Makers, held in May 1986, set up a Conflict Commission, charged with re-viewing the more than 200 banned films and assessing the possibility of their belated release. The work of the Conflict Commission, and the subsequent publication of documents and case histories, has provided an eloquent picture not just of the pervasiveness of cinematic censorship, but also of the image of the country cinematic bureaucrats and censors wished to impose upon audiences.[93] It is unsurprising that the treatment of sensitive periods of Soviet history should be particularly vulnerable to interdiction, and notable among the victims of shelving are a number of films commissioned to celebrate the fiftieth anniversary of the Revolution, including Aleksandr Askol'dov's *The Commissar* (*Komissar*), with its stress on the Revolution's merciless single-mindedness and the uncomprehending suffering experienced by ordinary people, and the portmanteau film *The Beginning of an Unknown Era* (*Nachalo nevedomogo veka*), which included versions of stories by Olesha and Platonov. Other periods were equally sensitive: Aleksei German's war films were temporarily shelved, as was Elem Klimov's treatment of the last years of the tsarist regime in *Agony* (*Agoniia*, 1975). Andrei Konchalovskii's picture of collective farm life in *The Story of Asia Kliachina, Who Loved But Did Not Marry* (*Istoriia Asi Kliachinoi, kotoraia liubila, da ne vyshla zamuzh*, 1966) was also too 'unvarnished' for the censor's taste, as were all the films of Aleksandr Sokurov, now the acknowledged master of Russian authorial cinema. The revelations and belated releases occasioned by the work of the Conflict Commission have redrawn the picture of the achievements of Soviet cinema in the Brezhnev period and suggested the ambitious path it might have taken. They also reveal the censorship to be motivated as much by aesthetic as by ideological considerations. A striking case is that of Kira Muratova's miraculously acute and moving account of the relationship of a divorced mother and her teenaged son in *The Long Farewell* (*Dolgie provody*, 1971), an achievement to set alongside the best work of Antonioni, shelved in part because its characters were found to be 'not cheerful enough' and to 'dance the wrong way'. The film contains a speech in which the young hero contrasts his desires as an individual (*lichnost'*) with those of society (*obshchestvennost'*), which can serve as a microcosm of the now enormous fissure between the private agendas of Soviet citizens, almost completely divorced from official ideology, and the artistic representations of their lives that would be tolerated. Other films

93 A comprehensive analysis of the workings of cinematic censorship in this period has emerged thanks to the Herculean efforts of a group of scholars at the National Film Research Institute (NIIK), headed by Valerii Fomin, first published in journals such as *Iskusstvo kino* and now collected in V. Fomin, 'Polka': *Dokumenty. Svidetel'stva.* Kommentarii (Moscow, 1992); V. P. Mikhailov (ed. and comp.), *Zapreshchennye fil'my: Dokumenty. Svidetel'stva. Kommentarii. 'Polka'.* Vyp. 2 (Moscow, 1993); and V. Fomin, *Kino i vlast'. Sovetskoe kino: 1965–1985 gody. Dokumenty. Svidetel'stva. Razmyshleniia* (Moscow, 1996).

were found to contain too much drinking, too much bad language, or too many jokes. Andrei Smirnov's *Autumn* (*Osen'*, 1973) was accused of containing too much bad weather, and permission had to be officially sought (and was officially given) to extend the agreed length of the film by shooting an additional scene in which the heroes took a sunlit walk in the woods.[94]

The 1980s

The early 1980s did see the release of some films that were ready to examine the Soviet past, and the Soviet present, with true fearlessness. Aleksei German's *My Friend Ivan Lapshin* (*Moi drug Ivan Lapshin*), first planned in 1969, eventually filmed in 1979–83, but shelved, was finally released in 1984. German's extraordinarily acute attention to the detail of life in the 1930s (to the sounds, the songs, the slogans, the perceptual clichés, as well as the visual patina), a concrete expression of his stated desire to 'make a film about the time', was so admired that in 1987 a critics' poll proclaimed it the best Soviet film of all time, and it had a great influence on other film-makers' attempts to grapple with Soviet history. Tengiz Abuladze's *Repentance* (*Pokaianie*, 1984), the first film released by the Conflict Commission, used allegory and farce to dissect the personality of a totalitarian leader. Rolan Bykov's *Scarecrow* (*Chuchelo*, 1983) used similar shock tactics in a tale of school bullying set in the present. But the early 1980s, and even the first year of the Gorbachev period, were in general a time of underachievement in Soviet cinema. It was the May 1986 Fifth Congress of the Union of Film Makers that threw the film industry into an initially utterly revivifying turmoil.

That the industry was in need of revitalization was obvious for a number of reasons. Attendances had continued to fall. Whereas, because of artificially low seat prices, a figure of 17 million viewers would be needed for a film to break even, more than 50 per cent of Soviet films were attracting fewer than 5 million, and the state was spending 78 million roubles a year in subsidies.[95] Students at VGIK, the State Film School, were in revolt.[96] The Fifth Congress signified its intent by removing two-thirds of the members of the board, including the First Secretary, and replacing them with younger directors whose films had been critical and often banned; this was true of most of the films of the new First Secretary, Elem Klimov. In addition to setting up the Conflict Commission, the Congress decided to take measures to overhaul the technical base of the industry, and to improve the career prospects of younger film-makers.[97]

94 V. Fomin, 'Vse nerazreshennoe— zapreshcheno', *Iskusstvo kino*, 5 (1989), 110–11.
95 See F. Albéra, 'Voyage dans un cinéma en mutation', *Cahiers du cinéma*, 395–6 (1987), 100.
96 See N. Laurent, 'La "Transparence" à l'épreuve: l'exemple du VGIK', *L'Autre Europe*, 14 (1987), 81–4, and the interview with Aleksandr Sokurov in E. Bokshitskaia, 'Pouchitel'naia istoriia studenta VGIKa, a vposledstvii kinorezhissera tret'ei kategorii Aleksandra Sokurova', *Iunost'*, 2 (1987), 9–13.
97 On the Congress, see 'V s"ezd kinematografistov . . .', *Iskusstvo kino*, 10 (1986), 4–133 (for the decisions of the Congress, see 121–5).

The late 1980s were certainly a time of great renewal in Soviet cinema. There was a new flowering of the work of documentarists, a new Kino-Pravda, which explored both the past, in such films as Marina Goldovskaia's *Solovki Power* (*Vlast' solovetskaia*, 1988), an examination of the history of a notorious island prison camp, and the present in a succession of films devoted to social analysis, particularly of the lives of young people. Notable in this context are a number of ever more subversive film investigations by the Latvian director, Juris Podnieks, beginning with his *Is it Easy to be Young?* (*Legko li byt' molodym?*, 1986).

The same double focus, on the past and the present, is visible in the feature films of the period. The *perestroika* years could be described as a time of the privatization of memory, as an entire society attempted to answer the question of what had brought it to its present crisis. The Stalin period in particular, but the Stalin period as lived through by ordinary individuals, became the subject-matter of films building on the achievement of *My Friend Ivan Lapshin* and *Repentance*, notably Vitalii Kanevskii's *Freeze, Die, Get Up Again* (*Zamri, umri, voskresni*, 1989). In the present, the lived lives and constrained aspirations of young people were the concern of several films, including a number starring hitherto marginalized rock musicians, such as Valerii Ogorodnikov's *Burglar* (*Vzlomshchik*, 1987), Sergei Solov'ev's *ASSA* (1987), and Rashid Nugmanov's *The Needle* (*Igla*, 1988). The sociological impulse was strongly apparent in Vasilii Pichul's *Little Vera* (*Malen'kaia Vera*, 1988), a tale of dead-end jobs and cramped lives in a Soviet industrial town.[98] The other major impulse of the time was towards a renewal of an authorial cinema which had not flourished on such a scale since the 1920s, apparent for example in a number of films (*Days of Eclipse* (*Dni zatmeniia*), 1988, *Save and Protect* (*Spasi i sokhrani*), 1989, *The Second Circle* (*Krug vtoroi*), 1990) by Aleksandr Sokurov. The key film of the period, combining sociological acuity with a brilliantly innovative authorial vision, is Kira Muratova's *The Asthenic Syndrome* (*Astenicheskii sindrom*, 1989), which presents the Soviet Union under *perestroika* as a place of neurosis and hysteria, its inhabitants cynical, hopeless, and bereft.[99]

The energy and achievement of these years, apparent both in production figures (which reached 300 in 1990) and in the originality of cinematic vision, was recognized by the frequency with which these films won prizes at Western festivals. But, as with *perestroika* as a whole, the seeds of renewal were also those of destruction, and clouds were gathering over the industry. Changes to the laws by which it was governed meant that new independent producers could now function outside the state system. The state industry itself was moved to a system of economic self-financing (*khozraschet*),[100] but a loosening

98 *Little Vera* attracted 54,900,000 viewers in its first year of release: see 'Sovetskie fil'my—absoliutnye chempiony prokata za chetvert' veka (1965–1988)', *Iskusstvo kino*, 6 (1990), 40.

99 For excellent surveys of the cinema of this period, see A. Lawton, *Kinoglasnost: Soviet Cinema in our Time* (Cambridge, 1992), and A. Horton and M. Brashinsky, *The Zero Hour: Glasnost and Soviet Cinema in Transition* (Princeton, 1992).

100 For the new model of the Soviet film industry, see Lawton, *Kinoglasnost*, 70–90.

of the distribution and exhibition system led to a huge inrush of American films, which proved extremely popular with audiences. In 1990, 215 Soviet and 178 foreign films were released in the Soviet Union,[101] and the favourite foreign actress of Soviet viewers was Michelle Pfeiffer for her role in Jonathan Demme's *Married to the Mob*.[102] Meanwhile the video industry was thriving, with video salons being set up to show (often pirated) copies of films that had sometimes not yet been cinematically released.[103] This, combined with the growth of cable TV channels, meant that audience figures continued to fall. Between 1986 and 1991 total attendances fell from 4,000,000,000 to 2,500,000,000, and it was estimated that there were 14,000,000 unsold seats every day.[104]

The Sixth Congress of the Union, held in June 1990, presided over its break-up into a Federation of Sovereign National and Territorial Organizations of Film Makers and introduced a system of guilds for directors, actors, and others. By now the Union was failing to keep up with industry developments and was beginning to seem irrelevant.[105]

Post-Soviet Cinema

A film made in 1991, the year of the Soviet Union's collapse, Nikita Mikhalkov's *Urga*, encapsulated the end of an era. Set in Mongolia, it told the story of a Soviet guest worker coming to terms with the realization that both he and the system he represented were no longer wanted. In a brilliant reversal of a central motif of classical Soviet cinema, the coming to consciousness of an outsider from East or West in the Soviet Union, the hero watches helplessly as Mongolia, Japan, and the United States combine to leave Soviet Russia on the scrap-heap of history.

Post-Soviet cinema faced all the problems being encountered by the society as a whole. Its audience had atomized into a number of small groups with contradictory tastes. In a country with a new name but little sense of identity, film-makers were uncertain what to say, how, and for whom. One of the solutions attempted was the internationalization of the industry. Films were made on Russian subjects with Western money, but the employment of Western stars as required by British or American co-producers (Anthony Andrews in Aleksandr Mitta's *Lost in Siberia* (*Zateriannyi v Sibiri*), Malcolm McDowell in Karen Shakhnazarov's *Assassin of the Tsar* (*Tsareubiitsa*), Tom Hulce in Andrei Konchalovskii's *The Inner Circle* (*Blizhnii krug*), all made in 1991) led to a skewing of the plot in the direction of a mythical international audience, and satisfied neither East nor West.

101 'Kinofil'my, vyshedshie na ekrany v 1990 godu', *Sovetskii ekran*, 18 (1990), 27–8.
102 'Konkurs "SE"-90', *Ekran*, 9 (1991), 12. Another eloquent sign of the Soviet film industry facing both East and West is provided by the marketing of the Clint Eastwood western *Pale Rider* under the title *Blednyi vsadnik*, a pun on the Russian title of Pushkin's poem *The Bronze Horseman* (*Mednyi vsadnik*).
103 On the role of video, see Lawton, *Kinoglasnost*, 99–106.
104 V. Demin, 'Veselo kak nikogda', *Ekran*, 8 (1991), 4.
105 For the materials of the Sixth Congress of the union, see 'VI s"ezd kinematografistov SSSR', *Iskusstvo kino*, 8 (1990), 3–6, and *Kino: Informatsionnyi biulleten'*, 5–6 (1990), 1–63.

A number of more artistically successful co-productions were made with French money.[106] Russian studio space was leased out and films by Western directors, such as Sally Potter's *Orlando* (1992), were made in Russia, until increased inflation made this no longer financially attractive. Many post-Soviet directors and actors began to live and work abroad, and Russian film-makers now often found it cheaper to film abroad.

Ambitious and innovative films continued to be made. Ivan Dykhovichnyi's *Moscow Parade* (*Prorva*, 1992) deepened the historical analysis by showing not just the terror but also the seedy glamour of Stalinist Russia. Kira Muratova's *The Sensitive Policeman* (*Chuvstvitel'nyi militsioner*, also 1992) continued her merciless dissection of the (now post-) Soviet psyche by showing her characters as infants and marionettes, ceaselessly parroting Soviet platitudes. Vladimir Khotinenko's *The Mussulman* (*Musul'manin*, 1995) showed the consequences of the return of a soldier captured in the Afghan war to his Russian village. And Sergei Bodrov's *Prisoner of the Caucasus* (*Kavkazskii plennik*, 1996) attempted to reveal the cancerous effect on Russian society of the Chechen and other wars.

Despite these achievements, inflation and further falls in attendances led to a vertiginous decline in the number of films made. From 300 in 1990 it plunged to forty-six in 1995, and was expected to fall further.[107] Some directors could still find the necessary funding and had enough sense of audience to play successfully to the international market. Nikita Mikhalkov's belated contribution to the great national retrospect on the Stalinist legacy, *Burnt by the Sun* (*Utomlennye solntsem*), won the Oscar for Best Foreign Language Film of 1994. In general, though, the Western vogue for Russian cinema had passed, supplanted by an enthusiasm for the emerging cinemas of Asia. Russian films were no longer winning prizes at (or even being granted showings at) Western film festivals, and this led to a rash of new festivals and prizes within the former Soviet Union, notably the Nikes, the Russian Oscars. A younger generation of film-makers, more equipped both practically and psychologically to work in the new conditions, was coming to prominence, a phenomenon noted at the Yalta Kinoforum of 1994 when Ivan Dykhovichnyi, Vladimir Khotinenko, Aleksandr Khvan, Sergei Sel'ianov, and Valerii Todorovskii were nominated as Directors of the Twenty-First Century. But the place to see the work of such directors was now on television, which was becoming increasingly ambitious in its support of serious cinema, on video, or at one of the many new festivals. For the cinemas that remained (the mass closure of cinemas was another phenomenon of the period) were now dominated by American products,

106 *Seans*, 9 (1994), contains a fascinating and diverse series of reports on the experience of this kind of co-production by directors including Kira Muratova, Nikita Mikhalkov, and Vitalii Kanevskii.
107 'Segida-info', 76. In the first nine months of 1996, only seventeen films were made: see *Seans*, 14 (1997), 107.

or by (usually unsuccessful) Russian imitations of these. In 1995, eighty-two Russian films were released on to Russian screens, and a further thirty-five from the former Soviet republics. The number of films from other countries, of which the overwhelming majority were American, was 169.[108] That the post-Soviet popular consciousness is now a confused amalgam of 'Soviet' and 'American' values was recognized by Dmitrii Astrakhan' in *Everything will be OK* (*Vse budet khorosho*), which cannily combines myths of worldly success in California with myths of traditional Russian community and the ability to endure. It was one of the biggest popular hits of 1995.

The readjustment of Russian cinema continues. The private money that flooded into the industry in the late 1980s, when it was one of the few areas where it could be set against tax and turned to profit, has now gone elsewhere. The state, which at the beginning of the decade, with the privatization of the studios, was almost entirely removed from production funding, is now crucial to its survival. Recent figures report that whereas of 394 films made in the Soviet Union in 1991 only nineteen attracted state funding, by 1995 out of fifty-one films being made in Russia, fifteen were fully funded and a further twenty partially funded by Roskomkino, the Russian State Cinema Committee.[109]

As so often before, the present state of the Russian film industry reflects the situation of the country as a whole. Ambitious and original films are being made against impossible odds, but audiences, impoverished and bewildered by recent events, are not always watching them.

108 'Khudozhestvennye fil'my, vyshedshie na ekrany v 1995 godu', *Ekran*, 1 (1996), 45–6.
109 V. Turovskii, 'Kino dolzhno byt' dorogim', *Izvestiia*, 31 May 1996, 6. The slight discrepancy between the production figures given here and those provided in *Iskusstvo kino*, 4 (1996), 76, can be explained by the fact that many films will have been made over part of two calendar years. By Sept. 1996 Roskomkino had received only 22.8 per cent of the budget allotted to it for that year: see *Seans*, 14 (1997), 107.

10

FRANK ELLIS

The Media as Social Engineer

The Creation of Homo Sovieticus, 1921–1953: Theoretical Background

> Sensible workers who follow Lenin should realize that a pitiless experiment is being performed on the Russian working class, an experiment which will destroy the best forces of the workers and will arrest normal development of the Russian Revolution for a long time to come.
>
> Maksim Gor'kii, 1917

Communication and the power of ideas are the engines of political change. Thus it could be argued that the most successful political parties are the most effective communicators. Yet this seemingly sensible argument is turned upside down by the success of Lenin's Bolsheviks. Political discourse in the liberal democracies concedes the possibility that a political party could fail to persuade the electorate, but in that case there can be no basis for power. Lenin, in marked contrast, saw political communication as a weapon for winning power, without the help of any electorate, and then retaining it in the face of opposition. Once in power with its rivals vanquished, the Party could then bring the full force of the mass media to bear on the population, in order to further its social and economic goals, launching, in effect, an unprecedented experiment in mass psychology.

Soviet media theory evolved from the principles of the revolutionary party prescribed by Lenin in the seminal work, *What is to be Done?* (*Chto delat'?*, 1902). Not far behind in canonical importance are 'Where to Begin?' ('S chego nachat'?', 1901) and 'Party Organization and Party Literature' ('Partiinaia organizatsiia i partiinaia literatura', 1905). Common to all these works is the conviction, explicit or implicit, that the creation of a new type of human being, one with a distinctive class psychology and cultural aspirations, was possible. To achieve these ambitious ends the Soviet media were to be deployed in educating, mobilizing, and indoctrinating the citizenry for its place in the new civilization. Whereas the media of the liberal democracies adhere to an ethos that is consensual, commercial, and empirical, the main task of the Soviet media was to propagate and to inculcate the Marxist-Leninist world-view to the exclusion of all others. From the beginning censorship was an indispensable and integral feature. The analysis of the Soviet media in their capacity of social engineer must, therefore, take cognizance of three factors: the nature of the relationship between the media and ideology; the aims of this relationship; and the degree of congruency between expectation and result.

Lenin's contribution to the theory and practice of the Soviet media—especially the press—was fundamental and enduring. For him, writing at the turn of the century, the primary task was quite obvious, as he observes in 'Where to Begin?': 'Above all we need a newspaper. Without it the systematic conduct of all-round propaganda and agitation, based on a consistent set of principles, is impossible.' As one might expect, Lenin was eager to spread the Party's message among the working class: 'We must actively initiate the political education of the working class, the development of its political awareness'.[1] A major theme is the concept of *soznanie* or *soznatel'nost'*, which in the lexicon of Marxism-Leninism means political awareness or consciousness. For the worker to possess *soznatel'nost'* meant to be aware of the iniquities perpetrated against the workers, to be able to explain, according to one's mastery of theory, the origins of these injustices and their solutions. Two additional tasks can be identified for the incipient agitation and propaganda apparatus: the first was to secure a dominant position among the competing voices opposed to tsarist rule; the second, which in part followed from the first, was to transmit Lenin's interpretation of Marx and Engels based on his analysis of Russia's social and economic conditions. A newspaper pursuing these ends would serve as a medium for educating the backward masses, preparing them for the forthcoming revolution. In a revealing statement Lenin commented that the paper would be 'a vital branch of our military activity'.[2] The networks through which the paper is to be distributed are clearly intended to assist an armed uprising and to function as a cover for the cadres of the new regime.

The ideas put forward by Lenin in 'Where to Begin?' are taken much further in *What is to be Done?* Three main questions are

1 V. I. Lenin, 'S chego nachat'?', in *Sochineniia*, v (Moscow, 1946), 8, and 'Chto delat'?', ibid. 371.
2 Lenin, 'S chego nachat'?', 9.

addressed: the character and content of Bolshevik agitation and propaganda; the Party's organizational tasks; and the plan for building up
an all-Russian fighting organization. In addition, we find the clearest
statements concerning the role of a revolutionary organization in the
phase before power is seized, the structure and aims of the press, and
the discussion of such vital questions as the freedom of the press and
the connection between revolutionary theory and practice.

Lenin attacked the notion of press freedom at every opportunity.
His main arguments against it can be summarized briefly. First, the
notion of a free press in the West is a fiction foisted on a gullible public to make them believe that the press and government are separate
institutions, and thus that what is written in the press does not necessarily reflect the views of politicians. Any notion of independence, it
would be argued, is illusory. Second, if only the wealthy can afford to
own and run printing equipment, then access to the press is rationed.
Freedom of expression is for the few. In 'Party Organization and Party
Literature' Lenin, addressing 'bourgeois individualists', argues:

Secondly, we must say to you bourgeois individualists that your talk about
absolute freedom is sheer hypocrisy. There can be no real and effective 'freedom' in a society based on the power of money, in a society in which the
masses of working people live in poverty and the handful of rich live like
parasites. Are you free in relation to your bourgeois publisher, Mr Writer, in
relation to your bourgeois public . . . ? . . . The freedom of the bourgeois
writer, artist or actress is simply masked (or hypocritically masked) dependence on the money-bag, on corruption, on prostitution.[3]

The Leninist analogy that private ownership of the press is a modern form of feudal monopoly undoubtedly has its attractions for the
advocates of class war, but it ignores the fact that sales of Western
papers and new types of media products and services reflect a genuine
demand, and that any paper is subject to the pressures of competition.
If nobody buys it, or it becomes too expensive to run (the fate of
Britain's *Today* in 1995), it goes to the wall. Lack of funds may inhibit
the publication of new papers, but the would-be proprietor is free to
raise capital for his venture and take a risk in the market-place. That
avenue remains firmly closed in Lenin's scheme of things. Furthermore, in a market economy where government censorship is not
excessively restrictive, newspapers can have a beneficial role as opponents of the ruling regime; they are not always simply (as Lenin
envisaged) the mouthpieces of their wealthy proprietors.

Another obvious benefit of a free press, which Lenin's ideologically
constrained model cannot tolerate, is a plurality of opinion. As far
as Lenin is concerned, too much choice in political matters is a

3 V. I. Lenin, 'Party
Organisation and
Party Literature', in
C. Vaughan James,
*Soviet Socialist Realism:
Origins and Theory*
(London, 1973), 105.

bad thing. The example of Gor'kii's paper, *Novaia zhizn'* (*New Life*), illustrates this point. In the immediate aftermath of the Revolution Gor'kii became one of Lenin's sternest critics on the subject of a free press, adopting a position that few today would dispute: 'Denial of freedom of the press is physical coercion, and this is unworthy of democracy.'[4] *Novaia zhizn'* was closed down on Lenin's orders in July 1918. Lenin regarded the freedom of criticism (*svoboda kritiki*) that went hand-in-hand with press freedom as an intellectual trend that would dilute the Party's zeal. But there was more to it than that. Freedom of criticism meant

the freedom to change social democracy into a democratic party of reform, the freedom to inculcate bourgeois ideas and elements into socialism . . . this pernicious freedom of criticism does not mean the replacement of one theory by another, but the freedom from any values and carefully thought out theory. It means eclecticism and lack of principles . . . Without a revolutionary theory there can be no revolutionary movement.[5]

Freedom of criticism would also inhibit the spread of *soznatel'nost'* among the working class, undermining their militancy. With typical aplomb Lenin argued that this would lead to a condition of *stikhiinost'* (spontaneity or elementalism) in which the working classes, distracted by short-term considerations and their passions, would fail to realize their historical destiny. The *soznatel'nost'*/*stikhiinost'* antithesis implied much more than the disciplined pursuit of the Party's goals and the acquisition of its canon. It demanded absolute intolerance towards other views, ideological exclusivity, and marked, at least as far as Lenin was concerned, the genesis of fundamental change in attitudes towards power relations.

Nor should we be misled by Lenin's contemptuous dismissal of freedom of criticism as just a 'fashionable slogan'.[6] The vitriol poured on those who advocated it and the energy expended on their ideological destruction suggest that Lenin saw freedom of criticism for what it was: a deadly threat to his monopoly of intellectual discourse within the ranks of the Party. The immediate background to the evolution of his ideas was, of course, the development of the print media in Russia during the late nineteenth century. Russian newspaper and journal readers at the turn of the century could select their organs of information from a wide political range, with legal Marxist, populist, and liberal, as well as pro-government views, all represented. In particular, Social Democrat propaganda had to struggle against, on the one hand, mass-circulation commercial papers, such as *Gazeta-kopeika* (*Copeck Paper*), which had a considerable following among the urban working classes, and on the other against the authoritative, but

4 M. Gorky, *Untimely Thoughts: Essays on Revolution, Culture and the Bolsheviks 1917–1918*, tr. H. Ermolaev (New York, 1968), 92.
5 Lenin, 'Chto delat'?', 328, 341.
6 Ibid. 368.

non-Marxist, social criticism offered by oppositional newspapers appealing to the intelligentsia, such as *Russkie vedomosti* (*Russian News*).[7] Lenin's views tacitly recognize the Social Democrats' impotence, under conditions of relative pluralism, in making their opinions carry weight.

'The newspaper', stated Lenin, 'is not only a collective propagandist and collective agitator, it is also a collective organizer'.[8] Agitation and propaganda are pervasive terms in Lenin's writings, and both fulfilled a specific function in Soviet media theory and practice. In the context of Western political systems, agitation and propaganda have acquired negative connotations: propaganda is the mask for lies and distortion, something we ascribe to our political opponents, whereas truth dwells with us. Such negative connotations are not implicit in the etymology of the word, or in its original usage (by the Catholic Church to describe its proselytizing activities during the Counter-Reformation). They are something which the concept has acquired in the twentieth century, epitomized above all in the activities of Joseph Goebbels, Hitler's masterful propaganda minister, and his equally effective, though largely unknown, Stalinist counterpart Willi Münzenberg. As Friedrich Hayek has noted, 'neither propaganda in itself, nor the techniques employed, are peculiar to totalitarianism, and . . . what so completely changes its nature and effect in a totalitarian state is that all propaganda serves the same goal, that all instruments of propaganda are co-ordinated to influence the individuals in the same direction and to produce the characteristic *Gleichschaltung* [forcible harmonization] of all minds.'[9]

This co-ordination of propaganda, and attempt to 'forcibly harmonize', was evident from a very early stage in the Bolshevik regime, one of whose earliest decrees, in November 1917, reintroduced press censorship, which had been abolished by the Provisional Government. Though oppositional papers could continue to publish outside Bolshevik-held territory during the Civil War, the Bolshevik victory in 1921 brought their existence to an end. From then on, newspapers and journals assiduously disseminated the Party line (though accommodating its sometimes abrupt and incongruous shifts and reversals as well). The most important vehicles of 'propaganda' were the flagship central organs, *Izvestiia* and *Pravda*. *Izvestiia* was founded in March 1917 as a Menshevik newspaper, but after the October Revolution was taken over by the Bolshevik leadership to stand alongside *Pravda*, which had been founded in 1912 as a successor to the earlier *Iskra*, and which was established on a firm footing after February 1917. Officially, *Izvestiia* represented the views of the government, *Pravda* those of

7 On the role of the press in relation to the intelligentsia's *mission civilisatrice*, and to political debate, in the late 19th and early 20th c., see L. McReynolds and C. Popkin, 'The Objective Eye and the Common Good', in C. Kelly and D. Shepherd (eds.), *Constructing Russian Culture in the Age of Revolution, 1881–1940* (Oxford, 1998), 71–2.
8 Lenin, 'S chego nachat'?', 10.
9 F. Hayek, *The Road to Serfdom* (London, 1993), 114.

the Party, but as was generally true of Soviet institutions, the nature of the one-party state made distinctions between the two newspapers very difficult, and in practice both offered from their inception a very similar mix of hortatory editorials, celebration of Soviet achievements, and heroically coloured or denunciatory human-interest stories. The same was true of the many republic and regional newspapers, which took their tone, and in some cases translated their material, from items published in the central press. Though some Soviet newspapers and journals were less earnest in tone than the mainstream central organs (for example, special-interest journals such as *Sovetskii sport* (*Soviet Sport*), news magazines such as *Ogonek*, or satirical magazines), all were overtly, and proudly, ideological, both in the coverage that they gave to items and in the manner in which they selected them. 'News', in the sense in which that is understood in the West, or in which *novosti* had been understood before the Revolution, i.e. the attempt objectively to record events as soon as possible after their occurrence, disappeared from Russian print culture for the best part of seven decades.

The widely held popular belief that the high circulation of *Pravda* and low availability of lavatory paper existed in some kind of correlation was probably a facetious myth, but it is clear from memoirs and literary treatments that the strictly propaganda side of newspapers' role—disseminating Party ideology—competed with a more homely function, with, for example, people proud that a family member or work colleague had got his or her 'picture in the paper', or devastated that some acquaintance had got involved in a scandal, much as would be true with many Western newspaper readers today. (One literary account which indicates this is Lidiia Chukovskaia's novel *Sof'ia Petrovna* (1939), in which the simple-minded heroine is delighted to see an illustrated article about her son's achievements as an engineer on the front page of *Pravda*.)

The divide between propaganda and its reception was especially sharp in the early years of the Soviet regime, since the learning and knowledge which characterized the Party élite separated it from the masses in whose name it claimed to speak, and particularly from the peasantry, whose very high rates of illiteracy barred the penetration of the Party's ideas at the most elementary level. This was where the function of 'agitation' (*agitatsiia*), as the supporter of 'propaganda', made itself felt. Outside the walls of Marxism-Leninism there seems to be no discernible difference between agitation and propaganda. Inside the fortress, however, another picture emerges. Lenin draws on the classic distinction given by Plekhanov:

He [the propagandist] must give 'many ideas', so many, in fact, that all these ideas in their sum total, will, at first, only be mastered by a small number (comparatively) of people. The agitator, speaking on the same question, will take the most outstanding example and the one most widely known to his listeners—let us say the death by starvation of a family without work or the increase of poverty etc., and using these examples, known to all, will direct all his efforts to give to the masses, who are familiar with the facts, *one idea*: the idea concerning the senselessness of the contradiction between the growth of wealth and the growth of poverty and will try *to arouse* dissatisfaction and indignation in the masses.[10]

The propagandist is concerned with written analysis and presentation, whereas the agitator relies on the spoken word. What Lenin proposes is, in fact, a neat solution to the problem of literacy dividing the Party élite from the masses. The propagandist concentrates on those members of society able to read, those who are accessible (or possibly vulnerable) to the Party's message. The agitator—some might say demagogue—spreads the message by word of mouth, deliberately seeking to exploit emotions and passions. Not surprisingly, agitation often comes close to violent coercion. Alex Inkeles understates this problem: 'The atmosphere of a discussion at a Soviet agitation session would not be regarded as "free" by Anglo-American standards. Any who persistently asked questions which indicated underlying opposition to the Party's programme would soon be exposed to police investigation.'[11]

The distinction made between propaganda and agitation in Leninist theory not only reflects the discrepancies in education between the Party élite and masses, but also reinforces it. Propaganda is an activity to be undertaken by the Party's theorists. Agitation is intended for the masses. If newspapers, magazines, and posters were the most important vehicles of propaganda, the means of agitation included such performative genres as the theatre sketch, the demonstration, the political meeting, and the collectively produced 'wall newspapers' (*stengazety*) that were created in every Soviet factory, office, and institution during the 1920s, 1930s, and 1940s. Of course, it is impossible wholly to separate agitation and propaganda, given that the two were different means of disseminating identical ideas, and that agitational genres could find their way into vehicles of propaganda—for example, the 'reader's letter', a supposedly spontaneous expression of grassroots views. But the essential distinction between propaganda as the exposition of dogma and agitation as the dynamic enactment of social solidarity remained in force throughout the Soviet period.

Besides convincing those hostile to Soviet ideology, such as peasants, of its political correctness, both forms of political communication

10 Lenin, 'Chto delat'?', 380.
11 A. Inkeles, *Public Opinion in Soviet Russia: A Study in Mass Persuasion* (Cambridge, Mass., 1950), 70.

were also intended to reinforce the message for those already converted, something especially important in the later years of Soviet rule. Confronted with the realities of power, Lenin, and even more Stalin, were, judged from the standpoint of orthodox theory, guilty of the most flagrant opportunism. The Party's propaganda and agitation apparatus had the vital role of accounting for these modifications of theory and abrupt changes in policy to the wider Party membership both at home and abroad. The task was not an enviable one. The propagandist and agitator had to operate in an ideological battlefield where the rules of engagement were liable to change at short notice. Both had to seek to convince an audience, to reinforce a set of beliefs, but within a circumscribed set of arguments. It is this ideological circumscription which imparted to so much of Soviet propaganda and agitation an atmosphere of intellectual insecurity and paranoia.

Agitation and propaganda gave rise to another peculiarity of the Soviet media. Even the most cursory reading of Lenin's works reveals a highly distinctive style, and one which was to have far-reaching consequences for the Russian language. Lenin effortlessly churns out pejorative neologisms which he hurls at his enemies. Clarity, precision, and brevity are frequently sacrificed to endless tautologies and periphrasis in an attempt to browbeat the ideological opponent.

One example must suffice. Throughout 'Where to Begin?' Lenin avails himself of every opportunity to refer to the 'all-Russian newspaper' or 'political newspaper'. Combined with military metaphors, the effect is one of barely controlled anger, determination and heroic struggle, and implacable resistance to all class enemies. Lenin not only imparts an idea—that of the all-Russian newspaper—but also seeks to impose a polemical style of writing and discussion, to make this the norm. The military metaphor is everywhere: the Party must be 'at its post'; there is talk of 'tactics'; the Party is 'in battle'; on the 'attack', or in 'defence'; 'terror' is a legitimate weapon. One might argue that all politicians, whatever their beliefs, exploit such images. But in the conditions that prevailed in Russia—certainly between 1917 and 1953—such language acquired an ominous significance. Let it be said that Lenin and his successors had no qualms about the use of terror to achieve political ends, and the Party-controlled media had their role to play. Violence in language precedes the physical violence meted out to 'enemies of the people'. The class struggle, it was implied, was not something that could be waged exclusively in the Party press. The various press campaigns against 'class enemies', 'rootless cosmopolitans', 'wreckers', and 'kulaks' created the necessary ideological justification *and* psychological preparation for the physical destruction of the class enemy, or any other obstacle blocking the path to the resolution of history. The peculiarities of the Soviet press meant that it became a powerful weapon of censure and, at the appropriate moment, an auditorium for the Party's executioners to pass sentence.

Refined and later applied to other media, such as radio, cinema, and television, Lenin's ideas on the press reflect the Party's ideological mission. Their salient points are as follows: first, the newspaper functions as a collective organizer, bringing together the best journalistic talents. During the underground phase the newspaper provides the nascent revolutionary organization with a theoretical forum for the discussion and dissemination of issues vital to the Party. Its secondary function is to serve as an underground headquarters, taking command of the revolution at the appropriate time. Propaganda and agitation are two important tasks of all Soviet media. As levels of literacy increase, the distinction between the two becomes blurred. Second, the Party press is designed to educate and to socialize the masses in accordance with the new ideology. There is, however, no role for the masses in the theoretical debate, which is strictly confined to the Party élite. Third, a major consequence of the penetration of ideology throughout all levels of Soviet society, and one that Lenin calls for in *What is to be Done?*, is the emergence of a new Party language. A new language equals a new way of perceiving the world. In this way, it is believed, the world can be changed. Fourth, Lenin regarded freedom of criticism as a pernicious influence on the ideological purity of the Party. The free press was a myth created by capitalist entrepreneurs in order to retain their monopoly of information and news. Hence the speed with which the Bolsheviks acted, after their rise to power, to suppress organs of information hostile to their own ideology.

Stalin and the Press

Without Stalin's absolute control of the press the administrative and physical terror and the carefully orchestrated atmosphere of mob rule—the hallmarks of the purges—would have been inconceivable. By the early 1930s this essential precondition had been achieved, and a well-drilled, obedient machine was at Stalin's disposal. The concentration of so much power and the threat it posed were only too clear to Martem'ian Riutin, who in June 1932, against the backdrop of the massive and violent collectivization campaign taking place in the countryside, circulated a comprehensive indictment of Stalin's rule. Among other things he noted: 'The press, a powerful means of communist education and weapon of Leninism, has, in the hands of Stalin and his clique, become a monstrous factory for lying and swindling, a device for terrorizing the masses.'[12]

Press control relied heavily on omission. One of the most striking and unnerving aspects of collectivization, an aspect also characteristic of the purges, was the total silence concerning the millions of victims. Behind the press façade of smiling, happy faces and the record-breaking feats of shock-workers and Soviet aviators was suffering on a scale never known before in Russia. In the words of Geoffrey Hosking, 'the mass arrests and the labour camps were never mentioned in the public media; but everyone knew, and the regime intended them to know, that people suddenly disappeared, that terrible things happened to them, and that many of them died'.[13] The suffering could not be totally hidden, but it could be ignored and a news black-out enforced.

Equally important for Stalin was the problem of deceiving the West about the genocide. As Robert Conquest suggests:

Stalin had a profound understanding of the possibilities of what Hitler approvingly calls the Big Lie. He knew that even though the truth may be readily available, the deceiver need not give up. He saw that flat denial on the one hand, and the injection into the pool of information of a corpus of positive falsehood on the other, were sufficient to confuse the issue for the passively uninstructed foreign audience, and to induce acceptance of the Stalinist version by those actively seeking to be deceived. The Famine was the first major instance of the exercise of this technique of influencing world opinion, but it was to be followed by a number of others such as the campaign over the Moscow Trials of 1936–1938, the denial of the existence of the forced labour camp system, and so on.[14]

Another success, and in some respects Stalin's greatest media coup, was the handling of the German–Soviet Non-Aggression Pact. On the face of it the Soviet media had an impossible task. From 1933 onwards Hitler was one of the main targets of Soviet propaganda. No effort was spared in his vilification. The rise of Hitler undoubtedly made Stalin's task of camouflaging the true extent of the collectivization and the purges that much easier. For his part Hitler made it clear that German expansion would have to be at the expense of the Soviet Bolshevik state. War alone could resolve this ideological rivalry.

The apparently non-controversial announcement in *Pravda* on 21 August 1939 that a Trade-Credit Agreement was to be signed by the two states studiously avoided any explanation for their sudden desire to improve bilateral relations.[15] However, the neutral tone of the article—*germanskii* replaced the by now standard epithet *fashistskii*—represented such a departure from the norm that the alert reader must have found it quite unusual. The signing of the Non-Aggression

12 M. Riutin, 'Prochitav, peredai drugomu', *Iunost'*, 11 (1988), 24.
13 G. Hosking, *A History of the Soviet Union* (London, 1985), 219.
14 R. Conquest, *The Harvest of Sorrow: Soviet Collectivization and the Terror-Famine* (London, 1986), 308.
15 'K sovetsko-germanskomu torgovo-kreditnomu soglasheniiu', *Pravda*, 21 Aug. 1939, 1.

Pact was announced in *Pravda* on 24 August 1939.[16] Earlier statements about a Trade-Credit Agreement can now be seen for what they were, a preface to or psychological softening up for the far more dramatic military pact. Viktor Kravchenko records that news of the pact left people 'stunned, bewildered and groggy with disbelief', and that after the pact had been signed 'any whisper against Germany, any word of sympathy for Hitler's victims, was treated as a new species of counter-revolution'.[17]

Another important function of the Soviet press, besides concealing the nature and motivation of government policy, was the targeting of Stalin's enemies, who were subjected, both before and after the War, to humiliating and vindictive attacks in stage-managed press campaigns. Campaigns of terror in the 1930s and 1940s were preceded by denunciations of victims, directly or obliquely, in *Pravda* and other press publications, right down to *stengazety*. An instance that indicates how the system functioned is the Doctors' Plot, initiated in January 1953 as one of Stalin's last acts before his death two months later. Though not an entire aberration in terms of Soviet history (it had been prefigured by attacks on prominent medical figures, such as Pletnev, in 1937, and also by the accusations of murder against Gor'kii's physicians when the writer died—of natural causes—in 1936, by the campaign against 'rootless cosmopolitans' in the late 1940s, and also by a number of murders of Jewish writers and actors in the period immediately before 1953), the campaign was new in the sense that overt anti-Semitism had traditionally been regarded by communists, both before and after the Revolution, as barbaric and uncultured, and characteristic of reactionary forces, such as the Black Hundreds of the early twentieth century.

The campaign was launched in earnest by a TASS announcement and an editorial in *Pravda* on 13 January 1953. Lidiia Timashuk, who worked in the Kremlin hospital, 'exposed' a number of Jewish doctors working there as participants in a plot to kill Stalin. The accusations were, of course, entirely without foundation, and the doctors were cleared of all blame shortly after the dictator's death. The tenor of the editorial, with its absence of any concrete evidence, is entirely characteristic of the way such campaigns were conducted:

The criminals' efforts were directed principally towards undermining the health of leading Soviet military cadres, taking them out of action and thereby weakening the country's defences. The arrest of the criminals frustrated their villainous plans and prevented them from achieving their monstrous ends.

Whose purposes, then, were these brutes serving? Who was directing the criminal terroristic and wrecking activity of these pernicious traitors to the

16 'Sovetsko-germanskii dogovor o nenapadenii', *Pravda*, 24 Aug. 1939, 1.
17 V. Kravchenko, *The Personal and Political Life of a Soviet Official* (London, 1949), 332, 335.

Motherland? What aim did they hope to achieve as a result of murdering active members of the Soviet government?

It has been established that all the members of the terrorist doctors' group were in the service of foreign intelligence agencies, to whom they had sold themselves body and soul, becoming their paid, their hired agents.[18]

The style of the piece is characteristic of Soviet denunciations: eschewing such niceties as evidence in favour of *ex cathedra* assertions ('it has been established'), it supports these with a familiar repertory of pleonasm, rhetorical questions, quasi-religious phraseology, and emotive collocations. This might well have distracted attention from the fact that at no point are the doctors directly accused of planning to murder Stalin, or that the anti-Semitic overtones, notwithstanding a reference elsewhere to a 'Zionist' group, are muted. In fact, with its emphasis on the group's alleged targeting of military cadres, the article can be read as pursuing the same objective of stirring up indignant patriotic pride as the Cold War propaganda in the coverage of the Korean War which dominated the front page of *Pravda* in the first few months of 1953.

However, the balance of nuance in the editorial was not directly reflected in the subsequent campaign. Iakov Rapoport, himself one of the 'guilty' doctors, has provided a detailed account of the campaign. His comments on public reaction are worth noting: 'Not surprisingly, most people, blinded as they were by Stalin's stupefying propaganda, took the TASS statement about the killer doctors on faith. They were inured to staggering revelations, but this one outshone by far all the previous concoctions.'[19]

Stalin's motives for the campaign are not clear. It has been seen as the prelude to the mass resettlement of Soviet Jews; as Rapoport has suggested, the Jews may have simply been convenient scapegoats, providing an outlet for people's frustration and anger. A by-product of the campaign, whether intentionally or unintentionally, was that Soviet scientists were terrorized into accepting scientific gibberish. Charlatans thrived in the poisonous climate of denunciation and suspicion, especially since one effect of the assaults on 'cosmopolitanism' was to induce a suspicion of scientific research outside the Soviet Union, and brand whole branches of endeavour, such as genetics and cybernetics, as 'bourgeois'. The career of the charlatan biologist Trofim Lysenko, whose crackpot theories of 'the inheritance of acquired characteristics' did enormous damage to Soviet agriculture, is well documented. But there were many others who seized their chance: for example, one Ol'ga Lepeshinskaia surfaced to preach the value of soda baths, claiming, without any verifiable evidence, that they could delay the onset of old age. The important point here is not

18 'Podlye shpiony i ubiitsy pod maskoi professorov-vrachei', *Pravda*, 13 Jan. 1953, 1.
19 Y. Rapoport, *The Doctors' Plot: Stalin's Last Crime*, tr. N. Perova and R. Bobrova (London, 1991), 78.

that such nonsense was propagated, but that its influence could not be challenged publicly and consigned to the intellectual rubbish dump. The result was a direct attack on the idea of objective truth and the scientist's professional training and experience: 'Her idea about soda baths was widely publicized, and baking soda disappeared from the shops. This was yet another manifestation of the mass hysteria of the times. Even critically minded people half-believed the propaganda and decided to make an attempt at rejuvenation.'[20]

The campaign against the Jewish doctors is instructive for other reasons. Violent or bizarre propaganda is subject to a law of diminishing return. The organizers of successive campaigns must invent ever more terrifying threats to the tranquillity of the socialist motherland in order arouse the hysteria of the masses, or run the risk of stagnation and apathy. But the other risk is that the regime, forced to depart ever further from the shores of probability, will lose control of its propaganda machine, exposing its mechanisms of control to scorn and ridicule. The end of the campaign was announced in *Pravda* on 4 April 1953 in a statement which admitted that there had been no basis for the accusations of 'wrecking, espionage, and terrorism'.[21] Rapoport notes that the arrangement of articles in both *Pravda* and *Izvestiia* was intended 'to tone down the sensational nature of both announcements, to make them look quite ordinary, nothing more than regular measures being taken by the new government . . . Still, these ruses could not conceal the importance of the two announcements, which were without precedent in the history of the Soviet state.'[22]

Radio

20 Rapoport, *The Doctors' Plot*, 260.
21 'Soobshchenie Ministerstva vnutrennikh del SSSR', *Pravda*, 4 Apr. 1953, 2.
22 Rapoport, *The Doctor's Plot*, 189.
23 For resolutions and plenary decisions relating to radio, cinema, press, and television, see R. H. McNeal, *Guide to the Decisions of the Communist Party of the Soviet Union 1917–1967* (Toronto, 1972). On cinema, see Ch. 9 above; on television, see below.

Once the Party's grip on the press had tightened it was a natural step to extend Lenin's proselytizing mission to the emerging media of radio, cinema, and eventually television. All three media were to have the core ideological tasks—with varying degrees of success—imposed upon them: the dissemination of political information; the education of the masses (to increase receptivity to the Party's ideas); the rallying of support for the Party's policies; and the provision of positive and constructive means of relaxation.[23]

Radio broadcasting was seen as especially useful in the early years of Bolshevik power. It promised enormous advantages for a state whose geographical range extended over eleven time zones, and the policy of *radiofikatsiia* or installation of radio was high on the list of the Party's priorities. As a policy, *radiofikatsiia* was concerned with the transmission of radio messages by signal, as well as messages relayed by wire and cable broadcasts within a local environment. The cable system or Radio-Diffusion Exchange (RDE, *radiotransliatsionnyi uzel*) was a closed system operated from a central command point. The system has the advantage that the listener hears only what the controllers wish him to hear. News is dispensed through a system of loudspeakers or *reproduktory* situated in public places: streets, hospitals, railway stations, and hotels. These loudspeakers feature prominently in the novels of Evgenii Zamiatin and Andrei Platonov, where they have Orwellian associations with thought control.

Regular radio broadcasting began in 1924, though radio had been used during negotiations at Brest–Litovsk with the aim of influencing German politicians.[24] Some of the first programmes were on art themes, broadcast under the title of 'Literature to the Masses'. Vladimir Maiakovskii was a regular speaker on the radio, successfully adapting his poetry to the new medium. In 1931 the All-Union Committee on Radio was formed, followed a year later by the creation of twelve local radio committees. The timing may be significant. By 1932 Stalin's modernization plans for the Soviet Union were well in hand. Radio, like television and cinema, was the symbol and substance of technological progress. But a more ominous cause may have been at work. A radio decree of 1931, 'On the Reconstruction of the Worker–Peasants' Correspondent Movement' ('O perestroike rabsel'korovskogo dvizheniia') recommended that forthwith the *rabsel'kory* (worker–peasant correspondents) should use radio more widely in their reporting activities, or 'raids', as they were known. With collectivization under way and the purges about to break, radio would be a useful weapon in Stalin's armoury for inducing terror and hysteria. In 1933 the administrative Radio Committee (Radiokomitet) became a firm fixture. By 1936 there were five radio programmes in operation which were adjusted for the country's time zones and various languages.

For all its propaganda advantages, however, short-wave radio broadcasting was in many ways a mixed blessing for the Party's media planners. True, radio gave the Party the potential to reach even the remotest regions of the Soviet Union—although even this was not without its disadvantages. One of the most famous broadcasts in the history of Soviet radio took place on 3 July 1941, when Stalin addressed a bewildered nation for the first time, eleven days after the German invasion. Many did not know how to take the speech. Stalin addressed his listeners as 'dear brothers and sisters, my friends'. This was not the harsh, aloof, infallible Stalin that people had come to know. For the first time there was a touch of humanity, some measure perhaps of just how bad things really were. Clearly, an address intended to reduce

24 B. Bridges, 'A Note on the British Monitoring of Soviet Radio, 1930', *Historical Journal of Film, Radio and Television*, 5 (1985), 185.

bewilderment served instead to sustain it: Viktor Kravchenko notes that people were baffled by Stalin's tone and the reasons given for the disastrous defeats.[25] Even more obviously on the down side, radio also allowed those Soviet citizens who were so inclined to listen in to Western radio stations. One of the first wartime decrees to be enacted was a ban on the possession of private radios. The alternative voice, new ideas, or simply hard news not transmitted from Moscow, could be received and disseminated by word of mouth. In the period after 1945 this would become an acute problem for the Party.

The Soviet Media's Mission Impossible

Regardless of who led it, the Party as constituted and forged by Lenin was itself the insurmountable obstacle to the moulding of the new Soviet man, at least in the utopian-inspired form. As Gor'kii warned in 1918, 'we should understand that the "new man" cannot be formed by politics alone, that by turning methods into dogmas we do not serve the truth but only increase the number of ruinous delusions which fragment our forces'.[26]

Nowhere were these delusions more evident than in the Party's ability to adapt to change. Qualities which made it eminently successful as an underground, subversive, paramilitary organization, united by a unique doctrine in the pursuit of power, did not lend themselves to peacetime construction. Indeed, given that its ideological analysis of the world told the Party that history was moving to a resolution of the struggle between capitalism and the international proletariat, then these qualities and attitudes could not be relinquished. Accustomed to settling its disputes by recourse to violent ideological polemics, the Party was not suited to the frustrations of democracy, compromise, or consensus. Ideology created the Party élite. With power won, ideology justified and perpetuated its survival. Without ideology there could be no Party and vice versa.

In fact some of the dangers had been foreseen by Lenin's political opponents at the time he was writing *What is to be Done?* Reservations about 'Where to Begin?', voiced in 1901 in *Rabochee delo* (*The Workers' Cause*) by a critic subsequently quoted by Lenin, pinpointed the dangers inherent in his plans for newspapers: 'A propagandistic organ will become an uncontrollable, autocratic legislator of the entire practical revolutionary struggle . . . What should our Party's attitude be towards its *total* subordination to an autonomous editorial board?'[27]

The question is a crucial one for what happens after the Party has seized power. Over ninety years later these concerns appear as grim

25 See Kravchenko, *The Personal and Political Life*, 366.
26 Gorky, *Untimely Thoughts*, 174.
27 Lenin, 'Chto delat'?', 461.

prophecy. In his reply Lenin argued that the principles of election and *glasnost'* would not work in tsarist Russia. Their implementation must be deferred until after the revolution, a pragmatic and perhaps not unreasonable view in the circumstances. Any practical objections to the implementation of election and full *glasnost'* should not, however, divert us from Lenin's intrinsic hostility to both concepts. The experience of organizations conceived and developed in secrecy shows that the habits of intrigue and suspicion very rarely disappear. Feeling itself surrounded on all sides by enemies, and taking major decisions behind closed doors, the Party was ill-equipped to perform in the full glare of *glasnost'* and accountability. Both were stillborn.

Other factors reinforced habits imposed by the need for conspiracy. Would a group of revolutionaries which has suffered long and hard not regard the fruits of victory as its legitimate prize? The two-tiered organization—the masses and the Party élite—also provided justification for the retention of power and the control of information and news. Both were too important to be shared with the inarticulate and ideologically impoverished masses. As Lenin argued, 'The "natural selection" of full *glasnost'*, election, and universal control will ensure that every member will eventually find his own level.'[28]

By the time of Stalin's death the Soviet media experiment had assumed huge proportions. Riutin's fears were thoroughly vindicated. What of the results? Had the psychology of pre-Soviet man undergone the transition to Homo Sovieticus? And if so, how did the results compare with the expectations? Writing during the Second World War, when pro-Soviet feelings were at their height, Arthur Koestler summarized the results of this experiment in vivid prose:

Based on the axiom that the end justifies the means, quickly tired of the inertia and dumbness of the peasant-masses, they [the regime] treated the living people as raw material in a laboratory experiment, working on the tender malleable mass with hammers, chisels, acids, and showers of propaganda-rays of ever varying wave-length. For the superficial observer the method worked. The people apparently believed all that was said to them, hailed their leaders, worked like robots, died like heroes—like the robots and heroes which the Germans and Japanese produced. But inside them the new springs had snapped and had to be replaced by the old ones, fetched from the dusty shelves of the lumber room.[29]

The subjects (in both senses) of the Soviet Union functioned despite as well as because of the official identities thrust upon them, thanks in large measure to continuity rather than rupture. Such failure of official policy to produce precisely the effects intended is also to be found in relation to the Soviet people's consumption of mass-media products, as we saw above in the case of the consumption of film.

28 Ibid. 446.
29 A. Koestler, *The Yogi and the Commissar and Other Essays* (London, 1945), 199.

The experiment as a whole, then, was a failure, but the Party could boast of some success. A state which exercises total control over the mass media, excludes all internal and external opposition, and reinforces messages with physical terror can make practically any absurdity appear normal. Such victories were, however, pyrrhic. When reason, common sense, and decency are assaulted often enough, then personality is crippled, and human intelligence disintegrates or is warped. The barrier between truth and lie is effectively destroyed; the idea of truth itself is discredited. Schooled in such a climate, fearful and deprived of any intellectual initiative, Homo Sovieticus could never be more than a mouthpiece for the Party's ideas and slogans, not so much a human being then, as a receptacle to be emptied and filled as Party policy dictated.

The Failed Experiment, 1953–1991

> But this attempt to exercise power over minds must destroy the last possibility of finding out what people really think, for it is clearly incompatible with the free expression of thought, especially of critical thought. Ultimately, it must destroy knowledge; and the greater the gain in power, the greater will be the loss of knowledge.
>
> Sir Karl Popper

The dissolution of the Soviet Union in 1991 marked, *inter alia*, the culmination of a series of incremental changes that started to affect the Soviet media after 1953. A significant development was the drive for convergence, in many ways spontaneous and home-grown, on the part of isolated unofficial groups and individuals, with norms of public and political discourse long accepted in the West, but officially reviled in the Soviet Union. The striving of individuals to be heard against the background ideological noise was, given the immense power wielded by the Soviet media apparatus, a remarkable feature of this forty-year period.

The challenge to the status quo emanated from two sources, one external, the other internal. Externally, the Party had to contend with many hours of Western radio-programming aimed specifically at the populations of Central and Eastern Europe.[30] The programming was perceived as hostile—intended, that is, to undermine the Party—and, worryingly for the Party, was listened to by large numbers of people. Another challenge, and one that the Soviet Union was ill-prepared to meet, was the proliferation of information technology (IT) and its effects on the dissemination of news. Soviet media structures were no

30 Regarding RFE's audience, J. Hale notes that 'in early 1974, 60 per cent of the population of Romania were listening to their broadcasts, 57 per cent in Poland, 55 per cent in Hungary, 43 per cent in Bulgaria and 39 per cent in Czechoslovakia—after a peak of 65 per cent in the aftermath of the 1968 invasion. . . . RL estimates 40 million listeners throughout the Soviet Union—a fifth of the population' (*Radio Power: Propaganda and International Broadcasting* (London, 1975), 40).

match for real-time news either in swiftness of response or in sheer volume. By the early 1980s this problem was starting to assume crisis proportions.

Internally, the pivotal point was Khrushchev's partial denunciation of his former boss, referred to obliquely as the 'cult of personality'. Slowly, the possibility of debate began to be felt in cultural and intellectual life. 'Violations of socialist legality' were condemned and prisoners were released. The decade after 1956 also saw the beginning of what later became the dissident movement, a phenomenon not confined to the Soviet Union. To this can be added greater efforts on the part of the regime to ensure the availability of consumer durables, which significantly accelerated the penetration of television. Accompanied by a marked rise in the number of people with higher technical education, the increase in television viewing helped to fuel dissatisfaction with Party propaganda, a largely unforeseen circumstance.

Radio after 1945

Soviet radio broadcasting faced two main tasks after 1945: the first was the need to counter the influence of Western radio stations; the second was to match the quality of Western programming, which, despite determined jamming, was reaching its target populations. Stalin ordered jamming of Voice of America (VOA) in 1948. Jamming of the BBC began a year later. Jamming was used by other Eastern-bloc states with varying degrees of success. Hungary stopped jamming in 1963, Romania in 1964. Poland halted jamming in 1956, reintroducing it at times of crisis, during the Baltic riots in the early 1970s, for example. Soviet jamming was not confined to Western radio stations. After the split with China both Radio Peking and Radio Tirana were jammed. As a policy jamming had disadvantages. Apart from the fact that it violated the United Nations resolution of 1950, it was largely ineffective, since it required two tiers to jam sky wave (international) and ground wave (local). It was also very expensive: in 1971 it was estimated that jamming operations cost the Soviet Union $300,000,000.[31]

By 1975 there were five main radio programmes catering for news, political discussion (First Programme), international broadcasting (Second Programme), educational matters (Third Programme), music (Fourth Programme), and a Fifth Programme catering for Soviet expatriates. Given the threat of Western radio stations, the task of *Maiak* (*Lighthouse*), a twenty-four hour programme of national and international news and light music founded in 1964, was the most important.

31 On the technical reasons for the expense of jamming, see ibid. 133; on the cost, see P. Lendvai, *The Bureaucracy of Truth: How Communist Governments Manage the News* (London, 1981), 167.

Statistics for the 1970s and early 1980s, when the Cold War was at its height, show that the Soviet Union was the largest purveyor of broadcast information in the world. Its broadcast schedule each week numbered 2,010 hours in 80 different languages, some of which, such as Quechua, are spoken by a very small minority of people. Some idea of the broadcasting effort can be seen from the fact that Soviet radio was transmitting in thirty-six languages not used by the West. In 1979 Moscow began its English-speaking service, Radio Moscow, which, with its imitation American accents, was irritating to British listeners, but which was aimed, in the first instance, at English-learners in the Third World.

In 1969 Boris Ponomarev, a Stalinist veteran, spoke of the need to break the class enemy's grip on the mass media, a brutally honest statement of intent which has frequently been ignored. As Paul Lendvai has noted, 'Sensitivity to the freer flow of information does not stem from the personal characteristics of the men in the Kremlin, as is sometimes thought by naive Western commentators. The total control over political communication is rooted in the very essence of the Communist regimes.'[32]

Ponomarev and his successors were quite right to fear the influence of Western radio stations. The influence was twofold. Most obviously, these stations could make direct appeals to the peoples of Eastern Europe. The full effect of this can be seen during the Hungarian uprising of 1956. Radio Free Europe (RFE) irresponsibly encouraged the subject people to believe—or gave strong hints, depending on one's interpretation—that Western military assistance was on offer. Large numbers of Hungarians took to the streets in the belief that the West would help them, a belief that turned out to be ill-founded. Thereafter the emphasis had to be on the provision of accurate information, and RFE sought to offer an alternative home service. It and other stations benefited from the ability of Western radio to challenge news and analysis from official Soviet-bloc sources by reporting events not covered in these, particularly natural disasters and accidents, and eventually the activity of dissidents, and other sensitive political matters.

In the 1970s the Soviet Union made determined efforts to exploit international agreements to limit the influence of Western radio. In 1979 the basis for a New World Order of Information was discussed at a conference in Tashkent. Manipulated by Soviet media specialists, the delegates were overwhelmingly hostile to the Western media, and above all to the free flow of information. Third World delegates complained of 'cultural imperialism' and wanted the flow of information from the West regulated. Regulation of the ether appealed to

32 Lendvai, *The Bureaucracy of Truth*, 225; Ponomarev's speech, first pub. 1974, is referred to on p. 190.

these governments, one suspects, because, like the Soviet regime, they were well aware of the dangers of alternative ideas, criticisms, and the exposure of human rights abuses. They had no wish to have their murderous and incompetent regimes exposed to too much analysis. Western television and radio programmes offered a standard of social, political, and economic comparison that embarrassed the representatives of certain African, Latin American, and Asian states.[33] Had some form of New World Information Order been enforced or adhered to during the 1970s and 1980s then a valuable lifeline for the people of Eastern Europe would have been severed. Pressures which led to *glasnost'* could have receded, or been less severe.

On the question of the objectivity and balance of Western radio stations, one can note that the prominent Brezhnev era dissidents Andrei Amal'rik, Vladimir Bukovskii, and Aleksandr Solzhenitsyn all criticized the Western stations for being too lenient in their reporting of Soviet human rights abuses. In 1980, for example, Solzhenitsyn accused the administration of VOA of being too sensitive to the concerns of the CPSU's Central Committee, and as a result too willing to censor items likely to give offence. He instanced two separate statements made by him in 1977, both dealing with abuses of human rights in the Soviet Union (the arrest of Aleksandr Ginzburg and the Sakharov Hearings in Rome). Both had been censored before being broadcast. Solzhenitsyn also levelled a second, and less serious, allegation: that the VOA's programming was unsuitable for the Russian listener, being too much occupied with 'trite and inconsequential drivel'.[34]

However, research carried out by RFE, and the many letters received by the BBC, suggest that Western radio broadcasts were more effective than Solzhenitsyn acknowledges, which would, of course, explain why the Soviet leadership allocated such huge sums to costly jamming operations. The personal testimony of other former Soviet citizens and East Europeans also makes a strong case for the effectiveness of the BBC in challenging and undermining official Soviet news. Even in the Stalin days, some Soviet citizens risked all to listen to Western radio. Leonid Finkelstein, who in 1947 was serving a sentence in one of Stalin's camps, speaks highly of Maurice Latey, one of Bush House's most influential commentators:

In 1947, like millions of my compatriots, I was arrested and sent to Gulag prison camps. In one of them, where I remained for several years, there was a skilful electrician named Fedorchenko. In his tiny workshop full of junk, amidst bundles of wire, discarded fittings, bulbs, old valves and the like, there existed a cleverly hidden receiver. He would invite me there, give me a single headphone—and there was Maurice talking![35]

33 Indonesia's Sukarno saw Hollywood's film-makers as revolutionaries because their films spread a message of consumerism that Asians wished to copy (M. McLuhan, *Understanding Media: The Extensions of Man* (London, 1987), 289).
34 A. Solzhenitsyn, 'Misconceptions about Russia are a Threat to America', tr. M. Nicholson and A. Klimoff, *Foreign Affairs*, 58 (1980), 823.
35 Cited in J. Tusa, 'Salvation on Short Wave', *The Times*, 11 Dec. 1991, 14.

We find the same determination to listen to the BBC in the recollections of Polish intellectuals imprisoned after the declaration of martial law in December 1981. Alexander Malachowski, who went on to become a member of the Polish parliament, used to listen to radio while others were taking exercise. Later, he would brief his friends on what he had heard from London. The murder of Bulgarian defector Georgy Markov by a secret-service agent wielding a specially adapted poisoned umbrella in London in 1978 offers dramatic confirmation of the BBC's power to strike at the foundations of totalitarian states via the airwaves. Markov's broadcasts to Bulgaria were obviously hitting home. The murder was, however, a propaganda disaster: it merely endorsed Markov's damning analysis of Zhivkov's Bulgaria, and, by association, the other totalitarian states of Eastern Europe.

Soviet and Western Views of Newsworthiness

Throughout the greater part of the Soviet period profound differences have separated Western and Soviet interpretations of newsworthiness. For the Western reader/viewer news means more than hard facts and the endless parading of expert opinion on any number of topics. Novelty is seen as part and parcel of the package. News is entertainment. We are titillated by sex scandals, fascinated by natural and man-made disasters, and rendered fearful by the latest crime statistics. Serial killers hypnotize us. Every age has its great worry, the all-pervading source of angst. Ours is the environment: ozone depletion, dolphins and seals dying of mysterious diseases, pollution, acid rain, over-population, all haunt and fascinate us. As far as the Western journalist or television programmer is concerned the possibilities inherent in newsworthiness are enormous.

In the Soviet media the interpretation was altogether more narrow. 'Newsworthy', as Ellen Mickiewicz puts it, 'is what reveals the underlying reality toward which history is tending.'[36] News which vitiated, was not germane to, or deemed to be unimportant for, the Party's goals was simply not news. For her part, Gayle Hollander detects a greater opportunism: 'Basically, anything which can be used to illustrate current Party policy or economic progress is considered worthy of publication, and almost anything else is considered unimportant or unworthy.'[37]

For the Soviet media specialist, capitalist countries were a rich source of negative news intended to underline the successes of socialism. Strikes, economic failure, and social unrest, undeniably present, were all grist to the mill, and ideally suited to reinforcing

36 E. Mickiewicz, *Split Signals: Television and Politics in the Soviet Union* (New York, 1988), 30.
37 G. D. Hollander, *Soviet Political Indoctrination: Developments in Mass Media Since Stalin* (New York, 1973), 39.

the Manichean vision of a world split into two camps, capitalist (reactionary) and socialist (progressive). Reporting of such matters sometimes had a factual basis, but was presented in a distorted manner to an audience denied information, for example, about the extensive welfare provision that existed in many Western states. Viewers were invited, by implication, to draw analogies between the plight of Western workers and that of Russian workers (who enjoyed none of these advantages) in pre-Revolutionary days.

Soviet definitions of newsworthiness affected the reporting of crime, human interest stories, and natural disasters at home too. For example, the absence of detailed reporting of crime suggested that the Soviet Union and its satellites were paragons of virtue, and that crime was something confined to the corrupt, capitalist West. No industrialized society is free of crime, and the Soviet Union was no exception to this rule. There were three standard Soviet responses to the existence of crime: first, to leave severe crime unreported (unless it occurred in the West, though this had the drawback of suggesting illicit parallels to the Soviet listener); second, to concede that some trivial or low-level crime existed; and third, where possible to blame Western influences such as radio, rock music, and the like for this. One of the most serious cases in recent years was that of the Moscow Ripper, who in October 1974 stalked the streets, killing at least seven women. But the killer's activities were not reported in the press—quite the reverse in fact. Viktor Pashkovskii, the then editor of *Moskovskie novosti* (*Moscow News*), went so far as to say that: 'no dangerous crimes had been committed in the city in the last ten days', which canny Muscovites took to mean the opposite.[38]

Why, then, were the Soviet media so reticent about crime? The existence of crime poses awkward questions for the underlying utopianism of Soviet ideology. Moreover, in any free and open forum on crime the nature of the regime itself would be called into question. It would be possible to turn Marxist-Leninist sociology on its head: if social milieu determines behaviour, then any serious crimes committed in the Soviet Union, for example the murders committed by the Moscow Ripper, would indicate that there is something drastically wrong with Soviet society. A more recent case in point is that of Andrei Chikatilo, better-known as the Rostov Ripper, who admitted after his arrest to killing some fifty-five people, many of them adolescents (of both sexes), whom he had stalked, then raped and killed with his teeth or with a knife. Chikatilo's Communist credentials were impeccable: a former Young Pioneer, he was a Party member and graduate of the Institute of Marxism-Leninism. He himself attempted to persuade the court that he was a victim of Soviet totalitarianism.[39]

38 See H. Smith, *The Russians* (London, 1977), 422–3.
39 Reuter, 'Rostov Ripper Admits to Being a Freak of Nature', *The Times*, 22 Apr. 1992, 8.

Finally, there was also the persistent notion that the task of propaganda was to provide incentive models of behaviour to be emulated. According to this view of information cause and effect, reportage of crime would simply encourage people to commit crimes.

A second category of news frequently absent from the Soviet media was the natural or man-made disaster. Aircraft crashes, industrial accidents, derailed trains, and perhaps the most notorious disaster of all, the explosion at the Chernobyl' nuclear power station in 1986, were often caused by human error and plain incompetence. Reporting on them might be damaging to Soviet scientific and industrial prestige, belying once again the picture of perfection and security cultivated in the Soviet media. Disasters on a large scale might also bring embarrassing offers of help from the West, the ideological rival. Finally, there was the problem of news-managing the unmanageable. Earthquakes and plane crashes may be statistically predictable, but the suddenness and ferocity with which calamity occurs takes us by surprise. In a world in which the unexpected occurs, how much credence should be given to those who proclaim that they know what is mankind's final goal, and exactly how to arrive at it?

It has sometimes been argued that these lacunae were one of a number of positive features of the Soviet press: 'Even if one assumes that the Soviet audience is no less interested in tales of death and destruction, heroism and valour, than those of capitalist countries, one can respect a system of news-values which down-plays such stories and does not rely on the manipulation of morbid curiosity to maintain viewing and circulation figures.'[40]

In fact Soviet audiences did not have to wait until the advent of *glasnost'* to have their morbid curiosity indulged. The Soviet media's news values were not always as ascetic as is suggested here. On occasion, the regime was able and willing to manipulate the 'morbid curiosity', and also the gullibility, of media consumers (both Soviet and Western). During the Solidarity crisis in Poland, for example, it was reported that a family in Baku had had a catastrophe with the pet lion they had reared for many years, which 'one fine day, in murderous fury, ate the son of the family and seriously injured the mother'. The incident was good for many days of diversionary coverage and debate.[41]

Granted, such items were never reported in order to increase viewing and circulation figures in pursuit of profit, but then this is hardly a material consideration where the state is the sole news provider. Certainly, Western tabloid journalism frequently breaches the accepted canons of good taste. It is anarchic and undoubtedly hunts out the sensational for profit; it is often trivial, and sometimes

40 B. McNair, *Glasnost', Perestroyka and the Soviet Media* (London, 1991), 65.
41 F. Thom, *Newspeak: The Language of Soviet Communism*, tr. K. Connelly (London, 1989), 67.

extremely funny. But for these very reasons it is not a reliable instrument for a repressive government. The very 'trite and inconsequential drivel' of which Solzhenitsyn complained underlines the difference in roles between the Western media and their Soviet counterparts. And, it might be added, the lighter items, such as chat shows or popular music, broadcast by Western radio stations, in particular VOA, however uncongenial they may have been to intellectuals such as Solzhenitsyn, were precisely what drew many younger listeners to tune into these stations, rather than into, say, *Maiak*, whose tame programmes of *estrada* music (balalaika choruses, war ballads accompanied by full orchestra, officially sponsored soft rock) did not succeed in drawing away this target audience.

Television and its Audience

In 1940 there were approximately 400 television sets in the entire Soviet Union.[42] By 1950 the number had risen to 10,000 sets, reaching 4.8 million by 1960. By 1976 the Soviet Union was producing some 7 million sets every year. In 1986 it was estimated that 93 per cent of the population possessed a television set. During the 1960s television ranked third—behind radio and the press—as the main source of information. By the middle of the 1980s television was the main source of news for most people. By any standards this represents a massive shift in the consumption of news and information.

Soviet television, like the press, was modelled on central, republican, and local networks. Central television consisted of six programmes, two of which reached the outer edges of the Soviet Union. All Soviet media functioned according to an overall operational plan: a long term plan of five years; an eighteen-month plan; a quarterly plan; and the plan for what is currently in progress. Quarterly plans were put together in the ten days before the beginning of the quarter. Secrecy surrounded the final choice of tasks. Only in the last two days before the beginning of the quarter were detailed tasks and targets allocated. The emphasis on planning the news and the application of the need-to-know principle suggest an intelligence agency not a television network.

Television news made greater demands on the propagandist than other media. It permitted the broadcast of instant bad news from the capitalist world, but because of the all-too-frequent discrepancy between propaganda and reality in the Soviet Union, it aroused indifference and even anger towards the media planners, who were seen to be patently out of touch with what was going on around the viewer.

42 Mickiewicz, *Split Signals*, 3.

This risk was present in the press and radio but was enhanced by television, given that spontaneity and immediacy are important conventions, or pretensions, of the medium.

Like the other Soviet media, Soviet television tried to change the moral and ethical nature of the population, bringing about 'the socialization of the person'.[43] Like other media, too, it was supposed to inspire the population to take an active part in the fulfilment of the Party's economic goals. But the nature of the medium forced Soviet television-programmers to reconsider, or at the very least, to pay more attention to what is understood by the term 'newsworthy'. Definitions of newsworthiness, as applied to the press, were largely inadequate when applied to the television.

Foreign criticism of the Soviet Union was, by and large, not something that the Soviet media broadcast. When it was transmitted it was accompanied by lengthy explanation and refutation. However, more neutral or supportive comments by foreign observers were sometimes broadcast, with the foreigners concerned given airtime to speak in their own language before the voice of the interpreter took over.[44] Such a procedure helped to convince the Soviet audience that what they were hearing in Russian translation was authentic. Moreover, it created an illusion of objectivity and thus legitimized the Soviet media's interpretation of the comments: 'Even if only a few in the television audience can follow the foreign sound track, there may well be the sense among many more that the statements attributed to others can be verified independently.'[45] If independent verification, or merely the illusion of it, is something at which the producers of the programme are consciously aiming, then objectivity would appear to be something that has intrinsic value. This represents a move away from the Leninist doctrine, which regarded objectivity as at best superfluous, or as a bourgeois ploy. The need to support a case with corroborating viewpoints or arguments can be seen as a concession to a competing world-view; tacit recognition that authority alone cannot guarantee that something will be believed. It bears witness to the existence of a more sophisticated audience. Even if the objectivity was largely illusory, it nevertheless indicated acceptance of the fact that objective arguments were more likely to convince than those which contain identifiable bias. For the Soviet viewer, if not for some of the producers of Soviet programmes, objectivity, however flawed, had become a desideratum.

Two theories of communication dominated Soviet media theory and practice following Lenin's *What is to be Done?*: the hypodermic effect model, and the two-step flow theory. Information, according to the first theory, is received in the form it is given. The main flaw here

43 Mickiewicz, *Split Signals*, 26.
44 Ibid. 147.
45 Ibid.

8 Cartoon satirizing Soviet telemania, published in the humorous magazine *Krokodil*, February 1971.

After the museum closes, figures from famous paintings, such as Repin's *Tsarevna Sophia* (just left of centre, with her arms folded), and Ivan the Terrible cradling his murdered son (right foreground) crowd round the set to watch an ice-hockey match. The cartoon not only indicates the importance of television in most ordinary Soviet citizens' lives from the late 1960s onwards, but also illustrates how selected texts from nineteenth-century high culture had become so familiar through school education, postage stamps, popular books, postcards, etc. that they were part of the nation's common currency.

lies in the failure to take cognizance of differing levels of ability among the population to read, to interpret, and to evaluate information. Yet even official Soviet sources indicate that there were often leakages and slippages in reception of information by the Soviet population owing to widely differing levels of knowledge. For example, a survey conducted in a medium-sized Soviet city during the 1970s uncovered some astonishing results. It was established that 25 per cent of the sample did not know what was meant by 'colonialism'; 66 per cent did not understand what 'leftist forces' were; and 75 per cent could not distinguish between 'liberal' and 'reactionary'.[46] For the Soviet media specialist these results must have been very worrying. The state permitted no independent dissemination of news, views, or information, and since the earliest days of the regime had gone to amazing lengths to inculcate a uniform world-view among the Soviet population. That a quarter of this population did not know what colonialism was could only raise serious doubts about the effectiveness of the Soviet media.

Similar findings have been made in Britain. A survey of television viewing habits has challenged many of the assumptions of advertising executives. The study (for which unobtrusive, easily ignored cameras were fitted in people's living rooms) showed that actual ratings for many programmes may be much lower than the BBC and ITV would publicly admit, and that audiences are far less passive than is thought to be the case. If they do not like what is on, then sets are switched off or programmes are ignored. Among the findings based on 7,000 hours of videotape and 100 British homes were that top-rated shows such as *Eastenders* and *Coronation Street* often played to nobody, and that viewers would read newspapers instead of watching *Neighbours*.[47] Could it be that the 25 per cent of the Soviet sample who did not know what colonialism was did not want to know, that ignorance was their form of rebellion against non-stop political indoctrination?

The two-step model was predicated on the assumption that educated people, i.e. those with higher education or specialized training, were more exposed to the media, because they were better qualified to understand the information and hence likely to be more interested in it. They passed on their news and interpretations of news to others. In effect they served as conduits of new information and as opinion-formers. The opinion-former continued to work after the news had been broadcast, filtering and interpreting information. Once again, however, the empirical case is weak, since it was precisely the better-educated who tended to be most critical of the Soviet government, and most active in organizing opposition to it.

Indeed, the power of the two-step theory and still less sophistic-ated hypodermic model lay in the force of dogma, rather than the

46 See Mickiewicz, *Split Signals*, ch. 5, which also contains a detailed discussion of the two dominant Soviet theories of communication.
47 See J. Miller, 'Home Truths TV Doesn't Want You to See', *Sunday Times*, 19 Jan. 1992, 4.

niceties of practical evidence. Both owed much to Lenin's views on propaganda and agitation, which made little or no provision for differentiation between consumers, for the discrete viewer or the niche audience. Yet the Soviet television audience, even in the 1960s, while clearly a mass audience, was also one in which individual viewers were sharply differentiated from one another for a whole variety of reasons: not only education, but also economic privilege, place of residence (whether in Russia or another republic, town, or village), sex, age, and so on. Furthermore, the context for television agitation was quite different. Television operates in a private setting, in the home (unlike the radio, the medium is wholly unsuited to broadcasting on the street or at the workplace). Accordingly, the peer pressure and fear of being singled out that were such powerful forces in suppressing dissent at mass meetings held in the workplace were hardly operational. The awkward questions that could not be asked in traditional *agitatsiia* situations might rise up unhindered, and even, in select company, be voiced openly.

This is not to say that television viewing is always an inflammatory or subversive activity. In the West, and also in post-*glasnost'* Russia, television has often been criticized as a social narcotic, locking people into their private predicaments, making them spectators rather than doers. In any case, in many Russian homes (as in British working-class homes, too, to judge by the survey referred to above) television has tended to be used as a kind of wallpaper, with the set kept on constantly during mealtimes etc., but watched only fleetingly and inattentively. By no means every message gets through.

In short, television meets a host of needs, among which the acquisition of information is only one. Among the most important is escapism, as convincingly demonstrated in the *glasnost'* and post-*glasnost'* periods by the runaway successes of soap operas, of which the low-budget 1970s Mexican production, *The Rich also Cry* (*Bogatye tozhe plachut*) was market-leader. Though some escapist Soviet programmes, such as the television adaptations of Iuliian Semenov's thrillers *Seventeen Moments in Spring* and *Tass is Authorized to Announce* (in 1973 and 1984 respectively) achieved large viewing figures in their day, neither they nor anything else on Soviet or post-Soviet television dominated the market to the extent of this soap (shown when viewers had a much wider choice of material on offer), which had Russians glued to their sets week after week. Collective farm-workers demanded that the soap be shown in the evening because they did not have videos. Managers of businesses wanted it stopped because workers were not turning up for shifts. Old people, worried that they might not live to see the end, wanted the episodes to be shown more frequently. And in crime-ridden Bishkek, the capital of Kirgyzstan, the police chief advised people that the safest time to walk the streets was the thrice-weekly slot when *The Rich also Cry* was shown. When Veronica Castro, who played Mariana, the main character, paid a visit to the Bol'shoi Theatre, she was mobbed by fans. All the standard ingredients of the genre were present: divorce, abortions, adultery, and suicides galore. Market research showed that some 43 per cent of Moscow's population watched every episode. Across the territory of the former Soviet Union viewers were estimated at some 100,000,000. (The American soap, *Santa Barbara* achieved much lower ratings; the relatively gritty Australian soaps, such as *Neighbours*, hugely popular on British television, have yet to make it to Russian TV, whose viewers watch soaps for glamour rather than for verisimilitude.)

The phenomenon of soaps and their power to disrupt lives is something that is well-established in the West. Before the market-based reforms of Soviet television, commentators on both sides of the Iron Curtain would cite the popularity of soaps as an example of Western decay. What this ignored is that Soviet viewers were never given the opportunity to watch them. Russian audiences have demonstrated the same kind of compulsive behaviour that had Western viewers transfixed by episodes of *Dallas* and *Dynasty* in the 1980s. More importantly, their addiction to *The Rich also Cry* underlines the total failure of some seventy years of Marxist-Leninist indoctrination. It marks an affirmation of shared humanity with all its absurdities, contradictions, strengths, and weaknesses over the dehumanizing effects of Soviet ideology, and of 'vulgar', tear-jerking melodrama, of the kind so popular before the Revolution and in the 1920s, and so detested by the Bolsheviks, over the dramas of socialist realism, or indeed traditional high culture.

Glasnost' and Dissolution

If television played a crucial role in undermining Soviet values, the final blow to the Soviet system's ability to insulate itself from Western influences was struck in the 1970s and 1980s with the rapid spread of information technology (IT). IT permeated and revolutionized every facet of Western society from videos to combat aircraft. Furthermore, the order of magnitude of change brought about by the information revolution was (and is) continually expanding.

IT deployed two potent weapons against the Soviet media structure: speed and volume. Speed exposed the weakness of a media policy whose day-to-day operational running relied too much on planning and secrecy. Where a plan exists, the need for individual initiative is minimal. In the electronic environment the flexibility with which a media system reacts to the unexpected, especially to bad news, becomes an important criterion for assessing its effectiveness. Secrecy imposes additional layers of control, which, in turn, impede flexibility. Where rival systems operate with the same disadvantages then the margin of effectiveness between the two is reduced. In the absence of any compensatory limitation, however, the side that cannot react as quickly, or as flexibly, as its opponent is severely disadvantaged. The Soviet débâcle in reporting the Chernobyl' disaster is a textbook example of such failure. Joined with the huge increase in the volume of news, which IT makes possible, the effect of speed was overwhelming. Unable to cope, Soviet delivery systems, domestic and international (TASS and APN), lost the initiative and found themselves on the defensive. The ability of the new electronic media to seep through just about any barrier, and, no less important, their ability to impose a new *modus operandi* on the dissemination of news, meant that the Soviet Union had, whether the Party liked it or not, been drawn into a global media structure, in which the West was setting the agenda. This situation marks the prelude to the Gorbachev reforms and the policy of *glasnost'*.

Through *glasnost'* Gorbachev confronted the fact that the Party's monopoly of the media had been gravely weakened, hoping in some way to be able to limit the damage, or even, as he believed initially, to manipulate the new environment with the aim of preserving the Party's unique position. It is difficult to say precisely at what stage Gorbachev lost control of this situation. Certainly, the Chernobyl' fiasco and its aftermath seem to be an obvious, if involuntary, Rubicon. In any case, the increasingly open reporting of Soviet history and current events from 1987 made it impossible to preserve the myth of smooth progress to an ever-brighter future, negate the reality of dissent, or maintain the fiction that the Soviet population lived a peculiarly privileged existence. Instead, catastrophe after catastrophe, official misdeed after official misdeed, were ruthlessly exposed. Where Khrushchev's denunciation of Stalin had reached tens of thousands, television programmes such as Aleksandr Nevzorov's sensational *600 Seconds* (*600 sekund*) confronted millions with abuses of authority and modes of living formerly suppressed by the authorities. Moreover, news coverage gave increasing emphasis to dissent in the various republics, and to its brutal, and highly unpopular, suppression by the authorities in some places (in January 1991, Nevzorov's energetic support for Gorbachev's attempt to put down the independence movement in Lithuania led to a slump in the authority of his programme). Instead of passively endorsing, or actively ignoring, what was broadcast, people became passionately involved, fiercely debating the issues raised before their eyes. As the organizers of the August 1991 coup found to their cost, it was no longer possible to restore Soviet-style media manipulation. The official announcements on television and in *Pravda* were almost immediately contested by unofficial media sources, from pirate radio stations to handbills to leaflets, and also in many newspapers, notably *Izvestiia* and local newspapers. Even the representations on official television rapidly expressed a growing hostility to the perpetrators of the coup, which was made clear in the subtleties of filming and interviewing technique.[48]

The very fact that *glasnost'* became official policy was, despite Gorbachev's assurances to the contrary, a public retreat from Leninist principles, the painful and humiliating recognition that the Soviet experiment was beyond redemption; the admission of the policy also contributed substantially to the collapse of Party control. Since Yeltsin took power, the media have continued to act as social critics and fora for debate, a role sometimes challenged, but not yet seriously assaulted, by an increasingly conservative President who querulously, and at times far from ineffectually, asserts his need for their support.

48 See V. E. Bonnell and G. Freidin, 'The Role of Television Coverage during Russia's 1991 Coup', in N. Condee (ed.), *Soviet Hieroglyphics: Visual Culture in Late Twentieth-Century Russia* (Bloomington, Ind., 1995), 22–51.

11

Creating a Consumer: Advertising and Commercialization

CATRIONA KELLY

The Rebirth of Advertising

Following the dissolution of the Soviet Union, advertising, like eroticism, has arrived explosively on the Russian scene, and, like explicit coverage of sex, seems to some an assault on cherished assumptions about the nature of Russian culture, and particularly about the elevated, didactic character that all the arts, but especially print culture, are expected to have. As the director of one successful advertising agency, Roman Frolov, put it recently: '[Russian] people shouldn't trust advertising as much as they tend to at the moment.'[1] Though the idea of reading between the lines of a text, or indeed rejecting it altogether as false, was perfectly familiar to Russian audiences in Soviet days, the process of adopting a new, self-conscious attitude to advertisements is slow and painful. They are seen as a Western product; since many Russians idealize Western culture, they find it hard to associate the 'crude' and 'aggressive' *reklama* now being foisted on them with the perceived sophistication of Western culture (though in fact many of the Western-made advertisements used in Russia are exactly the same as those used for Western audiences). At the same time, anger is inspired by Western advertisements that fail to register the specificities of Russian culture—ubiquitous advertising of pet-food far beyond the means of most households (the slogan 'vasha kiska kupila by Viskas'—'your cat would buy Whiskas'—invites the riposte that the cat is the only member of the household who could be naïve enough to waste money on that stuff), or publicity for a combined *shampun'-koditsioner* whose authors had failed to realize that the

1 'Vashe blagorodie, gosphozha reklama . . .', Ogonek, 27/28 (1994), 25.

Russian for 'conditioner' is in fact *bal'zam*, so that what they were actually advertising was shampoo with a built-in air conditioner. All this combines to mean that, according to a survey of 1994, the primary emotion inspired in 73 per cent of Russians by advertising is irritation.[2]

Confusion and alienation are perfectly understandable reactions, given that one of the aspects of Soviet culture that struck Western visitors to the country most forcefully was the extremely circumscribed part played there by advertising. From the end of NEP in 1928 until the beginning of the privatization campaign in the late 1980s, the absence of hard-sell commercial art was an indication of how consumer demand was constructed in the centralized economy, of the fact that, in this consensual culture, aspirations and desires might only be invoked in a safely educational context. As Ellen Mickiewicz rightly observed in her 1988 study of Soviet television, *Split Signals*, advertising was 'used not for the creation of needs, but rather to supplement policy (for example, touting fruit juices as part of the campaign to limit alcohol consumption) and steer patterns of buying in order to compensate for snags in the distribution system'.[3] Or, as stated by a 1941 article from the *Great Soviet Encyclopedia*:

In the conditions of socialist society, advertising is fundamentally different in content and form from that found in capitalist countries. The task of advertising in the USSR, given centralized planning of the economy and the extinction of capitalist competition, consists in the broad dissemination of information about new products and goods, new types of services, and the correct hygienic and aesthetic exploitation of all the many benefits which are made available to the labouring people of the USSR, in order that their material circumstances may be still further improved.[4]

In other words, advertising either followed the time-honoured traditions of *agitprop*—though usually adopting far more conservative imagery than would have been current in the 1920s—or alerted customers to new Soviet wonder products that had just come on to the market, and to the virtues of established ones (especially *dostatochnye tovary*, goods not in short supply, or *firmennye tovary*, 'branded goods', i.e. goods made and/or sold by the élite state companies that were often the descendants of former private ones). Whether they were Cold War caricatures directed at the imperialist aspirations of Western countries, exhortations to adopt hygienic habits, celebrations of the post-war Soviet answer to the Volkswagen, the Pobeda (Victory) sedan, or of Soviet ice-cream, the artistic aspirations of advertisements were generally modest (though some were remarkably striking given the constraints), and production values were low. Exceptions to these generalizations were items of peace propaganda mainly produced for export (such as the ubiquitous poster reproduction of Picasso's *Dove of*

2 Ibid. 24–5.
3 E. Mickiewicz, *Split Signals: Television and Politics in the Soviet Union* (New York, 1988), 29.
4 *Bolshaia sovetskaia entsiklopediia*, 1st edn., xlviii (1941), 557–8, headword *reklama torgovaia*.

9 'A Bravo a Day Helps You Work, Rest and Play'. Advertisement hoarding, St Petersburg, 1997.

In the mid-1990s, Russian advertising began to be 'naturalized', with home-produced advertisements running alongside translations of Western copy. The poster reproduced here, for a brand of ready-mixed cocktails in cans, advertises a product unknown in Russia before the collapse of the Soviet Union with a humorous reference to one of the sacred texts of Soviet culture. The slogan used, 'Grazhdane Rossii imeiut Bravo na otdykh i Bravo na trud', translates literally as 'The citizens of Russia have Bravo for rest and Bravo for work'. It puns, however, on a line from 'Song of the Motherland', a hit from Aleksandrov's 1936 film *The Circus*: 'Chelovek vsegda imeet pravo | Na uchebu, otdykh, i na trud' ('A person always has the right to study, to rest, and to work'). Though the production values of advertising remain relatively low, by comparison with those of the West (photomontage is rough-and-ready, and colour printing not always of a high standard), the use of word-play and in-jokes is now common: other examples from the late 1990s include a poster designed for trains operating services to resort areas around St Petersburg, and advertising an instant breakfast cereal with the slogan, 'Udachnyi vybor' ('A good choice', but also, 'A choice for the dacha').

Peace on relatively high-quality shiny paper), and posters advertising exhibitions, which were often produced with considerable imaginative creativity. Street posters for blockbuster movies (*kassovye fil'my*) conformed more to the dictates of folk art than of high art, but their lurid composition and colouring certainly made them eye-catching and noticeable. In fact, from the early 1960s, the Soviet regime had made some efforts to encourage advertising for consumer goods, as part of Khrushchev's targeting of 'rational consumption norms', supposed to ensure parity with the West by 1980. These efforts were co-ordinated through a variety of institutions subordinated to the Mezhduvedomstvennyi sovet po reklame (Inter-Authority Council on Advertising), but brochures, shop-window display, catalogues and posters, newspaper announcements, television and radio voice-overs were still the main methods, and strategies were generally unsophisticated (a food product would almost uniformly be described as *vkusno i polezno*, tasty and nutritious).[5] Standards in the unofficial economy were still more modest: advertisements for flat exchanges or the sale of second-hand goods consisted of no more than a scrawled description of the item concerned on a small piece of paper, sometimes with a fringe of tear-off telephone numbers round the outside.

At the end of the 1980s, however, with the coming of private enterprise, there was an explosion of advertising in every form, from magazine advertisements and small-ad freesheets pushed into the letter-boxes of apartment blocks to radio and television advertisements and vast roadside billboards. The old public-service tradition has not vanished entirely, however. In late 1994, for example, *Ogonek*, whose back cover had since 1990 always carried a full-page advertisement of one kind or another (in the early days usually inviting subscriptions to the magazine, now almost invariably for some commercial organization), devoted a spread to an international contest for AIDS propaganda video shorts. In the centre was a striking (if rather puzzling) photograph of a man and a woman's hands handcuffed together with a condom as padlock, but about half the page was taken up with practical details of the contest. But such advertisements have now been pushed to one side by a host of material that has no educational purpose, and which, unlike old-style Soviet advertising, does aim at precisely the 'creation of needs'. Many images are borrowed from the West, sometimes in a manner that seems (even if one is not a Russian nationalist) tactlessly obvious—for instance, a 1993 television commercial for cigarettes that used the *American* space programme in order to suggest the glamour and excitement of the brand. Indeed, the unadapted appropriation of Western material seems to be the norm in cigarette advertising (one reason, perhaps, why Boris Yeltsin

5 For an excellent discussion of post-Stalin advertising and its economic context, see P. Hansen, *Advertising and Socialism: The Nature and Extent of Consumer Advertising in the Soviet Union, Poland, Hungary and Yugoslavia* (London, 1974), 1–74. A close reading of one of its products is given in A. Zholkovsky, '19 oktjabrja 1982 g., or the Semiotics of a Soviet Cookie Wrapper', *Wiener Slawistischer Almanach*, 11 (1983), 341–54.

decreed in 1996 that this be banned from Russian television). This is also the case with the advertising of other products, such as branded foods, perfumes, and consumer hardware, where Western-made items have higher reputations for quality of manufacture or for reliability. However, there is now a fair amount of home-produced advertising, much of which displays a sturdy and refreshing independence in its choice of material, and which is an interesting reflection, in various ways, of the state of Russian commercial culture.

Unlike Soviet *agitprop* and product information, where centralized control ensured a high degree of stability in the imagery employed, so that it was often hard to spot the difference between shop-signs, packaging, and posters produced in the 1940s and those produced in the early 1980s, post-Soviet advertising now seems bewilderingly varied, at least at first sight. The impression of confusion partly comes from the fact that niche marketing does not yet seem particularly well-developed. So, for example, a general news magazine such as *Ogonek* may carry advertisements for specialized medical equipment (kidney dialysis machines manufactured by the German company Fresenius were advertised several times in 1993–4), or, more startlingly, a medley on peak-time television in 1994 included, between advertisements for biscuits, banks, and cigarettes, footage of tanks, aeroplanes, and heavy artillery which turned out to be advertising, not after-shave or some other such product needing a macho image, but the weapons themselves—it ended with the telephone number which you needed to ring in order to buy an armoured car or medium-range missile. Though advertisers, as in the West, do prefer peak-time slots (there is little advertising mid-afternoon), there does not seem to be, as yet, much sense of keying product to 'under-24s', 'over-60s', or any other such demographic category. (However, Roman Frolov does advocate niche marketing,[6] and occasional signs of it are evident already: for example, *Kommersant (Businessman)* magazine has a predominance of office equipment advertisements, alongside luxury goods, etc.)

It is fair to say that, compared with Western countries, and perhaps especially Britain, where advertising sometimes seems to absorb all the country's creative talents, Russian advertisement designers and commercial directors aim their sights relatively low. One finds very little of the self-referentiality of Western advertising (one advertisement used to parody another, for instance); informativeness is much more highly valued than free flights of creative fantasy. However, there is some evidence that even Western audiences, with their constant exposure to the medium, find the more pretentious advertisements baffling, or at the very least find it hard to remember which products to associate the more striking images with, so that some

6 See 'Vashe blagorodie'.

advertising agents now feel that emphasis on zanily memorable images has gone too far.[7] If Russian street billboards tend to be slogan-dependent, as Svetlana Boym has recently argued,[8] so, too, do many of the most successful advertisements and commercials in the West (if by 'successful' one means mnemonic in terms of the product's name). And, as Boym has also pointed out, Russian advertisements also have their own forms of esotericism. The 'products' of the financial services industry (which take up most advertising space—not surprisingly, given that banking is perhaps the only major growth industry in Russia today) are often presented with an emotive allusiveness that is much more like the packaging of perfume or cigarettes than the sober functionalism of their Western equivalents (whose standard motif of the friendly bank official—'capitalism with a human face'—works in order to play down mystique). Though savings companies may advertise fantastic and unsustainable interest rates on the Metro, those graduating to the media give no such practical information, concentrating not on the benefits, but on the glamour that is promised by accounts held with them.

Furthermore, Russian advertisements themselves display a fairly wide range of sophistication, with the small ads in local freesheets at one end and television commercials, especially those for banks and financial services at the other. There has also been a shift, during the last few years, from description of a product pure and simple (the newspaper advertisement with photograph and specifications, the television shot with voice-over) to the use of eye-catching techniques. In print advertising, slogans are often effective and memorable (e.g. a 1993 advertisement in *Ogonek* which screeched 'Our carpets can cope with any pets', featuring a photograph of two tigers lying on one of them, or a 1994 spread devoted to the Stolichnyi Bank credit card, with the admonition 'Cash is old-fashioned; pay more elegantly with the STB-card', and a glossy image of the card lying amongst various luxury items for women—a designer handbag, lipstick, perfume bottle, etc). Standards of photography, layout, and graphics have also risen over the last few years. Likewise, television advertisements now more frequently employ such techniques as computer graphics and animation, or use little dramatized scenes in order to introduce some product or service. Part of the huge initial success of the MMM savings bank, which went spectacularly bankrupt in 1994, was attributable to its enormously popular television advertisements, the central figure of which, a drunken layabout by the name of Lenia Golubkov, became a folk hero with Russian television audiences.[9]

A particularly striking feature in many recent advertisements, especially but not only television commercials, has been their use of

7 See e.g. T. Brignull, 'The Me is the Message', *Guardian*, 29 May 1995, and D. Sudjic, 'Selling Art and the Art of Selling', *Guardian*, 7 July 1995.
8 See S. Boym, *Common Places: Mythologies of Everyday Life in Russia* (Cambridge, Mass., 1994), 271–82.
9 See V. Permiakov and A. Pylaev, *Kak ia stal Lenei Golubkovym* (Moscow, 1994), and V. Dubitskaia's interview with the commercials' director Bakhyt Kilibaev in *Iskusstvo kino*, 1 (1995), 13–19.

knowing and often ironical references to Russian history. One could even speak of a sort of post-Soviet 'retro-chic' in advertisements such as that for Red October chocolate (*Ogonek*, 17 (1993)), 'a tried and tested brand', in which advertisements from 1923 and 1953 were used as insets; or for a savings bank on television in 1994, where the figures of two traditional Russian merchants (bearded, with long hair) were seated at a table whose elaborate turn-of-the-century banquet dishes were transformed by computer graphics into images of the property investments (factories, apartment blocks) in which the company specialized. As these two examples suggest, the commercial culture of the early twentieth century and the imagery of the Stalinist period are equally attractive to advertisers, and both are always employed tongue-in-cheek (this was particularly clear in an advertisement for Radost' fur hats, in which much play was made of the very Soviet-looking label, and where a slick young man in an elegant Western suit (but no hat) implausibly assured viewers 'I've got two myself'). This technique, known in marketing jargon as 'refreshing brand values', is currently fashionable in the West as well; clearly, it is particularly effective in a society where so many quality Soviet goods, from yoghurt to chocolate, are now challenged by often inferior foreign competitors.

Unfortunately, the humorous side to advertising is not always so obvious; very often, too, the serious assumptions behind the images are disturbing or even distasteful. To an even greater extent than in the West, the key selling point is a pretty girl in fashionable and sometimes revealing clothes (rather like the bikini-clad motor-show models of the 1970s), or a prosperous nuclear family in which Mama is busy in the kitchen while Papa sits at the table with his offspring or inducts his children in the new technology. There is a quite casual use of violence in order to sell some goods (for instance, a Rambo-style muscleman complete with pump-action shot-gun appeared in a 1994 television advertisement—selling, of all things, contact lenses). But perhaps the most worrying tendency is the advertisement in veiled form. Ball-point pens, ashtrays, and keyrings with company logos are innocent enough, but commercial sponsorship of children's pro-grammes has led to some invidious types of subliminal advertising: a programme about Lego plastic bricks showing children playing with top-of-the-range models expensive even by Western standards, or a quiz for little girls in which the camera dwells lingeringly on the prizes, all supplied by the toy company that sponsored the pro-gramme, in their branded boxes.[10] On the other hand, there is no doubt that the prevalence of advertising in Russia is still relatively restricted (if one compares the country with, for instance, the United

10 On packaging as advertising, see also N. Condee and V. Padunov, 'The ABC of Russian Culture: Readings, Ratings and Real Estate', in Condee (ed.), *Soviet Hieroglyphics: Visual Culture in Late Twentieth-Century Russia* (Bloomington, Ind., 1995), 130–72.

States). Television films are not yet interrupted for advertising slots; magazines (with a few exceptions, such as the American-controlled women's magazine *Cosmopolitan*, an extremely highly priced glossy aimed at a readership who can afford $200 for a pair of shoes) carry little advertising; hoardings and neon lights are massed in certain parts of the big cities (such as the road in from the airport and Okhotnyi Riad in Moscow) but entirely absent from others. It remains to be seen whether advertising will really take off in Russia as it has, over the last thirty years, in the West, or whether the long history of hostility to commercialism will mean that commercials and print advertising alike will continue to occupy a niche that, while larger than that allowed to them under Soviet culture, is still not particularly expansive.

The latter prediction may seem to carry more weight, given that there have recently been suggestions that advertising should be censored; not only misleading or mendacious statements would be banned, but also material 'not conforming to accepted standards of morality'.[11] Again, as with the debates around erotica, there is widespread support for regulation of 'mass arts' among those who would protest against the censorship of 'élite' art forms. Advertising, too, has still to make an impact on other genres of communication. No Russian director, for example, has yet followed Luc Besson and shot his or her films in advertisement-style. It is clear that advertising will continue to be disseminated in Russia for the foreseeable future (proposals to ban it from television are naïve, since commercial sponsorship, in one form or another, is essential to the medium's survival). But it is much harder to predict what developments the future holds, and in particular whether commercial art will become a major source of inspiration (if only through irritation) to the producers of high culture, as it was in the early twentieth century.

Leaks in the System: Commercialism in High Culture before 1991

It would be misleading to suggest that the creeping commercialization of Soviet popular culture which took place in the post-Stalin years, long before the advent of Western-style advertising, made no impact at all on high culture. Indeed, although the Writers' Union continued to issue calls distantly echoing the strident commands of the cultural revolution by exhorting its members to pay study visits to factories and to orient their work to the tastes of working people, the production novel as such went into an apparently terminal decline after 1953. Evident throughout Soviet culture was an elevation of

11 'Vashe blagorodie', 24. Information on the costs of advertising is hard to come by, partly because of spiralling inflation, and partly because of the leeway for negotiation, rake-offs etc.

10 'The friendship of nations': front cover of *Ogonek* magazine, 1957.

This image of Indian, Chinese, and Russian girls embracing was published to celebrate the Festival of Youth held in Moscow, September 1957. Though the image now seems sentimental and patronizing, both it and the festival represented a watershed in East–West relations, as the threat of real war was replaced by propaganda conflict, and direct confrontation by uneasy and cantankerous coexistence. The Festival of Youth has survived in oral history as a key experience of the Khrushchev thaw; among other things, it was marked by a large exhibition of work by young foreign painters that was rapturously received by Soviet artists starved of contact with artists outside the Soviet bloc for more than twenty years.

the formerly despised topic of *byt*—daily life, domesticity—which was dissected in many works of all kinds, particularly from the early 1960s. One direction was exemplified in the resurgence of an explicitly feminine, if not feminist, approach in the journalism and fiction of women writers. As perhaps the most disagreeable boulder making up the Sisyphean 'double burden', shopping was widely represented; Russian women produced some stark depictions of the procedures for, and effects of, negotiating with the 'market'. Natal'ia Baranskaia's *A Week Like Any Other* (*Nedelia kak nedelia*, 1969), and stories by Maia Ganina and Irina Grekova, and more recently Viktoriia Tokareva, Nina Katerli, and Liudmila Petrushevskaia, all showed women struggling to squeeze shopping into full working days, and to cope with shortages and queues. Tat'iana Tolstaia's 'The Circle' ('Krug', 1987) was a quirky variation on the 'woman as commodity' notion, showing a man who acquires new sexual partners by using the seven-figure inventory numbers on sheets fresh back from the laundry in order to organize his own personal telephone-dating service. Women poets, too, have sometimes (though less often, given the metaphysical bent of most recent Russian poetry) given space to such themes: in the striking opening of 'Reflection in the Mirror Opposite' (1983), Iunna Morits speaks of 'heaving on my hunched back | many things: sacks of potatoes, logs and bundles, | children, cripples and water-pipes.' (The rest of the poem rather conventionally juxtaposes this image to the 'unbending' nature of the poet's inner self, but the strength of the opening lines stands.)[12]

Such representations have been widely discussed recently in the context of the growing interest, among Western feminist critics, in Russian women's writing, particularly of the last three decades. A rather less well-known development of the 1970s and 1980s, though, is the appearance of the first Soviet 'shopping novel', Il'ia Shtemler's *Department Store* (*Univermag*, 1983). Western readers should not be misled into imagining anything like Judith Krantz's bedroom-and-boutique saga *Scruples*. Disappointingly, *Department Store* is an extremely dreary chronicle of life in a big Moscow shop from the inside out, a sort of factory novel translated to the retail sector, in which honest Soviet souls struggle to assert their morality in the face of self-serving colleagues, and indeed customers. That said, however, the narrative is not unconcerned with the new consumer ethic of the 1970s. In one scene, the poor quality of a new batch of footwear is extensively discussed,[13] and the activities of 'speculators' (i.e. black-market dealers trading in scarce goods) form quite a busy sub-plot. And whatever its interest to the Western reader, *Department Store* enjoyed quite a high degree of popularity in Russia: it created

12 Iu. Morits, 'I otrazilos' v zerkale naprotiv', in *Na etom berege vysokom* (Moscow, 1987), 50.
13 I. Shtemler, *Zavod: Roman. Univermag: Roman* (Moscow, 1988), 345–6; the novel paired with *Department Store* is in fact that very rare bird, a recent factory novel.

something of a stir when first published in *Novyi mir*, while the edition of 1988 had a print-run of 100,000 copies.[14] If 'commercial' literature in the last years of the Soviet Union did not always have 'commercial' themes, there were occasions when the two kinds of commercialism came into some kind of conjunction.

Another commercial, in the sense of popular, and officially well-favoured, way of addressing the increasing commercialism of Soviet society was what one might (by analogy with Catherine the Great's Russia) describe as Soviet 'court satires': prose, drama, and verse pouring scorn on the developing Soviet bourgeoisie. Soviet novels of the 1940s, as Vera Dunham demonstrated in her classic study *In Stalin's Time* (1976), treated aspirations to acquire material goods, provided these were seen as the props of *kul'turnost'*, with approbation, though in reality the goods described were often unavailable. In the 1960s, 1970s, and 1980s, by contrast, material goods could be obtained much more easily, even if they were *defitsitnye*, but the disintegration of universal measures of sufficiency led to anxiety about how much one could own and still be considered *kul'turnyi* (or *intelligentnyi*, the new catch-word). The ambiguity of official attitudes to consumerism —seen as a necessary, but hardly commendable, and indeed dangerous, phenomenon—was dutifully reflected in the 1970s work of Evgenii Evtushenko, whose poetry both made clear the increasing well-being that Soviet citizens could now expect, and cautioned against over-indulgence in this:

> Все на счетах высчитывая,
> нас,
>   как деток больших,
> покупает вещичками
> компромисс-вербовщик.
> Покупает квартирами,
> мебелишкой,
>   тряпьем,
> и уже не задиры мы
> а шумим—если пьем.
> Что-то—
>   вслушайтесь!—
>   щелкает
> в холодильнике «ЗИЛ».
> Компромисс краснощекенький
> зубки в семгу вонзил.
>
> [Doing his sums on the abacus
> Kompromiss buys us
>   like kids,

14 On publication, see K. Mehnert, *The Russians and Their Favorite Books* (Cambridge, Mass., 1983), 11; for print-run see Moscow 1988 edn.

offering glittering baubles
that we can't seem to resist.
He buys us with nice new apartments,
with furniture,
   or with clothes:
we don't fight him, or keep apart from him
but remember him in our toasts.
Listen,
   you hear something clonking
   inside
the new Zil fridge?
It's rosy-cheeked Kompromiss gnawing
on juicy smoked-salmon bits.][15]

Despite his use of the universal 'we', Evtushenko manages to suggest that he has escaped the clutches of Kompromiss Kompromissovich, if only by avoiding the invitation to muffle his social criticism that this devilish male muse has made at the beginning of the poem (' "Go on, why be capricious? | Just tinker a bit with that line." '). For the oppositional intelligentsia, on the other hand, Evtushenko's work was unpalatable precisely because of the 'compromised' position of the poet himself, whose Peredelkino dacha boasted far less accessible luxuries than a Zil fridge, just as his 'clothes' ran more to German linen shirts than Soviet nylon ones. More important, though, given Russian literature's long tradition of demarcating, as with Catholic priests, office and person, so that it is seen as perfectly acceptable for writers to sermonize on vices they themselves are known to have, was the wretched inadequacy of Evtushenko's stylistic resources, here and in other of his 'court satires'. Adopting Maiakovskii's *lesenka* (ladder) form as a mannerism, he achieved no discernible semantic or syntactic effects by it, and the Maiakovskian approximate rhymes do not conceal that the bland diction totally lacks the master's own populist gusto.

    Attempts to address Soviet commercialism by official writers, then, did not on the whole lead to much memorable work, certainly nothing above the level of the run-of-the-mill satire published in the comic weekly *Krokodil* (*Crocodile*), whose post-Stalin targets included 'shoddy goods and services'.[16] Nor were other 'commercial' efforts much more productive. Philip Hansen has recorded that in the 1970s, well-known Soviet poets were invited to write slogans for advertising milk products in the media and in film trailers, but this collaboration appears to have produced no household catchwords.[17] Painters had greater opportunities for inventiveness in some areas of the Soviet commercial arts, such as exhibition posters, but the traditions alluded

15 E. Evtushenko, *Sobranie sochinenii v 3 tomakh*, iii (Moscow, 1984), 452.
16 R. Stites, *Russian Popular Culture: Entertainment and Society since 1900* (Cambridge, 1992), 136.
17 Hansen, *Advertising and Socialism*, 55.

to here were usually non-Soviet (folklore or pre-Revolutionary art), and served to heighten the distance between *kul'tura* and *tovary shirokogo potrebleniia* (goods for mass consumption).

Given the ironies that beset Soviet consumerism itself in the Khrushchev and especially the Brezhnev days, it was perhaps inevitable that most memorable work touching on it should be produced outside the official arts establishment. One important corpus of such work originated from the Third Wave emigration, the writers and painters (some, but not all, former dissidents) who left the Soviet Union in the 1970s and early 1980s. Though many of the emigrants were, according to their Soviet passports, of Jewish 'nationality', and were given their export visas on the assumption that they would emigrate to Israel, in fact a good many of them followed their predecessors of the 1940s and made their way to the United States, which was now unquestionably the main cultural centre of the Russian diaspora. Here they found themselves in a society that had been represented by generations of their compatriots, from Maiakovskii and Il'f and Petrov in the 1920s, as the mirror-image of Soviet reality, inspiring, like any mirror-image, simultaneous horror and the uneasy sense of narcissistic affinity.

The culture shock of encounters with the New World inspired various reactions. On the one hand, *émigrés* from the Soviet Union were sometimes better prepared to deal with life at the bottom of a new society than their predecessors of the First Wave, since negotiating with the Soviet authorities required a good deal more toughness than had ever been demanded from the upper classes under tsarism. However, this was generally more likely to benefit those who had left Russia to make their fortunes—the modern Ostap Bender, say, who opened a string of non-tax-paying garages, after deciding that the American tax authorities and police offered no sort of challenge compared with the KGB. For creative artists, the shock of leading a non-subsidized and, to Russian sensibilities, ill-regulated, existence could be extremely distressing. Often, the need to negotiate with American commercial culture produced frustration, with publishers' or gallery owners' lack of interest in work that would not 'sell' seen as a form of censorship no less rigid than that practised by the Soviet system (which, of course, in a sense it was). Marilyn Rueschemeyer has recorded some comments reflecting the culture-shock among *émigré* painters:

People talk over the decorating possibilities of what they see, how it would look over their sofa—it's depressing.

For American artists, art is business. They are other men, other human beings. You have to persuade others, and be a salesman.[18]

18 M. Rueschemeyer, I. Golomshtok, and J. Kennedy, *Soviet Émigré Artists: Life and Work in the USSR and the United States* (New York, 1985), 89, 114, 116.

However, as Rueschemeyer points out, there was often a note of admiration in such assessments (the second speaker goes on, 'Still, I admire their professionalism'). And some members of the Third Wave proved a good deal more adaptable than their predecessors in organizing contacts, finding translators, and establishing reputations. Vasilii Aksenov, Sasha Sokolov, Vladimir Voinovich, above all Joseph Brodsky, soon became far more prominent than any of their predecessors in the First Wave (even Nabokov was never so ubiquitous in his punditry as Brodsky).

There were various factors behind this new prominence. Talent in itself was not in short supply in the First Wave emigration, but there was undoubtedly a greater number of talented prose-writers among the Third Wave *émigrés*, which was an obvious aid both to translation and to promotion (the poetic path to fame being a notoriously steep and rocky one in the Anglo-American world). There was also the fact that Soviet *émigrés*, unlike their predecessors, came from a culture that the West was trying to make sense of, rather than from one that had been supplanted. Rather than the material for slightly kitschy nostalgia, they could be the sources of hard information about issues the Soviet Union did not want mentioned. Hence, any proclamations by insiders, however far removed from the actual centres of power in the Soviet Union, appeared to lift the official blanket of silence, and shake the foundations of the monolith. And it should not be forgotten that Soviet *émigrés* indeed were the source of vital information on such issues as the inner workings of the KGB, the political élite, and cultural censorship.[19] The high-minded asceticism, or alternatively aestheticism, of some *émigrés* also lent them authority: if Solzhenitsyn forfeited this in most quarters by his sweeping Slavophile condemnations of Western decadence, the more judiciously ironical comments of Brodsky were received with a good deal more reverence. Finally, there was interest in the contributions these outsiders, but European outsiders, could make to Anglophone culture. If Brodsky's intellectual, highly wrought, intensely personal, and yet hieratic work appeared to continue a 'great tradition' sacrificed by postmodern trivialization of the arts, some of the most notable prose-writers offered novel prisms through which Western culture itself might be seen.

There is no doubt that the greatest works produced by a Russian reacting to American culture are Nabokov's novels *Pnin* (1957), *Pale Fire* (1962), *Ada* (1969), and especially *Lolita* (1955). These were the products of a remarkable talent who saw everything, even what he hated, with intense clarity, who had an outstandingly good reading knowledge of English, and who, after nearly twenty years of life in America, could certainly have been said to know his enemy. There is

19 See M. Dewhirst and R. Farrell (eds.), *The Soviet Censorship* (Metuchen, 1973).

nothing by any Third-Wave writer which describes rented homes, provincial colleges, bus-stations, or motels with anything like the poetic intensity of *Lolita* or *Pnin*. However, Vasilii Aksenov, who had already produced quite an interesting travelogue about American life before leaving Russia, *Round the Clock Non-Stop* (*Kruglye sutki non-stop*, 1976), followed this, in 1987, with *Looking for Melancholy Baby* (*V poiskakh grustnogo bebi*), a long essay that wittily records the state of perpetual cultural jet-lag that a European visitor to America feels during the first dizzying encounters with the life of American streets, bars, and other public places. Aksenov's standpoint of relentless defamiliarization has been adopted by other writers, such as Sergei Dovlatov, who left hilarious aphoristic accounts of his time in charge of a Russian newspaper, *The New American* (*Novyi amerikanets*), sponsored by a monoglot American determined to impose cultural control. And outside America, one of the few writers settled in Britain, Zinovii Zinik, has cast a similarly alienated eye on British culture in *The Russian Service* (*Russkaia sluzhba*, 1983), and *The Mushroom Picker* (*Lesofobka i fungofil*, 1986), both of which have been translated into English, and in the latter case, filmed for British television.

Not only American (or Western) culture was defamiliarized by the new prose-writers, though. Many took exile as an opportunity to scrutinize the Soviet milieu from which they had come from a new perspective. As Sergei Dovlatov wrote in a moving passage of *Craft* (*Remeslo*), his bipartite collection of aphorisms on life in Russia and America:

Home is us. Our first toys. Our elder brothers' darned cardigans. Sandwiches wrapped in newspaper. Little girls in brown uniform skirts. Change from our father's pocket. Exams, *shpargalki* [cribs, notes of information for cheating in exams] . . . Dreadful, absurd poems . . . Thoughts of suicide. A tumbler of Agdam [Azerbaijani wine] in an entranceway . . . A roll-up of rough tobacco in the army . . . Our little daughter, mittens, leggings, the flopped-down side of a tiny boot . . . Lines crossed through with an oblique stroke [by the censor]. Manuscripts, the militia, OVIR. Everything that happened to us is our home. And everything that happened will remain [with us] for ever.[20]

For Dovlatov, the 'home' that 'will remain for ever' consists for the most part of private experiences and possessions: poems, cardigans, sandwiches, rather than of anything explicitly linked with Soviet reality as such. Subversive genres are preferred: (unpublishable) manuscripts, the political anecdotes whose structure and lexicon have dictated the formal features of Dovlatov's own aphoristic, anecdotal style, a montage of materials from international chestnuts ('How would you like your hair done, sir?' 'In silence'), to Jewish jokes, to subversive tales of the leaders like those so widely narrated, but never

20 S. Dovlatov, *Remeslo* (Ann Arbor, 1985), 168.

published, in the Brezhnev era, to anecdotes of the lives of famous contemporaries (Brodsky says to a militiaman behind the locked grille of the night-time Metro: 'Just freeze there a minute: I've never seen a cop behind bars before!')[21] A similar sense of recovering suppressed history is clear in the work of two other *émigré* writers of broader ambitions than Dovlatov (most of whose work consisted of bitterly humorous reportage). In *Hand* (*Ruka*, 1980), *Kangaroo* (*Kenguru*, 1981), *Little Blue Scarf* (*Sinen'kii skromnyi platochek*, 1982), and *The Carousel* (*Karusel'*, 1983), Iuz Aleshkovskii uses fictionalized oral history, anecdote, and the powerful effects of 'unprintable' gutter language to produce a carnival assault on the bland, heroic history created by the Soviet regime. The novels and stories of Sasha Sokolov include pseudo-autobiographical mythologized Kremlinology (in *Palisandriia*, 1985), as well as tales of those permanently marginalized by Soviet society (*A School for Fools* (*Shkola dlia durakov*, 1976), *Between the Dog and the Wolf* (*Mezhdu sobakoi i volkom*, 1980)). Though published after the emigration of the two writers (in 1979 and 1975 respectively), many of the texts were composed before Aleshkovskii and Sokolov had left, thus exemplifying another persistent factor in the Third Wave emigration: the cross-fertilization between work published in *samizdat* (underground) and *tamizdat* (abroad). There is, as yet, nothing of comparable quality by an *émigré* woman writer, or to match the Czech writer Zdena Tomin's *Stalin's Shoe*, but the novels of Alla Ktorova (pseudonym of Viktoriia Sandor) are interesting impressionistic montages of life before and after emigration.

There were obvious attractions for *émigré* writers in rewriting Soviet history from the bottom up, using *petit-bourgeois* folklore where possible. It would have been much more difficult for a Soviet *émigré*, or indeed unofficial writer, at least until the system collapsed and began to seem the stuff of safe nostalgia, to write a hymn to official Soviet literature or to parody the production novel, let alone to eulogize the kind of goods available at souvenir shops or kiosks, those gardens of Soviet kitsch in its fullest flower: Palekh enamel boxes, woollen shawls with lime-green, shocking-pink, and scarlet roses, cretinously smirking Olympic bears, plaster busts of Lenin or Pushkin, electrified, foot-tall models of the Ostankino television tower with flashing lights at the top, or miniature silver samovars.[22] As in the days before the Revolution, it has been the visual arts that have absorbed 'vulgar' material more easily. A tolerant, postmodern approach has been all the more likely here, given the history of assimilating borderline arts, such as sign-painting. And in fact such borderline arts have continued to be a major inspiration to all artists, not just poster-designers. In the 1960s and 1970s, the veteran painter

21 These examples are all taken from S. Dovlatov, *Zapisnye knizhki* (Moscow, 1990).
22 So far, this side of Soviet life has only come near to being accommodated in a piece of cultural criticism by a Russian-American, Svetlana Boym: see *Common Places*, chs. 1 and 2.

11 A selection of Soviet *suveniry*.

In the post-Stalin era, mass tourism became a major Soviet industry, with not only established resorts, such as those on the Black Sea and Baltic, but many 'backward' areas of Central Asia and the Caucasus opened up for activity holidays and sightseeing. Hotels, hostels (*turbazy*), and restaurants were constructed to serve visitors, who were also encouraged, like tourists everywhere, to commemorate their journeys by sending postcards and buying mementos. The quality of the latter varied widely, from mass-produced plastic ephemera to attractive replicas of traditional craft goods—ceramics, textiles, lacquer, woodcarvings, and metalwork. The items illustrated here include Gzhel china (a pre-Revolutionary industry revived in the 1940s), Georgian and Uzbek ceramics, Khokhloma and Palekh lacquer-work, and a South Russian painted tray. Goods like these were available not only in resorts, but also in special shops in the bigger Soviet towns; some better-off Soviet citizens, such as Moscow and Leningrad intellectuals, put together personal collections of certain items, e.g. Gzhel, Palekh boxes, and Eastern rugs.

Aleksandr Tyshler (1898–1980) produced a series of obsessive, haunting paintings in which female figures are combined with fairground theatres, peep-show boxes, and other artefacts from the suppressed commercial past; primitivist painting has resurfaced in the work of such painters as Elena Figurina (b. 1955) and the print-maker Valentin Gerasimenko, whose work includes a series of modern *lubki* fitting traditional texts to modern scenes.[23]

Before the collapse of the Soviet Union, and with it the never-suspended, though increasingly unimportant, ethic of socialist realism, adventurous work that could be legitimized as *narodnoe* (popular, reflecting national tradition) had a considerably greater chance of being exhibited publicly than abstract art, whose fate had been sealed, for the meantime, by Khrushchev's infamous outburst in 1962 labelling all modern painting *govno* ('shit') (see above in the discussion of cinema). (Unofficial avant-garde exhibitions were in fact held after 1962 on numerous occasions, and though these were sometimes closed down by the police, after 1976 the Moscow Municipal Committee of Graphic Artists came to a partial accommodation, according to which non-socialist-realist exhibitions recognized by its Painting Section could be held if they were not publicized. However, those who stepped outside the boundaries of the Committee's tolerance were subject to harassment, and many prominent figures were forced to emigrate. It was only with *glasnost'*, therefore, that avant-garde art could come out from the underground again.)[24] In any case, intelligent use of popular material was often a productive form of working, given the peculiar history of the Soviet Union, where modernist approaches, for instance abstraction, flourished to an extraordinary degree before 1930, only to vanish into obscurity for more than three decades. Cut off from its own past, and from direct contact with the West (the state did not sponsor exhibitions of recent Western avant-garde art, and serious discussions of it were impossible in official journals), relying on reproductions in journals and books to get an idea of avant-garde directions, Russian avant-garde painters ran a strong risk of, so to speak, reinventing the easel. And indeed, to the Western observers who controlled the international art markets, Soviet unofficial art of the 1960s and 1970s did usually seem at once derivative and naïve. While work by Rodchenko, Lissitzky, and especially Malevich began to fetch huge sums, few living abstract artists from Russia were able to make any kind of an impression, with rare, though significant, exceptions such as the sculptor Ernst Neizvestnyi (b. 1925) and the painter Dmitrii Plavinskii (b. 1937).[25]

In contrast, quite a lot of Western interest was aroused by the parody socialist-realist works of (Vitalii) Komar and (Aleksandr)

23 See E. Figurina: *Zhivopis'. Valentin Gerasimenko: Grafika*, ed. T. E. Shekhter (Moscow, 1990).
24 See Rueschemeyer, Golomshtok, and Kennedy, *Soviet Émigré Artists*, 48–9.
25 On Neizvestnyi see J. Berger, *Art and Revolution: Ernst Neizvestny and the Role of the Artist in the USSR* (London, 1969), and E. Neizvestnyi, *Space, Time and Synthesis in Art* (Oakville, 1990).

Melamid, a two-artist team whose portmanteau name was itself a parody of such socialist-realist art-by-committee teams as the Kukryniksy. Sometimes so close to the original in theme as to be scarcely detectable as parody (as in 'Stalin and the Muse of Socialist Realism'), their work more often broadens into the seaside-postcard humour of a Young Pioneer masturbating in front of a mirror, or Stalin posed with a dinosaur in uniform, with Hitler surreptitiously tip-toeing into the background.[26] Rather less broadly humorous, though alluding to a more vulgarly gaudy era of Soviet mass art, is the work of Erik Bulatov (b. 1933), whose massive canvas *Have a Nice Stay* (*Dobro pozhalovat'*) is a photo-realist representation of the Golden Fountain at the Exhibition of Economic Achievements (VDNKh), with a headscarfed 'real' *kolkhoznitsa* at one side to complement the golden statues of idealized peasants on the fountain itself.[27] The effect is uncannily close to an Intourist poster of the 1970s, right down to the exaggerated azure of the sky, like a postcard shot through too much blue filter. Like pop-artists in the West, Bulatov, Komar and Melamid, and others use mass-produced imagery less in order to create a new form of art than to create a new form of popular culture, which, like its predecessor of pre-Revolutionary days, pre-empts the possibility of ironization by being knowingly parodistic itself.

Closer to the 'home within' credo exposed by Dovlatov, though, is the work of installation artist Il'ia Kabakov.[28] (The observations here and below are not intended to suggest that installation art and parodies of commercial culture are the only, or even necessarily the most important, directions in the visual arts since 1953. Equally significant have been the production of religious or spiritual works, performance art, various forms of conceptualism such as 'found sculpture', etc., and postmodern revivalism, such as the idealized still-lifes of the St Petersburg Group (Iurii Ivachenko, Sergei Arkhipov, Valera Esaulenko, and Iusup Khanmukhamedov).)[29] Some women artists have been doing interesting work along these lines too, for example Larisa Zvezdochetova, who manufactures collages from mass-produced 'souvenirs', such as presentation rugs, juxtaposing 'domestic' items, such as panels of rose-embroidery, with glorious commemorative symbols from public life, such as sports medals. The 'Peppers' (another ironic portmanteau name masking the male-female team Mila Skripkina and Oleg Petrenko) have made installations to highlight issues of reproductive politics. Lidiia Masterkova combined iconic subjects with cloth and lace textures in her 1970s work; more recently, textile artists such as Tat'iana Ivanitskaia, Mariia Romanova, and Ol'ga Florenskaia have been using traditional techniques, such as patchwork and appliqué; Romanova's work, with its

26 See Komar and Melamid, *Fruitmarket Gallery* (Edinburgh, 1985).

27 See D. Elliott and V. Dudakov (eds.), *100 Years of Russian Art from Private Collections in the USSR* (London, 1989), 146–7.

28 *Ilya Kabakov: Ten Characters* (ICA, London, 1989); *Ilya Kabakov: am Rande* (Kunsthalle, Berne, 1985); and *Dislocations* (Museum of Modern Art, New York, 1991).

29 On the St Petersburg Group, see *Time Present and Time Past: An Exhibition of Contemporary Russian Still-Life Watercolours* (Colnaghi Gallery, London, 1995).

strange, ungainly representations of childhood bogeys and figments of nightmare working against the soft, cosy effects of her patchwork, is the most interesting of the three. Similarly unsettling use of apparently comfortable and safe material—childhood reminiscences, favourite pastimes—is also made in the films of Kira Muratova, where scenes of a character playing *estrada* tunes at home on her trombone are cut into a stream-of-consciousness narrative that makes no distinction, in value terms, between these scenes and those in which random violence against people and animals erupts.[30]

Yet for all the considerable contributions by *émigrés* on the one hand, and pictorial artists on the other, to reviving a fruitful dialogue between art and commerce, perhaps the most impressive commemorations of Soviet commercial culture are literary works by writers who never left the Soviet Union. Boris Vakhtin's *The Sheepskin Coat* (*Dublenka*, 1979), was a witty and touching reworking of Gogol's *The Overcoat* (*Shinel'*) portraying the quest of a minor Soviet official (a political 'instructor', or ideological supervisor) to acquire the prestigious garment in question in order to impress a talentless but beautiful unofficial poet with whom he has fallen in love. Apart from the central character, there is a whole snake-pit of types from semi-official commercial culture, above all a con-man and fixer rejoicing in the name of Biceps, who can find anything anyone wants, even a Zhiguli car the colour of *café-au-lait* and mother-of-pearl. Still more impressive was Venedikt Erofeev's short novel *Moskva-Petushki* (translated as *Moscow Circles*, 1973). Though the narrator here is so little in tune with Soviet life that he has never been able to bring himself to visit its Urheimat, Red Square, and though his tale abounds in buried references to the Bible and to Russian classics, *Moskva-Petushki*, with its refrain 'And then I had another quick one', is a hymn not only to the most enduring form of popular rebellion, loquacious drunkenness, but also to every form of horrible liquid available in Soviet cosmetic stores:

Even the recipe for *The Tear of a Komsomol Girl* is sweet-smelling. And the finished cocktail is so fragrant it might make you pass right out for a minute at least. It made me, anyway.

Take:

150 ml lavender water
150 ml verbena water
30 ml 'Forest' cologne
2 ml nail varnish
150 ml 'Elixir' mouthwash
150 ml lemonade

30 On women artists, see Boym, *Common Places*, 260–5; A. Hilton, 'Feminism and Gender Values in Soviet Art', in M. Liljestroom, E. Mantysaari, and A. Rosenholm (eds.), *Gender Restructuring in Russian Studies* (Tampere, 1993), 104–7; M. Tupitsyn, 'Unveiling Feminism: Women's Art in the Soviet Union', *Arts Magazine* (Dec. 1990), 63–7; and *Women of Russia in Art* (catalogue of festival held at the Conway Hall, London, 14–21 Apr. 1995). On Muratova, see J. Taubman, 'The Cinema of Kira Muratova', *Russian Review*, 52 (1993), 367–81.

Stir for twenty minutes with a spray of honeysuckle. Some people will tell you that you can use dodder instead, but that's not true, it's a crime. Cut me to pieces if you like, but I'll never use a piece of dodder to stir *The Tear of a Komsomol Girl*. No, it has to be honeysuckle. I just burst out laughing when I see someone using dodder, not honeysuckle, to stir their *Tear* . . .[31]

Such repellent cocktails are the apt metaphors of an alchemy whereby the indigestible products of Soviet commercialism can be transformed into the intoxicating elixirs of a true artist.

The division between Soviet and *émigré* literature, never as great as in the 1920s, 1930s, and 1940s, since many *émigrés* already had some kind of a reputation with the Soviet public when they left, seemed about to be bridged altogether in the late 1980s and early 1990s. Writings by *émigrés* were ubiquitous in the Soviet press, prominent *émigrés* were canvassed for their views on the state of the nation, and a procession of former exiles returned, some, such as Sasha Sokolov and later Solzhenitsyn, to live permanently. There was also increasing traffic the other way, as passport regulations were relaxed, and Russian intellectuals hastened to travel abroad, and indeed to earn money there while they could. Though travel abroad continued in the mid-1990s (by 1995 there were about 70,000 Russians living semi-permanently in the UK alone), the sense of intense interest in *émigré* communities died down to a large degree. It had become increasingly obvious by 1993, when Yeltsin launched his assault on the Russian parliament, and when inflation began to spiral uncontrollably, that the post-Soviet experience was exceptional not only in terms of Russian history, but in terms of Western history too. The advice of *émigrés* seemed irrelevant even in the area where they were apparently best qualified to offer aid, the market for cultural products. Experience of Western publishers helps little when dealing with privatized Russian publishers, who work in a far more volatile market. The presence of mafia interests is one complication: a certain respectable reference book was published in 1993–4 behind the 'front' of a clothing firm in order that gangs would not learn of its presence and demand dues. Another is the amorphousness of the book-market, so that sure-fire sellers can become pulp material in a matter of months or even days, as the public moves on to some other taste. Hence, in a reversion to early nineteenth-century practices, some writers began, as the private book-market got underway, to pay for the publication of their own books, taking a risk that outgoings would be covered by profits. It is unclear how successful a strategy this has been.

Artists' circumstances were, as of the mid-1990s, equally uncertain. The international market maintained its preference for avant-garde

31 V. Erofeev, *Moskva-Petushki* (Paris, 1981), 65–6. For a wide-ranging and fascinating study of the more 'serious' cultural material on which Erofeev draws, including Russian icons, see S. Gaiser-Shnitman, *Venedikt Erofeev: Moskva-Petushki, ili 'the rest is silence'* (Berne, 1989).

classics above all, with icons, early twentieth-century figurative art, and nineteenth-century realism also fetching reasonable prices at auction. Again judging by auction prices, the Russian new rich, who became increasingly prominent buyers at auction from late 1993 onwards, have tastes that incline to Fabergé, porcelain and ormolu vases, malachite tables, and other opulent pieces of decorative art, as well as paintings representing picturesque Russian scenes in the mainstream realist manner (pine forests by Shishkin, fairground scenes by Makovskii, and so on).[32] They are clearly unlikely, for the meantime, to sponsor demanding excursions into abstract art, let alone conceptualism or performance art. If Russia does develop a post-Soviet tradition of corporate art, then, a mercantile direction of sponsorship to replace the city authorities and trade unions formerly commissioning heroic workers and peasants, it may well be a revival of early twentieth-century *style russe*. Or on the other hand, given the huge wealth accumulated by some new Russian millionaires (and billionaires), a significant patron of Western art, a distant successor to Shchukin, may perhaps emerge at the stage when the country does finally settle down.

[32] These assertions are based on the sales figures for the Icons, Russian Pictures and Works of Art auctions at Sothebys, London, 1991–5; see also D. Staunton, 'Loaded Russians March into Europe', *Observer*, 13 Aug. 1995.

Suggested further reading

Cinema:

Attwood, L. (ed.), *Red Women on the Silver Screen: Soviet Women and Cinema from the Beginning to the End of the Communist Era* (London, 1993).

Cherchi Usai *et al.* (eds.), *Silent Witnesses. Russian Films 1908–1919*, research and co-ordination by Y. Tsivian (London, 1989).

Goodwin, J., *Eisenstein: Cinema and History* (Urbana and Chicago, 1993).

Horton, A., and **Brashinsky, M.**, *The Zero Hour: Glasnost and Soviet Cinema in Transition* (Princeton, 1992).

Kenez, P., *Cinema and Soviet Society, 1917–1953* (Cambridge, 1992).

Lawton, A., *Kinoglasnost: Soviet Cinema in our Time* (Cambridge, 1992).

—— (ed.), *The Red Screen: Politics, Society, Art in Soviet Cinema* (London, 1992).

Lenin, Stalin, Partiia o Kino (Leningrad, 1938).

Leyda, J., *Kino: A History of Russian and Soviet Film* (London, 1960; repr. 1983).

Shklovskii, V., *Eisenstein, Vertov* (Moscow, 1927).

—— *Za sorok let* (Moscow, 1965).

Sovetskoe kino (1917–1978). Resheniia partii i pravitel'stva o kino. Sbornik dokumentov, i. 1917–1936 (Moscow, 1979).

Stites, R., *Russian Popular Culture: Entertainment and Society Since 1900* (Cambridge, 1992).

Taylor, R., *Film Propaganda: Soviet Russian and Nazi Germany* (London, 1979).

—— *The Politics of Soviet Cinema, 1917–1929* (Cambridge, 1979).

—— and **Christie, I.** (eds.), *The Film Factory: Russian and Soviet Cinema in Documents 1896–1939* (London, 1988).

Taylor, R., and **Christie, I.** (eds.), *Inside the Film Factory: New Approaches to Russian and Soviet Cinema* (London, 1991).

Taylor, R., and **Spring, D.** (eds.), *Stalinism and Soviet Cinema* (London, 1993).

Tsivian, Y., *Early Cinema in Russia and its Cultural Reception* (London, 1994).

Youngblood, D., *Soviet Cinema in the Silent Era, 1918–1935* (Ann Arbor, 1985; repr. Austin, Tex., 1991).

—— *Movies for the Masses: Popular Cinema and Soviet Society in the 1920s* (Cambridge, 1992).

· Media:

Barghoorn, F., and **Remington, T. F.,** *Politics in the USSR*, 3rd edn. (Boston, 1986).

Buzek, A., *How the Communist Press Works* (London, 1964).

Conquest, R., *The Harvest of Sorrow: Soviet Collectivization and the Terror-Famine* (London, 1986).

—— *Tyrants and Typewriters: Communiques in the Struggle for Truth* (London, 1989).

Counts, G., and **Lodge, N.,** *The Country of the Blind: The Soviet System of Mind Control* (Boston, 1949).

Dewhirst, M., and **Farrell, R.** (eds.), *The Soviet Censorship* (Metuchen, 1973).

Gorky, M., *Untimely Thoughts: Essays on Revolution, Culture and the Bolsheviks 1917–1918*, tr. H. Ermolaev (New York, 1968).

Graffy, J., and **Hosking, G. A.** (eds.), *Culture and the Media in the USSR Today* (London, 1989).

Hale, J., *Radio Power: Propaganda and International Broadcasting* (London, 1975).

Hayek, F., *The Road to Serfdom* (London, 1993).

Heller, M., *Cogs in the Soviet Wheel: The Formation of Soviet Man*, tr. D. Floyd (London, 1988).

Hollander, G. D., *Soviet Political Indoctrination: Developments in Mass Media Since Stalin* (New York, 1973).

Inkeles, A., *Public Opinion in Soviet Russia: A Study in Mass Persuasion* (Cambridge, Mass., 1950).

Koestler, A., *The Yogi and the Commissar and Other Essays* (London, 1945).

Kravchenko, V., *The Personal and Political Life of a Soviet Official* (London, 1949).

Lendvai, P., *The Bureaucracy of Truth: How Communist Governments Manage the News* (London, 1981).

McLuhan, M., *Understanding Media: The Extensions of Man* (London, 1987).

Milosz, C., *The Captive Mind*, tr. J. Zielonko (Harmondsworth, 1981).

Popper, K., *The Poverty of Historicism* (London, 1991).

Rapoport, Y., *The Doctors' Plot: Stalin's Last Crime*, tr. N. Perova and R. Bobrova (London, 1991).

Remington, T. F., *The Truth of Authority: Ideology and Communication in the Soviet Union* (Pittsburgh, 1988).

Smith, H., *The Russians* (London, 1977).

Solzhenitsyn, A., 'Misconceptions about Russia are a Threat to America', tr. M. Nicholson and A. Klimoff, *Foreign Affairs*, 58 (1980), 797–834.

Thom, F., *Newspeak: The Language of Soviet Communism*, tr. K. Connelly (London, 1989).

Tusa, J., *Conversations with the World* (London, 1990).

Advertising:

Boym, S., *Common Places: Mythologies of Everyday Life in Russia* (Cambridge, Mass., 1994), 271–82.

Condee, N., and **Padunov, V.**, 'The ABC of Russian Consumer Culture: Readings, Ratings and Real Estate', in Condee (ed.), *Soviet Hieroglyphics: Visual Culture in Late Twentieth-Century Russia* (Bloomington, Ind., 1995), 130–72.

Hansen, P., *Advertising and Socialism: The Nature and Extent of Consumer Advertising in the Soviet Union, Poland, Hungary, and Yugoslavia* (London, 1974), 1–74.

Permiakov, V., and **Pylaev, A.**, *Kak ia stal Lenei Golubkovym* (Moscow, 1994).

Zholkovsky, A., '19 oktjabrja 1982 g., or the Semiotics of a Soviet Cookie Wrapper', *Wiener Slawistischer Almanach*, 11 (1983), 341–54.

Visual arts and commercialism:

Berger, J., *Art and Revolution: Ernst Neizvestnyi and the Role of the Artist in the USSR* (London, 1969).

Bird, A., *A History of Russian Painting* (Oxford, 1987), ch. 15.

Bown, M. C., *Contemporary Russian Art* (London, 1988).

—— and **Taylor, B.** (eds.), *Art of the Soviets: Painting, Sculpture and Architecture in a One-Party State* (Manchester, 1993).

Boym, S., *Common Places: Mythologies of Everyday Life in Russia* (Cambridge, Mass., 1994), ch. 4.

Condee, N. (ed.), *Soviet Hieroglyphics: Visual Culture in Late Twentieth-Century Russia* (Bloomington, Ind., 1995).

Dodge, N. (ed.), *Russian New Wave* (Contemporary Russian Art Center, New York, 1981).

—— and **Hilton, A.**, *New Art from the Soviet Union* (Washington, 1977).

Elliott, D., and **Dudakov, V.**, *100 Years of Russian Art 1889–1989: From Collections in the USSR* (London, 1989).

Golomstock, I., and **Glezer, A.**, *Soviet Art in Exile* (New York, 1977).

—— **Rueschemeyer, M.**, and **Kennedy, J.**, *Soviet Émigré Artists: Life and Work in the USSR and in the United States* (New York, 1985).

Nathanson, M., *Komar/Melamid: Two Soviet Dissident Artists* (Carbondale, Ill., 1978).

Rosenfeld, A., and **Dodge, N. T.** (eds.), *Nonconformist Art: The Soviet Experience* (London, 1995).

Émigré literature:

Karlinsky, S., and **Appel, A.** (eds.), *The Bitter Air of Exile: Russian Writers in the West, 1922–72* (Berkeley, 1977).

McMillin, A. (ed.), *Under Eastern Eyes: The West as Reflected in Recent Russian Writing* (London, 1991).

Smith, G. S. (ed.), *Contemporary Russian Poetry: A Bilingual Anthology* (Bloomington, Ind., 1993).

Part 4

Identities: Populism, Religion, Emigration

The Retreat from Dogmatism: Populism under Khrushchev and Brezhnev

CATRIONA KELLY

In order to understand popular feeling in the years after Stalin's death, it is important to grasp two contradictory elements in Party policy under Khrushchev and his successors. While central elements of top-down governance remained in place until the collapse of Party rule in 1991—constitutional recognition of the Party's 'leading role' in political and social life, the mechanisms of the command economy, the agglutination of legislative and executive powers in Moscow under the democratic centralist system—subtle shifts in ideology and cultural regulation led to changes in perception of the 'the people' or 'the masses' as a symbolic entity. Though laws against mass resistance—strikes and uprisings—remained in place, and the Ministry of Internal Affairs retained wide-ranging powers against dissent, a growing recognition was given, in official policy and planning, to the practical causes of discontent (such as problems with the supply of food, consumer goods, and housing). In the late 1960s, the term 'mass culture' started to be applied, for the first time, to Soviet society as well as to Western societies, signalling a new, more complex and ramified, comprehension of the tastes and ideas of 'the people'.[1] Though the lower classes, for reasons which will be explained below, did not have the intelligentsia's enhanced possibilities of negotiation with the authorities, which facilitated the expression, on some occasions, of open dissidence, ordinary people's experience of Soviet life went through changes that were no less significant, even if they were not always so obvious.

1 See e.g. N. M.
Zorkaia, *Na rubezhe
stoletii: U istokov
massovogo iskusstva v
Rossii 1990–1910 gg*
(Moscow, 1976). See
also the journal
Dekorativnoe iskusstvo.

The pyramidal nature of Khrushchev's reforming programme
was made evident, in 1956, by the fact that the leader's famous de-
Stalinizing speech was given *in camera*, and then released to Party
committees at regional and district level. Though details of the document quickly became known among non-Party members of the
intelligentsia, many working-class Russians, especially those living in
the capitals, were more directly affected by the results of the Twenty-
Second Party Congress in 1961, at which Khrushchev's assault on 'the
cult of personality' was followed not only by the removal of the dead
dictator's embalmed corpse from the Lenin Mausoleum, but by the
toppling of statues and renaming of streets all over the Soviet Union.
The mass of the population was not consulted about the changes,
which at least in certain cases—such as the renaming of the hero city
Stalingrad as Volgograd—represented a potentially inflammatory
attempt to erase from history every aspect of the Stalin period,
however important its place in local and national pride. Remote from
the rationale behind such changes, those outside the élite were also
unlikely to benefit from Khrushchev's attempts (bumbling but at least
partly genuine) to institute a politics of consultation, as expressed, for
instance, in the discussions he held with literary and cultural figures
during 1960 and 1961.

Among intellectuals, the demystification of the Party leadership
just as often led to cynicism as to renewed fervour and respect.
For Boris Pasternak, Khrushchev was nothing more than a vulgar
peasant, less wicked than Stalin maybe, but also infinitely less
impressive. Vladimir Tendriakov, author of 'On the Blessed Island
of Communism' ('Na blazhennom ostrove kommunizma', 1974), a
viciously sarcastic memoir about a banquet organized for distinguished members of the Union of Writers at Khrushchev's dacha,
portrays Khrushchev as a not unlikeable, but deeply immature
individual, desperately anxious to impress his sophisticated guests,
and making a fool of himself over a game of plate-shooting. When
he finally managed to shoot enough plates to win a goody, perhaps through 'a nimble underling's trick', Khrushchev, according to
Tendriakov, first manifested infantile delight, then equally jejune
disappointment when realizing his prize was not the best one:

He was exhibiting pure childish glee in winning: he had shot down the
saucers and proved his dexterity, and how! Yeah, yeah, yeah!

People rushed up to hand him his china prize. He received it with
dignity—even the gravitas becoming a figure of State—and . . . glanced
across at Mzhavanadze's prize. Mzhavanadze was in seventh heaven, beam-
ing with joy—thank God, it had passed off all right!—and looked adoringly
into Khrushchev's eyes . . .

The smile left Mzhavanadze's face; he interpreted the boss's glance and lowered his eyes to his own prize, which he was still awkwardly clutching with both hands to his private parts. Oh dear, oh dear, there had been a small blunder: Mzhavanadze's ornate little statuette clearly had the more gilt on it ... Khrushchev scrutinized more closely the prize he had not been given.

And Mzhavandze jumped to it and hastened to proffer it to him.

'Let's swap, Nikita Sergeevich.'

No, I'm not inventing a single word for the sake of a story; it was all just as I'm telling you, please believe me. Yes, yes, Khrushchev did a swap: took Mzhavanadze's prize, which had more gilt on it. And both were clearly content with their exchange.

If Tendriakov's essay, for all its sustained ridicule, expresses some admiration, by the way, for Khrushchev's persistence, for the ends achieved by his 'sublime stupidity', and an ironic enjoyment of the fact that 'the butcher's judge was a man that Stalin considered a clown',[2] it also unambiguously indicates why it was that no one who had met Khrushchev in such circumstances, or even heard tenth-hand accounts of his behaviour, could ever feel the chilly terror that was inspired by equally well-worn accounts of Stalin's midnight cat-and-mouse games with frightened functionaries in the Kremlin.

Both Khrushchev's amnesty for political prisoners, and his blustering efforts at consultative politics, emboldened the intelligentsia. From the late 1950s, there was a massive growth of oppositional groups, especially, but not exclusively, in the capitals. Groups remained small, clandestine, and subject to police crackdowns. Prison sentences were still imposed against 'undesirables': the Moscow writers Andrei Siniavskii and Iulii Daniel' were sentenced to terms of 7 and 5 years' hard labour in 1966, the Siberian writer Leonid Borodin to 6 years in 1967, and a further 10 years in 1983, and the poet Irina Ratushinskaia to 7 years, also in 1983. Besides imposing prison terms, the government revived a form of repression first used against the philosopher Chaadaev in the 1830s: dissidents might be declared insane. However, modern dissidents, unlike Chaadaev, risked not genteel house arrest, but treatment with powerful psychotropic drugs for their 'schizophrenia'. This particularly brutal form of punishment was imposed on large numbers of younger intellectuals, from Joseph Brodsky in 1964 to Natal'ia Gorbanevskaia, participant in the Red Square demonstration against the invasion of Czechoslovakia, to Vladimir Bukovskii in the 1970s. Those not subjected to prison or mental hospital sentences could be exiled (from the Soviet Union, as with Solzhenitsyn in 1974, or within it, as with Sakharov in 1980). Lower-level action included all kinds of *nepriiatnosti* ('unpleasantnesses'): brow-beating interviews with the so-called 'First Section'

2 V. Tendriakov, 'On the Blessed Island of Communism', tr. M. Duncan, in O. Chukhontsev (ed.), *Dissonant Voices* (London, 1991), 101, 76.

(KGB officials), summary dismissal from one's studies or employment, telephone-tapping, tracking by agents in the street, and apartment searches.

In such circumstances, anonymity was the only sure means of
survival for dissidents; there could be no equivalent of the more
broadly-based East European protest movements, such as the pacifist campaigns in East Germany, or Charter 77 in Czechoslovakia.
However, the Helsinki accord of 1975, in which the Soviet Union
committed itself to international co-operation, including the observation of human rights, strengthened the determination of dissident
groups to compel the regime to heed its own declarations, and to
bring abuses to the notice of Western diplomats and journalists.
Though the chilling of East–West relations after the Soviet Union's
invasion of Afghanistan also meant that dissidence was treated more
harshly, there was no attempt to revive the mass purges of the Stalin
era. Apart from human rights generally, intellectuals in republican
capitals (particularly in the Caucasus, the Ukraine, and the Baltic
States) were active from the 1960s in the cause of national liberation from central control. The area of personal rights also attracted
occasional protesters: in 1980, for example, pioneering women in
Moscow and Leningrad formed the first feminist associations since
pre-Revolutionary times, only to have their activities brutally curtailed by the authorities after a matter of months.

Outside the intelligentsia, the boundaries of protest were differ-
ently set. Those outside the cultural élite might have less reason to
ridicule Khrushchev than metropolitan intellectuals, but they also
had a good deal less cause to feel personal affection for him, since
many key events of his leadership did nothing to humanize Party
authority over the masses. Manifestations of mass resistance were
brutally crushed, whether they occurred in the Soviet Union (as with
the Novocherkassk strikes of 1962) or in the Warsaw Pact countries
(as with unrest in Hungary, East Germany, and Poland during the
mid-1950s). Even according to the liberalized Criminal Code of 1960,
sentences of up to 15 years' imprisonment could be imposed for the
organization of 'mass unrest' (article 79).[3] Nor did the law-abiding
necessarily escape official bullying. The *trudovaia knizhka* (workers'
identity papers) system remained in force as a punishment for those
who had infringed work discipline, and the villages continued to suffer the caprice of geographically and culturally remote bureaucracy,
as maize monoculture was introduced to large areas of European
Russia, and so-called 'futureless villages' (*besperspektivnye derevni*)
closed down, their populations transferred to larger settlements
whether they liked it or not. Though some collective farm-workers

3 See Zh. Rossi,
Spravochnik po GULagu
(London, 1967), 505.

now had the right to leave the villages, those who did were denied full residency rights in the cities. Penned up in substandard housing beyond the city boundaries, the *limitchiki* did unskilled, low-paid, and low-status heavy work, becoming the backbone of the construction, motor, tanning, and rubber industries, and taking jobs as cleaners and catering workers.

The creation of a new industrial underclass was accompanied by the further enrichment of those who were already comparatively well off. While Khrushchev made some token gestures against nest-feathering by Party officials in the mid-1950s, the campaign against privilege was half-hearted and short-lasting. Indeed, social stratification not only continued, but was further entrenched, during his leadership, by measures such as the legalization of co-operative housing (a system by which the well-off could buy themselves out of the housing queue by paying a substantial subvention towards the construction costs of a new block), the encouragement of private trade through the establishment of collective farm markets, where peasants sold produce from their own allotments, and the proliferation of special schools, teaching languages, maths, science, or sport to particularly gifted children.[4] Social stratification was encouraged under Brezhnev's dominion, when the slogan 'stability of cadres' signified the development of a complex network of patronage by Party officials who, no longer fearing routine purges, began to build power networks within their district, region, and republic.

The 'workbook' system meant that workers and peasants depended to a far larger degree on the goodwill of management than did members of the 'free professions'. Publicizing abuses was therefore harder. A free trade union founded in 1977 was closed down in a matter of months; its successor, SMOT (the Free Interprofessional Association of Labourers) survived as a watchdog rather than a campaigning group. Though strikes and spontaneous demonstrations did occasionally take place in the 1960s, 1970s, and 1980s, as they had in the 1930s and 1940s, they were still not publicized. As in the 1930s and 1940s, open political resistance was much less common than manipulation of work conditions through absenteeism, pilfering, lengthy tea-breaks, go-slows, and other manifestations of a far from Protestant work ethic.[5] The fact that rigid planning targets remained in force, but so too did goods shortages and distribution hiccups, meant that the pre-modern alternation between 'storming' (working flat out to finish targets before the deadline) and idling was still the primary rhythm of all Soviet factories.

The Khrushchev and especially the Brezhnev years also saw a mushrooming of the unofficial economy, another effect of the

4 See M. Matthews, *Privileges in the Soviet Union: A Study of Elite Lifestyles under Communism* (London, 1978), and *Poverty in the Soviet Union: The Lifestyles of the Underprivileged in Recent Years* (Cambridge, 1986); and D. Filtzer, *Soviet Workers and De-Stalinization: the Consolidation of the Modern System of Soviet Production Relations, 1953–1964* (Cambridge, 1992), 29–30, and *Soviet Workers and the Collapse of Perestroika: The Soviet Labour Process and Gorbachev's Reforms, 1985–1991* (Cambridge, 1994), 27–31.

5 On popular resistance in the 1930s and 1940s, see C. Kelly and V. Volkov, 'Directed Desires: *Kul'turnost'* and Consumption', in Kelly and D. Shepherd (eds.), *Constructing Russian Culture in the Age of Revolution, 1881–1940* (Oxford, 1998), 307–13.

decreased fear of Party purges. The obtaining of work, goods, and favours *nalevo* ('on the left', i.e. on the sly) and *po sviaziam* (through connections) became ubiquitous, and *blat* (graft) became the predominant *modus operandi* of large sectors of the Soviet population. Entire factories, especially in the Caucasus, operated profitable sidelines running up consumer goods illegally; collective and state farms 'lost' part of their production to shady entrepreneurs; black market rings imported and distributed everything from videos to heroin. While some Soviet citizens (usually top Party officials) plunged wholeheartedly into corruption, and made their fortunes from it, others (often minor functionaries, such as beat policemen) expressed open nostalgia for the supposedly more wholesome days of 'the boss', Stalin. But for the vast majority of people, who had always lived with *blat*, the expansion of the alternative economy, and its increasing prominence, represented a change of degree, rather than of kind, from what they had known before, the cause of grumbling and minor squabbles, rather than of riots or serious violence.

In any case, there was now more to be obtained by *blat*, given that living standards rose significantly in the 1960s and 1970s. Crash building programmes gave thousands of city-dwellers, including some of the new incomers, their first opportunity to live in a separate family flat, rather than in a communal flat or a factory barracks. Production of consumer goods was stepped up; it gradually became possible for at least some to acquire refrigerators, cars, new furniture, televisions, even if quality remained low and supple erratic. Efforts were made to improve the supply of services as well as goods: new residential building was organized in satellite suburbs, microdistricts (*mikroraiony*), each with its own shopping, transport, and recreation facilities.[6] Sports facilities were improved—a landmark was the construction of the Moskva swimming pool in central Moscow, on land cleared by the demolition of the Cathedral of Christ Redeemer in 1934, and originally intended as the site for the vast Palace of Soviets, a project itself symbolically abandoned in favour of a less august and more populist institution (no less symbolic is the pool's recent replacement by a rebuilt Cathedral). Tourism was encouraged, with the building of vast hotels along the Black Sea, and of smaller hostelries, rest homes, and holiday camps (*turbazy*) in resorts and out in the countryside. There was a self-conscious attempt to introduce new types of social ritual. In 1964, the first 'Palace of Nuptials' (*Dvorets brakosochetaniia*) was opened in Leningrad; thereafter, the new, more opulent form of registry office marriage, with white dresses, piped music, and elegant surroundings (some of the Palaces really were former palaces) became popular among many of the city-dwellers with access to it.

6 See J. Pallot and D. A. Ward, *Soviet Town Planning* (London, 1981), and W. C. Brumfield and B. A. Ruble (eds.), *Russian Housing in the Modern Age: Design and Social History* (New York, 1993).

Not only high days but ordinary days became less stressful. Bad harvests under Khrushchev and Brezhnev meant that precious hard currency was spent on buying grain, but peasants no longer starved to death on their collective farms. The average village still lacked sanitation, metalled roads, and adequate shopping, cultural, or medical facilities, but agricultural workers were now paid a wage rather than being paid on results, so that consumer goods could be bought to improve conditions. As all over rural Europe, television, once introduced, became a main recreation for many villagers. In the cities, living space might still be cramped, and mechanization of housework extremely limited, but the average family could rely on a network of facilities—laundries, heating, lighting, public transport, cinemas, theatres—that functioned reasonably well and at a very low cost, as well as others—repairs, dry-cleaning, public catering—whose standards were variable and operations erratic, but where a larger than average cash outlay could sometimes ensure better quality. When purchasing food, for example, items that were scarce could be bought at a collective farm market or in the carry-out section of an expensive restaurant or high-quality grocery (such as the Metropole in Leningrad, or the Gastronome no. 1—still popularly known as Eliseev's—in Moscow). Though only the rich could shop in these places regularly, those above or even on the breadline might visit before a public holiday or a family birthday, to ensure there was a good spread for their guests. The dreary diet available in state shops might also be supplemented by the food packages given out at places of work, and including scarce items such as oranges, sausages, or ham, as well as samples of unpopular ones needing off-loading. And, as in the 1930s, but less furtively, a vast private-exchange system operated, according to which allotment tomatoes were swapped for vodka, which in turn paid, say, for repairs to a leaking lavatory. Beyond this again were the many illegal markets for prized deficit goods, such as scarce books, foreign clothes, drugs, and parts for cars or machines. Occasionally the police would raid one of these in order to make a point, but for the most part they operated regularly and without hindrance.

The problem for the Soviet government, then, was not the fact of shortages, which people found ways of getting round, than the fact that people now expected not to experience shortages. With increasing mobility, too, more and more of the population became aware that 'shortages' meant something different if you lived in a village (where there might be nothing at all to buy in the local shop), a small provincial town (where bread and stale cheese might be the only items available), a large town (where meat and full-fat butter were permanently 'deficit', and milk seasonally so), or Moscow (where the queues noticed by visiting foreigners in fact meant that there was plenty of almost every basic food). Moreover, in this hierarchical society, where workers, cities, and factories all had rankings, the top of the hierarchy exemplified, to many ordinary Russians, the truth of the Russian saying *s zhiru besiatsia* ('living off the fat of the land makes you crazy'). The more obvious the corruptibility of Party officials became, the more ludicrous appeared calls to self-denial on the part of the administration.

From the mid-1950s, therefore, the revolutionary ascetism of the past was conclusively abandoned, and a new Soviet ethos created that reinforced, yet subtly altered, the symbolic realities of the 1940s. A new, outward-oriented and competitive nationalism, forward- rather than backward-looking, replaced the blinkered chauvinism of Stalin's last days, when scientific research had been at a near-standstill, but the telephone, the radio, and other such key inventions had been credited to Russian pioneers. Under both Khrushchev and Brezhnev, the Soviet Union's world-power status was consolidated. The Cuban missile crisis in 1962 drew attention to the muscle that could be exercised by one of the world's two most important nuclear states. The building of the Berlin Wall in 1961 was a tangible symbol of the East–West separatism pursued by the Soviet State, which suspended its policy of hardline intervention in the internal affairs of Warsaw Pact countries only in the late 1980s. Outside the Warsaw Pact, from Vietnam to Mozambique, the Soviet Union nurtured dependent states as export markets for arms, consumer goods, and expertise, and as sources for cheap imports, particularly of food.

But it was not only foreign policy through which prestige was sought. Experimental science was once again lent ideological and financial support, leading to a scientific renaissance like that at the end of the nineteenth century. Apart from defence-linked research, a crucial area for investment was the space-travel programme, which handsomely recouped the outlay with a series of remarkable pioneering achievements in the late 1950s and early 1960s, including the launch of the first manned space rocket. Certainly, the government remained conservative in its funding policies; the development of some areas, notably cybernetics, was hindered. Narrow-minded official controls on the sciences meant that several notable dissidents, including Zhores Medvedev and Andrei Sakharov, came from the science establishment. But for all that, Soviet scientists now gained international acclaim for some of their projects, particularly in theoretical physics and mathematics. And the 1960s and 1970s saw a huge rise in popular interest in the sciences, manifested both in the subscription rates to journals such as *Nauka i zhizn'* (*Science and Life*), and in the flowering of science fiction, which in the hands of writers such as Boris Strugatskii (an astrophysicist) and his brother Arkadii could also become the vehicle of concealed social criticism.[7]

Apart from science, the key locus of post-Stalinist nationalism was sport. From the early 1960s right up to the collapse of the old order, Soviet and Warsaw Pact sportsmen maintained irresistible dominance, particularly in athletics and gymnastics, through an enormously efficient programme of state sponsorship, covering a network of special schools offering intensive training to talented children and first-class training facilities for adults whose 'amateur' status was usually a question of notional affiliation to a workplace where they had never in fact done a day's labour.[8]

Expanded media services (see Ch. 10) brought news of all these successes to bigger and bigger numbers of Soviet citizens. Where nationalism of the 1940s had stressed the irrelevance of foreign achievements to Soviet reality, nationalism after 1953 emphasized the Soviet Union's capacity to take on the West. Or indeed overtake it: *dogonim—peregonim Ameriku!* ('let us catch up with and overtake America!') was a ubiquitous slogan of the post-Stalin era.

Not every area of Soviet life inclined to nationalistic grandiosity. Public housing projects had become more modest and functional than in the days of high Stalinism (as indeed they needed to be, considering the new influx to the cities). Khrushchev's proclamation of a more cost-conscious ethic, with 'effective use of new materials', in 1954, was followed by a law of November 1955 prohibiting 'decorative excesses in architectural design and building'.[9] The high-profile projects of the Stalin years—imposing neo-classical turrets in the manner popularly known as vampire style—disappeared. The most characteristic form of housing in the late 1950s and early 1960s was low-rise (5-storey) boxy apartment blocks jokingly referred to as *khrushchoby* —a pun on Khrushchev and *trushchoba*, slum. In the mid-1960s, pressure on space dictated a turn back to medium-rise blocks again; these systems-built constructions, often coloured white and blue, and each containing dozens of rabbit-hutch flats, were too nondescript to attract any nicknames at all.

Even the prestige buildings of the Khrushchev and Brezhnev years were generally less pretentious (and also less well-constructed—cost-cutting had its drawbacks too) than their Stalinist predecessors. The lavish, stone-faced Palace of Soviets in the Kremlin was very much an exception; more typical were the Rossiia hotel nearby, a vast and ugly collapsed blue box, or its equally uncomely Leningrad sibling in the second capital. These typical buildings of the Brezhnev days were

7 On science, see S. Fortescue, *Science Policy in the Soviet Union* (London, 1990), and L. R. Graham, *Science in Russia and the Soviet Union: A Short History* (Cambridge, 1993).

8 On sport, see J. Riordan, *Sport and Soviet Society: The Development of Sport and Physical Education in Russia and the USSR* (Cambridge, 1977; repr. 1985).

9 Quoted in C. Cooke, 'Socialist Realist Architecture: Theory and Practice', in M. C. Bown and B. Taylor (eds.), *Art of the Soviets: Painting, Sculpture and Architecture in a One-Party State* (Manchester, 1993), 103–4.

12 Artist's impression of a family house to be built in the prestige new town for Soviet scientists, Akademgorodok, close to Novosibirsk (*Ogonek*, 28 (1958)).

One of Khrushchev's main concerns as Party leader was to develop outlying parts of the Soviet Union; he accordingly espoused a plan to relocate the Institute for Nuclear Physics in Siberia. As the space scientist Roald Sagdeev recounts in his memoirs, *The Making of a Soviet Scientist*, Soviet scientists themselves welcomed the move from the centre because '[we] hoped very much that by coming to virgin land we could start everything from scratch, according to international scientific standards' (p. 119). This hope was to be disappointed: by 1970, conditions in Akademgorodok were not much less claustrophobic than those in metropolitan institutes. However, as an experiment in bringing high culture to the Soviet wastelands, Akademgorodok remained unique, and a series of international conferences held in the 1960s made it, and its inhabitants, famous throughout the world scientific community. The generous scale of the family house here shows how privilege was increasingly not only accepted, but paraded, as an essential feature of the Soviet system.

more notable in terms of size and position than of architectural distinction (they practised an anodyne, watered-down-modernist glass, concrete, and girder style like that used for mediocre hotels and office buildings in the West). New Metro stations were also austere when compared with their Stalinist predecessors: cream tiles and simple lettering replaced the exuberant bronze sculpture galleries to be found in 1940s stations such as those on the Circle Line in Moscow, or Ploshchad' Vosstaniia Station in Leningrad.

History as Legitimation: Monumentalism after 1953

Despite the new emphasis on practicality, the practice of funding monumental constructions as a symbolic indication of the country's *puissance* did continue, particular attention being given to culture parks and monuments. In 1958, the Stalinist All-Soviet Agricultural Exhibition was closed, to be reopened in 1959 as the larger and more spectacular Exhibition of Economic Achievements (VDNKh), with pavilions dedicated to aviation and space travel as well as agriculture and industry. Further enlargements and improvements to VDNKh were made for the sixtieth anniversary of the October Revolution, in 1967, and for the Moscow Olympics, in 1980. The latter additionally required construction of a complex of enormous stadia and ceremonial arenas all over Moscow, including a vast equestrian sports complex at Bittsevskii Park. Monuments to space flight and its pioneers (the first cosmonaut, Iurii Gagarin, became a national hero on his descent from space in 1961) were constructed in Moscow and all over the Soviet Union; so, too, were commemorations of Soviet successes in aviation, such as notable jets in the IL- and TU- series.

Not only the present, but also the past was the subject of monumentalization. The statues of Stalin might disappear, but the de-Stalinizing era saw the creation of dozens of new memorials to Lenin. In Moscow, statues were placed outside Luzhniki Stadium (1958), the Supreme Soviet Building (in 1967), and on the Garden Ring near Oktiabr'skaia Metro Station (in 1985); a main thoroughfare in the capital, Bol'shaia Kaluzhskaia Street, was renamed Leninskii prospekt in 1957, on the occasion of the fortieth anniversary of the Revolution. The cult of Lenin was propagandized assiduously in nursery schools, schools, and pioneer camps, with episodes from the leader's childhood an obligatory part of all early-reading courses. And the commemoration of selected Old Bolsheviks, radical thinkers, and key events of revolutionary history was testament to the Party's desire to set up an alternative, non-Stalinist, history of the Communist Party.

13 The Pioneer Palace. Illustration from a children's book, *Our Leningrad*, 1958.

The emphasis on peace, plenty, and security, and on the importance of collective ritual, is characteristic of material aimed at children throughout the Soviet period, as is the overt use of political propaganda in teaching material from elementary to graduation levels. In the post-Stalin era the vacuum left by the disappearance of the Stalin cult was filled by a greater emphasis on Lenin, the Revolution, and on Russian history (the text accompanying this image informs the child reader that the Pioneer Palace is located in the former Anichkov Palace, a place to which ordinary people would not have been admitted before 1917, and that the Pioneer Palace was opened there in 1937).

For example, monuments to Krupskaia (1980) and Dzerzhinskii (1958) were set up in Moscow, while in Leningrad the famous Aurora cruiser, from which the first shots of the Revolution were (or alternatively, were not) fired, was retrieved from Oranienbaum, towed to the centre of the city, and opened as a museum in 1956. This recovery of suppressed aspects of the revolutionary past continued into the Gorbachev era, when, at the eleventh hour of the Communist Party, in the late 1980s, Bukharin, unmentionable under Khrushchev as well as Stalin, was finally rehabilitated as a model of the alternative, more humane ideologies that the Communist Party might have espoused, had Stalin not corrupted it.

Revolutionary history was by no means the only era of 'history of the fatherland' to be honoured. In 1954, the site once occupied by a monument to the Soviet Constitution (set up in 1919, and taken down in 1939) was filled by a pompous new equestrian statue of Prince Iurii Dolgorukii, by legend the founder of Moscow. A panorama of the Battle of Borodino painted by F. A. Roubaud in 1912, and long left neglected, was restored and reopened to the public in 1962. These small gestures towards conservationism were followed, in the Brezhnev years, by a much more wide-ranging campaign for the restoration of the past. A new law of 1976 gave official protection to ancient monuments, halting the indiscriminate demolition that had taken place since the 1930s. The 1970s and 1980s also saw the restoration of numerous churches in Moscow, and the promotion of the Golden Ring (historic towns within easy travelling distance of Moscow) as a major attraction for Russian and foreign tourists. Historical novels (such as Valentin Pikul''s *The Favourite* (*Favorit*, 1984), a sensational evocation of Catherine II's court) and historical films (from Iurii Bondarchuk's *War and Peace*, 1966, to the much less serious *Hussar's Ballad* (*Gusarskaia ballada*, 1962), a musical about the 1812 Patriotic War) came to be among the most popular genres of the 1960s, 1970s, and 1980s. Fantasy evocations of history figured widely in the official painting of the period, most famously in the massively popular images of Old Russian subjects created by Il'ia Glazunov.[10]

But the most strenuous efforts of all went into the commemoration of what was invariably referred to officially (in order to evoke the Patriotic War against Napoleon) as The Great Patriotic War of 1941–5. Between the mid-1950s and the mid-1970s, war memorials were constructed in numbers unparalleled in Russian history, and indeed in the history of most other countries.[11] From small, relatively unpretentious memorials in remote places (such as one or two burnt-out tanks set on a concrete platform, with inscription) up to vast, metropolitan complexes such as the Piskarevskoe Memorial Cemetery for victims

10 On popular historical fiction, see K. Mehnert, *The Russians and their Favorite Books* (Stanford, Calif., 1983); on painting see S. Reid, 'The "Art of Memory": Retrospectivism in Soviet Painting of the Brezhnev Era', in Bown and Taylor (eds.), *Art of the Soviets*, 161–87.

11 Some war memorials were constructed in 1940s—e.g. Victory Park in Leningrad, part of a complex that includes an earlier nationalist edifice, the aptly named Triumphal Gates of 1838—but the building programme began in earnest during the late 1950s. On memorials and rituals, see also R. Sartorti, 'On the Making of Heroes, Heroines and Saints', and N. Turmakin, 'The War of Remembrance', in R. Stites (ed.), *Culture and Entertainment in Wartime Russia* (Bloomington, Ind., 1995), 176–93, 194–207.

14 Statue of a woman holding a shell, Victory Park, Leningrad (St Petersburg), late 1940s.

Victory Park, which began to be laid out in 1945, is one of the largest memorial complexes in any Soviet city: it includes an avenue with busts of war heroes, pavilions decorated with statues such as the one pictured here, boating lakes, and shady walks. The woman holding a shell is typical of Soviet war memorials in that her bearing emphasizes resolution and confidence, rather than suffering or uncertainty. Moreover, the fact that she appears to be a factory-worker rather than a fighter (hence her civilian dress), with a shell fresh off the assembly line, is in accordance with official imagery that generally distinguished between the front (dominated by men) and the home front (dominated by women and children). Faintly visible on the wall behind the statue is a graffito, 'Yeltsin is a Fascist'; this defacement is an indication that war mythology has lost its power as a legitimation of political authority, or indeed a focus for social consensus.

of the Leningrad Blockade (opened on Victory Day in 1960), or the Tomb of the Unknown Soldier in Red Square (unveiled in 1967), countless shrines were now erected to the fallen, on the sites of battles and in cemeteries and town centres. The most usual pattern was a colossal statue or group of statues—Mother Russia was an especially popular subject—with an Eternal Flame (i.e. gas beacon) at its foot, guarded by ceremonially goose-stepping Young Pioneers or occasionally soldiers.

After 1953, the 'Great Patriotic War', became the key symbol of a national identity whose internationalism still had a strong undertow of defensiveness. The memorials, as well as war films and commemorative propaganda, stressed the messianic role of the Soviet Union in liberating Europe from fascism, and emphasized that the huge losses had not been in vain, since they had ensured victory. They communicated that this had been a victory, above all, on the part of the 'Great Russian People' toasted by Stalin on Victory Day, 1945—the Soviet Jews who had died in Nazi atrocities were not separately commemorated, the part played by non-Russian nationalities in defeating the Germans was played down. But the dreadful losses suffered by the Soviet Union during the war were also used, particularly in the Brezhnev years, to emphasize the country's status as a non-aggressive regulator of international affairs, and to stand as metaphor for a national identity based on *dolgoterpimost'* (endurance, sufferance), as well as *otvaga* (valour, or hurrah-patriotism). Predictably, masculine, militaristic images were used in order to capture the latter intonation, images of maternity, most particularly vast colossi of Mother Russia, to suggest endurance.

There is no doubt that war imagery represented an enormously successful crystallization of popular reactions to the aftermath of a painful and costly victory, the inspiration both of pride and of intense sadness. As any visitor to the country in the 1970s or 1980s will testify, toasts to 'peace and friendship' were an essential ritual at any official banquet. But the fact that officialdom was thoroughly in tune with popular feeling here was also indicated by the fact that artless protestations of the Soviet Union's non-belligerent intentions were frequent during unofficial encounters with ordinary Soviet people as well. Similarly, official war memorials not only acted as reminders of official nationalism; unlike most other memorials, they inspired genuine affection. The millions of brides and grooms (hotfoot from Palaces of Nuptials) who had themselves photographed on their 'big day' in front of war memorials were going through a ritual that bore some relation to traditional rites of respect for the dead (such as picnicking by graves on All Souls' Day). And if Victory Day was the occasion for sometimes uproarious celebration by veterans, Remembrance Day meetings, as Natal'ia Baranskaia's novel *Remembrance Day* (*Den' pominoveniia*, written in the 1970s, but not published until 1989) reveals, were a time for quiet reflecton on the part of war widows and the many other Soviet citizens who had lost relatives, as well as for official parades. Privileges awarded to war veterans—queue-jumping as well as enhanced pensions—were not resented, but seen as perfectly proper in a culture where wartime heroism was an irrefutable testimony of moral probity.

The ambiguity at which even war memorials and official commemorations hinted was evident, too, in artistic representations of the war. Though attacks on artists for 'excessive pessimism' in handling war themes were sometimes made, particularly between 1946 and 1953, from 1941 until 1986 representing the Second World War was one of the few ways in which writers, painters, film-makers, and musicians could give voice to the tragic aspects of Soviet history and Soviet reality. Anna Akhmatova's cycle 'In Praise of Peace', one of the few of her works published after Zhdanov's denunciation of her in 1946, illustrates how official populism and the populism of élite literature could, when war was the theme, be at one:

> Где елей искалеченные руки
> Взьвали к мщенью—зеленеет ель,
> И там, где сердце ныло от разлуки,—
> Там мать поет, качая колыбель.

> [Where the crippled arms of firs
> Demanded vengeance, a fir is growing green,
> And where a heart sorrowed in parting
> A mother sings and rocks her baby's cradle.][12]

Like the Blockade poetry of Ol'ga Berggol'ts or Vera Inber, Akhmatova's evocations of wartime suffering spoke in the voice of Mother Russia herself.

Lamentation was not the only possibility for those who wanted to write about the war. Texts such as Viktor Nekrasov's *In the Trenches of Stalingrad* (*V okopakh Stalingrada*, 1946), Evgenii Evtushenko's *Babii Iar* (1961), or films such as Grigorii Chukhrai's affecting *Ballad of a Soldier* (*Ballada o soldate*, 1959), Nikolai Gubenko's autobiographical account of war orphans *Winged Birds* (*Podranki*, 1977), or Elem Klimov's lurid, but intermittently powerful *Come and See* (*Idi i smotri*, 1985), were all notable examples of how the canonicity of war thematics facilitated unusually gritty and plausible portrayals of ordinary Soviet lives. But licence was not unlimited. Topics that might have been seen to

12 A. Akhmatova, 'Proshlo piat' let' (1950), in *Stikhotvoreniia i poemy* (Leningrad, 1977), 231. The poem was first published in *Ogonek* in 1950, but was not repudiated by Akhmatova when the Stalin era ended—it was reprinted in her *Stikhotvoreniia* (1958).

undermine the status of the military command or political authorities —the disaster-hit early campaigns of the Red Army in the months after the German invasion, or the collaboration of some Soviet citizens with the occupying forces, or revelations that the system of privileges according to rank had persisted even during the Blockade in Leningrad—remained taboo, in fiction as in journalism, until the height of *glasnost'* in 1989–90.[13]

War mythology was in many ways a supremely efficient basis of national identity in the post-Stalin era. Unlike the history of the Communist Party or even revolutionary history, it invoked what was universally perceived as a just cause: the righteousness of the war was never questioned, even in private, and up to the present day the appropriation by Soviet forces of 'trophy art' and other kinds of war booty (from trains to toothbrushes) is seen by most Russians as rightful recompense for their sufferings during the Occupation. War mythology tapped private as well as public sensibilities: the enormous casualties suffered by the Soviet Union after 1941 meant that no family was left untouched: as in Britain, France, and Germany after 1918, much of an entire generation of women was left widowed or single. Furthermore, bereavement for those who had died in ways that could not be mentioned (in the purges or famines) could be tapped by the very public parade of grief for war victims. Yet war mythology also carried the seeds of its own destruction as a consolidating force. Though official commemorations could, and often did, adequately express private feelings, the clichés of official propaganda were so melodramatically overstated, and so often repeated, as to invite ridicule to which the war itself would never have been subjected —as, for instance, in the following ironical *chastushka*:

> Звездочка с неба упала
> Прямо милому в штаны.
> Ну пусть все там оборвала,
> Лишь бы не было войны.

[A star fell down from the skies above
Straight into the pants of my dear sweet love.
Hell, who cares what it tears apart,
So long as a new war doesn't start?]

And in a ballad by the popular guitar-poet Aleksandr Galich, 'How Klim Petrovich Spoke at a Meeting in Defence of Peace', the first-person hero, a much-decorated master workman, is handed a speech which he to his horror realizes has been written for someone quite different:

13 On war films, see A. Lawton, *Kinoglasnost: Soviet Cinema in Our Time* (Cambridge, 1992). On war literature, see E. J. Brown, *Russian Literature since the Revolution*, 2nd edn. (Cambridge, Mass., 1982); D. Piper, 'Soviet Union', in H. Klein (ed.), *The Second World War in Fiction* (London, 1984), 131–72; and G. Hosking, *Beyond Socialist Realism: Soviet Literature since Ivan Denisovich* (London, 1980).

«Израильская, говорю, военщина
Известна всему свету.
Как мать говорю, и как женщина
Требую их к ответу!

Который год я вдовая—
Все счастье—мимо,
Но я стоять готовая
За дело мира!

Как мать я заявляю и как женщина . . . »
Тут отвисла у меня прямо челюсть—
Ведь бывают такие промашки!
Этот сучий сын, пижон-порученец,
Перепутал в суматохе бумаги.

['The war-mongering by those Israelis—
The whole world knows it.
As a woman, as a mother, I say—
"Let them answer for it."

'For years now I've been widowed,
My joys are long past,
But I'll stand up and be counted
For Peace, our great cause!

As a woman I tell you, and as a mother . . .'
And I caught my breath.
These cock-ups do happen!
That idiot messenger, the tosser,
Had given me the wrong text!]][14]

Klim Petrovich need not have worried, however; his speech was so formulaic in its sentiments as to be well-received even when recited by a strapping middle-aged man.

The Decline of Soviet Mythology: From Stagnation to Social Collapse

14 A. Galich, 'Istoriia o tom kak Klim Petrovich vystupal na mitinge v zashchitu mira', in *Pokolenie obrechennykh* (Frankfurt am Main, 1972), 264. For the *chastushka* quoted and many others, see *Nepodtsenzurnaia russkaia chastushka*, ed. V. Kabronskii (New York, 1978).

The appropriation of war mythology by the Party, and especially by the officially sponsored peace movement, exposed this aspect of national ideology to the same dangers as Party rhetoric more generally. As the population became more cynical about the Party, so it became more cynical about its pronouncements, and especially about public commemorations of its leading role. The regimes of Khrushchev and his successors saw an explosion of political jokes, many of them aimed directly at the leadership and at the Party. The triumphant political slogan *Lenin umer, a delo ego zhivet!* (Lenin has died, but his works live on!) was reapplied to an increasingly geriatric Party leader as *Brezhnev umer, a telo ego zhivet* (Brezhnev has died, but his waterworks live on).[15] By the late 1970s, the 'demonstrations' held for 7 November and 1 May (the prestige events in Red Square excepted), inspired a marked lack of enthusiasm in many people, who attended only because of the fear of *nepriiatnosti* (reprisals against them) at work. The parades had become openly lackadaisical and disorganized, with marchers falling out of step and doing all they could to skive off early. Though the festivities for 9 May had a more celebratory air, this was more to do with the likelihood of good weather than with deep feeling for the official side of the celebrations. And constant references to the role of the Red Army in saving the Soviet Union in the 1940s could not save rising discontent with the modern military command over its role in the disastrous Afghan War (begun in 1980), and its collusion in the appalling conditions suffered by conscripts undergoing compulsory military service—bullying, starvation rations, exposure to harmful levels of radiation. Sergei Kaledin's documentary story 'Stroibat' ('The Construction Battalion'), published in *Novyi mir* in 1990 but set in the 1970s, offers a harrowing description of life in a particularly unpleasant, but not untypical, section of the army, to which conscripts were relegated because of health or behavioural problems, and where drug abuse was as regular an event as *dedovshchina* (tormenting new boys).[16]

War mythology also had another kind of built-in obsolescence, since it was so heavily dependent on the folk memory of those who had actually lived through the experience. War films, war museums, and war literature all recalled a time of deprivation without parallel in the present; but the comparison, valid for those who could remember the 1940s, was a good deal less effective for their children and grandchildren. For them, the far-off days of social solidarity and self-sacrifice were not even a distant memory, and certainly not sufficient to prevent their becoming dissatisfied with the poor quality and scarcity of Soviet-made goods, most particularly consumer durables, as Western products leaked through on the black market. Increasingly, too, Western mass culture seemed more attractive than the Soviet *estrada*, a fact reflected not only in the high prices fetched on the black market by smuggled records, bootleg tapes and videos, posters, t-shirts, and jeans, but also by the assimilation of 'American' influences in Soviet mass culture itself. Goods manufactured in 'fraternal' socialist nations, such as East Germany and Yugoslavia, began to be marketed in special shops, which attracted massive queues; Pepsi Cola was manufactured and distributed under contract; and the government encouraged the development of a genre that could be

15 For further Brezhnev jokes, see Iu. Borev (ed.), *Fariseia: Poslestalinskaia epokha v predaniiakh i anekdotakh* (Moscow, 1992) (also includes urban myths).
16 The story put into print material circulating widely in oral tradition in 1980 when the present writer was a student in Russia.

termed 'rock-*estrada*', as Soviet groups produced diluted versions of Western popular music, some of which, such as the work of the group Time Machine, did have genuine appeal to Soviet young people. And naming patterns, which had formerly reflected popular solidarity with political leaders, now began to indicate disaffection with the Soviet past: there was a dramatic rise in popularity of Old Russian names (Rodion, Iaroslav, Viacheslav, Boleslava, Alevtina) and also of Russified Western names (Antuan, Teodor, Richard, Anzhelika, Paola, Linda, Liutsella), while Mariia and Aleksei, unpopular in the past because of their religious connotations (Aleksei was associated with St Alexis, was a popular peasant name, and was also the name of the last, murdered, tsarevich), also became considerably commoner.[17]

Such developments, though, could only foster the split between aspirations in different age-groups. So much is made painfully clear, for instance, by the very interesting memoirs of a Southern Russian working-class woman, Evgeniia Kiseleva, published in *Novyi mir* during 1991, but covering the years 1941 to 1980. Kiseleva's life-story is not narrated at all in the manner of official history—she is frank about the difficulties she endured in order to keep her family together during and after the war. Deserted by her first husband, she then married a hard-drinking, skirt-chasing second husband, being forced to *spekul'nut'* (deal on the black market) to raise money, and to see off her rivals, spitting full in the face of one, 'an ugly, toothy, gammy-legged hussy, with a mouth fit to split her face in half', and kicking another 'in the belly and in her privates'. Generally, her story is concerned with personal affairs, untouched by political history. Yet when she describes her life at the time of writing, in 1980, a didactic note enters the tale:

I almost feel like kissing everyone in the security department, that they've taken me on to work there, I'm no good I know, just a sick penniless old woman, who needs me, I know that! . . . Thanks be to the Soviet Authorities and to the Great Communist Party and Comrade Brezhnev the leader for the laws that let us invalids work when we're no good. Thanks be to them for looking after us old people. . . .

I'm proud of the leaders of our country. You see Brezhnev come into a meeting proud and upright, smiling, never mind he's seventy years old, pride and skill make him confident—think of all those countries he's conquered without tears or blood, just by kisses and hugs. Our dear Leonid Il'ich Brezhnev, I know as I sit here writing my book that Hitler drank up seas of blood and oceans of blood. I know that in 1942 in Pervomaisk those Germans drove a whole lot of prisoners, our soldiers, into a club and put a guard on it and boarded up the windows so those boys died of hunger . . . But now the young people, the ones the age of them soldiers, they don't know they're born: they've got plenty of clothes, and shoes, and plenty to eat, all paid for

17 See A. V. Suslova and A. V. Superanskaia, *O russkikh imenakh* (Leningrad, 1991), chs. 4 and 8. The authors of the book express mild disapproval about the popularity of foreign names (p. 81).

with their own money—all they've got to do is work and enjoy themselves! People here, especially young people, aren't pleased that the government gives so much away abroad, that they're helping Cuba and Vietnam and Romania and Hungary and lots more countries, I can't remember them all, I often quarrel with them, listen, young comrades, I say, that's our politics, as Lenin said and wrote, we have to share what we have with any country and be friendly so that we have peace, not war, that dreadful thing.[18]

By the late 1970s, it had become obvious that the 'young people' of whom Kiseleva spoke felt increasing cynicism, not only about the Soviet Union's foreign policy, but about a good many other aspects of Soviet society. Official Soviet mass culture was increasingly challenged, in their affections, by Western popular culture, and indeed by Soviet counter-culture, especially the songs of the 'bard' (guitar-poet) Vladimir Vysotskii, monuments to the shared experiences of ordinary Soviet young men (military service, drinking, love affairs, sport). The Party, not only an élite organization, but one dominated by the middle-aged and elderly, had little influence on most young people's lives; on the other hand, the Komsomol, diluted by mass membership, had long ceased to be a positive force of activism, though its members could still be subjected to damaging sanctions such as expulsion from educational institutions. As for compulsory tuition in dialectical materialism and history of the Communist Party at universities and institutes, this was treated by students with about as much fervour as the compulsory lectures in theology by their turn-of-the-century predecessors.

The growing disaffection among young people was to be expressed both in the birth of a separate youth culture (see Ch. 17) and in the high level of participation, among young people, in the informal political and cultural associations permitted by Mikhail Gorbachev in the late 1980s. The granting of permission to informal organizations also initiated the development of oppositional movements that were far more broadly based, in class terms, than the Russian dissident groupings of the 1960s and 1970s, where intellectuals had played a key role. Further impetus was given to discontent by clumsy attempts at marketization: the introduction of *khozraschet* (individual budget control by enterprises) in 1986 broke down old systems of distribution without facilitating new ones, leading to increasing chaos in industry, while the legalization of worker councils at factories gave workers no real control. Resentment against local and national management was increased by widespread fears of mass unemployment, lashed up by a law of 1991 permitting employees to be made redundant. Miners' strikes in 1989 and 1991 were part of a rush of events in which the Russian masses came out on to the streets, for the first time since

18 E. Kiseleva, 'Kishmareva, Kiseleva, Tiuricheva', *Novyi mir*, 2 (1991), 17–18, 22.

the late 1920s, in order to demand change, and to voice grievances over matters ranging from food and goods shortages to exploitation at work to pollution and other ecological issues.

The exasperation caused by shortages was further exacerbated by the conspicuous failure of the Gorbachev regime's bungled campaign against alcohol abuse, launched in the spring of 1985. As Stephen White has shown in his recent study of the campaign, it 'showed not just the limitations of a policy that was determined without the participation of ordinary citizens, but more generally the limitations of a system of government that denied them a share in the management of the society in which they lived'. The structure of the campaign had three parts, according to the classic model of a top-down initiative in the post-Stalin Soviet Union: first the identification of 'serious shortcomings' in the system, accompanied by 'a flood of real or if necessary fabricated letters in the press from ordinary citizens'; second, 'the adoption of a resolution promising to eliminate the shortcomings that had been brought to the leadership's attention in this way'; and finally, a 'turning point' in which local leaders reported great successes in implementing the campaign, and 'the central authorities, confirmed in their wisdom by these reports, are encouraged to raise their original objectives'.[19] In fact, in this as in other cases, such 'successes' were largely illusory. Despite some grassroots approval (particularly among women, who, although female alcoholism had also risen in the post-Stalin era, were still more likely to suffer the consequences of heavy drinking at second hand, as the partners and family members of violent drunks), the campaign quickly lost momentum under the weight of its own stupidity, with local leaders' efforts to follow the campaign leading to such unplanned and disastrous consequences as the uprooting of whole vineyards in wine-growing areas of the Union.

Resistance to the 'demi sec law' (*polusukhoi zakon*) soon took hold, therefore; the Party leader was dubbed Gensok (Gensek, General Secretary, the second element replaced with *sok*, fruit juice), and all sorts of methods of avoiding drinking the soft drinks promoted by the government evolved. While drink disappeared from diplomatic receptions, for instance, it was still possible for serious addicts to acquire their poison in the form of, say, spiked orange juice, or home-distilled hooch (*samogon*), whose production rocketed, precipitating a shortage of sugar in its turn. Vodka and *samogon* not only began to fetch huge prices on the black market, but became the standard form of currency for many transactions, being known jocularly as 'liquid cash' (*zhidkaia valiuta*). At least one works collective nominated its most notorious drunkard as convenor of the anti-alcohol campaign.

19 S. White, *Russia Goes Dry* (Cambridge, 1995), 189, 85.

The campaign concluded with heavy drinking and alcoholism still further entrenched than before it began; spirituous liquors, usually of poor quality and often contaminated, remain one of the most successful products of mafia-run factories.

The failure of the campaign resulted, as much as anything else, from a huge underestimation by Gorbachev and his associates of the importance of drinking to many Soviet citizens. Not only was drinking the main leisure activity in many provincial towns; it was also one of the only forms of cross-class bonding agent in an increasingly stratified society; moreover, drunkenness counted as a kind of free cultural space, a sort of 'tax haven' for social criticism. In the post-1953 era, cutting remarks could be make when drunk of a kind that would never have been tolerated in a sober speaker, a fact evident in the careers of some flamboyant drinkers, such as the poet Ol'ga Berggol'ts. However, the frightening dominance of alcohol as social lubricant was most obvious in working-class and peasant homes. While this had been true in pre-Revolutionary times as well, and throughout the Stalin era, the extent of consumption had now got quite out of hand, even during working hours. This is evident not only from literary texts, such as Sergei Kaledin's *The Humble Cemetery* (*Smirennoe kladbishche*, 1987), the tale of 'Sparrow', an alcoholic gravedigger, but also from factual accounts, such as the anthropologist Bruce Grant's recent description of his fieldwork on Sakhalin island. In the fish-packing factory where he spent time working as a casual labourer during the annual fish-run, drinking began at 11 a.m., when the factory opened, first with vodka ('following a consumption hierarchy that opened with the best first'). It then continued throughout the day until 2 a.m.:

The fish was not on schedule. The ladies in the cleaning section were having their own problems staying vertical, hence the first conveyor belt did not roll in until approximately two [p.m.], after what was two and a half hours of concerted resting. With the first fish, there was a lethargic twenty-minute display of worker honor, followed by a forty-five minute rest and the sampling of the atrocious Azerbaijani wine *Agdam*. We returned to work for thirty-five minutes, then rested for another thirty. This continued more or less until five, when we parted for an hour for dinner. On a more auspicious day the work would have been long completed.

By six o'clock the fish was on its eighth hour and indeed a great deal had accumulated over the course of the day. This began a somewhat stricter regime with more sporadic breaks, marked by the consumption of quantities of beer obtained over the dinner hour. By eleven the stalwart had graduated to the graver heavy-duty rot gut, *Samogon*, and at 11:30 P.M. an upper-lever supervisor from the cleaning section made her first belated appearance of the day to castigate the churlish, many of whom were by then contemplating the most extreme rung on the beverage totem, beer complemented by a judicious bug spray accent. By this time the better part of the still untreated fish had begun to sour in an unpleasant manner. A great post-midnight push concluded the task at 2.00 A.M., whereby the brigade retired to the bathhouse for our weekly washing in rusty orange hot water.[20]

The scenes described date from 1990. Although the village under observation was Nivkh rather than Russian, the vignette could have been sketched, *mutatis mutandis*, almost anywhere in the Russian Federation then or now. It illustrates how the work-to-rule atmosphere that prevailed in Soviet factories, with alternate idling and storming filling up long compulsory shifts, spiralled out of control once planned targeting had disintegrated.

Despite the conspicuous failure of the anti-alcohol campaign, the Gorbachev regime, especially in its later stages, did give ordinary Soviet citizens space to express their concerns about issues not previously debated openly in the public sphere, most notably environmental concerns, or complaints about food supply and wage levels. Also, for the first time since 1917, candidates from outside the Communist Party were allowed to stand in elections, giving those outside the Party élite the chance to nominate representatives. The impetus for the formation of grassroots protest organizations which gave somewhat more coherent voice to protest was undoubtedly stepped up by widespread reporting, in the Soviet media, of the activities of nationalist movements in the other republics, in some of which—notably the Baltic States and the Caucasus—dissidence had become an almost universal activity, and one which the authorities were now impotent to stifle. The high point of popular and intellectual consensus was marked by the aborted coup of August 1991, in which thousands poured out on to the streets to express their disapproval of the would-be dictators, and their support for democratic change, personified in the figure of Boris Yeltsin, a genuine folk hero for the meanwhile.

Since 1991, however, the momentum of mass participation has slowed down again. The harsh side-effects of accelerated privatization have created a new class of conspicuous Russian consumers, some of them beneficiaries of the *blat* system who have turned their previously illegal fortunes into legal dollar millions, some of them young entrepreneurs in growth areas (computer technology, financial services, protection rackets). At least two-thirds of Russian society, though, struggles to stave off penury: it is not only women now who are working 'double shifts', since many Russians of both sexes have to hold down two or even three paying jobs in order to survive. The fact that property is the only secure investment has meant that

20 B. Grant, *In the Soviet House of Culture: A Century of Perestroikas* (Princeton, 1995), 25.

families with the resources can make a reasonable living by letting out property (a married couple may move back in with one set of parents, say, leaving their two-roomed flat to be let), but on the other hand has made those living in fashionable areas of central Moscow extremely vulnerable to forced eviction by mafia gangs wanting to clear buildings for redevelopment. As inflation spirals, but wages in state institutions fail to keep pace, few have the time to attend political meetings or discuss current events. In any case, activism now seems pointless, as Yeltsin, like Gorbachev before him, becomes increasingly committed to reaction at home, and chauvinism abroad (the Chechen invasion, costly, bloody, and exceedingly unpopular, became an Afghan War of the mid-1990s). Popular interest in political participation has slumped: falling turn-outs in elections are among the indications of how lack of confidence in the capacity of politicians to provide solutions has grown (a point recognized by the new Russian constitution, which stipulates a minimum required turn-out of just 25 per cent for national elections). On the other hand, however, the dramatic success of nationalist and communist candidates in the 1995 parliamentary elections was an index of the strength of nostalgia for the Soviet past, especially outside the metropolitan centres.[21]

Yet for all that, one effect of *perestroika* and *glasnost'* persists: the views of those outside the élite have become more prominent, if not more influential. Old prejudices about the *narod* have come under pressure as it is realized that workers and peasants do not form an inert mass, but a range of widely differing groups, some of whom may support chauvinist associations, such as Pamiat' or Zhirinovskii's Liberal Democratic Party, the rump of the Communist Party, or monarchist caucuses, but the vast majority of whom are moved only by local causes, forming an enormous pool of floating voters, or non-voters, whose decisions may influence the future of an at least superficially democratic new Russia. A concomitant effect has been to bring about a crisis of identity not so much on the part of Party officials, who have generally been able to exploit their connections in order to survive the transition to free-market (or flea-market) economics, but on the part of those who traditionally shared their leading role in Soviet society—the Russian intelligentsia.

21 There are few studies to confirm the extent of this nostalgia. See, however, Grant, *The Soviet House*. On voting patterns, see L. Halligan and B. Mozdrukhov, *A Guide to Russia's Parliamentary Elections: CTE Briefing*, 1 (Dec. 1995).

13

Religion and Orthodoxy

JANE ELLIS

The Russian Orthodox Church, 1921–1953

The Bolsheviks lost no time in beginning their attack on the Russian Orthodox Church. Though the Church had been able to open a National Council in 1917 following the February Revolution (the first for 200 years, since the Church's governing structure had been suppressed by Peter the Great), after the October Revolution the Bolsheviks issued a series of decrees disestablishing the Church, secularizing schools, and confiscating its property.[1] Their Marxist ideology led the Bolsheviks to believe that property was an essential support for the Church and that its confiscation would inevitably lead to the Church's downfall: time was to prove them wrong.

In 1918 the aged Metropolitan Vladimir of Kiev was assassinated and the popular Metropolitan Veniamin of Petrograd was tried and executed (both were among the first martyrs of the Soviet period to be canonized in 1992). This was the start of a wave of persecution which lasted through the 1920s and 1930s, when hundreds of thousands of bishops, clergy, and laity were sent to the Gulag, where many of them perished or were shot. All religions and denominations suffered, but the sufferings of the Orthodox were on a larger scale, partly because of the sheer weight of numbers, and partly because of their connection with the overthrown tsarist regime.[2]

In 1918 Patriarch Tikhon anathematized those who

persecute [the] truth and are trying to ruin Christ's work. Echoes reach us every day of horrible and cruel massacres whose victims are innocent people, and even those lying on a bed of a sickness whose only fault was that they had honestly done their duty to their country and worn themselves out in the service of God and the people . . .

Foolish men, return to your senses and cease your massacres . . . by the authority committed to us by God, we forbid you to approach the mysteries [sacraments] of Christ, we anathematise you, you who at least still bear Christian names and, though it be only by your birth, belong to the Orthodox Church.[3]

It is difficult nowadays to recall that at that time it was by no means clear that the Bolsheviks would continue to rule for long or be able to extend their authority throughout the country.[4]

The atheism of Marxist materialist philosophy was intensified by the atheism of the Russian intelligentsia. From the mid-nineteenth century most intellectuals had turned their backs on the Church, which, they thought, offered no creative solutions to the problems facing Russia. Caricatures of ignorant, venal, and drunken priests were commonplace (and widely used in Soviet atheist propaganda). The publication of Landmarks (Vekhi) in 1909, including essays by Berdiaev, Bulgakov, Frank, Struve, and others was, however, a sign that some formerly Marxist thinkers had returned to traditional values and embraced the Church and, in Bulgakov's case, the priesthood. They were to become important in the development of Orthodox theology in the emigration after 1922, and many significant works were published in Paris.[5]

From 1922 anti-religious propaganda began in earnest. At Christmas a carnival mocking the nativity of Christ paraded through Moscow, and at Easter the carnivals were extended to all large towns: effigies of 'gods', from the God of Israel to Buddha, were burned. In 1925 the League of Militant Atheists was founded by Emil'ian Iaroslavskii. It published Bezbozhnik, a campaigning journal, and Anti-religioznik, a review of science and methodology for an educated readership. In 1929 it issued a Five-Year Plan, which was not realized but achieved impressive results: for example, by 1932, though the membership target of 17 million members had not been reached, it did claim over 5 million members. The even more ambitious Second Five-Year Plan aimed to eradicate all religion by 1937.[6]

Lenin's personal hostility to religion is well-known. He called it 'spiritual booze', an even harsher term than Marx's 'opium of the people'. Other Bolsheviks, however, had a different attitude to religion, notably the writer Maksim Gor'kii and the first People's Commissar for Enlightenment, Anatolii Lunacharskii, who became known as 'god-builders'. They argued that, since there was no god outside humankind, people must build their own god through the community by disregarding personal interests and focusing their creative

1 See N. Struve, Christians in Contemporary Russia (London, 1967), 25 ff., and Francis House, The Russian Phoenix: The Story of Russian Christians AD 988–1988 (London, 1988), 55 ff.
2 House, Russian Phoenix, 55–6.

3 Quoted in Struve, Christians, 28.
4 See House, Russian Phoenix, 56.
5 See J. Sutton, 'Fr Sergi Bulgakov on Christianity and Judaism', Religion, State and Society (RSS), 20 (1992), 62–7, esp. 62, and W. Van Den Bercken, 'Postcommunism avant la lettre: Russia's Religious Thinkers on Communism in 1918', RSS 20 (1992), 345–59.
6 See Struve, Christians, 54–6.

efforts on the building-up of the collective, which would become the common god. This *bogostroitel'stvo* foundered because of Lenin's opposition: he wrote to Gor'kii that 'every religious idea, every idea of God, even flirting with the idea of God' was 'unutterable vileness of the most degrading kind, a contagion of the most abominable type'.[7]

Lenin's anti-religious virulence was also expressed in the affair of the church valuables. In 1922 famine struck as a result of the Civil War, and Patriarch Tikhon called upon the faithful to surrender valuable church articles, except those consecrated for sacramental use, to be used to buy grain abroad. However, the government then ordered the surrender of *all* church valuables, hoping to portray the Patriarch as indifferent to the fate of the starving. People defending church valuables in the town of Shuia were shot, and fifty-four were tried, of whom eleven were executed. Following the affair, Patriarch Tikhon was arrested, but was suddenly released in 1923 following pressure from foreign governments, including the British. He issued a confession whose validity was disputed, as was an even stronger statement calling upon the clergy to recognize the Soviet government and issued over his signature as he was dying in 1925. Lenin's determination to use the affair for his own ends was revealed in a secret letter, excluded from his *Complete Works* and published eventually in Paris in 1970. He wrote to the Politburo: 'The more representatives of the bourgeoisie and the reactionary clergy that we manage to shoot the better.'[8]

The succession to Tikhon, in a process whose precise nature is still disputed, fell upon Metropolitan Sergii who, after a period of imprisonment, issued a declaration of loyalty to the Soviet government. This did not bring about the government concessions in the short term for which Sergii may have hoped, but his supporters argue that in the long term he acted in the only way possible to save the Church. The present patriarch, Aleksii II, repudiated Sergii's declaration in 1991, while acknowledging the impossible circumstances in which he had issued it.[9] Many church members went underground in response to Sergii's declaration: they became known as the True Orthodox or Catacomb Church, and re-emerged only from 1990 onwards.

Earlier the Soviet government had backed a reform movement within the Church known as the Living Church or Renovationists (*obnovlentsy*). They supported reforms such as a married episcopate which were debated at the 1917–18 Council, but were also openly pro-Soviet and took advantage of the hounding of the patriarchal Church to further their own ends. Many parishes initially went over to them, but most of the faithful remained loyal to Tikhon. The Living Church movement petered out when the Soviet government found that it could achieve its aims through the patriarchal Church and no

7 Lenin cited in House, *Russian Phoenix*, 55. On the revival of god-building in Soviet literature in the 1980s, see I. Maryniak, 'Truthseekers, Godbuilders or Culture Vultures? Some Supplementary Remarks on Religious Perspectives in Modern Soviet Literature', *Religion in Communist Lands (RCL)*, 16 (1988), 227–36.
8 For an account of the affair, see D. Pospielovsky, *The Russian Orthodox Church under the Soviet Regime 1917–1982* (Crestwood, Tenn., 1984), 93–7. On Patriarch Tikhon's arrest and confession, see Struve, *Christians*, 39–41. Lenin's letter of 18 Mar. 1922, 'TOP SECRET. To Comrade Molotov for Members of the Politburo', is cited in *RCL* 7 (1979), 46–8.
9 Patriarch Aleksi II, 'I Accept Responsibility for All that Happened', *RSS* 20 (1992), 241–2 (first pub. in *Izvestiia*, 10 June 1991, 2).

longer needed it. The patriarchal Church however continued to be denounced for alleged compliance with the regime by the *émigré*, pro-monarchist Karlovtsy Church (founded in Karlovci, Yugoslavia, in 1921), later known as the Russian Orthodox Church Abroad (or in Exile), which now has its headquarters in New York state.

In 1929 the Law on Religious Associations was adopted. This severely restricted the activities of all religious groups, whose only right now was to worship within the walls of a building registered for the purpose. All outside activities and social involvement were forbidden, and the number of places of worship was kept drastically low by simple refusals by local authorities to grant registration. This law (with minor amendments in 1975) was not superseded until 1990.

Propagation of scientific atheism continued throughout the education system and through cultural outlets and the media on a massive scale which was to come to an end only after Gorbachev's proclamation of *glasnost'*. Every factory, trade union, social club, and school had its 'atheist corner' or 'red corner', ironically replacing the former *krasnyi ugol* or icon corner found in the homes of the devout by exploiting the fact that the adjective *krasnyi*, which had formerly meant 'fair' or 'beautiful', now had a more politically amenable sense. Compulsory examinations on atheism were the norm in schools and institutes of higher education. Their impact, however, was probably no greater than that of any compulsory subject in any country, and indeed stimulated searching minds to embark on a religious quest, on the principle that if the regime was against religion there must be something to it. Museums of atheism were opened throughout the USSR, the best-known being housed in Leningrad's Kazan Cathedral. Opened in 1932, it included primitive anti-religious exhibitions offensive to believers. Gone were the days when the Kazan Cathedral could be used to perform requiems for the victims of Soviet terror, as it had been in August 1921, when the poet Gumilev and sixty-one others shot for alleged political crimes were commemorated by a service held there.[10]

The Greek author Nikos Kazantzakis, who wrote *The Last Temptation of Christ*, was one of many Western intellectuals fascinated by the Soviet experiment who visited the USSR, but possibly the only one with an Orthodox background which helped him empathize with the people he was meeting. He wrote in elegiac style of the abandonment of the old formal religion: 'God is wandering in the streets, homeless, jobless, persecuted like a bourgeois', but was equally repelled by the staff of the weekly journal *Ateist*, whom he watched producing satirical popular anti-religious articles and caricatures with a zeal amounting to religious fervour, and their director, 'his nose

10 See M. Elliott, 'The Leningrad Museum of the History of Religion and Atheism', *RCL* 11 (1983), 124–9, and N. Berberova, *The Italics are Mine*, tr. P. Radley (London, 1969), 129.

dripping with poison'. The old religion might be withering but only to be replaced by the fanatical religion of atheism with its own mysticism and dogmatism.[11]

Church members continued to be brutally persecuted throughout the 1930s as the mantle of Stalin's Great Terror was spread across the whole of the Soviet people. On the eve of the Great Patriotic War only four bishops remained at liberty and very few, possibly as few as a hundred, of the thousands of churches remained open for worship. Theological education, publication, and monasticism had long ceased. This situation was reversed by an unforeseen historical event: Hitler's invasion of the USSR on 21 June 1941. Stalin, taken unawares, remained silent, and the first to speak out was Metropolitan Sergii, who without, astonishingly, waiting for any declaration of government policy, issued a pastoral letter that same day: 'Our Orthodox Church has always shared the destiny of her people. She has suffered with them in their trials and has been consoled by their successes. And today, no less surely, she will not forsake her people. She gives her heavenly blessing to this sacrifice now to be made by the whole nation ... May God grant us victory.' Stalin's first appeal to the people, issued only ten days later, included in its opening sentence the words always used at the opening of an Orthodox sermon: 'Comrades, citizens, *dear brothers and sisters*, my friends'.[12]

Stalin found that he needed the support of Church leaders to kindle patriotic fervour for an unexpected war. Despite persecution Orthodoxy had remained alive in the hearts of the faithful. The Church contributed 150 million roubles to the war effort, including a tank division named after prince Dimitrii Donskoi (to be canonized in 1988). The future Patriarch Aleksii I refused to leave blockaded, starving Leningrad, where he sustained the people's morale by his preaching and by sharing their privations.[13]

In 1943, Stalin summoned the three Orthodox bishops remaining at liberty to a meeting where he asked them to name their requests for their Church. Metropolitan Sergii asked for mass reopening of churches, convening of a Church Council, and the renewal of seminary training for future priests. According to earlier (and sometimes inconsistent) reports of this conversation, Stalin asked why there were no 'cadres' to supply the shortage of clergy. Everyone knew that the 'cadres' had perished in the Gulag, but Metropolitan Sergii replied: 'There are all sorts of reasons why we have no cadres. One of the reasons is that we train a person for the priesthood, and he becomes the Marshal of the Soviet Union.' Stalin, evidently enjoying this allusion to his years in a Georgian seminary, began reminiscing, and the conversation lasted until 3 a.m.[14]

11 See W. Alexeev and T. G. Stavrou, *The Great Revival: The Russian Church Under German Occupation* (Minneapolis, 1976), 1–5.
12 See Struve, *Christians*, 59–61.
13 See Pospielovsky, *Russian Orthodox Church*, 200, and House, *Russian Phoenix*, 73.
14 See House, *Russian Phoenix*, 74 ff., and Pospielovsky, *Russian Orthodox Church*, 201–2.

Archival information which has only recently come to light records that Molotov, the foreign affairs commissar, who was present, asked Sergii when his Church would be able to host a high-level Anglican delegation headed by the Archbishop of York. The Anglican Church had been requesting the Soviet government to allow such an official visit for some time, presumably hoping to strengthen the Russian Church's position and perhaps to reassure members of the British public uneasy about Soviet–British friendship. Stalin was then, in advance of the Tehran Conference, putting pressure on the British to open the second front against Hitler to relieve pressure on the USSR. Later, Molotov was in no hurry to allow a return visit to the British as they had still not opened the Normandy front. This new information indicates the central influence of foreign policy in determining the Church's role from the very beginning of its wartime restoration.[15] The Moscow Patriarchate's usefulness to Soviet foreign policy was a major, perhaps the major factor in allowing such freedoms as it enjoyed in the post-war period.

The survival of Orthodox faith among the people became clearest of all in the territory occupied by the Germans, where churches and monasteries were reopened and people flooded back to them, celebrating belated baptisms and religious weddings. This temporary (1941–4) phenomenon was none the less so strong that it has been called 'the second baptism of Russia'.[16] Orthodox life persisted similarly in western territories of the USSR annexed after the war. In the Baltic area especially monastic life had continued, and the convent in Pyukhtitsa, Estonia, survived incorporation into the Soviet Union and still flourishes to the present day, preserving a strongly Russian atmosphere despite its geographical location. In nearby Pskov, which had been incorporated into the Estonian republic in 1918, there still functions the only monastery on Russian soil not to have been closed since its foundation in 1472.[17]

Realizing that his pre-war policy of eradicating religion had failed, Stalin decided to keep it above ground but within strict limits. Churches, monasteries, and seminaries reopened, and publication of Scriptures and prayer-books recommenced, but all this was contained not only within the bounds of the restrictive 1929 law but also by the watchdogs of the Council for Russian Orthodox Church Affairs (CROCA), whose commissioners in every *oblast'* of the USSR kept close watch on every bishop, priest, and pastor, and in many cases openly and illegally interfered in Church life. The life of Orthodox believers was hard, and many were broken by imprisonment or by being forced into informing on their fellow-believers, but the Church's traditions survived.

15 See D. Pospielovsky, 'The "Best Years" of Stalin's Church Policies (1942–1948) in the Light of Archival Documents', paper given at the 5th ICSEES World Congress, Warsaw, Aug. 1995, forthcoming, 9–11.
16 Alexeev and Stavrou, *Great Revival*, p. xii.
17 See J. Ellis, *The Russian Orthodox Church: A Contemporary History* (London, 1986; repr. 1989), 127, 129.

Undoubtedly there was a measure of anticlericalism, as in any industrialized, modernizing society, but much of the enforced anti-religious sentiment fell upon stony ground. Ignorance rather than hostility was the Church's adversary, an ignorance which persists to this day. None the less, a groundswell of popular piety remained. For many years this was dismissed as being the sentimental preserve of ageing *babushki*, but as decades passed even hardened opponents were forced to admit that there was a never-ending supply of them. It is generally accepted, though, that well into the post-war period the transmission of faith from grandmother to grandchildren—while mother was out at work—was the most widespread means of perpetuating it. It is also clear from memoir history and oral history that nannies and child-minders, many of whom were devout peasant women, could play a similar role in initiating children into religious faith. One Russian woman, now in her late fifties, for instance, recounts that when she reached the age of four, her nanny secretly had her christened, her agnostic parents having failed to perform the rite.[18]

Another indication of popular piety was the status and reverence accorded to the *startsy*, a tradition which survived the harsh years of the 1920s and 1930s when such men lived in deep secrecy, succoured by a few faithful 'spiritual children'. A *starets* is an elder or holy man (no women *startsy* are known of) who after many years of prayer, solitude, and a rigorously ascetic way of life is recognized as a person of deep insight, capable of guiding and counselling the faithful. *Startsy* are not appointed officially by the Church to their position, but acclaimed by the people who come to seek their counsel. Generally they are prescient (*prozorlivye*), that is, they know people's thoughts before they are uttered. Spiritual sons or daughters would place themselves in complete obedience to their *starets*. The best-known historical examples are St Serafim of Sarov and St Amvrosii of Optina, who was visited by Dostoevskii, Tolstoi, Gogol', and others.

In the Soviet Union, *startsy* became generally known of only after their deaths. One such was Fr. Zachariah, the last monk to leave the Holy Trinity Monastery of St Sergii at Zagorsk when it was closed by force, who lived in secret until his death in 1936, drawing to him people to whom he imparted spiritual strength:

After a little while people sensed the grace that dwelt in the elder and began to come to him in his cell. . . . A grief-stricken person had only to talk to the elder for a few minutes and suddenly all his depression and grief would vanish, and tranquillity would be established in his heart; his mind saw God, and such a good, childishly clear and pure feeling came over his heart, as it does on Easter night to a happy child, surrounded by the love of all those

18 C. Kelly, personal information, Moscow, 1991.

near and dear to him, a child who has not tasted grief, who has not known passions and sins. The elder seemed to resurrect and renew the soul that turned to him.[19]

Another elder, Tavrion (Batozsky), born in 1898, spent the years from 1928 to 1956 in camp or exile, which he later described in his sermons as the best days of his life, when he felt happy and praised God. From 1968 to his death in 1978 he became the spiritual father of a convent near Riga, which

was transformed into a place of pilgrimage, bursting with tens of thousands of believers from every part of [the USSR]. Drawn by tales of this extraordinary *starets*, they flocked from the spiritual desert of contemporary life as to a fount of 'living waters': the sick; the old; intellectuals from the big cities; peasants; engineers; hippies; workers—all the suffering people. . . . Many youngsters from Moscow have learnt here for the first time how to sing the psalms and services correctly.[20]

The link between past and present was shown also by a prediction made in the 1930s by the elder Serafim, living in secrecy near Zagorsk, who foresaw a great future for the 4-year-old son of a recent convert to Orthodox Christianity. The boy grew up to become the priest Aleksandr Men', the gifted preacher who transformed the lives of many before his brutal murder in 1990.[21]

A powerful example of the survival of Orthodox piety among the ordinary people, and especially a reverence for the Mother of the God (*Bogoroditsa*) is to be found in the survival of the legend *The Pilgrimage of the Mother of God Among the Torments*, which is mentioned by Dostoevskii's Ivan Karamazov. One of many narratives composed in the first Christian centuries dealing with the fringes of the Gospel story, its oldest known Slavonic version has been dated to the twelfth or thirteenth century. The considerable number of Slavonic versions dating from the fourteenth to nineteenth centuries attest to its popularity, though the Russian intellectual world discovered it only in 1857. The *Pilgrimage* recounts how the Archangel Michael and his angels conduct the *Bogoroditsa* to Hell and show her the different torments endured by those who have committed all manner of sins. She is then lifted up to Heaven where she pleads for mercy for the sinners, begging to be allowed to be tormented with them and calling upon the Archangels Gabriel and Michael with the angels and all the saints to join her entreaties. In response, God grants a remission of their suffering from Holy Thursday until Pentecost every year, at which (in Ivan Karamazov's version) they cry out from the depths of Hell: 'Thou art just, O Lord, thou hast judged aright!' Pierre Pascal writes in his commentary:

19 *An Early Soviet Saint: The Life of Father Zachariah*, tr. J. Ellis (London, 1976), 53–4.
20 'Russia's Spiritual Traditions Live On', *RCL* 10 (1982), 97–8.
21 *I bylo utro . . . : Vospominaniia ob ottse Aleksandre Mene* (Moscow, 1992), 109.

If the *Pilgrimage* is intended to suggest to the faithful a solution to the difficult problem of reconciling God's justice and his mercy, when the Church (after hesitating over the interpretation of the evangelical texts) had decided on the eternity of the pains of Hell, it is clear that the Mother of God has the necessary authority for obtaining this compromise solution, a sign of indulgence from God. Thus, two themes are conflated in the narrative—the glorification of the Mother of God for her potent intercession, and a modification of the uneasily tolerated doctrine of an eternal Hell.

He adds: 'It is unquestionably the problem of evil which, in the thought of Karamazov, establishes a relation between our apocryphon and the Legend of the Grand Inquisitor.'[22] Pascal uses the *Pilgrimage* to link the first and third parts of his book, dealing respectively with the nature of Russian religious belief and resistance to (Soviet) persecution. He relates accounts of martyrdom in the labour camps by nuns and others who in their acceptance of suffering for their faith recall the torments of those for whom the *Bogoroditsa* pleaded to God.

Devotion to the *Bogoroditsa* survived also in popular legend, for example one aetiological myth recorded in central Russia, which explains the origin of a shingle bank: 'When they started to pull the churches down in Stalin's time, the Virgin Mary came out and went to seek shelter in that village on the far side of the lake. The shingle bank marks where she went over the sea.'[23] Such legends indicate how attachment to Christian figures continued, as in the past, to exist alongside layers of secular practice and belief that the Church might have endorsed only reluctantly. In the same way, celebration of Easter with special foods (sweet curd cheese *paskha* and rich *kulich* loaves) and with painted eggs was current in many families whose knowledge of the theological and liturgical import of the festival was at best rudimentary.

The Russian Orthodox Church since 1953

Following Stalin's death Church life continued by force of inertia with no major policy decisions. Khrushchev's thaw, signalled by his 'secret speech' to the Twentieth Party Congress of 1956, began a general opening-up of the society within which the Church existed. Many human rights activists of the 1960s and 1970s date the awakening of their independent political consciousness to this event, including some who were to become campaigners for religious freedom. However, in sharp contrast to his image as a liberalizer, Khrushchev, largely on his own initiative, launched an all-out assault on religion

22 P. Pascal, *The Religion of the Russian People* (London, 1976), 57–81, 82, 83.
23 Quoted in J. Vytkovskaya, 'Slav Mythology', in C. Larrington (ed.), *The Feminist Companion to Mythology* (London, 1992), 115.

from 1959 to 1964. Believers were vilified in the Soviet press, and the Orthodox, though not more severely persecuted than other denominations, had a higher profile, especially among the clergy, with some well-publicized cases of apostasy by clerics who then joined in the hounding of the Church. Numerous believers were imprisoned. More than half of all Orthodox churches, between 10,000 and 12,000, were closed or destroyed. (Khrushchev was repudiated by his successors after his ousting in 1964, but they made no attempt to reopen these churches.) There was a flood of atheist propaganda. Khrushchev's antireligious persecution could perhaps have resulted from his need to show himself as a strong man in one area while he liberalized in others, but more probably the authorities had been alarmed by the Church's resilience and recovery after the decades of persecution intended to destroy it.[24]

Khrushchev's religious persecution prompted a few brave souls to stand up openly in defence of their faith. The Baptists were first into the fray in 1961 and 1962, with public appeals to cease interfering in Church affairs which swiftly led to the imprisonment of their leaders. A few Orthodox spoke out in the new medium of *samizdat*. Khrushchev's sudden fall was followed by a period of political uncertainty which bolder spirits saw as their chance to agitate for real freedom in every sphere of Soviet life.[25] Thus was born the human rights movement, including the campaign for religious freedom, as well as self-sacrificing efforts by writers, artists, and film-makers to break free of the confining ideological bonds of socialist realism (see Chs. 2 and 9).

The influence of Orthodoxy in art has been strong throughout the centuries. All forms of art have been imbued with Orthodox values and imagery. The beauty and haunting quality of icons continued to capture the imagination of even unbelieving artists in the USSR. Orthodox influence has also been apparent in music and architecture, with many ancient churches being the object of public preservation campaigns. These influences began to make themselves felt in various art forms during the 1960s and 1970s. Geoffrey Hosking has shown how, even within the limits imposed by socialist realism, writers such as Vladimir Tendriakov showed their protagonists seeking for (though not finding) faith in God. 'Village writers' (*derevenshchiki*) such as Vasilii Belov and Valentin Rasputin rediscovered values from a past way of life, sometimes including religious ones.[26] Later, under *glasnost'*, Chinghiz Aitmatov published his controversial novel The *Scaffold* (*Plakha*, 1987), whose hero is a young Christian who sacrifices his life in a struggle against the forces of evil. In an interview, Aitmatov, a self-proclaimed atheist, said:

24 See M. Bourdeaux, 'The Black Quinquennium: The Russian Orthodox Church 1959–1965', RCL 9 (1981), 18.
25 See A. Blane, 'A Year of Drift', RCL 2 (1974), 9–15.
26 See G. Hosking, Beyond Socialist Realism: Soviet Fiction since Ivan Denisovich (London, 1980), 68–70, 78–80, 92–7, 100.

The legendary figure of Christ, which was very likely invented by men, is still a living figure for us today, one which teaches us a lofty and unforgettable lesson of personal courage and nobility. After Christ there were great men in all walks of life . . . but Jesus has outlived them all, appealing equally to men of the second and twentieth centuries.[27]

As Mary Seton-Watson has shown, Aitmatov was much criticized in the Soviet press for the religious elements in his novel, but he and other writers had shown that the religious dimension could no longer be ignored in serious literature. However, Irena Maryniak showed that the element of 'god-building' was present in many of these works:

The religious elements to which Mary Seton-Watson points actually serve to bear the a-religious message that in order to improve the standard of social ethics it may be useful to create or 'build' a god. A rediscovery of religious culture and of the principle of faith, Aitmatov suggests, could help to give necessary guidance to Soviet society today . . . it is difficult to deny that in some recent writing, religious references have shown ways in which Christian culture, philosophy and history can be appropriated by ideology to establish cultural identity and to promote a set of ethical values for reference, with a view to making Soviet society stronger and more stable.[28]

In other writings, such as those of Vladimir Soloukhin (*Letters from the Russian Museum* (*Pis'ma iz russkogo muzeia*, 1966)), support for the Church also had layers of ambiguity: Orthodoxy was important here more as a symbol of national cultural achievement than as a spiritual force, Church buildings being only some of the traditional objects and practices whose preservation was advocated. A far more explicitly religious stance was taken by dissident writers, notably Leonid Borodin, whose novels *Partings* (*Rasstavan'e*, 1984) and *The Third Truth* (*Tret'ia pravda*, 1981) had priests and religious believers among their characters, and represented overtly Christian concepts of guilt, sin, and conscience.

In cinema, John Dunlop has shown how directors Andrei Tarkovskii and Andrei Konchalovskii struggled for years to express religious views in their films, both working for long periods abroad.[29] The film *Repentance* (*Pokaianie*) by the Georgian director Tengiz Abuladze, released in 1987, a moving exposure of Stalinism, had a powerful religious motif, and its closing words, 'What good is a road that does not lead to the church?' quickly entered daily parlance.

In painting, religious themes were to be found in works of a number of nonconformist artists of the 1970s. The infamous 'bulldozer exhibition' of 1974, when the Soviet authorities levelled an

27 Ch. Aitmatov, 'Kak slovo nashe otzovetsia', *Druzhba narodov*, 2 (1987), 237.
28 Maryniak, 'Truthseekers, Godbuilders or Culture Vultures?', 233, 236; Maryniak is responding to M. Seton-Watson, 'Religious Themes in Recent Soviet Literature', *RCL* 16 (1988), 117–25.
29 See J. Dunlop, 'Religious Themes in Recent Soviet Cinema', *RCL* 16 (1988), 210–16.

independent open-air art exhibition, included such works, some of which featured in the Image of Modern Russia exhibition of Russian religious art in London shortly afterwards.[30] The sculptor Ernst Neizvestnyi, though not a religious believer, produced studies of the Crucifixion which 'seem to recreate the link between the human condition and Christianity . . . the Cross lies at the centre of his system of images, expressing the Russian experience in spiritual terms'.[31] The Orthodox monk Vitalii Linitskii was sent out from his monastery to express his Christian vocation through his painting: his overtly Christian painting cycles *Apocalypse* and *The Seasons*, and his many paintings of small isolated churches and of angelic beings descending upon Russia, were to become popular in the West.[32] These predated the first official exhibitions of Il'ia Glazunov in 1978 and 1979, which attracted huge interest, not least because they included overtly Christian motifs: but although Glazunov's popularity grew, and his works were praised by Orthodox patriots Vladimir Osipov and Fr. Dimitrii Dudko, his vast canvases degenerated into a crude, overblown nationalism.[33]

Christian themes have been strong in poetry in the post-Stalin period. Irina Ratushinskaia's openly religious poetry contributed to a lengthy prison sentence from which she was released only after international protest in 1986, on the eve of the Gorbachev–Reagan summit in Reykjavik. The Nobel Prize winner Joseph Brodsky, who died at an early age in January 1996, though not formally a Christian, and a Jew by birth, was described as a 'Christian poet' by Lev Pokrovskii, and W. H. Auden noted the importance to Brodsky of the question of Christianity and culture. For Brodsky and his generation, and for younger poets such as Ol'ga Sedakova, the inspiration of Anna Akhmatova, a steadfast Christian resolutely opposed to political terror as well as a major poet, was crucial in finding expressions of belief that went beyond facile pieties.

The importance of the religious theme in culture has been well described by one of the generation of young intellectuals who rediscovered Orthodoxy in the 1970s, Tat'iana Goricheva:

It is only five years since the 'bulldozer exhibition', but it seems like decades. So much has happened, and our 'unofficial' culture, which came into existence so recently, already has a whole history of experience behind it.

There have been pictures, texts, seminars, journals—but that is not all. There have been demonstrations, arrests, trials—but that is not all either. The existential status of life has changed; the cultural atmosphere has been purified; new people have appeared—a new type of man.

Today I want to stress the fact that this renaissance has not just been a cultural one, but a spiritual one as well.

30 See A. Glezer, 'Religion and Soviet Non-Conformist Artists', *RCL* 4 (1976), 16–19.
31 M. Kalinovska, 'The Mystical Language of Ernst Neizvestny', *RCL* 4 (1976), 12.
32 See 'Creation not Destruction' [interview of 1977 with V. Linitskii, with colour photographs], *RCL* 10 (1982), 10–22.
33 See Ellis, *Russian Orthodox Church*, 297.

Goricheva epitomized the rediscovery of the Church following its rejection by both the nineteenth-century intelligentsia and the twentieth-century Communist Party: 'As it enters the Church, the Russian intelligentsia is flowing into the main channel of Russia's great culture; the prodigal son is returning to his Father and discovering in our Lord Jesus Christ the solution to all his problems.'[34]

As important as the emergence of Christianity in unofficial culture was its role in the human rights movement, where freedom of religion was one of several major goals. In 1965 two Orthodox priests, Gleb Iakunin and Nikolai Eshliman, published two open letters, one to the Patriarch and the second to the Chairman of the Supreme Soviet, detailing the repressive measures against the Church and the latter's lack of apparent resistance to them.[35] This act of unprecedented boldness first alerted the outside world to the problems of the Russian Orthodox Church. Both nationalists and liberals within the Church contributed to the struggle for religious freedom. The best-known voice to join their ranks belonged to Aleksandr Solzhenitsyn, a baptized member of the Church whose religious faith as evidenced in his writings has been much commented upon. His 'Lenten Letter' of 1972 bitterly criticized the Patriarch for subservience to the Soviet regime. In taking this stance, Solzhenitsyn distanced himself from the nationalists with whom he was later to be somewhat facilely compartmentalized by many Western commentators, and who had a much more favourable attitude to the Orthodox leadership. Nearly twenty years later, in Rebuilding Russia (Kak nam obustroit' Rossiiu?) his view of the hierarchy had altered scarcely at all.[36]

Solzhenitsyn was the editor of a seminal collection of essays by seven very different Orthodox writers published in 1975, From Under the Rubble (Iz-pod glyb). Its authors believed that Christianity in its Orthodox form held the clue to the future of Russia, and were united by a deep patriotism which avoided narrow nationalism. The contents of the book as well as its title consciously linked it with Landmarks, published in 1909, and its sequel De Profundis (Iz glubiny), published in 1918. It was the first time that Orthodox thinkers had been able to revive the ideas of the beginning of the century whose development had been so abruptly truncated by the Revolution. The theme of the need for national repentance, which was to become widespread during the period of glasnost', was raised here for the first time.[37]

Not only overtly protest activity was repressed. Fr. Dimitrii Dudko, a parish priest who held an unprecedented series of question-and-answer sessions after church services in 1974, when previously taboo subjects were aired, suffered all manner of harassment, culminating

34 T. Goricheva, 'The Religious Significance of Unofficial Soviet Culture', RCL 8 (1980), 230–2.
35 See M. Bourdeaux, Patriarch and Prophets (London, 1975), 189–238, and Ellis, Russian Orthodox Church, 292–5.
36 See A. Solzhenitsyn, Rebuilding Russia: Reflections and Tentative Proposals (London, 1991), 46–7.
37 See A. Solzhenitsyn, 'Repentance and Self-Limitation in the Life of Nations', in Solzhenitsyn et al., From Under the Rubble, tr. A. M. Brock et al. (London, 1975), 105–43.

in his arrest and imprisonment in 1980, during which he was pressurized into making a public, televised recantation of his activities (though not of his faith). Throughout the 1970s and into the 1980s the number of known prisoners of the faith was between 300 and 400—'known' prisoners being generally believed to be only the tip of the iceberg. They included those incarcerated indefinitely in psychiatric hospitals and forcibly injected with harmful drugs.

The main thrust of the campaign for religious freedom among all denominations, including the Orthodox, was a series of *samizdat* documents addressed to the Soviet authorities, and, as they failed to produce any changes, to international political and religious figures and bodies. Some of these responded, and a number of national parliaments and Churches made representations which had their effect, though often in a piecemeal way, such as the release of especially well-known prisoners on high-profile international occasions. The biggest disappointment in this area was the failure of the World Council of Churches to take any significant public action during the course of at least two decades. Its spokesmen repeatedly claimed that it preferred 'silent diplomacy' to public actions: and the very nature of silent diplomacy of course rendered it insusceptible to reliable evaluation. An open letter to the WCC's Nairobi Assembly in 1975 from Gleb Iakunin and Lev Regelson was debated in open session as a result of the determination of some delegates, but the machinery set up to monitor susbequent developments was not effective, and a similar open letter to the WCC's Vancouver Assembly in 1983 did not produce anything like the same effect. The WCC was to some extent a prisoner of its own bureaucracy: it had a principle of never making public statements about human rights matters in any country without consulting member Churches, and the Russian Orthodox Church, which had joined the WCC in 1961, always blocked any such attempts. Here we see the importance of foreign policy in the Soviet government's attitude towards the Russian Orthodox Church. The Soviet government's decision to allow the Church to join the WCC in 1961 (sharply reversing previous policy), served to distract international attention from the antireligious campaign; and its position as a WCC member (by far the largest in terms of Church membership), enabled the Soviet authorities to influence that body's decisions on matters throughout the world. The Russian Orthodox Church was, in fact, an important component of the attempt to impose a *Pax Sovietica* in the Cold War period.

The Soviet regime's pressure on the Church leadership imposed a gulf between it and those members of its flock who were campaigning for religious freedom. Statements about religious persecution by

Church dissidents were publicly denied by the leaders of the Moscow Patriarchate. Throughout this period the Church was speaking with two voices: the voice of internationally known prelates speaking through government microphones, and the faint but inextinguishable voices of *samizdat* and the Gulag.

The latter represented chiefly those whose instinctive weapon for achieving their ends was the written word: writers and intellectuals. Certainly some workers joined them, and many more shared their views, but Orthodox dissent can in no way be described as a workers' movement, in contrast to Russian and Ukrainian Protestants, for example, or Lithuanian Catholics, who derived the bulk of their members from the working class. The many millions of Orthodox believers (who ranged from the deeply devout to the merely nominal —the most generally accepted estimate of their number is 50 million) were largely passive, going to churches where they were open and suffering in silence where they were not. Against this general trend, however, must be noted a number of widely scattered campaigns at village and town level to reopen closed churches, attested to by many hundreds of pages of *samizdat* protests and appeals: these, however, became known of only when their cause was taken up by urban intellectuals and activists from the mid-1970s, as part of the campaign to implement the 1975 Helsinki Accords on, *inter alia*, human rights, which the USSR had signed.

If the writer Aleksandr Solzhenitsyn and the scientist Andrei Sakharov represented the twin poles of the human rights movement, then two priests, Gleb Iakunin and Aleksandr Men', were the figure-heads of the two schools of independent thought and action within the Russian Orthodox Church. Iakunin has been in the forefront of the movement for religious freedom within his Church for over thirty years, including eight years in the Gulag (1979–87). In 1990 and 1993 he was elected to the Russian Duma, where he continued to speak out as before. As a result, the Holy Synod unfrocked him in November 1995. Even among the many in a conservative Church who disapprove of his open political activisim, few deny his courage and consistency. Along with fellow Christian Democrats in parliament, he was instrumental in achieving the adoption of the Law on Religious Freedom in 1990, which realized virtually all the freedoms for which he and others had campaigned for so long.

Fr. Aleksandr Men''s approach was quite different, that of a parish priest and scholar. He and Iakunin were students together in Irkutsk as young men, when Men' helped Iakunin back to the Church after the latter had encountered difficulties with his faith. Though their paths later diverged, and were believed by some to be incompatible,

Men' told his spiritual children that Iakunin had a particular role to perform in the service of the Church and should not be criticized for his involvement in politics.

Aleksandr Men' was a uniquely gifted individual. He was an erudite and widely read scholar who could write illuminatingly on any level. A distiller of others' works rather than an original thinker, he made the fruits of numerous authors in several languages available to fellow-Russians starved of Christian literature. At the same time, he had the gift of getting on with people from every walk of life. Serious and totally dedicated to his ministry, he was by no means solemn or starchy, with a ready laugh. Unusually in a conservative Church, he was ecumenically minded and known for his openness to Catholicism. He was never a dissident, but there were many dissidents who came to him for spiritual succour. After the change in religious policy from 1988 onwards, he took full advantage of the new opportunities, visiting hospitals and schools, preaching to large crowds—he was a compelling public speaker—setting up an open Orthodoxy University, and still with time for his parishioners and the numberless spiritual children who had come to the faith under his guidance. The latter never understood how he found time for everything. He radiated energy.

Fr. Aleksandr Men' was brutally murdered with an axe early on the morning of 9 September 1990 in the woods around his village home as he was on his way to church. KGB involvement was immediately suspected, as was that of those in the Church hostile to him both for his ecumenical stance and for his Jewish descent. Over seven years later no suspect has been discovered, and few now believe that the murder will ever be solved. The impact of his murder is difficult to overemphasize. Though he had never sought publicity, he had become known over the years by word of mouth as a fearless priest, one of the few ready to baptize children secretly at a time when severe penalties could be incurred for doing so. In the last few years of his life his stature had become widely acknowledged. There is a general expectation now that he will be canonized as a saint; the only question is when.

In discussing these two significant figures, it has been necessary to run ahead of our chronological framework on religious policy; just as it was necessary to jump ahead to the post-*glasnost'* period when discussing cultural changes. We must now return to the changes on religious policy begun after Mikhail Gorbachev's accession to power in 1985, and especially to consider the significance of the Church's Millennium celebrations in 1988.

Gorbachev did nothing about religious policy during his first few years in power. Religious believers did, however, benefit from his changes on policy on dissent, which led to early release from imprisonment for many prisoners for the faith; on *glasnost'*, which meant that believers alongside others had greater freedom to express their views; and on democratization, which meant that they were no longer to be regarded as second-class citizens. The policy of *perestroika*, restructuring of the economy, did not affect the Church directly, but the millions of believers' votes were required to implement it.

The need for the Party to consider the Russian Orthodox Church's role in society was forced upon it by a historical event: the celebration of the thousandth anniversary of Christianity in Russia, Ukraine, and Belorussia in 1988. The celebrations of summer 1988 were therefore on a far greater scale, and with greater publicity, than anyone had envisaged even shortly before. This was partly necessitated by the presence of many foreign guests, and by Western media interest. There were, however, no legal or other guarantees that the more relaxed attitude to the Church would persist once the public celebrations were over. Contemporary commentary was marked by suspicion that the Soviet authorities would milk the Millennium events for every drop of favourable publicity before returning to the *status quo ante* once they were over. In the event, however, the Millennium was to mark a total volte-face in Soviet religious policy. This resulted from the remarkable historical coincidence of a thousand-year tradition with a three-year reform movement.

The first public sign of change came on 29 April 1988, when Gorbachev met Patriarch Pimen and members of the Holy Synod in the Kremlin. It was the first meeting of a Soviet head of state with religious leaders since Stalin's in 1943. 'We have a common history, a common motherland and a common future', Gorbachev told the Orthodox leaders, obliterating in one sentence seventy years of attempts to marginalize and ultimately eradicate religion. He called the Millennium 'a significant milestone' in the history, culture, and development of Russia, and hailed believers as 'Soviet people, working people, patriots', reversing former Party assertions that religious believers were 'not Soviet people'. He said that the legislation on religion would be revised: unfulfilled statements to this effect had been circulating for some time, but Gorbachev's public commitment to it would be hard to rescind.[38]

The main Millennium events took place in both Church and state premises in June 1988, first in Moscow and then in Leningrad, Kiev, and other centres. President Gromyko held a question-and-answer session for over 700 participants, including foreign guests, on 11 June, but most of them were dissatisfied and felt that he was not forthcoming in his replies, an indication that the 'old guard' in the Soviet

38 *Keston News Service*, 300 (12 May 1988), 16–18, and *Official Moscow Patriarchate Press Release on the Millennium*, 11 (13 June 1988), 5.

Politburo was still firmly in place. The most important concession to the Church was permission to hold a National Council (*Pomestnyi Sobor*): it was only the fourth in the Soviet period (the others had been in 1917–18, 1945, and 1971). Normally another *Sobor* would not have been expected until it became necessary to elect a new Patriarch. There was an atmosphere of far greater freedom than at previous *Sobory*, and some genuinely open debate occurred, though the presence throughout of state officials was a reminder that not everything had changed. They key development of the *Sobor* was the adoption of a new Statute (*Ustav*) regularizing Church life. It greatly expanded the restrictive 1945 Statute (*Polozhenie*), and repealed restrictive regulations on parish life passed by the Church under duress in 1961.[39]

Both before and after the Millennium there was some evidence of new thinking on religion in Party circles. Some of it came in public statements by the Chairman of the Council for Religious Affairs (CRA), Konstantin Kharchev, who had been appointed in December 1984 (i.e. in the pre-Gorbachev period), and who initially followed the restrictive line of his predecessors. In 1988 he gave two interviews which indicated a greater awareness of the need to recognize and grant believers' rights, though these were at variance with private speeches in which he asserted the need to continue strict state control over the Church.[40] The Academy of Sciences began a major study of religion throughout the world, excluding the USSR, based on the premiss that by the year 2000 an estimated three-quarters of the world's population would adhere to some kind of religious belief.

There was a pragmatic motive for the Party to take religion seriously, as noted above, but there were also signs that some elements in the Party were beginning to acknowledge that religion had some inherent value and usefulness. It was recognized that religion could motivate people to do things which otherwise they would not choose to do, and if so, it could be a force to get the country moving again. Religion, under the careful supervision of the Party, could help to promote morality and hope in the future and to fill the spiritual vacuum which communism had failed to fill. This, then, was god-building (*bogostroitel'stvo*), not god-seeking (*bogoiskatel'stvo*), as noted in our discussion of literature above. At this period, it was not true freedom of religion that was being considered, but a different method of using state-controlled religion for Party purposes.[41] In fact, however, the pace of events accelerated beyond the expectations of Party theorists, who viewed religion only as a combination of a set of ideas and more or less influential institutional bodies. This view proved inadequate, and the removal of restrictions on religion was to show that faith in action developed a momentum of its own.

39 See H. Bell and J. Ellis, 'The Millennium Celebrations of 1988 in the USSR', *RCL* 16 (1988), 292–328.

40 Interviews with A. Nezhnyi in *Ogonek*, 21 and 50 (1988), 2–5 and 26–8. His private speech to the Higher Party School in Moscow, Mar. 1988, was leaked to the Paris-based newspaper *Russkaia mysl'*, 20 May 1988, 4.

41 See J. Ellis, 'New Soviet Thinking on Religion', *RCL* 17 (1989), 100–11.

Kharchev's third and frankest interview came in the October 1989 issue of *Ogonek*, after he had been ousted from office. His increasingly open advocacy of believers' rights had brought him into conflict with the Ideology Commission of the Central Committee of the Communist Party (which was thus revealed for the first time to exercise control over religion, a matter previously shrouded in secrecy, though the Ideology Commission's role and its oversight of the CRA hardly came as a surprise). What was a surprise was that one of the reasons for Kharchev's dismissal vouchsafed to him by Vadim Medvedev, the chairman of the Ideology Commission, was that he had 'not found a common language with the ideological *apparat*, the "neighbours" [the CRA's term for the KGB] and the leadership of the Russian Orthodox Church'. This followed persistent rumours that Orthodox hierarchs had complained about Kharchev's interference in Church affairs, and also revealed close contacts between the Church leadership and the KGB which were to be reinforced by subsequent revelations. The Moscow Patriarchate had thus gained the power to influence political and Party developments only a short time after its new public status was proclaimed. Kharchev himself attributed these developments to 'the growing power struggle within the leadership of the Church', adding: 'I suspect that some members of the Synod, from force of habit, have counted more on the support of the authorities than on their own authority in the Church.'[42] This view was shared by internal Church critics: it is possible that Church leaders had been further angered by the fact that Kharchev had met a group of them, including Iakunin, thus admitting that their views were of interest to the state.

The change in religious policy meant vast new opportunities in the institutional life of the Church. These may be divided into two categories: expansion of formerly legal but highly restricted activities, and involvement in previously outlawed areas. In the former category, the Church was able to reopen huge numbers of churches and monasteries. The number of churches, 6,893 in 1988, quickly doubled and continued to grow, making it difficult to keep track of figures, especially as there were some disputes over Church buildings. The total of seventeen monasteries in 1988, none of which were east of Moscow, grew to 208 by September 1993. The Church's three theological seminaries and two academies for more advanced training quickly grew to a dozen, and a new type of institute, the *uchilishche* for training of psalm-readers, choir-directors, and other non-clergy personnel opened in several dioceses. Publishing activities, limited to production of small editions of Bibles, New Testaments, and service books, and a handful of regular publications, including the monthly

42 Interview with Nezhnyi, *Ogonek*, 44 (1989), 10–11.

Zhurnal Moskovskoi patriarkhii (*Journal of the Moscow Patriarchate*), were now increased, though the cost of paper and the absence of the Church's own printing press continued to hamper work.

In all these areas, however, the ideological barrier was replaced by a new but equally daunting one, finance. The copecks donated weekly by millions of faithful had previously been adequate for the Church's limited expenditures, leaving an abundance for lavish entertainment of foreign guests and for supposedly voluntary donations to the Soviet Peace Fund. Now, however, the Church's income was stretched to its limits and beyond. The thousands of churches and monasteries handed back by the state were in ruins, requiring a vast amount of labour and materials. The expansion in numbers of theological students and of publications all had to be paid for. This constraint applied also to the two previously forbidden areas of Church activity, education and charitable or welfare work. It was now possible for Sunday schools, Orthodox schools, or *lycées* offering a general education, and even universities to open, which they did both under the Patriarchate's auspices and also independently. In the field of charitable work, the Church, alongside other religious bodies, was called upon to meet the deficiencies of the Soviet welfare system in hospitals, orphanages, homes for the elderly, prisons, and elsewhere. Church resources were drawn into fighting new developments such as AIDS, care for Afghan veterans and refugees, and aftermaths of disasters such as the Chernobyl' explosion of 1986 and the Armenian earthquake of 1988. Not only did all these ventures demand literally endless amounts of money, they also required trained personnel and suitable premises which were sadly lacking.

The Church's growing role in public life was heightened by the attention given to its public statements during the failed coup of August 1991 and by the prominent public role of mediator which it took on during the armed conflict between President Yeltsin and the Russian Parliament during September–October 1993. This meant that no politician could afford to ignore the Church by the mid-1990s, leading to scepticism over the appearance of political leaders at church services. It is of interest that, while Gorbachev made no secret of his atheism, Yeltsin is on record as saying that his mother was 'deeply religious' and her attitude had remained with him. He added: 'I have great respect for religion. Perhaps, gradually, this will grow into greater religiosity. Possibly.'[43]

However, dissatisfaction with the Church leadership because of their past compromises continued. The Russian Orthodox Church was the only major institution in the former Soviet Union which had not experienced total changes in its top personnel. This was

43 *Survey of World Broadcasts* (SWB), SU/1850 B/6 (BBC Monitoring Service; 19 Nov. 1993).

compounded by revelations of documented collaboration between Church leaders and the KGB published in January 1992, after a parliamentary commission including Gleb Iakunin had been given access to the Lubianka archives following the failed 1991 coup. In a sense they contained nothing new in that it was common knowledge that Church leaders, like others, could not have continued in their posts unless they had co-operated with the KGB, and some of the more sensationalist reports in the Western press therefore have to be treated with caution. However, there was now incontestable proof from primary sources of the extent this collaboration had reached, and of the surveillance and other intrusive measures practised upon believers.

This distrust of the leadership was the chief reason why forty or so Orthodox parishes broke from the Moscow Patriarchate and joined the Russian Orthodox Church Abroad. The schismatic tendencies in Ukraine, complicated by nationalist aspirations and the legalization in 1989 of the outlawed Ukrainian Greek-Catholic (Uniate) Church previously claimed by the Moscow Patriarchate, reached an incredible pitch of confusion by the mid-1990s, when three or four jurisdictions were competing for the allegiance of the faithful. At the moment of its triumphal restoration, then, the Church was, ironically, prey to divisive and schismatic tendencies suppressed for decades.

The defensive mentality this encouraged can be seen also in the Orthodox attitude to Catholics and Protestants. Centuries of Orthodox—Catholic hostility came into play as the Roman Catholic Church under a Polish Pope was thought to be harbouring predatory intentions towards Holy Russia. The appointment of five Catholic bishops to sees within the Soviet Union without prior consultation deeply offended the Orthodox, already nettled by legalization of the Uniates in 1989. This meant a great setback in talks with the Vatican, which continued, but only with extreme difficulty.

At least, however, the Catholics offered recognizable entities and a structure with which dealings could be had, which was far from the case where Protestants were concerned. The bilateral relations the Orthodox had been conducting with various mainline Protestant Churches in the West, as well as its participation in the Protestant-dominated World Council of Churches and Conference of European Churches, took on a new lease of life in the freer conditions, but they had no basis for dealing with the flood of foreign Protestant and evangelical missionaries into their country. The majority, and certainly the richest and most conspicuous, were American, but there were also Europeans and South Koreans. They represented churches and parachurch organizations, international missions, and missions aimed specifically at the Soviet Union or communist countries in general, large internationally known organizations and preachers, and small denominations and local fellowships scarcely known to outsiders even in their own countries. Added to them were post-Christian or pseudo-Christian bodies which had strained relations with the Christian community, including Mormons, Jehovah's Witnesses, Moonies, Scientologists, and many others. Non-Christian emissaries such as Krishnaites and devotees of the Japanese sect Aum Shinrikyo quickly gained a following. The New Age movement gaining ground in the West also found a resonance in the former Soviet Union, where it shared similarities with some indigenous sects and movements influenced by extrasensory perception, hypnotism, and other phenomena, dating back for centuries: a new manifestation, in some ways, of the *dvoeverie* (double-faith, sometimes referred to as *mnogoverie*, multiple faith) which had persisted after the adoption of Christianity in Kievan Rus' (medieval Russia).

It was clearly very difficult for the Orthodox to distinguish even among the various Christian groups, let alone the others. The insensitive attitude of some foreign evangelists aroused great antipathy among the Orthodox population, who resented the assumption that they belonged to a non-Christian country. They thought that foreign Christians too readily accepted that the Soviet Union had in truth been an atheist country, as its propaganda had claimed. They found also that many evangelicals did not accept the Orthodox as true fellow-Christians, believing that their emphasis on ritual and tradition blinded them to the truth of the Gospel. Since there is in fact a good deal of nominalism and ignorance about the basics of the faith in the Russian Orthodox Church (as its own internal critics admit), the argument has been a complex and emotionally charged one. A further cause of grievance has been that foreign missionaries had financial resources far in excess of those of the Orthodox and other Russian Churches, and could afford to buy radio and television time and hire stadia to reach audiences denied to indigenous Christians. All this underlay attempts by the Moscow Patriarchate and others to amend the 1990 Law on Religious Freedom to favour it and other indigenous religions such as Islam at the expense of foreign missionaries.[44]

This cultural clash also heightened existing tensions between, on the one hand, conservatives and nationalists, and on the other, reformers and democrats in the Church. They were sharply divided in their attitude to Western Christians and to the West in general. Conservatives wanted to keep intact the proud traditions of their Church, preserved through the years of persecution, while reformers believed that changes, above all in Church government but also in

44 The developments from Gorbachev's accession to power to this point summarized here are covered in greater detail in J. Ellis, *The Russian Orthodox Church: Triumphalism and Defensiveness* (London, 1996), which covers the period 1985–94.

liturgical practice and theological training, were essential to meet the challenges of a new society. This dichotomy can be found in virtually any Church in the world, and to this extent the Russian Orthodox Church can be said to have become normalized. This tension was a genuine one under the Soviet regime, one which would have existed even without state manipulation of the Church. Dispute had also existed between nationalists and democrats in the Church, but became sharper once the latter were able to campaign openly for their views, and even form political parties. This made the already hardline nationalists even more virulent. Though the categories of conservative and nationalist, reformer and democrat, inevitably overlap to a large extent, they are by no means identical. It is for example perfectly possible to be a thoughtful conservative on matters of Church doctrine and practice without espousing the anti-Westernism and anti-Semitism of the nationalists. Patriotism, moreover, is by no means a monopoly of the right-wing, and Church reformers and democrats can be intensely patriotic in a way which sometimes surprises their Western counterparts.

Broadly speaking, the Church at present is divided between those who believe that the Russian Orthodox Church's current position as something close to a state church is its rightful one, and those who believe in equality before the law for all religions; those who base their vision of the future on close adherence to Russian values and traditions, and those open to what is best in the experience of fellow Christians abroad and of Western political achievements; those content to preserve their Church unchanged in its thousand-year-old tradition, and those who believe that unless it develops a prophetic voice challenging present complacency it will have nothing to say to the next generation of Russians.

14

Russian Culture and Emigration, 1921–1953

CATRIONA KELLY

The defeat of anti-Bolshevik forces in the Russian Civil War began a diaspora radically different in scale and character to anything that had occurred previously in Russian history. Before the Revolution, the numbers of Russians living outside their country's borders were not large. The massive landlocked empire absorbed the energies that in other colonial countries—France, Britain, Germany—surged into the conquest of territory overseas. Indeed, during the nineteenth century, the Russian Empire's most prominent *émigré* community was made up of Poles displaced by the Russian Empire's territorial gains, rather than by Russians themselves. Granted, there were some vocal groups of political exiles—Herzen in the 1850s and 1860s, Lenin and other leading Bolsheviks in the 1900s and 1910s—but their numbers were small, and their efforts concentrated on preaching to soulmates inside Russia. And, though the European Grand Tour was a vital experience for many Russians from the late eighteenth century until the early twentieth, from Princess Dashkova and Nikolai Karamzin to Anna Akhmatova and Aleksandr Blok, the most stable and long-lasting communities were those of expatriates rather than travellers or exiles—the diplomats, absentee landlords, and refugees from scandal whose main aim was to blend with their fellows in their new, vocational homelands, rather than preserve their Russianness come what may.

By contrast, the population displacement after 1921 involved millions of Russians from all classes (peasants and workers, intellectuals

15 Advertisement for German-made Russian vodka, from the Berlin Russian glossy *Zhar-ptitsa* (*Firebird*), 1921.

The image piquantly illustrates how goods packaged *à la russe* for the Western market (the bottle-label here shows a *polovoi*, waiter in national dress from a pre-Revolutionary Russian restaurant, and stresses its use of a 'genuine Muscovite' recipe) were then sold back to the Russian *émigré* community. The latter, too small to support its own factories and advertising agencies, still contained, in the early 1920s, enough big spenders to be targeted by luxury-goods manufacturers advertising champagne, furs, fashions, and sports cars in Russian as well as in German and French.

and artists, as well as the impoverished aristocrats who were to become, to partly informed Westerners, the best-known members of the emigration). The refugees poured over the borders of the former Russian Empire into Turkey, Finland, Poland, and China, settling thereafter in places as remote from their homeland and each other as Rio de Janeiro, Buenos Aires, Sofia, Belgrade, Harbin, Dublin, and New York, as well as Helsinki, Riga, Tallin, London, Prague, and especially Paris and Berlin. Although the individuals displaced by the deluge always kept a weather eye on the country to which many at first anticipated returning in a matter of months, the size of the population movement, and the very diverse forces that it involved, meant that internal differences and disputes soon became nearly as important as polemics with the common enemy, the new, Communist Russia.

Every strand of opposition to the Bolsheviks was represented in the new communities, from monarchists and former courtiers through ex-ministers, conservative and liberal, to Socialist Revolutionaries, anarchists, and Social Democrats of various hues. Those who supported a full restoration of the regime were especially well represented in Serbia and Bulgaria (then Orthodox monarchies), but were also to be found in Paris, Helsinki, and the other centres, where they lived in circles quite distinct from those in which the more radical elements mixed. Among the latter, some (the *Smenovekhovtsy*—signpost-changers, and the Eurasian movement) came to favour dialogue with the USSR (only to come under suspicion, in fact not unjustified in some cases, of collaboration with the regime). Others, however, continued to believe in the possibility of a democratic third way for Russia, supporting neither communism nor autocracy. The sputtering cauldron of incompatibilities and enmities was stirred by the activities of the Soviet government itself, which encouraged some prominent *émigrés* (such as the realist writer Aleksandr Kuprin) to return, and gave covert sponsorship to certain organizations, besides instigating a number of more squalid deeds, such as the assassination of prominent opponents (most famously, of course, Trotskii). There was also a large contingent of *émigrés* that refused to toe any particular line, which included many of the painters and musicians, as well as a smaller number of writers (Vladimir Nabokov, Vladislav Khodasevich, Marina Tsvetaeva), though this did not stop them being associated with particular groupings through their relatives and friends, or by those who wished to attack them.

Inevitably, the cultural life of the Russian emigration was subject to much the same fragmentation and contention as its political existence: here again attitudes to the Soviet Union were crucial. In the early 1920s, contacts between some *émigrés* and Soviet writers

and artists were close. Well-known Soviet writers and painters—
Maiakovskii, Erenburg, El Lissitzky, Pavel Kuznetsov—made well-
publicized visits to Paris and Berlin. But the detailed and accurate
information about Soviet political and cultural oppression that was
published in general monthlies such as *Sovremennye zapiski* (*Contemporary Annals*, Paris, 1920–40) provided liberals with ammuni-
tion against any *rapprochement*, to which the post-acmeist aesthetic
tastes of the most influential *émigré* critics—Georgii Adamovich,
Vladislav Khodasevich, Iurii Mandel'shtam—were also inimical.
Though two key journals—the Prague-based *Volia Rossii* (*Russia's
Freedom*, 1922–32) and *Sovremennye zapiski*—made strenuous efforts to
treat Soviet literature seriously during the 1920s, attempts at detachment were bedevilled by the hardening of attitudes in the Soviet
Union itself, as manifested in the institution of the cultural revolution in 1928, and the inauguration of socialist realism from 1932. Even
so, the view that the Soviet Union represented the culture of the
future was fairly widely held among at least younger *émigrés*; indeed,
one of the sad ironies of the 1930s, if not the 1920s, was the disparity
between *émigré* critics' faint praise for new work by diaspora writers,
and the confident trumpeting by Soviet journals of what was often far
inferior material.

   As the product of displaced societies in which the sense of what
was Russian to a large extent depended on memory, and which also
self-consciously defined itself in opposition to prevailing Soviet tastes,
Russian *émigré* culture could not be as diverse as Soviet culture in at
least some respects. There was, for instance, no proletarian poetry
and no peasant poetry (despite the presence of apparently suitable
class representatives in the emigration). On the other hand, this
was not a purely élite tradition either. Probably the most popular
émigré writers were purveyors of middlebrow fiction such as the historical novelists Mark Aldanov and (before his re-immigration in
1923) Aleksei Tolstoi, or the short-story writer Boris Zaitsev. There
were even bedroom novels, as provided by the minor poet Ekaterina
Bakunina, whose explicit, if gauche, descriptions of a married
woman's capers with her lovers, *The Body* (*Telo*, 1933) and *Love for
Six People* (*Liubov' k shesterym*, 1934) made her notorious throughout
the Paris emigration. A large readership also enjoyed the intentional
humour of Nadezhda Teffi, who masked ruthless exposés of *émigré*
anxieties under a studiedly artless, rather Nancy Mitfordish manner.
In her most popular collection, *The Little Town* (*Gorodok*, 1927), the
faux-naïf introduction sets out a picture of Paris life that confirms all
the worst fears that emigration means loss of dignity and national
identity:

The inhabitants gathered in two main population clusters: Passy and the Rive Gauche. They occupied themselves with various trades . . . Those of mature years ran restaurants and worked as Gypsy or Georgian waiters (if they had dark hair) or Ukrainians (if they were blondes).

The women spent their time dressmaking and running up little hats for each other. The men spent their time running up debts.

Apart from males and females, the population consisted of ministers and generals. Hardly any of these worked as taxi drivers; most of them lived off memoirs and loans . . . The inhabitants of the little town spoke a peculiar patois in which, however, philologists could easily discern Slavonic roots.[1]

But if the emigration had its own popular culture in the sense of shared jokes and nightmares, the published evidence of this was relatively sparse. There was no *émigré* cinema as such (i.e. a cinema made by Russians for Russians), though the Ermol'ev company, revamped after its purchase by Noë Bloch and Alexandre Kamenko in 1922 as Films Albatros, made notable contributions to the French cinema, including the Russian actor Ivan Mozzhukhin (Mosjoukine)'s innovative *Le Brasier ardent* (1923). And a good many writers, such as Nabokov, shared the pre-Revolutionary modernists' enthusiasm for the art.[2] Though commercial artists of Russian origin, such as the fashion illustrator Erté, achieved success in Western enterprises, the *émigré* communities were not large or rich enough to generate an independent commercial tradition. On the whole, then, the Russian emigration's contribution to popular culture was indirect, and came about through Westerners' preoccupation with the exoticism of a life that seemed still more attractively remote now that it had apparently been destroyed by the Revolution. Cossack uniforms and dancers, troikas, flaming kebabs on sabres, glasses smashed after toasts had been drunk, high-cheekboned women in gauzy dresses or furs— all these manifestations of *style russe* could be found in films (Greta Garbo as Anna Karenina), to ballets (*Petrouchka*, in particular, was to become a well-loved mainstay of the ballet repertoire, while Anna Pavlova's Dying Swan routine became so famous that her floating tutu even inspired a New Zealand meringue pie), to music (the concertos and symphonies of Rachmaninov, used as the sound-tracks to films, including the famous British weepie *Brief Encounter*), to clothes (frogged overcoats and fox-fur hats), but especially in the Russian restaurants of Paris and New York.

Such commercialization of Russian culture was not, unfortunately, always accompanied by enthusiasm for the high-cultural products of the Russian emigration. Certainly, painters, theatre activists, and musicians found their way into the mainstream of European modernism with relative ease. Kandinskii, Naum Gabo, Goncharova,

1 N. A. Teffi, *Gorodok* (New York, 1982), 5–7.
2 On Nabokov, see A. Appel, *Nabokov's Dark Cinema* (New York, 1974). On the Ermoliev company and Films Albatros, see R. Abel, *French Cinema: The First Wave (1915–1929)* (Princeton, 1984), 19–25, and F. Albéra, *Albatros des russes à Paris* (Milan, 1995).

16 Photograph of Michel Fokine (Mikhail Fokin, dancer and choreographer, collaborator of Diaghilev, whose creations include *Petrushka*, *Le Spectre de la Rose*, and *Daphnis and Chloe*) doing a Russian dance (published in *Zhar-ptitsa*, 1921).

Ballet and cabaret, especially but not exclusively if of Russian interest, found a ready audience not only among Russians, but among Westerners attracted by the acrobatic skills and sumptuous costumes on display. Diaghilev's Ballets Russes, and later its successors such as the Ballet Russe de Monte-Carlo, exemplified Russian culture for generations of Europeans, especially Britons, hostile to the Soviet Union itself; designers such as Goncharova, Benois, and Bakst, and choreographers such as Massine (Leonid Miasin) and Bronislava Nijinska (Nizhinskaia) were key influences in the formation of the London Royal Ballet in the 1940s.

Larionov, Aleksandra Ekster, Aleksandr Benois, Il'ia Zdanevich, Stravinsky, Prokof'ev, Kreisler, Artur Rubenstein, Ol'ga Slobodskaia, Chaliapin, quickly acquired fame among lovers of the arts all over Western Europe. Diaghilev's Ballets Russes, famous before the Revolution, upheld its reputation with productions such as *Les Noces* (1923), *Les Biches* (1924), *Le Train bleu* (1924), *Apollon Musagète* (1928), and *Le Fils prodigue* (1929), many of which were staged with the participation of well-known Western European artists, such as the composer Francis Poulenc and the painters Picasso and Rouault. If representations of a raw, pagan Russia (such as Goncharova's designs for *Les Noces*, or Stravinsky's score for the same piece) were received with enthusiasm as a new and promising contribution to neo-primitivism, presenting oneself as the colourful Other was by no means the only way in which a painter or composer could find an enthusiastic audience. But writers faced an almost insuperable language barrier. If industrious communists and fellow-travellers could be found to render Soviet writers such as Maiakovskii, Leonov, or Vsevolod Ivanov into French or English, even the better-known *émigré* writers generally remained untranslated until the 1950s and 1960s. Nabokov's *Mashenka* and *King, Queen, Knave* both appeared in German translations soon after their first publication in 1926 and 1928, but his later *émigré* novels were not translated until after the Second World War. Tsvetaeva was forced to translate her own work—with a conspicuous lack of success—into French. Even Russian *émigré* literature's greatest coup—the awarding of the Nobel Prize to Ivan Bunin in 1933—did not raise its profile significantly, or stimulate extensive translation.

Part of the cause for this may have lain in the parochial character of diaspora writing, and in the conservatism of some older writers (Merezhkovskii, Gippius, Aldanov, or Zaitsev). However, the lineaments of the *émigré* situation—alienation, disorientation, the need to rely on the patently unreliable evidence of memory—were thoroughly in tune with European modernism's preoccupation with the instability of identity. In the work both of Nabokov and his contemporary Nina Berberova, the idea of 'Russia' signifies as much the attempt to recapture the lost certainties of childhood, the pursuit of the 'naïve' from a position of wounded sentimentality, as a search for the actualities of history before 1917. The same is true in the work of some *émigré* poets, many of whom—both established figures such as Khodasevich or Georgii Ivanov, and post-1921 beginners such as Boris Poplavskii, Anatolii Shteiger, Valerii Pereleshin, Anna Prismanova, Raisa Blokh, or Vera Bulich—were far closer to the spirit of European modernism than their predecessors among the Russian futurists and acmeists. There was also an emphasis on craft which, if it constrained some *émigré* poets—Adamovich or Iurii Mandel'shtam—into elegant vacuity, made others more self-conscious in their self-fashioning, more careful in their choice of language, than all but very few of their Soviet contemporaries. If the Russian *émigré* establishment's answer to socialist realism could often be aesthetic genteelism, the saving grace was that many journals were in the hands of working journalists rather than literary critics, and that ideological fragmentation could generate reluctant pluralism as well as defensive proscriptiveness (many of the groups were simply too small to fill journals month by month on their own).

Despite chronic lack of funds, a shrinking readership (those who emigrated as adolescents or children tended, notwithstanding their parents' best efforts to the contrary, to assimilate into countries that had received them, particularly in Britain and France), and a nagging lack of confidence, *émigré* literature remained a significant force until the onset of the Second World War, when most of the major journals were forced to close, and publishing operations contracted drastically. The years after the war saw something of a revival, with some journals, such as *Vozrozhdenie (Rebirth)*, reopening, and the surviving First Wave writers joined by a number of individuals who had escaped from the Soviet Union during the war (such as Ivan Elagin and Ol'ga Anstei). But the axis had shifted from the European capitals to New York, with *Novyi zhurnal (New Review*, founded in 1942) now the most important forum for literature published in Russian. American literature proved still less receptive to the Russian sensibility than the European literatures had (with the signal exception of Vladimir Nabokov, now remade as a writer in English), and it was through scholarship rather than literature that the Russian emigration made its mark on the far side of the Atlantic, as theorists, historians, and literary critics both contributed to the development of Slavic studies (Fedotov, Vernadsky, Raeff, Markov, Karlinsky), and made international reputations in other disciplines (Roman Jakobson, the ancient historian Mikhail Rostovtseff).

Suggested further reading

Populism:

Dissidence, informal political movements

Bonnell, V. E., Cooper, A., and **Freidin, G.** (eds.), *Russia at the Barricades: Eyewitness Accounts of the August 1991 Coup* (New York, 1994).

Bukovskii, V., *To Build a Castle: My Life as a Dissenter* (London, 1978).

Clarke, K., and **Posadskaia, A.**, *Women in Russia: First Feminist Samizdat* (London, 1980).

Funk, N., and **Mueller, M.** (eds.), *Gender Politics and Post-Communism: Reflections from Eastern Europe and the Former Soviet Union* (New York, 1993).

Gorbanevskaia, N., *Red Square at Noon*, tr. A. Lieven (Harmondsworth, 1972).

Hosking, G., Aves, J., and **Duncan, P.** (eds.), *The Road to Post-Communism: Independent Political Movements in the Soviet Union, 1985–1991* (London, 1992).

Orlova, R., and **Kopelev, L.**, *My zhili v Moskve, 1956–1980* (Ann Arbor, 1988).

Ratushinskaia, I., *Grey is the Colour of Hope*, tr. A. Kojevnikov (London, 1988).

Rossi, Zh., *Spravochnik po GULagu* (London, 1987).

Sakharov, A., *Sakharov Speaks*, ed. H. E. Salisbury (London, 1974).

Shelley, L. I., *Policing Soviet Society: The Evolution of State Control* (London, 1996).

Solzhenitsyn, A., *et al.*, *From Under the Rubble*, tr. A. M. Brock *et al.* (London, 1975).

Soprotivlenie v GULage (Moscow, 1992–).

Cultural politics, official populism, popular culture

Bown, M. C., and **Taylor, B.** (eds.), *Art of the Soviets: Painting, Sculpture and Architecture in a One-Party State* (Manchester, 1993).

Brumfield, W. C., and **Ruble, B. A.** (eds.), *Russian Housing in the Modern Age: Design and Social History* (New York, 1993).

Cherednichenko, T., *Tipologiia sovetskoi massovoi kul'tury: Mezhdu 'Brezhnevym' i 'Pugachevoi'* (Moscow, 1994).

Cohen, S., and **vanden Heuvel, K.**, *Voices of Glasnost: Interviews with Gorbachev's Reformers* (New York, 1989).

Condee, N. (ed.), *Soviet Hieroglyphics: Essays on Late Twentieth-Century Russian Visual Culture* (Bloomington, Ind., 1995).

Fitzpatrick, S., *The Cultural Front: Power and Culture in Revolutionary Russia* (Ithaca, NY, 1992).

Fortescue, S., *Science Policy in the Soviet Union* (London, 1990).

Frankel, E. R., *Novy Mir: A Case Study in the Politics of Literature, 1952–1958* (Cambridge, 1981).

Graffy, J., and **Hosking, G.** (eds.), *Culture and the Media in the USSR Today* (Basingstoke, 1989).

Graham, L. R., *Science in Russia and the Soviet Union: A Short History* (Cambridge, 1993).

Grant, B., *In the Soviet House of Culture: A Century of Perestroikas* (Princeton, 1995).

Gubareva, O. E., *Preimushchestvennoe razvitie tiazheloi industrii i sozdanie izobiliia predmetov potrebleniia* (Moscow, 1960).

Johnson, P., *Khrushchev and the Arts: The Politics of Soviet Culture, 1962–1964* (Cambridge, Mass., 1965).

Lane, C., *The Rites of Rulers: Ritual in Industrial Society: The Soviet Case* (Cambridge, 1981).

Mehnert, K., *The Russians and their Favorite Books* (Stanford, Calif., 1983).

Nove, A., *Glasnost' in Action: Cultural Renaissance in Russia* (Boston, 1989).

Riordan, J., *Sport and Soviet Society: Development of Sport and Physical Education in Russia and the USSR* (Cambridge, 1977; repr. 1985).

Spechler, D., *Permitted Dissent in the USSR: Novy Mir and the Soviet Regime* (New York, 1982).

Stites R., *Russian Popular Culture: Entertainment and Society since 1900* (Cambridge, 1992).

Suslova, V. A., and **Superanskaia, A. V.**, *O russkikh imenakh* (Leningrad, 1991).

Thompson, T., and **Sheldon, R.** (eds.), *Soviet Society and Culture: Essays in Honour of Vera S. Dunham* (Boulder, Col., 1988).

White, S., *Russia Goes Dry* (Cambridge, 1995).

Lifestyles, personal attitudes

Birman, I., *Personal Consumption in the USSR and the USA* (London, 1989).

Bridger, S., *Women in the Soviet Countryside: Women's Roles in Rural Development in the Soviet Union* (Cambridge, 1987).

—— and **Riordan, J.** (eds.), *Dear Comrade Editor: Readers' Letters to the Soviet Press under Perestroika* (Bloomington, Ind., 1992).

Brine, J., **Perrie, M.**, and **Sutton, A.** (eds.), *Home, School and Leisure in the Soviet Union* (London, 1980).

Filtzer, D., *Soviet Workers and De-Stalinization: The Consolidation of the Modern System of Production Relations, 1953–1964* (Cambridge, 1992).

—— *Soviet Workers and the Collapse of Perestroika: The Soviet Labour Process and Gorbachev's Reforms, 1985–1991* (Cambridge, 1994).

Lapidus, G. (ed.), *Women in Russia* (New York, 1978).

Matthews, M., *Privileges in the Soviet Union: A Study of Elite Lifestyles under Communism* (London, 1978).

—— *Poverty in the Soviet Union: The Lifestyles of the Underprivileged in Recent Years* (Cambridge, 1986).

McAuley, A., *Economic Welfare in the Soviet Union: Poverty, Living Standards and Inequality* (Madison, Wis., 1979).

—— *Women's Work and Wages in the Soviet Union* (London, 1981).

McCauley, M. (ed.), *Khrushchev and Khrushchevism* (London, 1987).

Ruthchild, R. G., *Women in Russia and the Soviet Union: An Annotated Bibliography* (New York, 1993).

Vasil'eva, L., *Kremlevskie zheny* (Moscow, 1992) (abridged tr. by C. Porter as *The Kremlin Wives* (London, 1994)).

Zemtsov I., *Partiia ili mafiia? Razvorovannaia respublika* (Paris, 1976).

The Church and religion:

Alexeev, W., and **Stavrou, T. G.**, *The Great Revival: The Russian Church under German Occupation* (Minneapolis, 1976).

Davis, N., *A Long Walk to Church: A Contemporary History of Russian Orthodoxy* (Oxford, 1996).

Ellis, J., *The Russian Orthodox Church: A Contemporary History* (London, 1986; repr. 1989).

House, F., *The Russian Phoenix: The Story of Russian Christians AD 988–1988* (London, 1988).

Pascal, P., *The Religion of the Russian People* (London, 1976).

Pipes, R., *Russia under the Bolshevik Regime* (London, 1994), ch. 7.

Pospielovsky, D., *The Russian Orthodox Church under the Soviet Regime 1917–1982* (Crestwood, Tenn., 1984).

Roberts, E., and **Shukman, A.** (eds.), *Christianity for the Twenty-First Century: The Life and Work of Alexander Men* (London, 1996).

Struve, N., *Christians in Contemporary Russia* (London, 1967).

Émigré culture:

Albéra, F., *Albatros des russes à Paris* (Milan, 1995).

Beaujour, E. K., *Alien Voices: Bilingual Russian Authors of the 'First' Emigration* (Ithaca, NY, 1989).

Benois, A., *Reminiscences of the Russian Ballet* (London, 1941).

Berberova, N., *The Italics are Mine* (London, 1969).

Beyssac, M., *La Vie culturelle de l'émigration russe* (Paris, 1971).

Borovsky, V., *Chaliapin, a Critical Biography* (London, 1988).

Buckle, R., *Diaghilev* (London, 1979).

Chamot, M., *Natalia Gontcharova* (London, 1979).

Foster, L. Z., *Bibliography of Russian Émigré Literature, 1918–1968* (2 vols.; Boston, 1970).

Hardeman, H., *Coming to Terms with the Soviet Regime: The 'Changing Signposts' Movement among Russian Émigrés in the Early 1920s* (DeKalb, Ill., 1994).

Hirsbrunner, T., *Strawinsky in Paris* (Laaber, 1982).

Johnston, R. H., *New Mecca, New Babylon—Paris and the Russian Exiles, 1920–1945* (Kingston, 1988).

The Letters of D. S. Mirsky to P. P. Suvchinskii, 1922–31, ed. G. S. Smith, Birmingham Slavonic Monographs, 26 (Birmingham, 1995).

Odoevtseva, I., *Na beregakh Seny* (Paris, 1983).

Raeff, M., *Russia Abroad: A Cultural History of the Russian Emigration, 1919–1939* (New York, 1990).

Stolypin, A. P., *Na sluzhbe Rossii: Ocherki po istorii NTS* (Frankfurt am Main, 1986).

Stravinsky, I., *An Autobiography* (London, 1975).

Struve, G., *Russkaia literatura v izgnanii*, 2nd edn. (Paris, 1984).

Williams, R. C., *Culture in Exile—Russian Émigrés in Germany, 1881–1941* (Ithaca, NY, 1972).

Zil'bershtein, I. S., and **Samkov, V. A.** (eds.), *Sergei Diagilev i russkoe iskusstvo: Stat'i, otkrytye pis'ma, interv'iu. Perepiska. Sovremenniki o Diagileve* (2 vols.; Moscow, 1982).

Sexuality, Gender, Youth Culture

15

Sexuality

MARK BANTING

CATRIONA KELLY

JAMES RIORDAN

The history of sexuality after the Russian Revolution well illustrates the conflicts and contradictions that beset this period of Soviet history. Even if the Bolsheviks' plans for cultural revolution had been coherent and straightforward, they would have had difficulty in imposing uniformity on the huge and diverse territory that they were attempting to control. The former Russian Empire was a patchwork of ethnic groups and creeds, of settled and nomadic populations, of big industrialized cities, small workers' settlements, villages touched by migrancy and untouched by migrancy, and outlying small farms. There was also a massive range of life patterns and moral perceptions: both homosexuality and polygamy were tolerated in large stretches of central Asia, while within Russia itself, heterosexual relations ranged from the dynastic alliance of traditional peasant households, based on property held in common and shared labour, to the occasional alliances of factory workers constantly unsettled by their movement back and forth to the villages, to the more or less long-term affective unions of the upper middle classes and intelligentsia, which themselves might be sanctioned or not by a church ceremony (though the institution of civil marriage, *grazhdanskii brak*, had no legal validity, it carried wide symbolic and moral authority among the increasing numbers of intellectuals who contracted such unions).

The situation was further complicated by the fact that Bolshevik, and later Soviet, attitudes to marriage, the family, and sexual relationships were always torn between two conflicting imperatives inherited from the European socialist theories that they had espoused. The impulse to intervene in and regulate private behaviour, to emphasize the individual's necessary commitment to the state in order to combat 'bourgeois individualism' vied with the perception that cultural relations were necessarily subordinate to economic relations, and that attempts to regulate private behaviour were misguided. Throughout the 1920s and 1930s, a struggle between priorities was in evidence; only after the Second World War, as the Stalinist regime battled to overcome the population losses and social upheavals brought by four years of all-out fighting, was there an unambiguous commitment to pro-natalist policies, and to the propagandization of the nuclear family. However, even at this point the need to increase the population at all costs forced the government to take a softer line on extramarital liaisons (tolerated where they led to the birth of children) than might have seemed in strict logical accordance with its moralistic emphasis on the sanctity of the family.

Our discussion here is set out in three sections. The stops and starts, upheavals and discontinuities of Soviet policy on and attitudes to sex and the family up to the death of Stalin will be the subject of a short general history. This is followed by a more extended analysis of the history of homosexuality after 1917, as an exemplification of the problems and uncertainties of Soviet sexual revolution. Finally, we consider attitudes towards the body and its cultural representations, returning to late-Soviet and post-Soviet attitudes towards homosexuality as exemplary of the problems besetting any attempt to assert new identities.

Theory and Policy on Marriage and the Family, 1917–1953

Like all other political parties of the early twentieth century, the Bolsheviks prior to 1917 had no clear-cut programme in the area of sexual politics. The sex issue was perceived as a primarily economic and socio-political one, and discussion, in the wake of Friedrich Engels's *The Origin of the Family, Private Property and the State* (1884), concentrated on marital and affective relationships as a product of property relations. Though Marx himself had described male–female relationships as a crucial measure of the extent to which 'a person's natural behaviour has become human',[1] a rigid historical sequentialism constrained diversity of discussion. This was particularly true in Russia, where debate on personal rights was associated with liberalism and with bourgeois feminism. Though the activist

1 K. Marx and F. Engels, *Early Works* (Moscow, 1961), 587.

Aleksandra Kollontai had produced a schematic critique of sexual relations in 'Love and the New Morality' (1911), 'The Relations between the Sexes and Class War' (1911), and 'The New Woman' (1913) (all of which were later republished in her *The New Morality and the Working Class*, 1918), she was, when these essays were first published, a marginal figure in the Russian Social Democratic movement whose views were neither particularly representative nor particularly influential. More typical was the attitude of Lenin to sexual revolution, which he saw as inevitable but made clear, by his phrasing, that he feared and mistrusted:

An individual's feelings will swiftly change in an epoch when powerful states are crumbling, when the old relations of domination are withering on the bough, when an entire social world is starting to perish. *Whipped-up frenzy for variety and enjoyment easily acquires unrestrained power.* The forms of marriage and communion between the sexes in bourgeois society no longer satisfy people. A revolution is close in the sphere of marriage and sexual relations, in keeping with proletarian revolution.[2]

After the Revolution, too, Lenin's comments on sexual activities usually had a fastidious, even disdainful, tone; he certainly never endorsed liberty for its own sake.

Nor was libertarianism the purpose of Bolshevik family policy, which was intended to liberate citizens, particularly women, from the shackles of patriarchy, and grant them full rights in the new egalitarian society. Equal rights within marriage (including the criminalization of polygamy and of the betrothal of young girls in the Islamic territories of the former Russian Empire) were a natural parallel to equality before the law in terms of rights to property and representation. Women were given the right to their own surname, place of residence, and civil status (formerly surrendered on marriage, when a wife became her husband's dependant). Legislation on the right to work was accompanied by measures ensuring paid maternity leave. To relieve women of onerous 'domestic servitude', the state began to establish a network of crèches, nurseries, and communal food kitchens. Medical service for mothers and children was expanded and improved, and became entirely free. The work was headed by the educated and courageous Commissar for Health, Nikolai Semashko.[3] Visitors to the Soviet Union in the early 1920s, not all of them by any means Bolshevik supporters, commented with approbation and astonishment on what was then the most progressive set of social measures anywhere in the world.

However, the many splendid beginnings and projects proved impossible to carry through. Shortage of funds meant that the

2 C. Zetkin, 'From Notebooks', *Reminiscences of Lenin*, v (Moscow, 1979), 45, emphasis added.
3 See S. G. Solomon, 'Social Hygiene in Soviet Medical Education, 1922–30', *Journal of the History of Medicine and Allied Sciences*, 45 (1990), 607–43.

numbers of canteens, nurseries, crèches, and other facilities were never adequate, and standards were not always high. The economic catastrophe brought about by the Civil War, exacerbated by mass famine in large areas along the Volga in 1921 and a major food shortage in the cities, placed the Soviet Union at the mercy of foreign aid in order simply to feed its population. *Besprizornye* (orphan children) poured into the cities, where severe accommodation shortages made communal life more a matter of stark necessity (ten primuses in the kitchen of a professor's confiscated flat) rather than a utopian vision come to life.[4] The state had no funds to cope with the many broken relationships, fatherless families, and deserted children that had resulted both from war and from its well-meaning assault on the traditional marriage, nor with the associated ills of venereal disease and prostitution.

All these phenomena were recorded in the many social surveys that make this period one of the best documented in Russian history. There were studies of schoolchildren, prostitutes, VD-sufferers, and students, as well as of 'normal' adults. At first glance, all the results testify to social problems and sexual dissolution. Premarital and extramarital sex was common among young workers and students. According to Sergei Golod's estimates, aggregating the results of several large-scale surveys in the 1920s, between 85 per cent and 95 per cent of men and 48 per cent and 62 per cent of women had engaged in premarital sex. On average men began their sexual lives at 17, and roughly a quarter of those surveyed had lost their virginity before their sixteenth birthday. Women commenced their sex lives rather later than men, but the gap was steadily diminishing. Extramarital sex was also quite common; according to a survey carried out by Golosovker, about a third of the student women he surveyed had themselves engaged in it, and half of all respondents approved of it on principle. As is scarcely surprising, the abortion rate was extremely high: 102,709 legal abortions were carried out in Russian hospitals in 1926, 39 per cent in the two capitals, 46 per cent in regional centres or small towns, and only 15 per cent in villages; in other words, the 17 per cent of Russia's women who lived in cities or towns accounted for 85 per cent of the abortions.[5] VD was also rife, and doctors were concerned not only by its spread, but also by the general ignorance among sufferers of the nature, causes, and treatment of the disease. According to a survey of VD patients undertaken in 1925 in Moscow, as many as 45 per cent of the men and 81 per cent of the women had no knowledge of the nature and treatment of VD. What is more, between 54 per cent and 88 per cent of all those infected with the disease traced its source back to prostitution.[6]

4 On the *besprizornye*, see A. M. Ball, *And Now My Soul is Hardened: Abandoned Children in Soviet Russia, 1918–1930* (Berkeley, 1994).
5 See W. Z. Goldman, 'Women, Abortion and the State, 1917–1936', in B. E. Clements, B. A. Engel, and C. D. Worobec (eds.), *Russia's Women: Accommodation, Resistance, Transformation* (Berkeley, 1991), 249–50; see also the same author's *Women, the State and Revolution: Soviet Family Policy and Social Life, 1917–1936* (Cambridge, 1993).
6 See N. A. Vein, 'Osnovnye faktory, vliiaiushchie na rost i rasprostranenie venericheskikh boleznei', *Venerologiia i dermatologiia*, 6 (1925), 133–6.

Were these circumstances, seen in their historical context, so novel and sensational as to warrant talk of a sexual revolution? In Golod's interpretation, the empirical material shows the destruction of traditional norms and values rather than the emergence of new ones. The 'sexual freedom' brought by revolution was for the meantime merely 'freedom from', not 'freedom to'. People sensed that former constrictions had vanished, but they still did not know what to do with that freedom. The result was an incomplete, negative freedom—like the freedom of a thirsty man to wander in the desert. But Sheila Fitzpatrick, in her analysis of statistics on the social behaviour of Soviet students in the 1920s, comes to the different conclusion that norms were not even much disrupted by revolutionary change: 'The reported behaviour of Soviet students provides more evidence of the persistence of traditional sexual patterns—including male machismo and prudent female chastity—than of liberating sexual revolution.'[7]

The two theses are not, of course, incompatible. Some pre-Revolutionary commentators, such as census data-collectors, noted that many Russian factory workers were living in unformalized alliances well before 1917; the pattern of the 'bigamous' male factory worker, with an 'official' wife at home in the country, and a companion in the city, was fairly common, and so too was the phenomenon of the woman worker with several children by different male partners.[8] Whether individual subjects perceived the conditions of the 1920s as 'revolutionary' would therefore have depended on their personal experiences (as partners or children) before 1917. There does seem to be some evidence, though, that attitudes if not behaviour had accommodated some of the new 'cultural revolution' rhetoric. For example, though only 44 per cent of Odessa students said they believed in the existence of true love, 63 per cent claimed to have experienced it.[9]

It is not surprising that young adults should have recorded diverse and even contradictory ideological promptings, given that the Bolshevik establishment of the early 1920s was itself divided about the nature of the ideal sexual relationship. Aleksandra Kollontai, whose position as Commissar of Public Welfare made her views vastly more influential after the Revolution than before, argued in her sensational article 'Make Way for Winged Eros!' (1923) for the importance of emotional, serious, and loving relationships, opposing herself to 'sexual fetishism' and hedonism, and contemptuously terming the casual relations of the Civil War years manifestations of the sex instinct unworthy of true Bolsheviks.[10] It was Kollontai's fate to be denounced on the one hand for sentimentality, and on the other (much more unfairly) for advocating random sexual promiscuity, a charge that was

7 S. Fitzpatrick, 'Sex and Revolution: An Examination of Literacy and Statistical Data on the Mores of Soviet Students in the 1920s', *Journal of Modern History*, 50 (1978), 271.

8 See 'M.' and 'O.', 'Tsifry i fakty iz perepisi Sankt-Peterburga v 1900 godu', *Russkaia mysl'*, 11 (1902), 92, and R. Glickman, *Russian Factory Women: Workplace and Society 1880–1914* (Berkeley, 1984).

9 Fitzpatrick, 'Sex and Revolution', 275, 277.

10 A. Kollontai, 'Dorogu krylatomu Erosu! Pis'mo k trudiashcheisia molodezhi', *Molodaia gvardiia*, 3 (10) (1923), 111–13.

borne out neither by this essay nor by her collection of short stories *The Love of Worker Bees* (1923), in which sexual freedom is advocated only to the extent that it does not interfere with the greater aim, 'to work and love life'.

A different and much more dogmatic stance was adopted by Aron Zalkind, author of such popular books as *Youth and Revolution* (1924), *Sexual Fetishism: A Review of the Sex Question* (1925), and *The Sex Issue in Soviet Social Conditions* (1926). Zalkind admits the existence of a biological sexual attraction between human beings, and acknowledges the harm of repression ('sexual self-corking'). At the same time, he proposes wholly to subordinate sexuality to the proletariat's class interests. In the preface to his 'Twelve Sexual Commandments for the Revolutionary Proletariat', he prescribes a curious form of ideological sex sublimation: 'Sexual life is permissible only in so far as it encourages the growth of collective feelings, class organization, creative efforts at work, and militant activity . . . Because the proletariat and the labouring masses allied to it comprise the great bulk of humanity, *revolutionary expedience is the best biological expedience*, the best biological blessing.'[11]

Although this now sounds like a parody, at the time Zalkind's 'Twelve Commandments' carried enormous conviction. The male revolutionary who subordinated his sexuality to his role in the Party, but who (in contrast to his usual countertype, the wilting bourgeois *byvshii*, 'ex') exuded potency, was a familiar figure in literature of the time. Indeed, the literature of the time commonly if not uniformly represented sexual activity as squalid and 'animal' in nature, opposing to it manly self-restraint on the one hand, and sexual liberation for women up to a specific point (not such as to alienate and threaten men) on the other. In Anna Karavaeva's construction novel *The Sawmill* (*Lesozavod*, 1928), the emotional side of sexual relationships is entirely the province of the novel's heroine, whose incipient conflict with her lover, Ognev, the resolute action man of Party policy, is evaded through her willingness to recognize that Party work is his primary social duty. Revolutionary politics could reinforce, or indeed exaggerate, the perception that sex was an essential physical need for a man, and love an essential emotional requirement for a woman. And, since guilt-free, if not random and 'animal', sexual activity was an important signifier of liberation for women, the woman activist who renounced her sex life in favour of the revolution was not really a possibility.

At the same time, the limited free market in cultural products that operated under NEP allowed large Soviet audiences to enjoy books and films that perpetuated the 'decadent' sexuality of

11 A. Zalkind, *Revoliutsiia i molodezh'* (Leningrad, 1924), 69, emphasis added.

pre-Revolutionary days. Though Anastasiia Verbitskaia, the best-selling writer of the 1910s, was denounced as 'vulgar', and appeared in LEF's rogues' gallery of counter-revolutionary horrors, her best-known novel, *The Keys of Happiness* (*Kliuchi schast'ia*, 1908–13) was still widely read by working-class women and girls. By keeping such books out of print, the Soviet authorities could reduce their potential audience; the problem of what to do with 'trivial' films was more difficult, since the state-run cinemas could not keep afloat by showing even the most popular ideologically correct films, such as Eisenstein's *Strike* (*Stachka*, 1924). It was possible to prevent the more unsophistic-ated rural audiences from seeing trash, since village cinemas were run as public-service facilities rather than profit-making enterprises, so that didacticism could be assured. But until the end of NEP, when the Party Conference on Cinema Affairs proclaimed an end to 'bourgeois vestiges', economic realities dictated that Soviet cinema activists had either to subsidize serious films by means of Western-made erotic melodramas and light comedies, or to make their own melodramas and comedies in order to compete. The latter course was adopted in Konstantin Eggert's film *The Bear's Wedding* (*Medvezh'ia svad'ba*, 1926), scripted by Lunacharskii from a story by Merimée, which depicts the alliance of a were-bear Count with a glamorous blonde lady whom he gnaws to death on her wedding night. Lun-acharskii attempted to lend respectability to the subject by means of references to the decline of the degenerate aristocracy (the were-bear is finally hunted down by his own irate peasants). But this did not in any way impede the overweeningly frivolous momentum of *The Bear's Wedding*, which, while no great film, does hit the spot in a properly populist manner, particularly in its closing scenes, shot in a Gothic half-light that communicates a powerful and creepy eroticism.

Though censorship existed from early days, then (the literary and theatrical censorship, Glavlit and Glavrepertkom, were instituted in 1922 and 1923 respectively), its achievements were for the time being less than overwhelming. Libraries might be purged, and the publica-tion of unsuitable books (such as pre-Revolutionary potboilers) prevented, but the performance arts were harder to regulate. Soviet commentators certainly thundered against decadence: in 1924, a joint circular issued by Glavlit and Glavrepertkom attempted to dis-courage the then popular foxtrot, shimmy, and other Western dances which were being copied by Soviet young people: 'Being a product of Western restaurant life, these dances are oriented toward the very basest instincts . . . They are essentially a salon imitation of the sex act and all manner of perversion . . . Within the working atmosphere of the Soviet Republic, which is reconstructing life and sweeping away *petit-bourgeois* decadence, dancing should be quite different—exhilarating, joyful, ennobling.'[12]

But only after 1928, when restaurants and dance-halls all came into the hands of the state, could bans on such 'salon imitations of the sex act' be effectively applied. Thereafter, multiple measures came into force whose final effects, by the late 1930s, would be to make Russian society far more sexually conservative. These included not only measures specifically directed at sexual activity—the outlawing of homosexuality in 1934 and of abortion in 1935, and the tighter regulation of divorce from 1936—but also the increasingly heavy censorship of works of art. At the 1934 Soviet Writers' Congress, it had been stated that socialist realism was on no account to be identified with 'physiological naturalism', as exemplified in Joyce's *Ulysses*. Though the question of what socialist realism was remained, as we have seen (see Ch. 2), elusive (at least during the Congress), the question of what it was not—sexually (or indeed excretorily) explicit—had been made perfectly clear. A year later, on 17 October 1935, was passed the USSR Law 'On Responsibility for Preparing, Keeping, and Advertising Pornographic Publications'. The law was sufficiently vaguely formulated to make the most innocent materials indictable, and to allow imprisonment on the most ridiculous of charges. In the new climate, Shostakovich's *Lady Macbeth of Mtsensk* (*Ledi Makbet Mtsenskogo uezda*) could be denounced because the music was held to evoke the creaking of bedsprings too naturalistically, and many literary and filmic texts of the 1920s were to disappear from view for decades.

Changes in institutional regulation were accompanied by assiduous propagandization of the nuclear family and increasingly heavy insistence on traditional roles within the house, if not on the factory floor. The Soviet Union might still vaunt its women aviators for propaganda purposes, but they now often wore lipstick (state cosmetics factories having been set up in the mid-1930s), and women's magazines gave increasing attention to the joys and duties of homemaking. In the 1940s, divorce regulations were further tightened by the Family Law of 1944, which attached financial penalties to childlessness and to divorce, abolished the legal recognition of *de facto* marriages introduced in 1918, and offered financial incentives to especially fecund mothers and to single mothers who chose not to sue for paternity. Social engineering by law was underpinned in Party ideology and propaganda, and by openly coercive measures, which included the public dressing-down of individuals who had engaged in immoral behaviour at Party meetings and at the political training sessions held in all Soviet places of work.[13] (Dressings-down continued well into the post-Stalin period: a 1963 story by Iulii Daniel' contains an

12 Quoted in I. Kon, *Sexual Revolution in Russia* (New York, 1994), 155.
13 On the 1944 Family Law, see M. Buckley, *Women and Ideology in the Soviet Union* (Hemel Hempstead, 1989), 133–5; on its effects, see R. Orlova, *Vospominaniia o neproshedshem vremeni* (Ann Arbor, 1988), 110–11.

exquisite parody of a denunciation for 'antisocial behaviour', detailing how, instead of attending a lecture on the socialist political economy, 'Comrade Zalesskii was disrupting the virtue of the Soviet family, being in a completely undressed condition, with the exception of a sleeveless knitted sports shirt'.[14] The practice spread to foreign communist parties. Jim Riordan, a long-time member of the British Communist Party, was voted upon for expulsion following his divorce in 1965—he was 'saved' by one vote!)

Yet for all the growing sexophobia of Soviet culture in the late 1930s, which was to reach its culmination in the 1940s, the Soviet system never managed to wipe out 'illegitimate' sexual activity; and the transition from the 1920s to the 1930s was complex. In order to form a more detailed appreciation of that complexity, let us turn now to the question of homosexuality.

Homosexuality and the Sexual Landscape of Stalinism

At first sight, changes in the legal status of homosexuality after 1917 appear to confirm the totalitarian model of Stalinism as a radical break with the past, a period of repression hitherto unforeseen, brought about by a new and effective regulation of public and private behaviour. But the history of its regulation is marked by the same contradictions as the history of sexuality in general.

Bolshevik legislation on homosexuality had been considerably more permissive than tsarist legislation, placing no prohibition on consensual homosexual acts (homosexual rape was forbidden). In March 1934, however, after several months of OGPU pogroms against homosexuals, and of purges in the army on the pretext of 'orgiastic behaviour', espionage, and counter-revolutionary behaviour, a new law forbidding consensual male sexual intercourse was placed on the statute books. The project for the law came from G. G. Iagoda, who, in a letter sent to Stalin, spoke of 'an organization [ob"edinenie] of homosexuals in Moscow and Leningrad'. Stalin agreed that 'these scoundrels must be punished in exemplary fashion'.[15] Homosexuality was now explicitly linked with fascism—'eradicate the homosexual, and fascism will disappear', proclaimed Maksim Gor'kii—and its suppression justified as an indication of the worker state's commitment to social and sexual hygiene.

As has been indicated above, the assault on homosexuality was one of a package of measures aimed at establishing the monogamous nuclear family as the Soviet social norm, which can be traced back to

14 Iu. Daniel', 'Chelovek iz MINAPa', in *Govorit Moskva* (Moscow, 1991), 149.
15 See 'Primerno nakazat' etikh merzavtsev', *Istochnik*, 5–6 (1993), 164–5.

a spate of attacks in 1928, in *Pechat' i revoliutsiia* (*Press and Revolution*) and other journals, on the '*petit-bourgeois* bohemianism' of free-living intellectuals, and to Stalin's declaration in 1930 that the Zhenotdely, Party women's sections, could be closed because 'the woman question has been solved'—in other words, there was no further need for equal-opportunities campaigns. Describing early twentieth-century morals in 1928, for instance, M. Reisner wrote, 'And Russia, like the West, saw a "flowering of passions", free marriages with incessant divorces, every possible type of monogamy, polygamy, polyandry, *right up to overt same-sex love*. So a certain talented poet and writer, now dead, was forever proudly touting about to excited admirers his wife of the male sex, who used this protection to make a literary reputation for himself too.' The 'poet' mentioned is almost certainly Mikhail Kuzmin, who in fact lived on until 1936.[16]

The increasing insistence of the Soviet State on regulating private behaviour can also be seen as a consequence of the Central Committee's acceptance, in June 1925, of the doctrine of 'socialism in one country', a doctrine whose defeated antagonist was Trotskii's theory of world revolution. With the Soviet Union's internationalist aspirations ended in practical, if not propaganda, terms, international capitalism was replaced as the regime's bugbear by the shadowy figure of the 'enemy within'. As Stalin rose to power, and his political opponents, real and fictional, were subjected to more and more savage reprisals, the family (an entity towards which nineteenth-century socialists had felt suspicion if not hostility, seeing it as the repository and instrument of bourgeois property rights) began to be propagandized as a *iacheika* (cell organization), occupying a key position in the socialist political structure. Parents were responsible for *vospitanie*, the moral indoctrination of the young; all members, not only parents, had to ensure each other's conformity to political and ideological rectitude. The figure of Pavlik Morozov, a Young Pioneer murdered by his parents after he had denounced them to the authorities, was held up to generations of young people as a model for their behaviour.

There is thus a striking distinction between the Soviet Union's politicization of the personal, intended to make private space subject to the campaigns that were transforming public politics and industrial relations in the 1930s, and the late twentieth-century Western 'gay pride' movement's declarations that 'the personal is political', whose ultimate aim was freeing private relations from public legal regulation, with public activism as a means to this end. But when one compares Soviet policy with that obtaining in Western countries during the 1920s, 1930s, and 1940s, a rather different picture emerges. The Bolsheviks' advocacy of decriminalization of homosexuality

16 *Pechat' i revoliutsiia*, 5 (1928), 90, emphasis added. On the rise of the nuclear family generally, see above; I. Kon and J. Riordan, *Sex and Soviet Society* (London, 1993); and Buckley, *Women and Ideology*, ch. 3.

17 Detail of a portrait of the Young Pioneer hero Pavlik Morozov.

Murdered by his father and stepmother in 1932 for denouncing them as kulaks to the Soviet authorities in his village, Pavlik was an important symbol of how Soviet citizens were expected to carry *bditel'nost'* (watchfulness, awareness of 'enemies of the people') into their own families. While his example did not result in floods of accusations by children against their parents, it did make many parents wary of expressing anti-Soviet views, or even mildly criticizing Party policy, in their children's presence. The myth of Pavlik Morozov also stressed that ordinary forms of seniority, such as that of parents over children, or teachers over pupils, might be overturned by the overweening authority of the state, thus preventing minor authority-figures from exercising too much control over young minds. In the post-Stalin period, the cult of Pavlik Morozov lost much of its power, but important anniversaries were still commemorated (the picture reproduced here appeared in *Ogonek* in May 1962, on the thirtieth anniversary of his death).

was in line with radical and liberal views both in Western Europe and in Russia itself (the Social Democrats everywhere had broadly supported decriminalization, while the liberal Kadet Party and the Anarchists had pressed for it in Russia), the historical accident that brought them to power meant that decriminalization was achieved much earlier in Russia than elsewhere (where in most cases, legal tolerance was only achieved after the Second World War). Conversely, Russian legislation and attitudes after 1934 were not markedly more hostile than those in several Western countries—not only in the 'totalitarian' regime of the Third Reich, where homosexuals were subject to mass incarceration and extermination, but also in Britain and America (where radical medical treatments such as castration and testicle transplantation were practised, eugenic theories of human development taken seriously, and where the liberation of Nazi Pink Triangle camps was carefully concealed, lest it inspire sympathy for 'deviants'). It is surely not accidental that the recriminalization of homosexuality in Russia came soon after Hitler's accession to power in 1933; having lost its most powerful overseas ally, the German Left, the Soviet administration no longer needed to take into account that ally's strong support for the decriminalization of homosexuality. Hence, Stalinist policy, rather than being a brutal local aberration, represented an extreme version of the post-Enlightenment state's attempt to exercise control over physical processes by a combination of legal regulation and insistent propaganda.[17]

The local-historical context also needs to be considered. The character of the 1934 legislation was in some respects remarkably close to that of pre-Revolutionary anti-homosexual legislation. Both the 1934 law, and the 1845 law which first explicitly outlawed homosexual acts, used the ambiguous term *muzhelozhstvo* (literally 'lying with a man') to describe the forbidden behaviour; both distinguished between the less heinous offence of a consensual act—for which both parties might be indicted—and the more serious one of an act accompanied by force (*nasilie*) or whose victim was a minor (*maloletnii* in the 1845 law, *nesovershennoletnii* in the 1934 one), or other dependent person (the 1845 law specified only *slaboumnye*, persons of feeble mind, while the 1934 law spoke more broadly of 'acts involving the exploitation of the sufferer's dependent position'). The 1845 law was more openly sententious in its phrasing, stating that 'a person discovered in the unnatural vice of *muzhelozhstvo* is subject to loss of all property rights and exile to Siberia [after 1900, this was changed to 'up to 5 years in corrective institutions'] plus religious penance, if he is a Christian', while the Soviet law stated more neutrally 'the sexual intercourse of a man with a man (*muzhelozhstvo*) is punishable by deprivation of

17 See W. Reich, *The Sexual Revolution* (New York, 1945), and K. A. Martin, 'Gender and Sexuality: Medical Opinion on Homosexuality 1900–1950', *Gender and Society*, 23 (June 1993), 17–29. Cf. the reports of the World League of Sexual Reform Congresses for 1928, 1929, and 1930. A letter to Stalin from the British Communist Harry White protesting at the recriminalization of homosexuality, written in May 1934, appears in *Istochnik*, 5–6 (1993), 185–91.

liberty for a period of up to 5 years'. The Soviet law drew a less firm distinction between consensual and non-consensual acts (punishing the latter by a sentence of up to 8 years, while the 1845 legislation dictated 10–12 years' hard labour). But the restored use of the traditional (indeed religiously coloured) term *muzhelozhstvo*, and the similar punishments attached to its practice pre- and post-Revolution, could only enhance the widely attested tendency of many Soviet citizens to interpret the outwardly 'repressive' measures of the 1930s as a welcome return to normality after the revolutionary upheavals, and anti-traditionalist social policies, of the 1920s.[18]

The grounds for such an interpretation are made firmer by the character of the Bolshevik decriminalization of homosexuality, which as described by its advocates emerges less as an active gesture of emancipation, than as a passive decision not to prohibit homosexuality as new legislation was drawn up *ex nihilo* after 1917. In G. A. Batkis's assertion that '[Soviet legislation] declares the absolute non-interference of the state and society into sexual matters . . . concerning homosexuality, sodomy and other forms of sexual gratification which are set down in European legislation as offences against morality. Soviet legislation treats these in exactly the same way as so-called "natural" intercourse', the phrase 'non-interference' is indicative.[19] Certainly, homosexuality was at no stage openly approved by even the most forward-thinking Soviet leaders of the 1920s. The most prominent theorist of sexual relations, Aleksandra Kollontai, was wholly heterosexist in her approach (and also inclined to idealize motherhood); not even lesbianism figures in her feminist visions of 'new morality', let alone male homosexuality. Kollontai was here continuing the tradition of the more romantic Russian radicals of the nineteenth century, such as Chernyshevskii, who had also glorified heterosexual relations (in this case, non-procreative ones) as the pinnacle of human happiness. For his part, Lenin (notwithstanding his own well-recorded and rather Victorian prudery concerning such matters) conformed to the alternative radical tradition according to which public debate on sexual matters (as opposed to family relations) was seen as silly if not improper: 'There is no room', he declared, 'for [the discussion and theorizing of sex] among the class-conscious fighting proletariat!'[20] Many 1920s Bolsheviks saw themselves as heirs to Chernyshevskii's Rakhmet'ev, the superman who had suppressed all human weakness, to a tradition where, as Aileen Kelly has put it, 'the revolutionary was [supposed] to turn himself into a flawless monolith by suppressing all private emotions, interests and aspirations which stood in the way of the total and unhesitating subordination of his reason and will to a doctrine of revolutionary change'.[21] In this

18 *Polnoe sobranie zakonov Rossii*, xx (St Petersburg, 1846), no. 19283, 839; *The Penal Code of the Russian Socialist Federal Soviet Republic: Text of 1926 (with Supplements to 1934)* (London, 1934) (for the Russian text of the law, see *Ugolovnyi kodeks RSFSR 1960 g.*, article 121); and *Ugolovnoe zakonodatel'stvo Soiuza SSSR i Soiuznykh Respublik*, i (Moscow, 1963), 119. On pre-Revolutionary legislation, see also L. Engelstein, *The Keys to Happiness: Sex and the Search for Modernity in Fin de Siècle Russia* (Ithaca, NY, 1992), ch. 2.
19 G. A. Batkis, quoted in *Socialist Review*, 167 (1993), 13; see also his 'Sexual Reform in the USSR', in *Proceedings of the the World League for Sexual Reform Congress, Copenhagen, 1–5 December 1928* (Copenhagen, 1929), 37. Cf. the account of a homosexual patient given in the venereologist L. Fridland's *Za zakrytoi dver'iu: Zapiski vracha-venerologa* (Paris, 1927), 10–20.
20 See C. Zetkin's 'Recollections', in the appendix to *The Emancipation of Women from the Writings of V. I. Lenin*, with an Appendix, 'Lenin on the Woman Question', by Clara Zetkin (New York, 1984), 101.
21 A. Kelly, 'Self-Censorship and the Russian Intelligentsia', *Slavic Review*, 1 (1987), 194.

perspective, homosexuality was just as dangerous as any other form of sexual attraction, and acceptable only in so far as it permitted an individual's full involvement in the revolutionary social collective.

For the younger generation of Bolsheviks who did believe in the necessity of sexual activity, the so-called 'physiological' school, the male heterosexual drive was the most important representation of the natural forces that dictated and legitimized the sexual act. Surveys of sexual attitudes and behaviour reveal that many young men in the 1920s firmly believed that abstinence was the cause of psychological disturbance and sexual dysfunction (it might provoke persistent impotence). Though some realized that women might have sexual needs too, their suggestions for alleviating sexual problems indicate that only heterosexual intercourse occurred to them as a possible solution for either sex. These suggestions included the idea that women should make themselves available for the sexual relief of unmarried men two or three times a year; that women and men should freely engage in sexual relations; and that the state should (as a temporary measure) open brothels to both sexes 'according to their needs'.[22] Though surveys do not indicate students' attitude to homosexuality as such, their general disapproval of masturbation makes it unlikely that other 'unnatural' practices would have appealed, and the incidence of declared homosexual behaviour was extremely low.

As for medical opinion, that, in line with Western scholarship since the late nineteenth century, viewed homosexuality as an 'illness', to be checked, if not cured, by considerate treatment. As M. Sereiskii wrote in an article for the first edition of the *Great Soviet Encyclopedia*, published in 1930, and representing Soviet medical orthodoxy in the 1920s, homosexuality was an 'unnatural' form of sexual activity, caused by a pathological condition with various other undesirable symptoms, both physiological ('eunuchization' and feminization of the secondary sexual characteristics) and psychological (hysteria, impressionability, self-hatred). But homosexuals were not to be blamed for their pathological condition, a factor recognized in Soviet law's decriminalization of homosexuality:

Understanding the defectiveness of the homosexual's development, [Soviet] society does not and cannot apportion blame for this defectiveness to the person characterized by such peculiarities. And thus the barrier that naturally arises between the homosexual and society, forcing the former into himself, is to a high degree broken down. Emphasizing the significance of the sources from which this anomaly arises, our society sets in place a variety of therapeutic and sanitary measures to ensure homosexuals all the necessary conditions so that their life conflicts are as painless as possible, and so that the estrangement proper to them is healed within the new collective.[23]

22 S. Fitzpatrick, 'Sex and Revolution', in *The Cultural Front: Power and Culture in Revolutionary Russia* (Ithaca, NY, 1992), 80–1, 88–9.
23 *Bol'shaia sovetskaia entsiklopediia* (*BSE*), xvii (Moscow, 1930), 593–7; see also D. Healey, 'The Russian Revolution and the Decriminalisation of Homosexuality', *Revolutionary Russia*, 6 (1993), 26–54.

All in all, then, attitudes among experts and the lay public alike were wary at best, with a degree of suppressed hostility sometimes making itself evident. No wonder that most evidence suggests open homosexuality to have been confined to the sort of élite intelligentsia circles where it had been current before the Revolution, and where the Oscar Wilde trial had been received as a shocking indication that England, the supposed home of democratic freedom, was in fact the capital of hypocrisy and intolerance. Certainly, the most prominent homosexuals and lesbians in Soviet culture—the poets Nikolai Kliuev, Mikhail Kuzmin, Sofiia Parnok, and Poliksena Solov'eva—had all been 'out' well before the Revolution. Conversely, the new measures did nothing to decrease residual intolerance among even some intellectuals: one of the reasons for Anna Akhmatova's strong dislike of Kuzmin, frequently referred to in her conversations with Lidiia Chukovskaia, was certainly Kuzmin's sexual tastes—Akhmatova always maintaining a judicious silence about the exact nature of her own 'triangular' relations with the composer Artur Lourie and society beauty Ol'ga Glebova-Sudeikina. (In contrast to this, the cultural theorist Mikhail Bakhtin, in his 1973 interviews with Viktor Duvakin, reveals an evidently relaxed attitude towards the sexuality of Kuzmin and others whom he had encountered in the 1920s, referring matter-of-factly to Kliuev's apparent assertion that Christ was homosexual, and speaking sympathetically of the views of an unnamed German specialist who visited Russia to collect information about homosexuality and wrote a 'huge book' arguing that 'there are no norms of sexual life which should be banned or subject to persecution'. It is only the description of the book as being 'about these perversions' that betrays a residual negative view.)[24] Lesbianism continued to provoke as strong or indeed stronger mistrust, though it had never been illegal (and was not banned even in 1934); the inoffensive, even affectionate term *goluboi* ('blue') used for male homosexuals has no equivalent for women, who had to (and still must) be described either by the rather clinical denomination *lesbiianka* or by such circumlocutions as 'she doesn't much like men'. Though Soviet intellectual culture was no more, and perhaps less, prejudiced against (at least male) homosexuality than Western European or American culture of the day, the fact that homosexuals were extremely well-represented among Russian *émigrés* (Diaghilev, Sudeikin, Somov, and Nijinsky being only the most famous examples) also suggests that the Soviet Union was never perceived as an ideal homeland of sexual toleration.

Nor was there an explosion of gay writing, at any rate for print, in the 1920s. Though Mikhail Kuzmin did include veiled descriptions of

24 See *Besedy V. D. Duvakina s M. M. Bakhtinym* (Moscow, 1996), 179–80.

homosexual encounters in his last collection, *The Trout Breaks the Ice* (*Forel' razbivaet led*), published as late as 1929, Kliuev's more explicit and original erotic poems created unease even at an earlier stage. His remarkable tribute to a fellow-poet, friend, and probably also lover, *Lament for Esenin*, was suppressed soon after its publication in 1926; unsurprisingly, given the homoerotic intensity of many passages, celebrating Esenin in Kliuev's unmistakable folk-inspired idiom:

> Рожоное мое дитятко, матюжник милый,
> Гробовая доска—всем грехам покрышка,
> Прости ты меня борова, что кабаньей силой
> Не вспоил я тебя до златого излишка! . . .
>
> С тобою бы лечь во честной гроб,
> Во желты пески, да не с веревкой на шее!
> Быль иль не быль то, что у русских троп
> Вырастают цветы твоих глаз синее?
>
> [My prickly child, my sweet rebel,
> The coffin lid shuts off all sins:
> Forgive me, the old boar, that I didn't use my strength
> To fill your throat till gold drops ran over! . . .
>
> Let me lie down with you in the grave of honour,
> In the yellow sands, but with no rope round your neck!
> Is it truth or legend, that by Russian paths
> Grow flowers still more blue than your eyes?][25]

In the pages of his *Literature and Revolution* (1923) that Trotskii devoted to Kliuev's *The Fourth Rome*, the work's explicitly homoerotic fusions of landscape and the body (Kliuev's promised land is 'a coast of nipples, of sultry buttocks | a valley of loins, a plateau of knees, a bog of thighs')[26] were passed over in (embarrassed?) silence; Trotskii inaccurately interpreted the work as an assault on the 'urbanized' poetry of Esenin.

Similar sexually explicit references, such as 'the meadow of raging members', were censored out of Kliuev's lyric 'Voyage' ('Puteshestvie') when this was published in 1928. The fairly restricted limits of toleration meant that some of the most remarkable evocations of same-sex desire were composed for private consumption. Sofiia Parnok's late lyrics to her lover Nina Vedeneeva were written without the possibility or even the hope of publication; additionally, her friend Lev Gornung recalled in a memoir that she had imagined some poems which she felt were too explicit even to be written down.[27]

When homosexuality was mentioned by critics and historians, a note of disapproval was usually to be heard. For example, the notes to the 1928 edition of memoirs by a well-known nineteenth-century

25 N. Kliuev, *Plach o Esenine* (New York, 1954), 12.
26 N. Kliuev, *Chetvertyi Rim* (Petrograd, 1922), 11.
27 See N. Kliuev, *Sochineniia*, i (Munich, 1969), 554; S. Parnok, *Polnoe sobranie stikhotvorenii* (Ann Arbor, 1979); and L. Gornung, 'Sofiia Parnok', *Nashe nasledie*, 2 (1989), 88. On Parnok, see also D. Burgin, *Sophia Parnok: The Life and Work of Russia's Sappho* (New York, 1994).

homosexual, F. Vigel', contrive to refer disapprovingly to the memoirist's sexuality on at least one occasion.[28] It is one of the sad ironies of Soviet sexual politics in the 1920s that homosexual writings of talent were less acceptable to contemporary tastes than lurid and melodramatic descriptions of the sexual exploitation of women by men, including explicit depictions of rape. The aggressive machismo of the 1920s was no doubt partly a reaction to the new legally registered equality of women, an assertion of men's symbolic status in compensation for their perceived (never actual) loss of political power; it was also inherent in the revolutionary rhetoric and representations that the Bolsheviks enthusiastically borrowed from the French revolutionaries, their mythic ancestors. If homosexuality was permissible in Russia, it was still illegal in Georgia and in Azerbaijan, Turkmenia, and Uzbekistan; if homosexuals could not be prosecuted for sexual activities as such, they could on charges of 'disorderly behaviour' (as in fact happened in 1922 when a gay *priton* ('den') was subjected to a police crackdown).[29]

But if the cultural revolution was less than successful in terms of providing a congenial society for homosexuals (and often for heterosexual women as well), it would also be wrong to overlook the fact that the 1934 law, like the pro-family measures of 1936, did represent real changes in official attitudes. As Batkis had asserted, early Soviet legislation had been relatively symmetrical on gender grounds, outlawing both heterosexual and homosexual rape, but granting freedom to both heterosexual and homosexual consenting acts (though, in the 1926 Criminal Code, 'coercion into sexual intercourse' and 'enticement to prostitution' were constructed as offences whose victims could only be female). The 1934 law, however, singled out male homosexual acts for censure. This was not simply because the law was silent on female homosexuality, but also because the crime of rape as such could no longer have a male victim: male rape was assumed to be an aggravated form of homosexual intercourse, rather than a separate crime. Furthermore, in terms of legal practice, post-1934 law was more repressive even than that which obtained prior to 1917, when the crime of *muzhelozhstvo* had carried (in practice rather than the letter of the law) a strict interpretation as anal intercourse between men, and when other acts of 'perversion', notably 'the equally unnatural vice of bestiality', had also been subject to punishment under criminal (as well as clerical) law. In Soviet law, on the other hand, 'other perversions' were not punishable unless they involved a minor.[30] Though the perpetrators of other forms of sexual immorality, notably adultery, risked denunciation at the collective gatherings organized at all Soviet places of work to keep citizens in

28 A note to F. F. Vigel', *Zapiski*, ii (Moscow, 1928), 108, refers to the imprisonment of a young aristocrat for *muzhelozhstvo*, adding that this was 'a vice from which Vigel' himself suffered'.
29 See Healey, 'The Decriminalisation'.
30 See *Kommentarii k Ugolovnomu kodeksu RSFSR 1960 g.* (Moscow, 1962), 238, and contrast 'Muzhelozhstvo', in *Entsiklopedicheskii slovar' Brokgauza i Efrona*, xx (St Petersburg, 1897), 110.

line, and though they might risk dismissal as well as humiliation, they did not face a stretch in a labour camp.

What was more, Soviet official sources missed no opportunity to ram home the 'unnatural', antisocial, and morally reprehensible character of homosexuality. In contrast to the relatively benign tone of the *Great Soviet Encyclopedia*'s first edition, the second edition's entry on homosexuality (which was now seen as the product of 'decadent social forces') was extremely censorious; in a total reversal of pre-1934 ideology, the harsh legal treatment of homosexuality was now seen as an indication of Soviet law's unique wisdom: 'In Soviet society, with its healthy morality, H[omosexuality], as a sexual perversion, is considered disgraceful and criminal. It is punishable under Soviet law, with the exception of those cases where it is a symptom of psychological disturbance . . . In bourgeois countries, where H. is an expression of the moral decadence of the ruling classes, it is *de facto* not punishable.'[31] Earlier in the article, the anonymous author asserted that 'the overwhelming majority' of homosexuals were not suffering from any psychological disturbance, and that 'perversions cease as soon as the subject is placed in a suitable social environment'.

There is a huge irony in this assertion, given that, as in most masculinist patriarchal societies, the legal tabooing of homosexuality in Stalinist Russia paradoxically also contributed to the fetishization of this 'vice', so that male homosexual activity, including homosexual rape, functioned as a weapon of power in all-male institutions: schools, the army, and especially in prison camps. The powerful culture of *dedovshchina* (subordination of junior males to *dedy*, 'grandads', i.e. senior males) could be—and often was—reinforced by sexual relations constructed on the familiar dominant/subordinate, active/passive, enhanced masculinity/effeminacy paradigm. The obscene slang of Russian prison camps is extraordinarily rich in terms for the two partners in such homosexual relations. The 'male' partner may be named as *govnomes* (shit-stirrer), *kochegar* (stoker), or *zhopochnik* (arse bandit); the 'female' as *zheniva* (wife), *dashka*, *marusia* (from common women's names), *petushok* (cockerel), *kozel* or *kozlik* (billy-goat), *gomo* or *gomik* (homo). Of these latter only *kozel* has masculine connotations; the vastly greater number of names for the 'passive' partner suggests that it is the 'aberrant' status of the unmanly man that needs to be particularized. Conversely, among women there is apparently no special term for the 'passive' partner, but a considerable variety for the 'active'—*kobel* and *kobla* (male dog: the latter feminized in terms of grammatical gender), *kovyrialka* (from *kovyriat'sia*, to wank), *volodia* (from a common man's name). Homosexual relations in the camps replicated 'ordinary' sexual

31 *BSE*, 2nd edn., xii (Moscow, 1952), 35.

relations, with the *zheniva* adopting the victimized status which women having affairs with men also espoused. Sexual relations became an expression of power in the most brutal sense: a strongman's capacity to rape a reluctant woman (a common boast was 'she scratched my face to bits') or to subdue another man and then become his protector, were comparable matters of pride.[32]

Clearly, a prison camp was the very furthest thing from a suitable environment in which to be 'cured' of homosexuality; which did not, of course, make it a congenial environment for actual homosexuals. But it is possible to speculate that some of these did become involved in relationships as a way of protecting themselves from random intimidation or gang-rape, of obtaining favours, and/or of satisfying sexual and emotional needs (motivations all recorded in the case of women prisoners engaging in sexual relations with men). Since homosexual encounters are always described at second hand, it is hard to tell. A very rare recorded instance of a homosexual relationship formed in the camps is represented by the case of the poet Anna Barkova, who lived for some years with a fellow-inmate after the two of them had been released. For Barkova, the relationship was just as intense, committed, and creatively stimulating as that between Evgeniia Ginzburg and her second husband Anton Walter, but she, unlike Ginzburg, left no direct account of it—though some love poems survive, and it is likely that in her unfinished narrative poem, *The First Woman, and the Second: A Poem about Two Camp Inmates* (*Pervaia i vtoraia: Poema o dvukh arestantkakh*) (1954), Barkova intended to represent a lesbian affair between incarcerated women.

How many homosexuals sent to camps after the 1934 law were in fact exposed to 're-education' in the camps is hard to say, given the secrecy that hung over prosecutions for sex crimes. Figures from the end of the Soviet period suggest that prosecutions generally took place in cases involving venereal disease and the corruption of minors. But the fact of the legislation put an end to the limited tolerance of 'abnormal' sexuality that had obtained between 1890 and 1934; overt expression of gay identity would resurface only five and a half decades later, in the latter stages of the Gorbachev regime.

The 'Normalization' of Sexuality, 1934–1953

As the expression of a desire not harnessed to procreative impulses, or subject to legal control except by absolute prohibition (homosexual marriage not being a possibility that entered anyone's head), homosexuality became the ultimate taboo for Soviet society as it attempted

32 See Zh. Rossi, *Spravochnik po GULagu* (London, 1967), keywords *govnomes*, etc., and *ebat'sia*.

to make monogamy, construed as a breeding ground for new citizens, the sole legitimate form of sexual self-expression. As any unmarried male might now be the object of suspicion, marriage or cohabitation was institutionalized as the social norm. According to estimates made by I. P. Il'ina, in 1939 as many as 78.7 per cent of Soviet women between the ages of 25 and 29 were married, and 81.8 per cent of those between 30 and 34.[33]

While not able to ensure the stability of monogamous heterosexual relations (marital breakdown remained common), Stalinist laws were able to make marriage both ubiquitous and prominent in symbolism. Public culture now presented a bland image of sexual propriety: not only promiscuity, but also nudity (except in such strictly sex-segregated places as public bathhouses and changing-rooms, or used as a device for the psychological torture of prisoners) was frowned on; overt expression of sexuality was taboo. Sculptured or painted figures were almost always draped, or dressed in trunks and tunics; even that traditionally naughty genre, the novel, confined premarital sexual activity among positive heroes and heroines to a quick peck on the cheek. (Among married heroes and heroines, only the results of sexual activity—a procession of perfect babies—might be shown.) A limited amount of counselling on pregnancy, childbirth, and child-rearing was available, but sex education (beyond warnings on the dangers of abortion and VD) was not. One amusing instance of public puritanism is the fact that the rules of culture clubs in the late Stalin period dictated that dance partners should hold hands only through the sterilizing barrier of a handkerchief; girls had to wear special underskirts lest their underwear become visible as they spun round on the dance-floor.[34]

Yet references to sex did not disappear from Soviet culture. The pro-natalist policies of the 1940s—when women were rewarded for their fecundity by decoration as 'hero mothers'—required the publication of handbooks on child-bearing and -rearing, usually under the title *Mother and Child*, wherein reference had to be made (in however veiled and oracular a manner) to human reproductive biology. Even eroticism could not be entirely expunged. The 'natural' passions of heterosexual men might be stirred by the sight of lightly-clad gymnasts taking part in the sports parades that were such a familiar feature of Soviet life, or by the pictures of bosomy young girls in gauzy dresses that were churned out by official painters in the 1940s; women might feast their eyes on images of fully clothed, but muscular, young men of clean-cut, Arian good looks. Soviet fashion remained roughly in step with trends in other countries, so far as material conditions allowed; therefore, women and men in the cities, at least, were

33 I. Il'ina, 'Vliianie voin na brachnost' sovetskikh zhenshchin', in A. G. Vishnevskii (ed.), *Brachnost', rozhdaemost', smernost' v Rossii i v SSSR* (Moscow, 1977), 50–61.
34 S. Geisser-Schnittmann, 'Frauenbild und Frauenlos in der Stalin-Ära', *Neue Zürcher Zeitung*, 19–20 Feb. 1994, 25, and personal information.

18 What the elegant Soviet lady was wearing, Autumn 1949: two outfits from the popular illustrated magazine *Ogonek*.

Even at the most xenophobic period of Soviet history, contact with the West was not completely cut off; as this picture shows, styles of dress remained roughly similar on both sides of the Iron Curtain. Soviet women were not encouraged to wear the New Look triumphing in Paris during the late 1940s and early 1950s (probably because of the extravagant amounts of material required to make circular skirts). However, the big-shouldered three-quarter-length coats, nylon stockings, Cuban heels, tight bodices, flared skirts, and sausage curls under saucer-shaped felt hats are in tune with what was being worn by many women in America and Western Europe at the time. The diagrams inset into the photographs are pattern outlines for sewing workshops or home dressmakers, allowing them to copy the new designs.

dressed in clothes that their pre-Revolutionary ancestors would have thought shockingly clinging and revealing. Below the surface, too, 'illegitimate' sex continued to exist, with prostitution, like crime and drug and alcohol abuse, leading an underground existence. Even in public culture, illegimate behaviour occasionally surfaced, if only in propaganda admonitions: homosexuality might be invoked in denunciations of fascism, or loose-living 'bourgeoises' appear briefly in Soviet novels as foils to the clean-living heroines. Such glimpses of prohibited worlds can scarcely have added to the well-being of those for whom philoprogenitive monogamy was not the ideal, but they did contribute to the often startlingly decadent atmosphere surrounding élite Soviet culture in the 1930s and 1940s. There is evidence, in oral history, that *café-chantant*-style entertainments were on offer to high officials in Leningrad and Moscow after the Second World War. Lavrentii Beria, the head of the NKVD and vicious architect of the purges, is said to have cruised Moscow at night looking for suitable women who might be inveigled (usually against their will) back to his flat and forced into sex.[35] Similar rumours circulated about Stalin who, despite his ascetic public image, was alleged to take part in 'orgies with naked Bacchic figures all around, a big walrus phallus hanging from the ceiling, and Stalin taking girls like the mythical dragon'.[36]

True or false, such stories at the very least indicate some Soviet citizens' appreciation of the deep divisions in their culture, of the repressed promiscuity and hedonism that was the inevitable under-side of puritanical myth. Yet at the same time, this myth was accepted at face value by other Soviet citizens, perhaps the majority, who believed passionately in the innocence, decency, and 'humanism' of their culture, so that they would later attribute any relaxation of the proprieties to the result of the West's insidious influence. Even Evgeniia Ginzburg, one of the victims of Stalinism, and also one of its ablest critics, was to assert in the 1960s that not every form of 'Bolshevik' control should be rejected: 'You can go too far like that. Justifying homosexuality or marijuana, for instance. In the camps, I had more sympathy with the women who slept with the guards than I did with the lesbians or pederasts.'[37]

Glasnost' and the 'Sex Boom': Expressions of the Body before and after 1988

For most Russians, apart from those who do not believe that sexual behaviour and representations should be regulated in any way (a

35 There is a circumstantial if rather sensationalized account of Beria's activities in L. Vasil'eva, *Kremlevskie zheny* (Moscow, 1992).
36 Iu. Borev (comp.), *Staliniada* (Moscow, 1990), 84, 153–4. More mundanely, Stalin had a well-attested penchant for pretty young opera singers, such as Natal'ia Shpiller and Vera Davydova, a taste shared by many of his contemporaries and successors into the Brezhnev days (see A. McMillin, 'Natalia Shpiller: Songs for Stalin', obituary in *Guardian*, 21 Oct. 1995, and G. Vishnevskaia, *Galina: A Russian Story* (London, 1986), 127–31).
37 Quoted in R. Orlova and L. Kopelev, *My zhili v Moskve, 1956–1980* (Ann Arbor, 1988), 326.

19 Naming ritual for infants initiated by the Leningrad Palace of Nuptials (*Dvorets brakosochetaniia*) in the early 1960s.

The late Stalinist era had seen some degree of *rapprochement* with traditional religious ritual, which was invoked, where convenient, as a prop to nationalism. The Khrushchev regime, however, saw a reversion to the anticlerical spirit of the 1960s, with churches and monasteries suppressed, and a concerted effort to introduce secular rituals of social solidarity. The Palaces of Nuptials, set up in the late 1950s as alternatives to church weddings for those alienated by the brisk unceremoniousness of ordinary marriage registrations, began to encourage parents to return and register their offspring in a ceremony invoking the contribution of the new citizen to the socialist collective, and his/her inheritance of revolutionary traditions: babies were presented with certificates and with medals decorated with imagery (such as the Aurora and Lenin at the Finland Station) invoking Leningrad as the 'cradle of the Russian Revolution'.

small if sometimes vocal minority), the issue of where to draw boundaries of tolerance was no less controversial in the mid-1990s than it was in the late 1980s, at the moment when Gorbachev's liberalization of print censorship first allowed the publication of much more sexually explicit material than Soviet censorship would have allowed into the public domain. Certainly, before that, as was pointed out by N. Petrova, a contributor to a round-table debate organized by *Ogonek* in order to discuss the Ministry of Internal Affairs' late-1993 indictment, on grounds of pornography, of the magazine *Eshche* (*More*), sexual expression was far from unknown in Russia:

Colourful (I'd even say elegant) erotic journals from abroad would do the rounds by some unfathomable means, in my youth I read Maupassant and Zheromskii (in strict secrecy from my parents), and some dreadfully pornographic (at least, we thought so) story by Aleksei Tolstoi, we wore minis and platforms exactly like today's young people, and we drank too (and no less than they do, if I remember rightly), but . . . so what has changed? What annoys us all so much? And my generation in particular?[38]

Petrova's answer is to give a prolonged analysis of an article by a certain Iaroslav Mogutin, writing in *Novyi vzgliad* (*New View*) in which he lambasts several famous women, including Nadezhda Krupskaia, as frigid, ugly old maids. She cogently argues that Mogutin's misogyny is the product of 'an entire philosophy—there's no place for women in politics', and calls women to put the situation right themselves— 'men will never help us'. Her letter is an unusually clear articulation of why it is that Russian women should be more disinclined to welcome the liberalization of erotic expression than men: because so much of it is designed to cater for men's tastes. As we will see below, this is true even of anti-AIDS propaganda, and although serious Russian newspapers and magazines are now less inclined to demonstrate their daring by plastering their pages with naked bodies (the ubiquity of commercial representations having made what seemed brave in 1990 seem banal in 1995), images of women's bodies are still on extremely wide display in Russian society. The contexts in which they are visible vary from those that are familiar to any Western European or American (soft- and hard-core porn magazines, porn videos, girly calendars and posters, topless bars, stripteases, massage parlours, and other sex joints) to those in which they are not (both Sergei Govorukhin's 1990 documentary *We Can't Live Like This* (*Tak zhit' nel'zia*) and Andrei Nevzorov's sensational news-slot *600 Seconds* (*600 sekund*), hugely popular in the same year, employed close-up images of the naked and mutilated victims of psychopathic sex killers, something that would have been censored on legal, let alone aesthetic, grounds in the West).

38 *Ogonek*, 17–18 (1994), 15.

This last case illustrates that there is nothing simple or easily solvable about the predicament of Russian society, a point that is widely recognized now that most people have overcome their naïve assumption that the opposite of Soviet censorship, with its many and obvious constraints, including the prohibition of an elastically defined 'pornography', meant no censorship. A central problem is the unusual reverence that print culture has traditionally inspired: it is significant that the Ministry of Internal Affairs selected a magazine editor, rather than a film, theatre, or floorshow director, as the target of its pornography crackdown. This local tradition sharpens the edge of debates round the erotica/pornography, serious art/titillation, quality/rubbish dichotomies that are so familiar in contemporary Western societies as well. The most explicit material produced within Russian culture during the 1970s and 1980s was work by intelligentsia writers, of whom the most famous are Eduard Limonov and Viktor Erofeev. Though Erofeev, and a much less explicit woman writer, Valeriia Narbikova, came in for criticism on the part of conservative critics around 1990, attacks in the liberal press have been muted by the assumption that censorship against the arts is a 'respectable' issue only among far-right nationalists. Attacks on 'pornographic trash', on the other hand, come from much more diverse quarters. The defence of *Eshche* made by several of the intellectuals called together by *Ogonek* to discuss the paper was based not on the rights of the magazine's gay producers and consumers, but on aesthetics. It was argued that the images in the magazine—a photograph of a man with a large cucumber in his anus, or balancing a prize watermelon on his erect penis—were not mindless porn, but knowing and intelligent parodies of 1970s Soviet propaganda, with its cliché portraits of muscular hero workers.

The fear (among male writers at least) that criticizing any representation of sexual material that appeals to any intellectuals may seem reactionary is understandable, but it has some unfortunate consequences. One is that very few representations of sexuality come to terms, in any sense, with the dangers of sex. As in the early twentieth century, it is left to investigative journalists to write about such subjects as child prostitution, or even prostitution more generally. Recent documentary exposés of sexual exploitation—for example, the story of a rent-boy (working dressed as a girl) and his companion who were severely beaten and hideously assaulted by thugs in Moscow (the companion died in hospital after having his genitals cut off and receiving three stab wounds), or a sober-minded account of a back-street brothel which described racketeers beating a prostitute who had failed to satisfy requirements—have not so far made their way into literature or film.[39] The current distaste for critical realism is

39 See *Ogonek*, 2–3 (1994), 22–3, and 8 (1994), 26–8.

some explanation of this (there is a feeling that *chernukha*—verismo —is old hat, since it is associated with the first denunciations of the Brezhnev days in the late 1980s). But the tendency to portray sex simply in terms of safe (if by post-Soviet standards shocking) fantasy (almost always, violence is directed against women, leaving the assumed male reader protected) makes a good deal of contemporary art both superficial and ephemeral. It either violates old prohibitions, or marks time until there are new prohibitions to violate—even if some of the newly published material, such as Viktor Erofeev's 'Persian Lilac' ('Persidskaia siren''), about a woman whose vagina acts as an oracle, or the stories of Marina Palei, represent women using their bodies in a refreshingly energetic and guilt-free manner.

But the borderline between exposition (of particular psycho-pathologies or perceptions) and exploitation (i.e. the representation of these in order to titillate the reader or viewer) is particularly hard to draw in a society where unpredictable violence and commercialized sexual activity have become so prominent (as a discussion topic if nothing else) that representations of them, unless unusually lurid, are likely to attract no attention whatsoever. The days are long past when even considered depictions of sexual activity, such as Vasilii Pichul's film *Little Vera* (*Malen'kaia Vera*, 1988), could excite outrage (here it was not the grim and all too convincing portrayal of a provincial town that raised hackles, but shots of Vera and her boyfriend having sex with Vera on top).[40]

If adults are by now inured to eroticism, however, it is not clear that children necessarily are. The issue of how harmful the proliferation of erotica is to children is experienced particularly painfully, both because of an ingrained tradition of idealizing childhood, and because there is no organized system of sex education. A survey conducted recently in Moscow indicated that only a third of parents ever provide their children with any form of sex education, and that only 17 per cent of schools make up the deficiency—and this in the relatively sophisticated conditions of a major city. Since the sole initiative to set up formal sex-education programmes, the Centre for the Formation of Sexual Culture, founded in Moscow in 1989, closed in 1992, children are mostly now left to learn the 'facts of life' from other children, books, or the media—from which about 50 per cent of children acquire enlightenment about such issues as contraception. The almost complete dearth of suitable educational books and programmes means that fiction, soap operas, pornographic magazines, newspapers, videos, and smutty jokes (now available in printed collections, such as *Jokes about Sex* (*Seksual'nye anekdoty*), or published as supplements to popular newspapers) are children's likeliest guides

40 On the reception of *Little Vera*, see the readers' letters quoted in M. Khmelik, *Malen'kaia Vera* (Moscow, 1994); abbreviated English versions of some letters are given in her *Little Vera*, tr. C. Porter (London, 1990).

to sexual relationships—a situation that clearly does not aid the acquisition of detached and well-informed appreciations of these. Furthermore, all the evidence indicates that those from the least economically and educationally privileged backgrounds are the most likely to engage in sexual activity early in their lives. If in the past (according to some reports) large numbers of Soviet citizens were unaware of the existence of the female orgasm, now they are confronted with utterly unrealistic descriptions of this unfamiliar phenomenon, which naturally only add to the anxieties of many Russian women, among whom stress and poor health, especially gynaecological problems exacerbated by the extremely high abortion rate, make the idea of any physical pleasure seem illusory and even insulting, or of Russian girls, among whom the fear of pregnancy, sexual disease, and abuse is also all too well-founded.

The new prominence of sex in post-Soviet society is not experienced, then, as a joyful free-for-all, a long-awaited upsurge of repressed feeling. Rather, it is the product of an inevitable crisis brought about by the contradictions in official policies since Stalin's death, as successive regimes eased the legal regulation of private activity, and permitted increased contact with the West, yet attempted to preserve intact the old ideals of the well-regulated family. During the Khrushchev thaw, there was both a pragmatic acceptance of the need to legislate for, rather than against, urban reality (abortion was legalized once more in 1955, and regulations on divorce relaxed). Furthermore, the leader's acknowledgement, in 1956, that the woman question had not been solved after all, that social problems continued, allowed issues such as marital breakdown, pre- or extramarital intercourse, and illegitimate births to be discussed more openly. Such issues could also be represented by the artistic works of the time, as they were in the work of well-regarded writers, for example the woman writer Irina Grekova. Rape or child abuse, however, were still heavily censored topics, though there is every reason to believe that they were common in Soviet society (in the absence of proper surveys, concrete evidence is hard to find). The sensibility of the time, with its emphasis on the continuing viability of 'Soviet' ideals, including the puritanical cult of the hygienic, athletic body, also precluded much consideration of sexual pleasure, as opposed to (the aftermath of) sexual activity. No professional sexual literature was published, nor was foreign literature imported; such sexological treatises as had been purchased in earlier periods (the 1920s and early 1930s, and the pre-Revolutionary era) remained under lock and key in the *spetskhrany* (special closed sections of libraries and institutes), where material was available only to those who could demonstrate to the custodians (employed to act as vigilant censors) a *bone fide* professional or academic need to consult it.

But, as contacts with the West became easier, Soviet scientists came into closer touch with their foreign colleagues, getting to hear of such landmark surveys as the Kinsey Report. Soviet young people, also now aware of the rather freer mores of the West, began to be more demonstrative; it became clear that their values and sexual conduct were moving in the same direction as those of their peers elsewhere. (The International Festival of Youth, held in Moscow in 1957, is widely supposed to have been a turning-point, as Soviet young people mingled—in every sense of the word, it is alleged—with visitors from dozens of foreign countries.) By the early 1960s, a few pioneers were even embarking on sexological research. The first of these, Sergei Golod, a postgraduate student of Igor' Kon's at Leningrad University, presented his thesis, based on data from surveys begun in the early 1960s, for examination in 1969. Alas, the First Secretary of the Komsomol Central Committee, I. M. Tiazhel'nikov, personally refused permission for it to be heard, calling it 'an ideological diversion contrary to the spirit of Soviet youth'. Golod was forced to compose another thesis, this time on 'working women' (i.e. women in industry), who, it was considered self-evident, could not possibly have time to think about sex . . .

If analysis of empirical data was still frowned on, the Brezhnev period of 'stagnation' was, however, to see the rebirth of medical sexology, or *seksopatologiia*—the Russian term used signifies the emphasis on the problematic, morbid nature of 'abnormal' sexual phenomena that the revived discipline shared with its 1920s predecessor. In the early 1970s, Professor Abram Sviadoshch set up the first Sexological Centre in Russia, a voluntary (i.e. unfunded) institution attached to the city health department in Leningrad. His book *Female Sexopathology*, first published in 1974, is still a standard source of reference, and popularizing distillations of it bring Sviadoshch's work to an even wider audience. The rigid demarcation of traditional gender roles in Sviadoshch's work—'Children should see that there is a difference between men's work and women's work, though the impression should not be created that the world is divided into two hostile camps'[41]—was entirely in the spirit of the Brezhnev government's sex-role socialization programme, a response to the 'demographic crisis' (i.e. the falling birth-rate in European Russia) that sought to impress the joys of motherhood on women, a fact that certainly facilitated the publication of this study on the taboo area of sex. Sviadoshch's views on homosexuality are equally conventional: he recommends aversion therapy and hypnotherapy as well as psychotropic drugs to cure the

41 A. M. Sviadoshch, *Zhenskaia seksopatologiia*, 3rd edn. (Moscow 1988), 161.

condition. Similarly, the first sex teaching aids, written by Antonina Khripkova, Vice-President of the USSR Academy of Pedagogical Sciences, and Dmitrii Kolesov, head of the Age Physiology Institute, *Girl—Adolescent—Young Woman* (*Devochka—Podrostok—Iunosha*, 1981) and *Boy—Adolescent—Young Man* (*Mal'chik—Podrostok—Iunosha*, 1982), both with a print-run of over a million copies, were a ridiculous hotch-potch of physiological information and primitive moralizing dressed up as hygienic prescriptions. Igor' Kon's own *Introduction to Sexo-logy* (*Vvedenie v seksologiiu*), written in 1979, was published in various East European countries (East Germany, Czechoslovakia, Hungary) shortly after its completion, but not until 1988 in the Soviet Union, though Kon's books on adolescent psychology, *Adolescent Psychology* (*Psikhologiia rannei iunosti*, 1979) and *Psychology of Older Schoolchildren* (*Psikhologiia starshikh shkol'nikov*, 1980) did go into print, becoming the first systematic studies of the subject to appear in Russia for more than fifty years. In 1986 they were followed by *The Psycho-Hygiene of Sex among Children* (*Psikhogigiena pola u detei*), authored by the Leningrad psychiatrists Isaev and Kagan. Two years later came the first concerted effort to provide sex therapy to the Soviet public, as the USSR Health Minister, under pressure from Soviet psychiatrists and clinical psychologists, set up specialized 'family advice' clinics in most larger cities. Soviet citizens could now present themselves for psychological counselling and practical advice at the hands of clinical psychologists who often took a direct and serious interest in the methodology and procedures of their Western colleagues. In the late 1980s also, doctors and educationists, despairing of the likelihood of state intervention, began to set up voluntary organizations in order to impart 'the culture of sex' to the Soviet public. The first such organization to come into being was the Health and the Family Association (with assistance from the Health Ministry); then came the Children's Fund and the Committee of Soviet Women (which was reformed, after December 1991, as the Russian Family Planning Association), the Association for Combatting AIDS and the Association for Combatting Sexually Transmitted Diseases, among various others.

Yet such efforts, for all that they represent some kind of an effort to come to grips with the problems of a society at once promiscuous and sexually ignorant, have been able to achieve little. Under-funding has limited capacities to propagandize their efforts and to offer practical aid (for example, available contraceptives are far outstripped by the numbers of the sexually active, so that abortion still remains the main method of contraception). Properly trained personnel are also scarce. Furthermore, some of the old attitudes persist: in V. Vladin and D. Kapustin's *The Harmony of Family Relations* (*Garmoniia semeinykh otnoshenii*), for example, first published as recently as 1988, men are assumed to be the initiators of sexual relations, who arrange the sexual education (*vospitanie*), of their wives (*sic*) until the latter can overcome their sexual shyness and be brought to experience the sexual excitement that is necessary to their husbands' serenity as well as their own. Though some of the advice given in Vladin and Kapustin's book depends on an eminently practical recognition of the actual circumstances of (post-)Soviet life—much emphasis is placed, for instance, on the dangers of excessive alcohol consumption before sexual intercourse—the fact that references to female 'modesty' have an ideological as well as pragmatic content is suggested by the same book's guidelines on bringing up your daughter:

As girls grow up, they must have feelings of personal dignity, maidenly honour [*devich'ia chest'*], and modesty instilled in them. Unfortunately these are quite complex concepts . . . if on the one hand they do not 'get through' sufficiently, then nothing will remain sacred for the girl . . . if they 'get through' too successfully, then one builds up the foundations for future marital conflicts . . . Exactly like boys, although much less frequently, girls may sometimes engage in masturbation. One should not make a drama out of this, but it is essential to understand the causes behind the occurrence of this phenomenon, and to take steps in order to stamp it out from the girl's earliest childhood.[42]

By contrast, it is only 'excessive masturbation' in boys that is frowned on, and the cure in each case differs. Girls are to be 'inculcated into' getting up early and engaging in healthy sporting pursuits (p. 102); boys are also to be 'encouraged' (note the difference in phrasing!) to undertake sports, and their parents are to beware offering them 'exaggerated' physical gestures of affection, which may increase the urge to self-abuse (p. 87).

The sexual double standard that prepares girls for their envis-aged life as 'guardians of the family hearth' (p. 98), surrendering their 'maidenly honour' only for their husbands (who are respectfully appreciative of the gesture), is not the only evidence that sexologists continue to propagandize the pro-family and pro-natalist ideologies of the Brezhnevite 'demographic crisis'. The advice on contraception is so inaccurate that one suspects its authors of a hidden desire to increase the birth-rate rather than to aid women in controlling their fertility. It is (wrongly, according to Western research) suggested that the coil and the rhythm method are safe methods of contraception, while barrier methods (effective not only in contraceptive terms, but in combating sexually transmitted diseases) find considerably less favour; women are advised that the cap or condom may inhibit the beneficial effects of sperm on their internal organs. If couples insist on

42 V. Vladin and D. Kapustin, *Garmoniia semeinykh otnoshenii* (Petrozavodsk, 1991; repr. of Moscow, 1988 edn.), 99, 102; subsequent refs. in text. Similar views are expressed in V. I. Zdravomyslov, Z. E. Anisimova, and S. S. Libikh, *Funktsional'naia zhenskaia seksopatologiia* (Alma Ata, 1985), and Sviadoshch, *Zhenskaia seksopatologiia*. On sex-role socialization generally, see L. Attwood, *The New Soviet Man and Woman: Sex Role Socialization in the USSR* (London, 1990).

using condoms, and 'despite the fact that many medics (including us) are actively engaged in a campaign against too great an enthusiasm for condoms, they have still not lost their popularity', they are advised to smear them with vaseline (which causes rubber to perish!) in order to avoid 'unpleasant friction' in use (pp. 125–6).

If much Soviet 'medical' writing on sex is characterized by disinformation, myth-making, and prudery, such 'Victorian' hypocrisy is seriously out of step with the highly urbanized society that it addresses, where social relations are close to those prevailing in most Western countries. The Soviet Union indeed saw a significant drop in the birth-rate (from 2.8 children per woman in 1958–9 to 2.45 per woman in 1988, and 2.1 per woman in the Russian Federation). But the birth-rates in some other European countries have dropped still more dramatically, and the current rate, even in European Russia, is still higher than in Scandinavia, Germany, or Italy, and not much lower than that in Britain. Panic about the extinction of the Russian race would seem to be premature, therefore, while the customary Western anxieties about the burden of an ageing population are at the moment curtailed by the relatively low life expectation, especially among men (which stood at 62 in 1993, and has since dropped to 57). Similarly, while divorce rates have risen substantially over the last thirty-five years (from 6.5 per 1,000 married couples in the RSFSR in 1958–9 to 17.5 in 1978–9) the rate of marital breakdown (around half of all marriages) is comparable with that in the USA, Britain, or Scandinavia. A recent survey suggests that the sexual behaviour of young people is also closely parallel to that of their peers in Western Europe and America.[43] The demography of personal relationships in Russia, then, does not differ starkly from that in other industrialized countries. The difference at present is the almost total inadequacy of the welfare safety-net protecting the many single mothers in the population, and the dearth of practical measures, as opposed to ideological pronouncements, devoted to their situation.

The famous comment of a woman participant in one of the first Soviet–American satellite link-up discussions, 'There is no sex in the Soviet Union', was a self-evident absurdity in practical terms, however well it encapsulated the self-righteous puritanism with which the state had characterized itself after 1935. And in fact even this self-righteous puritanism had begun to alter significantly during the late 1960s and early 1970s. This was not only because *apparatchiks* of the Khrushchev and Brezhnev eras were often just as corrupt in sexual terms as they were in financial terms, engaging in a promiscuity that far outdid the self-conscious left-bank bohemianism of the Russian avant-garde.[44] It was also because official culture, especially 'mass

43 Birth-rate and divorce statistics taken from *Demograficheskii entsiklopedicheskii slovar'* (Moscow, 1985), 359, and *Novaia Rossiia: Informatsionno-statisticheskii al'manakh* (Moscow, 1994), 122–31.
44 See I. Kon, *Sexual Revolution in Russia* (New York, 1994), 201.

culture' (a term that began, during the 1970s, to be used in the context of Soviet society as well as in denunciations of the 'decadent' West) had begun to express much less 'healthy' and restrained sexual interests than had been evident in the 1940s, 1950s, and early 1960s. While the representation of nudity and any kind of copulation, however 'normal' and heterosexual, remained taboo in literature and on film, there were often surprisingly overt depictions of erotic behaviour. In *The Gypsy Camp Goes to Heaven (Tabor ukhodit v nebo)*, for example, a 1976 *kassovyi fil'm* (film anticipating a mass audience, a blockbuster) directed by Emil Lot'ianu, and loosely based on a Gor'kii story, there was a startling scene in which the hero ripped off the heroine's blouse before kissing her passionately on the breasts.

Indeed, the increasing importance of the notion of the 'mass audience' artefact could lead to some baffling clashes of permissiveness and non-permissiveness. In 1980, about a year before *The Gypsy Camp* was given a repeat run in the large provincial city of Voronezh, south of Moscow, the arts institute in the town had been the victim of a police pogrom, accompanied by denunciations in the local newspaper, *Kommuna (Commune)*. Besides unpatriotic behaviour (a student pianist was arraigned for playing programmes in international competitions that did not include work by Soviet composers), the accusations made included indecency and pornography, which had (so informed gossip related) been provoked by a lecturer on Impressionism who used Renoir nudes in order to illustrate his lectures. Increasingly, as Western erotic art (girlie magazines and videos) was smuggled into Russia and made its way on to the black market, there was pressure on Soviet mass culture to accommodate at least part of the new ethos of sexual hedonism. Certainly, sexually explicit literature in Russian could only be published abroad (for example, the confessional works of the writer—since turned fascist— Eduard Limonov, most famously his quasi-autobiographical *Rake's Progress*-cum-*Candide* in America, *It's Me, Eddie (Eto ia, Edichka*, 1979; translated as *Fuck Off, America*, 1982). But such works also made their way back illegally to Russia itself, fuelling the underground literature and arts tradition that had existed since the Khrushchev thaw.

Like many of Gorbachev's policies, then, the tolerance of publications concerned with sexuality was an acceptance of the inevitable: in this case, an admission to the public domain of material that had long circulated underground. The fact remains, though, that the ubiquity of nudity and crudity (competitions for the man with the 'largest member', cheap and badly printed porno magazines, topless calendars) has come as a huge shock in a society in which the naked body was on general public display only in strictly sex-segregated, 'hygienic' contexts such as bath-houses and changing rooms. Tensions are further increased by the widespread belief that the last few years have brought about the end of sexual prohibitions that characterized not only Soviet culture specifically, but Russian culture more generally. Even well-informed and well-read Russians will often assert, quite wrongly, that there has never been a pornographic tradition in Russia, forgetting the notorious salacities of the eighteenth-century poet Ivan Barkov or the 'underground' works of Pushkin and Lermontov, to name only the most 'elegant' examples.[45] Other difficulties are that the flood of titillatory publications has not been accompanied by notable progress in the field of sexual education; that the pornography —and such educational materials as there are—is generally stridently sexist and heterosexist; and that the traditions of élite erotic writing are still underdeveloped, advertising an iconoclasm to which they could only pretend in a society whose traditions are less than broad minded. Add in the fact that the supposed 'deluge of pornography' has become a key target of right-wing statements, from those of the August 1991 coup leaders to those of Zhirinovskii, and it is easy to see why sexual matters should continue to create much conflict, anxiety, and unhappiness in post-Soviet Russia today.

Blue Si(gh)tings: Homosexuality in Late- and Post-Soviet Culture

Same-sex relations are an area of sexuality that defines the limits of acceptability in Russian society, a fact of which Russian comment-ators are conscious, whether they think that homosexuality should be banned, freely tolerated, or accepted subject to certain restraints. At least three of the participants in the *Ogonek* round-table on *Eshche* made this point. For the psycholinguist Iurii Sorokin homosexuals were less culpable than feminists, if only because the former were con-demned by their 'genotype' (a sociobiologistic term that has become a topos of recent discussions of just about every moral issue in Russia), while the latter were wilfully attempting to impose their authority on men. For two other commentators, however, it was precisely the openness of homosexuality that illustrated things had gone too far. The writer and president of the Harmony feminist group, Mariia Arbatova, brandished the Russian 'view that homosexuality and lesbianism are part of the struggle for human rights' as a sign of the embarrassing infantilism and intellectual redundancy of members of the 'underground'. Most curiously of all, the writer and journalist Aleksandr Shatalov represented historical Russia as swinging violently

45 See e.g. K. Chukovskii, *Zhivoe o zhivom* (Moscow, 1963), 105–6: 'Our literature is one of the most chaste in the world. The deep seriousness of the aims that it sets itself excludes all lightweight and frivolous themes.' An indicative collection of 19th-c. Russian scabrosities that gives the lie to this statement is *Russkii erot, ne dlia dam* (n.p., 1879).

between homosexual eras, in which heterosexuals were marginalized and put to death (the eras of Ivan the Terrible and Pushkin), and heterosexual ones, in which homosexuals were the victims (the eras of Lermontov and Stalin).[46]

So far as the specific legislation on homosexual behaviour was concerned, the situation in the Soviet Union remained stable for a long time after Stalin's death. The 1934 law forbidding *muzhelozhstvo* remained on the statute books. It was not until the status of the RSFSR Criminal Code itself was questioned by Mikhail Gorbachev in the late 1980s that homosexual law reform again came on to the Soviet political agenda. With discussions of the possible content of a new Code, however, came the question of whether Article 121 should be renewed or not, with liberals pressing for decriminalization, and right-wingers voicing their hostility to reform in terms recalling the rhetoric of the Stalin years. Both Gorbachev's government and that of his successor Boris Yeltsin therefore stalled on giving a final commitment to decriminalization. However, in April 1993, Article 121 section 1 (forbidding consensual sexual relations between men) was finally repealed, though Article 121 section 2 (forbidding rape, violence, coercion, and sex with minors) remains in force.[47]

Even before the repeal of Article 121/1, doubts about the status of the Criminal Code offered gay men some respite from the law. Since the late 1980s, therefore, gay men in Russia have begun to live openly, indeed in some cases prominently, and a number of campaigning and lobby groups have been set up to represent their interests. Lesbians have also been involved in the movement from the earliest stages. (Although lesbianism as such has never been illegal under Russian law, lesbians whose sexual preferences came to the attention of the authorities could be made to submit to enforced psychiatric treatment, and debarred from certain professions (e.g. teaching), supposedly to stop them from corrupting minors.) The earliest lobby group, the Moscow Sexual Minorities Association, founded in 1989, was quickly succeeded by the Gay and Lesbian Alliance, headed by Roman Kalinin and Evgeniia Debrianskaia. Since then, groups have been formed in other cities, with particularly active groups in St Petersburg, Sverdlovsk, Kazan, Rostov-on-Don, and Altaiskii krai. Many groups publish their own newspapers, the best-known of which are *Tema* (*Theme*), published in Moscow until it closed down in 1993, *Gei Slaviane* (*Gay Slavs*) of St Petersburg, edited by Ol'ga Zhuk, Oleg Ul'ba, and Sergei Shcherbakov, and *Eshche*, published in Latvia but widely circulated in Russia.[48]

Like the comparable associations of Russian feminists (which, however, keep their distance from gay issues), gay and lesbian groups

46 *Ogonek*, 17–18 (1994), 15–17.
47 See C. Williams, 'Singing the Blues: The Russian Gay Movement in the 1990s', *Perversions: The International Journal of Gay and Lesbian Studies*, 4 (1995), 133–4.
48 Here and below see Williams, 'Singing the Blues', 136–9; Igor Kon, 'Sexual Minorities', in Kon and J. Riordan (eds.), *Sex and Russian Society* (London, 1994), 89–115; and J. Riordan, 'Coming Out: The Gay Community in the USSR', *Slovo*, 3 (1990), 51–66.

remain small and volatile (as will be explained later, infighting between radicals and liberals has characterized the movement from its early days). Their publications, like those of the feminists, are barely solvent, failing to reach more than a fraction of their potential constituency (it has been estimated that around 5 million Russians may be gay or lesbian, but the highest recorded circulation for a gay newspaper is around 30,000). Hence, they are bedevilled by financial problems, often relying on subsidies from Western gay and lesbian groups to keep going, and translating much of their material from Western sources as well. Still, the fact that these groups exist at all is a tribute to the energy and courage of their organizers, given the long history of discrimination against homosexuals, both legal and cultural.

Between the recriminalization of homosexuality in 1934 and the late 1980s, almost the only gay men who could live openly (a few famous dancers and artists apart, who were in any case always at risk of exposure should they come into official disfavour) were Soviet spies. The one gay café in Moscow tolerated by officialdom was kept open by and on behalf of the KGB as a means of recruiting foreign diplomats through blackmail; the system also guaranteed the loyalty of the Soviet agents themselves, since any misdemeanours were certain to bring hard labour in the Gulag. Homosexuality remained taboo in medical circles: in the 1970s and 1980s, Soviet psychiatric clinics 'cured' homosexuals by offering them therapy which could involve exposing them to heterosexual erotica. The development of Soviet psychotherapy (in which Academician Igor' Kon was one notable pioneer) placed therapists in an impossible position: aware that Western psychotherapy now accepted homosexuality, they still felt in duty bound to counsel patients against behaviour that was illegal and therefore dangerous, and to attempt to cure them of their condition. As for gay men (and women) themselves, they lived very discreetly: because of this, evidence of their activities is very hard to trace. But it seems certain that they, like many other kinds of fugitives and marginals, relied on a network of safe houses giving them escape routes from the militia and the KGB. As the unofficial economy expanded under Brezhnev, and as the puritanism of Stalinist culture gradually relaxed (by the early 1970s the representation of at least 'normal' sexual behaviour had become much more openly tolerated), homosexuals benefited indirectly, though there were still many dangers. In particular, infection with venereal disease (the concealment of which merited a prison sentence) could make a man's homosexuality evident, and so cause him to be imprisoned on that ground: hence the saying that from the doctor's surgery to the prison cell was only one step for a gay man.[49] Once a homosexual had been

49 In fact, 264 men in 1991 and 185 in 1992 made this 'one step', according to Russian Home Office Statistics: see Wilson, 'Singing the Blues', 134.

discovered, the KGB would work diligently in order to trace other 'criminals' among his contacts. Just as in other homophobic cultures, the pick-up places used by homosexuals, such as public toilets and parks (the Aleksandrovskii sad in Moscow, the garden outside the Malyi Theatre in Leningrad), were also often infiltrated, making arrests a constant risk.

Among non-homosexuals, there was an overwhelming ignorance that could sometimes have its fortunate side. In 1991, one leading activist, whose lover had recently been murdered by blackmailers, reflected that gay life had been easier in the Brezhnev years, when it was not recognized: parents would not see anything wrong in a son sleeping with his best friend, assuming this to be ordinary male friendship (in Russian culture, it is much more common for friends of the same sex to hold hands in the street, kiss each other, and engage in other forms of public physical contact).[50] Where evidence of homosexuality was available, reactions were diverse and often contradictory: on the one hand, a common view among Soviet men was (and is) that homosexuals are not 'real men'; on the other, a Russian woman recently described her husband's desertion of her for his male lover as a typical illustration of how men lived 'following their animal sex drives'.[51]

A further contradiction is that the crisis in the legal status of homosexuality coincided with the first large-scale panics in the Soviet Union about the AIDS epidemic, so that the pressure for democratization on one side was met on the other by fears that sexual liberalization would be linked to a mass outbreak of the disease in Russia. When news of the world epidemic first broke in the mid-1980s, AIDS was treated in Soviet sources as purely a Western problem; indeed, the Health Ministry even accused the Pentagon of having created AIDS in chemical weapon experiments. The dangers to the Soviet public were smugly downplayed by officials passing off puritanical ideology as reality: 'We do not have the conditions conducive to the spreading of this disease in this country: homosexuality is a grave sexual perversion punishable by law, and we are constantly engaged in explaining the harm that comes from taking drugs. Nor do we have excessive contacts with foreigners.' And similarly: 'AIDS . . . is largely a social disease, since it is connected with sexual promiscuity; this is tolerated in certain circles in the West, but it is unnatural in our society.'[52]

In actual fact, as anyone who spent time there in the 1970s or 1980s will attest, promiscuity was rife in the Soviet Union, particularly among young people; but public prudery and xenophobia alike combined to give assertions to the contrary a broad currency with

50 Personal interview with M. Banting, 1991.
51 Ibid.
52 N. Burgasov, 'SPID v SSSR', *Literaturnaia gazeta*, 7 May 1986.

the Soviet population. Prejudice appeared confirmed when the first person to test positive in the Soviet Union was a foreign national, the second a Soviet citizen who had been working in Africa. When 200 children at the Elitsa hospital contracted AIDS from unsterilized syringes, campaigns for practical action were initiated, and the Soviet press acquired another theme—the incompetence of low-level medical workers. But the main emphasis, in anti-AIDS propaganda and official comments alike, continued to be placed on AIDS as a manifestation of corrupt, non-Russian sexuality. All foreigners became suspect (in the early 1990s AIDS tests were imposed upon all long-stay visitors, an imposition that remains in force, though in practice the requirement for the tests is often waived, for Westerners at least). And two other groups that have come under suspicion, in coverage that mixes horror and prurience, are hard-currency prostitutes and homosexuals.

The cult of the *interdevochka* (literally 'international girlie') is one of the most revealing aspects of Soviet and post-Soviet culture. One of the smash hits of the late Soviet period, both as book and film, was *Interdevochka*, a film recounting the life of Tania Zaitseva, which sensationally dwelt on the material benefits of this new form of the oldest profession (clothes, money, marriage to a well-off Swede) before imposing a properly tear-jerking and moralistic ending, as Tania discovered that dull bourgeois prosperity in Sweden was no kind of a life compared with the impecunious vitality of Russia, but was killed on her way back to the airport and life in the motherland. Shortly after the film was released, a widely reported poll among adolescent Russian schoolgirls revealed that a high proportion of them saw hard-currency prostitution as the most attractive job they could aspire to. But it was not only popular culture that focused on such women. The newspaper *Sovetskaia Belorussiia* (*Soviet Belorussia*) reported that Soviet prostitutes had posed in a Western porn journal as 'Russian slave girls', an action the paper described as a slander of the Soviet system or even treachery.[53] Appropriately, such treacherous individuals were regarded as conduits for AIDS into Russian culture: as a group of army personnel put it in a letter to *Komsomol'skaia pravda*: '[Hard-currency prostitutes] don't give a damn about what they hold dear, they are bringing AIDS into this country like a fifth column. We are going to use every means at our disposal to combat prostitution . . . for the sake of Russia's honour.'[54]

Yet at the same time the hard-currency prostitute was revered and respected as the symbol of a new entrepreneurial culture, and not without cause; since privatization the majority of new jobs for women, apart from those few who have the resources to set up their

53 See V. I. Pokrovskii, 'SPID', *Komsomol'skaia pravda*, 27 Aug. 1987.
54 Readers' letters page, *Komsomol'skaia pravda*, 27 Aug. 1987.

own businesses, have been in 'glamorous' professions where good looks and the promise of sexual availability are demanded. Soviet small businesses regularly advertise not for secretaries, but for 'young, attractive, broad-minded female secretaries', and the director of a 'charm school' for highly-paid PAs in Moscow confirmed that advice on how to deal emolliently with sexual advances is an important part of the course.[55]

If discourses on AIDS led to a paradoxical reintegration into mainstream (post-)Soviet thinking and symbolism of the long-marginal figure of the prostitute, the situation with homosexuals was more complex. The early anti-AIDS propaganda worked by reaffirming the place of 'natural' heterosexual (male) desire: medical advice was heavily diluted by articles whose tone was lubricious, and whose illustrations were sexually explicit.[56] A comparable absorption of homosexual desire was not possible, given that paternal masculinity had been essentialized in the patterns of political and social relations, with absolute phallic power located in the Party leadership. Imagery of Stalin, the most successful exploiter of this power, as 'father of the nation', whose paternal authority trickled down to the male heads of every important Soviet organization (women being accepted as directors only in organizations of low status, such as nurseries and canteens), and the emphasis on reproductive biology (enhanced by the 1970s and 1980s propaganda campaign to halt the 'demographic crisis'—that is, raise the birth-rate in European Russia) made acceptance of fluid and different desires impossible for officialdom. With denunciations of homosexuals for immorality on the one hand, sometimes even accompanied by demands for their isolation or liquidation, it is scarcely surprising that homosexual activists themselves graduated to the relatively benign biologistic definitions of their identity. Explanations by specialists that 'their hypersexuality is the result of faulty biology' were apparently accepted by liberal gays, who declared: 'We are not seeking to convert anyone to our ways. We are what nature made us.'[57]

Characterizations of bisexuality were, if possible, even more offensive than those of homosexuality, because of its dangerous ambiguity: rather than being outside the borders of heterosexual behaviour, it threatened to transgress these, and to undermine heterosexuality by infiltration. As one medical specialist, Professor A. Rakhmanova, put it in a letter to the Leningrad City Council in 1990, 'concealment [of sexual orientations] is particularly dangerous in the case of bisexual persons, because it promotes the transition of the disease [AIDS] from a small limited community into the sphere of heterosexual relations'.[58] Bisexuals can 'pass' as straight, because they are apparently 'healthy',

55 'Natasha v poiskakh referenta', Ogonek, 24–6 (1994), 22–3.
56 See L. Kirkham-Lebel, 'The Politics of Alienation: Current Women's Issues in the Soviet Union', M.Phil. thesis (Oxford, 1991).
57 A. Novikov, 'Sindrom trekh obez'ian', Molodoi kommunist, 12 (1988), 75, and A. Zubov, 'Is It Easy To Be Gay?', New Times, 43 (1990), 46–7.
58 Quoted in SPID, seks, zdorov'e, 2 (1993), 42.

yet they also, like homosexuals, have an excess of 'sexual passion'. This makes them a particularly effective 'fifth column' against 'normal' heterosexuals.

The centrality of sexual politics to the movement against democratization is nowhere more explicit than in the declaration made by the Emergency Committee responsible for the coup of August 1991:

Crime is growing fast, it is becoming organized and politicized. The country is sinking into an abyss of lawlessness. Never in the history of the country has the propaganda of sex and violence had such scope, threatening the life and health of future generations . . . We intend to declare a merciless war on the criminal world and to root out shameful manifestations which discredit our society and humiliate Soviet citizens.[59]

The threat was immediately recognized by gay activist groups, especially as there had already been signs of a backlash. In June a vice department had been set up by Colonel Aleksandr Chekalin. He was equipped with lists of prostitutes, drug users, and homosexuals, and his reported aim was 'to stop the dirt'. Lists were pooled with the medical authorities; it was declared that 'criminal plagues connected with psychological anomalies come to life rapidly at times of economic and social chaos', and that one of these plagues was 'anal sex between men'. On the first day of the August coup, 'unnamed' officials turned up at Moscow AIDS clinics and demanded lists of patients.[60]

Outside the White House, gay activists assembled and distributed condoms to the other protesters, an act intended to symbolize that people's ability to take charge of their own bodies was part of the democratization process. In the Soviet Union, where condoms and other contraceptives had always been of poor quality, when available at all, the gesture also effectively conveyed contempt for the ruling authorities: the people were taking over the government's distributive powers.

But homosexual activism has not always so effectively harnessed the potential powers of democratization. As mentioned earlier, many activists have been concerned to defuse hostility by alluding to the naturalness of homosexual contact. Sometimes, as in a recent article by A. Zubov, this assimilation is further justified by suggesting that, on the one hand, homosexuals themselves would escape from blackmail, intimidation, and violence if they joined the mainstream, and on the other hand, that their own 'excessive' desires might be curbed by contact with the civilizing, 'familial' forces of the larger social order.[61] Among homosexual activists, the fear has been expressed that a discourse on sex as sex will simply confirm this stereotype of dangerous

59 Sovetskaia Rossiia, 20 Aug. 1991; see also J. L. Black (ed.), USSR Documents Annual 1991: Disintegration of the USSR, ii (Gulf Breeze, 1993), 177.
60 See Gay Times (Aug. 1991), 16, and ibid. (Sept. 1991), 5.
61 See Zubov, 'Is It Easy To Be Gay?'.

desires: 'While discussing relations between men and women, people understand that it is not only sex, but also love, friendship, marriage and many other things as well. Homosexuality is thought of as if it were only unusual and dangerous sex.'[62] In deconstructing the last-mentioned stereotype, the writer fails to deconstruct the equally stereotypical ideas in the previous sentence; homosexuality is domesticated by reference to very traditional notions of heterosexuality.

The anxieties behind such declarations were vehemently articulated in the backlash against Roman Kalinin, a populist and radical gay activist who adopted a different strategy from other activists. The text in which he caused greatest uproar was one in which he sought to acknowledge the realities of sexual activities, referring to paedophilia and necrophilia and other such practices as well as intercourse between adult men.[63] While reactionary nationalists, such as the writer Valentin Rasputin, seized on such assertions as confirmation of their worst fears about homosexuality, homosexual activists accused Kalinin of threatening the progress of gay rights by drawing attention to taboo expressions of desire. Kalinin's choice of sexual preferences was undoubtedly misguided, since both paedophilia and necrophilia are hard to defend as consensual activities. But responses to his article displayed no sensitivity to the honesty of his attempt to confront sexual realities, or to the subtlety of his argument that the consensuality of acts was more important than their harmonization with supposed public tastes, an argument that recentres sex in the democratic discourse by positing individuals as free to express their desires equally in the community, but without being subject to community control.

Instead of deconstructing the sexual establishment as Kalinin did, late- and post-Soviet gay activism has generally preferred to form its own establishment, to set up public or semi-public fora where the morality of the majority can assess and define a suitable gay behaviour, separate from, but similar to, heterosexuality. Homosexuals now have an existence in the semi-public domain, but one subject to spatial denomination and distinction. 'Blue dens' are given special protection by the police, a fact that ensures their survival, but also their 'difference', and this paradoxical situation is well conveyed in the frustrated comment of a far from sympathetic police official: 'Even if we know about a "blue den", we have no right to accuse them of anything [HIV dissemination? depravity?] because as a rule they've turned into legal clubs.'[64] Safe from harm for the meanwhile, the 'blue dens' will be exceedingly vulnerable to crackdown if there is a change in the official policy of non-interference; prominent police protection also signifies that their entry into public culture remains only partial.

62 I. Kon, 'Coming Out into Chaos', paper given at the International Conference on Sexuality (Free University, Amsterdam, June 1994), 13.
63 R. Kalinin, 'Seks men'shinstva i Mossovet', Sem'ia, 47 (1990), 2.
64 Quoted in M. Kirtser, 'V Moskve nachalas' epidemiia SPIDa sredi gomoseksualistov', Kommersant, 17 Nov. 1993.

In the same way, emphasis on the naturalness of homosexuality perpetuates the standard categorizations of Soviet medicine, ensuring that binary definitions and geographies go unchanged. The plurality of everyday sexual activity, Kalinin's attempted agenda, has been ignored in favour of a straightforward us–them paradigm, which in turn discourages the many (post-)Soviet men (and women) whom the history of discrimination against homosexuals has made reluctant to describe themselves as 'gay'. At the same time, as a formerly oppressed and silent community emerges at last from its particularly constrictive closet into a society rife with prejudice, it is perhaps hard to pronounce on what the most appropriate strategy for representing collective identity might be, most particularly since the gay literature and publishing, gay art, gay cinema and theatre that might provide striking and imaginative visions of alternative lifestyles have still to make any impact in Russia. Here too, the situation of the gay movement in Russia resembles that of the various feminist lobby groups, whose demands often seem conservative when viewed from a Western perspective, though these at times simply express a pragmatic appreciation of majority attitudes in a country where sexual intolerance and ignorance is widespread, and concepts of gender roles have still to go through full de-Stalinization.

16

LYNNE ATTWOOD

Gender Angst in Russian Society and Cinema in the Post-Stalin Era

After Stalin's death, the rapid industrialization and militarization of society were no longer the paramount concerns. The excessive work-load which had been placed on women, the concomitant erosion of traditional gender roles, and the negative effect this had had on the birth-rate, now became subjects for both journalistic and cinematic contemplation. The model Soviet woman who successfully juggled professional and domestic roles was increasingly portrayed as a fiction, someone who existed only on cinema screens and in the press. In real life she was overworked, exhausted, and unable to perform either of her roles adequately.[1] Something had to go. Some commentators suggested that women should be able to choose whether to prioritize work or family.[2] However, with the emphasis now firmly on innate differences between the sexes, there was a distinct subtext. This was that women placed undue emphasis on their professional work because of decades of erroneous upbringing, and that it was in their own interests, as well as those of the family and society, for them to concentrate their attention on the family.

Furthermore, the resurrection of 'family values' under successive leaders from Brezhnev to Gorbachev, while characteristic of the unpredictable U-turns that Soviet policy on gender rights had manifested throughout its history, was not simply a top-down measure imposed on a passive population. The reinforcement of rigid gender roles also bore witness to a general recognition (albeit one that was to remain tacit until the Gorbachev era) that the employment-, education-, and political participation-led drive to make women equal with men had not succeeded even in the terms of its own rhetoric. Certainly, in higher education, things did not look too bad. In 1965, for example, women made up 44 per cent of students at tertiary institutions, and 54 per cent and 66 per cent respectively of those attending the most prestigious variants of these, medical and academic institutes (i.e. pedagogical institutes and universities). However, once women graduated to employment, they earned on average less than two-thirds of what was earned by men. This was partly because a skilled/unskilled dichotomy had persisted in industry, with many low-prestige occupations almost totally feminized (e.g. catering and other service industries). It was also because, in white-collar jobs, there existed a more or less impenetrable 'glass ceiling' preventing women's promotion to higher grades of employment. Again in the mid-1960s, women made up about 50 per cent of junior academic staff, but only 8 per cent of university professors and academicians; 87 per cent of school teachers for the lowest years but only 21 per cent of secondary school heads; 59 per cent of factory technicians but only 6 per cent of factory directors; 82 per cent of copy- and sub-editors but only 35 per cent of senior editors and writers.[3]

Furthermore, the 'double shift' worked by most women, as full-time workers and homemakers, might be facilitated by the provision of full-time child-care during working hours, but child-care at other times, besides every other area of home management from shopping to clothes-washing to cleaning, was a private matter. In the vast majority of households these tasks were carried out by women without the aid of their male partners or of machinery, though some fortunate individuals could rely on a woman relative, usually their own mother (the *babushka* support network), and a privileged minority on paid help. No wonder that women had at their disposal less than two-thirds of the free time available to men. The low quality of the average woman's life, even in the relatively halcyon days of the late 1960s and early 1970s, before serious food shortages still further increased the load, is evident in Natal'ia Baranskaia's story *A Week Like Any Other* (*Nedelia kak nedelia*, 1969), which shows a woman running from home to work to shops (in her lunch hour) and back to work, then back home again and so on.

Beyond such pressures, which were quite widely discussed from the moment that Khrushchev admitted, in 1956, that the 'woman question' had not been solved after all, lay other difficulties that could only be hinted at in official Soviet publications until the late 1980s. These included, after the prohibition of abortion was reversed in 1955, an astronomical abortion rate (early 1980s estimates ranged as high

1 Elena T., 'Svobodna ot chego?', *Rabotnitsa*, 4 (1984), 29.
2 V. Stolin, 'Vybiraia—vybirai', *Rabotnitsa*, 9 (1985), 27.

3 Figures taken from I. A. Kurganov, *Zhenshchiny i kommunizm* (New York, 1968), 26–8, 42–4; see also R. Stites, *The Women's Liberation Movement in Russia: Feminism, Nihilism, and Bolshevism, 1860–1930* (Princeton, 1978), 398–400, and J. Shapiro, 'The Industrial Labour Force', in M. Buckley (ed.), *Perestroika and Soviet Women* (Cambridge, 1992), 14–38.

as an average of twelve per woman); widespread alcoholism in the male population, with a concomitant incidence of domestic violence and child abuse; and an extremely high rate of infant mortality. Accordingly, the idea of liberation from work and into full-time housekeeping and childbearing attracted many women, while many also welcomed the end of old attitudes that had been manifested, for instance, in the use of the insulting term *izhdiventsy sem'i* (dependants) to describe full-time housewives. Celebration of the delights of femininity in ideology and media imagery was some consolation for the exploitation that large numbers of women experienced at work and in the family, having much the same effects as the bouquets with which Soviet women were presented by gallant husbands and work colleagues once a year, on International Women's Day (8 March). As more explicit discussion of women's hardships began during the Gorbachev years, such idealizations became more frequent, and many women proved receptive to new Western imports such as beauty contests, romantic novels, and expensive cosmetics.[4] This background meant that the notion of the country's dire social problems being largely or partly traceable to a 'feminization' of men and 'masculinization' of women was held by very large numbers of people, many of whom would not consciously have endorsed ideas that they felt to emanate from official ideology.

It is important here to bear in mind the fact that institutionalized feminism is an unfamiliar phenomenon in Soviet and post-Soviet society. The new feminist pioneers in the 1970s—Tat'iana Mamonova, Iuliia Voznesenskaia, Tat'iana Goricheva, and Natal'ia Malakhovskaia, the leaders of a small Leningrad group—were savagely hounded by the Soviet authorities; the group was disbanded, and they were forced to emigrate. The groups that have emerged since *glasnost'* have not been subject to such pressures, but the feminist network is still far from large (maybe a few thousand women at most in a number of major cities), and its influence extremely limited, partly because there is no funding for mass publications. The Russian version of the American magazine *Cosmopolitan* is probably at least as influential as the much more cheaply produced feminist newsletters, xeroxed in small numbers. Besides, as unemployment and social deprivation become increasingly pressing problems, the key area for feminists is seen to be welfare work of various kinds (sex education campaigns, lobbying Duma members, organization of charity relief), rather than ideological proselytism. Accordingly, most Russian women, including writers and film directors, have little awareness of feminism as anything more than an irritating Western irrelevance.

4 See M. Buckley, *Women and Ideology in the Soviet Union* (Hemel Hempstead, 1989), 200–9, and Buckley, 'Introduction: Women and Perestroika' and B. Heldt, 'Gynoglasnost: Writing the Feminine', in Buckley (ed.), *Perestroika and Soviet Women*, 1–13, 160–75.

Nevertheless, the redefinition of their role has not gone unchallenged by women, who are, of course, well aware how overburdened women had become: publicist Larisa Kuznetsova suggested that taking on traditionally male functions in addition to their unrevised female roles had turned them into a 'third sex', a hybrid containing the features and traits of the other two.[5] All the same, a number of women academics and journalists protested that forcing women back into the family was no solution. Paid work was essential for them no less than for men, not only for economic reasons but also because it provided them with a source of personal fulfilment.[6] What was necessary was to find a more equitable way of sharing the work-load between men and women which was not based on an outmoded understanding of gender difference. The discussions which figured so prominently in the press and in academic discourse were also reflected in the cinema, with a glut of films exploring the clash between women's social and familial roles with a vigour that makes these films perhaps the most rewarding and revealing cultural expressions of a key set of problems.

Such studies of stress and conflict were also facilitated by the fact that the Soviet cinema, like other areas of cultural life, underwent a relaxation of censorship regulations after 1953, so that some surprisingly tough and gritty realism began to be produced. However, that such tolerance had its limits was manifested, for instance, in the shelving of two early films by a highly talented woman director, Kira Muratova: *Brief Encounters* and *Long Goodbyes* (*Korotkie vstrechi*, 1968, and *Dolgie provody*, 1971), which were released only in the *glasnost'* period (in 1988 and 1987 respectively).

We will look now at six films, made from the late 1960s to the 1990s, which explored the consequences of changing gender roles. The first four, dating from the 1960s and 1970s, focus on the clash of roles experienced by women in Soviet society, with their engagement in traditionally male activities (the military and/or professional work) preventing them from carrying out their traditional female functions (motherhood and family). The last two, made in the 1990s, focus on men whose manhood is in some way threatened. We shall be arguing, however, that even where there was a female protagonist, the real agenda was the challenge the non-traditional woman presented to the status and self-image of Russian men. Four of these films were directed by male and two by female directors, and we will be suggesting that the latter take a rather different approach to the subject. Both the films by female directors were made in the Brezhnev era. We were unable to find a recent film by a woman which explored gender relations. This is partly because there are far fewer female than male

5 L. Kuznetsova, 'Tretii pol?', *Novoe vremia*, 9 (1988), 46.
6 See e.g. N. Maslova and E. Novikova, 'Parametry "zhenskogo voprosa" ', *Novoe vremia*, 11 (1987), 28.

directors: in the catalogue of Russian films made between 1991 and 1994, 390 male directors are listed and only eighteen female. However, we shall also be arguing that women are generally less concerned about the maintenance of rigid gender roles; perhaps this makes female directors less inclined to explore the subject in their films, unless, as in the Brezhnev era, there is intense social interest in the subject. There is also a strong concern amongst most female directors in Russia not to make films which could be described as 'women's cinema', a term which is still thought to brand the product as inferior.[7] This might also make them less inclined to explore the subject of gender relations.

Representations of Women in Men's Films of the 1960s and 1970s

In Aleksandr Askol'dov's *The Commissar* (*Komissar*, made in 1967, but not released until 1988), the protagonist, Klavdiia Vavilova, has entered that most masculine of all domains, the military. As one scholar has argued, the military has traditionally provided men with a role 'as male-defining as child-bearing is female-defining':[8] the female soldier is, then, the classic 'masculinized woman'. Vavilova (as she is usually referred to) is both soldier and mother during the course of the film, placing this clash of identities in particularly sharp focus. The film is set in the Civil War, which facilitates comparison between Vavilova and that other famous female soldier, Ania in the Vasil'ev 'brothers'' 1934 classic *Chapaev* (see above Ch. 9). While Ania's femininity remained intact despite her army experiences, Vavilova proves herself to be as tough and ruthless as any man. Yet she is still a woman, capable of giving life as well as taking it.

The film is replete with images that contrast the military and motherhood. In the opening scene, the Red Army rides past a statue of the Madonna, while a lullaby plays on the soundtrack. A deserter is captured, and is sentenced to death by firing squad; he is clutching a jug of milk (the essence of maternal sustenance), and when he falls it is the milk which pours across the ground instead of his blood. While Vavilova is in the agony of labour, she has hallucinations of battle scenes. As the child is born, she dreams of his father being killed in battle. Vavilova herself is the instrument of both life and death. Although it is not she who actually shoots the deserter, she opens her mouth just as the gunfire starts, and the burst of noise appears to come from inside her. She has also attempted to destroy the life inside her, even threatening the doctor with a gun when he refuses to perform a late abortion.

7 See e.g. interviews with K. Kamalova in L. Attwood, 'Some Interviews on Personal Questions', in Attwood (ed.), *Red Women on the Silver Screen* (London, 1993), 231–5.
8 J. H. Stiehm, quoted in S. Jeffords, *The Remasculinization of America: Gender and the Vietnam War* (Bloomington, Ind., 1989), 92.

The masculinization of Vavilova is emphasized by the contrast between her and Mariia, the woman with whose family she is billeted. Mariia is the epitome of femininity, as indicated by her total commitment to her family. In the short story on which the film is based ('In the Town of Berdichev', by Vasilii Grossman) Mariia is called Bela; in changing her name Askol'dov has turned her into motherhood incarnate, the Madonna statue come to life. She has six children, but remains improbably beautiful and slim. She is shown in almost constant contact with her children, washing them, holding them, playing with them, talking to Vavilova about them. Vavilova, in contrast, is more concerned with guns, incessantly inspecting and cleaning them, at least until her own child is born. The gun is, of course, a classic phallic symbol, and in case we do not recognize this fact we are given a number of nudges. A cannon is rolled through the village and passes in front of three of Mariia's children, playing naked in the street; their genitals, the two penises and the 'castrated' pudenda of the girl, are clearly visible behind the cannon. When Vavilova is in labour she dreams of embracing her lover during a lull in the fighting; her hand simultaneously strokes the barrel of a cannon. By association with the gun, then, Vavilova is represented as having become a virtual man. This is emphasized by her size: she towers over the diminutive Jewish father, Magazanik, whose slippers are even too small for her enormous feet.

Motherhood seems at first to feminize Vavilova. Perhaps, as Freud would have claimed, the child functions as penis substitute. As Kaplan explains in her study of representations of motherhood in American culture, 'the child represents the longed-for penis and signifies the end of women's envy . . . The mother is happily passive, receptive to her child's needs, and without her own desire.'[9] Vavilova fusses over the child 'like a Jewish mother', as Mariia observes; she dresses in a frock and a headscarf and even starts to scrub the floor. (It is useful to note here the importance of the water motif. Before the birth Vavilova was associated with images of wild, turbulent water, which for Freud symbolized sperm. For Mariia, water was used for quiet domestic purposes. When Vavilova begins using water in the same way, this denotes that she has become a 'real' woman.) 'What did you think?', says Magazanik, when Mariia expresses surprise at this transformation. 'If you dress a woman in leather breeches, does she turn into a man?' Yet at the end of the film Vavilova abandons her child, pulls her greatcoat over her dress (a suggestion that she is now half man, half woman—Kuznetsova's 'third sex'), and returns to battle. She has rejected the private domain, traditionally the preserve of women, in favour of the public world of men; she has placed social duty and

9 E. A. Kaplan, *Motherhood and Representation: The Mother in Popular Culture and Melodrama* (London, 1992), 46.

abstract ideals above her own child. The implicit message is that Soviet society, in demanding such duty and self-sacrifice from women, has distorted female nature.

The same could be said of the protagonist of Gleb Panfilov's *I Wish to Speak* (*Proshu slova*, 1976). This time the clash comes not between the military and motherhood, but between professional and family duties. Elizaveta Uvarova (who, like Vavilova, is generally referred to by her surname) is the mayor of a provincial city. She is a fine, committed person, dedicated to improving the lives of its people. She aims to construct enough new housing over the next ten years to give every family its own apartment; to this end she plans to build a bridge across the river and turn the undeveloped left bank into a modern residential district. The project is laudable but unrealizable. Bureaucracy, inertia, and incompetence hinder her at every turn (the existing housing is so shoddily built that cracks begin appearing as soon as it is completed). Yet Uvarova's commitment to her civic duties so dominates her life that there is no time left for family concerns. She has a husband, Sergei, and two teenage children, but at times seems almost unaware of their existence: when a work colleague asks her to convey his greetings to Sergei, she asks absently: 'Sergei who?'

The film begins with the death of Uvarova's son in a shooting accident. He has found a gun in the snow, and cannot get it to work; it goes off suddenly while he is trying to repair it. The rest of the film is a flashback of events leading up to the death. Beginning with the courtship of Uvarova and Sergei, it traces her growing estrangement from her family as public life takes over. She was once a champion shooter, and shooting remains her only hobby; hence although her son has killed himself, the link between Uvarova and guns makes her neglect the symbolic cause of his death. This point is emphasized when we discover that the tools with which he was repairing the gun were a gift from her. If the gun is seen as a phallic symbol, Uvarova, like Vavilova, is portrayed as a surrogate man. She is rarely depicted at home, and when she is, it seems little more than an extension of the workplace: she uses her family as a trial audience for her latest speech. On the wall behind her desk is a series of family photographs, but with a portrait of Lenin in the centre; when she gazes at the pictures it is on Lenin that she focuses. At her son's funeral she remains dry-eyed (unlike her husband), and even goes straight back to work; the news of Salvador Allende's death, in contrast, reduces her to uncontrollable grief. In short, she has cut herself off from private matters; all her drive, and even her emotion, is reserved for the public world, for public service. The bridge has acquired a symbolic meaning. Her desperation to unite the two banks of the river contrasts with the collapse of the link between her and her family. As with *The Commissar*, the message is that Bolshevism, through its stress on social duty above all else, has distorted female personality.

Films Made by Women in the 1960s and 1970s

A rather different message emerges from films about women's roles made by female directors. Françoise Navailh, exploring the representations of women in four films of the 1970s and early 1980s, apparently sees little difference between Lana Gogoberidze's approach and those of the three male directors whose work she looks at: 'A disappointing job and a shattered family—such are the two main lines of those films.'[10] We wish to argue, on the contrary, that a quite different attitude towards the female protagonist can be discerned in accordance with the director's gender.

Nadezhda Petrukhina, the central character in Larisa Shepit'ko's 1966 film *Wings (Kryl'ia)* is another military woman, a former fighter pilot in the Great Patriotic War. She is now back in civilian clothes and serving as the director of a technical school. She is also the mother of an adopted daughter a little older than her pupils, who has recently married and left home. Nadezhda is undergoing a personal crisis brought on by her daughter's departure. She is clearly an unhappy woman, out of step with her times. She was reared in an era when social duty was elevated to the status of a moral absolute. Now more traditional roles are expected of women, and Nadezhda does not know how to perform them. She is contrasted continually with a new breed of women—the giggly schoolgirls who think they will attract boys by acting stupid, the journalist who comes to interview Nadezhda wearing narrow high heels, the daughter she confronts across a gaping generation divide.

Tania is a child of the 1960s who cannot understand her mother's sense of duty. She urges her to give up her job and devote time to herself. Nadezhda, in turn, is appalled at her daughter's lack of social conscience. Tania seems to have little interest in anything beyond her marriage. Although we learn from her mother's conversations with others that Tania is a maths student at the university, this is not something she talks about herself; it seems to have little importance to her.

Nadezhda is not comfortable in the private space, that traditional female domain. She is almost always pictured at work, in the streets, on public transport, and, in her imagination, flying through the sky. When she is at home, she seems anxious to get out of it. Yet she is not welcome in the public sphere. This is a man's world, whatever the

10 F. Navailh, 'The Image of Women in Contemporary Soviet Cinema', in A. Lawton (ed.), *The Red Screen: Politics, Society, Art in Soviet Cinema* (London, 1992), 215.

Soviet insistence on women's equality. When Nadezhda decides not to waste any more Sundays peeling potatoes and to eat in the local restaurant instead, she is refused admittance; although the Bolsheviks once intended public dining facilities to free women from the kitchen, now women are not allowed in unaccompanied after 6.00 p.m. Nadezhda goes instead to a beer bar, where apart from the waitress she is the only woman, and is hassled by a drunken male customer. When she and the waitress later discover a common bond and begin spontaneously to sing and dance together before the bar opens, they are brought to an abrupt halt by the astonished stares of the men waiting outside. Men can find pleasure in each other's company, but for two women to do so is seemingly unacceptable. When Nadezhda visits her daughter in her new flat, she finds it full of her husband's male friends; she and Tania are excluded, shown looking in from the other side of a glass door.

Yet these men, with all their social advantages, come nowhere near Nadezhda in terms of strength and capability. Her male assistant, Boris Grigor'evich, is awkward and inept, unable to show any initiative himself and scarcely capable of carrying out Nadezhda's instructions. The men she meets in Tania's flat, although supposedly intellectuals, talk inanities.

Neya Zorkaya has described Nadezhda as 'the tragic product of a certain period of Soviet history' which promoted a type of female heroism which has become obsolete. Oksana Bulgakova is still more negative: for her, Nadezhda is 'shrivelled, set and old fashioned . . . a non-modern woman who has blundered into modern life'.[11] This, we would argue, is not the impression Shepit'ko intended. Nadezhda is certainly out of step with her times, but Shepit'ko does not suggest that the roles now on offer to woman are an improvement. Tania's life is hardly an attractive alternative. Social duty has been replaced by duty to an individual man; her marriage is based on a hierarchy of roles in which she is clearly the subordinate partner. Nadezhda's relationship with her wartime lover, Mitia, shown to us in dream-like flashbacks, was, in contrast, one of comradeship and equality. So too is her close but platonic friendship with the museum director, Pasha. Nor has Nadezhda turned her back on maternal pursuits, like Vavilova and Uvarova. Her relationship with her daughter may not be easy, but Nadezhda loves her and tries to establish intimacy. She also looks after a neighbour's children, and clearly gets pleasure from their company. This is not a one-dimensional woman, then, but one who has managed to juggle different roles, however hard this has proved.

Throughout the film there is a sense that society has placed barriers around people, especially women—that they are in some way

11 N. Zorkaya, *The Illustrated History of the Soviet Cinema* (New York, 1989), 253–4, and O. Bulgakova, 'The Hydra of the Soviet Cinema', in Attwood (ed.), *Red Women*, 171.

trapped. When Nadezhda goes to the flat of a disgraced student, the only person she finds there is a lonely old woman, virtually imprisoned since she is unable to undo the chain on the door. While Nadezhda dreams of flying through the open sky, the camera shows her packed tightly into a crowded bus. The film ends with her returning to the airfield where she once trained, and her old colleagues let her get into a plane as they push it towards the hangar; just as they are about to go inside she starts the engine and takes off. In the final shot she is back in the sky, in her element. She is free at last of the constraints placed on women.

The Georgian director Lana Gogoberidze takes a similarly sympathetic view of her heroine in *Some Interviews on Personal Questions* (*Neskol'ko interv'iu po lichnym voprosam*, 1979). (Since Gogoberidze is Georgian, discussion of her work in a book on Russian culture requires some explanation. It is justified because Gogoberidze was one of the best-known Soviet directors of the late Brezhnev era, and the films she made about the lives of urban women, although set in Tbilisi, clearly had as much relevance to Russian as to Georgian viewers. As she explained in a personal interview with Lynne Attwood in July 1989, after the release of *Some Interviews* she received hundreds of letters from women from all parts of the Soviet Union. 'And the letters all began with this phrase', she explained: "This film is about me". The women asked me how I could have known what their lives were like . . .')[12]

Sofiko is a journalist working in the letters section of a local newspaper. She is currently conducting a series of interviews with local women who have written to the paper about their family problems, and their stories form the backdrop to her own unfolding domestic crisis. Sofiko's life has long been a frantic race between work and family; she also makes time to visit two elderly aunts who used to look after her when her mother was in a Stalinist labour camp. Her husband, Archil, feels neglected, and when a less demanding secretarial job becomes free at her newspaper he urges her to take it. She is appalled at the suggestion. Archil proceeds to find himself a younger woman who is more willing to make him the centre of attention. When Sofiko learns of the affair she makes a vain attempt to win him back, trying to brighten up her appearance and take a greater interest in family affairs. This all fails, however, and in the end she accepts the inevitability of divorce.

Some Soviet critics held Sofiko to blame for the breakdown in the marriage. L. Mamatova, for example, criticized her for being so absorbed in her job that she does not notice how weary Archil has become of her neglect of the home.[13] However, this is surely not the

12 For more on this, see the interview with L. Gogoberidze in Attwood, 'Some Interviews', 226–31.

13 L. Mamatova, 'Internatsional'noe i natsional'noe v sovetskom kino', in *Sovetskoe kino: 70-e gody* (Moscow, 1984), 179–80.

message Gogoberidze intended. The director makes it clear that, despite Archil's complaints about Sofiko's neglect of the home, the entire domestic workload rests on her shoulders. When she is at home she is always dressed in an apron, preparing food, getting the children ready for school, tending her elderly mother. It is she who does the shopping, standing in endless queues composed entirely of women. When Archil invites a group of male friends to dinner, Sofiko has to cook and wait on them; yet when she dares to dance with the guests (still wearing the apron) Archil glares at her with the same male disapproval which confronted Nadezhda and her dancing partner in *Wings*. He then leaves Sofiko to do the clearing up. When he tells her he cannot go on living like this, he is sitting at the kitchen table doing nothing while she bustles round preparing the family's meal. Like Shepit'ko, then, Gogoberidze makes it clear how partial women's equality has been in Soviet society.

Although Sofiko is committed to her job, she has not cut herself off from family life. Indeed, she is at the centre of a network of family relations, as daughter as well as mother. Archil, on the other hand, seems more a spectator of family life. As Françoise Navailh notes, at one point he is pictured watching Sofiko laughing and playing with the children on the other side of a glass door.[14] If the women were closed out of social life by a glass door in *Wings*, here the same barrier stands between men and their families.

Unlike the protagonists of the previous films we have looked at, Sofiko neither loses nor abandons her children; they will stay with her, not Archil, after the divorce. She tells Archil that they are old enough now to cope with the separation. The implication is that he will leave the family. Gogoberidze makes it clear that Archil is the unreasonable party who is responsible for the break-up of the family by refusing to accept a more egalitarian relationship with his wife. The problems women have combining their roles cannot be resolved by putting them back in the kitchen. Despite her sadness at losing Archil, in effect their separation is, like Nadezhda Petrukhina's flight in the plane, a liberation.

In short, it can be argued that Shepit'ko and Gogoberidze are rather less concerned than their male colleagues about the blurring of boundaries between gender roles. The protagonists of *The Commissar* and *I Wish to Speak* are portrayed as having distorted, damaged female identities, indicated by their obsession with public duty and their failure as mothers. In *Wings* and *Some Interviews*, however, the heroines do manage to combine professional and maternal roles, however difficult this may be. Neither abandons nor withdraws from the family. At the same time, reproduction is not presented as woman's

14 Navailh, 'The Image', 213.

362   Lynne Attwood

only real purpose in life. Both Nadezhda and Sofiko are physically attractive, and neither is depicted as mannish (even if Nadezhda does favour suits and sensible shoes). Neither is contrasted with an idealized feminine woman living an appropriately traditional life: on the contrary, Nadezhda's daughter does not seem happy in her patriarchal set-up. The solution to the conflict between women's roles is not for them to return to full-time domesticity and embrace some essential femaleness; it is for society—and men—to accommodate more flexible gender roles. In these films, then, we find resistance to society's promotion of more traditional gender roles. Although Shepit'ko has consistently been described as a 'manly' director,[15] we would argue that these two films constitute what Kaplan has called a 'female' discourse. Kaplan differentiates this from a '(patriarchal) "feminine" discourse', promoting some notion of essential femaleness. On the contrary, it is a 'struggle against dominant discourses which position women in oppressive ways'.[16]

Gender Issues in Films of the *Glasnost'* and Post-*Glasnost'* Era

Concern about women's roles in Soviet society was not brought to an end with the changes initiated by Gorbachev. Indeed, Gorbachev himself argued that women's professional achievements had left them with insufficient time 'to perform their everyday duties at home' and insisted that ways were being discussed to return them to their 'purely womanly mission'.[17] In fact, the transition to a market economy provided an additional reason for doing so: if women could be persuaded to leave the workforce voluntarily, this would ease the growing threat of unemployment.

With the collapse of socialism, attention has been paid to the supposedly negative influence it had on male personality. The market which has taken its place is said to require personality traits traditionally associated with men: entrepreneurship, self-confidence, individual responsibility, and initiative. State socialism, on the other hand, promoted 'feminine' qualities such as 'collective responsibility, implementation [of state decisions], an instrumental attitude towards work, conservatism'.[18] While socialism resulted in a distortion of both male and female personalities, it was particularly damaging for men since it stifled their masculine traits. Accordingly, the move to the market has been accompanied by calls for more rigid gender roles and a more determined process of gender socialization.

15 See M. Zak, 'Opyt kinorezhissury', in *Sovetskoe kino*, 225, and K. Kamalova, interviewed in Attwood (ed.), *Red Women*, 232.
16 Kaplan, *Motherhood*, 16.
17 M. Gorbachev, *Perestroika* (London, 1987), 117.
18 Iu. E. Aleshina and A. S. Volovich, 'Problemy uslovleniia rolei muzhchiny i zhenshchiny', *Voprosy psikhologii*, 4 (1991), 74–82.

Cinema has, again, reflected these concerns. The blatant explorations of women's roles which were so prominent in cinema of the Brezhnev era have given way to a more subtle discourse on gender which forms a subtext in films within a wide range of genres. Adventure films in particular, usually involving Russia's new organized crime rings, give film-makers the chance to portray a tough new society in which men have been forced to reclaim their masculinity from the feminizing influence of state socialism. They cannot start too young: in *In Order to Survive* (*Chtoby perezhit'*, Vsevolod Plotkin, 1993) a soft, city-spoiled teenager learns the hard way to abandon his feminine ways and toughen up when he is kidnapped by a mafia gang. These new heroes are strong and ruthless, rugged individuals looking out for themselves. Power in this new world rests exclusively with men, backed up by a range of firearms, with the usual Freudian connotations.[19]

You are My Only One (*Ty u menia odna*), a popular comedy/melodrama of 1993 by Dmitrii Astrakhan', comes closer to the domestic dramas of the Brezhnev era, but this time the focus is on a man rather than a woman. Like many films of the late and post-Soviet era, it is ostensibly about the lure of the West, and the need to resist this: the Russian soul can only be nourished in its own soil. However, there is an underlying message: that men need to re-establish themselves as patriarchs, reclaim their rightful place in the family and society. The protagonists are a couple called Natasha and Evgenii (Zhenia), who live with their teenaged daughter, Olia, in a one-room apartment. Natasha is a sex therapist who spends her working days telling confused couples how to improve their sex lives: an indication, perhaps, that she has usurped the masculine, sexually active role. She is certainly the more active partner in the marriage, manipulating all around her in an attempt to improve their lot. Zhenia is an engineer, but the firm he works with is planning to merge with an American company, which will result in the loss of many jobs. The representative of the American company turns out to be a Russian *émigrée*, Ania, whom Zhenia and Natasha knew when they were teenagers, and who was in love with Zhenia. Natasha insists that he exploit this connection. At first he refuses, but, at least partly to spite Natasha, he goes on to have an affair with Ania. She decides to take him back to the States with her, and takes him to an expensive foreign-currency store to get him appropriately clothed. He sheepishly submits as two female shop assistants undress and dress him, and watches uncomfortably as Ania counts out hundred-dollar bills. Later he arrives at Ania's hotel at the same moment as a transvestite prostitute turns up to meet a client. This hybrid of a person, neither man nor woman, takes out a wad of

19 See L. Attwood, 'Men, Machine Guns and the Mafia: Post-Soviet Cinema as a Discourse on Gender', *International Women's Studies Forum*, 18 (1995), 513–21.

money to tip the doorman, and Zhenia recalls the pile of dollars Ania spent on him earlier that evening. In shame he turns round and sets off back home. This experience is a turning point for Zhenia. He now rejects the 'feminized' part of himself, and is able for the first time to deal with the young neighbours whose incessant parties he has suffered for so long, and then go on to re-establish his pre-eminence in the family. By the end of the film Natasha is clinging to him and begging for his forgiveness; Olia joins them, completing the perfect patriarchal family tableau. We are not suggesting that this film is entirely about the resurrection of masculinity. The title of the film has a *double entendre* which hints at one of its themes: the hero eventually turns his back on the West and commits himself to Russia, which, like his wife, is his 'only one'. Like the 1989 hit *Intergirl* (*Interdevochka*), then, this film is concerned with the danger of the lure of the West, and of Russia prostituting itself to the West. But gender angst is certainly one of its main themes.

Sergei Livnev's *Hammer and Sickle* (*Serp i molot*, 1994) is set in the early years of Stalinism, and uses allegory to explore the supposed distortion of gender identity. His protagonist undergoes an actual sex-change operation; Evdokiia Kuznetsova becomes Evdokim Kuznetsov. This literal 'new man' is then turned into the symbol of the 'new Soviet man'. 'He' becomes a Hero of Socialist Labour and marries Varia, a key woman worker in the Metrostroi (Metro construction organization), and the couple becomes the model for Vera Mukhina's famous statue of the male industrial worker and the female collective farmer. The couple then adopt a child, Dolores, a refugee from the Spanish Civil War. Yet Evdokim begins to feel manipulated, and to question the values of the new society. An unsuccessful attempt on Stalin's life results in him being shot and paralysed; but for propaganda purposes his act of rebellion is presented to the public as an heroic defence of the leader. He is set up in a museum reminiscent, as Elena Plakhova points out, of Lenin's Mausoleum,[20] a living corpse visited by worshippers, until he is shot dead by his young daughter.

Livnev is clearly intent on playing games with Soviet and, particularly, Stalinist mythology. At the same time he has produced a latter-day version of the Frankenstein story, in which the monster is the 'new Soviet person', who, he suggests, was a mutant, neither man nor woman. Evdokim is manipulated both by the state and by his wife. He is not a 'real' man either physically or figuratively; in all senses he is impotent. Despite the pretty, feminine dresses Varia wears when she is not at work, she is more forceful than her husband; by the end of the film she has assumed total control over him, even clambering on top

20 See E. Plakhova, 'Eto nash sovetskii gerb', *Iskusstvo kino*, 1 (1995), 52–7.

of him to satisfy herself sexually. Since he is totally incapable of movement, there is clearly nothing he can contribute—the implication is that women in Stalin's Russia took on so many of men's roles that they had no need of men at all. Indeed, the film abounds in images of powerful and sometimes aggressive women. Most significantly, the doctor who performs the sex change operation is female. Evdokim is, on the one hand, the ultimate 'masculinized woman', yet he is also the feminized man supposedly produced by Soviet society: impotent, paralysed, incapable of independent action.

The 'Crisis of Masculinity'

As noted earlier, despite the concentration in the Brezhnev era on the 'masculinized' woman, Soviet socialism is now said to have had a still more pernicious effect on men and on masculinity. It could be argued, however, that men are in general more concerned about the preservation of gender roles. As suggested earlier, the two female directors whose work we have looked at were rather less worried about the blurring of gender boundaries than were their male counterparts.

A greater male insecurity about gender is not unique to Russian society. Sociologist Christine Williams, in her study of the self-image of male nurses and female marines in the United States, argues that men 'have more at stake emotionally than women in preserving and maintaining gender differences'. The male nurses she interviewed tried continually to reaffirm their manhood, 'often emphasiz[ing] their masculinity and attempt[ing] to distance themselves from their female colleagues'. Women in the marines, however, were much more relaxed about their female identities, even in gruelling combat conditions. Williams concludes that: 'Unlike men's masculinity, women's femininity does not seem to be threatened when they engage in nontraditional activities.'[21]

Williams explains this by reference to psychoanalysis, and in particular Nancy Chodorow's psychoanalytic approach to gender development in infants. Since women in US society are generally in charge of child-care, children of both sexes have their first emotional bond with their mother. Both are initially 'feminine-identified'. This makes gender development more problematic for boys than for girls, since they have to reject this feminine identification in order to assume a masculine identity. As Chodorow explains, 'A boy, in order to feel himself adequately masculine, must distinguish and differentiate himself from others in a way that a girl need not—must categorize himself as someone apart. Moreover, he defines masculinity negatively as that

21 C. L. Williams, *Gender Differences at Work* (Berkeley, 1989), 11, 3.

which is not feminine.'[22] This results in adult men being more concerned about the preservation of strong gender identities.

If this is one possible explanation of male gender anxiety in Russia as well as the United States, it has been compounded by a number of other crucial factors unique to Russia. The disproportionate number of men killed in the war or in Stalinist camps led to a demographic imbalance which meant that the mother was not only the primary, but in many cases the only, upbringer. In addition, there is a widespread belief amongst Russians that the country was historically a matriarchy in which women always held the pre-eminent position. The writer Tat'iana Tolstaia, for example, talks of 'the powerful female principle that suffuses the Russian universe. Home, hearth, household, children, birth, family ties, the close relationship of mothers, grandmothers, and daughters: the attention to all details, control over everything, power, at times extending to tyranny—all this is Russian woman.'[23]

This supposed male oppression at the hands of women was exacerbated by the oppression exerted by the state. On the one hand, the Soviet Union's extensive welfare system, which met all of its citizens' basic needs, stifled their drive and initiative. At the same time, it exerted such tight control over their behaviour that it destroyed their independence and autonomy. Damage to Soviet manhood is said to have been particularly acute in the Stalin era. Even though the image of the muscle-bound Stakhanovite seems to glorify masculinity, the state was at its most intrusive, and men at their most impotent. Furthermore, as Elena Stishova has argued, there was room for only one male role model in that era (and, we could add, only one patriarch)—Stalin himself. This, she continues, led to a collapse of male self-confidence, which continued beyond Stalin's death.[24]

Yet despite the contention that Russia has always been a matriarchy, being a male in Russia has, as we saw above, carried many of the same rights and privileges in relation to women that it has done in all patriarchal societies: more status, better pay, better opportunities. Soviet proclamations about women's equality did little to alter this pattern. At the same time, men have been able to call on women to provide them with a range of domestic services that the Soviet state, despite its earlier promises, failed to deliver. Men clearly have many practical reasons to fear the erosion of gender difference. The representations of gender relations looked at here, with the exception of those in the work of the two female directors, could be described as a promotion of patriarchal relations whenever changes in economic and demographic priorities made this possible, in which women's main function was presented as bearing children and tending the family hearth.

22 Quoted ibid. 13.
23 T. Tolstaya, 'Notes from Underground', *New York Review of Books*, 37 (1990), 4.
24 L. Attwood, personal discussion with film critic E. Stishova, Apr. 1994.

17

HILARY
PILKINGTON

'The Future is Ours': Youth Culture in Russia, 1953 to the Present

The history of the study of youth culture in Russia clearly illustrates the way in which academics in the USSR and the West have failed to talk cross-culturally. Whilst generally simply working in different paradigms from which meaningful communication was impossible, the two sides, on occasion, have come into direct conflict. The clearest example of this was the post-1968 disagreement on the very existence of a youth culture as a unique phenomenon separating youth from the adult world and expressing a subcultural resistance to adult norms. Western academics (those, ironically, adopting a Marxist analytic framework) were accused by their Soviet counterparts of falsely imputing to youth both class interests and a consciousness of them. Interestingly, in the sphere of youth cultural studies at least, there has been no outright victory of Western over Soviet paradigms. Indeed in both cases, the 1980s marked a fundamental shift in the way youth cultural practice was framed, as a result of which Western researchers have virtually abandoned the notion of youth culture. This does not mean to say that they have adopted Soviet alternatives (which are described in detail below) or that they have ceased to acknowledge the role of youth cultural practice altogether. Rather it is that this practice is now considered as the meeting of two moments: youth's positioning in discourse (produced by ever-changing media, academia, and state and social agencies); and youthful negotiations of this positioning, the creation and reworking of identities. Thus, in this exploration of the changing nature of youth culture in the post-war period in

Russia, the object of study is considered by the authors to be, first, texts, cultural products and artefacts, and media forms (music, film, video, computer games) which shape youth styles and position young people as subjects; second, practices of consumption (shopping, watching, listening, eating), leisure activities, style creation, music and dance, media use, language; and third, the interaction between the above, which is precisely where youthful subjectivities are created and recreated.

What will be charted below, therefore, are the changing forms of youth cultural practice and their sociocultural context as well as the paradigms within which youth cultural practice has been considered in the Soviet Union from 1953. The question of to what extent youth cultural practice in Russia has been moulded by processes of globalization and to what extent it has remained rooted in the 'local' will be considered. Finally new areas demanding research attention will be suggested, as well as the implications of existing research for informing cultural studies in general.

Youth in the Post-War Period: Demobilization or Remobilization?

The early Soviet period had been dominated by a vision of the nation's youth as the 'constructors of communism'. Youth had been portrayed as the avant-garde of the cultural assault on illiteracy, backwardness, and superstition among the rural population, and as the most enthusiastic participants in the giganticist construction projects of the industrialization drive begun at the end of the 1920s. As a consequence little, if any, attention had been paid to young people's localized cultural activities. Although the constructors-of-communism paradigm continued into the post-war period, a new dimension of the debate emerged which was to generate an interlocking paradigm within which the youth question was framed. The Soviet Union had emerged out of the Second World War as a global power, but one whose presence for the Western world was perceived as threatening. This was because not only had the USSR proved its military power during the war, but in a changed political climate in the West, socialism was beginning to enter the mainstream political agenda, most obviously in the development of the welfare state. For the Soviet Union itself, the new status also brought threats of an ideological kind. Increased openness to, and growing contacts with, the West led to exposure to 'decadent' cultural forms (in particular rock 'n' roll and jazz) which were taken up, and reworked, by Soviet young people.

Manifestations of such ideological deviation were ascribed to Western propaganda and attempts by intelligence organs to win over Soviet youth, just as in the pre-war period they had been blamed on vestiges of the capitalist past. However, any self-respecting Marxist would have been aware that these new music and dance forms, and their resonance among Soviet youth, had their roots in material culture. Like Western societies, the Soviet Union experienced a post-war 'boom' which expressed itself in the most comprehensive urbanization drive to date, the reduction, by the end of the 1960s, in the working week (in the towns) from six to five days, and a greater emphasis on the development of leisure time and the cultural sphere. Moreover, the cultural thaw associated with the Khrushchev period reduced the political costs of non-sanctioned cultural activity. The combined impact of these three factors was a burst of youth cultural activity finding expression in unsanctioned poetry readings, folk clubs, rock 'n' roll music and dance styles (led by so-called *stiliagi*), the bard movement, participation in ecological organizations (such as the Nature Protection Volunteers) and historical associations. At the same time groups formed to 'struggle against' those youth activities that were seen to be ideologically subversive and culturally negative. The informal communards movement emerged to combat the power of territorial gangs, while patrols of the official Communist Youth organization (the Komsomol) cut the trousers and hair of *stiliagi* in a number of cities.

Thus, the growing urbanization of Soviet society, its greater affluence and openness to the West produced in the post-war period a flourish of non-sanctioned youth activity. Like the early dissident circles, however, these pockets of activity were limited. They were confined to the main urban centres, to student or other intellectually oriented sections of society, and largely closed to those devoid of such cultural capital. Indeed, for those other than the cultural intelligentsia, the Khrushchev period may have been experienced less as one of cultural relaxation allowing greater artistic freedom than as one of the renewal and reinforcement of campaigns designed to create a uniform mass of people matching the ideals of socialist society. In particular the Komsomol rallied young people to take part in new construction campaigns as well as the Virgin Lands project which enabled vast sections of the steppe to be turned to agricultural production. In addition, the Komsomol was required increasingly to assume responsibility for the educational achievement and ideological conviction of young people. As a result, by the end of the Khrushchev period, the Komsomol was no longer the expression of the avant-garde of youth but a mass organization (of 20 million members) which had begun to appear almost as an organ of social control of youth by young people themselves.

The Soviet Way of Life: Ideology and Reality Part Company

In the period of high Sovietism, youth cultural groups did not disappear, but rather became an increasingly everyday phenomenon of Soviet society. The material base for this was continued urbanization, the extension of the average period of education (leading young people to enter paid employment and start their own families later), an increasingly leisure-oriented society and, not least, a flourishing second economy. But despite the proclaimed intention to promote Group B (consumer and service) industries over those of Group A (production of the means of production) in the Brezhnev period, the switch to 'post-industrial' modes of production was never really achieved. The result was a permanent deficit of consumer goods and extremely poor provision of leisure and entertainment facilities and virtually no recognition of consumer differentiation. Consequently, artefacts of Western youth culture became key units of currency (home-produced recordings, blue jeans, bell-bottoms, badges, and Western rock albums) and their exchange and sale became a central part of Soviet youth cultural practice. It was during this period that an established, core youth slang was developed, drawing on criminal argot, foreign borrowings (especially from English), and traditional Russian obscenities (*mat*), as well as neologisms developed to express young people's own cultural practice. Examples of youth slang originating in criminal argot include *ksiva* and *ksivnik* (the former meaning 'passport, documents' and the latter meaning the pouch often hung around the neck in which you carried these—standard wear for hippie types from the 1970s onwards), *ment* ('policeman'), and a number of words for money such as *katia* (100 roubles), and *chirik* or *dichka* (10 roubles). English borrowings include *men* and *gerla* (meaning 'bloke' and 'chick'), *khairatyi* ('hairy one' i.e. hippy), *ringat'* ('to ring'), *drinchit'* ('to drink'), and *naitat'* ('to spend the night').

The chief medium of youth culture in the 1970s, however, was probably rock music, and it was in this period that 'Soviet rock' took shape. At the beginning of the 1970s, over 250 rock bands were known in and around Moscow alone. Although youth cultural groups, by their very existence, were perceived to be making political statements, their actual political engagement waxed and waned. The height of such politicking was after the crushing of the Prague Spring in 1968, when the hippies in particular became highly politicized and a central part of the pacifist movement in the USSR. But the clamp-down on dissent in general from 1972 pushed them into a more closed and ritualized existence until a new wave of hippies emerged in the final years of the Brezhnev regime. In general, political engagement was less central to Soviet hippies than to their Western brethren and was secondary to music, style, and pleasure in their cultural practice.

How was this youth cultural activity recorded and interpreted in Soviet society at the time? It was in the late 1960s and the 1970s that Soviet sociology came of age and the recognition of 'socio-demographic peculiarities' of young people allowed specific research on youth to be conducted. However, the ideological domination of sociological research meant that the exercise was subordinated to the overriding task of providing evidence of the superiority of the Soviet way of life. As such, surveys of young people's values and attitudes emphasized the commitment of Soviet youth to collectivism, communism, patriotism, internationalism, and hard work. These values, together with the sociopolitical activeness of Soviet youth (measured via figures on Komsomol membership) became the official description of 'youth culture'. This is important because it signified a rejection of contemporary Western (bourgeois) notions of youth culture. Those engaged in theorizing youth activity rarely ventured beyond the critique of bourgeois theories of youth (counter-)culture which, it was argued: falsely posited style and lifestyle as a site of protest; erroneously suggested youth had class interests of their own; effectively neutralized the real political protest of youth by channelling young people's energies into mindless pop music; and misinterpreted the significance of youth counter-culture which was, in fact, the manifestation of the crisis of capitalist society.

Soviet theorists, though, failed to develop a really effective alternative theory of youth cultural practice and, by default, adopted and employed, rather paradoxically, structural-functionalist explanations of youth culture which, in the West, were considered to be the tools of the 'right'. Such explanations were premised on the fundamental stability of society, and saw youth culture as one element in the necessary socialization process of young people into the adult world. In serious Soviet sociological literature issues such as the maladjustment to urban lifestyle and a range of problems of the micro-social sphere were considered. But for ideologues such issues constituted ideological struggles, and the 'deviations' recognized in the youth world were posited as the result of the subversive activities of the West. Thus, the inevitable consequences of the transfer to intensive economic development and the official promotion of a more consumer-based society for youth cultural practice were neither fully recognized nor sensibly addressed.

The only theoretical development in this sphere was the adoption of the concept of the 'rational use of free time'. This theory attempted to show the difference between cultural relations in socialist and capitalist versions of modernity. Whilst in both societies emphasis was placed on high standards of living and development of consumer industries, Soviet society, it was claimed, was characterized by rational consumption and not cheap consumerism. But concern was expressed about young people's attitudes to their leisure. First, it was suggested, they tended to consume, rather than create, their own entertainment; this was a problem because it disrupted the dialectic of the 'construction of communism' by breaking the link between active physical involvement and ideological engagement. But second, the content of that which they were passively consuming was perceived as fundamentally opposed to, and subversive of, the socialist personality (*lichnost'*). Consumption was not interpreted as an evil in itself, therefore. Indeed the consumption of spiritual and leisure artefacts (cinema, concerts, theatre, and fashion) was considered a normal part of responsible free-time activity (and reflected the much propagandized rapid rise in the material well-being, level of education, and culture of young people). Consumption, however, was sharply contrasted to consumerism, which represented the disharmony of material and spiritual demands and which turned people into the slaves of things. The development of rational needs was the way in which consumption in socialist society was differentiated from consumerist psychology alien to socialism. Rational needs did not express narcissistic pleasure principles based on the use of particular commodity forms for self-gratification but rather allowed for the all-round harmonious development of the individual without contradicting the social good.

The Komsomol remained the organization entrusted with ensuring that free time was used rationally, and right up until the eve of Gorbachev's ascension to power campaigns were conducted to achieve the goals set. In 1984, for example, the Ministry of Culture issued a particularly harsh directive including black lists of bands and songs not to be played at discos (empowering Komsomol detachments to raid discos to enforce this). As part of the cultural onslaught it was stipulated that at least 80 per cent of material played by Soviet rock groups must be written by members of the Union of Composers, and a commission was established to review these groups (leading to about one third to one half being disbanded). That this was deemed necessary reveals the concern about the messages fed to youth in the process of consumption. Rock, it was claimed, had been primarily designed to help destroy rationality as well as the ability to appreciate 'real' culture, by inculcating blind consumerism, and it encouraged social passivity through a process of gradual stupefaction (*effekt oglupleniia*). Western rock was particularly condemned for its anti-Soviet nature; it was declared to constitute psychological warfare against the Soviet Union that had been targeted specifically at youth since they were a psychologically and emotionally susceptible section of the population.

Thus on the eve of *perestroika* a binary pair of interlocking paradigms was being employed by Soviet academics and youth practitioners in order to understand the phenomenon of youth cultural activity. On the one hand Soviet young people were portrayed as qualitatively different from their Western counterparts: not oppressed and duped by the capitalist system and its cultural doping, but socially and politically active members of society, at the forefront of the construction of the new society, in its latest stage of development. The susceptibility of youth to the subversive tactics of the West was also recognized, however; after all, the ideological struggle between socialism and capitalism took place primarily in the cultural sphere and, it was claimed, youth had been targeted for special attention by the West because of its vulnerability. In other words, Soviet young people were also the 'victims of Western influence', something which manifested itself in their blind copying of decadent Western cultural forms (music, style, dance and movement, trends, and political apathy).

The Reconstructors of Communism? Youth Cultural Practice in the *Perestroika* Period

The policy of *glasnost'* promoted by the reformist Gorbachev leadership transformed the discussion of youth in the mid- to late 1980s. But it would be misleading to suggest that *glasnost'* simply revealed the gap between ideology and the reality of young people's lives. Rather, *glasnost'* increasingly generated its own agenda. Thus in the first period of *perestroika* (1985–6) the key themes of youth as constructors of communism and youth as prone to diversion by Western consumerism were left very much intact; they were played out and reworked via a limited exposé of the 'real conditions' of Soviet society. The idea that the problems illuminated by the spotlight of *glasnost'* could be put in order through an improvement in the ideological work of the Komsomol and the encouragement of youth into more active forms of leisure pursuits was not subjected to critique.

The Soviet state faced a new challenge in the *perestroika* period, however, since youth cultural activity by this time had emerged from its bunkers and was visible to all as a plethora of youth cultural groupings gathering on the streets, in Metro stations, in basements of blocks of flats, and in parks and squares of urban districts. This was reflected in a radical change in the press debate on youth during the middle period of *perestroika* (1987–9), when a new object of press debate emerged, the *neformaly* (non-formal groups). These groups were alternative cultural formations formed outside official institutions (ranging from youth cultural groups such as bikers, punks, and hippies to embryonic political parties and social movements), and the discussion of their activity was pursued with the aim of devising means by which the official institutions they had escaped could rekindle contacts with them and guide them in a socially positive direction. This was evident in the elaboration of what became known as the 'differentiated approach' to the *neformaly* which was employed by Komsomol officials and academics alike in order to classify the multifarious non-formal groups as 'positive' (ecological, pro-*perestroika*), 'neutral' (dance, movement and music fans, punks, hippies, bikers), or 'negative' (anti-*perestroika* political groups, neo-fascists, 'delinquent' groups). Towards the end of this period, concern over the 'cancerous' spread of negative (politically antagonistic or delinquent) groups was replacing fascination with the neutral (spectacular subcultural) groups as the chief focus of the *perestroika* youth debate. In particular, coverage of the phenomenon of teenage gangs in Russia's provincial cities verged on promoting a nationwide moral panic.

The *neformaly* debate was thus a specific *perestroika* agenda born of the perceived need to redefine a new relationship between the Komsomol and its members as well as between the Komsomol and the state. This, in turn, reflected the redefinition of the role of the Communist Party. The debate was one over the right to a monopoly of organized sociocultural activity which appeared to have been challenged by non-formal youth cultural groups. Youth issues were thus lent a pseudo-political significance in the *perestroika* period, while little attention was given to the actual nature of youth cultural activities and their real significance. Micro-level studies of youth cultural practice in Russia in this period, on the other hand, suggest a youth cultural scene clearly differentiated by strategies reflecting not political persuasion (for or against *perestroika*), nor even general ideological positions (such as neo-Slavophile, neo-Stalinist, or Westernizer). As in the adult world, relations of domination and subordination were reflected in hierarchies of age, space (class), and gender, and these shaped positions and strategies in the youth sphere.

20 New recruits to the *stiliagi* at one of their regular meeting places—the Catacombs—in central Moscow, 1991.

The *stiliagi* are revivalist rock 'n' roll fans taking their names from their predecessors, Soviet 'teds' of the early 1950s. The new *stiliagi* emerged as fans of two popular bands of the 1980s, Bravo and Brigada S, and prided themselves on their style (*stil'*), the smartness of which was meant to symbolize their clean-living and cultured way of life. In contrast to many other youth cultural groups, the revivalist *stiliagi* attracted a large number of young women. This was both because of the striking role model provided by Zhanna Aguzarova (at one time the lead singer of Bravo) and because of the respectable image of the *stiliagi* which did not compromise the girls' femininity.

21 Russian punks taking a break from band rehearsals near their homes in a working-class high-rise district of Moscow in 1991.

Apart from their musical activities, the main aims of these punks were to avoid military service and waged labour; all lived off disability pensions. The downside of this strategy was compulsory treatment for their supposed psychiatric disorders; one member of the band was still undergoing treatment at the time this photograph was taken.

In the large western Russian cities youth culture during the *perestroika* period was dominated by the *tusovka*, a distinct and fluid youth cultural grouping linking a specific set of people to a certain gathering place. *Tusovki* were often music-, dance-, or style-based, although not necessarily so, and by the end of the *perestroika* period the term *tusovka* had come to be widely used to denote any group of friends. Indeed within each style-based *tusovka* (punks, hippies, revivalist *stiliagi*, skateboarders, heavy metallists, etc.) there were sub-*tusovki* based on district, age, or other criteria. What was significant about the *tusovka* was its form of activity. Whilst commonly interpreted in the *neformaly* debate as a 'harmless' but 'useless' way of spending free time, *tusovka* life for young people meant a new, more meaningful form of communication experienced though the employment of dance, music, dress, play, and language.[1]

Tusovka slang is a particularly useful source of evidence about the content of youth cultural practice, since it reveals the borrowings and neologisms employed by youth to express those activities, emotions, and sensations not fully articulated in mainstream linguistic practice. Such language *names* things particularly important to youth cultural practice such as 'having a laugh' (*prikolot'sia/prikalyvat'sia*, from the noun *prikol*, meaning 'a joke'), or 'being sussed' (e.g. *vrubat'sia*, *v"ekhat'*, meaning 'to get your drift' or 'know what one is talking about'). Youth slang also *colours* language by inventing words which give a new tone to concepts for which conventional terms already exist. The most obvious example of the latter is the term *sovok*, meaning 'Soviet Union', 'Soviet citizen' or, in its adjectival form *sovkovyi*, 'reflecting Soviet mentality'.[2]

Outside the main cities, whether on their periphery or in provincial towns, however, a different basic unit of youth cultural formation is in evidence: territorially based groups or gangs. Such groups (originally forming around blocks of flats, courtyards, or schools) were looked down on by the *tusovki*, who referred to them as *gopniki* or *urla*, and there were incidences of attacks by the latter on the former, as well as organized fights between different territorial groups. The gap between provincial and capital youth cultures suggests the impossibility of talking about 'Soviet youth' as a single category. While it is difficult to talk about 'class' differences in the experience of youth in the Soviet period in a classical Marxist sense, society was nevertheless clearly stratified. Spatial stratification was particularly important in Soviet society, and consumption and access to leisure facilities was (and is) determined above all by place of residence (village, small town, regional centre, republic capital) and by access to foreign countries or visitors. Hence, since the 1950s there has been talk of a 'golden

1 For a more detailed discussion of *tusovka* practice in the late 1980s and early 1990s, see H. Pilkington, *Russia's Youth and Its Culture: A Nation's Constructors and Constructed* (London, 1994).
2 For a fuller analysis of Russian youth cultural slang, see H. Pilkington 'Tusovka or Tu-sovka? What Does Youth Slang Tell us about Contemporary Russian Youth Culture?', *Rusistika*, 9 (1994), 10–21.

youth', a privileged group of young people whose parents' positions and access to the West had allowed them a very different lifestyle from other young people. In the 1980s such people were known as the *mazhory*, and defined as the sons and daughters of high-ranking officials, distinguished often by their sporting of Western clothes and their ownership of Western consumer goods (especially audio and video equipment). The youth cultural practice of such people was obviously wholly different from those in rural areas or on the periphery of towns (often first- or second-generation urban residents). Rapid urbanization in the post-war period was not supported by infrastructural development, which led to the creation of urban ghettoes extremely poorly provided for in terms of sports and leisure facilities. With not even a mall to hang around, it is not surprising that territorial gang structures quickly developed and structured extra-institutional life for young people.

Of course not all young people were drawn into these courtyard (*dvor*)-based groupings, and one common way out of provincialism was through further or higher education. In prestigious institutes in the main cities student ways of life in many ways reflected that of the 'golden youth'; the two were equated in many criticisms of youth culture in the post-war press. Indeed many *stiliagi* went on to become the creative intelligentsia of the later Soviet period. However, many educational institutions in the capitals or regional centres were filled by students from rural and small towns. This was particularly true of vocational colleges, which found it difficult to recruit the youth 'élite' of the major urban centres into non-prestigious professions. Provincial young people often continued to live peripheral lives in cramped student hostels on below-subsistence-level grants. Moreover, the relations of domination and subordination, hierarchy, ritual, and humiliation of the *dvor* gangs was not always evaded. Hostels for both students and young workers were notorious for their institutionalized hierarchies in which money and obligations might be extorted from new students by older ones in a not dissimilar way from the practice of *dedovshchina* (bullying, tormenting new boys) among conscripts in the armed forces.

A third broad area of youth cultural activity has been centred around semi-legal or illegal economic activity. Although most youth cultural groups used the second economy to access the cultural artefacts and consumer goods they required, some young people's lifestyles were centrally focused around second-economy strategies. These were people who dealt with foreign currency, buying and selling Western goods, and hard-currency prostitutes. Increasingly, racketeering impinged on this strategy, although it became a real issue only after the collapse of the Soviet Union and the process of privatization had begun.

Another area of youth cultural activity obscured in the press and academic debates of the *perestroika* period is the participation of young women. Official versions of youth culture under *perestroika* made it appear a wholly masculine affair. Where girls were discussed they were treated only as the most irrational consumers of Western goods or as victims of male consumption (portrayed as being prepared to exchange access to their bodies for expensive gifts or as girls abused by the male members of territorial gangs). In fact girls actively participate in youth cultural groups, and on their own terms. Some groups, especially those associated with specific music or dance trends, indeed may be dominated by girls (as in the case of revivalist *stiliagi* of the mid-1980s). Most girls become involved in youth cultural groups either independently or via other female friends, and space is found even in such closed, fraternal groups as the bikers to 'be yourself'. While girls who are active on the youth scene are well aware of the fine line they often tread in terms of independence and dependency, sexual use and abuse, and control and insecurity, they develop strategies to negotiate these problems (problems, incidentally, which they no doubt confront in their 'other' lives at home, in the workplace, and in personal relationships). These strategies differ widely, leading to the labelling of some girls as 'slags' by other girls and revealing the ultimately male-determined environment in which youth cultural identities are constructed. None the less, to reduce the experience of young women on the youth cultural scene to that of objects of sexual abuse by aggressive male youth would be to blindly accept the 'truth' of the media debate emergent from the late 1980s.

By 1990 the centrifugal forces pulling the Soviet Union apart, together with deepening economic and social crisis, increased the state's concern with securing its national future. This meant that it paid additional attention to the material position of young people as well as to solving those 'youth problems' (drug addiction, alcoholism, juvenile crime) that threatened the health and strength of the future nation. Such a dramatic change could not be contained within the old paradigms of the youth debate, and what emerged to replace it was a familiar (to Western ears) discourse of social control, which posited youth, first and foremost, as an object of social policy. Thus by the beginning of 1992 youth cultural groups began to be interpreted as evidence of youth's peripheral social position, and youth as a whole was seen no longer as the vanguard of the 'construction of communism' but as a social metaphor for a collapsing society. Thus at the close of the twentieth century youth are being seen not as the constructors of the 'bright future' but as a 'lost generation' which has neither present nor future.

Youth Cultural Debates and Practices in Post-Soviet Russia

In the harsh reality of post-Soviet Russia, youth cultural practice has disappeared from official and academic youth agendas. Instead youth is portrayed as a vulnerable section of society whose position may lead them into politically or socially dangerous acts. In particular, the problem of unemployment is stressed, together with the accompanying loss of belief among youth in the value of education. Those who choose to drop out (or are thrown out of schools) often find themselves on the street with no agency but the police obliged to deal with them. This, it is suggested, is creating a new wave of homeless children (*besprizorniki*)—reminiscent of the most traumatic and destabilized periods of Russian history—and a growing pool of juvenile criminals. There is also significant concern over surveys suggesting that young people are inclined towards violence as a means of resolving conflicts, and are generally intolerant, especially towards ethnic minority groups. This trend, in contrast to the West, however, is generally blamed not on exposure to violent films, but on the legacy of the past and the unstable and brutal present. In terms of the kind of academic work undertaken on youth, the appearance of these new themes has led to fewer studies of the general value systems and political engagement of young people (although these continue) alongside a greater role for social psychology in the study of youth experience. Particularly noteworthy are studies of young people's own experience of violence, their familial situation, the kinds of interpersonal relations formed, and the problems encountered in these by young people.

Judging from the Moscow youth cultural scene as it looked in 1994, it would indeed appear that Russia is moving not only into a post-Soviet but also into a post-*tusovka* world. This world has been defined by the processes of marketization (and the concomitant emergence of new Russians and new mafias); globalization (often experienced as 'Westernization' or 'Americanization'); the brutalization of politics, and, in particular, the emergence of chauvinist street politics; the sexualization of the youth sphere; and the impact of drugs on youth cultural practice. For movers on the youth cultural scene, the market has meant, on the one hand, new opportunities to exploit the overlap between formal and informal spheres, and many would like to see their future in business linked to their youth cultural interests. However, the form that privatization and marketization has taken has also shut down many spaces for young people. Control by racketeers and mafias makes it a brutal world to which, in particular, young women's access is extremely circumscribed. The new space for commercial activity, together with the force of Western images of youth cultural practice, has also meant the emergence of a club scene. Whilst on the one hand this is welcomed, the cost is prohibitive for most young people. Clubs are thus essentially for the new rich (if entrance fees are paid) or the old *tusovka* hands (who can use the cultural capital accumulated from their former 'underground' days to gain free admission). Meanwhile the formalization and commercialization of the youth cultural scene has effectively destroyed much of the alternative communication which was so valued by *tusovka* members in their old forms of practice.

Post-*tusovka* identities among young people therefore are being taken up against a backdrop of the rapid incorporation of at least the major Russian cities into the sphere of influence of the Western mass media and the global economy (including the global drugs market), alongside an increasingly exclusionist national politics emanating from above. This is not surprising, given that globalization is experienced unevenly: while MTV may be received and watched avidly by Moscow teenagers, large parts of the country receive only the two Federal Russian channels and one or more regional channel. Indeed, it would not be at all surprising if the globalization of some did not lead to the localization or parochialization of others. Just as in the past, when the perceived privileges of the few in the centre often drew the wrath of those on the periphery (manifested in raids by gangs of suburban or provincial city youth on central Moscow youth groups), so now there are regionalist and nationalist reactions to the perceived Western or dollar mentality of the new rich of the post-Soviet period. In many provincial cities the rejection of 'Moscow' fashion continues; indeed many of the recent trends in Western style make no sense in contemporary Russia. Movement towards natural fibres, ethnic Third-World styles, and androgynous haircuts is appealing only to a tiny minority; the majority choose overtly feminine or masculine styles, ostentatious jewellery, and indiscreet make-up. In the last few years there has also been a move away from English texts and back to Russian lyrics in popular and rock music. This has certainly been encouraged by the emergence of domestic record companies and promotion agencies (finally breaking the Melodiia monopoly), but it also reflects the continued popularity of traditional Russian pop (*estrada*) alongside a flourishing rap, hip-hop, and traditional rock scene.

It is as yet difficult to define fully the new contours of post-Soviet youth cultural practices. They will undoubtably be shaped by the dual processes of globalization and localization (the emergence of locally based, bodily and territorially rooted identities) which are shaping cultural development across the globe. What is certain, however, is that Russian youth are not simply being duped by Western consumerism; indeed the deficit in the past plus the present low buying-power of the rouble makes Russian youth extremely choosy and sophisticated consumers who can spot a Chinese or Korean copy in an instant. Yet very significant differences remain within Russian youth, and further research especially needs to be done on attitudes towards Western/American images, role models, and styles among rural, capital, and provincial urban youth. Clearly many young people's reference point is other Western youth today rather than the Russian young people of previous generations, whose experience was wholly different from their own. Nevertheless this does not mean they do not imbue what they adopt at the level of style with their own, locally rooted meaning. It is these meanings that must be uncovered and explored by those seeking to understand contemporary Russian youth culture.

Conclusion

Approaches to the understanding of youth issues in the Soviet period have been constructed around an interplay of biological and social understandings of what constitutes 'youth'. Youth was attributed specific psychological traits which set it apart from the adult population, but the primacy of class analysis meant that young people appeared as a demographic stratum of separate classes (both within Soviet and between Soviet and Western, capitalist societies) rather than as a class in itself. As such, the possibility of a distinct youth culture was rejected, since in a non-antagonistic society the socialist way of life was common to all. More important than the class (or rather non-class) position of youth, though, has been the role it was seen to play in the historical process. The 'continuity of generations' in a non-antagonistic society replaced the struggle between classes as the motor of history. History became the renewal of generations in a linear march towards communism. This meant that drive for ideological purity among youth was greater than among the adult population, since evidence of a generation gap would wreck the very means of the development of socialist into communist society; it would disrupt the laws of history themselves.

This created a need for the affirmation of the loyalty of youth, and sociologists were set the task of testing the success with which this had been achieved. The results of thirty years of the sociology of youth was summed up by Blinov as leaving 'no doubt that contemporary Soviet youth is characterized by remarkable ideological and moral qualities—fidelity to the ideals of communism, devotion to the interests of Soviet society and an ever-increasing social activism'.[3] This was evidenced in the high levels of participation in the Komsomol (over 41 million by 1982) and in the purposeful nature of youth activity (study and self-education, sport, artistic clubs, socially useful activity, participation in socialist competition, 'shock' construction work for the Komsomol, and student work-brigades). This was the culture of Soviet youth, and it was contrasted to the crisis of bourgeois culture which had led youth into illusory forms of lifestyle revolution. This is not to say that 'negative tendencies' in young people's behaviour were never mentioned. But when they were, they were treated almost solely at the ideological level and attributed to the harmful influence of Western propaganda or, where a deeper sociological approach was attempted, temporary problems arising as first and second generations adapted to urban culture or particular micro-environmental dislocations (especially divorce).

The *perestroika* period opened up for discussion a different cultural practice rooted in the real experience of youth in the post-war period. This practice was borne of key sociocultural processes and tensions: formal versus non-formal cultural activity; strategies expressed through style; and the competing processes of globalization and localization. In the post-Soviet period youth has ceased to be an object of overt political struggle, and youth culture as a thing in itself has become difficult to separate out from other aspects of youth experience. However, it remains important to recognize youth practice outside work, school, and family, as well as the significance of horizontal links and references to a wider (global) youth world via cultural artefacts and media. In the post-1991 period Russia has been opened to a whole host of new media and sites of cultural production which position young people and help shape their identities. These include Western images transferred by film, satellite and cable television, fashion, magazines, advertising, pornography, beauty shows and quiz shows, and the impact of the information explosion. It is the study of these media and processes which should guide the research agenda on Russian youth culture (and not only youth culture) in the future. Not only will this create a much needed, culturally sensitive picture of the actual cultural practice of young people in contemporary Russia,

3 N. Blinov, 'The Sociology of Youth: Achievements and Problems', *Soviet Sociology*, 21 (1983), 6.

but it may inform wider debates on the local reworkings, if not subversions, of global messages.

Suggested further reading

Gender and sexuality:

Bauer, R. A., *The New Man in Soviet Psychology* (Cambridge, Mass., 1952).

Buckley, M., *Women and Ideology in the Soviet Union* (Hemel Hempstead, 1989).

Burgin, D., *Sophia Parnok: The Life and Work of Russia's Sappho* (New York, 1994).

Clements, B. E., *Bolshevik Feminist: The Life of Aleksandra Kollontai* (Bloomington, Ind., 1979).

Costlow, J., Sandler, S., and Vowles, J. (eds.), *Sexuality and the Body in Russian Culture* (Stanford, Calif., 1994).

Farnsworth, B., *Aleksandra Kollontai: Socialism, Feminism, and the Bolshevik Revolution* (Stanford, Calif., 1980).

Fitzpatrick, S., *The Cultural Front: Power and Culture in Revolutionary Russia* (Ithaca, NY, 1992).

Gessen, M., *The Rights of Lesbians and Gay Men in the Russian Federation*, bilingual Russian and English edn. (San Francisco, 1994).

Goldman, W., *Women, the State and Revolution: Soviet Family Policy and Social Life, 1917–1936* (Cambridge, 1993).

Healey, D., 'The Russian Revolution and the Decriminalisation of Homosexuality', *Revolutionary Russia: Journal of the Study Group on the Russian Revolution*, 6 (1993), 26–54.

Karlinsky, S., 'Russia and the USSR', in W. R. Dynes (ed.), *Encyclopedia of Homosexuality*, ii (New York, 1990), 1133–8.

—— 'Russia's Gay Literature and Culture: The Impact of the October Revolution', in M. B. Duderman, M. Vicinus, and G. Chauncey, Jr. (eds.), *Hidden from History: Reclaiming the Gay and Lesbian Past* (Harmondsworth, 1991), 347–65.

Kirkham-Lebel, L., 'The Politics of Alienation: Current Women's Issues in the Soviet Union', M.Phil. thesis (University of Oxford), 1991.

Kon, I., *Sexual Revolution in Russia* (New York, 1994).

—— and Riordan, J. (eds.), *Sex and Society in the Soviet Union* (London, 1993).

Kozlovskii, S., *Argo russkoi gomoseksual'noi subkul'tury: Materialy k izucheniiu* (Benson, Vt., 1986).

Liljestroom, M., Mantysaari, E., and Rosenholm, A. (eds.), *Gender Restructuring in Russian Studies* (Tampere, 1993).

Marsh, R. (ed.), *Women in Russia and the Ukraine* (Cambridge, 1996).

Moss, K., *Out of the Blue. Russia's Hidden Gay Literature: An Anthology* (San Francisco, 1997).

Naiman, E., *Sex in Public: The Incarnation of Early Soviet Ideology* (Princeton, 1997).

Posadskaya, A., *Women in Russia*, tr. and ed. K. Clarke (London, 1995).

Riordan, J., 'Coming Out: The Gay Community in the USSR', *Slovo*, 3 (1990), 51–66.

Shcherbakov, S. P., 'On the Relationship between the Leningrad Gay Community and the Legal Authorities in the 1970s and 1980s', in T. Veispak and

U. Parikas (eds.), *Sexual Minorities and Society: The Changing Attitude towards Homosexuality in 20th Century Europe* (Tallinn, 1991).

Stites, R., *The Women's Liberation Movement in Russia: Feminism, Nihilism and Bolshevism, 1860–1930* (Princeton, 1978), chs. 10 and 11.

—— *Russian Popular Culture: Entertainment and Society since 1900* (Cambridge, 1992).

Stone, D., 'Gay Life in the USSR', *Gala Review*, 10 (1987).

Tuller, D., *Cracks in the Iron Closet: Travels in Gay and Lesbian Russia* (London, 1996).

Williams, C., 'Singing the Blues: The Russian Gay Movement in the 1990s', *Perversions: The International Journal of Gay and Lesbian Studies*, 4 (1995), 128–48.

Cinema and gender:

Attwood, L. (ed.), *Red Women on the Silver Screen: Soviet Women and Cinema from the Beginning to the End of the Communist Era* (London, 1993).

Horton, A., and **Brashinsky, M.**, *The Zero Hour: Glasnost and Soviet Cinema in Transition* (Princeton, 1992).

Lawton, A., *Kinoglasnost: Soviet Cinema in our Time* (Cambridge, 1992).

—— (ed.), *The Red Screen: Politics, Society, Art in Soviet Cinema* (London, 1992).

Youth culture:

Pilkington, H., *Russia's Youth and Its Culture: A Nation's Constructors and Constructed* (London, 1994).

—— 'Tusovka or Tu-sovka? What Does Youth Slang Tell us about Contemporary Russian Youth Culture?', *Rusistika*, 9 (1994), 10–21.

Conclusion: Towards Post-Soviet Pluralism? Postmodernism and Beyond

CATRIONA KELLY

DAVID SHEPHERD

STEPHEN WHITE

That the last Part should have ended with a consideration of youth in post-Soviet Russia may seem, if not an inevitable, then at least an appropriate ending to an account of culture which has sought to stress its unfinalized, constantly developing character. It also, of course, mimics a key aspect of the continuity with the past that has been a constant accompaniment to that development. The investment (whether sincere or cynical) of hope in successive generations of youth in the Soviet period looks set to continue, as in the following conclusion to the post-Soviet textbook on 'culturology' quoted in our Introduction:

[After every setback in Russia's history] the country arose from the ashes, gathered its strength, restored what had been destroyed, acquired a new social memory and spiritual culture, and continued to develop, because at the basis of all the achievements of culture is the human being, who determines the meaning and purpose of the historical process and preserves and develops the values of culture, and is the principal keeper of its achievements.

The future of Russia is in the hands of the younger generation [*podrastaiushchee pokolenie*], it is this generation that will determine Russia's fate, its sociocultural processes, and its relationships with the other peoples of the Earth.[1]

This optimistic anticipation of what might once have been termed a 'radiant future' is in fact, if we disregard its rather embarrassing grandiloquence, little more than a truism combined with homiletic pieties of a thoroughly Soviet (but not only Soviet) kind. While acknowledging the historical character of cultural activity and human

1 V. V. Agenosov *et al.*, *Kul'turologiia: Teoriia i istoriia kul'tury* (Moscow, 1996), 270.

agency alike, it simultaneously threatens to cast both into the limbo between cyclical recurrence and teleological progression.

Limbo, the ultimate *bezvykhodnoe polozhenie*, might seem an apt designation of the current state of Russian society and culture as the new millennium approaches, preceded in Russia as elsewhere by tedious speculation about what it might promise or portend. One lesson that can surely be drawn from the history of twentieth-century Russian culture is that allegedly key dates do not necessarily possess the watershed significance ascribed to them. Yet 1991, the year of the Soviet Union's dissolution, seems just as surely to have marked the beginning of a phase of prolonged uncertainty about identity and cultural value. In what follows we seek to outline some of the forms taken by that uncertainty, in the hope that this will allow us to discern the boundaries between the Soviet and the post-Soviet, and to gain some sense of their (im)permeability.

Changing Identities in the 1990s[2]

It used to be easy to establish who was a Russian—and, less easily, what it meant. For most of the pre-Revolutionary period, to be a Russian was to be a member of the Orthodox faith: indeed that was the description of nationality that appeared in the internal passport, and it was a part of the celebrated trinity that was put forward by Count Uvarov, education minister in the 1840s: *samoderzhavie, pravoslavie, narodnost'* (Autocracy, Orthodoxy, and Nationality). In the Soviet years there was no problem either, as Russians became the 'elder brother' in a system that reflected their predominance, although it limited their capacity for self-expression. The Russian capital was the Soviet capital; Russian was the state language; Russians predominated in the ruling Party, though not in parliament. And although the new regime was an atheist one, when a reconciliation came in the late 1980s it was with the church of Russian believers. Symptomatically, when the republics declared independence in 1990 and 1991 there was one exception: the Russian republic, which declared its sovereignty. It would have been meaningless for Russia to declare its independence of the USSR when it accounted for about three-quarters of its territory and more than half of its population.

There had, in fact, always been ambiguities about a Russian identity, particularly an enduring controversy about whether Russians were Europeans or Asians, or whether they had their own unique identity that required special forms of politics and society for its expression. Russia, after all, was an Asian as well as a European

2 This section was written by Stephen White.

22 Building work in progress on the new Cathedral of Christ Redeemer, August 1995.
The original Cathedral of Christ Redeemer, finished in 1883, was a sumptuous commemoration of Russia's victory over Napoleon in 1812. It was demolished in 1934, as
part of the remodelling of Moscow as Soviet capital. The grandiose Palace of Soviets
intended to replace it was never built, as the site proved too waterlogged to take its
foundations. In 1958, an open-air swimming pool was opened in its place (an event
popularly held to be the ironic fulfilment of a nineteenth-century prophecy: 'nothing
can replace the cathedral but water'). In the early 1990s, the pool was closed, and work
began in 1995 on a new cathedral, which has become the focus of intense controversy.
For nationalists, it is a welcome symbol of Russia's return to Orthodox conservatism;
for liberal intellectuals, the expenditure on this concrete pastiche seems obscene,
given that medieval buildings all over Russia are in a dangerous state of decay
owing to lack of funds for restoration work.

power—more European in terms of population numbers, but more Asian in terms of territory. After 1917, that special role appeared to be institutionalized as the USSR became the core of an international state system and a wider network of communist parties. It was the second superpower, a world leader in science and space exploration, and one of the biggest medal-winners at the Olympics—especially in 1980, when most of the Western nations boycotted the Moscow games. Including the Chinese, something like a third of humanity shared the Soviet view that 1917 had been not just a Russian revolution but the decisive turning-point in world history.

In the post-Communist 1990s things looked very different. Gone, for a start, was superpower status, with the dissolution of the Warsaw Treaty Organization and of the wider network of international alliances with fraternal states. And gone, with the 'end of history', was the notion that the Communist-ruled states had a social and economic system that was inherently superior to the class-divided societies of the capitalist West. The Soviet state itself disappeared, although 76 per cent of those who voted in the referendum that took place in March 1991 had wanted to maintain a 'reformed' USSR; and post-Soviet Russia itself came under threat from minorities within its own territory, above all the Chechens. National income fell by about a half in the first half of the 1990s; crime was rampant; life expectancies were down. And although Russia was still overwhelmingly Russian, with more than 80 per cent of all Russians living within its borders, as many as 25 million found themselves living in the neighbouring states of what became known as the 'near abroad' (see Table 1).

Russians, in the 1990s, were confused, angry, and alarmed by these far-reaching changes in their environment. And they were unclear about the place they occupied as a people or as a state in the rather different international community of which they were now a member. For some foreign observers, Russians were still outside the 'common European home' of which they had been the first to speak. Their democracy was uncertain, and their economy was ailing. More fundamentally, they were part of a different cultural tradition, one that had not experienced Roman law and feudalism, with their notions of private property and limited government.[3] But for others, Russians shared their Christian religion with the Western nations; their language was a part of the Indo-European family; and they had been a member of the European state system since the eighteenth century. Indeed, they were allies of the Western powers in both the world wars, losing more of their own population as part of the Western alliance against Nazi Germany than any major country has ever lost in armed conflict.[4]

3 For Ralf Dahrendorf, for instance, 'Europe ends at the Soviet border, wherever that may be' (*Reflections on the Revolution in Europe* (London, 1990), 110). Or, in the words of a Lithuanian quoted by Slavenka Drakulic, 'Europe is . . . not Russia!' (*Café Europa: Life after Communism* (London, 1996), 31).
4 A recent survey-based investigation, for instance, finds no discontinuity between Russian attitudes east and west of the Urals, and that there are many similarities between Russian and West European (though not always American) values: see W. L. Miller, S. White, and P. Heywood, *Values and Political Change in Postcommunist Europe* (London, 1997). Russians' own ambivalent views are considered in I. B. Neumann, *Russia and the Idea of Europe* (London, 1995).

Table 1: Russians in the former Soviet republics (percentage of all Russians living in Russia and other republics, 1989 census)

	Russians (m.)	% of all Russians	% of republic population
Russia	145.2	82.6	81.5
Ukraine	11.4	7.8	22.1
Kazakhstan	6.2	4.3	37.8
Uzbekistan	1.7	1.1	8.3
Belarus	1.3	0.9	13.2
Kyrgyzstan	0.9	0.6	21.5
Latvia	0.9	0.6	34.0
Moldova	0.6	0.4	13.0
Estonia	0.5	0.3	30.3
Azerbaijan	0.4	0.3	5.6
Tajikistan	0.4	0.3	7.6
Lithuania	0.3	0.2	9.4
Georgia	0.3	0.2	6.3
Turkmenia	0.3	0.2	9.5
Armenia	0.0	0.0	1.6

Source: *Rossiiskii statisticheskii ezhegodnik: 1996* (Moscow, 1996), 49.

Russia, for Winston Churchill in 1939, was a 'riddle wrapped in a mystery inside an enigma'. But it was less of a mystery than it had been by the late 1980s, as an opinion-poll industry began to establish itself and (after 1989) publish its findings in a regular bulletin.[5] The polls, admittedly, could get things wrong: the success of Zhirinovskii's Liberal Democrats in the December 1993 elections, in defiance of unimpressive predictions, was nothing less than a 'fiasco', in the words of one senior pollster, Boris Grushin.[6] But they gradually improved in the accuracy of their predictions, and the availability of surveys

5 For a review, see M. Wyman, *Public Opinion in Postcommunist Russia* (London, 1997).
6 *Mir mnenii i mneniia o mire*, 5 (1994), 4.

—domestic and foreign, by telephone or door-to-door, commercial or political, professionally conducted or otherwise—was itself a factor of some importance in breaking down the notion of a monolithic 'public opinion' that had prevailed in the Communist past, rejecting the pursuit of a homogeneous Homo (Post-)Sovieticus (see Introduction), and opening the way to an exploration of identities in terms that individuals, or groups of various kinds, could choose themselves.

The existence of surveys over a reasonably extended period, moreover, made it possible to assess the extent to which mass opinion had also been changing. And generally, those changes were less dramatic than a wholesale transition might have suggested. What, for instance, did Russians think was their homeland five years after the USSR had disappeared? For the largest single group (28 per cent) it was still the Soviet Union; the next largest group (27 per cent) thought of Russia; but nearly as many (25 per cent) thought of the region in which they lived, or in which they had grown up (another 17 per cent). A large majority (71 per cent) thought it a great misfortune the Soviet Union no longer existed; and even more (76 per cent) thought Russia should unite with its largest neighbour, Ukraine (Ukrainians themselves were less enthusiastic).[7]

How did Russians think they had changed themselves after the change of regime? Rightly or wrongly, they thought they were more 'industrious' or 'energetic' in 1994 than they had been in 1989; but in other respects there were few differences. Russians still thought their main characteristic was that they were 'open and unpretentious' (72 per cent took this view in 1994); they also thought they were 'hospitable' (67 per cent), 'patient' (62 per cent), and 'peaceable' (52 per cent), but also 'impractical' (39 per cent). It was freedom of speech, for ordinary Russians, that had been the most welcome of the changes that had taken place since the end of Communist rule. The institution of multi-party politics, by contrast, was thought to have been a change for the worse; so too was the introduction of the right to strike; and the break-up of the USSR itself was condemned by an overwhelming 75 per cent.[8]

Where did Russians place themselves, in the world of post-Communist states that they inhabited after 1991? Did they, for instance, think they were Europeans? In 1996, according to another source, 9 per cent of Russians did so 'often' and 14 per cent 'sometimes'; but 17 per cent did so 'rarely' and much the largest group, 59 per cent, were 'never' inclined to do so.[9] Equally, there was strong support for the proposition that Russia should move forward in accordance with its 'own path' rather than a European or American model. Did Russians, for instance, think they had the same values

7 US Information Agency, *Opinion Analysis*, 23 Dec. 1996, 1–3.
8 *Segodnia*, 24 Jan. 1995, 10.
9 R. Rose, *New Russia Barometer*, v. *Between Two Elections* (Glasgow, 1996), 71–2.

and interests as people in the West? Only a minority (21 per cent) thought they had; a much more substantial 78 per cent disagreed, with little difference across the generations.[10] There was particular mistrust of 'foreign organisations and experts advising our government'; many thought privatization would mainly benefit foreigners;[11] aid from Western countries was 'aimed at making us dependent';[12] and there was strong opposition to foreign ownership of industry, land, or shops and cafés, or to any other form of foreign investment.[13]

Who, in these new circumstances, could be considered a Russian? Was it all who lived in Russia and thought of themselves as Russian, or was it a matter of genetic descent? The All-Russian Centre for the Study of Public Opinion found that 55 per cent agreed with the first, more inclusive view, but 36 per cent thought Russians were an ethnic group and that they were defined by their ancestry and not simply their place of residence. Of all the characteristics that might identify a Russian, the most important was that they shared the 'traditions of the Russian people' (54 per cent), and that they were native speakers of the language (53 per cent). A further 40 per cent thought it was essential to subscribe to the 'moral ideals of Russia'; but membership of the Orthodox faith, which had virtually defined a Russian in the pre-Revolutionary years, was mentioned by just 19 per cent.[14]

Being a Russian was also a matter of shared experience, and of a shared perception of that experience. Of what periods in their historical past, according to the surveys, were Russians in fact the proudest? By a considerable margin it was their victory in the Second World War, or 'Great Patriotic War' as it is still known (43 per cent); in second place came the 'great patience of the Russian people' (39 per cent), and in third place their literature (19 per cent). The great majority were largely (25 per cent) or entirely (63 per cent) in agreement with the proposition that Russia was a great country, and that Russians had nothing in their past of which they need feel ashamed. Why, then, did they live so badly? About a quarter (24 per cent) thought seventy years of Communist rule had ruined the country; but just as many thought it had suited Western countries to keep Russia backward, and rather more (30 per cent) blamed the support that earlier governments had offered to the developing or socialist countries.[15] A bitter, resentful attitude towards the West was strengthening in the late 1990s as former allies in Eastern Europe were admitted into NATO, and as evidence mounted that the forms of economic management that had been supported by Western governments were leading Russia into a deepening recession.

Identities were of concern to individual citizens, confused about their place in the world and in their own country after the end of

10 Ibid. iv. *Survey Results* (Glasgow, 1995), 50.
11 Ibid. iii. *The Results* (Glasgow, 1994), 33, 45.
12 US Information Agency, *Opinion Analysis*, 3.
13 Rose, *New Russia Barometer*, vi. *After the Presidential Election* (Glasgow, 1996), 16.
14 *Ekonomicheskie i sotsial'nye peremeny: Monitoring obshchestvennogo mneniia*, 5 (1996), 79.
15 Ibid. 80, 84, 80–1.

Soviet rule; they were also of concern to government, to parties and movements, and to political élites. A common element, in the late 1990s, was that government itself should be strengthened, that Russian foreign policy should be independent of Western influence, and that integration with the other former Soviet republics should be accelerated. The government party, Our Home is Russia, for instance, called for the 'unity and integrity of the Russian state' in the manifesto that it produced for the December 1995 Duma elections, and promised to support the rights of fellow nationals in the countries of the 'near abroad'. The centrist movement, Women of Russia, was another that favoured a strong state and the collective security of the former Soviet republics, as well as friendly relations with the Western powers. A hardline grouping, Communists—Working Russia—For the Soviet Union, called more directly for the restoration of the USSR and of the Soviet system itself; it took 4.5 per cent of the national party vote, just behind Women of Russia.[16]

The Communist Party of the Russian Federation stopped short of demanding the restoration of Soviet rule, but it pointed to the efforts of a 'fifth column' to persuade the country to adopt forms of government and economic management that were alien to its nature, and called instead for the defence of the 'national-state interests of Russia' and the gradual, voluntary re-establishment of a unitary state.[17] Party leader Gennadii Ziuganov was one of the most determined advocates of the view that Russia was a 'special kind of civilization' and the core of a 'Eurasian continental bloc', whose interests were opposed to those of the 'ocean power' (the USA) and the other parties to the Atlantic alliance. For Ziuganov and his colleagues, Russia had its own distinctive values, which were collectivism, statehood, goodness, and justice. It rested, equally, on the Orthodox religion, and on the unity of the Slavic nations.[18]

Shortly after his re-election in 1996 Boris Yeltsin asked Russian scholars to think up a 'national idea' that could help to consolidate a divided and fractious country. There was some agreement, in opinion surveys, that Russians were 'returning to their spiritual origins'. But what, in the late 1990s, could serve to unite them? For some, like the distinguished literary scholar Dmitrii Likhachev, the whole notion of a 'national idea' was not just a 'stupidity, but a very dangerous stupidity'.[19] And there was no indication, if the surveys again were any guide, that any kind of public philosophy would be found around which Russians—and all who lived in Russia but who might not be Russian by nationality—would be able to unite. Only one idea emerged clearly, according to the surveys that were conducted in 1996: nearly half those who were asked (46 per cent) thought a strong

16 See *Predvybornaia platforma Vserossiiskogo obshchestvenno-politicheskogo dvizheniia 'Nash dom Rossiia'* (Moscow, 1995); *Programma politicheskogo dvizheniia 'Zhenshchiny Rossii'* (Moscow, 1995); and *Predvybornaia pozitsiia izbiratel'nogo bloka 'Kommunisty—Trudovaia Rossiia—Za Sovetskii Soiuz'* (Moscow, 1995).
17 The Communist electoral programme was printed in *Dialog*, 10 (1995), 3–9.
18 G. A. Ziuganov, *Rossiia—rodina moia* (Moscow, 1996), 50.
19 *Izvestiia*, 29 Nov. 1996, 5.

Russian state was the best means available of restoring the national spirit. But very few thought there was much future in reviving the influence of the Church, or establishing a powerful all-Russian political party, or attempting to limit the place that foreigners had come to occupy in Russian life. A few more favoured restricting the powers of officialdom (16 per cent); otherwise, the most general response was 'don't know' or 'no reply'.[20]

Britain, it was suggested in the 1960s, had lost an empire and not yet found a role. Russians, by the late 1990s, had lost an ideology and not yet found a focus for their various identities beyond a powerful state that was likely to leave very little space in which they could find expression. Indeed, the search for identities seemed premature so long as there was no organized network of social interests—or 'civil society'—with which they might be associated. From this point of view, a powerful state made it more likely that the society would remain 'primordial and gelatinous', in the words that the Italian Marxist Antonio Gramsci had used to distinguish East from West many years earlier.[21] More promising was the development of associations that embodied the interests of workers and capitalists, of regions and the nationalities, of genders and generations.[22] It seemed possible, though not certain, that these could gradually assemble the support of those they claimed to represent; and that, if they did, they could encourage the formation of a variety of corporate identities that would take the place of the single and compulsory identity that had been imposed upon all of the Soviet nations in the recent past.

Post-Sovietism and Postmodernism

The privileging of variety over singularity, and of freedom over obligation, might be said to be among the key tenets of that elusive yet ubiquitous category of recent discourses on culture, the postmodern. In our discussion of recent Russian literature we saw how postmodernism has been explicitly promoted as the only relevant tendency of recent years, but implicitly demoted by the resurgent popularity of realistic fiction and documentary prose (see Ch. 3). Apologists of the concept might, of course, claim this very state of affairs as proof of the continuing vitality of perversely polymorphous postmodernism. And it does seem as mandatory for surveys of Russian culture to end with a nod in the direction of postmodernism as it is to express confidence in imminent cultural renaissance or the reconstructive capacities of youth.

One such survey, I. V. Kondakov's *Introduction to the History of Russian Culture* (published in 1997 with a title-page boast that it is

20 *Ekonomicheskie i sotsial'nye peremeny*, 5 (1996), 85.
21 A. Gramsci, *Note sul Machiavelli, sulla politica e sullo stato moderno* (Turin, 1966), 68.
22 For a discussion of some of these themes, see H. Pilkington (ed.), *Gender, Generation and Identity in Contemporary Russia* (London, 1996). On the related issue of loss of identity, see T. McDaniel, *The Agony of the Russian Idea* (Princeton, 1996).

'recommended by the State Committee on Higher Education of the Russian Federation as a textbook for institutes of higher education'), concludes with a 'Glance at the History of Russian Culture as a Whole' in terms of ' "Chaos and Order" '. The persistence of this and other binary oppositions is seen as the principal stumbling block to the maturation of Russian culture into the kind of 'ternary' system characteristic of the West:

the issue at the current stage in the historical development of Russian culture is as far as possible to smooth out, attenuate, damp the explosive processes which are taking place at the present moment; to find forms of 'switching' a binary system to a ternary one, to develop a 'language' for translating the dichotomous logic of cultural-historical development into a trichotomous one; to find forms for the self-consciousness of Russian culture which do not keep reproducing the same mechanisms of uncompromising party struggle, axiological polarization, ethical maximalism, harsh confrontationalism, radical reorganization of society, and so on.[23]

The transition from an all-or-nothing dynamics to an evolutionary, genuinely pluralistic mode will be possible, in Kondakov's optimistic argument, thanks to the 'non-standard approaches and solutions' made necessary in the study of Russian culture by 'the absence of boundaries between cultural and social phenomena in Russia, the overlapping of various historical stages and developmental tendencies' (p. 667). Although this syncretism is seen as characteristic of Russian culture and society throughout their history, it finds its clearest expression in the 'post-totalitarian' period, that is, after 1991. In what might be read as a feeble postmodernist flourish, Kondakov describes the resulting space in which the shift from a binary to a ternary model might be taking place not in the concluding chapter from which we have been quoting—whose sub-subtitle is '(In Place of a Conclusion)'—but in the one preceding it, ' "The Postmodernist Paradigm" of Contemporary Culture'.

In this chapter, Kondakov contends that 'phenomena of culture that are incompatible in meaning and in origin are now conjoined in our consciousness as values', thus producing a perfect model of

'postmodernist discourse': the cultural life of the country stands before the gaze of the culturologist as a work of *sots-art* [socialist art]: we have the clichés of socialist realism, and the playful [*ernicheskii*] context in which they are inscribed, and the ironic-wistful distantiation of author and spectator from the resulting 'monster', and the serious understanding that what we see is no more than an *artistic project*, and not life in itself, 'ready to use', but a kind of *simulacrum*, a 'non-functional machine'. (p. 632)

Paradoxically (how else?), salvation from the nostalgia for *state cultural paternalism*, from the tragic combination of 'mass *intolerance*'

23 I. V. Kondakov, *Vvedenie v istoriiu russkoi kul'tury* (Moscow, 1997), 663–4; subsequent refs. in main text.

with 'general *all-is-permittedness* [*vsedozvolennost'*]', of which this post-modernism is a symptom lies in the 'zone of indifference' to which it gives the clearest cultural expression. It is this zone, this 'accumulation of all the hopes and disappointments built up over the period of reform' which 'is today blocking the processes of confrontation and schism so characteristic of Russia'; and 'the fact that almost a third of society (especially among young people) is consuming this specific "middle culture", which acts as a buffer between polarized tendencies, gives cause for hope' (pp. 634–5).

Youth and postmodernism thus come together in an alliance that offers the best promise for the future at a time when 'the study of Russian culture as a world-class phenomenon [*iavlenie mirovogo poriadka*] is only just getting properly started' (p. 667). It is in the nature of Kondakov's survey that his assertions about the post-modernist moment in Russian culture should remain generalizations. For more detail of Russian postmodernism's specific character, and of the extent to which it is coterminous with the post-Soviet period, we should turn to the work of its most vigorous Russian chronicler, Mikhail Epstein (Epshtein), founder of the Laboratory of Modern Culture in Moscow, who emigrated in 1988 and currently holds an academic post in the United States. Epstein offers theoretically sophisticated, yet fairly accessible, accounts of postmodern trends in recent Russian culture, most notably Conceptualism, Metarealism, and Presentism, arguing that the postmodern has been present in Russian culture no less than in Western since the 1960s.[24] Epstein's comparisons between the Russian versions of postmodernism, such as the 'conceptualism' of Dmitrii Prigov, and Western variants have been questioned,[25] and he does himself insist that there are two major differences between Russian and Western postmodernism. First, 'In the Soviet Union, a postmodern relativity of ideas arose from its own ideological, not economic, base, as an extension of the logic of "late communism" [as opposed to late capitalism], a condition in which all elements of reality acquire the form of ideas and all ideas become "acceptable", "manageable" and "exchangeable"' (pp. 157–8). Second, 'There are two essential aspects to Western postmodernism: the actual substance of postmodernism, and the interpretation of this substance in postmodern terms. In the Soviet Union, these two aspects developed separately' (p. 208).

Epstein's principal concern is to overcome this disjuncture, and to bring postmodern theory to bear on Soviet practices and phenomena hitherto unrecognized as postmodern. Like Kondakov, he follows Jean Baudrillard in basing his understanding of postmodernism on the notion of 'simulation', whereby 'models of reality replace reality

24 See M. Epstein, *After the Future: The Paradoxes of Postmodernism and Contemporary Russian Culture*, tr. and ed. A. Miller-Pogacar (Amherst, 1995), 19–50; subsequent refs. in main text.

25 See M. Perloff, 'Russian Postmodernism: An Oxymoron?', *Postmodern Culture*, 3 (1993), no pagination; see also the 'Symposium on Russian Postmodernism' in the same issue (URL http://jefferson.village. virginia.edu/pmc/ contents.all.html).

itself, which then becomes irrecoverable' (p. 189). It is not just that there is no direct, unmediated access to the real; rather, all that we can ever have access to are the models or representations which make up 'hyperreality'. This opens the way for a coruscating interpretation of Soviet Marxism as 'postmodern pastiche' (p. 153), 'totalitarian because it erases the difference between idea and reality, as well as that between opposing conceptions' (p. 155). The Soviet 'postmodern relativity of ideas' reached its apogee 'in the Brezhnev era, when the difference between facts and ideas was virtually erased' (p. 159). Thus *subbotniks* (leisure days 'voluntarily' given up to labour for the collective good) 'were examples of hyperevents, simulating "the celebration of labor" . . . No labor was recognized in the Soviet Union except this artificial communist enthusiasm.' Similarly, 'the presence of the idea of a sausage [a favourite metonymic denotation of material well-being in the late Soviet period] confronts the absence of real meat therein . . . Cheese or sausage in Russia, far from being material facts, turned into Platonic ideas' (pp. 194–5). It was in this world that there appeared the ultimate simulacrum—Brezhnev himself, universally recognized to have been vacuous, but surely never more strikingly characterized than in Epstein's intellectual redaction of the jokes popular in the time of 'Il'ich', as the would-be 'continuator of Lenin's cause' liked to style himself: 'a postmodern surface object, even a kind of hyperreal object, behind which stands no reality' (p. 95). The post-Soviet world, too, is for Epstein one in which 'in the long run Yeltsin or another leader will manage to create a simulated market economy in Russia' (p. 197).

There is no doubting the wit of Epstein's account of Soviet 'hyperreality', but there is a sense in which it reproduces the very tendencies it identifies, coming perilously close to Baudrillard's notorious and irresponsible questioning, both before and after the event, of the reality of the Gulf War (see Ch. 2). Such hyperbole may induce hypertension or worse in those who were forced to carry out officially unrecognized labour, or who now find that the materialized 'Platonic idea' has been placed beyond their grasp by an inflation that is more than rhetorical.

There are potential problems, too, with some of Epstein's discussion of the cultural manifestations of the postmodern mentality. Thus 'what is called postmodernism in contemporary Russia is not only a response to its Western counterpart but also represents a new developmental stage of the same artistic mentality that generated socialist realism' (p. 189). Notwithstanding the writings of Boris Groys discussed earlier (Ch. 2), this yoking of postmodernism and socialist realism retains a salutary capacity to shock and to disrupt established literary-historical patterns—but it also, ironically, recalls Soviet literary history in those dire Stalinist moments when, in defiance of temporal and spatial distance, it uncovered the germ, or even the buds, of socialist realism as far afield as mid-nineteenth-century English fiction. Moreover, to Groysian *épatage* is added a statement evincing a will to structuralist totalization characteristic of Iurii Lotman and the Moscow–Tartu school, whose influence Epstein readily acknowledges: 'Further, both of these movements, socialist realism and postmodernism, are actually components of a single ideological paradigm deeply rooted in the Russian cultural tradition' (ibid.). This, together with a broad-brush account, complete with diagrams, of the history of Russian literature from Kievan Rus' to the present in terms of a recurrent cycle of four phases (social, moral, religious, aesthetic), seems to threaten a dispiriting victory for a dehistoricizing view of cultural development, a collapsing of distinctions not only within the Soviet period, but also between that and the periods preceding and following it.

However, Epstein sees the trap and sets about side-stepping it. Noting, in a comment whose relevance to his own approach he cannot have failed to spot, that 'the Russian philosophical tradition places a premium on wholeness, which has played a number of cruel tricks on the events of Russian history and spawned a political totalitarianism that ironically tried to envelop all of life into a single ideological principle' (p. 301), he describes a set of current practices and principles which would both honour and overcome this tendency, a series of 'experiments in the building of an antitotalitarian totality that includes the postmodern play of difference and simultaneously creates a realm that differs from and is beyond the province of play itself' (pp. 328–9).

First among the practices is essayism, hardly something new, but now especially timely because, as a kind of ' "humanistic mythology" ', it 'does not erase the boundaries between image, concept, and experience; on the contrary, it sharpens them to re-create the full multidimensionality of the human phenomenon' (p. 249). Alongside this is the 'lyrical museum', which, by displaying 'the things of everyday life, lacking any material, historical, or artistic value . . . things of universal distribution that are available anywhere' (pp. 253–4), likewise moves us beyond the hyperreality of postmodernism 'out into trans-semiotic space where signs . . . point to something external to themselves, something unconditionally existent', in which 'reality is restored to its rights' (pp. 278–9). For the analysis of culture there is not only 'culturology', that peculiarly Russian version of cultural studies born of the Moscow–Tartu school, but also 'transculture'.

This diverges from Russian tradition (and, says Epstein, from Western multiculturalism) in its privileging of a Bakhtinian 'outsideness' ('finding one's place on the border of existing cultures' (p. 298)), in its 'assumption that every particular culture is incomplete and requires interaction with other cultures' (p. 303); but it remains traditionally Russian and culturological in its 'attempt to attain a free multidimensional totality opposed to totalitarianism' (p. 301).

Epstein is not only confident of his vision of the past, but also bullish about the future, echoing, but with an optimistic inflection, Evgenii Zamiatin's 1921 warning that the future of Russian literature lay in its past: 'the cultural past of all humanity is now our only future' (p. 295). This future is not the age of post-Sovietism, or of post-postmodernism, or of any multiple of that prefix, but the age of a new, original prefix, 'proto-', 'the epoch of ever-changing projects, whose realization becomes not a transfiguration of reality, but the simple fact of their proposal' (p. 338).

The fact that Epstein's vision of future cultural theory and practice in the era of 'proto' is articulated from a Western rather than a Russian institutional positioning, and that much of the discussion of Russian postmodernism has been conducted in the cyberspace of the internet, is an index of the extent to which the traditional remoteness of the Russian 'intelligentsia' from the Russian 'people'—for all the recent changes in the identity of these two groups signalled by the quotation marks—remains in this case undiminished. Moreover, Epstein's emphasis on a project whose fulfilment is subject to endless deferral may at first sight seem rather more British (what counts is the taking part, not the winning) than Russian. However, it not only recalls Soviet attitudes, whether regretful or ironic, towards the ever-deferred goal of Communism, but also reminds us of the fact that the Russian intelligentsia has always been able only to dream of solving problems in practice rather than in theory, and that it never had any choice but to eat dinner before it had decided the question of God's existence. Perhaps, however, this postponement is a luxury that can no longer be afforded, an ill-advised attempt to resist those quotation marks in a country which insists that they be inscribed, weary as it is of deferral, and still exercised by the mundane but pressing question of where the next dinner is coming from.

Chronology of Events from 1917

This chronology is not intended to be exhaustive, and emphasizes cultural rather than political history, chronologies of which are relatively widely available—see e.g. G. Hosking, *A History of the Soviet Union: Final Edition* (London, 1992). Unless otherwise stated, the organization within years is thematic rather than chronological, such that major national and international political events are followed by changes in domestic and cultural policies, important events in the arts and popular culture, etc.

1917 Food riots in Petrograd initiate revolution

Abdication of Nicholas II; formation of the Provisional Government (February)

Women granted the vote (March)

Lenin returns from exile (April)

1st All-Russian Congress of Soviets (June)

'July days' in Petrograd (July)

Bolsheviks take control; 2nd All-Russian Congress of Soviets (October–December)

Decrees on peace (October: armistice with Germany instituted in December), land ownership (October), Rights of the People of Russia (November), workers' control (November), reintroduction of press censorship (abolished by the Provisional Government: November), civil marriage (December)

Institution of Cheka (Emergency Committee for the suppression of counter-revolution) (December)

Creation of Narkompros (People's Commissariat of Enlightenment); Anatolii Lunacharskii becomes Minister of Culture (December)

New orthography made mandatory for all state and government organizations (December)

1918 Socialist revolution in Germany and proclamation of the Republic there

Secession of Ukraine, Georgia, Armenia, Azerbaidjan

Beginning of Russian Civil War

Suppression of the Constituent Assembly (January)

Separation of Church and State

Proclamation of Red Terror

First revolutionary festivals (celebrations for May Day, anniversary of the
  October Revolution)
Introduction of Gregorian calendar
New orthography made mandatory for all state press (October)
Blok, *The Twelve* (*Dvenadtsat'*)
Lenin's *Plan for Monumental Propaganda* (statues of revolutionary and cultural
  figures)
Art schools liquidated; VKhUTEMAS (Higher Art Workshop) set up
Protazanov, *Father Sergius* (*Otets Sergii*, film of Tolstoi story)
Birth of Solzhenitsyn

1919   8th Party Congress; Politburo and Orgburo set up
Anti-Soviet forces press forward in Civil War
Abolition of Academy of Arts
Nationalization of film industry
Emigration of Gippius, Merezhkovskii, Nabokov, Protazanov

1920   9th Party Congress
Red Army starts to make headway in Civil War
Reorganization of Narkompros into three sections; Agitprop and
  Glavpolitprosvet (Directive of Political Education) set up
Proletkul't brought under Narkompros umbrella
Storming of Winter Palace, spectacle to commemorate 3rd Anniversary of
  Revolution
Tatlin, *Monument to the Third International* (the Tatlin Tower)
Emigration of Bunin, David Burliuk
Founding of the Russian *émigré* journal *Sovremennye zapiski* (*Contemporary
  Annals*) in Paris

1921   Creation of Gosplan
10th Party Congress; New Economic Policy (NEP) inaugurated
Red Army invades Georgia
Popular unrest in Petrograd; mutiny at Kronstadt
Beginning of serious famine on the Volga (lasts into 1922)
Foundation of VAPP (All-Russian Association of Proletarian Writers)
Journals *Krasnaia nov'* (*Red Virgin Soil*) and *Pechat' i revoliutsiia* (*Press and
  Revolution*) founded
Execution of the poet Nikolai Gumilev
Death of Blok
First Working Group of Constructivists inaugurated
Gor'kii leaves Russia for 'health reasons'
Emigration of Remizov, Belyi, Kandinskii

1922   Cheka reorganized as GPU
Stalin becomes General Secretary
Repression of Patriarch Tikhon and other churchmen
Formation of USSR
Foundation of Glavlit (literary censorship organization)
Foundation of Goskino (State Film)

Pil'niak, *The Bleak Year* (*Golyi god*) hailed as the first revolutionary novel
Meyerhold's landmark productions of *The Death of Tarelkin* (*Smert' Tarelkina*)
   and *The Magnanimous Cuckold* (*Velikodushnyi rogonosets*)
Emigration of Tsvetaeva and Khodasevich; expulsion of many intellectuals

1923   12th Party Congress
USSR Constitution published
Institution of Glavrepertkom (theatre censorship authority)
Foundation of LEF (Left Front of the Arts)
Belyi returns to Russia
Protazanov returns to Russia

1924   Death of Lenin
Petrograd renamed Leningrad
Death of Briusov
Sovkino replaces Goskino
Protazanov makes *Aelita*
Eisenstein, *The Strike* (*Stachka*)

1925   Trotskii forced to stand down as War Commissar
14th Party Congress: 'Socialism in one country' declared
Central Committee Resolution on Literature
Journal *Novyi mir* (*New World*) founded
Suicide of Sergei Esenin
Soviet exhibits create a stir at the Paris Exhibition of Decorative Arts
Eisenstein, *Battleship 'Potemkin'* (*Bronenosets Potemkin*)

1926   Trotskii expelled from the Politburo
Increasingly vicious power struggles within VAPP and against other literary
   groups
Pudovkin, *The Mother* (*Mat'*)

1927   15th Party Congress: collectivization of agriculture
Celebrations for 10th Anniversary of October Revolution
Kliuev reads his anti-Soviet lament for the Russian village, *Scorched Earth*
   (*Pogorel'shchina*) at private gatherings
Eisenstein, *October* (*Oktiabr'*)

1928   Onset of 'cultural revolution', 'class war', and campaigns against
   'bohemianism'
Beginning of First Five-Year Plan
VAPP reformed as RAPP
Party Conference on Cinema Affairs declares an end to 'bourgeois vestiges'
Sovkino replaced by Soiuzkino
Glaviskusstvo (centralized directorate for all the arts) set up

1929   Start of forced mass collectivization
Defeat of 'Right Opposition'; Bukharin expelled from Politburo
Lunacharskii removed from Narkompros

1930   Stalin's *Pravda* article, 'Dizzy with Success', attacks overzealous officials
Stalin declares 'the woman question' solved

Construction of permanent stone mausoleum for Lenin's body on Red
  Square
Suicide of Maiakovskii
RAPP becomes most powerful literary organization
Pechat' i revoliutsiia closed down

1931 Trial of Mensheviks
Construction work begins on White Sea Canal
Glavlit's powers extended
Gor'kii returns permanently to USSR

1932 Reintroduction of internal passport system
Famine in the Ukraine and elsewhere (continues until 1934)
Opening of Dneprostroi hydroelectric scheme
Central Committee resolution 'On the Reformation of Literary and Artistic
  Organizations': RAPP and other 'proletarian' organizations closed down
  and Union of Writers, Union of Composers set up

1933 Start of Second Five-Year Plan
Opening of White Sea Canal (largely constructed with forced labour)
Death of Lunacharskii
Glaviskusstvo replaced by UTZP (Directorate of Theatre and Performance
  Enterprises)

1934 17th Party Congress
GPU reorganized as NKVD
Assassination of Kirov
Male homosexuality outlawed
Sentence of 10 years for 'failure to denounce' political misdemeanours
  introduced
First Congress of Soviet Writers and declaration of socialist realism as official
  artistic method
Extension of powers of Glavrepertkom (theatre censorship organization)
Mandel'shtam arrested and sentenced to 3 years' internal exile
Demolition of Cathedral of Christ Redeemer
'Brothers Vasil'ev', *Chapaev*, a hit with film audiences
Prokof'ev returns to Russia from Paris
Titles Hero of the Soviet Union and Master of Sport introduced

1935 Stalin declares 'life has become better, life has become jollier' (*zhit'
  stalo luchshe, zhit' stalo veselee*)
Introduction of 'Stakhanovite' celebrations of super-productive workers
Outlawing of pornography
First line of Moscow Metro completed
Soviet Film-makers' Congress
Rationing of meat, fish, sugar, fats, and potatoes, and later bread and flour,
  ends

1936 New family law: divorce now significantly more difficult
Outlawing of abortion
Promulgation of Stalin Constitution

Trial of Zinov'ev, Kamenev, and others
Ezhov becomes head of NKVD
Foundation of Committee on Artistic Affairs to replace UTZP
Many early Soviet films blacklisted
'Formalism' denounced in a series of *Pravda* articles
Aleksandrov's *Circus* (*Tsirk*) a hit with film audiences
Shostakovich's *Lady Macbeth of Mtsensk* (*Ledi Makbet Mtsenskogo uezda*) denounced in *Pravda*

1937   Height of the Purges: trial of Radek, Piatakov, and others
Execution of Marshal Tukhachevskii
Execution of Kliuev
Reconstruction of Gor'kii Street begins
Centenary of Pushkin's death celebrated by publication of academic edition of his works, festivals, renaming of streets

1938   Start of Third Five-Year Plan
Stalin, *A Short Course in the History of the Communist Party*
Purges continue: show trials of Bukharin, Rykov, Iagoda, and others
Beria becomes head of NKVD
Reintroduction of labour books (*trudovye knizhki*, personal work records) for workers
Execution of Pil'niak
Mandel'shtam rearrested; later dies in imprisonment
Closing of Meyerhold Theatre
Television centre opens in Moscow

1939   18th Party Congress
Nazi–Soviet Pact; invasion of Eastern Poland ('liberation of Western Ukraine')
Finno-Soviet War begins
Fadeev becomes Secretary of the Writers' Union
Arrest of Babel'
Return of Tsvetaeva to Russia
Arrest and execution of Meyerhold
Stalin Prizes inaugurated

1940   Defeat of Finland
Annexation of Baltic States
Assassination of Trotskii
Introduction of fees for higher and upper secondary education
Reintroduction of officers' ranks in armed forces
Sovremennye zapiski closes in Paris
Execution of Babel'
10th anniversary of Maiakovskii's death commemorated by evening in the Bol'shoi Theatre and erection of monument on Maiakovskii Square

1941   German invasion of USSR; at first German forces make significant inroads
Beginning of Leningrad Blockade
Evacuation of Moscow

Fall of Kiev

Stalin makes first broadcast (3 July)

Lateness for work becomes criminal offence

Suicide of Tsvetaeva in evacuation (August)

1942   Wehrmacht reaches Stalingrad (September) and is encircled by Red
Army (November)

Restoration of full officer status in Red Army

Krasnaia nov' closed down

Foundation of New York *émigré* monthly *Novyi zhurnal* (*New Journal*)

1943   Surrender of German 6th Army at Stalingrad

Battle of Kursk

Moscow Patriarchate re-established; Orthodox Church encouraged as patriotic focus

1944   Lifting of Leningrad Blockade

Establishment of Second Front in France

Warsaw Uprising

'The Internationale' replaced by new Soviet national anthem

1945   Yalta Conference (February): Stalin, Roosevelt, and Churchill agree
'spheres of influence'

Surrender of Germany (9 May)

Stalin toasts 'the Great Russian People' at victory celebrations in Moscow
(24 May)

Potsdam Conference (July–August): denazification, demilitarization, and
decentralization of Germany agreed

1946   Fourth Five-Year Plan

Famine in Ukraine (lasts into 1947)

Repatriation (often forcible) of Soviet 'displaced persons'

Central Committee decree *On the journals 'Zvezda' and 'Leningrad'* denouncing Akhmatova and Zoshchenko, and *On the Repertoire of Dramatic Theatres*,
demanding 'conflictless' theatre

Fadeev becomes General Secretary of Writers' Union

Foundation of *émigré* journal *Grani* (*Facets*) in Frankfurt

1947   Beginning of campaign against 'rootless cosmopolitans' (i.e. Jews)

Rearrest of many victims of 1930s purges

Censorship of books on nationalist grounds initiated

Re-establishment of Academy of Arts

Stalin meets Eisenstein and Cherkasov to discuss *Ivan the Terrible* (*Ivan Groznyi*)

1948   Communist coup in Czechoslovakia

'Lysenkoism' becomes official ideology in biological sciences

Death of Zhdanov

Decree of Soviet of Ministers on widening of the activities of consumer
co-operatives

1949   Closure of Moscow Jewish State Theatre

Closure of Pushkin Museum of Fine Arts (the only showcase for Western
classical art in Moscow)

1950 Stalin attacks the formerly canonical linguistic theories of Nikolai Marr
Tvardovskii appointed editor of *Novyi mir*

1951 Fifth Five-Year Plan

1952 19th Party Congress

1953 Discovery of 'Doctors' Plot' (alleged scheme of Jewish doctors to murder top Soviet officials) announced
Death of Stalin
Revolt in Norilsk labour camp
Soviet troops suppress workers' uprisings in East Germany
Khrushchev confirmed as First Secretary of the Communist Party
Death of Prokof'ev

1954 Pospelov Commission begins investigation of repressions under Stalin
Revolt in Kengir Labour Camp
Virgin Lands campaign for volunteer labour in Central Asia begins
Attacks on Stalinist literary policy in *Novyi mir* are followed by dismissal of Tvardovskii as editor
Second Writers' Union Congress
Fadeev replaced by Surkov as General Secretary of the Writers' Union

1955 Establishment of Warsaw Pact
Leningrad Metro opens
Pushkin Museum of Fine Arts reopened
Relegalization of abortion

1956 20th Party Congress: Khrushchev denounces some of Stalin's crimes, and also reopens the debate on 'the woman question'
Amnesty for many political prisoners
Serious unrest in Poland and Hungary put down by Soviet troops
Abolition of fees for higher and upper secondary education
Dudintsev, *Not by Bread Alone* (*Ne khlebom edinym*)
Kalatozov, *The Cranes are Flying* (*Letiat zhuravli*)

1958 Educational reform
Publication of new criminal code
Pasternak awarded Nobel Prize for Literature and expelled from Writers' Union
Tvardovskii reappointed editor of *Novyi mir*
'Moskva' swimming pool opened on site of Cathedral of Christ Redeemer

1959 Start of Seven-Year Plan
Khrushchev launches campaign for mass planting of maize
Chukrai, *Ballad of a Soldier* (*Ballada o soldate*)

1960 Death of Pasternak

1961 First manned Soviet space flight
Building of Berlin Wall
Closure of Monastery of the Caves, Kiev, signals new anti-Church campaign
22nd Party Congress: denunciation of 'the cult of personality'
Stalin removed from Lenin Mausoleum

1962   Cuban Missile crisis

Workers' strikes and riots in Novocherkassk brutally suppressed

Solzhenitsyn, *One Day in the Life of Ivan Denisovich (Odin den' Ivana Denisovicha)*

1963   Khrushchev warns Writers' Union of dangers of 'bourgeois influences'

1964   Khrushchev deposed and replaced by Brezhnev (August)

The poet Joseph Brodsky tried for 'parasitism' and sentenced to 5 years' hard labour (February)

1966   23rd Party Congress

Trial of Siniavskii and Daniel'

Death of Anna Akhmatova

1967   Arab-Israeli War: Soviet Union takes pro-Arab line

Celebrations for 50th anniversary of Revolution

Iurii Andropov becomes head of KGB

1968   Dubcek's declaration of 'Communism with a human face' is followed by invasion of Czechoslovakia

Red Square protests against invasion followed by severe reprisals against participants

1970   Removal of Tvardovskii from *Novyi mir* editorship

Solzhenitsyn awarded Nobel Prize for Literature

1971   Ninth Five-Year Plan

24th Party Congress

Mass Jewish demonstration at Supreme Soviet followed by beginning of large-scale emigration to Israel

1972   Unrest in Lithuania

Crackdown on dissidence in the Ukraine

Expulsion of Brodsky from USSR

1974   Deportation of Solzhenitsyn

Foundation of third-wave *émigré* journal *Kontinent (Continent)* in Paris

1975   Helsinki accord

Sakharov awarded Nobel Peace Prize

1976   25th Party Congress

Tenth Five-Year Plan

Formation of Helsinki Watch groups

1977   Brezhnev becomes President of USSR

Publication of new Soviet constitution

1978   Unrest in Georgia

Trial of Anatolii Shcharanskii

1979   Soviet invasion of Afghanistan

Brezhnev awarded Lenin Prize for literature

Samizdat literary almanac *Metropol' (Metropolis)* prepared in Moscow and soon published abroad; participants, including Aksenov, Bitov, Lisnian-skaia are sharply criticized and some subjected to sanctions

1980 Olympic Games held in Moscow and boycotted by many Western countries
Sakharov exiled to Gorky
Formation of Solidarity trade union in Poland

1981 Jaruzelski declares martial law in Poland
26th Party Congress
Eleventh Five-Year Plan
Expulsion of Aksenov from USSR

1982 Soviet Union stations SS-21 missiles in GDR
Last Helsinki Watch group disbanded
Death of Brezhnev; Andropov becomes General Secretary of CPSU

1984 Death of Andropov; Chernenko becomes General Secretary

1985 Chernenko dies and is replaced by Gorbachev

1986 27th Party Congress
Explosion at Chernobyl'
Sakharov allowed to return to Moscow

1987 New law allowing budget freedom to Soviet enterprises (*khozraschet*)
Brodsky awarded Nobel Prize for Literature

1988 Gorbachev elected President of USSR
Serious unrest in Armenia over the Nagorno-Karabakh district; Azerbaijanis carry out pogrom against Armenians in Sumgait
Celebrations of Orthodox Millennium
Authors allowed to self-publish books

1989 Elections to Congress of People's Deputies
Serious unrest all over Soviet Union and Eastern Europe
Fall of Berlin Wall (November)
Velvet Revolution in Czechoslovakia (November)

1990 Reunification of Germany
CPSU renounces its 'leading role' (February)
Lithuania declares independence (March)

1991 Soviet forces attempt to 'restore order' in Vilnius and Riga (January)
Yeltsin elected president of Russia (June)
Defeat of coup attempt organized by General Emergency Committee; Communist Party suspended (August)
Most Republics declare independence
USSR disbanded (December)

1992 Abkhazian–Georgian War
First Booker Prize for the Russian Novel

1993 Anti-homosexuality legislation repealed (April)
Yeltsin orders military assault on Russian parliament, forcing it to dissolve against its will (September)
New constitution published (December)
Right makes significant gains in parliamentary elections

1994   Return of Solzhenitsyn to Russia

Collapse of the MMM Bank

Invasion of Chechenia

1995   Assassination of television chief Vladimir List'ev (March)

Right-wingers, including ex-Communists, make further gains in parliamentary elections (December)

1996   Resignation of reformist Foreign Minister Andrei Kozyrev; he is replaced by hardliner Evgenii Primakov (January)

Chechen rebels take hostages in Pervomaiskoe, Dagestan; Russian forces capture settlement after all-out attack

Russian Communist Party selects Gennadii Ziuganov as its presidential candidate (February)

Yeltsin re-elected President

Death of Brodsky

Analytical Index of Names and Places

Note: Personal names are glossed only in the cases of those individuals whose contribution to the development of Russian culture is discussed in the text. The category of 'places' includes important named sites of cultural activity, such as theatres. Movements and associations are listed in the Subject Index.

Efros, A., theatre director 95–6, 101, 104–5
Egg, K., film director 171, 172, 317
Eiges, K., pianist 111
Eikhenbaum, B. M., formalist critic 25
Eisenstein [Eizenshtein], S., avant-garde film director 58, 92, 101, 117, 169–70, 174–5, 176, 177, 178, 180, 182, 317
Ekk, N., film director 172, 175, 177, 178
Ekster, A., artist, cinema and theatre set designer 99, 139, 172, 303
El'tsin, B., see Yeltsin, B.
Elagin, I., writer 304
Engels, F. 193, 312
Engelstein, L. 17
Epstein [Epshtein], M., theorist of postmodernism 12–13, 397–400
Erenburg, I., writer, memoirist 58, 300
Ermler, F., film director 173, 178, 180
Erofeev, Venedikt, writer 70, 242–3
Erofeev, Viktor, writer 76, 335, 336
Erté [Romain de Tirtoff], fashion illustrator 301
Esaulenko, V., painter 241
Esenin, S., peasant poet 326
Eshliman, N., Orthodox priest 286
Eshpai, A., composer 126, 136
Estonia 279
Etkind, E., critic, writer 70
Evreinov, N. N., avant-garde theatre director 92
Evtushenko, E. A., poet 61, 121, 183, 233–4, 264
Ezhov, N. I., head of OGPU 50

Fadeev, A., writer, Chairman, Soviet Writers' Union 51
Fairbanks, D. 171
Falk, R., constructivist artist 143
Favorskii, V., painter 139
Fedotov, G. P., historian, religious thinker 304
Feinberg, S., composer 110, 112–13, 117
Feklistov, A., actor 107
Figurina, E., painter 240
Filonov, P., avant-garde painter 139, 141, 144, 151 n. 14
Filozov, A., actor 106
Finkelstein, L., prisoner under Stalin 211
Finland 146

Firsova, E., composer 119, 129
Fitzpatrick, S. 17, 38–9, 315
Fletcher, G. 1
Florenskaia, O., textile artist 241
Fogel, V., film actor 168
Fokin, M., dancer, choreographer 302
Fokin, V., theatre director 107, 108
Fomenko, P., theatre director 107, 108
Fomin, V., film director 186
Frank, S. L., philosopher 29, 275
Freud, S. 357, 364
Frolov, R., advertising executive 223, 227
Frow, J. 6
Furmanov, D., writer 176

Gabo, N., artist 138, 301–3
Gagarin, Iu., first man in space 259
Gaidai, L., film director 185
Gaidar, A., children's writer 178–9
Galanskov, Iu., dissident 62
Galich, A., guitar-poet 69, 265–6
Gan, A., constructivist artist 144
Ganina, M., writer 232
Garbo, G. 301
Gardin, V., film director 167
Gastev, A. K., proletarian poet 32–3, 34
Gelovani, M., film actor 182
Genet, J. 108
Georgia 327, 361
Gerasimenko, V., painter 240
Gerasimov, A., socialist realist painter 139, 147–53
Gerasimov, S. A., film director 178
German, A., film director 185, 186, 187, 188
Gershkovich [Herschkowitz], F., composer 119, 125, 129, 131
Ginzburg, A., dissident 62, 211
Ginzburg, E., memoirist 329, 332
Gippius, Z., mystical symbolist writer 303
Gladilin, A. T., writer 61
Glazunov, A., composer 115
Glazunov, I., painter 136, 261, 285
Glebova-Sudeikina, O., society beauty 325
Glière, R., composer 115
Glinka, M., composer 127, 134, 136, 137, 181
Goebbels, J. 158, 196
Gogoberidze, L., film director 359, 361–3
Gogol', N. V., writer 106, 107, 115, 169, 242, 280
Golden Ring 261

Goldovskaia, M., film director 188
Goldschmidt, A. 154
Golod, S., sexologist 314, 315, 338
Goncharova, N., avant-garde painter 138, 139, 301–3
Gor'kii, M., proletarian writer 165, 178, 202, 342
as figurehead of Soviet literature 43, 77
opposition to Bolshevik regime 75–6, 192, 195, 206
and religion 275–6
and sexuality 319
and socialist realism 46, 48
Gorbachev, M. S., last Soviet leader (1985–91) 11, 57, 61, 65, 122, 124, 261, 273, 285, 352–3, 354, 373
and anti-alcohol campaign 159, 270–2
and cinema 187–9
and glasnost' and perestroika 67–8, 73–85, 221–2, 269, 334, 363, 373
and intelligentsia 71–4
and religion 289–91, 293, 295 n. 44
and sexuality 329, 342–3, 344
and theatre 91, 96
Gorbanevskaia, N., writer 251
Goricheva, T., feminist writer and activist 67, 285–6, 354
Gorky, see Nizhnii Novgorod
Gornung, L., memoirist 326
Gorodinskii, V., musicologist 128
Gould, G. 131
Govorukhin, S., documentary film-maker 334
Gramsci, A. 395
Granin, D., writer 59, 65
Grant, B. 271–2
Grebenshchikov, Iu., actor 106
Grekova, I., writer 232, 337
Grishin, V., politician 96 n. 6
Gromyko, A., politician 290–1
Grossman, V. S., writer 58, 70, 75, 77, 357
Grotowski, J. 108
Groys, B., literary critic 40–1, 45–6, 398–9
Grushin, B., opinion pollster 391
Guazzoni, E. 170
Gubaidulina, S., composer 119, 121, 127, 129, 135
Gubenko, N., film director 264
Gubenko, N., politician 75, 97
Gumilev, N., acmeist poet 74, 277

Hansen, P. 234
Hayek, F. 196

Heartfield, J. 158
Herschkowitz, F., *see* Gershkovich, F.
Herzen [Gertsen], A. I., liberal thinker, émigré 297
Hindemith, P. 110, 113
Hingley, R. 5
Hitler, A. 75, 158, 196, 201, 202, 241, 278, 279, 322
Hollander, G. 212
Hollywood 167, 168, 179, 181, 185, 211 n. 33
Honegger, A. 113
Hosking, G. 201, 283
Hrabovsky, L., composer 119
Hulce, T. 189

Iagoda, G. G., head of OGPU 319
Iakovlev, A., politician, ideologist of *perestroika* 71, 74, 96 n. 6
Iakovlev, B., socialist realist painter 147, 152
Iakunin, G., Orthodox priest 286, 287, 288–9, 292, 294
Ianchuk, N., musicologist 111
Iaroslavskii, E., founder of League of Militant Atheists 275
Igumnov, K., pianist 111
Il'f, I. and Petrov, E., satirical writers 235
Il'ina, I. P. 330
Inber, V., poet 264
Inkeles, A. 198
Ioganson, B. V., constructivist artist 143, 152
Ioseliani, O., film director 185
Iskander, F. A., writer 61, 67, 71
Iugov, A., historical fiction writer 81
Ivachenko, Iu., painter 241
Ivan IV (the Terrible, ruled 1547–84) 344
Ivanitskaia, T., textile artist 241
Ivanov, G., poet 303–4
Ivanov, Viktor, poster artist 158–9
Ivanov, Vsevolod, writer 303
Ivanov-Boretskii, M., musicologist 111
Ivashkin, A., cellist 127, 132
Izmailovo Park (Moscow) 62

Jacoby, G. 181
Jakobson, R., linguist 304
Jameson, F. 83
Joravsky, D. 26
Joyce, J. 62, 318

Kabakov, I., installation artist 241
Kabalevskii, D., composer 115, 126

Kafka, F. 62, 107
Kalatozov, M., film director 178, 183
Kaledin, S., writer 267, 271
Kalinin, R., gay activist 344, 350–1
Kamenko, A., film producer 301
Kancheli, G., composer 134
Kandinskii, V., avant-garde painter 138, 140, 151, 301–3
Kanevskii, V., film director 188, 190 n. 106
Kant, I. 27
Kaplan, E. A. 357, 363
Kapustin, D., author of sex manual 339–40
Karamanov, A., composer 130 n. 18
Karamzin, N. M., historian, writer 297
Karatygin, V., music critic 110, 111
Karavaeva, A., writer 316
Karetnikov, N., modernist composer 124, 129, 130 n. 18, 131, 135
Kariakin, Iu., literary scholar 73
Karlinsky, S., literary critic 304
Kassil, L., children's writer 58
Kastalskii, A., musician 111
Kataev, V., writer 178–9
Katerli, N., writer, memoirist 59–60, 77 n. 23, 232
Kaufman, M., cameraman 168–9
Kazan Cathedral (St Petersburg) 277
Kazantzakis, N. 277
Keaton, B. 171
Kedrov, M., theatre director 99
Kelly, A. 323
Kemp-Welch, A. 29
Khachaturian, A., composer 115, 117, 118, 120
Khanumkhamedov, Iu., painter 241
Khanzhonkov, A., film producer 165, 166
Kharchev, K., Chairman of Council for Religious Affairs 291–2
Kharms, D., absurdist writer 125
Kheifits, I., film director 182–3
Khlebnikov, V., futurist poet 140
Khmelko, M., painter 152
Khodasevich, V., poet 299, 300, 303–4
Khokhlova, A., film actress 168
Kholodnaia, V., film star 166
Khotinenko, V., film director 190
Khrennikov, T., composer, General Secretary, Soviet Composers' Union 117, 118–19, 124, 125, 126–7, 131

Khripkova, A., author of sex manuals 339
Khrushchev, N. S., Soviet leader (1954–64) 74, 226, 235, 249–69, 353
  attacks on artists 61–2, 240
  and cinema 182–4
  corruption under 253–4, 341
  and cultural thaw 57, 60, 65, 123, 231, 282, 337, 342, 370
  and denunciation of Stalin / de-Stalinization 57, 59, 60, 183, 209, 221, 250, 282
  and music 130
  and religion 282–3, 333
  and theatre 91
  as viewed by intelligentsia 250–1, 252
Khutsiev, M., film director 182–3, 184
Khvan, A., film director 190
Kiev 129, 274, 290
Kiritsyn, V., theorist of postmodernism 83
Kirov, S. M., Bolshevik politician, assassinated 1934 80, 178
Kirpotin, V. Ia., literary critic 94
Kiseleva, E., memoirist 268–9
Kleberg, L. 106
Klimov, E., film director 183, 186, 187, 264
Kliuev, N., peasant poet 325, 326
Klutsis, G., poster artist 158
Knebel', M., theatre director 95, 105
Kochergin, E., theatre set designer 101
Kochergin, N., poster artist 157
Koestler, A. 207
Kolesov, D., author of sex manuals 339
Kollontai, A., Social Democrat, feminist 312–13, 315–16, 323
Komar, A., artist 71, 240–1
Komarov, S., film director 168, 171 n. 38
Kon, I., sexologist 338, 339
Konchalovskii, A., film director 185, 186, 189, 284
Kondakov, I. V. 395–7
Konenkov, S., sculptor 151 n. 14
Kornilov, B., poet 63
Korovin, K. A., impressionist painter 148
Kosmodem'ianskaia, Z., resistance heroine 180
Kozintsev, G., film director 169–70, 178
Krantz, J. 232

Krasin, B., musician 111
Kravchenko, V., Soviet official 202, 206
Kremlin (Moscow) 182, 202, 210, 251, 257, 290
Krenek, E. 110, 131
Krestinskii, V., historical fiction writer 81
Kriuchkov, N., film actor 180
Krivulin, V., avant-garde writer 76
Krupskaia, N., leading Bolshevik 334
Ktorova, A. [pseud. of V. Sandor], writer 238
Küchelbeker, W. [Kiukhel'beker, V.], romantic writer, journal editor 121, 137
Kukryniksy, collective name of three cartoonists, M. *Kupriianov*, P. *Krylov*, and *Nikolai* Sokolov 158, 241
Kuleshov, L., film theorist and director 168, 169–70, 174–5
Kupchenko, I., actress 107
Kuprin, A. I., realist writer 299
Kurchatkin, A., writer 67
Kustodiev, B., avant-garde painter 155
Kuzmin, M., poet 320, 325–6
Kuznetsov, P., post-impressionist painter 145, 300
Kuznetsova, L., publicist 355, 357

Ladynina, M., film actress 176, 179, 180
Lamm, P., composer 111, 112
Larionov, M. F., avant-garde painter 138, 139, 303
Latey, M. 211
Latvia 344
Lavrenev, B. A., writer 95
Le Corbusier, H. 144
Lebedev, E., actor 101
Ledenev, R., composer 130 n. 18, 136
Legoshin, V., film director 178–9
Leibowitz, R. 130
Leite, A. 155
Lelevich, G., proletarian cultural theorist 31–2, 36, 37, 55
Lendvai, P. 210
Lenin, V. I., Bolshevik politician and theorist, first leader of Soviet Union 2, 69, 103, 269, 297, 398
    criticism of 75
    cult of 70, 144, 158–9, 178, 182, 238, 259, 260, 266–7

views on culture 21–4, 27–8, 32, 43, 55, 109; on cinema 92, 167, 170, 181; on literature 24–5, 37, 40; on music 112; on press 192–6, 199–200, 204, 206–7, 216–18, 222; on propaganda 197–9, 219; on religion 275–6; on sexuality 313, 323; on theatre 91
Leningrad, *see* St Petersburg
Leonov, L. M., writer 303
Leontiev, K. N., writer, critic, philosopher 8
Lepeshinskaia, O., medical charlatan 203–4
Lermontov, M. Iu., writer 343, 344
Leskov, N. S., writer 116
Liatoshinskii, B., composer 120, 129
Ligachev, E., politician 96 n. 6
Likhachev, D., literary scholar 394
Limonov, E., writer 70, 75, 335, 342
Linitskii, V., Orthodox monk 285
Lipatti, D. 130
Lissitzky, El. [Lisitskii, L. M.], avant-garde painter 139, 140, 240, 300
Lithuania 221–2, 288
Liubimov, Iu., theatre director 95, 96, 97, 101–4, 105
Livnev, S., film director 365–6
Lorca, F. G. 121
Losskii, N. O., philosopher 29
Lot'ianu, E., film director 342
Lotman, Iu. M., cultural semiotician 2, 12, 64, 399
Lourié [Lur'e], A., composer 110–11, 112, 325
Lubianka (site of Cheka headquarters, Moscow) 294
Lukács, G. 6
Lukov, L., film director 180
Lumière brothers 165
Lunacharskii, A. V., first Commissar of People's Enlightenment 114, 145, 317
    views on culture 28–9, 37, 110, 140; on cinema 167; on music 112; on religion 275–6; on theatre 92, 93; on visual arts 148
Lyotard, J.-F. 83
Lysenko, T., charlatan biologist 203

McDowell, M. 189
Macherey, P. 25–6
Mahler, G. 110
Maiakovskii, V., futurist poet and dramatist 94, 98, 140, 142, 154, 157, 205, 234, 235, 300, 303

Makanin, V., writer 67
Makovskii, K., painter 244
Maksimov, V. E., writer, dissident 60 n. 7, 70, 75
Malachowski, A. 212
Malakhovskaia, N., feminist activist 354
Malevich, K., constructivist painter 139, 140, 141, 144, 151, 240
Maliavin, F., World of Art painter 138
Malov, O., pianist 136
Mamatova, L. 178, 361
Mamonova, T., feminist writer and activist 67, 354
Mandel'shtam, Iu., poet, literary critic 300, 304
Mandel'shtam, N., memoirist 69
Mandel'shtam, O. E., acmeist poet 58, 62, 74
Manège Exhibition Hall (Moscow) 61
Mann, T. 106
Mansurian, T., composer 130 n. 18
Mansurov, P., artist 138
Marchenko, A., writer 70
Markov, G. 212
Markov, G., socialist realist writer 64, 76, 81
Markov, V., literary critic 304
Marx, K. 193, 275, 312
Maryniak, I. 284
Massine [Miasin], L., choreographer 302
Masterkova, L., artist 241
Matiushin, M. V., avant-garde artist 144
Mausoleum (Red Square, Moscow) 144, 250, 365
Medtner, N. K., composer 110
Medvedev, R., Marxist historian 68
Medvedev, V., politician 292
Medvedev, Zh., scientist, dissident 256
Medvedkin, A., film director 176
Melamid, A., artist 71, 240–1
Men', Fr. Aleksandr, priest 281, 288–9
Men'shikov, O., actor 107
Men'shov, A., film director 64–5, 185
Merezhkovskii, D., mystical symbolist writer 29, 303
Merimée, P. 171, 317
Messiaen, O. 130
Metro 375
    Moscow 144–5, 228, 259
    St Petersburg 259
Metropolitan Sergii 276, 278

Sereiskii, M. 324
Serov, V. G., painter 148
Seton-Watson, M. 284
Shakhnazarov, K., film director 189
Shalamov, V., writer 69
Shaporin, Iu., composer 115, 117, 120
Shatalov, A., writer, journalist 343–4
Shatrov, M., playwright 66, 74, 105
Shauro, V., politician 96 n. 6
Shchedrin, R., composer 125
Shcherbachev, V., composer 111
Shcherbakov, D., actor 106
Shcherbakov, O., editor, *Gei Slaviane* 344
Shchukin, I., industrialist, collector of art 244
Shebalin, V., composer 113, 118
Shepit'ko, L., film director 184, 185, 359–61, 362–3
Sheremet'evo airport (Moscow) 230
Shishkin, I., realist painter, member of Wanderers movement 244
Sholokhov, M. A., writer 77
Shostakovich, D. D., composer 63, 113, 115–16, 117–18, 119, 120–3, 125–7, 128–9, 130, 133, 135, 136, 318
Shteiger, A., poet 303–4
Shtemler, I., writer 232–3
Shterenberg, D., avant-garde painter 145
Shukshin, V. M., village prose writer, film director 65, 183
Shumiatskii, B., Old Bolshevik, head of Soiuzkino 174, 175–6, 179
Shvarts, E., writer 76
Siberia 258, 322
Sidorov, E., politician 76 n. 20
Sil'vestrov, V., composer 119, 130 n. 18, 134, 136, 138
Simonov, R., theatre director 99
Simonovich-Efimova, N., constructivist artist 143
Siniavskii, A. D., writer 52, 57, 59, 62, 70, 74, 251
Skriabin, A. N., composer 110, 113, 127, 128
Skripkina, M., *see* 'Peppers'
Slavkin, V., playwright 67, 105–6
Slobodskaia, O. 303
Smirnov, A., film director 187
Smirnov, D., composer 129
Sokolov, Sasha, writer 70, 236, 238, 243
Sokurov, A., film director 186, 188

Soloukhin, V., writer 284
Solov'ev, S., film director 188
Solov'eva, P., modernist poet 325
Solov'ov, Vsevolod, historical fiction writer 81
Solzhenitsyn, A. I., writer, critic of Soviet system 57, 60–2, 68–9, 70, 75–6, 77, 78, 79, 83, 184, 211, 215, 236, 243, 251, 286, 288
Somov, K., artist, founder member of World of Art movement 325
Sorokin, Iu., psycholinguist 343
Stadniuk, I. F., writer 64
Stalin, I. V., Bolshevik, Soviet leader (1924–53) 2, 45, 58, 61, 73, 75, 118, 139, 188, 211, 229, 230, 234, 239, 250, 251, 256, 261, 263, 278, 320, 322 n. 17
and cinema 146, 167, 174, 176, 179, 181–2
cult of 11, 151–2, 158, 181–2, 199, 209, 259, 260
cultural policies of 43, 116, 128
death of (as culturally significant moment) 15, 57, 58, 99, 115, 119, 120, 126, 182, 202, 207, 249, 264 n. 12, 265, 270, 271, 282, 312, 321, 337, 344, 352, 367
denunciations of 57, 59, 60, 84, 95, 183, 209, 221, 250, 282
jokes about 237–8
and media 200–4, 205–6
and music 116, 122, 131, 134
nostalgia for days of 254
and penal system 69
and religion 278–9, 282, 290
rehabilitation of 64, 69
representations of 241, 348
and sexuality 319, 330, 332, 344, 345, 367
and terror 278
and theatre 91
and visual arts 141, 146
Stalingrad 250
Stanislavskii, K., theatre director 92, 93, 94, 95, 98–9, 100, 101
Starewicz, W., film animator 166, 167
Stein, P. 108
Steiner, R., leader of anthroposophy movement 99
Stenberg brothers, constructivist artists, theatrical set designers 99, 143
Stepanova, V., avant-garde artist 98, 143
Stishova, E. 367

Stites, R. 17, 23–4, 27, 30
Stolper, A., film director 179, 180
Stolypin, P., Prime Minister (under Nicholas II) 79
Strauss, J. 181
Strauss, R. 110
Stravinsky, I., composer 110, 111, 122, 128, 129, 131, 138, 303
Strehler, G. 108
Strugatskii brothers (A. N. and B. N.), science fiction writers 70–1, 257
Struve, P., anti-radical thinker 275
Sukhovo-Kobylin, A. V., playwright 99
Suslin, V., composer 129, 133
Svilova, E., film editor 168–9
Sviridov, G. [also Iu.], composer 136–7
Szymanovski, K. 113

Taganka Theatre (Moscow) 95, 96, 97, 98, 101–4, 105–6
Tairov, A. Ia., avant-garde theatre director 94, 99
Tarkovskii, A., film director 183, 184, 185, 284
Tarsis, V., writer 70
Tartu 64
Tashkent 210
Tatlin, V., avant-garde painter 139, 140–1
Tavrion (Batozsky), elder (*starets*) 281
Tchaikovsky, P. I., composer 136, 182
Teffi, N., writer 300
Tendriakov, V. F., writer 65, 250–1, 283
Termen, L. [Theremin, Leon], acoustic engineer 112
Theremin, Leon, *see* Termen, L.
Tiazhel'nikov, E., politician 96 n. 6
Tiazhel'nikov, I. M., Komsomol leader 338
Timashuk, L., Kremlin hospital worker 202
Todorovskii, V., film director 190
Toidze, I., poster artist 158
Tokareva, V., writer 232
Tolstaia, T., writer 67, 76 n. 20, 232, 367
Tolstoi, A., historical fiction writer 300
Tolstoi, L. N., writer 25, 101, 166, 280
as model for Soviet writers 35, 39
Tomashevskaia, Z. 123
Toscanini, A. 117

Tovstonogov, G., theatre director 95, 96, 100–1, 104
Trauberg, L., film director 169–70, 178
Tret'iakov, S., avant-garde writer 42–3
Trifonov, Iu. V., urban prose writer 65, 66
Trotskii, L., Bolshevik political and cultural theorist 28, 35–6, 105, 157, 167, 299, 320, 326
Tseitlin, L., violinist 111
Tsvetaeva, M., modernist poet 123, 299, 303
Turkmenia 327
Turovskaia, M. 178
Tvardovskii, A. T., poet, editor of *Novyi mir* 57, 60, 74, 77
Tverskaia ulitsa (ulitsa Gor'kogo), main Moscow boulevard 100
Tynianov, Iu., formalist theorist and literary historian 169
Tyshler, A., avant-garde artist 139, 238–9

Ukraine 252, 288, 290, 294, 392
Ul'ba, O., editor, *Gei Slaviane* 344
Ulanovskaia, B., writer 76, 77 n. 23
Ul'ianov, M., actor 107
Ulitskaia, L., writer 76, 77 n. 23
Urusevskii, S., cameraman 183
Ustvol'skaia, G., composer 135–6
Uvarov, S., Minister of Education (under Nicholas I) 388
Uzbekistan 327

Vaginov, K. K., writer 39
Vakhtangov, E. B., theatre director 93, 98–9, 101
Vakhtin, B., writer 242
Valkenier, E. 147
Varèse, E. 112
Vasil'ev 'brothers' (G. and S., actually unrelated), film directors 176–8, 179, 356
Vasiliev, A., theatre director 105–7, 108

VDNKh (Vystavka dostizhenii narodnogo khoziaistva, Exhibition of Economic Achievements, Moscow) 241, 259
Vedeneeva, N., physicist, lover of S. Parnok 326
Verbitskaia, A., writer 317
Vernadsky, G., historian 304
Vertov, D., avant-garde film director 144, 168–70, 172–3, 174–5
Victory Park (St Petersburg) 261, 262
Vigel', F., memoirist 326–7
Viktiuk, R., theatre director 108
Virta, N., writer 95
Vitebsk 140
Vladimov, G. N., writer 75, 84
Vladin, V., author of sex manual 339–40
Voinovich, V. N., satirical writer 70–1, 75, 83, 236
Volga 314
Volgograd, *see* Stalingrad
Volkonskii, A., composer 129–30, 131
Volkov, S. 121
Voronezh 342
Voronov, Iu., politician 96 n. 6
Voronskii, A. A., literary critic, editor of *Krasnaia nov'* 35, 36, 46
Voznesenskaia, Iu., feminist writer and activist 67, 354
Voznesenskii, A. A., poet 61, 96, 105, 183
Vustin, A., composer 119
Vvedenskii, A., absurdist writer 125
Vysotskii, V., guitar-poet, actor 69, 96, 104, 269

Webern, A. 119, 129, 130, 131, 134
White House (Moscow) 72, 73, 349
White, H. 322 n. 17
White, S. 270
Williams, C. 366
Wyshnegradsky, I., composer 112

Yeltsin [El'tsin], B., Russian President (1991–) 96 n. 6, 222, 226–7, 243, 262, 272, 273, 394
and intelligentsia 72, 73
and religion 293
represented in literature 81
and sexuality 344
Youngblood, D. 17

Zachariah, Fr., elder (*starets*) 280–1
Zagorsk 280–1
Zaitsev, B., writer 300, 303
Zakharov, M., theatre director 105, 108
Zakharov, V., politician 67, 96 n. 6
Zakhava, B., theatre director 99
Zalkind, A., sexologist 316
Zalygin, S. P., novelist 61
Zamiatin, E., 'neo-realist' writer 34, 74, 77, 205, 400
Zbruev, A., actor 107
Zdanevich, I., painter 303
Zetkin, C. 167
Zhdanov, A. A., Communist Party spokesman on cultural matters 11, 50, 118, 126, 180–1, 264
Zheliabuzhskii, Iu., film director 171, 172
Zhigulin, A., memoirist 74
Zhirinovskii, V., nationalist politician 273, 343, 391
Zhuk, O., editor, *Gei Slaviane* 344
Zimianin, M., politician 96 n. 6
Zimin, P., musicologist 111
Zimmerman, B. A. 132
Zinik, Z., writer 85, 237
Zinov'ev, A., philosopher, writer 70–1, 75
Ziuganov, G., leader of Russian Communist Party 394
Zolotonosov, M., writer 76, 84
Zorkaya, N. 360
Zoshchenko, M., satirical writer 50, 51
Zubov, A. 349
Zvezdochetova, L., artist 241

Subject Index

abortion 314, 318, 330, 337, 339, 353–4
absenteeism 253
absurd, theatre of 104
Academy of Arts 139, 146, 147
Academy of Sciences 291
acmeism 300, 303–4
adventure fiction 81
advertising 218, 223–30, 234, 298, 384
Afghan war 159, 190, 252, 267, 273, 293
agitation 91, 154, 167
  and theatre 91–2, 98
  and propaganda 193–4, 196–200, 219
  see also *agitprop*
agitprop 224, 227
  see also agitation; propaganda
AIDS 159, 226, 293, 334, 346–9, 350
alcoholism, *see* drinking
AKhRR (Assotsiatsiia kudozhnikov revoliutsionnoi Rossii, Association of Artists of Revolutionary Russia) 144, 145–7
Anarchists 322
anthroposophy 99
anti-cosmopolitan campaigns 95, 181, 199, 202, 203
  see also anti-Semitism
anti-Semitism 75, 79, 84–5, 95, 181, 202, 203, 296
  see also chauvinism; racism; xenophobia
APN 221
architecture 15, 138, 257–9, 283
  avant-garde 29, 144
  constructivism in 143
  Stalinist 2, 145, 257
atheism 275–8, 283–4, 293, 295, 388
audience, *see* reception

August 1991 coup 72, 75, 222, 272, 293, 294, 343, 349
Aum Shinrikyo sect 295
avant-garde 341
  and architecture 29, 144
  and cinema 166
  and literature 45–7, 52, 76; *see also* LEF; postmodernism
  and music 112, 113, 123–8
  and visual arts 138–45, 240–1
  see also constructivism; futurism; modernism
aviation 259

ballet 302, 303
Ballets Russes 303
banking 228, 229
Baptists 283
bards, *see* guitar-poetry
BBC 209, 211, 218
beauty contests 354, 384
Berlin Wall 156
beskonfliktnost' (conflictlessness) 51, 95, 99
besprizorniki (homeless children) 314, 381
best-sellers 78, 81–2
bikers 375, 380
billboards 225, 226, 228, 230
bisexuality 348–9
  see also homosexuality; lesbianism; sexuality
Black Hundreds 202
black market 80, 232, 253–4, 267, 268, 270, 342, 345, 379–80
blat 97, 254, 272–3
body, representations of 15, 312, 332–43, 349
bogoiskatel'stvo (god-seeking) 291
bogostroitel'stvo (god-building) 275–6, 284, 291

Bolshevik Revolution, *see* Revolutions, Russian: 1917 (October)
Bolsheviks 21–2, 220, 297, 299, 311, 315, 323
  'Old' 80, 259
  see also Communist Party
Booker Prize 83, 84
bourgeois attitudes 9, 14, 312, 332
  see also bourgeoisie
bourgeoisie 22, 28, 233
  see also bourgeois attitudes
Brest–Litovsk Treaty 205
bytovaia proza, see everyday prose

capitalism 11, 21, 206, 212–13, 224, 320, 370, 371, 374, 390
cars 224, 254, 255
Catacomb Church 276
Catholicism 288, 289, 294
censorship 30, 235, 236, 237, 318, 335
  cinema 174, 175, 180–1, 184, 185–7, 318, 335, 355
  literary 5, 24, 27–9, 51, 55, 65, 69, 317, 318, 337
  media 193, 211, 230
  press 28, 194, 196, 200
  relaxation of 334
  theatrical 93, 95–6, 107
central planning 224, 249, 272
  see also collectivization of agriculture; five-year plans; industrialization
charity:
  Orthodox Church and 293
  women and 354
charlatanism in science 203
chastushka 265
chauvinism 381
  see also anti-Semitism; racism; xenophobia
Chechen war 190, 273, 390

cult of personality:
  of Lenin 70, 144, 158–9, 178, 182, 238, 259, 260, 266–7
  of Stalin 11, 60, 151–2, 158, 181–2, 199, 209, 250, 259, 260
cultural heritage 74
  assimilation of 33–5, 36, 110–11
cultural policy, *see* Communist Party, policy on culture of
cultural politics 23–5, 46, 77
cultural revolution 84, 311, 315
  Leninist model of 21–3
  1928–31: 38–43, 146, 173–5, 230, 300
cultural semiotics, *see* Tartu school
culture:
  binary models of 1–4, 5, 6, 52, 64, 374, 396
  commercial 229, 230; *see also* commercialism
  and economic sphere 6–7, 9
  see also Communist Party, policy on culture of; intelligentsia; *kul'turnost'*; mass culture; popular culture; youth, culture
culturology 10, 12–13, 387, 399–400
Czechoslovakia, invasion of (1968) 57, 68, 208 n. 30, 251, 371–2

dance 317–18, 330, 369, 370, 374, 375, 378, 380
Decembrists 137
dedovshchina (tormenting new boys) 267, 328, 379
demographic crisis 338, 340, 348
demonstrations 44, 253, 267, 269–70, 285
denunciation 202, 203, 318–19
design 138
de-Stalinization 57, 59–62, 183, 250, 259–61, 351
detective fiction 64
détente 66
didacticism 140, 223, 317
disasters:
  man-made 210, 212, 221, 293
  natural 210, 212, 213, 293
dissidence 60, 235, 249, 251–2, 256, 269, 272, 289–90, 370, 372
  literary 59, 62, 68–71, 84
  political 68, 209, 210, 211
divorce 318, 337, 341, 384
  see also family
Doctors' Plot (1953) 202–3
domestic violence 354
dress, *see* clothes
drinking 159, 269, 332, 340, 354, 380
  regulation and prohibition of 224, 270–2

drugs 159, 254, 332, 346, 349, 380
dvoeverie (double faith) 295

education 198, 217, 370, 373, 381
  further 379
  higher 72, 218, 277, 370, 379, 396; *see also* universities
  increased access to 78, 209, 371
  moral (*vospitanie*) 320
  Orthodox Church and 293
  peasantry and 8, 23
  as policy objective 21–2
  self- 384
  theological 278, 292, 295–6
  workers and 8, 23
  see also literacy; schools; science; sex education; universities
elders, see *startsy*
elections 273, 394
emigration 57, 297–304, 325
  and cinema 167, 185–6
  and commercial culture 235–8
  and feminism 354
  and literature 69, 70, 71, 74–5, 82, 84, 235, 236–8, 242, 243, 299, 300, 303–4
  and music 299, 301
  and national identities 300–1
  and religion 275
  and visual arts 138, 235–6, 242, 299, 300, 301–2
environmentalism 159, 270, 272, 370, 375
Ermol'ev film company 301
erotica 70, 83, 223, 230, 335, 336, 342, 343, 345
  see also pornography
estrada (light music) 125, 215, 242, 267–8, 382
ethnic relations 159
Eurasianists 299
evangelical Christianity 294–5
everyday prose (*bytovaia proza*) 66
ezhovshchina 49

Fabergé 244
family 371
  Communist Party policy on 311–20, 327, 337, 338–9, 340, 352, 355
  nuclear 229, 312, 318, 319–20
  see also divorce; gender roles; motherhood
famine 157, 170, 201, 255, 265, 276, 314
fascism 68, 263, 319, 332, 375
fashion 143, 330–2, 373, 382, 384
  see also clothes

FEKS (Factory of the Eccentric Actor) 169
fellow-travellers:
  musicians 109
  writers 36–7, 39, 47, 303
feminism 252, 312, 343, 344–5, 351, 354
  and literature 66–7, 232
  see also 'woman question'; women
festivals:
  film 175, 182, 190
  street 15
film, *see* cinema
Films Albatros 301
financial services 228, 272
First Five-Year Plan 14, 173, 182
First World War 155, 165–6
five-year plans 158, 275
folk music 111, 114, 117
folklore, visual arts and 139, 226, 235
formalism 25, 113, 114, 115, 118, 126
futurism 34, 113, 138, 139, 303–4
  see also avant-garde; modernism

gay and lesbian activists 344–5, 346, 349–51
gender roles 229, 316, 318, 338, 351, 375, 376, 395
  represented in cinema 173, 180, 352–67
  see also family; motherhood; sexuality; women
German–Soviet Non-Aggression Pact 201–2
glasnost' 5, 11, 57, 58, 68, 70, 71–83, 84, 91, 96–7, 105–6, 159, 207, 211, 214, 219, 221–2, 240, 265, 273, 277, 283–4, 286, 289–90, 334, 354, 355, 363–4, 374
  see also *perestroika*
Glavlit (literary censorship body) 28, 317
Glavpolitprosvet (Department for Political Education) 93
Glavrepertkom (theatrical censorship body) 28, 93, 95, 317
globalization 6, 369, 381, 384
god-building, see *bogostroitel'stvo*
god-seeking, see *bogoiskatel'stvo*
Gosizdat (Gosudarstvennoe izdatel'stvo, State Publishing House) 29, 110, 113–14, 149
Goskino (Central State Cinematic Enterprise) 170
graffiti 262
grazhdanskii brak, *see* marriage, civil

limitchiki 253
literacy 22
drives for 9, 27, 157, 369
levels of 154, 197–8, 200
peasantry and 27, 197
see also education; reading
literary criticism 38–9, 63–4
literature 2, 4–5, 21–85, 316–17,
325–6, 330, 332, 335–6, 337, 342,
351, 399
and commercialism 232–4,
236–8, 242–3
Communist Party policy on
36–8, 50, 52, 58, 67–8
and emigration 69, 70, 71, 74–5,
82, 84, 235, 236–8, 242, 243, 299,
300, 303–4
functionality of 25, 40
and identities 24, 31–8, 40, 66
institutions of 24–5; censorship
5, 24, 27–9, 51, 55, 65, 69, 317,
318, 337; publishing 27, 29, 30,
38–9, 61, 79, 81–2, 83, 243, 351;
readership 29, 76; *see also*
journals; literary criticism
and journalism 40
modernism in 62, 70, 74, 303–4
and national identities 393
professionalization of 54
realism in 35, 39–40, 46–7, 61, 70,
76, 84, 145, 299, 395
and religion 283–4, 285, 291
and romanticism 53–4
as social commentary 25, 234, 257
socialist realism in 24, 43–52,
60 n. 7, 64–5, 76, 84, 283–4, 318,
398–9
translated 62, 78, 82
underground 65, 67, 68, 342
women and 66–7, 76, 232, 238, 353
see also adventure fiction;
children's literature; cruel
prose; detective fiction;
dissidence, literary; erotica;
everyday prose; fellow-
travellers; guitar-poetry;
historical fiction; horror
stories; literary prizes;
literaturnost', *lubochnaia
literatura*; memoirs; poetry;
popular literature; proletarian
writers; romantic fiction;
science fiction; thrillers;
village prose; war literature;
youth prose
literature of fact, *see* LEF
literaturnost' 25
see also literature
Litfront 39–40

Living Church 276–7
localization 5, 384
lubochnaia literatura (penny
dreadfuls) 27
see also popular literature
lubok (popular prints) 240
see also visual arts

mafia 81, 243, 273, 381–2
magazines 198, 384
humorous 217, 234
illustrated 148, 298; see also
Ogonek
pornographic 334, 335, 336, 342,
343, 347
women's 230, 318, 354
see also journals; newspapers;
press
magnitizdat 69, 104
Maiak (radio station) 209, 215
makulatura scheme 78
MAPP (Moskovskaia assotsiatsiia
proletarskikh pisatelei,
Moscow Association of
Proletarian Writers) 32
market 6, 14, 55, 82–3, 97–8, 269,
273, 363, 381–2, 398
see also black market; New
Economic Policy;
privatization
market research 220
marriage 350
civil (*grazhdanskii brak*) 311, 318
policy on 311–19, 330
Marxism 31, 195, 378, 398
and culture 6, 7, 9, 10, 21, 368, 370
Marxism-Leninism 115, 118, 193,
197, 213, 220
mass culture 6, 27, 77–83, 230, 241,
267, 269, 341–2
see also popular culture
mass song 114
masturbation 340
maternity leave 313
media 5, 11, 24, 193–222, 228, 234,
257, 272, 336, 354, 368, 369, 382,
384
censorship of 193, 211, 230
Communist Party policy on 65,
192–200
and identities 192–200, 204,
206–9, 216, 218
theory of 216–19
see also *glasnost'*; journals;
magazines; newspapers; press;
radio; television
memoirs 69–70
Mensheviks 21
mentalities, *see* identities

metarealism 397
middle classes, *see* bourgeoisie
missionaries 294–5
MMM savings bank 228
mnogoverie (multiple faith) 295
modernism 9
in literature 62, 70, 74, 303–4
in music 110, 111–12, 113–14, 115,
116, 125, 128–33, 134, 136
in visual arts 139, 142, 145, 240,
301–3
modernization:
belief in 9–12, 21
as explanatory model 4, 5, 6
monasticism 278, 292, 333
montage:
in cinema 168–9, 175
in photography 158, 225
in theatre 101
monuments 259–66
Moonies 295
Mormons 295
motherhood 263, 323, 338, 357
see also family; gender roles;
sexuality; women
museums 151, 261, 399
of atheism 277
and identities 10
war 267
music 109–37, 264
avant-garde in 112, 113, 123–8
Communist Party policy on 109,
110–11, 112, 114–15, 116, 117, 118,
119, 122–3, 128
constructivism in 113, 144
and emigration 299, 301
modernism in 110, 111–12, 113–14,
115, 116, 125, 128–33, 134, 136
and national identities 134–7
religious 134–6, 283
socialist realism in 114, 126, 131
see also *estrada*; guitar poetry;
jazz; mass song; popular
music; popular song;
proletarian musicians; rock
music
music-hall 169
Muzo (music division of
Narkompros) 110–11
muzhelozhstvo (sodomy) 322–3, 327,
344

names 268
Narkompros (Narodnyi
komissariat prosveshcheniia,
People's Commissariat of
Enlightenment) 27–8, 29, 32,
92, 110–11, 112, 113, 114, 143, 145,
167

narod (people) 249
  and intelligentsia 3, 8, 28, 56, 72, 73, 400
  representations of 273
  see also identities, national; *narodnost'*; peasantry; populism; workers
narodnost' 48, 388
  see also identities, national; nationalism
nationalism 68, 73, 74, 79, 84–5, 226, 256–7, 263–6, 285, 286, 295–6, 333, 335, 350, 382, 389, 394–5
  see also identities, national
nationalities, demands for autonomy of 221–2, 272
NATO 393
neformaly 269, 375, 378, 381
neo-primitivism 139, 240, 303
NEP (Novaia ekonomicheskaia politika, New Economic Policy) 14, 26–31, 36, 38, 45, 93, 109–10, 114, 171, 173, 223, 316–17
New Age movement 295
New Economic Policy, *see* NEP
'new' man and woman 5, 207–8, 365–6, 392
  see also identities, programmes for formation of
'new' Russians 244, 381–2
news, Soviet conception of 197, 208–9, 210, 212–15, 216
newspapers 82–3, 157, 193–4, 195–7, 198, 199–200, 206, 222, 334, 336, 342, 344–5, 347
  mass-circulation 195–6
  see also *Izvestiia*; journals; magazines; media; *Pravda*; press
NKVD 332
Nobel Prize for Literature 75
Novyi mir (literary journal) 57, 58, 61, 68, 77, 184, 232–3, 267, 268

objectivity 43, 46, 216
obnovlentsy, *see* Living Church
occultism 80–1
ocherk (sketch) 40
October Revolution, *see* Revolutions, Russian
Ogonek (illustrated magazine) 77, 197, 226, 227, 228, 229, 231, 258, 292, 321, 331, 335, 343
  see also magazines, illustrated
OGPU 319
'Old' Bolsheviks, *see* Bolsheviks, 'Old'
Olympic Games (Moscow, 1980) 96, 259

opinion polls, *see* surveys
Orthodox Church 148, 274–96
  Communist Party and 78, 274–80, 289–93, 296, 388
  and charity 293
  and education 293
  Millennium celebrations of (1988) 289–91
  and national identities 278–9, 284, 296, 395
  see also Orthodoxy
Orthodoxy, national identities and 68, 388, 389, 393, 394

pacifism 372
painting, *see* visual arts
Pamiat' (nationalist movement) 273
parki kul'tury i otdykha, *see* Parks of Culture and Rest
Parks of Culture and Rest (*parki kul'tury i otdykha*) 44, 259
parties, political 273, 394
  see also Communist Party
partiinost' (Party-mindedness) 24, 48
Party, *see* Communist Party
Party-mindedness, *see partiinost'*
patriarchy 313
patriotism, *see* identities, national
patronage 244
peasant poets 300
peasantry:
  culture of 21
  and drinking 271
  and literacy 27, 197
  representations of 159
  and workers 28, 273
  see also intelligentsia; *narod*; workers
penal institutions 293
  see also prison camps
penny dreadfuls, see *lubochnaia literatura*
people, the, see *narod*
People's Commissariat of Enlightenment, *see* Narkompros
Peredvizhniki, *see* Wanderers
perestroika 11–12, 39, 58, 71, 73, 74–5, 77, 82–3, 96–7, 105, 141, 155, 159, 188, 221, 273, 290, 374–81, 384, 396
  see also *glasnost'*
Pereval 46
performance art 241, 244
pets 80–1
photography 144
  see also montage

Pioneers 213, 241, 259, 260, 263, 320, 321
poetry 61, 285, 303–4, 370
polygamy 311, 313
popular culture 15, 30, 73–4, 269, 347
  and élite culture 5, 6, 47–8, 230
  see also mass culture; popular literature; popular song
popular literature 217
  see also *lubochnaia literatura*; popular culture
popular music 15, 112, 117, 215, 267–8, 369, 370, 372, 375, 378, 380, 382
  see also rock music
popular piety 280–2
popular song, 180, 225
populism 8, 39, 195, 249–73
  see also identities, national; *narodnost'*; nationalism
poputchiki, *see* fellow-travellers
pornography 27, 81, 116, 318, 334–5, 342–3, 384
  see also erotica
positive hero 48, 330
postcards 217
posters 144, 154–9, 198, 224–6, 227, 234–5, 267
postmodernism 6, 12, 57, 83–4, 236, 238, 241, 395–400
Pravda (newspaper) 61, 116, 122, 167, 176, 179, 196–7, 201–3, 204, 222
presentism 397
press 193–204, 215, 375
  campaigns in 202, 270, 347
  censorship of 28, 194, 196, 200
  freedom of 24, 194–5, 200
  see also journals; magazines; media; newspapers
prison camps 60, 61, 69, 70, 75, 158, 187, 201, 211, 274, 278, 281, 282, 288, 328–9, 345, 367
private enterprise 226
privatization 155, 191, 224, 272, 347–8, 382, 393
privilege 253, 258, 264, 265
prizes, cinema 190
prizes, literary:
  Booker 83, 84
  Lenin 66
  Nobel 75
  Stalin 51
production, cultural 4–5, 6, 13, 14, 24, 31–2, 37, 243
  see also consumption; reception
production novels 40, 230, 232 n. 13, 238, 316
projectionism 143–4

village prose 61–2, 66, 84, 283
virgin-lands campaign 183, 370
visual arts 57, 58, 61, 138–53, 231, 251,
    261, 264
  avant-garde and 138–45, 240–1
  and commercialism 234–6,
    238–42, 243–4
  Communist Party policy on
    50–1, 62, 138, 146
  constructivism in 29, 140, 141,
    142, 143–5
  didacticism in 140
  and emigration 138, 235–6, 242,
    299, 300, 301–2
  and folklore 139, 226, 235
  institutions of 139–40
  modernism in 139, 142, 145, 240,
    301–3
  and national identities 148
  neo-primitivism in 139, 240,
    303
  realism in 139, 140, 144, 145–6,
    244
  and religion 241, 283, 284–5
  socialist realism in 71, 139,
    146–53, 240–1, 283
  stylization in 141
  utilitarianism in 140–1, 142
  see also icon; lubok;
    projectionism; suprematism;
    Wanderers
Voice of America (VOA) 209, 211,
    215
vospitanie, see education, moral

wall newspapers, see stengazety
Wanderers (Peredvizhniki), school
    of realist painters 139, 144,
    146
war films 179–80, 181, 183, 185, 186,
    263, 264, 265 n., 267
war literature 65–6, 264–5, 267
war memorials 261–4
war mythology 261–8
WCC, see World Council of
    Churches
welfare services 293, 341, 354, 367,
    369
  see also charity; public health
Westernizers 3, 8, 375
'woman question' (zhenskii vopros)
    320, 337, 353–4
  see also feminism; women
women:
  and charity 354
  and cinema 359–63
  as commodities 380
  and consumption 380
  'double burden' of 159, 232, 272,
    353
  and education 353
  and employment 353, 355
  and equal rights 313, 320, 352–5,
    367
  and literature 66–7, 76, 232, 238,
    353
  see also feminism; 'woman
    question'
Women's Sections, see Zhenotdely

workbooks (trudovye knizhki) 252,
    253
workers 15, 250
  and drinking 271
  and peasantry 28, 273
  and political consciousness 195
  representations of 159
  and sexuality 316
  see also industrialization; narod;
    peasantry; urbanization
World Council of Churches (WCC)
    287, 294
World of Art movement 109–10,
    138, 145, 148

xenophobia 346–7

youth 395, 396
  as constructors of communism
    174, 369–71, 373, 374, 380, 383
  culture 61, 81, 231, 268, 269,
    368–85, 387
  and identities 368–9, 372, 380, 384
  slang 371, 378
youth prose 61

zhdanovshchina (1946–8) 50–2, 58,
    95, 99, 116, 118, 180–1
Zhenotdely (Party Women's
    Sections) 2, 320
zhenskii vopros, see 'woman
    question'
zhestokaia proza, see cruel prose
zhiznestroenie (life-building) 34, 45